INFORMATION INDIA: 1992-93

CONCEPTS IN COMMUNICATION
INFORMATICS & LIBRARIANSHIP
(CICIL)

For a list of titles in this series,
see pp. 653-56 at the end of the book

ABOUT THE AUTHORS

S.P. AGRAWAL (*b.* 1929) was Director, National Social Science Documentation Centre, ICSSR, and Member Secretary, Indian Association of Social Science Institutions. He was also the Vice-Chairman of the Asia and Pacific Information Network in Social Sciences (APINESS). In 1988 he was awarded the degree of Doctor of Philosophy in Education (*Honoris Causa*) by International University Foundation. Presently, he is Member, IFLA Round Table on Research in Reading and Member, International Committee for Social Science Information and Documentation. He is also Member of Board of Studies of National Archives of India and Member, Hindi Advisory Committee, Ministry of Coal, Government of India. Born and brought up in the cradle of freedom movement which he joined at the tender age of twelve, he gained an insight into political problems and developed a sense of responsibility which bore fruit as an information scientist committed to Gandhiji's philosophy and action-plan in the field and its social concept. He has written extensively on various aspects of education, Indian Polity and Library and Information Science.

J.C. AGGARWAL (*b.* 1928), former Deputy Director of Education/Executive Director of Delhi Bureau of Textbooks, Delhi Administration has a varied experience in the field of education. He has singly/jointly authored about 130 books on Education, Social Sciences and Current Problems. In collaboration with S.P. Agrawal, he has written *Documentation Encyclopaedia of UNESCO* and Education (in two parts); *Women's Education in India; National Policy on Education: Agenda for India 2001*; and *Vocational Education in India.*

His other recent publications include: *Yearbook of Indian Education, 1991; World Overview; Ramamurti Report 1990 on National Policy on Education in India; and Survey of Educational Documents in the World Since 1983,* etc.

Concepts in Communication
Informatics & Librarianship—62

General Editor: **S.P. Agrawal**

INFORMATION INDIA: 1992-93

GLOBAL VIEW

S.P. AGRAWAL
former Member Secretary
Indian Association of Social Science Institutions
NEW DELHI

J.C. AGGARWAL
former Executive Director
Delhi Bureau of Textbooks, Delhi Administration
NEW DELHI

CONCEPT PUBLISHING COMPANY, NEW DELHI 110059

ISBN 81-7022-538-8

First Published 1994

Published and Printed by
Ashok Kumar Mittal
Concept Publishing Company
A/15-16, Commercial Block, Mohan Garden
NEW DELHI 110059 (India)

Lasertypeset by
Printing Express
H-13, Bali Nagar
NEW DELHI 110015

GENERAL EDITOR'S INTRODUCTION

Information India was first brought out in 1989 by the Publisher under CICIL series which covers a wide range of disciplines – interrelated but at the same time including a very wide stretch of topics for investigation, research and study. It is of great consolation that previous editions of *Information India* placed in the hands of the discerning readers as also reviewers have been received well. In all humility, we assume that these annuals have fulfilled a long felt need.

The focus of the present volume is on India as it was in 1992. As many as 36 out of the total of 49 chapters, under suitable divisions, are devoted to various aspects of the country. The chapters are, by and large, a combination of descriptive accounts and vital statistics. *Information India* is now accompanied by 3D companion volume – *Development/Digression Diary of India*.

S.P. AGRAWAL

PREFACE

In this compilation it has been endeavoured to give all important facets of not only India but also the world as a whole.

A comparative study of the indicators of development with regard to 170 countries including populous and less populous countries, as also developed, developing and under-developed countries have been included.

Relating to India, it has been attempted to provide almost all embracing facts and figures with regard to various sectors of development since 1947. A detailed account has been given about important aspects, as well as other topical areas which are of significance in any discussion on India.

As a matter of fact, the book includes a panoramic view of almost everything important that happened in India during the period under review.

It is observed that data collected by various national and international organisations from different sources and also used here, do not necessarily relate to the same year in a few cases.

S.P. AGRAWAL
J.C. AGGARWAL

CONTENTS

Part II : *India 1992-93*

PART ONE

WORLD OVERVIEW

1

ENVIRONMENT AND DEVELOPMENT

1.1 United Nations Conference on Environment and Development: The Earth Summit, June 1992

Introduction

The United Nations Conference on the Environment and Development (UNCED), the largest inter-governmental Conference ever held, concluded in Rio de Janeiro, Brazil on June 14, 1992. After 12 days of meetings and two-and-a-half years of preparation, the Conference adopted and recommended for endorsement by the UN General Assembly at its next regular session: (i) The Rio Declaration on Environment and Development; (ii) Agenda 21; and (iii) a Statement of Principles on the Management, Conservation and Sustainable Development of All Types of Forests. Also the Conventions on Biological Diversity and Climate Change were both opened for signatures during UNCED. Agenda 21 and the Forest Principles were still under negotiation even as the Conference began and all three documents were part of an "Earth Summit" that was, in fact, many conferences in one: a negotiating conference, Conventions being signed, future conventions being put in a place, a plenary of the presentation of ideas and imperatives for action, a hoped-for pledging conference, Brazil negotiating with the IMF, a media event and the largest gathering of Heads of State and Government in history.

The summit segment of the UNCED proceedings took place on June 12-13, 1992. This two-day session was addressed by 118 Heads of State and Government and included a meeting around a huge round-table especially constructed for the purpose. The summit segment helped to focus massive media attention on UNCED and forced national leaders to address their constituencies on issues of environment and development; however, opinion is divided on the quality of the results of "the largest international Summit meeting in history".

Plenary

The main deliberative body in Rio was the Plenary which finally adopted the Rio Declaration, Agenda 21 and the Forest Principles, and where the General Debate was conducted. It was chaired by the President of Brazil and heard statements by 135 nations, many delivered at the Ministerial level, 13 United Nations specialized agencies, 23 inter-governmental organizations, 16 non-governmental organizations, 13 United Nations organs and four observer delegations — for a grand total of 204 speakers. The Plenary set up a Main Committee to finalise the work on the Rio Declaration, Agenda 21 and the Forest Principles and deal with the remaining major areas of contention. This Main Committee (a *de facto* PrepCom V) was chaired by Tommy Koh

(Singapore), who divided the items into eight contact groups representing most of the negotiating work not completed by the preparatory committee: Atmosphere, Biodiversity/Biotechnology, Finance, Forests (including the Forest Principles and the Agenda 21 chapter on combating deforestation). Freshwater Resources, Institutions, Legal Instruments and Technology Transfer. He retained the remaining items and the Rio Declaration for the Main Committee.

Finance

The agreement on financing Agenda 21 and the work of the Conventions represented the most politically difficult set of negotiations of UNCED and, for most governments, the most significant. Those observers, including NGOs, who do not view money as the solution to development and environmental problems, nevertheless recognise that financial contributions by the industrial countries measure their commitment to address the problems. It is not clear how much has been pledged that is "new and additional". Estimates hover around $2-5 billion. A minimum of $10 billion had been viewed as the yardstick of success.

Institutions

The first contact group to conclude its work was that on international institutional arrangements. The main outstanding item was on the inter-governmental arrangements to be adopted to monitor the implementation of Agenda 21. Much work had been undertaken, especially by NGOs, in the period before Rio to strengthen the commitment for a high-level Commission on Sustainable Development to be set up and this option was quickly accepted in Rio. Many delegations used that this Commission report to the top political body in the UN — the General Assembly. Most major industrialised governments opposed this approach as being incompatible with their objective of revitalising the Economic and Social Council (ECOSOC) and insisted, successfully, that the new Commission report to ECOSOC. The International NGO Taskforce on Institutional and Legal Matters had ensured that the institutions chapter call for an expanded role for NGOs and will monitor the 47th General Assembly where the details and terms of reference of the commission will be determined.

Rio Declaration

The Rio Declaration is a set of 27 principles to govern the economic and environmental behaviour of both nations and individuals.

Agenda 21

Agenda 21 is UNCED's blue-print for action to the 21st century. It is unique in its extensive coverage of environment and development issues, even though much of its content is not new and, in some places, its text is actually weaker than that of existing agreements. Described as "a voluminous programme of action", the proposals of Agenda 21 are divided into four sections, 40 chapters and more than 100 programme areas. Its ambitious goal is to cover all areas where environment and development intersect and major social groups are affected. Its final chapters on the financing of its implementation and follow-up to UNCED are considered by many to be the most important.

The first section of Agenda 21 looks at the social and economic dimensions of sustainable development, with chapters on sustainable development in developing countries, poverty, consumption patterns, demographics, health, human settlements and integrating environment and development in decision-making. More than any other section, this one examines the linkages between environment and development, focusing both on the impacts of human activities on the environment and on the impact of environmental degradation on human living conditions. This section expands upon the relationship between poverty and environmental degradation which was outlined at the 1972 World Conference on Environment. It also addresses the negative impact which affluence, though unsustainable consumption patterns, has on the environment — a dimension which has been virtually ignored in the past.

The relative impact of poverty and affluence became a point of contention in this section. An agreement was finally reached which stated:

> While poverty results in certain kinds of environmental stress, the major cause of the continued deterioration of the global environment is the unsustainable pattern of consumption and production, particularly in industrialised countries, which is a matter of grave concern aggravating poverty and imbalances.

The second section of Agenda 21 deals with the conservation and management of resources for development. It addresses protection of the atmosphere, oceans, and freshwater; combating deforestation and desertification; conservation of biodiversity; promoting sustainable agriculture; and management of fragile ecosystems, biotechnology, toxic chemicals and hazardous, solid, and radioactive wastes. International commitment to launch a process of negotiation on a convention to combat desertification was a major priority for the Africa Group, a priority which met with success after lengthy negotiations.

Although many of the chapters in this section have developmental dimensions, they are primarily environmental issues. The length of the section, approximately that of all of the other sections together, is illustrative of the concern of many developing countries and NGOs, that environment received more attention in this conference than development.

The chapters on deforestation, biological diversity and the atmosphere were influenced by related conventions which were negotiated in other fora.

The third section, Strengthening the Role of Major Groups, is the most extensive and formalised recognition in a UN document of the potential and actual contributions of NGOs and other independent sectors. The nine chapters in this section are on women, children and youth, indigenous peoples, NGOs, local authorities, workers and trade unions, business and industry, the scientific and technological community, and farmers. Each chapter outlines the contributions of one of the Major Groups and examines ways to strengthen the group and further incorporate it into a governmental and international work on environment and development. The chapters also address the responsibilities and, in some cases, the rights and vulnerabilities of the different sectors. The text provides the basis for increased collaboration among the various sectors, governments and international agencies.

The fourth and final section of Agenda 21, on means of implementation, includes chapters on financial resources and mechanisms; transfer of technology; science; education, training and pubic awareness; capacity building in developing countries; international institutional arrangements; regional organizations; international legal instruments and mechanisms; and data and information.

Statement of Principles on Forests

These Principles, which are the "first global consensus on forests', affirm the importance of forest management and conservation for sustainable development". The negotiations on forests illustrated the great inter-linkages between issues and the potential conflicts between environmental protection and economic development.

Many factors contributed to the controversy of this issue. Claims of national sovereignty over natural resources contrast with calls for forests to be the common heritage of humankind. The dependence of economies on harvesting forest resources, particularly in developing countries, makes the prospect of internationally imposed limits in the absence of compensation unacceptable. The resistance to adopting similar restrictive measures for car emissions, while emphasising the importance of carbon sinks, undermines the climate for international agreement.

Conventions

The Conventions on Biological Diversity and Climate Change were opened for signatures during the Conference. They were negotiated by two separate Intergovernmental Negotiating Committees (INC). The first of these, under the sponsorship of the United Nations Environment Programme (UNEP), had the Convention on Biological Diversity under deliberation for nearly, four years. It was adopted on the May 22, 1992 and, as of June 14, 1992 had been signed by 153 States (and the EEC). The Convention on Climate Change, 15 months in preparation, was adopted on May 9, 1992 and has also been signed by 153 States (and EEC).

I. *Biological Diversity Convention*: The Biological Diversity Convention asserts that industrialised countries must assist developing countries both financially and with the transfer of technological know-how. While the primary responsibility for setting up protected areas rests with individual nations, the first beneficiaries should be the indigenous peoples and rural groups whose patterns of sustainable use have preserved these ecosystems for centuries.

II. *Framework Convention on Climate Change:* The Climate Change Convention calls for the protection of the earth's atmosphere from the "greenhouse effect", caused by the build up of anthropogenic gases that trap heat from the sun. The return by industrialised nations to their 1990 levels of greenhouse gas emissions by the end of the decade, had been targeted as an initial goal. The final document does not provide any specific timetables or indicate what will happen in respect of emissions after the year 2000, but does provide for a Conference of the Parties (signatory countries) to take subsequent steps and for at least two reviews before the year 2000. Several countries chose to show their disappointment with the Climate Convention and the position of the U.S. Government by starting initiatives including an elaboration of protocols to the convention, which contain the timetables and targets which did not survive the Convention negotiations.

Source: *E & D File*, No. 31, July 1992. United Nations Non-Government Liaison Service, New York.

1.2 Text of Declaration

Recognising the integral and independent nature of the earth, our home, we proclaim that:

Principle 1: Human beings are at the centre of concerns for sustainable development. They are entitled to a healthy and productive life in harmony with nature.

2. States have, in accordance with the Charter of the United Nations and the principles of international law, the sovereign right to exploit their own resources pursuant to their own environmental and policies, and the responsibility to ensure that activities within their jurisdiction or control do not cause damage to the environment of other States or areas beyond the limits of national jurisdiction.

3. The right to development must be fulfilled so as to equitably meet developmental and environmental needs of present and future generations.

4. In order to achieve sustainable development, environmental protection shall constitute an integral part of the development process and cannot be considered in isolation from it.

5. All States and all people shall cooperate in the essential task of eradicating poverty as an indispensable requirement for sustainable development.

6. The special situation and needs of developing countries, particularly the least developed and those most environmentally vulnerable, shall be given special priority. International actions in the field of environment and development should also address the interests and needs of all countries.

7. States shall cooperate in a spirit of global partnership to conserve, protect and restore the health and integrity of the earth's ecosystems. In view of the different contributions to global environmental degradation, States have common but differentiated responsibilities. The developed countries acknowledge the responsibility that they bear in the international pursuit of sustainable development in the view of the pressures their societies place on the global environment and of the technologies and financial resources they command.

8. To achieve sustainable development and a higher quality of life for all people, States should reduce and eliminate unsustainable patterns of production and consumption and promote appropriate demographic policies.

9. States should cooperate to strengthen indigenous capacity-building for sustainable development by improving scientific understanding through exchanges of scientific and technological knowledge, and by enhancing the development, adaptation, diffusion and transfer of technologies, including new innovative technologies.

10. Environmental issues are best handled with the participation of all concerned citizens, at the relevant level. At the national level, each individual shall have appropriate access to information concerning the environment that is held

by public authorities, including information on hazardous materials and activities in their communities, and the opportunity to participate in decision-making processes. States shall facilitate and encourage public awareness and participation by making information widely available. Effective access to judicial and administrative proceedings, including redress and remedy, shall be provided.

11. States shall enact effective environmental legislation, environmental standards, management objectives and priorities should reflect the environmental and developmental context to which they apply. Standards applied by some countries may be inappropriate and of unwarranted economic and social cost to other countries, in particular developing countries.

12. States should cooperate to promote a supportive and open international economic system that would lead to economic growth and sustainable development in all countries, to better address the problems of environmental degradation. Trade policy measures for environmental purposes should not constitute a means of arbitrary or unjustifiable discrimination or a disguised restriction on international trade. Unilateral actions to deal with environmental challenges outside the jurisdiction of the importing countries should be avoided. Environmental measures addressing transboundary or global environmental problems should, as far as possible, be based on an international consensus.

13. States shall develop national law regarding liability and compensation for the victims or pollution and other environmental damage. States shall also cooperate in an expeditious and more determined manner to develop further international law regarding liability and compensation for adverse effects of environmental damage caused by activities within their jurisdiction or control to areas beyond their jurisdiction.

14. States should effectively cooperate to discourage or prevent the relocation and transfer to other States of any activities and substances that cause several environmental degradation or are found to be harmful to human health.

15. In order to protect the environment, the precautionary approach shall be widely applied by States according to their capabilities. Where there are threats of serious or irreversible damage, lack of full scientific certainty shall not be used as a reason for postponing cost-effective measures to prevent environmental degradation.

16. National authorities should endeavour to promote the internationalisation of environmental costs and the use of economic instruments, taking into account the approach that the polluter should, in principle, bear the cost of pollution, with due regard to the public interest and without distorting international trade and investment.

17. Environmental impact assessment, as a national instrument, shall be undertaken for proposed activities that are likely to have a significant adverse impact on the environment and are subject to a decision of a competent national authority.

18. States shall immediately notify other States of any natural disasters or other emergencies that are likely to produce sudden harmful effects on the environment of those States. Every effort shall be made by the international community to help States so afflicted.

19. States shall provide prior and timely notification and relevant information to potentially affected States on activities that may have a significant adverse transboundary environmental effect and shall consult with those States at an early stage and in good faith.

20. Women have a vital role in environmental management and development. Their full participation is therefore essential to achieve sustainable development.

21. The creativity, ideals and courage of the youth of the world should be mobilised to forge a global partnership in order to achieve sustainable development and ensure a better future for all.

22. Indigenous people and their communities, and other local communities, have a vital role in environmental management and development because of their knowledge and traditional practices. States should recognise and duly support their identity, culture and interests and enable their effective participation in the achievement of sustainable development.

23. The environment and natural resources of people under oppression, domination and occupation shall be protected.

24. Warfare is inherently destructive of sustainable development. States shall therefore respect international law providing protection for the environment in times of armed conflict and cooperate in its further development as necessary.

25. Peace, development and environmental protection are interdependent and indivisible.

26. States shall resolve all their environmental disputes peacefully and by appropriate means in accordance with the Charter of the United Nations.

27. States and people shall cooperate in good faith and in a spirit of partnership in the fulfilment of the principles embodies in this declaration and in the further development of international law.

Source: *Earth Summit*, June 1992, UNCED.

1.3 **Agenda 21**

Population appears in various parts of *Agenda 21*, the non-binding action plan for sustainable development approved in June at the Earth Summit (formally, UNCED or the United Nations Conference on Environment and Development) in Rio de Janeiro. The following excerpts are taken from the chapter on "Demographic dynamics and sustainability":

"Reproductive health programmes and services, should as appropriate, be developed and enhanced to reduce maternal and infant mortality from all causes and enable women and men to fulfil their personal aspirations in terms of family size, in a way in keeping with their freedom and dignity and personally held values."

(Paragraph 5.49)

"Governments should take active steps to implement, as a matter of urgency. . . measures to ensure that women and men have the same right to decide freely and responsibly on the number and spacing of their children, to have access to the information, education and means, as appropriate, to enable them to exercise this right..."

(Paragraph 5.50)

"Governments should take active steps to implement programmes to establish and strengthen preventive and curative health facilities that include women-centred, women-managed, safe and effective reproductive health care and affordable, accessible services, as appropriate, for the responsible planning of family size, in keeping with freedom, dignity and personally held values and taking into account ethical and cultural consideration."

(Paragraph 5.51)

"...UNFPA and other relevant agencies should strengthen the coordination of international cooperation activities with recipient and donor countries in order to ensure that adequate funding is available to respond to growing needs."

(Paragraph 5.55)

(Source: *Populi*, July-August 1992.)

2

HUMAN DEVELOPMENT

2.1 Human Development Report, 1992

Human development, or the process of enlarging the range of people's choices, has become central to the global development debate, says the *Human Development Report 1992*, third in an annual series, published for the UN Development Programme (UNDP) on April 23, 1992.

Human development is now the core of the United Nations International Development Strategy for the 1990s. It is a key element in discussions on international development assistance. It is also increasingly being reflected in the national development plans and strategies of developing countries from Bangladesh to Ghana and from Pakistan to Colombia.

UNDP, along with UNICEF, is working with more than 20 countries that have requested assistance in formulating comprehensive human development strategies. "Understanding and accepting the human development concept alone will not revolutionalize development practice. The concept must be translated into concrete action in order to ensure more positive, realistic and sustained development in future".

The report suggests three ways to go about this:

* All countries, rich and poor, will have to set national human development goals and strategies. To attain those goals, it will be necessary, especially for those developing countries starting at the lowest human development levels, to make fundamental and even unpopular policy and institutional changes.

  Industrialized countries will have different priorities. But they, too, will need to spell out their objectives and develop new approaches "to confront such intractable problems as homelessness, drug addiction and urban violence". The challenge for these countries will be to strike a balance between market efficiency and social compassion.
* New people-oriented criteria for project appraisal will have to be developed. Experience has shown that even the most technically and economically sound development projects can result in considerable social and political damage — including increased disparities between urban and rural areas or between ethnic groups or between men and women. Yet most appraisal formulae used today are more concerned with the technical, financial and economic feasibility of projects and less with their impact on people.
* Foreign aid will have to be restructured in order to address both poverty and human development concerns. Currently, only 27% of foreign aid is earmarked for the poorest nations, and an even smaller proportion — 6.5% — is allocated to human needs around the world.

"The concept of human development has lent new vigour to the development debate in the 1990s". "What is important is to put the concept into practice. Human destiny rests on choice, not chance."

The *Human Development Report* notes that restricted and unequal access to the world's financial, trade and labour markets costs developing nations and their poor populations $500 billion annually — or nearly 10 times what they receive in foreign aid — and calls for dramatic changes to open up global markets, create more job opportunities, overhaul international institutions and strike a "global compact" between rich and poor nations to promote an equitable and peaceful world.

Such a compact would ensure that by the year 2000 developing attain their essential human goals, reduce absolute poverty by at least 5%, create sufficient jobs to absorb current unemployment and new additions to the labour force, and accelerate GDP growth rate to achieve these objectives. It would ensure at the same time implementation of such shared global objectives as controlling drug trafficking and pollution, containing immigration pressures and encouraging nuclear non-proliferation policies. A four point strategy to fund such a global compact is suggested:

* Reduce military expenditures by 3% a year through the 1990s to create a peace dividend of $1,500 billion - $1,200 billion in the industrial nations and $300 billion in the developing countries;
* Open up global markets, particularly in the labour-intensive exports of developing countries such as textiles, clothing, footwear, agricultural and tropical products;
* Reform foreign aid, the system of official development assistance (ODA), both to increase its volume and to distribute it more efficiently. The report suggests that at least two-thirds of ODA should be channelled to the poorest nations, compared with the present one-quarter, and at least 20A% should be devoted to human priority expenditure, compared with the present 7%.
* Strike a new global debt bargain to halt the current net transfer of $50 billion a year from developing to industrial countries.

Many developing countries should reform themselves for human development, too, says the report, it calls for more open governments, better economic management and massive investment in people and technology. A restructuring of budget priorities in the developing countries, particularly through reductions in military spending and privatization of inefficient public enterprises, can provide sufficient resources for the human capital formation they need for future growth.

The report also calls for major changes in the functioning of the World Bank, IMF, GATT, the Global Environment Facility (GEF) and UN programmes to ensure better management of the global economy in the interests of all nations and all people, particularly to promote greater access of the developing countries to opportunities of global markets.

It breaks ground in urging a Development Security Council within the United Nations. The Council would provide a prominent and powerful forum for global policy coordination, trusted by both industrial and developing countries. The Council would tackle all important issues on the global policy agenda, from food security to ecological security, from development assistance to humanitarian assistance, from debt problems to commodity problems, from drug trafficking to technology transfers. It would provide a policy framework for the work of international development and financial institutions. The Council should consist of 22 members — 11 permanent and 11 rotating. The permanent members would include China, France, Germany, Japan, Russia, United Kingdom, and United States, as well as the four most populous countries from each developing region: Brazil, Egypt, India and Nigeria.

Human Development Reports in 1990 and 1991 introduced the Human Development Index (HDI), which ranks countries not by gross national product but by combined rates of life expectancy, education and basic purchasing power. The reports concentrated on how developing nations and their aid donors could better mobilise their efforts for comprehensive human development strategies. To date, 20 developing countries have requested UNDP assistance to formulate their own human development strategies.

While this third report focuses more on the global dimensions of human development — how international trade, immigration and financial policies contribute to human development and income disparities between rich and poor nations — it also continues improving the HDI, updating the statistics from the 1984-85 range to 1990.

In 1992, Canada displaced Japan at the top of the HDI for industrial countries, while Romania stays at the bottom. Among developing countries, Barbados remains at the top, while Guinea has replaced Sierra Leone at the bottom.

In 1991, the report introduced a new human freedom index. Subsequent data showed that much more conceptual and methodological work was required to measure freedom. This year, a new methodology is suggested to construct a political freedom index based on generally accepted concepts and values. The major components of the political freedom index are personal security, rule of law, freedom of expression, political participation and equality of opportunity.

One of the preliminary findings of the report is that human development and political freedom seem to move in tandem: countries with high human development levels have an average political freedom ranking of 84%, while those with a low HDI rank have an average freedom index of 48%.

Source: *Go-Between*, Special Insert, May 1992. Based on a press kit prepared for the *Human Development Report 1992*.

3

ADVANCEMENT OF WOMEN: Highlights and Issues

3.1 Women in Politics and Economic Power: ILO Report

Despite performing exceptionally well in all areas of governance, women's accession to higher echelons of political and economic power is extremely slow and at today's pace would take five centuries to be at par with men.

As things stand at present, only six of the 179 stated members of the United Nations are governed by a woman. Women occupy barely 3.5 per cent of the ministerial cabinet posts.

Ninety-three countries have men heading their Ministries exclusively, says an International Labour Organisation (ILO) release entitled, "*Women in authority: the ideal and the reality*".

Most of the women in the leading positions in Government have broken new ground in education, culture, social welfare and women's issues.

The areas of activity in which women are most commonly accepted are actually "extensions" of the traditional roles that, throughout the world, the woman assumes in the family.

Public opinion is still surprised by the appointment of a woman to high office, especially so if this happens in spheres historically associated with supposed "male vocations".

Almost everywhere in the world, women have the vote and account for over half of the electorate, but with rare exceptions, however, their political activities are restricted to anonymous and informal roles in local communities. They hover at the margins of the higher levels of trade union, political, governmental and corporate life, and of interest groups.

Until 1987, women occupied barely 10 per cent of parliamentary seats, with the northern and eastern European countries taking the lead.

Recent political restructuring in Eastern Europe and in the former Soviet Union has brought with it a sharp fall in women's representation in those parliaments.

The same holds true for the trade union memberships.

This pattern of inequality is mirrored, indeed accentuated, in the employers' organizations where women are practically absent.

The "invisibility" of women in public life, and consequently in political, economic and professional activity, is both the cause and consequence of their being consistently barred from positions of authority.

The cultural and social models repeat themselves and creates a setting that is hardly conducive to women progressing much beyond the limits of their homes.

Enmeshed in a tangle of little encouragement and probable reprobation, women are hesitant about struggling to advance in profession or political careers, as to do so would frequently put at stake their role within the family circle.

On the other hand, as they hardly manage to participate fully in the decisions affecting their lives and families, it will prove difficult for them to breakout of the vicious circle.

The ILO release deals with the question of decision-making from three points of view.

First, as a question of human rights: Women make up half the population and more than one-third of the workforce and so their right to full citizenship and equality of opportunity and treatment in employment must be clearly expressed by their participation at all levels.

Secondly, as a matter of social justice to combat discrimination against women, which is very harsh when it comes to employment.

Thirdly, as an essential requirement for the acceleration and effectiveness of development, as women are capable of providing a different sort of ability and creativity, which has not so far been tapped, and they can ensure a better balance in the allocation of resources and distribution of the benefits of progress.

(Source: *Hindustan Times*, March 10, 1993)

3.2 **Women in the Government of the 150 Countries with Parliaments**

TABLE 3.1: Women in the Government of 150 Countries as on October 31, 1991

				Member of national government		
Country	Date of validity	Head of State	Head of govern-ment	Minis-ter(s)**	Deputy Minis-ter(s)	Other mini-sterial functions
1	2	3	4	5	6	7
Afghanistan*	06/91	No	No	2(?%)	No	Dept. Heads
Albania*	07/91	No	No	—	—	—
Algeria*	07/91	No	No	2(?%)	No	No
Angola*	07/91	No	No	—	—	—
Antigua and Barbuda	07/91	No	No			
Argentina*	07/91	No	H.S.			
Australia*	08/91	No	No	3(?%)	No	No
Austria*	06/91	No	No	2(?%)	No	1 s.s
Bahamas	07/91	No	No	—	—	—
Bangladesh*	07/91	No	Yes	—	—	—
Barbados	04/91	Yes	No	No	1(?%)	No
Belgium*	06/91	No	No	No	No	3 s.s (23%)
Belize	07/91	Yes	No	—	—	—
Benin	07/91	No	No	—	—	—
Bhutan	07/91	No	No	—	—	—
Bolivia*	07/91	No	H.S.	—	—	—
Botswana	05/91	No	H.S.	1(?%)	No	No
Brazil*	07/91	No	H.S.	—	—	—

1	2	3	4	5	6	7
Bulgaria*	07/91	No	No	1(?%)	—	—
Cameroon*	06/91	No	No	1(?%)	No	No
Canada*	06/91	No	No	7(?%)	No	6 p.s.
Cape Verde*	07/91	No	No	—	—	—
Cent. African Rep.*	03/91	No	No	1(?%)	1(?%)	No
Chile*	06/91	No	H.S.	1(?%)	—	5 sub-s.s.
China*	07/91	No	No	—	—	—
Colombia*	11/91	No	H.S.	1(?%)	—	—
Comoros	07/91	No	H.S.	—	—	—
Congo*	11/91	No	No	—	—	—
Costa Rica*	07/91	No	H.S.	—	—	—
Côte d'Ivoire*	07/91	No	No	—	—	—
Cuba*	06/91	No	H.S.	—	—	—
Cyprus*	06/91	No	No	No	No	No
Czechoslovakia*	07/91	No	No	—	—	—
Dem. People's Rep. of Korea*	07/91	No	No	2(?%)	2(?%)	—
Denmark*	05/91	Yes	No	4(21%)	No	No
Djibouti*	07/91	No	No	—	—	—
Dominica	07/91	No	Yes	No	No	No
Dominican Republic*	07/91	No	H.S.	—	—	—
Ecuador*	07/91	No	No	—	—	—
Egypt*	07/91	No	No	1(?%)	No	No
El Salvador*	07/91	No	H.S.	—	—	—
Equatorial Guinea*	07/91	No	H.S.	1(?%)	No	No
Estonia*	11/91	No	No	—	—	—
Ethiopia*	11/91	No	No	—	—	—
Finland*	07/91	No	No	—	—	—
France*	06/91	No	Yes	4(21%)	2(20%)	1 s.s. (6.25%)
Gabon*	07/91	No	No	3(1.1%)	No	1 s.s.
Gambia	07/91	No	H.S.	—	—	—
Germany*	06/91	No	No	5(7%)		3 s.s.
Greece*	06/91	No	No	1(?%)	1(?%)	3 u.s.s.
Grenada	07/91	No	No	—	—	—
Guatemala*	07/91	No	H.S.	—	—	—
Guinea-Bissau	07/91	No	H.S.	—	—	—
Guyana	05/91	No	No	6(30%)	No	No
Haiti	07/91	No	No	—	—	—
Honduras*	07/91	No	H.S.	—	—	—
Hungary*	07/91	No	No	2(6%)	2(?%)	No
Iceland*	07/91	Yes	No	—	—	—
India*	**05/91**	**No**	**No**	**1(?%)**	**No**	**No**
Indonesia*	06/91	No	H.S.	2(?%)	No	No
Iran (Isl. Rep. of)*	07/91	No	No	No	No	No
Iraq*	07/91	No	H.S.	—	—	—
Ireland*	07/91	Yes	No	—	—	—
Israel*	05/91	No	No	No	No	No
Italy*	07/91	No	No	2(6%)	No	3 sub-s.s. (4.5%)

1	2	3	4	5	6	7
Jamaica*	07/91	Vac.	No	—	—	—
Japan*	06/91	No	No	1(?%)	No	No
Jordan*	07/91	No	No	—	—	—
Kenya*	07/91	No	H.S.	—	—	—
Kiribati	07/91	No	H.S.	—	—	—
Kuwait*	11/91	No	No	No	No	No
Lao People's Dem. Republic*	07/91	No	No	—	—	—
Latvia*	11/91	No	—	—	—	—
Lebanon*	07/91	No	No	—	—	—
Liberia*	11/91	No	NO	—	—	—
Libyan Arab Jamahiriya*	07/91	No	H.S.	—	—	—
Liechtenstein	07/91	No	No	—	—	—
Lithuania*	11/91	No	—	—	—	—
Luxembourg*	07/91	No	No	No	No	1 s.s.
Madagascar*	07/91	No	No	—	—	—
Malawi	07/91	No	H.S.	—	—	—
Malaysia*	07/91	No	No	—	—	—
Maldives	07/91	No	H.S.	—	—	—
Malta*	07/91	No	No	—	—	—
Mauritius	07/91	No	No	—	—	—
Mexico*	07/91	No	H.S.	—	—	—
Monaco*	07/91	No	H.S.	—	—	—
Mongolia*	06/91	No	No	No	—	—
Morocco*	06/91	No	No	No	No	No
Mozambique*	07/91	No	No	—	—	—
Namibia*	07/91	No	No	2(?%)	1(?%)	No
Nauru	07/91	No	H.S.	—	—	—
Nepal*	07/91	No	No	—	—	—
Netherlands*	07/91	Yes	No	—	—	—
New Zealand*	06/91	Yes	No	3(11.5%)	No	No
Nicaragua*	05/91	Yes	No	No	No	No
Niger*	07/91	No	H.S.	—	—	—
Norway*	06/91	No	Yes	9(47%)	Various	No
Pakistan*	07/91	No	No	—	—	—
Panama*	07/91	No	H.S.	No	No	No
Papua New Guinea*	07/91	No	No	—	—	—
Paraguay*	07/91	No	H.S.	1(?%)	No	No
Peru*	07/91	No	No	—	—	—
Philippines*	07/91	Yes	No	1(3.6%)	No	32(20.5%)[1]
Poland*	06/91	No	No	1(?%)	No	No
Portugal*	07/91	No	No	—	—	—
Republic of Korea*	07/91	No	No	1(?%)	No	No
Romania*	07/91	No	No	No	No	No
Rwanda*	04/91	No	H.S.	No	No	No
Saint Kitts and Navis	07/91	No	No	—	—	—
Saint Lucia	04/91	No	No	No	No	No
Saint Vincent and the Grenadines	07/91	No	No	—	—	—
San Marino*	07/91	No	H.S.	1(?%)	No	No
Sao Tome and Principe	07/91	No	No	—	—	—

1	2	3	4	5	6	7
Senegal*	04/91	No	No	2(9.5%)	No	No
Seychelles	06/91	No	H.S.	3(30%)	No	No
Sierra Leone	07/91	No	H.S.	—	—	—
Singapore*	07/91	No	No	—	—	—
Solomon Islands	07/91	No	No	—	—	—
South Africa	05/91	No	No	1(?%)	No	No
Spain*	07/91	No	No	—	—	—
Sri Lanka*	07/91	No	No	1(3.8%)[2]	—	—
Suriname*	07/91	No	No	—	—	—
Swaziland	07/91	No	No	—	—	—
Sweden*	07/91	No	No	—	—	—
Switzerland*	07/91	No	H.S.	—	—	—
Syrian Arab Republic*	07/91	No	No	1(?%)	No	No
Thailand*	07/91	No	No	—	—	—
Togo*	08/91	No	No	—	—	—
Tonga	07/91	No	No	—	—	—
Trinidad and Tobago	07/91	No	No	—	—	—
Tunisia*	07/91	No	No	No	No	No
Turkey*	03/91	No	No	1(?%)	No	No
Tuvalu	07/91	No	No	—	—	—
Uganda*	04/91	No	H.S.	4(?%)	4(?%)	No
Union of Soviet Socialist Rep.	6/91	No	No	2(?%)	1(?%)	No
United Arab. Emirates*	07/91	No	No	—	—	—
United Kingdom*	06/91	Yes	No	4(13.8%)	No	No
United Republic of Tanzania*	07/91	No	H.S.	—	—	—
United States of America*	05/91	No	H.S.	—	—	—
Uruguay*	07/91	No	H.S.	—	—	—
Vanuatu	04/91	No	No	No	No	No
Venezuela*	07/91	No	H.S.	—	—	—
Viet Nam*	06/91	No	No	No	2(?%)	No
Western Samoa	07/91	No	No	—	—	—
Yemen*	07/91	No	No	—	—	—
Yugoslavia*	06/91	No	No	No	No	No
Zaire*	07/91	No	No	—	—	—
Zambia*	07/91	No	H.S.	—	—	—
Zimbabwe*	06/91	No	No	3(0.6%)	6(?%)	No

1 *Philippines*: Deputies, Under-Secretaries, Assistant Secretaries.

2 *Sri Lanka*: 1 (out of 26) Cabinet Ministers: (3.8%); 2(out of 23) Ministers not in the Cabinet: (8.7%); 3 (out of 29) Ministers of State: (10.3%).

* Parliament represented in the Inter-Parliamentary Union as on 31-10-91

** Excluding Head of Government when she is the Prime Minister

— No information available

H.S. There is no Prime Minister and the Head of State is the Head of the Government

p.s. Parliamentary Secretary

s.s. Secretary of State

sub-s.s Sub-Secretary of State

u.s.s. Under Secretary of State

vac. Vacant

(Source: *Inter-Parliamentary Union, Women and Political Power,* Series "Reports and Documents", No. 19, Geneva, 1992, p. 163)

3.3 Data on Women[1]

TABLE 3.2: Data on Women

Item	Year	India	Country with best position	No. of countries for which data available	**India's position in the world**
1. Adult literacy rate as % of males	1990	**55**	Venezuela (103)	89	**66**
2. % of pregnant women immunised against Tetanus	1990-91	**80**	Korea, Dem. Rep. (99)	83	**22**
3. % of contraceptive prevalence	1990-92	**43**	Belgium (81) Hong Kong (81)	109	**54**

3.4 Convention on the Elimination of All Forms of Discrimination against Women

The Convention on the Elimination of All Forms of Discrimination against Women was adopted on December 18, 1979 and entered into force on September 3, 1981. The success of the Convention is reflected in the 114 ratifications and accessions received by May 14, 1992.

The Convention recalls that discrimination against women violates the principles of equality of rights and respect for human dignity, is an obstacle to the participation of women, on equal terms with men, in the political, social, economic and cultural life of their countries, hampers the growth of the prosperity of society and the family and makes more difficult the full development of the potentialities of women in the service of their countries and of humanity. The text of the Convention contains universal and inalienable rights that are already embedded in the Charter of the United Nations. It is an internationally binding legal instrument, which sets international standards for the treatment of women in all areas of life and guarantees their rights to a life of full equality, to self-development and to full participation in all aspects of society. The existence of inconsistencies between customary and State laws is a common problem in many developing countries. Customary laws are often recognized particularly when they do not seem to conflict with State laws.

Measures provide for women equal rights with men in political and public life; equal access to education and the same choice as men of curricula; non-discrimination in employment and pay; and guarantees of job security in the event of marriage and maternity. The Convention underlines the equal responsibilities of men and women in the context of family life. It also stresses the social services needed, especially child-care facilities, to enable family obligations to be combined with work responsibilities and participation in public life. Additional articles of the Convention call for non-discriminatory health-care services for women, including those related to family planning, the accordance to women

1. *See also* Chapter 7, Section 8 for detailed Data.

of a legal capacity identical to that of men, and requires that States parties agree that all contracts and other private instruments that restrict the legal capacity of women "shall be deemed null and void". Article 5 requires States parties to modify the social and cultural patterns of conduct of men and women with a view to achieving the elimination to prejudices and customary and all other practices that are based on the idea of the inferiority or the superiority of either of the sexes or on stereotyped roles for men and women.

Under article 18, States parties undertake to submit a report within one year of ratification of the Convention, and thereafter at least every four years, on the legislative, judicial, administrative or other measures that they have adopted to give effect to the provisions of the convention and on the progress made.

By becoming a party to the Convention, a State makes an international commitment to the principle of the dignity and worth of all its citizens and to the eradication of all discrimination that precludes women from the enjoyment of their human rights and fundamental freedoms. The legal obligations under the Convention are threefold: first, the Convention addresses the removal of discriminatory laws and obstacles to equality; second, it promotes equality by affirmative action; and third; it aims at eliminating attitudes, conduct, prejudices and practices that are based on the inferiority or superiority of either sex.

The Convention can only take effect, however, if it reaches all levels of society. Attitudes must be changed at the grass-roots level, inside families and throughout society at large in order to end discrimination.

3.5 **Committee on the Elimination of Discrimination against Women**

The Committee on the Elimination of Discrimination against Women was established in accordance with article 17 of the Convention. It meets annually to examine reports submitted by States parties under the terms of article 18.

The Committee is composed of "twenty-three experts of high moral standing and competence in the field covered by the Convention". The experts are elected by the States parties from among national candidates and serve in their personal capacity. Consideration is given to equitable geographical distribution and to the representation of different forms of civilization as well as the principal legal systems.

The experts who have served on the Committee for the first 10 years have indeed reflected these ideals. While most have been lawyers, judges or legal scholars, they have also included specialists in economics, diplomacy, mass communications and sociology.

During the consideration of country reports, the Government representative and the Committee members engage in a constructive dialogue, an exchange of ideas and experiences, in order to identify gaps and obstacles to achieving equality and to encourage new endeavours. Questioning during the presentation of a country report has even provoked occasional minor changes in national law and at least a few parties have appeared willing to use their dealings with the Committee as an occasion for a genuine review and re-examination of national laws, policies and practices.

3.6 **Fourth World Conference on Women, 1995**

The Fourth World Conference on Women: Action for Equality, Development and

Peace will be held at Beijing, China, from 4 to 15 September 1995.

The Commission on the Status of Women is the preparatory body for the Conference and, as such, discussed organizational and substantive issues pertaining to the Conference and its preparations at its thirty-fifth and thirty-sixth sessions. In order to provide readers with the current status. Commission resolutions 35/4 and 36/8 as well as decision 35/101 are reproduced below in full.

Resolution 35.4. Preparations for the World Conference on Women in 1995

The Commission on the Status of Women,

Bearing in mind General Assembly resolution 45/129 of 14 December 1990, in which the General Assembly endorsed Economic and Social Council resolution 1990/12 of 24 May 1990 recommending that a world conference on women should be held in 1995.

Taking into account Economic and Social Council resolution 1990/15 on the recommendations and conclusions arising from the first review and appraisal of the implementation of the Nairobi Forward-looking Strategies for the Advancement of Women to the year 2000.

Considering that the world conference on women should result in the full implementation of key aspects of the Forward-looking Strategies up to the year 2000.

Considering also that the world conference on women should focus world attention on the situation of women and should result in a renewal of political commitment:

1. *Decides to* prepare for consideration by the world conference on women in 1995 a programme of action comprising a limited number of issues that have been identified as representing a fundamental obstacle to the advancement of the majority of women;
2. *Decides also* that, within the programme of action, goals should be established, if possible in quantitative terms, and concise, action-oriented guidelines should be provided to accelerate the implementation of the Nairobi Forward-looking Strategies for the Advancement of Women;
3. *Decides further* that the programme of action should continue to focus on equality, development and peace and should include the following elements:

    (a) The strengthening of efforts at the national and international levels, taking into account the circumstances in each country, to increase awareness among men and women of women's rights under international conventions and national law;

    (b) The implementation of special measures to increase the proportion of women involved in decision-making in the economic, social and political spheres;

    (c) The strengthening of world-wide efforts to end illiteracy among women and girls by the year 2000;

    (d) The establishment of specific programmes for improving the conditions of women and girls living in poverty, particularly those living in extreme poverty, by *inter alia*, adequate training to develop their skills and capabilities;

(e) The establishment of specific programmes aimed at improving women's and girls' health by ensuring them access to adequate maternal health care, family planning and nutrition;

(f) The implementation of policies to prevent, control and reduce violence against women and girls in the family, the workplace and society;

(g) The establishment or strengthening of national institutional mechanisms for the advancement of women;

(h) The establishment of special programmes aimed at meeting the specific needs of refugee, displaced and migrant women and girls and those living in conflict areas;

(i) The elaboration of ways and means of using new and high technologies; as well as scientific research, to benefit women;

4. Requests the Secretary-General to submit to the Commission on the Status of Women, as its thirty-seventh session, a report on existing technical and financial cooperation targeting programmes in favour of women, as well as guidelines for a comprehensive plan to overcome constraints and increase such cooperation with regard to the elements set out above;
5. Requests the Secretary-General to submit to the Commission at its thirty-sixth session a draft report to serve as a working document for the elaboration of the programme of action, based on existing United Nations data, bearing in mind that the programme of action should be concrete and concise, capable of leading to feasible, effective and immediate action, as well as awareness and political will on the part of Governments and governmental and non-governmental organizations;
6. Requests the bodies, regional commissions, specialized agencies and other organizations of the United Nations system, as well as the non-governmental organizations concerned, to contribute to the preparations for the world conference on women in 1995;
7. Requests the Secretary-General to report to the Commission at its thirty-sixth session on the contribution of bodies, regional commissions, specialized agencies and other organizations of the United Nations system, as well as the non-governmental agencies concerned, to the preparations for the conference.

Resolution 36/8. Preparations for the Fourth World Conference on Women: Action for Equality, Development and Peace

The Commission on the Status of Women,

Recalling the Nairobi Forward-looking Strategies for the Advancement of Women,[2] endorsed by the General Assembly in its resolution 40/108 of 13 December 1985,

2. *Report of the World Conference to Review and Appraise the Achievements of the United Nations Decade for Women: Equality, Development and Peace, Nairobi, 15-26 July 1985* (United Nations Publication, Sales No. E.85.IV.10), Chap. I, Sect. A.

Recalling also Economic and Social Council resolution 1987/20 of 26 May 1987, in which the Council decided that the Commission on the Status of Women should be designated as the preparatory body for world conferences on women,

Recalling further Economic and Social Council resolution 1990/15 of 24 May 1990, on the recommendations and conclusions arising from the first review and appraisal of the implementation of the Nairobi Forward-looking Strategies for the Advancement of Women to the year 2000.

Recalling also its resolution 35/4 on preparations for the world conference on women in 1995 and decision 35/101 on the title of the Conference,

A

Organization of the Conference

Noting with appreciation the offers made by the Governments of Austria and China to act as host for the Fourth World Conference on Women: Action for Equality, Development and Peace, and the forum for non-governmental organizations,

Taking into consideration General Assembly resolution 46/98 of 16 December 1991, in which the Assembly requested the Commission to decide on the venue of the Fourth World Conference on Women not later than at its thirty-sixth session, in accordance with Commission decision 35/102, bearing in mind that preference should be given to the region that had not yet hosted a world conference on women,

Considering the duration of previous world conferences on women, as well as similar United Nations conferences,

Bearing in mind that the Conference in 1995 coincides with the fiftieth anniversary of the United Nations,

Affirming the importance to the success of the Conference of the maximum participation of Governments at the highest possible level, of intergovernmental organizations, organizations of the United Nations system and interested non-governmental organizations, as well as other regional organizations acting through their representatives of the Commission,

Recalling that the General Assembly, in its resolution 46/98, requested the Secretary-General to appoint not later than 1992 the Secretary-General of the Conference,

Recalling its resolution 35/4, in which it decided to prepare programme of action for consideration by the Conference,

1. *Decides*

(a) To accept the offer of the Government of China to act as host for the Fourth World Conference on Women: Action for Equality, Development and Peace, in accordance with General Assembly resolution 40/243 of 18 December 1985;
(b) That the Conference should be of a duration of ten working days;
(c) That the Conference should be held at Beijing from 4 to 15 September 1995;

2. *Also decides* to recommend that participation in the Conference should be

open to:

(a) All States Members of the United Nations or of any of the specialized agencies or of the International Atomic Energy Agency;

(b) Representatives of organizations that have received a standing invitation from the General Assembly to participate in the sessions and the work of all international conferences convened under its auspices in the capacity of observers to participate in the Conference in that capacity, in accordance with General Assembly resolution 3237 (XXIX) of 22 November 1974 and 43/177 of 15 December 1988;

(c) Representatives of the national liberation movements recognized in its region by the Organization of African Unity to participate in the Conference in the capacity of observers, in accordance with General Assembly resolution 3280 (XXIX) of 10 December 1974;

(d) The executive heads of the specialized agencies and the International Atomic Energy Agency, as well as interested organizations of the United Nations system;

(e) Other interested intergovernmental organizations, to be represented by observers at the Conference;

(f) Interested non-governmental organizations in consultative status with the Economic and Social Council, to be represented by observers at the Conference;

(g) Individuals who, in recognition of their personal contributions to the advancement of women, are invited by the Secretary-General;

(h) Members of the Committee on the Elimination of Discrimination against Women;

3. *Requests* the Economic and Social Council to request the Committee on Non-Governmental Organizations to consider on a priority basis, in advance of the Conference, the granting of consultative status to more non-governmental organizations concerned with the advancement of women, with particular attention being given to applications from non-governmental organizations from developing countries, and also requests that the Committee on Non-Governmental Organizations be provided with additional resources to deal with the additional workload;

4. *Recommends* that the arrangements for consultation with non-governmental organizations, as approved by the Economic and Social Council in its resolution 1296 (XLIV) of 23 May 11968, be reviewed to make consultative status more accessible to non-governmental organizations, particularly those from developing countries;

5. *Recommends* that the Secretary-General appoint a woman as Secretary-General of the Conference, not later than 1992, who should have international stature in relation to the advancement of women and experience in the United Nations system, and who would assume primary responsibility for the preparation of the Conference;

6. *Also recommends* that, in appointing the necessary staff for the Conference, the Secretary-General include persons from the developing and the least developed countries, taking into consideration equitable geographical distribution;

7. *Decides* that the agenda for the Conference shall include:

(a) The second review and appraisal of the implementation of the Nairobi Forward-looking Strategies for the Advancement of Women to the year 2000;
(b) The Platform for Action;
(c) The main conclusions and recommendations of regional preparatory conferences;
(d) Institutional arrangements for the implementation of the Platform;

8. *Requests* the Secretary-General to submit a report to the Commission on the Status of Women, at its thirty-seventh session, containing a first draft, which will serve as a working document for the elaboration of the Platform of Action, taking as a basis all guidelines contained in Commission resolution 35/4, the impact of the changes that have taken place in the international community on the status of women, the importance of integrating gender perspectives in policy-making in all areas and at all levels, the need to give priority to the situation of rural women, in particular in developing countries, and differences in priorities among regions, based on a full input from the organizations of the United Nations system, as well as other regional organizations acting through their representatives to the Commission;
9. *Also requests* the Secretary-General to submit to the Commission at its thirty-seventh session a report containing (a) information on data that would be used in the formulation of the second report on the implementation of the Nairobi Forward-looking Strategies and (b) an outline of the second report, in which special emphasis should be given to the recommendations and conclusions arising from the first review and appraisal of the implementation of the Strategies, contained in the annex to Council resolution 1990/15, in particular those referring to the condition of women in developing countries;
10. *Further requests* the Secretary-General to prepare draft rules of procedure for consideration by the Commission at its thirty-eighth session.

B
Preparatory process

Emphasizing the importance of national preparatory activities in focusing national attention on the issue of the status and advancement of women for national machinery to assess the situation and mobilize national non-governmental organizations and individuals, with a view to improving national performance in the advancement of women,

Considering the importance of activities for the advancement of women that have taken place at the regional level since International Women's Year and recognizing the necessity of providing for an exchange of national experiences and the elaboration of regional priorities and perspectives for the Fourth World Conference on Women: Action for Equality, Development and Peace, and to the year 2000,

Recalling Economic and Social Council resolution 1990/9 of 24 May 1990 on the second report on the implementation of the Nairobi Forward-looking Strategies for the Advancement of Women,

Recognizing the importance of non-governmental organizations in the preparations for the Conference at the national, regional and global levels, especially the forum for non-governmental organizations, which will take place prior to and partially simultaneously with the Conference,

Acknowledging the important role of women entrepreneurs, notably in small and medium-sized enterprises, in mobilizing resources and in promoting economic growth and socio-economic development,

Convinced that promotion of the Conference requires the creative and effective use of public information,

1. *Recommends* that Governments establish a national committee or designate a national focal point to initiate and promote preparations for the Fourth World Conference on Women: Action of Equality, Development and Peace, by organizing and coordinating national activities, including assembling information and gender-disaggregated statistics for the elaboration of national reports on the situation of women, and increasing public awareness about the Conference, and requests that reports on such activities be made available to the Secretary-General;
2. *Urges* organizations of the United Nations system, at the national level, to cooperate with national efforts to prepare for the Conference and to coordinate their activities through the United Nations Resident Coordinator;
3. *Requests* the Secretary-General to inform Governments about the recommendation regarding national committees or focal points;
4. *Recommends* that the national reports cited in paragraph 1 above cover the period from 1985 to the present;
5. *Urges* the organizations of the United Nations system to provide support, on request, to the preparation of national reports;
6. *Recommends* that regional conferences already scheduled include in their agendas preparations for the World Conference and suggests that, in those regions that have not yet scheduled them, regional conferences to prepare for the World Conference be organized under the auspices of the corresponding regional commission;
7. *Requests* regional conferences to identify regional trends, priorities, obstacles and innovative suggestions for future action and that the results of those regional conferences be provided to the Commission on the Status of Women not later than at its thirty-ninth session;
8. *Recommends* that regional conferences include in their agenda the issue of women in public life, emphasizing their role in politics and decision-making;
9. *Requests* the Secretary-General to include in the preparations of the priority theme on peace, "women in international decision-making", for the Commission at its thirty-ninth session, information on women in public life;
10. *Recommends* that a public information strategy for the Conference be designed, using information mechanisms that reach the greatest number of people and based on the conference themes, in particular those related to development;
11. *Also recommends* that regional conferences include in their agenda the issue of entrepreneurship and the advancement of women, emphasizing the need to facilitate an overall entrepreneurial activity through appropriate economic policies, training, access to credit, information and other support systems;
12. *Requests* the Secretary-General to plan and implement an information

campaign and to issue a new bulletin entitled *Conference 95* twice a year to disseminate information on preparatory activities for the Conference at all levels in all official languages;

13. *Also requests* the Secretary-General to provide Governments with a concise set of guidelines for public information campaigns at the national level and with periodic information packages that can be made available to national mass media and non-governmental organizations;
14. *Further requests* the Secretary-General to report to the Commission at its thirty-seventh session on the planning and implementation of the complete information campaign, including its priorities and resource needs;
15. *Requests* the Secretary-General to include the Conference as part of the celebrations for the Fiftieth Anniversary of the United Nations.

C
Forum for non-governmental organizations

Recalling successful forums for non-governmental organizations held in Mexico, Copenhagen and Nairobi,

Acknowledging the offer by the host Government to all non-governmental organizations and individuals wishing to attend the forum in Beijing,

1. *Emphasizing* the importance of close proximity between the forum and the Fourth World Conference: Action for Equality, Development and Peace, as well as some concurrence in time;
2. *Invites* the committee of non-governmental organizations arranging the forum and national and regional activities to provide information, including media arrangements, to the Commission on the Status of Women through a report of the Secretary-General on preparations for the Conference;
3. *Emphasizing* the importance of unrestricted participation by the media in covering the forum;

D
Resources for the Conference and its Preparations

Recalling General Assembly resolution 46/98 of 16 December 1991, in which concern was expressed that the resources of the Fourth World Conference on Women: Action for Equality, Development and Peace, were not sufficient, and Assembly resolution 46/185 of 20 December 1991, in which the Assembly requested the Secretary-General to ensure that adequate resources are provided for the preparation of the Conference during the biennium 1992-93,

Desiring to ensure the maximum representation by Governments, especially of the least developed countries, in the regional preparatory process and in the Conference,

1. *Requests* the Economic and Social Council to reconsider the budget envisaged for the Fourth World Conference on Women: Action for Equality, Development and Peace, on the basis of a report of the Secretary-General outlining resource requirements for regional and interregional preparatory activities, public information activities and for the Conference itself;

2. *Urges* Governments, intergovernmental organizations, non-governmental organizations and individuals to contribute extrabudgetary resources to the trust fund established by the Secretary-General for the preparations of the Conference, especially for the participation of representatives of the least developed countries in regional meetings and in the Conference;
3. *Urges* Governments, international organizations and multilateral financial institutions to provide assistance to the least developed countries for their preparatory activities at the national level;

E

Documentation

1. *Decides* that the documentation for the Fourth World Conference on Women: Action for Equality, Development and Peace, will include:

* Report of the Secretary-General on the second review and appraisal of the implementation of the Nairobi Forward-looking Strategies for the Advancement of Women;
* Draft final document (Platform for Action);
* Update of the World Survey on the Role of Women in Development;
* Update of the World's Women: Trends and Statistics;
* Update compendium on the implementation of the Convention on the Elimination of All Forms of Discrimination against Women;
* Report of the Secretary-General on the outcome of regional preparatory meetings for the Fourth World Conference on Women: Action for Equality, Development and Peace;
* Relevant sections of final documents emanating from the United Nations Conference on the Environment and Development, the World Conference on Human Rights and the International Conference on Population and Development.

Decision 35/101. Title of the World Conference on Women in 1995

At its 13th meetings, on 8 March 1991, the Commission on the Status of Women decided:

(a) That the world conference on women in 1995 should be entitled "fourth World Conference on Women: Action for Equality, Development and Peace";
(b) That promotion of the world conference at the national level could also utilize additional formulations, such as the following sub-titles:

(i) Remove the Obstacles Now;
(ii) Women: Half the World — Half the Power;
(iii) Women: Mobilizing for Power — Acting for Change;
(iv) Social Justice for Women;

(c) That the results of the use of additional formulations at the national level should be made available to the Secretariat for inclusion in reports on the preparations for the world conference.

Non-governmental Organizations

Activities leading up to the World Conference and the NGO Forum are being coordinated by a Planning Committee which meets each year at the time of the Commission. The Steering Committee currently comprises the Coordinator, the presidents of the NGO Committees on Women in New York, Geneva and Vienna, the President of the Conference of Non-governmental Organizations in Consultative Status with the United Nations Economic and Social Council (CONGO). A Convenor has yet to be appointed. The Third Planning Committee Consultation took place on 9 and 10 March 1992. Topics discussed included budget and finance; media and public relations; and regional conferences. The following action plan was suggested to ensure the mobilization of national affiliates of international non-governmental organizations.

Suggested Action Plan

1. Contact national affiliates immediately with request/suggestion

   1.1 To begin establishment of national open to a broad variety of concerned organizations.
   1.2 To develop national priorities and to increase efforts to integrate women in all aspects of development such as positive action to implement the provisions of the Convention on the Elimination of all Forms of Discrimination against Women and the Forward-looking Strategies.
   1.3 To ask national affiliates to report back to international headquarters-even on an interim basis-about action taken.
   1.4 To send reports to Steering Committee at address of the secretariat, where a task force will receive the answers and prepare a report to the 1993 Consultation and Commission on the Status of Women.

2. Purpose

These coalitions should start the networking process by establishing contacts with governments and national machinery for the advancement of women

   2.1. In order to ensure NGO participation in national appraisal processes and
   2.2. To contribute to national reports and proposals for national platforms of action
   2.3. Once the structure has been established, national NGOs' concerns can be fed into the regional preparatory process.

3. Suggested timetable

March 1992: INGOs reach out to their national affiliates suggesting to establish national coalition.

March 1993: Reports received by Steering Committee will have been fed in to Secretary-General's report to the Commission on the Status of Women acting as preparatory body for the 1995 Conference.

During 1993: Regional NGO preparations will reflect national concerns and regional NGO Committees/Networks should be established.

March 1994: Final contributions to national report or write own NGO report and discuss with Governments.

During 1994:
(a) Organization of regional forums in conjunction with the United Nations regional meetings;
(b) Reporting back to Steering Committee, so that it can report to the Commission on the Status of Women at the last preparatory meeting in March 1995.

4

CHILD WELFARE AND DEVELOPMENT

4.1 The State of the World's Children, 1993

Amid all the problems of a world bleeding from continuing wars and environmental wounds, it is nonetheless becoming clear that one of the greatest of all human aspirations is now within reach. Within a decade, it should be possible to bring to an end the age-old evils of child malnutrition, preventable disease, and widespread illiteracy.

As an indication of how close that goal might be, the financial cost can be put at about $25 billion a year.[1] That is the UNICEF estimate of the extra resources required to put into practice today's low-cost strategies for protecting the world's children. Specifically, it is an estimate of the cost of controlling the major childhood diseases, halving the rate of child malnutrition, bringing clean water and safe sanitation to all communities, making family planning services universally available, and providing almost every child with at least a basic education.

In practice, financial resources are a necessary but not sufficient prerequisite for meeting these basic needs. Sustained political commitment and a great deal of managerial competence are even more important. Yet it is necessary to reduce this challenge to the denominator of dollars in order to dislodge the idea that abolishing the worst aspects of poverty is a task too vast to be attempted or too expensive to be afforded.

To put the figure of $ 25 billion in perspective, it is considerably less than the amount the Japanese Government has allocated this year to the building of a new highway from Tokyo to Kobe; it is two to three times as much as the cost of the tunnel soon to be opened between the United Kingdom and France; it is less than the cost of the Ataturk Dam complex now being constructed in eastern Turkey; it is a little more than Hong Kong proposes to spend on a new airport; it is about the same as the support package that the Group of Seven has agreed on in 1992 for Russia alone; and it is significantly less than Europeans will spend this year on wine or Americans on beer.

Whatever the other difficulties may be, the time has therefore come to banish in shame the notion that the world cannot afford to meet the basic needs of almost every man, woman and child for adequate food, safe water, primary health care, family planning, and a basic education.

---

1. In 1990, UNICEF estimated at $20 billion a year the extra financial resources needed to meet health, nutrition, education, and water and sanitation goals agreed at the World Summit for Children. Estimates for the additional resources required also to meet family planning goals have since become available and this has increased the overall estimate to approximately $25 billion a year.

Present Budget Allocation of Governments of Developing Countries

If so much could be achieved for so many at so little cost, then the public in both industrialized and developing countries might legitimately ask why it is not being done.

In part, the answer is the predictable one: meeting the needs of the poorest and the least politically influential has rarely been a priority of governments. Yet the extent of present neglect in the face of present opportunity is a scandal of which the public is largely unaware. On average, the governments of the developing world are today devoting little more than 10 per cent of their budgets to directly meeting the basic needs of their people. More is still being spent on military capacity and on debt servicing than on health and education.

Perhaps more surprising still, less than 10 per cent of all international aid for development is devoted to directly meeting these most obvious of human needs. And as total bilateral aid from the Western industrialized nations is now running at approximately $40 billion a year, this means the amount given for nutrition, primary health care, water and sanitation, primary education, and family planning, comes to about $4 billion a year. This is less than half as much as the aid-giving nations spend each year on sports shoes. It could therefore fairly be said that the problem today is not that overcoming the worst aspects of world poverty is too vast or too expensive a task; it is that it has not seriously been tried.

A Watershed

With the beginning of the 1990s has come new hope that the age of the neglect may be giving way to the age of concern.

The evidence for this new hope, amid all the seismic shifts in the political and economic landscape of recent years, is a series of quieter changes which have not made the nightly news but which have affected the daily lives of many millions of people.

The first of these changes is the entirely new priority that has been given to the task of immunizing the world's children. For a decade, national health services, UNICEF, the World Health Organization (WHO) and many thousands of individuals and organizations have struggled towards the goal of 80 per cent immunization, coverage in the developing world. In 1990, that goal was reached. The result is the saving of over 3 million children's lives each year, and the protection of many millions more from malnutrition, disease and disability.

The significance of this achievement goes beyond these extraordinary statistics. Eighty per cent immunization means that approximately 100 million children are being reached by a modern medical technique on four or five separate occasions during their first year of life. As a logistical achievement, it is unprecedented; and it shows beyond any doubt that the outreach capacity now exists to put the basic benefits of scientific progress at the disposal of the vast majority of the world's poor. Secondly, it demonstrates that progress can now be made towards basic social goals even by the poorest of developing countries. Over the last five years, immunization coverage has been lifted dramatically in many nations with per capita incomes of less than $500 a year.

Other advances in knowledge and technique are now lining up outside the door that immunization has unlocked. And the potential remains enormous.

Thirty-five thousand children under five die in the developing world every day. Almost 60 per cent of those deaths, and much of the world's illness and malnutrition, are caused by just three diseases — pneumonia, diarrhoea and measles — all of which can now be prevented or treated by means which are tried and tested, available and affordable.

Similarly, the Vitamin A deficiency which threatens up to 10 million of the world's children with death, serious illness, and loss of eyesight, could not be brought under control at a cost which is negligible in relation to the benefits it would bring.

Or to take another example, the iodine deficiencies that lower the mental and physical abilities to up to a billion people and are the world's single biggest cause of mental retardation could also now be eliminated at a total cost of approximately $100 million — less than the cost of two modern fighter planes.

Even those aspects of poverty which have traditionally been considered the most expensive and the most logistically stubborn — the lack of adequate nutrition, safewater supply, and basic education — are also now becoming susceptible to a combination of new technologies, falling costs, and community-based strategies. The cost of providing clean water in Africa, for example, has been halved since the mid-1980s and now stands at an average figure of about $20 per person per year. Similarly, countries such as Bangladesh and Colombia have demonstrated that a basic, relevant education can be provided at a cost of approximately $20 per child per year. Equally large-scale trials in Africa and in India have shown that the incidence of child malnutrition can also now be halved at a cost of less than $10 per child per year.

New Goals

These advances in technology and strategy, and the extraordinary potential they have revealed, were the principal concern of the World Summit for Children held at the United Nations in September 1990 — at about the same time as the immunization goal was being reached. The Summit was attended by approximately half the world's Presidents and Prime Ministers and resulted in a set of specific commitments which, if implemented, would indeed mark the beginning of a new era of concern.

Those commitments, designed to reflect the potential of the knowledge and the technologies now available, were expressed as a series of specific goals to be achieved by the end of the present century. These goals include: control of the major childhood diseases; a halving of child malnutrition; a one-third reduction in under-five death rates; a halving of maternal mortality rates; safe water and sanitation for all communities; universally available family planning services; and basic education for all children.

To give these commitments a more permanent purchase on political priority, the countries represented at the Summit, and the many more who have subsequently signed the Declaration and Plan of Action, also agreed to draw up detailed national programmes for reaching the agreed goals. As of September 1992, such plans have been completed in over 50 countries and are nearing completion in 80 others. In June 1992, the United Nations Secretary-General reported to the General Assembly that 31 countries have so far indicated they will restructure budgets to increase the proportion of government spending devoted to basic education, primary health care, nutrition, water and sanitation.

The drawing up and financing of such plans is inevitably a bureaucratic process, and too much should not be expected too soon. But most nations have made a start towards keeping the promises than have been made to the world's children. Immunization levels have been sustained and in some cases, notably in China, lifted above the new goal of 90 per cent (at which point very significant decreases in the incidence of disease can be expected). Polio has almost certainly been eradicated from Latin America and the Caribbean, where a year has now passed since the last confirmed case of virus. Reported cases of the main vaccine-preventable diseases are declining and WHO believes there is a reasonable chance that the 1995 goal of eliminating neonatal tetanus will be met. Countries such as Bangladesh, Bolivia, Ecuador, Malawi, Namibia, Sri Lanka, Tanzania and possibly Brazil have already begun serious efforts to halve the rate of malnutrition. Similarly, several countries are moving determinedly towards the goal of water and sanitation for all — including Bangladesh, Burundi, China, Ghana, India, Nigeria, Paraguay, the Sudan, Togo, Viet Nam, and virtually all the countries of Central America. And to achieve the Summit goal of empowering all families with today's knowledge about the importance of breastfeeding, hundreds of hospitals and maternity units have begun to change institutional policies and to use their enormous influence to reverse the trend towards the bottle-feeding of infants.

Not least, the promise of the Summit is being kept by the rapid spread of acceptance for the *Convention on the Rights of the Child*, which seeks to lay down minimum standards for the survival, protection, and development of all children. The *Convention* was adopted by the General Assembly of the United Nations towards the end of 1989 and came into force, with the necessary 20 ratifications, on the eve of the 1990 World Summit for Children. Usually, such conventions require many decades to achieve the stage of widespread international recognition; but in this case, the Summit urged all national governments to ratify as quickly as possible and more than 120 have so far done so.

Promises on Paper

The importance of the *Convention*, the Summit goals, and the national programmes of action that have been drawn up should neither be overestimated nor underestimated. At the moment they remain, for the most part, promises on paper. But when, in the mid-1980s, over 100 of the world's political leaders formally accepted the goal of 80 per cent immunization by 1990, that, too, was just a promise on paper. Today, it is a reality in the lives of tens of millions of families around the world.

One lesson to be learned from the achievement is that formal political commitments at the highest levels are necessary if available solutions are to be put into action on a national scale. But a second lesson is that such commitments will only be translated into action by the dedication of the professional services; by the mobilization of today's communications capacities; by the widespread support of politicians, press, and public; and by the reliable and sustained support of the international community. Most of the countries that succeeded in reaching the immunization goal succeeded primarily because large numbers of people and organizations at all levels of national life became seized with the idea that the goal could and should be achieved. Many developing countries could provide examples, but it will be sufficient to cite the case of Bangladesh;

against formidable difficulties, one of Asia's poorest and most populous countries succeeded in lifting its level of immunization coverage from only 2 per cent in 1985 to 62 per cent in 1990.

The question for the years immediately ahead is whether people and organizations in all countries and at all levels are prepared to breathe similar life into new goals that have been agreed on, and into the national programmes of action that have been drawn up for achieving them.

Many hundreds of organizations, especially in the developing world, are already beginning to respond to this challenge. In particular, many have come forward in support of the commitment made by their political leaders to achieve basic social goals by the end of this century. In some 70 countries, people's organizations of one kind or another have worked with governments in drawing up national programmes of action for achieving those goals.

These efforts are just a beginning; and when measured against the demands of the task in hand they are still only a very weak beginning. Not hundreds of organizations but thousands, not thousands of people but millions, will need to give their support to this cause if it is to become a matter of national and international priority.

To maintain the political momentum that has been generated, nothing less is now required than a worldwide strengthening of the basic needs movement to the point where it begins to exert the same kind of pressure as is today being brought to bear for the protection of the environment.

Such pressure will not be easy either to create or to sustain. A movement to overcome the worst aspects of poverty, and particularly to protect children, has no obviously powerful constituency and no immediate vested interest to appeal to. The environmental and women's movements are, in varying degrees, becoming everyone's concern, for the obvious reason that almost everyone is directly touched in one way or another by both of these issues. A movement to met basic human needs will not succeed unless it, too, becomes everyone's concern. And to achieve that, the complex realities of common cause must also become more widely known and understood. None of the great issues that are assuming priority today — the cause of slowing population growth, the cause of achieving equality for women, the cause of environmentally sustainable development, the cause of political democracy — will or can be realized unless the most basic human needs of the forgotten quarter of the earth's people are met. This cause, too, must therefore become the concern of all.

Only by this degree of popular participation, by the practical and political energies of literally millions of people and thousands of organizations, will the new commitments and the promises of the 1990s be given a priority in national life. And only by such means will a new age of concern be born.

Wider Changes

All of these developments, and the hopes to which they have given rise, come at a time of extraordinary change in world affairs. And it is possible to hope that the cause of overcoming the worst aspects of poverty will also draw sustenance, for the long haul ahead, from the changed political and economic environment of the 1990s.

At the moment, that environment remains extremely difficult for most nations of the developing world. There is as yet no sign that the ending of the cold war is leading to any increase in the resources available for development. Index, much of the developing world is today facing its worst financial famine of the modern era, starved of resources by its own high levels of military spending, by the continuing debt crisis, by the further falls in commodity prices, by the restrictive trade policies of the industrialized nations, by the lingering recession in large parts of the world, by the costs of post-war reconstruction in the Persian Gulf, and by the channelling of new aid, credit, and investment on the nations of Eastern Europe and the former Soviet Union.

But despite all of these problems, the prospects for progress have been profoundly improved by the enormous political and economic upheavels of recent years: the advance of democracy throughout Latin America; the liberation of Eastern Europe; the collapse of the Soviet Union; the ending of the cold war; the spread of democratic political reform through most of Africa (including the erosion of apartheid); the almost world wide retreat from the ideology of highly centralized government control over all aspects of economic life; and the growing acceptance of the necessity of joint international action in response to both humanitarian and environmental problems.

These changes amount to one of the most rapid transformations in history. And for all the suffering that is surfacing in the turbulent wake of these changes, from Somalia to the former Yugoslavia, it can still be said that this is a transformation which holds out new hope for world development. If the various forms of free market economic policies now being adopted are not crushed under weight of military spending, debt repayment, and trade protectionism, then there is real hope of achieving sustained economic growth. And if the steps now being taken towards democracy do not falter under the assault of continued poverty and social unrest, then there is also real hope that the poor will eventually begin to share more equitably in the benefits of that growth.

These developments are changing the overall environment in which the developing world must earn its living and within which its people must struggle to meet their own needs. Whether those needs are met or not depends, first of all, on whether families have jobs and incomes. Second, it depends on whether governments fulfil their responsibilities for providing the essential services and safety nets in support of families so that even the most disadvantaged do not suffer from preventable malnutrition, from disease borne by unsafe water and sanitation, or from the lack of even basic health care and education. The great changes of the last five years by no means make such progress inevitable or automatic; but they do make it more possible and more likely.

This coming together of both general and specific developments means that a new threshold in the struggle to overcome the worst aspects of poverty has been reached in the early years of the 1990s. Broad-scale political and economic change is creating an environment more conducive to a renewal of progress against poverty; and advances in technology, in strategy, and in political commitment to meeting basic social goals have given that challenge both a specific focus and new impetus.

Symptom and Cause

Putting into practice today's low cost methods of overcoming malnutrition, disease, and illiteracy, will not solve the problems of economic development; it will not remove the burden of debt or restructure economic relationships; it will not bring an end to oppression and exploitation or eradicate the many causes of unemployment and low incomes; nor will it meet the legitimate aspirations of hundreds of millions of people in the developing world who are not living in absolute poverty but who do no enjoy the amenities of life that are taken for granted in the industrialized nations. It has therefore sometimes been argued that such specific, targeted interventions address only the symptoms of poverty and leave the causes undisturbed.

This is an argument which is no longer deserving of the politeness extended to it in the past. For it is an argument which fails to recognize that frequent illness, malnutrition, poor growth and illiteracy, are some of the most fundamental causes as well as some of the most severe symptoms of poverty. It fails, for example, to take into account that the pulse of economic development is weakened when millions of children suffer from poor mental and physical growth; that the march toward equality of opportunity is slowed when the children of the very poor drop out of school and into a lifetime of illiteracy; that the productivity of communities is enervated by hours spent carrying water from unsafe sources and by the time, energy, and health that is lost to the diseases it brings; that the prospects of finding a job and earning an income are crushed by preventable disabilities such as polio or nutritional blindness; that a family's capacity to save and invest in the future is the less when a child is born mentally retarded by iodine deficiency; and that the contribution of women to economic development cannot be liberated if women remain chained to long years of child-bearing, long days of attendance on illness, and long hours devoted to the fetching and carrying of water and fuel.

In these and many other ways, the worst symptoms of poverty help to crush the potential of the poor, to reduce their control over circumstance, to narrow the choices available to them, and to undermine the long-term process of development.

The struggle for social justice and economic development, both within and between nations, must continue — just at the poor themselves will continue to struggle, as they have always done, to meet most of their own needs by their own efforts. But it is a tragic mistake not to recognize that those efforts can be enhanced by doing what can now be done to reduce disease, disability, malnutrition, illiteracy, and drudgery. Today's advances in knowledge and technology could therefore augment future prospects as surely as they could diminish present suffering. And the argument that making today's advances widely available is dealing only with symptoms is an argument as destructive to the future as it is insensitive to the present.

Finally, the great demographic change taking place in our times also adds its weight to the idea that the time is now right for a determined effort to overcome the worst aspects of poverty.

Fertility rates have fallen in almost every region of the world. In Latin America, the annual number of births has now begun to decline; in Asia, birth will reach a peak in the mid-1990s and begin to fall; even in South Asia, a peak will be reached within a decade. Only in Africa will the annual number births continue to rise until well into the next century. A historic turning-point in the modern era will therefore soon be reached. For once the annual number of births is stable or declining, any further investment in such services as health and education can be used to improve the quality of the services offered and to increase the proportion of people reached. In other words, the task of providing such services will no longer be a case of 'running to stand still', and the goal of meeting basic human needs will no longer be a target that is for ever moving away.

Required Allocation of Government Spending for Basics

As the end of the 20th century approaches, there is therefore an accumulation of reasons for believing that ending the worst aspects of poverty is an idea whose time may finally have come.

New strategies and low-cost technologies are available. Specific goals which reflect this potential have been agreed upon. The commitment to those goals bears the signatures of more Presidents and Prime Ministers than any other document in the history. The plans for achieving them have been or are being drawn up in most nations. And there is a growing acceptance of the idea that targeting some of these worse effects of poverty, particularly as they affect children, is an essential part of long-term development strategy.

In the wider world, the ground being gained by democratic systems means that the long-starved concerns of the poor may begin to put on political weight. At the same time, economic reforms may also create the kind of environment in which a new effort to meet basic human needs would have a much greater chance of success. Meanwhile, the powerful tide of demographic change is also beginning to turn.

For all of these reasons, a new potential now exists for moving towards a world in which the basic human needs of almost every man, woman and child are met. But it is equally clear that this attempt will not gather the necessary momentum unless the political commitment is sustained and the extra resources begin to be made available.

If advantage is to be taken of the political commitments that have been made, and of the national programmes of action that have been drawn up, then those extra resources must begin to become available in the next 12 months to two years.

Some nations have already begun the process of finding the necessary funds from their own resources. In most cases, this is almost certainly going to mean an increase in the proportion of government expenditures allocated to nutrition, primary health care, clean water, safe sanitation, basic education, and family planning services. UNICEF strongly supports the United Nations Development Programme's suggestion that at least 20 per cent of government spending should be allocated to these direct methods of meeting priority human needs. If implemented, such a restructuring of government budgets would enable the developing nations as a whole to find several times the $25 billion a year that is needed to achieve the agreed goals.

In practice, such a shift in present patterns of resource allocation will not be easy to bring about. All governments, however well-intentioned, have limited room for manoeuvre as political pressures push them against the walls of economic constraint. Currently, the governments of the developing world as a whole are spending over one-third of their combined budgets on the repayment of debt and on the financing of the military. Such distortions do not happen by accident. And the internal and external forces which have shaped such spending patterns will not disappear overnight. Nor will the pressure to devote disproportionate amounts of public resources to more advanced and more expensive health and education services for the wealthier and more influential sections of society.

But even in face of all such pressures, it should be possible to allocate 20 per cent of government spending to the task of helping the poor meet their needs for food, water, sanitation, basic health care, family planning, and the education of their children.

Restructuring Aid

There remains the question of whether the industrialized nations are prepared to assist in this effort. Following the commitment made at the *World Summit for Children*, every developing countries which draws up a detailed programme of action for reaching the agreed goals should now be able to expect that some proportion of the cost will be met by increased or reallocated aid. That proportion will vary from less than a quarter in East Asia and Latin America, to between a quarter and a half in South Asia, and up to two-thirds in the least developed countries and sub-Saharan Africa. For the developing world as a whole, the additional external assistance required will be in the region of an additional $8 billion a year.

So far there is no significant sign that the industrialized nations are prepared to make additional resources available on this scale. Aid continues to stagnate. And there have been few serious attempts to restructure existing aid allocations. Government-to-government assistance cannot easily shuffle off the coil of foreign policy considerations, economic vested interests, and historical associations, which means that the richest 40 per cent of the developing world's population receives twice as much aid per head as the poorest 40 per cent. More positively, it would be a mistake to imply that all the aid not used for directly meeting basic human needs is irrelevant to this cause. Roads also help to meet basic needs. Jobs even more so.

But again, it is not too much to expect that 20 per cent of development aid should be allocated to directly helping people to meet their most basic needs for food, water, health care, family planning and primary education. Such a restructuring of aid expenditures would, on its own, make available the extra $8 billion a year required. It would be an increase in the kind of aid that the majority of people in the developing world want to receive, and in the kind of aid that the majority of people in the industrialized world want to give. And it is an increase which should now be offered to any developing country that commits itself to a programme of action to meet basic human needs.

The same commitment must also be expected from the multilateral organizations which currently disburse approximately $12 billion a year. In particular, the United Nations could play an increasingly central role in international efforts to achieve agreed social goals and to lay a new foundation for human development in the 21st century. And it is a role that could also provide a focus for the impending reform of the United Nations system and lead to the kind of changes which would make sense to, and meet with the approval of, a worldwide public.

The Fading Excuse

This opportunity must not be allowed to evaporate into the perennial atmosphere of pessimism about the prospects for world development. The necessary task of drawing attention to human needs has unfortunately given rise to the popular impression that the developing world is a stage upon which no light falls and only tragedy is enacted. But the fact is that, for all the set-backs, more progress has been made in the past 50 years than in the previous 2,000. Since the end of the Second World War, average real incomes in the developing world have more than doubled: infant and child death rates have been more than halved; average life expectancy has increased by about a third; the proportion of the developing world's children starting school has risen from less than half to more than three quarters (despite a doubling of population); and the percentage of rural families with access to safe water has risen from less than 10 per cent to almost 60 per cent. Yet even these statistics cannot capture the true dimensions of the change that has occurred in only a few decades. Much of the world has also rid itself of colonialism, brought apartheid in all its forms to the edge of extinction, and largely freed itself from the iron grip of fascist and totalitarian regimes. And underlying all of these changes is the slow and even more fundamental change from a world organized almost exclusively for the benefit of a privileged 10 per cent or 20 per cent, in almost all societies, to a world in which the needs and the rights of all people are increasingly recognized. Only a few decades ago, it did not seem a matter of great concern that the poor majority had no right to vote, no freedom of expression or religion, no right to due process of law, or that their children were not educated or immunized and received little or no benefit from advances in hygiene and health care. In many nations, it even seemed natural that the children of the poor could be sold or bonded or made to work 14 hours a day in field or mine or factory. And 50 years ago, when more than a million people starved in Bengal famine, they died in a world which raised no murmur of protest.

Seen from this longer perspective, the fact that two-thirds of the world's people now have the right to vote, or that 80 per cent of the world's infants are immunized, or that there is such a thing as a worldwide Convention on the Rights of the Child, is a symptom of a remarkable change. And in the face of such progress, pessimism is a sign less of sagacity than of cynicism. In the decade ahead, a clear opportunity exists to make the breakthrough against what might be called the last great obscenity — the needless malnutrition, disease, and illiteracy that still casts a shadow over the lives, and the futures, of the poorest quarter of the world's children.

It is almost unthinkable that the opportunity to reach these basic social goals should be missed because the political commitment is lacking or because the developing world and the donor nations cannot, together, find an extra $25 billion a year.

In the industrialized world, neither recession nor competing claims on resources can justify the failure to find the extra $8 billion a year which would be required to support developing nations that decide to make meeting basic social goals into a national priority.

In the developing world, underdevelopment is a fast-fading excuse for failure to make that commitment and to begin mobilizing the necessary financial and human resources.

The difficulties are enormous. But they shrink beside the difficulties that can be and have been overcome in the course of all the many great achievements of our times.

It is time that the challenge replaced excuse. If today's obvious and affordable steps are not taken to protect the lives and the health and the normal growth of many millions of young children, then this will have less to do with the lack of economic capacity than with the fact that the children concerned are almost exclusively the sons and daughters of the poor — of those who lack not only purchasing power but also political influence and media attention. And if the resources are not to be made available, if the overcoming of the worst aspects of poverty, malnutrition, illiteracy and disease is not to be achieved in the years ahead, then let it now be clear that this is not because it is not a possibility but because it is not a priority.

Conclusion

In 1992, many specific tragedies have again assaulted the very idea of childhood in such places as Somalia and the former Yugoslavia. The response to these tragedies, wherever they occur, is a major part of the work of UNICEF and is addressed in many other UNICEF publications and statements during the course of the year.

But for more than 10 years, the *State of the World's Children* report has concentrated on issues which profoundly affect far larger numbers of children but which do not constitute the kind of news even which qualifies for the world's attention. This is tragedy which does not happen in any one particular place or time; it happens quietly in poor communities throughout the developing world. It is therefore not news, and so it slips from the public eye and from the political agenda. But it is nonetheless a tragedy far greater in scale than even the greatest of the emergencies which so often command the world's, and UNICEF's, concern. No famine, no flood, no earthquake, no war, has ever claimed the lives of 250,000 children in a single week. Yet malnutrition and disease claim that number of child victims *every week*. And for every one of those children who dies, many more live on with such ill health and poor growth that they will never grow to the physical and mental potential with which they were born.

When little or nothing could be done about this larger-scale tragedy, then neglect was perhaps understandable. But slowly, quietly, and without the world taking very much notice, we have arrived at the point where this tragedy is no longer necessary. It is therefore no longer acceptable in a world with any claim on civilization. The time has therefore come for a new age of concern.

Political and economic change in the world is beginning to create the conditions which, however difficult, offer new hope for overcoming the worst aspects of world poverty, particularly as they affect the world's children. The cost of providing health and education services in the developing world remains relatively low, and the gradual stabilization in the numbers of infants being born means that further investments in basic services can now begin to increase the proportion of the population served. Meanwhile, the technologies and strategies for controlling malnutrition, disease and illiteracy have been tried and tested and now stand waiting to go into action on the same scale as the problems they can so largely solve.

The convergence of all of these different forces means it is now possible to achieve one of the greatest goals that humanity could ever set for itself — the goal of adequate food, clean water, safe sanitation, primary health care, family planning, and basic education, for virtually every man, woman and child on earth. In 1990, this new potential for specific action against thes. worst aspects of poverty was formulated into a set of basic social goals which accurately reflect that potential and which have been formally accepted by the great majority of the world's political leaders. A start has been made, in many nations, towards keeping the promise of those goals.

We therefore stand on the edge of a new era of concern for the silent and invisible tragedy that poverty inflicts on today's children and on tomorrow's world. Whether the world will enter decisively into that new age depends on the pressure that is brought to bear by politicians, press, public, and professional services in all nations. And among the readers of this report, there is hardly any individual or organization that could not now become involved.

(Source: Summary of the *State of the World's Children 1993,* UNICEF, New York, 1993).

4.2 **Mortality Rate**

TABLE 4.1: Mortality Rate

	Item	Year	**India**	Country with best position	Number of countries for which data available	India's position in the world
1.	Infant Mortality Rate Under 1	1991	**84**	Sweden (4)	129	**87**
2.	Infant Mortality Rate Under 5	1991	**126**	Sweden (5)	129	**87**

5

ECONOMY: Global Perspective

5.1 Economic Environment

Aid for Basic Needs

In the industrialized world, those who support progress towards meeting basic human needs should also be aware that increase in aid are not enough. Two other changes are needed.

First, the proportion of aid given for the purposes of directly meeting the basic needs of the poor should be increased to at least 20 per cent.

Second, the flow and direction of aid should also be influenced by whether or not aid is likely to be used to bring additional benefits to the poorest quarter of the recipient countries' populations (as opposed to providing services for the not-so-poor or allowing governments to spend more of their own resources on prestige projects or on the military). One way of assessing that likelihood is by regularly monitoring progress towards the agreed basic needs goals.

Far from being too idealistic a notion, the idea that the flow of aid and loans should be heavily influenced by the likelihood of their being used to meet basic needs is an idea currently being considered by the institution that is the world's largest source of development finance. In October 1991, the President of the World Bank told the annual meeting of the International Monetary Fund/World Bank that poverty eradication should be the Bank's "overarching objective" and that the volume of Bank lending "should be linked to efforts to reduce poverty."

The evolution of such new criteria for aid and loans could both assist, and the assisted by, a greater public concern for aid in the industrialized world. Public support for aid is not dead. But it has been seriously wounded by the widespread and largely justified perception that aid is not primarily being used to meet the needs or enhance the capacities of the poorest, or to directly attack the worst aspects of poverty. Mobilizing public support for increases in aid therefore depends, in large part, on making aid programmes themselves more worthy of that support. And that responsibility is one which sits on both 'donor' industrialized nations and 'recipient' developing nations with equal weight.

International Trade

In addition to the potential reductions in military spending and the actual advances made by democracy, the collapse of the Soviet Union and the end of the cold war have also led to economic reform and to the adoption of 'market-friendly' policies in many countries that have long laboured under highly centralized economic regimes. The result is likely to be the demise of inefficient state-owned companies, more productive use of resources, and the liberation of people's energies and initiatives. This development, too, therefore holds out the hope of accelerated economic growth.

Yet for many nations, it may well prove a false hope. Market forces cannot conjure economic growth out of an investment vacuum. The developing world needs investment: in its peoples' health and education; in the infrastructure of transport, communications, and energy; and in its industrial enterprises. Yet large parts of the developing world, and especially the nations of sub-Saharan Africa, are unable to make that investment. And the cause is not only high levels of military spending.

This year, the developing world must devote 20 per cent of all its export earnings to servicing its debts. Those debts now total almost $1,300 billion. Each year, capital and interest repayments of $134 billion fall due. Such a sum — three times as much as all the aid received from all sources — cannot of course be repaid. The unpaid part is therefore added to the total debt.

Sub-Saharan Africa is particularly hard hit. Its total debt has tripled since 1980 and now stands at approximately $175 billion. This is less than 14 per cent of the total debt of the developing would, but it is too much for Africa's frail economies to bear. The countries of sub-Saharan Africa are now spending 50 per cent more on the servicing of their debts than on the health and education of their children. Yet even this sacrifice is only enabling those countries to pay about one third of the interest that falls due each year.

Investment in the future is therefore being undermined by the debts of the past. And without such investment, the coming of market-friendly economic policies is unlikely to fulfil the hopes that have been aroused for accelerated economic growth.

There has been much talk of cancelling or writing down debts, and numerous proposals have been debated and adopted at meetings from Toronto to Trinidad. Yet actual debt cancellations so far have reduced sub-Saharan Africa's annual payments by approximately $200 million per year on total 1991 payments of $10.6 billion a year — a reduction of approximately 2 per cent.

Instead, the policy that has been consistently urged on debtor nations is that they should increase their exports in order to earn their way out of debt. But because the developing world is still so dependent on a relatively small range of raw materials for its export earnings (Latin America remains two-thirds dependent on raw materials and Africa over 90%) the result has been an over-supply and a further collapse in price. Côte d'Ivoire and Ghana have boosted exports of cocoa. Tanzania has boosted exports of cotton. But to no avail. Prices for developing world's principal raw materials, which fell steadily in the 1980s, fell by another 20 per cent between 1989 and 1991 and are likely to remain at this depressed level for the foreseeable future. This solution has therefore conferred its main benefits on the industrialized nations in the form of cheaper commodities. Meanwhile, for the developing world, the debts have continued to mount.

The obvious answer is for developing nations to diversify their economies and begin exporting processed and manufactured goods in order to reduce dependence on commodities and to earn foreign exchange. But this requires both investment and access to markets. And in large measure, both of these are being denied to most of the countries of the developing world today. Investment from internal sources is, as we have seen, largely pre-empted by military spending and debt repayments. Investments and loans from outside have almost ceased as more than $100 billion has gone to Eastern Europe, to the task of easing Russia's re-entry into the world economy, and to reconstruction in the Persian Gulf. Bilateral aid stagnates. Private investment flows almost entirely to other industrialized countries or to a handful of nations in East Asia or Latin America.

Some developing countries are now beginning to acquire the technologies that, together with the advantages of low-cost labour and abundant raw materials, could enable them to increase exports and create the jobs and the incomes by which people can meet their needs. But that opportunity is being denied to them by the tariffs, quotas, and other restrictions imposed by the industrialized nations. Such barriers are today costing the developing world approximately $50 billion a year in lost earnings — as much as all the aid they receive. It is therefore also essential that the present round of discussions under the General Agreement of Tariffs and Trade (GATT) should reach the kind of agreement which will mean that economic opportunity is no longer restricted by the protectionism of those who have for so long preached free-market economics to the developing world.

Optimism at the spread of market-friendly economic policies must therefore be tempered by the fact that the rules of the international market-place are not neutral but are often heavily biased against the developing world. And those who seek to support the basic needs movement must also be aware that pressure for action on debt, aid and loans, and on trading relationships, will also be a necessary part of that struggle.

The Market and the Poor

For those who are involved or who may become involved in such movement, it is also important to be aware that economic growth, even if achieved, does not in itself mean that basic needs will be met. In a great many countries today, including many industrialized nations and many developing nations that have enjoyed rapid economic growth in the past, the poorest 20 per cent have not shared in the benefits of that growth. In the United Kingdom and the United States, for example, the 1980s were years of almost continuous economic growth in which the poorest of their people have shared not at all.

The recent return to growth in Latin America also illustrates the point. Economic reform in the late 1980s and early 1990s has helped to push GNP growth beyond 3 per cent a year in Latin America as whole. But in a nation such as Brazil, where the income of the richest 20 per cent is 33 times greater than that of the poorest 20 per cent, the benefits of a return to economic growth are shared so unequally that the poorest derive little or no benefit from the process. Similarly in Venezuela, where economic growth touched 9 per cent in 1991, the very poorest families have seen little improvement in their standard of living and many have found that the cost of meeting their basic needs has risen faster than their incomes.

The links between economic reform, economic growth, and the meeting of basic needs are therefore anything but automatic. Specific government policies are not only necessary to promote the right kind of growth but also to translate that growth into improvements in the lives of the disadvantaged. Market economics is not a panacea for social progress. And if governments abandon their responsibilities, then the result will be societies in which inequalities continue to increase and in which economic demand counts for all and human need counts for nothing. It is the responsibility of the government to support parents by investing in health and education for all children; to construct the safety nets which will mean that the minimum needs of the vulnerable are met; to make available to all the basic benefits of advances in human knowledge that are of little commercial interest; and to offset the inbuilt tendency of market forces to favour the already advantaged. Basic needs will not be met, and basic investments will not be made, by any visible hand.

The end of the cold war, the collapse of Soviet communism, the widespread movement towards political democracy and economic reform, have raised a worldwide hope that this century could end as optimistically as it began disastrously. It is an unprecedented opportunity which has so suddenly been presented. But it is no more than that — an opportunity — and it will not remain open forever. And it is now essential that the industrialized nations that have urged democratic politics and free-market economics on the developing world should now do everything in their power to create the international environment in which such policies can prove themselves.

If this can be done, then the economic and political reforms now being so widely implemented could engender the kind of progress from which the poor might also derive some benefit. By the advance of democracy, the poorest classes could begin to acquire a little more of the political influence which, in most cases, is the missing link between what could be done and what is being done to eradicate the worst of poverty; and by economic reform, increasing numbers of the poor should be able to meet their own needs by means of their own efforts and their own incomes.

Source: *The State of the World's Children, 1993*, UNICEF, 1993.

5.2 **Balance of Payments: International Monetary Fund Report**

The deficit of development countries widened to a whopping 81 billion US dollars in 1991 from a mere $12 billion in the previous year.

Further, the current account deficit of the industrial countries sharply nosedived to a mere 18.5 billion dollars in 1991 from a staggering $108.2 billion in 1990.

Among the developing countries, the oil exporting nations logged a deficit of 51.8 billion dollars in 1991 compared with a surplus of $10 billion in 1990, deflecting the persistent fall in the per barrel value of oil

On the other hand, the deficit of the non-oil developing countries increased slightly to 29.2 billion dollars in 1991 from $22 billion in 1990.

Pointing out that the current account deficit to the developing countries soared to 81 billion dollars in 1991, the Fund said this was largely attributable to a drop in the merchandise trade surplus to $11.7 billion from $57 billion.

The merchandise trade surplus of the oil exporting countries fell as the result of a reduction in exports that was greater than the fall in imports. By contrast, the deficit of the non-oil developing countries increased, despite an increase in their exports.

In contrast to the merchandise trade surplus, the deficit in other goods, services and income items remained persistently large, worsening by 46 per cent in 1991 to 104.9 billion dollars.

Among the major components of this category, only the travel item showed a marked surplus, while income showed a small but increasing surplus.

Long-term capital inflows to developing countries rose sharply to 108.9 billion dollars in 1991 from $21.6 in 1990, while the outflow of short-term capital increased slightly to $5 billion from $2.9 billion.

Their reliance on exceptional financing was reduced slightly to 40.4 billion dollars in 1991 from $41.3 billion in the previous year and reserved rose by $64.2 billion in 1991 compared with $40.8 billion.

Overall, capital movements for developing countries, including changes in reserves, showed a net inflow of 79.2 billion dollars in 1991, compared with an inflow of $18.8 billion in 1990.

Capital outflows representing net acquisition of financial assets abroad by developing countries fell to 91.5 billion dollars in 1991 from $07.1 billion in 1990, the Fund said.

Source : *BOP Statistics Year Book 1992,* International Monetary Fund, Washington, reported in *Hindustan Times*, February 6, 1993.

5.3 Debt Crisis

Ten years have passed since Mexico's inability to service its debts triggered a rapid succession of similar moratoria by other debtor countries and led to what has come to be known as the "debt crisis".

Lessons Learned

If the debt crisis has taught anything, it is the fallibility of forecasts. A sizable part of the world's financial and economic community believed in the late 1970s that sovereign countries did not go bankrupt. Even after the crisis broke, the pessimists did not predict the kind of stagnation suffered by the debtor countries during the 1980s and many people dismissed the disruption in payments as simply a liquidity problem. As recently as five years ago, few could have predicted that much of Latin America would today be wrestling with the question of how to manage large-scale capital inflows. In that spirit of humility, listed below are ten key lessons.

(1) Systemic thinking is crucial to avoiding bad lending decisions. For much of the 1960s and 1970s, the growth of income in most countries significantly exceeded interest rates. In this environment, it was difficult for a country to appear insolvent. Even nations that borrowed to pay all of their interest bills could have improving debt indicators. Neither lender nor borrower questioned what would happen if the international economic environment changed dramatically, as it did with the sudden and sharp disinflation in the industrialized world in the early 1980s.

One after another, countries to whom bankers had been eager to lend only months before ran into problems servicing their external obligations. Indeed, within two years of Mexico's default, 30 developing countries — representing half of developing country debt — were failing to service their debt as originally scheduled. The pervasiveness of debt problem is testimony to the dominant role played by a changed international economic environment. It also demonstrates the folly of assuming, as some prominent bankers did at the time, that simply spreading exposure across developing countries was an adequate way to diversify risk.

(2) Heavy borrowing that is not accompanied by productive investments is a disaster for creditor and debtor alike. If the money borrowed during the 1970s had been used widely — that is, to finance high-return investments, or underwrite necessary structural changes — debtor countries could have ridden out the disinflationary storm of the early 1980s. Indeed some countries— such as Korea, whose external debt went up nine-fold over the 1970s — followed precisely such a strategy and were able to stay their development course through the 1980s. Unfortunately, however, in too many other developing countries, the easy availability of international credit in the 1970s was used to postpone, rather than catalyze, necessary economic reforms.

Telltale signs that all was not well were rationalized by both borrowers and lenders in a willing suspension of disbelief. Neither side carefully examined what was happening to fiscal deficits and public enterprise losses; nor was the connection made between why residents were transferring funds abroad in ever increasing amounts, even as foreign creditors transferred resources in to shore up sagging public finances. The problem was exacerbated by the paucity of information and poor book-keeping on how the borrowed funds were actually being used. The net result was to build up the "liabilities" side of the debtor country's "balance sheet", without a commensurate increase in the stock of productive "assets". Sorting out this disequilibrium would preoccupy national policy-makers and international agencies for the subsequent decade.

(3) Countries that "opted out" of the international financial system have generally done worse as a result. During the last decade, a few countries tried at various times to resolve their debt problems unilaterally by opting out of the international financial system. They stopped servicing their external obligations and broke off relations with their creditors. Sometimes, this was preceded by a breakdown of negotiations on a stabilization and adjustment program with the international financial institutions. In the end, these actions have generally proved detrimental to the debtor country involved. One reason is that the financial costs associated with the building up of arrears has been added to the cost of delaying much needed adjustment — these costs include reduced trade and interbank credit lines, as well as higher prices (the "spreads") that have had to be paid for these lines. But even more important and damaging have been the adverse effects of isolationist action on domestic confidence. Trying to get the best deal within the mainstream, with the support of official development agencies, seems to be a more fruitful avenue for country action than trying to go it alone.

(4) Good national policies are the key to capital market access. The debt crisis was at least much a symptom as a cause of bad economic performance. It is important to emphasize that private capital has continued to flow during the 1980s to a number of developing countries, notably the prudently managed economies of East Asia. For that region as whole, net resource flows from private sources have been positive in every of the 1980s, and foreign equity flows have gone up eightfold over the decade. A more recent phenomenon is the return to capital market access of a number of the debt-distressed Latin American countries, including Argentina, Brazil, Mexico, and Venezuela. It is not a coincidence that among these, Mexico, the country with the strongest track

record in economic management in the region, is also by far the largest recipient of private portfolio flows to developing countries.

Underlying this widening access to international capital markets has been a revolution in economic policies across much of the developing world. Fiscal deficits and inflation are down, and exchange rates reflect market realities rather than national pride. Macro-economic stabilization has been accompanied by deep-rooted structural change. The role of government is being greatly curtailed, trade barriers have come down, and the privatization of public enterprises is underway in virtually every World Bank borrower. One of the painfully learned lessons of the last several decades is that sustained growth depends on governments choosing an appropriate economic role — doing those things that governments need to do, such as providing infrastructure and basic human services, but leaving to the market that which the market can do best.

(5) Economic adjustment takes time and things often get worse before they get better, so attention to the political and economic sustainability of reform is in the interest of both the creditors and debtors. It is now clear from the experience of Chile, Ghana and Mexico, among others, that market friendly policies can help to improve the economic performance of economies previously hamstrung by a plethora of controls and distortions. But dismantling controls and opening up an economy takes time and involves substantial dislocations. This means that output at first declines, before gradually increasing — a process that creates enormous political pressures to reverse reform policies. The situation is greatly exacerbated when adjustment coincides with import cutbacks, which are caused by the need to use scarce foreign exchange to service foreign debts.

For policy-makers, import compression during adjustment poses a cruel dilemma. either they can seek to maintain consumption and reduce capital goods imports, thereby compromising the long-run economic viability of reforms, or they can seek to reduce consumption, even as economic dislocations increase, thereby risking political instability. Since creditors have a strong stake in the success of reform efforts, it may well be in their collective interest to avoid import compression. Yet no individual private creditor has an incentive to accept debt reduction or to put in new money; each would prefer to "free ride" on the activities of other creditors. This where the presence of official lenders, with a longer-term stake in the debtor country, makes a vital contribution by limiting the need for initial cutbacks in consumption without distorting the short-term adjustment process to regain credit-worthiness.

(6) There is a compelling need for official action to overcome free rider problems that complicate debt reschedulings and reductions. The problems of free-riding and holdouts among the banks have exacerbated coordination difficulties that would have resulted simply from the number and diversity of lenders.. In purely domestic contexts, bankruptcy laws exist because of the recognized problem of dealing with conflicts among creditors, and between creditors and debtors. Without such laws regulating sovereign lending, there is a clear case for government action to overcome free-rider problems. The critical point was recognized when the crisis broke and the world financial system seemed to be at risk. But during the heyday of *laissez faire* enthusiasm during the mid-1980s, at least some officials lost sight of it.

The free-rider issue is well recognized in the structure of the Brady Plan, which has provided the framework for commercial debt reduction agreements since 1989. The "menu" approach enables creditors banks with different preferences to choose the debt reduction option most suited to their needs, while the comprehensive nature of these deals minimizes the possibility of free riding by a small group of creditors at the expense of the other participants.

This comprehensive approach is based on the recognition that market buybacks (the re-purchase for cash of debt) of only a small part of the outstanding debt stock, even at a discount to face value, generate few benefits for the debtor country, because they raise the probability that the country will repay its debt, and thus the market value of the country's remaining outstanding debt. Confronted with a steadily increasing price for their debt obligations, countries that are already financially strained will soon reach a point where further buybacks are economically unviable, rendering this mechanism unsuited for large-scale reductions in debt stock. In the same way, there is a real danger that partial debt-equity swaps may benefit creditors who hold on to their debt, without doing a great deal for debtor countries.

(7) Treating the debt crisis purely as a liquidity problem delayed the search for a stable and real solution. In the early years of the debt crisis, many observers felt that the indebted countries were suffering from a liquidity — rather than a solvency — problem, and thus the official workout strategy relied on providing new funds to overcome the temporary shortage of finance. But in many instances, commercial lenders were unwilling to provide these new funds, essentially because they were uncertain about the prospects of recovering this money even in the medium term. It was only the debt reduction deals under the Brady Plan that finally helped to reduce this uncertainty by removing one part of the contingent claims on future public finances. More generally, this experience has demonstrated the weakness of the basic liquidity-solvency distinction as applied to the debt crisis. This lesson is well learned now, but the cost of delay has been to put development on hold for a decade in many of these countries. A lesson for the future is the importance of acknowledging reality sooner.

(8) Debt reduction is sometimes necessary but only works well when accompanied by good economic policies. The main benefit of a Brady-type debt reduction deal for a debtor country is that it eliminated the contingent liability represented by the unserviced part of the old debt. The debt reduction thus reduces uncertainty about the returns to any new investment and helps to create the climate of confidence for the private sector to undertake new investments. These benefits are best captured in countries where an established track record of sound policies and prudent economic management have already lifted the other impediments to renewed private sector confidence. Such an established record does not yet exist in some of the severely indebted middle-income developing countries that have not concluded a Brady-type deal with their commercial creditors. Waiting until it does will maximize the potential benefits of the deal to the country and ensure the productive use of the resources needed to finance the transaction.

(9) Building risk-sharing contingencies into financial contracts is much less costly than renegotiating contracts when things go wrong. The essence of the workout process during the 1980s was to agree on the terms for the ex-port rewriting of loan contracts to share the losses associated with an outcome that had turned out to be worse than either lender or borrower had envisaged. The process was made more difficult by the fact that virtually none of the original loan contracts had such "downside" contingency clauses, meaning that all the contracts had to be renegotiated ex-post and without a frame of reference that

such a clause would have provided. Moreover, the predominance of syndicated lending to sovereign borrowers in the 1970s meant that the risk-sharing features of other forms of international finance, notably foreign direct investment and other equity flows, had been largely foregone.

The recent boom in portfolio flows to emerging stock markets in these countries shows that at least one set of international investors has learned from this experience. It is not clear, however, that many developing countries have fully realized either the potential for, or the implications of, using a more diversified set of financial instruments.

(10) External finance for investment in low-income countries must come largely from official sources. A key lesson of the debt crisis is that commercial banks are an inefficient instrument for channeling long-term investment finance to the poorest countries. During the next decade, their role in these countries is likely to focus on the provision of trade and short-term credit, and correspondent banking relationships to facilitate international trade arrangements, as well as limited-recourse project finance, where the repayments on the loan are linked to the success of the investment project financed by the money. Other commercial sources will also run up against internal, or externally imposed, regulatory or creditworthiness constraints.

Yet the financing needs of these countries continue to be pressing. During the past decade, per capita incomes in the severely indebted low income countries have fallen by a fifth to well short of a dollar a day in 1991. Raising incomes from these pitiful levels will require both better economic management and an injection of foreign capital for investment in economic development. Because many of the countries are not likely to be creditworthy for a long time, the real need is to increase concessional financing. A doubling of all the net resource flows to developing countries last year would add a little over $16 billion to the aid bill of the industrialized world — just 1 per cent of what the world spends on defense each year. It is also a small price to pay for reversing the decline in health, nutrition, and educational standards that has characterized so many of these countries during the 1980s.

Continuing Debt Crisis

The preceding lessons are vital not only to avoid future debt crises but also to tackle the substantial unfinished agenda from the 1980s. Certainly, considerable progress has been made. National and international actions have helped avert any serious damage to the international financial system, which was a real concern in the early aftermath of the crisis. With the recently announced commercial debt reduction agreements for Argentina and Brazil, the normalization of external creditor relations is now well advanced for the middle-income developing countries. And sustained official financial support on concessional terms has complemented the very limited domestic savings of the poorest countries, ensuring that their basic import needs have continued to be met.

But the debt crisis is far from over for more than 40 developing countries, which continue to have difficulties in servicing their debt as originally contracted. In particular, much remains to be done for the poorest developing countries, 26 of which are classified as severely indebted. For these countries — mostly in sub-Saharan Africa — official support has been strong through the 1980s, in terms of the provision of both new money and progressively more concessional debt relief. But external viability has remained elusive. On average, these countries have been allocating a quarter of their exports to debt servicing, although this still only enables them to pay half the scheduled amount.

Under any plausible future scenario, many of these countries will regain external viability only if some portion of their existing — largely official bilateral — debt is written down, reflecting the creditors' acceptance of a reduction in the stock of debt outstanding. Bringing scheduled debt-service payments to a level that can reasonably be expected to be paid would help reduce uncertainty and make new creditors feel more confident that their contractual arrangements were likely to be honored. Debt relief for these countries is thus a high-priority item. But the actual amounts required will have to be determined on a case-by-case basis and assessed within the context of the overall economic and structural adjustment program. It is clear, however, that in many countries, this relief will need to go beyond the 50 per cent reduction in the present value of debt service that has characterized some of the most recent agreements reached with official bilateral creditors under the auspices of the Paris Club.

As for the remaining severely indebted middle-income countries, the objective remains to restore access to private international capital markets. The recent experience of a number of major Latin American countries, including Argentina, Brazil, Chile, and Mexico, has shown that private capital can flow back in substantial amounts under the right national and international conditions. Foremost among these is a sustained track record of economic and structural reform. Investor confidence has also been helped by the successful completion — or imminent conclusion — of Brady-type agreements for reducing part of the existing commercial bank debt. A similar sustained track record of sound national policies, complemented, in some cases, by an agreement on commercial debt reduction, should facilitate the return to market access for the dozen or so middle-income countries still classified as severely indebted. The same considerations also apply to some of the states of the former USSR, whose current debt-servicing problems have sharply curtailed access to private international capital markets.

In sum, the debt crisis may no longer be the principal preoccupation of the international commercial banks, but it is far from over the many of the countries involved, among them, some of the poorest. For a number of these countries, a combination of growth and cash flow relief through rescheduling should result in a resumption of normal creditor relations by the mid-1990s. For others, however, a return to external viability can only be achieved in conjunction with some reduction of their existing debt obligations. For all of them, the key to both improved economic performance and continued support from the international financial community will be sound economic policies. And the importance of these policies will increase in the 1990s, as international capital markets remain tight and the competition for concessional finance becomes stronger. Moreover, the tolerance for wrong policies will be sharply reduced in a world where capital account liberalization and financial market integration make large sudden outflows of capital a real constraint on government action.

Sound policies need to be nurtured by a supportive international economic environment. This means that the developing world's recovery and growth prospects would be helped by reducing protectionism in the OECD countries. Cutting current levels of industrial country protection in half would lead to a $50 billion increase in developing country exports – not including the sizable benefits to consumers in the developed world. It also means that developing countries, as price takers in the international capital markets, would benefit from industrial country policies that would bring down real interest rates from their current high levels. As long as real interest rates are above the growth rates for some developing countries, any net borrowing must necessarily worsen their debt indicators. Thus, actions by the industrial countries to raise their own level of saving, thereby reducing pressure on international markets, would do much to improve the creditworthiness and financing prospects of the developing countries in the decade ahead.

Source: Masood Ahmed and Lawrence Summers, *Finance and Development*, September 1992.

5.4 Third World Output: International Monetary Fund Report

Output in the developing countries is expected to expand by an impressive 5 per cent in 1993 and 1994. The achievement is particularly commendable, given the weakness of activity in the industrial countries.

However, many countries had failed to register any meaningful improvement in economic conditions, particularly in Africa. In fact, some of the countries, per capita real incomes remained below the levels experienced 10 or even 20 years ago divergencies in growth among developing countries had tended to widen in recent years.

The stronger performers among the developing countries had higher saving rates, investment, efficiency of investment and overall productivity growth. Typically, they also financed a larger proportion of investment from domestic savings. When they had recourse to external saving, it was often in the form of foreign direct investment and equity capital rather than loans.

The better-performing countries were more outward-oriented with regard to trade links and also had greater economic ties with other developing countries. Their trade with other developing countries was able to mitigate the effects of the current sluggishness of growth in the industrial world.

The impressive growth record of many Asian countries illustrated the longer-term benefits from sustained stabilisation and reform efforts.

The experience of the past 40 years. offered strong evidence of a close linkage between liberal trade and exchange regimes and economic prosperity. Many developing countries had also increasingly moved to make their currencies convertible, to promote competition and to liberalise foreign trade, and this had helped them overcome the debt crisis of the 1980s and to sustain growth even in the face of weak activity in the industrial countries since 1990.

Yet the significant benefits from free trade now seem threatened. "The failure to conclude the Uruguay round is adding to trade tensions and is depriving the world of potentially large gains from further liberalisation of tariff and non-tariff barriers, from the extension of multilateral rules to new sectors, from a strengthening of rules and disciplines on anti-dumping, subsidies, and safeguards, and from a strengthening of the dispute settlement mechanism and of trade policy surveillance.

"The industrial countries are increasingly seeking recourse to countervailing and anti-dumping duties and to non-tariff barriers. Excessive focus on bilateral or even sectoral trade imbalances has led to a dangerous proliferation of managed trade agreements.

"Efforts to bring the Uruguay round to an early and successful conclusion and reverse the rise in protectionist barriers must be a central element of any cooperative effort to strengthen growth worldwide."

About the US, the most pressing priority of economic policy was the need to reduce the large federal budget deficit in order to strengthen saving and investment.

Recent economic developments suggested that the natural forces of recovery, aided by earlier monetary stimulus, were taking hold and that significant short-term fiscal stimulus was now less necessary than might have appeared earlier. In other words, President Clinton's stimulus package was not absolutely essential.

The $12 billion stimulus package amounted to a little less than one-fourth of one per cent of US gross domestic product, and a package of that magnitude would not have an appreciably large effect.

Source: *World Economic Outlook*, International Monetary Fund, Washington, 1993, reported by N.C. Menon in *Hindustan Times*.

6

EDUCATION

6.1 World Education Report, 1991

The World Education Report (1991), the first in the new biennial series of UNESCO, examines selected issues of education policy against the changing background of world education. It reviews the development of education at the global level over the past two decades, focusing mainly on access to and participation in the formal system even as it draws attention to regional variations especially in the poorest countries.

Report aims at presenting a broad but concise analysis of major trends and policy issues in education in the world today. Besides discussing the continuing challenges the face basic education, it also deals with the global prospects of education for all.

The total world expenditure on formal education increased to over a trillion dollars in 1988 — equivalent to around 5.5 per cent of the world's GNP. Of this, only one-eighth was spent in the developing countries of Asia, Africa and Latin America, which, nevertheless, account for three-fourths of the total world enrolment in formal education.

In 1988, India spend 8.5 per cent of the total Government expenditure on education. Among the 24 Asian countries out of 41 for which figures are available, only Sri Lanka and Laos fared worse.

India tops the list of ten countries with the largest number of illiterate adults in 1990. While China had 224 millions, India had a staggering 281 millions with the rest of the world accounting for 243 millions. The other eight nations on top of this list include Pakistan 43 million, Bangladesh 42 million, Nigeria 29 million, Indonesia 27 million, Brazil 18 million, Egypt 16 million, Iran 10 million and Sudan 10 million.

The regional averages mask important differences at the country level. Around three-quarters (705 million) of the world's adult illiterates in 1990 are accounted for by just ten countries. Future progress in increasing the global literacy rate depends largely on continuing progress in those countries. Nevertheless, the highest rates of illiteracy are generally to be found in the least developed countries.

The main obstacles to faster progress in improving world literacy are economic conditions in the majority of countries which have low literacy rates and social factors in most countries hindering the educational participation of women and girls.

Economic conditions, on which depend the possibility of major budgetary initiatives in support of national literacy campaigns and extensions of primary education, are important but not necessarily decisive. All but two of the seventeen countries, including three out of the ten large ones, which are projected to have adult literacy rates still below 50 per cent at the end of the century are least developed countries. On the other hand, another eleven least developed countries are projected to have literacy rates above 50 per cent by the end of the century, in some cases substantially so. For the remaining fifteen least developed countries though projections are not available, there is evidence that some of them have made substantial progress in recent years as a result of vigorous national literacy campaigns and efforts to provide for universal primary education.

However, if the figures are taken percentage-wise India is little better off (if only one can say that) than many other countries. While the illiteracy rate in the age-group of 15 years and over, for India is 51.8 per cent, Afghanistan with 70.6 per cent illiterates top the list with Pakistan (65.2%), Cambodia and Bangladesh (64.7 and 64.8% respectively) following closely. At the bottom of the list are countries like Jamaica and Italy with 1.6 per cent illiterate population and 2.9 per cent respectively.

While 66.3 per cent of Indian females in the same age group are illiterate, the percentage of illiterate males is 38.2. The illiteracy rate in the age group of 15-19 years is 34.4 per cent. The total change during the past two decades has been 26.8 per cent.

The report also gives some interesting figures on communications and media in India. First the daily newspapers. According to it, while the number of copies per 1,000 inhabitants was 21 in 1980 it rose to 31 in 1988. Similarly, while the consumption of printing and writing paper was 762 kilograms per 1,000 inhabitants in 1980, it rose to 1,105 kg in 1988. In 1988, the number of radio receivers per 1,000 inhabitants was 78 and that for television was seven in comparison to 13 in Pakistan, 400 in Bahrain, 589 in Japan, 731 in Malta, 740 in Oman, 759 in Germany and an all-time high of 768 in Monaco.

Contrary to the popular belief that a large portion of Indian students opt for science, medicine and engineering, it is the study of law, social science and humanities that predominates in the country. 38 per cent Indian students choose the humanities and 23 per cent law and social science as against 29 per cent who take the natural sciences, engineering and agriculture and only four per cent who go in for medicine.

(Source: *World Education Report, 1991*, UNESCO, Paris.)

6.2 **International Commission on Education**

An International Commission on Education has been set up at the initiative of UNESCO. The Commission will reflect on the aptitudes, know-how, competence and knowledge that individuals need to carry out their duties and realize their rights.

A mix of historians, ministers, writers, educators, and sociologists among others from fourteen countries round the world constitute the fourteen members of the Commission. It will be chaired by Jacques Delors, President of the Commission of the European Communities. Other members include Mr. Carlos Fuentes, Mexican writer and University Professor and the Rt Hon Michael Manley, university lecturer, author and former Prime Minister of Jamaica.

In view of the importance and range of its mandate, the Commission will be aided in specific aspects of its work by an international group of distinguished advisors known for their successful work in the area of educational policy.

Ms Gro Harlem Brundtland, Prime Minister of Norway, Sir Yehudi Menuhin, British violinist, David Suzuki, Canadian scientist and science populariser and winner of the 1986 Kalinga Prize and Sheikh Saki Yamni, former Saudi Arabian minister of Petroleum and Natural Resources are among those who will constitute this group. The Education Commission will present its report at the beginning of 1995.

(Source: *UN Newsletter*, February 27, 1993.)

7

ECONOMIC AND SOCIAL DEVELOPMENT: Comparative Country Profile (Other than Trade)

7.1 Introduction

The tables given in this Chapter cover a wide range of economic and social statistics on the development of the nations of the world and provide a comparative study of the various facets of life. The data derived by the United Nations Children Fund (UNICEF) from the following international agencies, among others assume a special significance (i) United Nations Population Division, (ii) United Nations Statistical Office, (iii) World Bank, (iv) United Nations Educational Scientific and Cultural Organisation (UNESCO), (v) World Health Organisation (WHO), (vi) Food and Agricultural Organisation (FAO), (vii) International Monetary Fund (IMF), (viii) Organisation for Economic Cooperation and Development (OECD), besides UNICEF's own divisions and offices.

Where possible only comprehensive or representative national data have been used. The data for infant mortality rates, life expectancy, crude birth and death rates, etc. are part of the regular work on estimates and projections undertaken by the United Nations Population Division. These and other internationally produced estimates are revised periodically which explains why some of the data will differ from those found in earlier publications.

New indicators which reflect the World Summit for Children Goals, have been included on breast-feeding and sanitation. New demographic estimates, first released by the United Nations Population Division in July 1992, have also been incorporated in the tables. Finally, the four U5MR group summaries have been changed from medians to weighted averages, and regional summaries have been added to the end of each of tables 1 to 7 and 10.

The value of 70 under five deaths per 1000 live births used to distinguish the two higher U5MR groups of countries from the two lower groups, in Tables 1 to 7 and 10, reflects the *World Summit for Children* mortality goal target. The U5MR goal aims at a reduction of the under-five mortality rate in all countries during the 1990s by one third or to 70 per 1000 live births, whichever is less. Hence, if all countries achieve the under-five mortality goal, by the end of the 1990s all countries should belong to the two lowest U5MR groups.

Major social and economic changes in Asia and Europe have led to the creation of a number of newly independent countries. But country infrastructures take time to adjust to the changed status and the currently available statistics on these newly independent countries are limited. Recognizing both the need for reporting on the situation of children and women in these countries, as well as the limited coverage of the statistics, a separate table (table 9) has been added.

Following signs have been used:

- NA Data not available.
- X Indicates data that refer to years/periods other than those specified in the column heading, differ from the standard definition, or refer to only part of the country.

7.2: **Basic Data**

TABLE 7.1 : Basic Data

	Under-5 mortality rate		Infant mortality rate (under 1)		Total population (millions)	Annual no. of births (thousands)	Annual no. of under-5 deaths (thousands)	GNP per capita (US$)	Life expectancy at birth (years)	Total adult literacy rate	% of age-group enrolled in primary school (gross)	% share of household income 1980-1988	
	1960	1991	1960	1991	1991	1991	1991	1990	1991	1990	1986-1990	lowest 40%	highest 20%
1	2	3	4	5	6	7	8	9	10	11	12	13	14
Very high U5MR countries	283	197	164	114	502	23629	4697	355	50	40	64	NA	NA
1 Angola	345	292	208	170	9.6	496	153	610[x]	46	42	93	NA	NA
2 Mozambique	331	292	190	170	14.6	672	209	80	47	33	68	NA	NA
3 Afghanistan	360	257	215	165	17.9	964	236	280[x]	43	29	24	NA	NA
4 Sierra Leone	385	253	219	146	4.3	206	53	240	42	21	53	NA	NA
5 Guinea-Bissau	336	242	200	143	1.0	442	10	180	43	36	59	NA	NA
6 Guinea	337	234	203	138	5.9	303	71	480	44	24	334	NA	NA
7 Malawi	365	228	206	144	9.9	539	123	200	45	NA	67	NA	NA
8 Mali	400	225	200	108	9.5	487	111	270	45	32	23	NA	NA
9 Niger	321	218	181	127	8.0	414	90	310	46	28	28	NA	NA
10 Chad	325	213	195	125	5.7	252	54	190	47	30	57	NA	NA
11 Ethiopia	294	212	175	125	51.5	2543	540	1220	46	NA	38	NA	NA
12 Somalia	294	211	175	125	9.0	457	95	150	46	24	15	NA	NA
13 Mauritania	321	209	191	120	2.1	97	20	500	47	34	51	NA	NA
14 Burkina Faso	363	206	205	120	9.3	435	89	330	48	18	36	NA	NA
15 Bhutan	324	205	203	133	1.6	63	13	190	48	38	26	NA	NA

Contd.

TABLE 7.1 *Contd.*

1		2	3	4	5	6	7	8	9	10	11	12	13	14
16	Zambia	220	200	135	112	8.4	394	82	420	45	73	95	11x	61x
17	Liberia	310	200	184	131	2.7	127	25	450x	55	40	34	NA	NA
18	Uganda	223	190	133	110	18.1	924	174	220	43	48	70	NA	NA
19	Rwanda	255	189	150	112	7.3	382	71	310	47	50	69	NA	NA
20	Nigeria	212	188	108	86	112.2	5181	1008	270	52	51	70	NA	NA
21	Cambodia	217	188	146	120	8.6	342	65	NA	50	35	NA	NA	NA
22	Senegal	299	182	172	82	7.5	330	61	710	49	38	58	NA	NA
23	Yemen	378	182	214	110	12.1	599	110	650x	52	39	86	NA	NA
24	Burundi	260	181	153	108	5.7	262	47	210	48	50	69	NA	NA
25	Zaire	300	180	174	117	38.7	1845	333	230	52	72	78	NA	NA
26	Central African Rep.	294	180	174	106	3.1	138	25	390	47	38	64	NA	NA
27	Tanzania	249	178	147	112	26.9	1299	230	120	51	91	64	NA	NA
28	Madagascar	364	173	219	113	12.4	569	97	230	55	80	92	NA	NA
29	Sudan	292	169	170	102	26.0	1111	189	420x	51	27	50x	NA	NA
30	Gabon	287	161	171	97	1.2	50.	8	3330	53	61	NA	NA	NA
31	Benin	310	149	184	89	4.8	235	34	360	46	23	66	NA	NA
32	Lao. Peo. Dem.	233	148	155	101	4.3	196	28	200	50	NA	110	NA	NA
33	Nepal	298	147	186	102	20.1	776	114	170	53	26	85	13x	59x
34	Togo	305	144	182	88	3.7	164	23	410	54	43	103	NA	NA
35	Iraq	171	143	117	111	18.7	735	106	2340x	66	60	96	NA	NA

Contd.

TABLE 7.1 *Contd.*

	1	2	3	4	5	6	7	8	9	10	11	12	13	14
	High U5MR countries	231	116	143	80	1672	53579	6176	525	59	54	93	18	44
36	Lesotho	210	137	149	82	1.8	63	9	470	60	NA	107	NA	NA
37	Haiti	270	137	182	89	6.6	236	32	370	56	53	84	6	48
38	Ghana	224	137	132	84	15.5	659	90	390	55	60	75	17	45
39	Pakistan	221	134	148	94	121.5	5044	671	380	58	35	38	19	46
40	Bangladesh	2247	133	151	101	116.6	4514	583	200	52	35	70	**24**	37
41	Cote d'Ivoire	300	127	165	93	12.5	624	77	730	52	54	70	13	53
42	**India**	**236**	**126**	**144**	**84**	**863.2**	**25654**	**3221**	**350**	**60**	**48**	**97**	**20**	**41**
43	Cameroon	270	126	163	66	11.9	489	60	940	55	54	101	NA	NA
44	Bolivia	282	126	167	89	7.4	258	32	620	60	78	82	12	58
45	Namibia	248	120	146	73	1.5	64	8	1030 x	58	NA	NA	NA	NA
46	Myanmar	237	117	158	85	42.8	1411	164	220 x	57	81	103	NA	NA
47	Congo	220	110	143	83	2.3	103	11	1010	52	57	NA	NA	NA
48	Libyan Arab Jamahiriya	269	108	160	72	4.7	201	21	5310 x	62	64	NA	NA	NA
49	Peru	240	97	142	68	22.0	652	63	1160	64	85	123	13	52
50	Guatemala	220	92	125	52	9.5	373	34	900	64	55	76	14 x	55 x
51	Morocco	265	91	163	72	25.7	853	77	950	63	50	68	23	39
52	Turkey	216	89	160	72	57.2	1633	146	1630	67	81	113	11	55
53	Zimbabwe	181	88	109	61	10.3	422	36	640	56	67	128	NA	NA
54	Indonesia	215	86	128	61	187.7	5104	437	570	62	77	118	21	41
55	Botswana	169	85	116	62	1.3	50	4	2040	60	74	115	9	59

Contd.

TABLE 7.1 *Contd.*

	1	2	3	4	5	6	7	8	9	10	11	12	13	14
56	Egypt	260	85	168	62	53.6	1735	146	600	61	48	97	21	41
57	Ecuador	184	82	124	58	10.8	329	27	960	66	86	118	NA	NA
58	Mongolia	185	82	128	62	2.3	78	6	780 x	63	NA	102	NA	NA
59	Nicaragua	209	81	140	58	3.8	160	13	830 x	65	NA	95	12	58
60	Papua New Guinea	248	79	165	55	4.0	134	10	860	55	52	73	NA	NA
61	Dominican Rep.	200	76	125	58	7.3	213	16	820	67	83	96	NA	NA
62	Kenya	202	75	120	52	24.4	1085	79	370	59	69	94	9x	60x
63	Honduras	230	73	160	62	5.3	201	15	590	65	73	109	12	59
64	South Africa	126	72	89	54	38.9	1237	88	2530	62	NA	NA	NA	NA
	Middle U5MR Countries	174	36	114	29	2226	50370	1804	1465	69	76	120	15	NA
65	Brazil	179	67	117	55	151.5	3668	247	2680	66	81	NA	8	63
66	El Salvador	210	67	130	50	5.3	180	12	1100	65	73	78	8	66
67	Iran, Islamic Rep. of	233	62	145	47	60.0	2437	149	2450	67	54	108	NA	NA
68	Algeria	243	61	148	50	25.7	886	53	2060	66	57	96	NA	NA
69	Paraguay	103	59	66	48	4.4	148	9	1110	67	90	106	NA	NA
70	Tunisia	254	58	159	45	8.2	228	13	1420	67	65	115	NA	NA
71	Viet Nam	219	52	147	39	68.1	2040	105	240 x	63	88	102	NA	NA
72	Syria	217	47	135	37	12.8	552	25	990	66	65	108	NA	NA
73	Jordan	180	46	135	39	4.2	165	7	1240	67	80	99	NA	NA
74	Lebanon	91	46	68	36	2.8	77	4	2150 x	68	80	100	NA	NA
75	Philippines	128	46	81	34	63.8	1975	90	730	65	90	111	14	52

Contd.

TABLE 7.1 *Contd.*

	1	2	3	4	5	6	7	8	9	10	11	12	13	14
76	Venezuela	114	43	81	34	19.8	528	22	2560	70	88	105	14	51
77	Saudi Arabia	292	43	170	33	15.4	560	24	7050	69	62	76	NA	NA
78	Oman	378	42	214	32	1.6	65	3	5220 x	69	NA	102	NA	NA
79	Mexico	138	37	97	30	86.3	2462	91	2490	70	87	117	13	NA
80	Romania	82	34	69	227	23.3	367	12	1640	70	NA	96	NA	NA
81	Korea, Dem. Peo. Rep.	120	34	85	25	22.2	533	18	970 x	71	[illegible]	107	NA	NA
82	Thailand	146	33	101	28	55.4	1169	338	1420	[illegible]	[illegible]	89	15 x	50 x
83	USSR (former)	53	31	38	23	282.8	4847	156	45[illegible]0x	[illegible]	NA	105	NA	NA
84	Albania	151	311	112	26	3.3	76	22	79[illegible]x	73	NA	99	NA	NA
85	Panama	105	30	69	21	2.5	63	2	1830	73	88	107	NA	NA
86	United Arab Emirates	239	29	145	24	1.6	35	1	198[illegible]	71	48	111	NA	NA
87	Mauritius	1104	28	70	22	1.1	20	1	2250	70	NA	103	12	46
88	China	205	27	133	22	1170.4	24592	661	370	70	73	135	22	38
89	Uruguay	57	24	51	21	3.1	54	1	2560	722	96	107	18	44
90	Argentina	70	24	59	22	32.7	673	16	2370	71	95	111	14	51
91	Trinidad and Tobago	69	23	56	20	1.3	30	1	3470	71	NA	97	13x	50x
92	Yugoslavia (former)	113	22	92	19	23.9	343	8	3060	72	93	95	17	43
93	Bulgaria	70	21	49	17	9.0	113	2	2250	72	NA	97	NA	NA
94	Chile	142	21	114	17	13.4	307	6	1940	72	93	98	13	54
95	Sri Lanka	130	21	90	16	17.4	371	8	470	71	88	108	13	56
96	Colombia	130	21	88	18	32.9	806	17	1240	69	87	107	13	53

Contd.

TABLE 7.1 *Contd.*

	1	2	3	4	5	6	7	8	9	10	11	12	13	14
	Low U5MR Countrjes	48	11	38	9	959	13428	144	17580	76	NA	103	18	41
97	Malaysia	105	20	73	15	18.3	541	11	2340	70	78	97	14	51
98	Jamaica	89	19	63	15	2.4	55	1	1510	73	98	105	15	49
99	Costa Rica	122	18	85	14	3.1	84	2	1910	76	93	100	12	55
100	Hungary	57	17	51	16	10.5	128	2	2780	70	NA	97	26	32
101	Poland	70	17	62	15	38.3	566	10	1690	71	NA	99	24	35
102	Kuwait	128	17	89	14	2.0	53	1	16150^x	75	73	100	NA	NA
103	Cuba	91	14	65	11	10.7	187	3	1170^x	76	94	103	NA	NA
104	Checho-slovakia	33	13	26	12	15.7	220	3	3140	72	NA	93	NA	NA
105	Israel	39	12	32	10	4.9	108	1	10920	76	NA	94	18^x	40^x
106	Portugal	112	12	81	10	9.9	117	1	4900	74	85	127	NA	NA
107	USA	30	11	26	9	252.6	4024	43	21790	76	NA	101	16	42
108	Greece	64	11	53	10	10.1	106	1	5990	77	93	102	NA	NA
109	Ireland	36	10	31	8	3.5	52	1	9550	75	NA	101	NA	NA
110	Singapore	50	10	36	8	2.7	44	0	12310	74	NA	110	15	49
111	Belgium	35	10	31	8	10.0	121	1	15540	76	NA	101	22^x	36^x
112	Australia	24	10	20	8	17.3	261	3	17000	77	NA	106	16	42
113	Italy	50	10	44	8	57.7	575	6	16830	77	97	96	19	41
114	New Zealand	26	110	22	8	3.4	59	1	12680	75	NA	106	16	45
115	Korea, Rep. of	126	10	88	9	43.7	714	7	5400	70	96	109	20	42
116	Canada	33	9	28	7	27.0	388	3	20470	77	NA	105	18	40

Contd.

TABLE 7.1 *Contd.*

	1	2	3	4	5	6	7	8	9	10	11	12	13	14
117	Germany	40	9	34	8	79.8	901	8	22320x	76	NA	103	20x	39x
118	Denmark	25	9	22	8	5.2	62	1	22080	75	NA	98	17	39
119	Switzerland	27	9	22	7	6.8	84	1	32680	78	NA	NA	17	45
120	France	34	9	29	7	56.9	772	7	19490	77	NA	113	18x	41x
121	United Kingdom	27	9	23	7	57.5	792	7	16100	76	NA	106	17x	40x
122	Austria	43	9	37	8	7.7	90	1	19060	76	NA	104	NA	NA
123	Spain	57	9	46	8	39.0	423	4	11020	77	95	111	19	40
124	Hong Kong	64	8	43	7	5.8	73	1	11540	77	NA	105	16	47
125	Netherlands	22	8	18	7	15.1	202	2	17320	77	NA	116	20	38
126	Norway	23	8	19	7	4.3	61	1	23120	77	NA	98	19	38
127	Finland	28	7	22	6	5.0	64	0	26040	75	NA	99	18	38
128	Japan	40	6	31	5	124.0	1384	9	25430	79	NA	102	22x	38x
129	Sweden	20	5	16	4	8.6	117	1	23660	78	NA	104	21	37
	Regional summaries													
	Least developed countries	286	180	172	115	519	22973	4128	240	50	47	66	NA	NA
	Developing countries	217	101	136	67	4147	123583	12523	805	61	65	100	NA	NA
	Developed countries	45	17	36	113	1213	17423	298	14710	74	NA	103	18	40

Contd.

TABLE 7.1 *Concld.*

1	2	3	4	5	6	7	8	9	10	11	12	13	14
Sub-Saharan Africa	261	180	151	103	515	23659	4299	490	51	54	68	NA	NA
Middle East & North Africa	246	90	157	66	332	11925	1075	1975	63	58	95	NA	NA
South Asia	238	131	147	89	1158	37386	4846	335	58	46	86	20	42
East Asia & Pacific	198	42	128	32	1700	38946	1641	650	68	76	125	20	42
Latin America & Caribbean	161	57	108	44	442	11667	662	2105	67	85	108	11	59

Countries listed in descending order of U5MR (shown in column 3).

7.3 **Demographic Data**

TABLE 7.2 Demographic Data

		Population (millions) 1991		Population annual growth rate (%)		Crude death rate		Crude birth rate		Life expectancy		Total fertility rate	% of population urbanized	Average annual growth rate of urban population (%)	
		Under 16	Under 5	1965-80	1980-91	1960	1991	1960	1991	1960	1991	1991	1991	1965-80	1980-91
	1	2	3	4	5	6	7	8	9	10	11	12	13	14	15
	Very high U5MR countries	276	106	2.6	3.0	26	16	50	47	39	50	6.6	25	5.9	5.3
1	Angola	5.5	2.2	2.8	2.9	31	20	49	51	33	46	7.2	27	6.4	5.9
2	Mozambique	7.7	2.9	2.5	1.7	26	18	47	45	37	47	6.5	25	11.8	8.8
3	Afghanistan	9.7	4.2	2.4	1.0	30	22	52	52	33	43	6.9	18	6.0	2.6
4	Sierra Leone	2.2	0.9	2.0	2.4	33	22	48	48	32	42	6.5	31	4.3	5.1
5	Guinea-Bissau	0.5	0.2	1.2	2.0	29	22	40	43	34	43	5.8	19	1.7	3.6
6	Guinea	3.3	1.3	1.9	2.6	31	21	53	51	34	44	7.0	25	6.6	5.6
7	Malawi	5.8	2.3	2.9	4.3	28	21	54	55	38	45	7.6	11	7.8	6.9
8	Mali	5.4	2.1	2.1	3.0	29	20	52	51	35	45	7.1	23	4.9	5.6
9	Niger	4.6	1.8	2.7	3.3	29	19	53	51	35	46	7.1	19	6.9	7.2
10	Chad	2.9	1.1	2.0	2.2	30	18	46	44	35	47	5.9	30	9.2	6.5
11	Ethiopia	28.2	11.2	2.7	2.6	28	19	50	49	36	46	7.0	12	6.6	4.2
12	Somalia	5.1	2.0	2.7	2.6	28	19	50	50	36	46	7.0	24	6.1	3.6
13	Mauritania	1.1	0.4	2.3	2.7	28	18	48	46	35	47	6.5	44	12.4	7.3
14	Burkina Faso	4.9	1.9	2.0	2.6	28	18	49	47	36	48	6.5	14	3.4	8.5
15	Bhutan	0.7	0.3	1.6	22.2	26	17	42	40	37	48	5.9	5	3.7	5.3

Contd.

TABLE 7.2 *Contd.*

	1	2	3	4	5	6	7	8	9	10	11	12	13	14	15
16	Zambia	4.8	1.8	3.1	3.5	22	17	50	47	42	45	6.5	42	7.1	4.0
17	Liberia	1.5	0.6	3.0	3.2	25	15	50	47	41	55	6.8	44	6.2	5.8
18	Uganda	10.4	4.1	2.9	2.9	21	21	50	51	43	43	7.3	11	4.1	5.4
19	Rwanda	4.2	1.7	3.3	3.1	22	18	50	52	42	47	8.5	5	6.3	4.8
20	Nigeria	62.5	23.4	2.5	3.3	24	14	52	46	40	52	6.6	334	4.8	5.9
21	Cambodia	4.1	1.5	0.3	2.5	21	15	45	40	42	50	4.5	11	1.9	3.8
22	Senegal	3.9	1.5	2.5	2.8	27	17	50	44	37	49	6.2	39	4.1	3.9
23	Yemen	7.2	2.7	2.3	3.5	28	14	53	49	36	52	7.3	28	6.4	7.1
24	Burundi	3.1	1.2	1.9	2.9	23	17	46	46	41	48	6.8	5	1.8	5.1
25	Zaire	22.1	8.6	2.8	3.3	23	15	47	48	41	52	6.7	28	7.2	3.1
26	Central African Rep.	1.6	0.6	1.8	2.6	26	18	43	45	39	47	6.2	46	4.8	4.6
27	Tanzania	15.4	6.0	3.3	3.4	23	15	51	48	41	51	6.8	20	8.7	6.8
28	Madagascar	6.8	2.6	2.5	3.2	24	13	48	46	41	55	6.6	23	5.7	5.8
29	Sudan	13.5	5.0	3.0	3.0	25	15	47	43	39	51	6.2	22	5.1	4.3
30	Gabon	0.5	0.2	3.5	3.6	24	16	31	41	41	53	5.2	44	4.2	6.0
31	Benin	2.7	1.1	2.7	2.9	33	18	47	49	35	46	7.1	37	10.2	4.8
32	Lao. Peo. Dem.	2.3	0.9	0.6	2.8	23	16	45	45	40	50	6.7	18	4.8	6.0
33	Nepal	10.0	3.4	2.4	2.7	26	14	46	39	38	53	5.6	10	5.1	7.9
34	Togo	2.0	0.8	3.0	3.0	26	13	48	45	39	54	6.6	28	7.2	5.2
35	Iraq	9.8	3.6	3.4	3.3	20	7	49	39	48	66	5.8	71	5.3	4.2

Contd.

TABLE 7.2 *Contd.*

1	2	3	4	5	6	7	8	9	10	11	12	13	14	15
High U5MR countries	707	244	2.5	2.3	21	10	44	32	44	59	4.2	30	4.1	3.8
36 Lesotho	0.8	0.3	2.3	2.7	24	10	43	35	43	60	4.8	19	14.6	6.5
37 Haiti	3.0	1.1	2.0	1.9	23	12	42	36	42	56	4.9	28	4.0	3.8
38 Ghana	8.3	3.0	2.2	3.3	19	12	48	42	45	55	6.1	34	3.4	4.3
39 Pakistan	61.8	22.5	3.1	3.2	23	11	49	42	43	58	6.3	31	4.3	4.6
40 Bangladesh	54.5	19.7	2.7	2.5	22	14	47	39	40	52	4.8	16	8.0	6.3
41 Cote d'Ivoire	7.4	2.9	4.2	3.8	25	15	53	50	39	52	7.4	40	8.7	5.3
42 India	**343.7**	**115.9**	**2.3**	**2.1**	**21**	**10**	**43**	**30**	**44**	**60**	**4.0**	**25**	**3.6**	**3.1**
43 Cameroon	6.1	2.3	2.7	2.9	24	13	44	41	39	55	5.8	39	8.1	5.4
44 Bolivia	3.4	1.2	2.5	2.5	22	10	46	35	43	60	4.7	50	2.9	3.9
45 Namibia	0.8	0.3	1.0	3.0	22	11	45	43	42	58	6.0	27	1.9	5.1
46 Myanmar	18.4	6.5	2.3	2.1	21	12	42	33	44	57	4.3	25	2.8	2.5
47 Congo	1.2	0.5	2.7	2.9	23	15	45	45	42	52	6.3	40	3.5	4.2
48 Libyan Arab Jamahiriya	2.6	1.0	4.6	4.0	19	8	49	43	47	62	6.5	81	9.7	5.6
49 Peru	9.0	3.0	2.8	2.2	19	8	47	30	48	64	3.7	69	4.1	3.0
50 Guatemala	5.0	1.8	2.8	2.9	19	8	49	39	46	64	5.5	39	3.6	3.5
51 Morocco	11.6	4.0	2.5	2.6	21	9	50	33	47	63	4.5	45	4.2	3.7
52 Turkey	22.2	7.8	2.4	2.3	18	7	45	29	50	67	3.6	59	4.2	5.5
53 Zimbabwe	5.4	2.0	3.1	3.3	20	11	53	41	45	56	5.5	28	7.5	5.8
54 Indonesia	71.5	23.5	2.3	2.0	23	9	44	27	41	62	3.2	28	4.7	4.6
55 Botswana	0.7	0.2	3.5	3.2	20	10	52	39	46	60	5.2	24	15.4	8.2

Contd.

TABLE 7.2 *Contd.*

	1	2	3	4	5	6	7	8	9	10	11	12	13	14	15
56	Egypt	23.5	7.8	2.4	2.5	21	10	45	32	46	61	4.2	44	2.9	2.5
57	Ecuador	4.6	1.5	3.1	2.6	15	7	46	30	53	66	3.8	55	5.1	4.4
58	Mongolia	1.1	0.4	3.0	2.8	18	8	43	35	47	63	4.7	57	4.5	3.8
59	Nicaragua	2.1	0.8	3.1	2.8	19	7	51	41	47	65	5.2	59	4.6	4.0
60	Papua New Guinea	1.8	0.6	2.3	2.3	23	11	44	34	41	55	5.0	15	8.4	4.3
61	Dominican Rep.	3.0	1.0	2.7	2.3	16	6	50	29	52	67	3.5	59	5.3	4.0
62	Kenya	13.9	5.2	3.6	3.5	22	11	53	44	45	59	6.4	23	9.0	7.3
63	Honduras	2.7	1.0	3.2	3.4	19	7	51	38	46	65	5.1	43	5.5	5.3
64	South Africa	16.9	5.8	2.4	2.5	17	9	42	32	49	62	4.2	49	2.6	2.8
	Middle U5MR countries	738	243	2.1	1.6	16	7	36	23	52	69	2.7	41	3.2	3.3
65	Brazil	55.3	16.9	2.4	2.0	13	7	43	24	55	66	2.9	74	4.5	3.3
66	El Salvador	2.5	0.9	2.7	1.4	16	8	48	34	50	65	4.2	44	3.5	2.1
67	Iran, Islamic Rep. of	32.2	11.6	3.2	3.9	21	7	47	41	50	67	6.1	56	5.5	5.2
68	Algeria	12.5	4.3	3.1	2.9	20	7	51	34	47	66	5.0	51	3.8	4.6
69	Paraguay	2.0	0.7	2.8	3.0	9	6	43	34	64	67	4.4	47	3.2	4.4
70	Tunisia	3.3	1.1	22.1	2.3	19	78	47	28	48	67	3.6	55	4.2	3.4
71	Viet Nam	28.9	9.6	1.0	2.2	23	9	41	30	44	63	4.0	20	4.1	2.5
72	Syria	7.4	2.7	3.4	3.5	18	6	47	43	50	66	6.3	50	4.5	4.3
73	Jordan	2.2	0.8	2.6	3.2	23	6	50	39	47	67	5.8	67	5.3	4.5
74	Lebanon	1.1	0.4	1.6	0.4	14	7	43	27	60	68	3.2	82	4.6	1.7
75	Philippines	28.1	9.4	2.9	2.5	15	7	45	31	53	65	4.0	42	4.0	3.8

Contd.

TABLE 7.2 *Contd.*

	1	2	3	4	5	6	7	8	9	10	11	12	13	14	15
76	Venezuela	7.9	2.6	3.5	2.5	10	5	45	27	60	70	3.2	90	4.5	3.3
77	Saudi Arabia	7.8	22.8	4.6	4.5	23	5	49	36	44	69	6.5	76	8.5	5.9
78	Oman	0.9	0.3	3.6	4.3	28	5	51	41	40	69	6.8	11	8.1	8.1
79	Mexico	35.7	11.9	3.1	2.3	13	6	45	29	57	70	3.3	72	4.5	3.2
80	Romania	5.6	1.8	1.1	0.4	9	11	20	16	65	70	2.2	53	3.4	1.3
81	Korea, Dem. Peo. Rep.	7.2	2.7	2.7	1.8	13	5	42	24	54	71	2.4	60	4.6	2.3
82	Thailand	18.2	5.6	2.7	1.5	15	6	44	21	52	69	2.3	21	4.6	4.2
83	USSR (former)	77.1	22.9	0.9	0.8	7	10	24	17	68	70	2.3	66	2.2	1.4
84	Albania	1.1	0.4	2.5	1.9	10	5	41	24	62	73	2.8	35	3.4	2.5
85	Panama	0.9	0.3	2.6	2.1	10	5	41	25	61	73	3.0	52	3.4	2.7
86	United Arab Emirates	0.5	0.2	16.1	4.3	19	4	46	22	53	71	4.6	80	18.9	5.5
87	Mauritius	0.3	0.1	1.6	1.1	10	7	44	19	59	70	2.0	41	4.0	0.7
88	China	357.2	120.4	2.2	1.5	19	7	37	21	47	70	2.3	25	2.6	4.4
89	Uruguay	0.8	0.3	0.4	0.6	10	10	22	17	68	72	2.4	88	0.7	1.0
90	Argentina	10.4	3.3	1.6	1.3	9	9	24	21	65	71	2.8	86	2.2	1.7
91	Trinidad and Tobago	0.5	0.1	1.3	1.3	9	6	38	24	63	71	2.8	65	5.0	1.6
92	Yugoslavia (former)	5.6	1.6	0.9	0.6	10	9	23	14	63	72	1.9	55	3.0	2.7
93	Bulgaria	1.8	0.5	0.5	0.1	9	12	18	13	68	72	1.9	67	2.8	1.1
94	Chile	4.6	1.5	1.8	1.7	13	6	37	23	57	72	2.7	84	2.6	2.1
95	Sri Lanka	5.9	1.8	1.8	1.5	9	6	36	21	62	71	2.5	21	2.3	1.5
96	Colombia	12.3	3.9	2.2	1.9	12	6	45	25	57	69	2.7	69	3.5	2.8

Contd.

TABLE 7.2 *Contd.*

	1	2	3	4	5	6	7	8	9	10	11	12	13	14	15
	Low U5MR Countries	**213**	**67**	**0.9**	**0.7**	**10**	**9**	**21**	**14**	**68**	**76**	**1.8**	**75**	**1.7**	**1.0**
97	Malaysia	8.0	2.7	2.5	2.6	15	5	44	30	54	70	3.7	42	4.5	4.8
98	Jamaica	0.8	0.3	1.5	1.2	9	6	39	23	63	73	2.5	51	3.4	2.4
99	Costa Rica	1.3	0.4	2.6	2.8	10	4	47	27	62	76	3.2	47	3.7	3.7
100	Hungary	2.1	0.6	0.4	-0.1	10	14	16	12	68	70	1.8	63	1.8	1.0
101	Poland	9.8	2.7	0.8	0.7	8	10	24	15	67	71	2.1	61	1.8	1.3
102	Kuwait	0.7	0.2	7.0	3.6	10	2	44	28	60	75	3.8	95	8.2	4.1
103	Cuba	2.7	0.9	1.5	0.9	9	7	31	17	64	76	1.9	73	2.7	1.7
104	Checho-slovakia	3.6	1.1	0.5	0.2	10	11	17	14	70	72	2.0	76	1.9	1.5
105	Israel	1.8	0.6	2.8	2.1	6	7	27	22	69	76	2.9	91	3.5	2.5
106	Portugal	2.0	0.6	0.6	0.1	11	10	24	12	63	74	1.5	33	2.0	1.4
107	USA	612	20.3	1.0	0.9	9	9	23	16	70	76	2.0	75	1.2	1.1
108	Greece	1.9	0.5	0.7	0.5	8	10	19	10	69	77	1.5	62	2.5	1.3
109	Ireland	0.9	0.2	1.2	0.3	12	9	21	15	70	75	2.2	57	2.2	0.6
110	Singapore	0.7	0.2	1.6	1.1	8	5	38	16	64	74	1.7	100	1.6	1.1
111	Belgium	1.9	0.6	0.3	0.1	12	11	17	12	70	76	1.6	96	0.5	0.2
112	Australia	4.2	1.4	1.8	1.5	9	8	22	15	71	77	1.9	85	0.2	1.4
113	Italy	9.6	2.9	0.6	0.2	10	10	18	10	69	77	1.3	69	1.0	0.6
114	New Zealand	0.9	0.3	1.3	0.9	9	8	26	17	71	75	2.1	84	1.5	0.9
115	Korea, Rep. of	11.3	3.5	1.9	1.2	14	6	43	16	54	70	1.7	70	5.7	3.6

Contd.

TABLE 7.2 *Concld.*

	1	2	3	4	5	6	7	8	9	10	11	12	13	14	15
116	Canada	6.3	2.0	1.3	1.1	8	8	26	14	71	77	1.8	77	1.5	1.3
117	Germany	14.8	4.6	0.2	0.2	12	11	17	11	70	76	1.5	85	0.9	0.5
118	Denmark	0.9	0.3	0.5	0.1	9	12	17	12	72	75	1.7	85	1.1	0.2
119	Switzerland	1.3	0.4	0.5	0.6	10	10	18	12	71	78	1.6	61	1.2	1.4
120	France	12.2	3.8	0.7	0.5	12	10	18	14	70	77	1.8	73	2.7	0.4
121	United Kingdom	12.1	4.0	0.2	0.2	12	11	17	14	71	76	1.9	89	0.5	0.2
122	Austria	1.5	0.5	0.3	0.2	12	11	18	12	69	76	1.5	58	0.1	0.9
123	Spain	7.3	2.1	1.0	0.4	9	9	21	11	69	77	1.4	78	2.4	1.1
124	Hong Kong	1.2	0.4	2.1	1.2	7	6	35	13	66	77	1.4	94	2.3	1.5
125	Netherlands	3.1	1.0	0.9	0.6	8	9	21	13	73	77	1.7	9	1.5	0.6
126	Norway	0.9	0.3	0.6	0.4	9	11	18	14	73	77	1.9	74	5.0	1.0
127	Finland	1.0	0.3	0.3	0.4	9	10	19	13	68	75	1.8	60	2.5	0.4
128	Japan	22.8	6.9	1.2	0.5	8	7	18	11	68	79	1.7	77	2.1	0.7
129	Sweden	1.7	0.6	0.5	0.3	10	11	15	14	73	78	2.0	84	1.0	0.4
Regional summaries															
	Least developed countries	270	102	2.6	2.7	25	16	48	44	39	50	6.0	19	6.4	5.2
	Developing countries	165	574	2.4	2.1	20	9	42	30	46	61	3.7	33	4.0	3.9
	Developed countries	277	86	0.8	0.6	9	10	21	14	69	74	1.9	73	1.7	1.0
	Sub-Saharan Africa	281	107	2.7	3.0	24	15	49	46	40	51	6.5	28	5.7	5.2
	Middle East & North Africa	159	56	2.9	3.0	21	8	47	36	47	63	5.0	52	4.9	4.6
	South Asia	486	168	2.4	2.2	21	11	44	33	43	58	4.4	24	3.9	3.5
	East Asia & Pacific	560	188	2.2	1.7	19	7	39	23	47	68	2.6	28	3.3	4.1
	Latin America & Caribbean	171	55	2.5	2.1	13	7	42	26	56	67	3.2	71	4.0	3.0

Countries listed in descending order of U5MR.

7.4 Economic Data

TABLE 7.3: Economic Data

	GNP per capita (US$) 1990	GNP per capita average annual growth rate (%)		Rate of inflation (%)	% of population below absolute poverty level 1980-89		% of central government expenditure allocated to (1986-91)			ODA inflow in millions US$ 1990	ODA inflow as a % of recipient GNP 1990	Debt service as a % of exports of goods and services	
		1965-80	1980-90	1980-90	Urban	Rural	health	education	defence			1970	1990
1	2	3	4	5	6	7	8	9	10	11	12	13	14
Very high U5MR countries	**355**	**2.4**	**-0.8**	**24**	**NA**	**NA**	**3**	**9**	**NA**	**12723**	**12**	**5**	**15**
1 Angola	610[x]	NA	6.1	NA	NA	NA	6	15	34	211	NA	NA	NA
2 Mozambique	80	NA	-4.1	37	50	67	5	10	35	923	76	NA	5
3 Afghanistan	280[x]	0.6	NA	NA	18[x]	36[x]	NA	NA	NA	172	NA	NA	NA
4 Sierra Leone	240	0.7	-1.5	56	NA	65[x]	8[x]	16[x]	4[x]	66	7	11	6[x]
5 Guinea-Bissau	180	-2.7	1.7	NA	NA	NA	1	3	4	118	67	NA	27
6 Guinea	480	1.3	NA	NA	NA	NA	NA	11	29	274	10	NA	6
7 Malawi	200	3.2	-0.1	15	25	85	7	9	5	450	27	8	19
8 Mali	270	2.1[x]	1.2	3	27[x]	48[x]	4	17	17	462	20	1	7
9 Niger	310	-2.5	-4.5	3	NA	35[x]	NA	NA	NA	357	15	4	4
10 Chad	190	-1.9	3.3	1	30[x]	56[x]	8	8	NA	314	29	4	2
11 Ethiopia	120	0.4	-1.2	2	60	65	NA	NA		871	14	11	31
12 Somalia	150	-0.1	-1.8	50	40[x]	70[x]	1	2	38	433	46	2	18[x]
13 Mauritania	500	-0.1	-1.8	9	NA	NA	4	23	NA	207	21	3	8
14 Burkina Faso	330	1.7	1.4	5	NA	NA	5	14	18	305	10	7	5
15 Bhutan	190	NA	7.4	8	NA	NA	5	12	NA	42	15	NA	NA

Contd

TABLE 7.3 *Contd.*

	1	2	3	4	5	6	7	8	9	10	11	12	13	14
16	Zambia	420	-1.2	-2.9	42	25		7	9	NA	430	13	6	11
17	Liberia	450[x]	0.5	5.2[x]	NA		23[x]		NA	NA	94	NA	8	NA
18	Uganda	220	-2.2	0.8	107			2	15	26	563	15	3	35
19	Rwanda	310	1.6	-2.2	4	30	90[x]	5	26	NA	281	13	1	11
20	Nigeria	270	4.2	-3.0	18	NA	NA	1	3	3	214	1	4	20
21	Cambodia		NA	NA	NA	NA	NA	NA	NA	NA	35	NA	NA	NA
22	Senegal	710	-0.5	0.0	7	NA	NA	NA	NA	NA	724	14	3	15
23	Yemen	650[x]	NA	NA	NA	NA	NA	NA	NA	NA	390	NA	NA	17[x]
24	Burundi	210	2.4	1.3	4	55[x]	85[x]	4	16	16	259	23	2	41
25	Zaire	230	-1.3	-1.5	61	NA	80[x]	4	6	14	816	10	4	6
26	Central African Rep.	390	0.8	-1.3	5	NA	91	NA	NA	NA	227	19	5	6
27	Tanzania	120	0.8	-0.7	26			6[x]	8[x]	16[x]	1155	42	5	18
28	Madagascar	230	-0.4	-2.3	17	50[x]	50[x]	NA	NA	NA	375	14	4	34
29	Sudan	420[x]	0.8	1.8[x]	34[x]	NA	85[x]	NA	NA	NA	768	NA	11	3
30	Gabon	3330	5.6	-2.6	-2	NA	NA				139	4	6	5
31	Benin	360	-0.3	-1.0	2	NA	NA	6	31	17	254	15	2	5[x]
32	Lao, Peo. Dem.	200	NA	0.7	NA	NA	NA	NA	NA	NA	150	18	NA	12
33	Nepal	170	NA	1.8	9	55[x]	61[x]	5	11	6	383	12	3	14
34	Togo	410	1.7	-1.7	5	42[x]	NA	5	20	11	205	14	3	10
35	Iraq	2340[x]	NA	NA	NA	NA	NA	NA	NA	NA	56	NA	NA	NA
High U5MR countries		**525**	**2.6**	**1.8**	**23**	**32**	**37**	**3**	**9**	**15**	**20609**	**3**	**15**	**20**
36	Lesotho	470	6.8	-0.9	13	50[x]	55[x]	7	16	10	138	17	5	2
37	Haiti	370	0.9	-2.3	7	65	80	NA	NA	NA	176	7	59	3
38	Ghana	390	-0.8	-.06	43	59	37	9	26	3	470	8	6	18
39	Pakistan	380	1.8	2.9	7	32[x]	29[x]	1	2	28	1108	3	24	17
40	Bangladesh	200	-0.3	1.0	10	86[x]	86[x]	5	11	10	2081	9	NA	16

Contd.

TABLE 7.3 *Contd.*

	1	2	3	4	5	6	7	8	9	10	11	12	13	14
41	Cote d'Ivoire	730	2.8	-3.7	2	30	26	4	NA	NA	674	8	7	13
42	**India**	**350**	**1.5**	**3.2**	**8**	**29**	**33**	**2**	**3**	**17**	**1550**	**1**	**22**	**20**
43	Cameroon	940	2.4	-0.3	6	15[x]	40[x]	3	12	7	475	4	3	13
44	Bolivia	620	1.7	-2.6	318	NA	NA	2	18	14	499	7	11	29
45	Namibia	1030[x]	NA	NA	13[x]	NA	NA	10	22	7	62	NA	NA	NA
46	Myanmar	220[x]	1.6	NA	NA	40[x]	40[x]	5	17	25	196	NA	12	29[x]
47	Congo	1010	2.7	-0.2	1	NA	NA	NA	NA	NA	208	9	12	15
48	Libyan Arab	5310[x]	0.0	-9.2	0	NA	NA	NA	NA	NA	11	NA	NA	NA
49	Peru	1160	0.8	-2.0	234	46	83	5	16	11	36	2	12	5
50	Guatemala	900	3.0	-2.1	15	17	51	10	20	13	191	2	7	10
51	Morocco	950	2.7	1.6	7	28[x]	45[x]	3	17	15	965	4	9	19
52	Turkey	1630	3.6	3.0	43	NA	NA	4	19	12	1259	1	22	25
53	Zimbabwe	640	1.7	-0.8	11	NA	NA	8	NA	17	336	5	2	19
54	Indonesia	570	5.2	4.1	8	20	16	2	8	8	1717	2	7	23
55	Botswana	2040	9.9	6.3	.12	40	55	5	20	12	151	6	1	4
56	Egypt	600	2.8	2.1	12	34	34	3	13	13	5584	18	38	21
57	Ecuador	960	5.4	-0.8	37	40	65	7	25	12	142	1	9	27
58	Mongolia	780[x]	NA	NA	-1	NA	NA	NA	NA	11	NA	NA	NA	
59	Nicaragua	830[x]	-0.7	4.7[x]	432	21[x]	19[x]	11	9	50	316	NA	11	3
60	Papua New	860	NA	-0.5	5	10[x]	75[x]	9	15	5	376	11	1	17
	Guinea													
61	Dominican Rep.	820	3.8	-0.4	22	45[x]	43[x]	10	9	5	93	2	4	6
62	Kenya	370	3.1	0.3	9	10[x]	55[x]	5	20	8	989	NA	6	21
63	Honduras	590	1.1	-1.2	5	31	70	NA	NA	7	445	15	3	32
64	South Africa	2530	3.2	-0.9	14	NA	NA	NA	NA	NA	NA	NA	NA	NA

Contd.

TABLE 7.3 *Contd.*

1	2	3	4	5	6	7	8	9	10	11	12	13	14
Middle U5MR Countries	21465	4.2	1.4	94	NA	NA	7	11	10	8706	1	12	16
65 Brazil	260	6.3	0.6	284	9	34	7	5	4	161	0	13	15
66 El Salvador	1100	1.5	-0.6	17	20	32	8	16	25	344	6	4	20
67 Iran, Islamic Rep. of	2450	2.9	-0.8	14	NA	NA	9	22	14	66	0	NA	NA
68 Algeria	2060	4.2	-0.3	7	20[x]	NA	NA	NA	NA	225	0	4	58
69 Paraguay	1110	4.1	-1.3	24	19[x]	50[x]	4	13	13	50	1	12	12
70 Tunisia	1420	4.7	0.9	7	20[x]	15[x]	6	16	7	310	3	20	22
71 Viet Nam	240[x]	NA	NA	NA	NA	NA	NA	NA	NA	164	NA	NA	NA
72 Syria	990	5.1	-2.1	15			1	9	41	645	5	11	25
73 Jordan	1240	5.8[x]	-3.9	NA	14[x]	17[x]	6	14	23	884	23	4	22
74 Lebanon	2150[x]	NA	NA	NA	NA	NA	NA	NA	NA	136	NA	NA	NA
75 Philippines	730	3.2	-1.5	15	52	64	4	17	11	1266	3	8	16
76 Venezuela	2560	2.3	-2.0	19	NA	NA	10	20	6	76	0	3	17
77 Saudi Arabia	7050	4.0[x]	-5.6	-4	NA	NA	NA	NA	NA	18	NA	NA	NA
78 Oman	5220[x]	9.0	7.1	NA	NA	NA	5	11	41	67	NA	NA	13
79 Mexico	2490	3.6	-0.9	70	NA	NA	2	14	2	130	0	24	18
80 Romania	1640	NA	1.1	2	NA	NA	9	3	10	NA	NA	NA	NA
81 Korea, Dem. Peo. Rep.	970[x]	NA	NA	NA	NA	NA	NA	NA	NA	6	NA	NA	NA
82 Thailand	1420	4.4	5.6	3	10	25	20	7	17	787	1	3	11
83 USSR (former)	4550[x]	NA	NA	NA	NA	NA	NA	NA	NA	NA	NA	NA	NA
84 Albania	790[x]	NA	NA	NA	NA	NA	NA	NA	NA	NA	NA	NA	NA
85 Panama	1830	2.8	-2.0	2	21[x]	30[x]	18	19	8	93	2	8	3

Contd.

TABLE 7.3 *Contd.*

1	2	3	4	5	6	7	8	9	10	11	12	13	14
86 United Arab Amirates	19860	NA	-7.2	1	NA	NA	7	15	44	4	0	NA	NA
87 Mauritius	2250	3.7	5.4	9	12x	12x	9	14	2	86	4	3	4
88 China	370	4.1	7.9	6	NA	13	NA	NA	8	2064	1	NA	9
89 Uruguay	2560	2.5	-0.9	61	22	NA	5	7	9	46	1	22	30
90 Argentina	2370	1.7	-1.8	395	NA	NA	2	9	9	173	0	22	25
91 Trinidad and Tobago	3470	3.1	-6.0	6	NA	39x	NA	NA	NA	10	0	5	13
92 Yugoslavia (former)	3060	5.2	-0.9	123	NA	NA	NA	NA	53	46	0	10	7
93 Bulgaria	2250	NA	2.3	2	NA	NA	4	6	7	NA	NA	NA	16
94 Chile	1940	0.0	1.1	21	12	20	6	10	8	89	0	19	15
95 Sri Lanka	470	2.8	2.4	11	NA	NA	7	10	7	659	8	11	10
96 Colombia	1240	3.7	1.1	25	32	70	NA	NA	NA	89	0	12	33
Low U5MR countries	**17580**	**NA**	**2.5**	**5**	**NA**	**NA**	**13**	**4**	**14**	**2578**	**NA**	**NA**	**10**
97 Malaysia	2340	4.7	2.5	2	13	38	NA	NA	NA	467	1	4	10
98 Jamaica	1510	-0.1	-0.4	18	NA	80	7	11	8	277	8	3	24
99 Costa Rica	1910	3.3	0.6	24	8	20	26	19	2	228	4	10	21
100 Hungary	2780	5.1	1.5	9	NA	NA	8	3	4	NA	NA	NA	43
101 Poland	1690	NA	1.2	54	NA	NA	NA	NA	NA	NA	NA	NA	4
102 Kuwait	16150x	0.6x	-2.2	-3	NA	NA	8	14	20	4	NA	NA	NA
103 Cuba	1170x	NA	NA	NA	NA	NA	23	10	NA	29	NA	NA	NA
104 Czechoslovakia	3140	NA	1.3	2	NA	NA	NA	2	7		NA	NA	9
105 Israel	10920	3.7	1.5	101	NA	NA	4	10	25	1374	3	3	NA
106 Portugal	4900	4.6	2.4	18	NA	NA	NA	NA	6	67	0	7	16

Contd.

TABLE 7.3 *Contd.*

	1	2	3	4	5	6	7	8	9	10	11	12	13	14
107	USA	21790	1.8	2.2	4	NA	NA	14	2	23	NA	NA	NA	NA
108	Greece	5990	4.8	1.5	18	NA	NA	NA	NA	NA	35	0	9	NA
109	Ireland	9550	2.8	1.1	7	NA	NA	13	13	3	NA	NA	NA	NA
110	Singapore	12310	8.3	5.7	2	NA	NA	5	18	22	-4	0	1	NA
111	Belgium	15540	3.6	1.2	4	NA	NA	12	2	5	NA	NA	NA	NA
112	Australia	17000	2.2	1.7	7	NA	NA	13	7	9	NA	NA	NA	NA
113	Italy	16830	3.2	2.2	10	NA	NA	11	8	4	NA	NA	NA	NA
114	New Zealand	12680	1.7	0.6	10	NA	NA	12	12	4	NA	NA	NA	NA
115	Korea, Rep. of	5400	7.3	8.9	18	18[x]	11[x]	2	20	26	53	0	20	6
116	Canada	20470	3.3	2.4	4	NA	NA	6	3	7	NA	NA	NA	NA
117	Germany	22320[x]	3.0[x]	2.2[x]	3[x]	NA	NA	19	1	8	NA	NA	NA	NA
118	Denmark	22080	2.2	2.1	6	NA	NA	1	9	5	NA	NA	NA	NA
119	Switzerland	32680	1.5	1.7	4	NA	NA	13[x]	3[x]	10[x]	NA	NA	NA	NA
120	France	19490	3.7	1.7	6	NA	NA	15	7	7	NA	NA	NA	NA
121	United Kingdom	16100	2.0	2.5	6	NA	NA	15	3	12	NA	NA	NA	NA
122	Austria	19060	4.0	2.0	4	NA	NA	13	9	3	NA	NA	NA	NA
123	Spain	11020	4.1	2.7	9	NA	NA	13	6	6	NA	NA	NA	NA
124	Hong Kong	11540	6.2	5.5	7	NA	NA	NA	17	NA	48	0	NA	NA
125	Netherlands	17320	2.7	1.4	2	NA	NA	12	11	5	NA	NA	NA	NA
126	Norway	23120	3.6	2.7	6	NA	NA	10	9	8	NA	NA	NA	NA
127	Finland	26040	3.6	3.1	7	NA	NA	11	14	5	NA	NA	NA	NA
128	Japan	25430	5.1	3.5	2	NA	NA	NA	NA	NA	NA	NA	NA	NA
129	Sweden	23660	2.0	1.8	7	NA	NA	1	9	6	NA	NA	NA	NA

Contd.

TABLE 7.3 *Concld.*

1	2	3	4	5	6	7	8	9	10	11	12	13	14
Regional summaries													
Least developed countries	240	-0.1	0.1	23	55	70	5	13	16	13894	15	7	10
Developing countries	805	3.7	2.2	62	27	31	5	12	12	43082	2	12	16
Developed countries	14710	NA	2.4	5	NA	NA	14	4	14	1534	NA	NA	NA
Sub-Saharan Africa	490	2.5	-0.9	17	NA	62	4	12	11	14316	10	5	14
Middle East & North	1975	3.8	-1.4	12	NA	NA	6	18	18	11392	2	NA	28
South Asia	335	1.5	3.0	8	33	39	2	4	18	5995	2	21	18
East Asia & Pacific	650	NA	6.8	9	NA	17	NA	15	14	7336	1	NA	11
Latin America & Caribbean	2105	4.1	-0.3	190	18	49	6	10	5	4043	0	14	18

Countries listed in descending order of U5MR.

7.5 **Educational Data**

TABLE 7.4: Educational Data

	Adult literacy rate				No. of sets per 1000 population 1989		Primary school enrolment ratio						% of grade 1 enrolment reaching final grade of primary school 1988	Secondary school enrolment ratio 1986-90 (gross)	
	1970		1990				1960 (gross)		1986-90 (net)		1986-90 (net)				
	male	female	male	female	radio	television	male	female	male	female	male	female		male	female
1	2	3	4	5	6	7	8	9	10	11	12	13	14	15	16
Very high U5MR countries	**30**	**14**	**59**	**37**	**128**	**17**	**39**	**19**	**73**	**54**	**52**	**41**	**55**	**22**	**13**
1 Angola	16	7	56	29	53	6	NA	NA	101	85	NA	NA	24[x]	17	9
2 Mozambique	29	14	45	21	41	2	60	36	76	59	49	41	39	7	4
3 Afghanistan	13	2	44	14	104	8	15	2	31	16	NA	NA	63	11	5
4 Sierra Leone	18	8	31	11	220	10	30	NA	65	40	NA	NA	NA	23	11
5 Guinea-Bissau	13	6	50	24	39	NA	NA	NA	76	42	52	29	8	9	4
6 Guinea	21	7	35	13	41	5	44	16	46	21	34	17	44	14	5
7 Malawi	42	18	NA	NA	237	NA	NA	45	73	60	52	49	47	6	3
8 Mali	11	4	41	24	39	0	14	6	29	17	23	14	40	9	4
9 Niger	6	2	40	17	59	4	7	3	36	20	NA	NA	75	8	3
10 Chad	20	2	42	18	237	1	29	4	79	35	52	23	71	12	3

Contd.

TABLE 7.4 *Contd.*

	1	2	3	4	5	6	7	8	9	10	11	12	13	14	15	16
11	Ethiopia	8	NA	NA	NA	188	2	11	3	46	30	32	24	44	17	12
12	Somalia	5	1	36	14	41	14	13	13	20	10	14	8	37	13	7
13	Mauritania	NA	NA	47	21	143	23	13	3	60	42	NA	NA	68	22	10
14	Burkina Faso	13	3	28	9	26	5	12	5	44	27	34	20	64	9	5
15	Bhutan	NA	NA	51	25	15	NA	5	NA	31	20	NA	NA	26	7	2
16	Zambia	66	37	81	65	74	25	51	34	99	91	81	79	64	25	14
17	Liberia	27	8	50	29	225	18	45	18	43	24	NA	NA	NA	NA	NA
18	Uganda	52	30	62	35	99	8	NA	32	76	63	57	50	76	16	8
19	Rwanda	43	21	64	37	59	NA	NA	NA	69	68	65	65	36	9	6
20	Nigeria	35	14	62	40	171	29	46	27	77	63	NA	NA	52	22	16
21	Cambodia	NA	23	48	22	107	8	NA	NA	NA	NA	NA	NA	50^{x}	45	20
22	Senegal	18	5	52	25	113	35	36	NA	67	49	55	41	85	21	11
23	Yemen	14	3	53	26	59	27	NA	NA	132	39	NA	NA	53	42	7
24	Burundi	29	10	61	40	57	1	27	9	77	60	55	46	83	5	3
25	Zaire	61	22	84	61	101	1	88	32	89	67	67	53	73	32	16
26	Central African Rep.	26	6	52	25	61	2	53	12	79	48	56	37	48	16	6
27	Tanzania	48	18	93^{x}	88^{x}	21	1	33	18	64	63	47	48	75	5	4
28	Madagascar	56	43	88	73	198	20	58	45	94	90	64	63	32	20	18
29	Sudan	28	6	43	12	235	61	35	14	58^{x}	41^{x}	23	17	76^{x}	23^{x}	17^{x}
30	Gabon	43	22	74	49	138	36	NA	NA	NA	NA	NA	NA	44^{x}	NA	NA

Contd.

TABLE 7.4 *Contd.*

1	2	3	4	5	6	7	8	9	10	11	12	13	14	15	16
31 Benin	23	8	32	16	89	5	38	15	87	44	69	36	40	23	9
32 Lao. Peo. Dem.	37	28	NA	NA	124	5	34	16	122	98	NA	NA	38	31	22
33 Nepal	23	3	38	13	33	2	19	1	112	57	84	43	27	42	17
34 Togo	27	7	56	31	210	6	63	24	126	80	85	58	46	33	10
35 Iraq	50	18	70	49	202	68	94	36	104	87	90	78	58	58	37
High U5MR countries	**50**	**25**	**65**	**41**	**113**	**39**	**77**	**42**	**103**	**82**	**NA**	**NA**	**59**	**49**	**31**
36 Lesotho	49	74	NA	NA	68	3	63	102	99	115	64	76	50	21	31
37 Haiti	26[x]	17[x]	59	42	5	50	42	86	81	44	44	9	20	19	
38 Ghana	43	18	70	51	295	15	52	25	82	67	NA	NA	87	49	30
39 Pakistan	30	11	47	21	86	16	46	13	49	27	NA	NA	51	28	12
40 Bangladesh	36	12	47	22	41	4	66	26	76	64	67	58	46	23	11
41 Cte d'ivoire	26	10	67	40	139	59	68	24	82	58	NA	NA	73	27	12
42 India	**47**	**20**	**62**	**34**	**78**	**27**	**80**	**40**	**112**	**82**	**NA**	**NA**	**53**	**54**	**31**
43 Cameroon	47	19	66	43	131	22	87	43	108	93	80	69	68	31	21
44 Bolivia	68	46	85	61	597	98	78	50	86	77	88	78	50	36	31
45 Namibia	NA	NA	NA	NA	133	16	NA	NA	NA	NA	NA	NA	NA	NA	NA
46 Myanmar	85	57	89	72	81	2	61	52	106	100	NA	NA	33[x]	25	23
47 Congo	50	19	70	44	109	5	103	53	NA	NA	NA	NA	62	37	14
48 Libyan Arab Jamahiriya	60	13	75	50	224	91	92	24	NA	NA	NA	NA	82[x]	NA	NA
49 Peru	81	60	92	79	251	95	95	71	125	120	NA	NA	70[x]	69	61
50 Guatemala	51	37	63	47	64	45	50	39	82	70	NA	NA	36	21	19

Contd.

TABLE 7.4 *Contd.*

1	2	3	4	5	6	7	8	9	10	11	12	13	14	15	16
51 Morocco	34	10	61	38	209	70	67	27	81	55	65	40	63	42	30
52 Turkey	69	34	90	71	161	174	90	58	117	108	NA	NA	97	63	39
53 Zimbabwe	63	47	74	60	85	27	NA	NA	130	126	100	100	74^{x}	49	42
54 Indonesia	66	42	84	62	144	55	86	58	120	115	100	97	79	52	43
55 Botswana	37	44	84	65	111	12	35	48	112	117	94	110	95	31	36
56 Egypt	50	20	63	34	322	98	80	52	104	89	NA	NA	95	91	71
57 Ecuador	75	68	88	84	314	82	87	79	118	117	NA	NA	63	55	57
58 Mongolia	87	74	NA	NA	131	38	79	78	100	103	NA	NA	NA	88	96
59 Nicaragua	58	57	NA	NA	247	61	65	66	90	100	71	76	29	28	46
60 Papua New Guinea	39	24	65	38	69	2	59	7	79	67	78	67	61	16	10
61 Dominican Rep.	69	65	85	82	168	82	99	98	95	96	NA	78	33	NA	NA
62 Kenya	44	19	80	59	95	9	64	30	96	92	NA	NA	62	27	19
63 Honduras	55	50	76	71	384	70	68	67	108	109	89	94	43	28	36
64 South Africa	NA	NA	NA	NA	324	101	94	85	NA	NA	NA	NA	NA	NA	NA
Middle U5MR countries	84	80	85	68	277	100	93	88	124	115	98	96	75	51	45
65 Brazil	69	63	83	80	373	204	97	93	NA	NA	NA	NA	22^{x}	32	42
66 El Salvador	61	53	76	70	403	87	NA	NA	77	78	69	71	27	26	26
67 Iran, Islamic Rep. of	40	17	65	43	245	66	56	27	115	101	99	90	91	62	44
68 Algeria	39	11	70	46	232	73	55	37	103	88	97	81	90	61	53
69 Paraguay	85^{x}	75^{x}	92	88	169	48	105	90	108	104	93	92	57	28	30
70 Tunisia	44	17	74	56	188	75	88	43	123	107	99	90	79	50	39

Contd.

TABLE 7.4 *Contd.*

	1	2	3	4	5	6	7	8	9	10	11	12	13	14	15	16
71	Viet Nam	NA	NA	92	84	107	38	NA	NA	105	99	NA	NA	57	43	40
72	Syria	60	20	78	51	248	59	89	39	114	1102	100	93	85	63	45
73	Jordan	64	29	89	70	252	77	94	59	98	99	88	88	96[x]	80	78
74	Lebanon	79[x]	58[x]	88	73	834	327	105	99	105	95	NA	NA	NA	57	56
75	Philippines	84	81	90	90	136	41	98	93	111	110	100	98	71	72	75
76	Venezuela	79	71	87	90	432	156	100	100	105	105	107	88	70	50	62
77	Saudi Arabia	15	2	73	48	280	277	22	NA	81	70	64	48	90	53	39
78	Oman	NA	NA	NA	NA	645	762	NA	NA	106	97	86	881	91	55	40
79	Mexico	78	69	90	85	242	127	82	77	118	115	NA	NA	70	53	53
80	Romania	96	91	NA	NA	195	194	101	95	96	95	NA	NA	94	84	92
81	Korea, Dem. Peo. Rep.	NA	NA	NA	NA	117	14	NA	NA	110	103	NA	NA	99	100	100
82	Thailand	86	72	96	90	182	109	88	79	89	88	NA	NA	59	32	28
83	USSR (former)	98	97	NA	NA	685	323	100	100	104	105	NA	NA	94	NA	NA
84	Albania	NA	NA	NA	NA	172	83	102	86	99	98	NA	NA	91	86	73
85	Panama	81	81	88	88	222	165	98	94	109	105	90	89	79	56	63
86	United Arab Emirates	24	7	58	38	322	109	NA	NA	111	110	100	100	96	60	69
87	Mauritius	77	59	NA	NA	354	215	103	93	102	104	92	94	98	53	53
88	China	NA	NA	84	62	184	27	NA	NA	142	128	100	100	81	50	38
89	Uruguay	93[x]	93[x]	97	96	600	227	111	111	107	106	NA	NA	93	68	76,
90	Argentina	94	92	96	95	673	219	98	99	107	114	NA	NA	NA	69	78

Contd.

TABLE 7.4 *Contd.*

1	2	3	4	5	6	7	8	9	10	11	12	13	14	15	16
91 Trinidad and Tobago	95	89	NA	NA	460	301	NA	NA	95	98	93	89	81	84	
92 Yugoslavia (former)	92	76	97	88	245	197	113	108	95	94	NA	NA	98x	82	79
93 Bulgaria	94	89	NA	NA	436	249	94	92	98	96	86	85	62	74	76
94 Chile	90	88	94	93	340	201	111	107	99	97	NA	NA	77	72	78
95 Sri Lanka	85	69	93	84	194	32	100	90	109	106	100	100	94	71	76
96 Colombia	79	76	88	86	167	108	77	77	106	108	72	74	56	52	53
Low U5MR countries	97	95	NA	NA	1148	521	108	106	103	103	97	98	95	90	92
97 Malaysia	71	48	87	70	428	144	108	83	97	96	NA	NA	96	58	59
98 Jamaica	96	97	98	99	409	124	92	93	104	1105	98	100	85	62	68
99 Costa Rica	88	87	93	93	259	136	97	95	101	99	86	86	77	41	42
100 Hungary	98	98	NA	NA	592	409	103	100	96	97	93	94	94	70	72
101 Poland	98	97	NA	NA	428	292	110	107	99	99	97	98	92	80	83
102 Kuwait	65	42	77	67	337	281	131	102	101	99	NA	77	90	93	87
103 Cuba	86	87	95	93	343	203	109	109	105	100	96	95	88	84	94
104 Czecho-slovakia	NA	NA	NA	NA	583	410	93	93	92	93	NA	NA	93	84	90
105 Israel	93	83	NA	NA	468	266	99	97	92	95	NA	NA	78	79	86
106 Portugal	78	65	89	82	216	176	132	129	131	123	NA	NA	NA	47	56
107 USA	99	99	NA	NA	2122	814	NA	NA	101	100	95	96	90	98	99
108 Greece	93	76	98	89	4119	195	104	101	101	102	97	98	100	99	94
109 Ireland	NA	NA	NA	NA	583	271	107	112	100	101	88	90	97	93	102
110 Singapore	92	55	NA	NA	306	372	121	113	111	109	100	100	100	68	71
111 Belgium	99	99	NA	NA	776	447	111	108	101	101	96	97	78	103	104

Contd.

TABLE 7.4 *Contd.*

1	2	3	4	5	6	7	8	9	10	11	12	13	14	15	16
112 Australia	NA	NA	NA	NA	1262	484	103	103	106	105	97	98	99	80	83
113 Italy	95	93	98	96	794	423	11	109	96	96	97	98	100	78	78
114 New Zealand	NA	NA	NA	NA	922	372	110	106	106	106	100	100	95	87	89
115 Korea, Rep. of	94	81	99	94	1003	207	99	89	107	110	100	100	100	88	85
116 Canada	NA	NA	NA	NA	1023	626	108	105	105	105	96	97	96	104	105
117 Germany	NA	NA	NA	NA	895x	378x	NA	NA	103	102	NA	NA	99x	92	88
118 Denmark	NA	NA	NA	NA	1012	528	103	103	97	98	NA	NA	99	106	107
119 Switzerland	NA	NA	NA	NA	851	406	1118	118	NA	NA	NA	NA	99x	NA	NA
120 France	99	98	NA	NA	895	400	144	143	114	111	100	100	96	93	100
121 United Kingdom	NA	NA	NA	NA	1145	434	92	92	015	106	97	97	NA	82	85
122 Austria	NA	NA	NA	NA	622	475	106	104	104	103	NA	NA	97	81	83
123 Spain	93	87	97	93	304	389	106	116	112	110	100	100	94	100	111
124 Hong Kong	NA	NA	NA	NA	634	260	93	79	105	104	NA	95	98	71	75
125 Netherlands	NA	NA	NA	NA	902	485	105	104	114	117	100	100	94	105	102
126 Norway	NA	NA	NA	NA	796	423	100	100	98	98	98	97	100	96	101
127 Finland	NA	NA	NA	NA	998	488	100	95	99	99	NA	NA	100	103	121
128 Japan	99	99	NA	NA	895	610	103	102	102	102	100	100	100	94	97
129 Sweden	NA	NA	NA	NA	885	471	95	96	104	104	100	100	100	89	93

Contd.

TABLE 7.4 *Concld.*

1	2	3	4	5	6	7	8	9	10	11	12	13	14	15	16
Regional summaries															
Least developed countries	36	18	58	36	93	8	44	23	74	57	54	44	52	21	12
Developing countries	53	33	75	55	174	51	75	49	108	92	87	82	64	47	35
Developed countries	98	96	NA	NA	1029	482	106	105	103	103	97	98	94	91	93
Sub-Saharan Africa	34	17	64	44	145	22	49	28	75	60	53	45	58	21	13
Middle East & North Africa	47	19	70	46	237	106	72	41	103	86	81	70	85	61	43
South Asia	44	19	59	32	76	23	74	36	99	72	NA	NA	52	47	27
East Asia & Pacific	76	56	85	66	1996	40	87	69	130	120	NA	NA	77	51	42
Latin America & Caribbean	76	69	87	83	335	156	91	86	108	107	83	79	47	46	51

7.6 **Health Data**

TABLE 7.5: Health Data

	% of population with access to safe water 1988-90			% of population with access to adequate sanitation 1988-90			% of population with access to health services 1985-88			% fully immunized 1990-91					
										1 year-old children				pregnant women	ORT use rate 1987-91
	total	urban	rural	total	urban	rural	total	urban	rural	TB	DPT	polio	measles	tetanus	
1	2	3	4	5	6	7	8	9	10	11	12	13	14	15	16
Very high U5MR countries	43	62	35	43	66	33	52	NA	NA	62	47	46	46	28	39
1 Angola	35	75	19	21	25	20	30[x]	NA	NA	54	27	26	40	36	48
2 Mozambique	24	44	17	21	53	12	39	100	30	63	42	42	50	30	30
3 Afghanistan	21	39	17	NA	5	NA	29	80	17	39	30	30	29	9	26
4 Sierra Leone	36	33	37	63	92	49	NA	NA	NA	71	56	57	54	77	60
5 Guinea-Bissau	27	17	30	21	29	18	NA	NA	NA	94	63	63	52	35	5
6 Guinea	51	78	42	6	22	1	47	100	40	47	35	35	33	25	65
7 Malawi	56[x]	97[x]	50[x]	84	100	881	80	NA	NA	96	81	78	78	76	14
8 Mali	41	53	38	19	90	3	15	NA	NA	68	34	34	39	9	NA
9 Niger	61	100	52	9	36	3	41	99	30	26	17	17	23	44	54
10 Chad	57	25	70	NA	NA	NA	30	NA	NA	27	12	12	21	4	15
11 Ethiopia	19	70	11	19	97	7	46	NA	NA	29	21	21	17	6	38
12 Somalia	37	50	29	18	44	5	27[x]	50[x]	15[x]	31	18	18	30	5	78
13 Mauritania	66	100	100	39	69	13	40	NA	NA	60	26	26	29	40	NA
14 Burkina Faso	69	44	72	NA	49	NA	49[x]	51[x]	48[x]	60	38	38	36	26	NA
15 Bhutan	32	60	30	9	50	7	65	NA	NA	81	79	77	82	43	65

Contd

TABLE 7.5 *Contd.*

1		2	3	4	5	6	7	8	9	10	11	12	13	14	15	16
16	Zambia	60	76	43	56	76	34	75X	100X	50X	97	79	78	76	68	89
17	Liberia	55	93	22	NA	NA	2	39	50	30	62X	28X	28X	55X	20X	9
18	Uganda	21	43	18	30	32	30	61	90	57	100	76	76	73	21	30
19	Rwanda	50X	79X	48X	57	77	55	27X	60X	25X	94	85	85	81	88	24
20	Nigeria	53	50	54	58	63	55	66	85	62	57	44	44	46	26	35
21	Cambodia	18	40	15	13	53	8	53	80	50	54	40	40	34	22	6
22	Senegal	47	84	25	53	86	36	40	NA	NA	69	51	51	46	33	27
23	Yemen	38	56	30	37	51	64	38	NA	NA	71	53	53	45	8	7
24	Burundi	38	100	34	10	80	5	61	NA	NA	88	83	89	75	56	49
25	Zaire	33	59	17	NA	NA	NA	26	40	17	65	32	31	31	29	45
26	Central African Rep.	26	32	21	NA	NA	48	45	NA	NA	42	25	26	25	87	24
27	Tanzania	56	75	46	68	93	58	76X	99X	72X	89	79	74	75	40	83
28	Madagascar	22	62	10	NA	9	NA	56	NA	NA	67	50	49	40	17	11
29	Sudan	46	55	43	71	89	66	51	90	40	66	63	63	59	116	37
30	Gabon	68	90	50	NA	NA	NA	90X	NA	NA	96	78	78	76	86	10
31	Benin	54	66	46	35	42	31	118	NA	NA	81	68	68	60	83	45
32	Lao. Peo. Dem.	35	50	32	13	49	5	67	NA	NA	34	22	22	20	13	30
33	Nepal	37	66	34	2	17	1	NA	NA	NA	81	74	74	63	17	14
34	Togo	59	76	53	22	56	10	61	NA	NA	79	61	61	51	81	33
35	Iraq	92	100	72	75	100	11	93	97	78	79	63	64	68	45	70

Contd.

TABLE 7.5 *Contd.*

1	2	3	4	5	6	7	8	9	10	11	12	13	14	15	16
High U5MR countries	75	83	71	23	56	10	61	NA	NA	886	80	80	76	65	26
36 Lesotho	48	59	45	15	22	14	80	NA	NA	76	75	74	76	NA	68
37 Haiti	36	59	27	21	42	13	50	NA	NA	72	41	40	31	23	20
38 Ghana	57	90	41	52	92	33	60	92	45	55	39	39	39	9	21
39 Pakistan	56	80	45	24	55	10	55	99	35	91	81	81	77	42	34
40 Bangladesh	81	76	81	16	57	8	45	NA	NA	86	60	60	53	78	26
41 Cote d'ivoire	76	70	80	60	73	51	30[x]	61[x]	11[x]	47	337	37	47	35	16
42 India	**86**	**87**	**85**	**16**	**53**	**2**	**NA**	**NA**	**NA**	**92**	**89**	**89**	**86**	**80**	**14**
43 Cameroon	42	46	39	46	100	1	41	44	39	48	34	34	35	35	84
44 Bolivia	53	77	27	27	40	13	63	90	36	67	58	67	73	52	63
45 Namibia	NA	NA	NA	NA	NA	NA	NA	NA	NA	68	87	82	71	52	NA
46 Myanmar	31	38	30	36	39	35	33	100	11	65	62	62	63	61	19
47 Congo	38	92	2	NA	NA	NA	83	97	70	88	74	74	64	60	26
48 Libyan Arab Jamahiriya	94	100	80	91	00	72	NA	NA	NA	91	62	62	59	18	60
49 Peru	61	78	10	59	76	20	75	NA	NA	78	71	74	59	12	NA
50 Guatemala	62	91	43	59	72	52	34	47	25	43	63	69	49	18	24
51 Morocco	61	100	25	NA	NA	16	70	100	50	92	81	81	80	64	13
52 Turkey	78[x]	95[x]	63[x]	NA	NA	NA	NA	NA	NA	52	72	72	66	20	NA
53 Zimbabwe	66	31	80	NA	NA	NA	71	100	62	87	83	81	83	60	77
54 Indonesia	58	72	51	39	51	33	80	NA	NA	87	83	82	78	52	45
55 Botswana	54[x]	84[x]	46[x]	42	98	20	89[x]	100[x]	85[x]	92	86	82	78	62	64

Contd.

TABLE 7.5 *Contd.*

1	2	3	4	5	6	7	8	9	10	11	12	13	14	15	16
56 Egypt	73	92	56	NA	NA	10	NA	NA	NA	93	93	87	90	71	58
57 Ecuador	58	75	44	67	98	38	75	92	40	83	59	62	54	5	70
58 Mongolia	65	78	50	NA	NA	NA	NA	NA	NA	92	84	85	86	NA	59
59 Nicaragua	54	78	18	27	30	16	83	100	60	75	71	833	54	25	40
60 Papua New Guinea	34	93	23	45	99	35	96	NA	NA	68	53	54	52	3	46
61 Dominican Rep.	63	86	28	28	41	10	80	NA	NA	45	47	64	69	24	31
62 Kenya	30x	61x	21x	34	89	19	NA	NA	NA	80	74	71	59	37	69
63 Honduras	65	86	48	58	79	42	66	80	56	99	94	93	86	16	70
64 South Africa	NA	NA	NA	NA	NA	NA	NA	NA	NA	85	67	69	63	NA	NA
Middle U5MR countries	76	89	67	67	83	48	87	NA	NA	93	87	92	89	54	55
65 Brazil	97	100	86	64	86	1	NA	NA	NA	80	75	96	83	62	62
66 El Salvador	48	84	19	58	86	36	56	80	40	66	60	60	53	19	45
67 Iran, Islamic Rep. of	89	98	76	63	86	32	80	95	65	91	88	88	84	77	71
68 Algeria	68x	85x	55x	57	80	40	88	100	80	99	89	89	83	27	26
69 Paraguay	34	65	7	86	89	83	61	NA	NA	93	79	79	74	54	42
70 Tunisia	92	97	86	96	98	94	90x	100x	80x	80	91	91	82	40	63
71 Viet Nam	42	50	40	62	70	60	80	100	75	91	88	88	88	14	53
72 Syria	70	90	50	85	85	84	75x	92x	50x	98	92	92	87	84	89
73 Jordan	99	100	98	61	92	NA	97	98	95	NA	91	91	83	47	77
74 Lebanon	92	95	85	NA	NA	NA	NA	NA	NA	4	85	85	51	NA	10
75 Philippines	81	93	72	67	83	63	NA	NA	NA	96	89	90	88	52	25

Contd.

TABLE 7.5 *Contd.*

1	2	3	4	5	6	7	8	9	10	11	12	13	14	15	16
76 Venezuela	90x	93x	65x	51	57	5	NA	NA	NA	83	54	63	61	NA	80
77 Saudi Arabia	94	100	74	NA	100	NA	97	100	88	97	96	96	90	62	45
78 Oman	55	100	49	48	75	45	91	100	90	92	94	94	96	97	19
79 Mexico	71	79	49	58	77	13	78	80	60	87	64	95	78	42	66
80 Romania	NA	NA	NA	NA	NA	NA	NA	NA	NA	90	96	92	89	NA	NA
81 Korea, Dem Peo. Rep.	NA	NA	NA	NA	NA	NA	NA	NA	NA	99	98	99	99	99	72
82 Thailand	93	97	92	91	79	95	90	90	90	99	90	91	79	76	43
83 USSR (former)	NA	NA	NA	NA	NA	NA	NA	NA	NA	90	67	74	85	NA	NA
84 Albania	NA	NA	NA	NA	NA	NA	NA	NA	NA	94	94	96	87	NA	NA
85 Panama	84	100	66	81	99	61	80x	95x	64x	87	82	80	27	55	
86 United Arab Emirates	95	NA	NA	77	93	22	99	NA	NA	96	84	84	81	NA	81
87 Mauritius	95	100	92	92	100	86	100	100	100	98	91	91	88	77	7
88 China	74	87	68	NA	NA	NA	90	100	88	96	95	96	95	NA	54
89 Uruguay	73	85	5	NA	NA	NA	82	NA	NA	99	88	88	82	13	96
90 Argentina	65	73	17	69	75	35	71	80	21	99	84	88	99	NA	70
91 Trinidad and Tobago	96	100	87	98	100	95	99	NA	NA	NA	73	74	81	NA	70
92 Yugoslavia (former)	NA	NA	NA	NA	NA	NA	NA	NA	NA	89	NA	86	88	NA	NA
93 Bulgaria	NA	NA	NA	NA	NA	NA	NA	NA	NA	99	99	99	98	NA	NA
94 Chile	89	100	21	85	100	4	97	NA	NA	90	91	91	93	NA	1
95 Sri Lanka	60	80	55	59	68	56	93x	NA	NA	85	83	83	76	50	76
96 Colombia	88	88	87	70	96	13	60	NA	NA	93	87	94	83	40	40

Contd.

TABLE 7.5 *Contd.*

1	2	3	4	5	6	7	8	9	10	11	12	13	14	15	16
Low U5MR countries	NA	NA	NA	NA	NA	NA	NA	NA	NA	77	89	88	78	NA	NA
97 Malaysia	79	96	66	76	100	60	NA	NA	NA	99	90	90	79	83	47
98 Jamaica	100	100	100	85	96	74	90	NA	NA	94	83	86	68	50	10
99 Costa Rica	92	100	84	94	99	89	80x	100x	63x	92	95	95	90	68	78
100 Hungary	NA	NA	NA	NA	NA	NA	NA	NA	NA	99	99	99	99	NA	NA
101 Poland	NA	NA	NA	NA	NA	NA	NA	NA	NA	95	98	99	96	NA	NA
102 Kuwait	NA	100	NA	NA	100	NA	100	NA	NA	3	92	92	93	22	10
103 Cuba	NA	NA	NA	NA	NA	NA	NA	NA	NA	98	99	97	99	88	80
104 Czecho-slovakia	NA	NA	NA	NA	NA	NA	NA	NA	NA	98	99	99	98	NA	NA
105 Israel	NA	NA	NA	NA	NA	NA	NA	NA	NA	NA	88	88	88	NA	NA
106 Portugal	NA	NA	NA	NA	NA	NA	NA	NA	NA	89	89	89	85	NA	NA
107 USA	NA	NA	NA	NA	NA	NA	NA	NA	NA	NA	NA	NA	NA	NA	NA
108 Greece	NA	NA	NA	NA	NA	NA	NA	NA	NA	56	NA	96	76	NA	NA
109 Ireland	NA	NA	NA	NA	NA	NA	NA	NA	NA	NA	65	81	78	NA	NA
110 Singapore	100	100	0	99	99	NA	100	100	NA	99	85	85	90	NA	NA
111 Belgium	NA	NA	NA	NA	NA	NA	NA	NA	NA	NA	94	95	75	NA	NA
112 Australia	NA	NA	NA	NA	NA	NA	NA	NA	NA	NA	90	90	68	NA	NA
113 Italy	NA	NA	NA	NA	NA	NA	NA	NA	NA	4	83	63	43	NA	NA
114 New Zea-land	97	100	82	NA	NA	NA	NA	NA	NA	20	90	90	90	NA	NA
115 Korea, Rep. of	100	100	100	100	100	100	93	97	86	76	80	79	96	NA	NA
116 Canada	NA	NA	NA	NA	NA	NA	NA	NA	NA	NA	85x	85x	85x	NA	NA

Contd

TABLE 7.5 *Contd.*

1	2	3	4	5	6	7	8	9	10	11	12	13	14	15	16
117 Germany	NA	NA	NA	NA	NA	NA	NA	NA	NA	84	94	94	59	NA	NA
118 Denmark	NA	NA	NA	NA	NA	NA	NA	NA	NA	NA	95	97	84	NA	NA
119 Switzerland	NA	NA	NA	NA	NA	NA	NA	NA	NA	NA	NA	98	94	NA	NA
120 France	NA	NA	NA	NA	NA	NA	NA	NA	NA	80	95	90	69	NA	NA
121 United Kingdom	NA	NA	NA	NA	NA	NA	NA	NA	NA	75	85	90	89	NA	NA
122 Austria	NA	NA	NA	NA	NA	NA	NA	NA	NA	97	95	95	74	NA	NA
123 Spain	NA	NA	NA	NA	NA	NA	NA	NA	NA	NA	73	73	84	NA	NA
124 Hong Kong	100	100	96	NA	100	NA	99[x]	NA	NA	94	90	90	42	NA	NA
125 Netherlands	NA	NA	NA	NA	NA	NA	NA	NA	NA	NA	97	97	94	NA	NA
126 Norway	NA	NA	NA	NA	NA	NA	NA	NA	NA	95	86	84	87	NA	NA
127 Finland	NA	NA	NA	NA	NA	NA	NA	NA	NA	91	90'	90	95	NA	NA
128 Japan	NA	NA	NA	NA	NA	NA	NA	NA	NA	85	90	90[x]	73	NA	NA
129 Sweden	NA	NA	NA	NA	NA	NA	NA	NA	NA	14	99	99	84	NA	NA
Regional summaries															
Least developed countries	47	61	42	29	57	22	45	NA	NA	68	51	51	48	42	35
Developing countries	72	84	65	38	71	22	75	NA	NA	84	78	79	76	57	40
Developed countries	NA	NA	NA	NA	NA	NA	NA	NA	NA	82	82	84	80	NA	NA

Contd.

TABLE 7.5 *Concld.*

1	2	3	4	5	6	7	8	9	10	11	12	13	14	15	16
Sub-Saharan Africa	44	60	37	43	69	32	52	NA	NA	63	48	48	47	31	43
Middle East & North Africa	74	93	56	67	89	37	77	NA	NA	82	81	80	77	48	51
South Asia	80	85	78	17	53	4	52	NA	NA	90	83	83	79	73	19
East Asia & Pacific	71	85	65	58	73	51	87	NA	NA	93	90	91	89	53	49
Latin America & Caribbean	80	89	57	62	81	18	72	NA	NA	82	72	87	77	47	58

7.7 **Nutrition Data**

TABLE 7.6: Nutrition Data

	% of infants with low birth weight	% of children (1986-91) who are			% of children (1986-91) suffering from				Average index of food production per capita (1979-81= 100)	Daily per capita calorie supply as a % of requirements	% of household income (1980-85) spent on	
		exclusively breast-fed (0-3 months)	breast-fed with complementary food (6-9 months)	still breast-feeding (12-15 months)	underweight (0-4) moderate & severe	underweight (0-4) severe	wasting (12-23 months) moderate & severe	stunting (24-59 months) moderate & severe			all food	cereals
	1990								1991	1988-90		
1	2	3	4	5	6	7	8	9	10	11	12	13
Very high U5MR countries	16	NA	NA	82	34	NA	15	NA	96	91	NA	NA
1 Angola	19	NA	NA	NA	NA	NA	NA	NA	80	80	NA	NA
2 Mozambique	20	NA	NA	NA	NA	NA	NA	NA	68	77	NA	NA
3 Afghanistan	20	NA	NA	61x	38	7	NA	NA	73	72	NA	NA
4 Sierra Leone	17	NA	NA	92x	23x	2x	14x	NA	84	83	56	22
5 Guinea-Bissau	20	NA	NA	98x	23x	NA	NA	NA	104	97	NA	NA
6 Guinea	21	NA	NA	85x	NA	NA	NA	NA	88	97	NA	NA
7 Malawi	20	NA	NA	96x	24x	NA	8	61	77	88	55	28
8 Mali	17	8	45	90	31x	9x	16	34x	97	96	57	22
9 Niger	15	NA	NA	15x	49	9	23x	38x	73	95	NA	NA
10 Chad	NA	NA	NA	NA	NA	NA	NA	NA	97	73	NA	NA

Contd

TABLE 7.6 *Contd.*

	1	2	3	4	5	6	7	8	9	10	11	12	13
11	Ethiopia	16	NA	NA	95[x]	38[x]	NA	19[x]	43[x]	87	73	50	24
12	Somalia	16	NA	NA	54[x]	NA	NA	NA	NA	81	81	NA	NA
13	Mauritania	11	12	39	89	48	23	18	65	75	106	NA	NA
14	Burkina Faso	21[x]	NA	NA	97[x]	NA	NA	NA	NA	118	94	NA	NA
15	Bhutan	NA	NA	NA	90[x]	38[x]	NA	4[x]	56[x]	94	128	NA	NA
16	Zambia	13	NA	NA	93[x]	25[x]	5[x]	10[x]	59[x]	98	87	37	8
17	Liberia	NA	15	56	67	NA	NA	NA	NA	63	98	NA	NA
18	Uganda	NA	70	67	86	23	5	4	25[x]	97	93	NA	NA
19	Rwanda	17	NA	NA	74[x]	33[x]	4[x]	1[x]	34[x]	86	82	30	11
20	Nigeria	16	2	52	86	36	12	16	54	124	93	52	18
21	Cambodia	NA	NA	NA	72[x]	20	3	NA	NA	140	96	NA	NA
22	Senegal	11	7	68	93	22[x]	6[x]	8	28[x]	96	98	50	15
23	Yemen	19	15	NA	NA	53[x]	NA	15[x]	NA	79	NA	NA	NA
24	Burundi	NA	89	66	96	38	10	10	60	88	84	NA	NA
25	Zaire	15	NA	NA	86[x]	NA	NA	NA	NA	94	96	55	15
26	Central African Rep.	15	NA	NA	NA	NA	NA	NA	NA	93	822	NA	NA
27	Tanzania	14	NA	NA	70[x]	48	6	NA	NA	81	95	64	32
28	Madagascar	10	NA	NA	85[x]	33[x]	8[x]	17	56[x]	83	95	59	26
29	Sudan	15	14	45	80	20	NA	13[x]	32[x]	76	87	60	NA
30	Gabon	NA	NA	NA	NA	NA	NA	NA	NA	85	104	NA	NA

Contd.

TABLE 7.6 *Contd.*

	1	2	3	4	5	6	7	8	9	10	11	12	13
31	Benin	NA	NA	NA	76^{x}	NA	NA	NA	NA	114	104	37	12
32	Lao. Peo. Dem.	18	NA	NA	NA	37	NA	20	44	110	111	NA	NA
33	Nepal	NA	NA	NA	82^{x}	NA	NA	NA	NA	124	100	57	38
34	Togo	20	10	86	95	24	6	10	37^{x}	87	99	NA	NA
35	Iraq	15	NA	NA	58	12	2	NA	NA	65	128	NA	NA
High U5MR countries		27	NA	NA	77	50	21	20	59	110	105	47	16
36	Lesotho	11	NA	NA	76^{x}	16	2	7	23	80	93	NA	NA
37	Haiti	155	NA	NA	29^{x}	3^{x}	17^{x}	51^{x}	83	89	NA	NA	
38	Ghana	17	2	57	94	27	6	15	39	105	93	66	NA
39	Pakistan	225	25	29	78	40	14	11	60	102	99	54	17
40	Bangladesh	50	NA	NA	82^{x}	66^{x}	27^{x}	16^{x}	65	96	88	59	36
41	Cote d'ivoire	14^{x}	NA	NA	78^{x}	12	2	17	20	93	111	40	14
42	**India**	**33**	**NA**	**NA**	**NA**	**63^{x}**	**27^{x}**	**27**	**65^{x}**	**116**	**101**	**52**	**18**
43	Cameroon	13	7	NA	NA	17^{x}	NA	2^{x}	43^{x}	79	95	24	8
44	Bolivia	12	59	57	73	13	3	2	51^{x}	125	84	33	NA
45	Namibia	12	NA	NA	73^{x}	29^{x}	6^{x}	9^{x}	30^{x}	92	NA	NA	NA
46	Myanmar	16	NA	NA	94^{x}	32	9	NA	NA	88	114	NA	NA
47	Congo	16	NA	NA	90^{x}	24	NA	13	33	97	103	42	19
48	Libyan Arab Jamahiriya	NA	NA	NA	NA	NA	NA	NA	NA	74	140	NA	NA
49	Peru	11	32	49	57	13^{x}	2^{x}	3	43	93	87	35	8
50	Guatemala	14	NA	NA	82	34^{x}	8^{x}	3	68^{x}	95	103	36	10

Contd.

TABLE 7.6 *Contd.*

1	2	3	4	5	6	7	8	9	10	11	12	13
51 Morocco	9	48	48	62	16^{x}	4^{x}	6	34^{x}	134	125	40	12
52 Turkey	8	NA	NA	63^{x}	NA	NA	NA	NA	99	127	40	8
53 Zimbabwe	14	11	94	90	12	2	2	31	76	94	40	9
54 Indonesia	14	39	82	82	40	NA	NA	NA	125	121	61	18
55 Botswana	8	41	82	77	15	NA	NA	NA	63	97	35	13
56 Egypt	10	38	52	77	10	3	4	32	106	132	50	10
57 Ecuador	11	31	31	51	17	0	4	39	99	105	30	NA
58 Mongolia	10	NA	NA	NA	NA	NA	NA	NA	76	97	NA	NA
59 Nicaragua	15	NA	NA	NA	11	1	0	22	62	99	NA	NA
60 Papua New Guinea	23	NA	NA	NA	35	NA	NA	NA	98	114	NA	NA
61 Dominican Rep.	16	14	24	23	13^{x}	2^{x}	3	26^{x}	81	102	46	13
62 Kenya	16	24	87	83	14^{x}	3^{x}	5^{x}	32^{x}	193	89	39	13
63 Honduras	9	NA	NA	24^{x}	21	4	2^{x}	34^{x}	81	98	39	NA
64 South Africa	NA	NA	NA	NA	NA	NA	NA	NA	81	128	26	NA
Middle U5MR countries	10	NA	NA	41	21	NA	9	36	122	116	42	NA
65 Brazil	11	4	28	25	7	3	2^{x}	15^{x}	115	114	35	9
66 El Salvador	11	NA	NA	55^{x}	NA	NA	3	36	103	102	33	12
67 Iran, Islamic Rep. of	9	NA	NA	51^{x}	443^{x}	NA	23^{x}	55^{x}	114	125	37	10
68 Algeria	9	NA	NA	NA	10^{x}	NA	4^{x}	13^{x}	104	123	NA	NA
69 Paraguay	8	7	61	40	4	1	0	17	116	116	30	6
70 Tunisia	8	21	53	57	10^{x}	2^{x}	4	23^{x}	102	131	37	7

Contd.

TABLE 7.6 *Contd.*

	1	2	3	4	5	6	7	8	9	10	11	12	13
71	Viet Nam	17	NA	NA	49^{x}	42	14	12^{x}	49^{x}	131	103	NA	NA
72	Syria	11	NA	NA	41^{x}	NA	NA	NA	NA	73	126	NA	NA
73	Jordan	7	32	NA	61^{x}	6	1	3	21	82	110	35	NA
74	Lebanon	10	NA	NA	15^{x}	NA	NA	NA	NA	132	127	NA	NA
75	Philippines	15	NA	NA	53^{x}	34	5	14	45	82	104	51	20
76	Venezuela	9	NA	NA	30^{x}	6^{x}	NA	4	7^{x}	99	99	38	NA
77	Saudi Arabia	7	NA	NA	NA	NA	NA	NA	NA	223	121	NA	NA
78	Oman	10	NA	NA	76	NA	NA	NA	NA	NA	NA	NA	NA
79	Mexico	12	38	36	32	14	NA	6^{x}	22^{x}	97	131	35	NA
80	Romania	7	NA	NA	NA	NA	NA	NA	NA	70	116	NA	NA
81	Korea, Dem Peo. Rep.	NA	NA	NA	NA	NA	NA	NA	NA	109	121	NA	NA
82	Thailand	13	4	69	58	26^{x}	4^{x}	10	28^{x}	109	103	30	7
83	USSR (former)	6	NA	NA	NA	NA	NA	NA	NA	96	132	NA	NA
84	Albania	7	NA	NA	NA	NA	NA	NA	NA	62	107	NA	NA
85	Panama	10	NA	NA	55^{x}	16	NA	7	24	81	98	38	7
86	United Arab Emirates	6	NA	NA	26	NA	NA	NA	NA	NA	NA	NA	NA
87	Mauritius	9	NA	NA	40^{x}	24	NA	16^{x}	22^{x}	94	128	24	7
88	China	9	NA	NA	NA	21^{x}	3^{x}	8^{x}	41^{x}	138	112	61	NA
89	Uruguay	8	NA	NA	NA	7^{x}	2^{x}	NA	16^{x}	108	101	31	7
90	Argentina	8	NA	NA	114^{x}	NA	4	NA	NA	95	131	35	4

Contd.

TABLE 7.6 *Contd.*

1	2	3	4	5	6	7	8	9	10	11	12	13
91 Trinidad and Tobago	10	10	39	30	7^x	0^x	5	4^x	87	114	NA	NA
92 Yugoslavia (former)	NA	NA	NA	NA	NA	NA	NA	NA	87	140	27	NA
93 Bulgaria	6	NA	NA	NA	NA	NA	NA	NA	88	148	NA	NA
94 Chile	7	NA	NA	20^x	3^x	0^x	1	10^x	118	102	29	7
95 Sri Lanka	25	14	47	71	29	2	21	39	89	101	43	18
96 Colombia	10	17	48	39	10	2	5	18	104	106	29	NA
Low U5MR countries	7	NA	NA	NA	NA	NA	NA	NA	02	133	15	3
97 Malaysia	10	NA	NA	19^x	NA	4	6	NA	146	120	30	NA
98 Jamaica	11	NA	NA	43^x	7	1	6	7	96	114	39	NA
99 Costa Rica	6	NA	NA	24^x	6	NA	3	38	90	121	33	8
100 Hungary	9	NA	NA	NA	NA	NA	NA	NA	114	137	25	NA
101 Poland	NA	NA	NA	NA	NA	NA	NA	NA	103	131	299	NA
102 Kuwait	7	NA	NA	12^x	6	NA	2	14	NA	NA	NA	NA
103 Cuba	8	NA	NA	NA	NA	NA	1^x	NA	96	135	NA	NA
104 Czecho-slovakia	6	NA	NA	NA	NA	NA	NA	NA	91	125	22	NA
105 Israel	7	NA	NA	NA	NA	NA	NA	NA	91	125	22	NA
106 Portugal	5	NA	NA	7	NA	NA	NA	NA	117	136	34	NA
107 USA	7	NA	NA	NA	NA	NA	NA	NA	94	138	13	2
108 Greece	6	NA	NA	NA	NA	NA	NA	NA	104	151	30	NA
109 Ireland	4	NA	NA	NA	NA	NA	NA	NA	118	157	22	4
110 Singapore	7	NA	NA	NA	14^x	NA	NA	NA	70	136	19	NA
111 Belgium	6	NA	NA	NA	NA	NA	NA	NA	110	149	15	2

Contd.

TABLE 7.6 *Contd.*

1	2	3	4	5	6	7	8	9	10	11	12	13
112 Australia	6	NA	NA	10	NA	NA	NA	NA	92	124	13	2
113 Italy	5	NA	NA	NA	NA	NA	NA	NA	99	139	19	2
114 New Zealand	6	NA	NA	NA	NA	NA	NA	NA	102	131	12	2
115 Korea, Rep. of	9	NA	NA	27^{x}	NA	NA	NA	NA	100	1120	35	14
116 Canada	6	NA	NA	NA	NA	NA	NA	NA	117	122	11	2
117 Germany	NA	NA	NA	NA	NA	NA	NA	NA	NA	NA	NA	NA
118 Denmark	6	NA	NA	NA	NA	NA	NA	NA	132	135	13	2
119 Switzerland	5	NA	NA	NA	NA	NA	NA	NA	100	130	17	NA
120 France	5	NA	NA	NA	NA	NA	NA	NA	106	143	16	2
121 United Kingdom	7	NA	NA	NA	NA	NA	NA	NA	108	130	12	2
122 Austria	6	NA	NA	NA	NA	NA	NA	NA	103	133	16	2
123 Spain	4	NA	NA	NA	NA	NA	NA	NA	111	141	24	3
124 Hong Kong	8	NA	NA	NA	NA	NA	NA	NA	111	125	12	1
125 Netherlands	NA	NA	NA	NA	NA	NA	NA	NA	103	114	13	2
126 Norway	4	NA	NA	NA	NA	NA	NA	NA	108	120	15	2
127 Finland	4	NA	NA	NA	NA	NA	NA	NA	98	113	16	3
128 Japan	6	NA	NA	NA	NA	NA	NA	NA	99	125	16	4
129 Sweden	5	NA	NA	NA	NA	NA	NA	NA	96	111	13	2

Contd.

TABLE 7.6 *Concld.*

1	2	3	4	5	6	7	8	9	10	11	12	13
Regional summaries												
Least developed countries	24	NA	NA	82	42	14	15	50	91	90	NA	NA
Developing countries	19	NA	NA	68	36	12	14	47	116	107	43	NA
Developed countries	6	NA	NA	NA	NA	NA	NA	NA	99	133	15	2
Sub-Saharan Africa	16	NA	NA	84	31	8	13	44	96	93	37	16
Middle East & North Africa	10	NA	NA	62	24	NA	NA	NA	106	123	NA	NA
South Asia	34	NA	NA	78	59	25	23	64	112	99	53	19
East Asia & Pacific	11	NA	NA	66	26	NA	NA	NA	130	112	49	NA
Latin America & Caribbean	11	NA	NA	33	11	3	4	23	104	114	35	8

7.8 **Women Data**

TABLE 7.7: Women Data

	Life expectancy females as a % of males 1991	Adult literacy rate females as a % of males 1990	Enrolment ratios females as a % of males 1986-90		Contraceptive prevalence (%) 1980-92	Pregnant immunized against tetanus 1990-91	% of births attended by trained health personnel 1983-91	Maternal mortality rate 1980-90
			primary school	secondary school				
1	2	3	4	5	6	7	8	9
Very high U5MR countries	106	62	74	58	6	28	33	640
1 Angola	107	52	84	53	1x	36	15	NA
2 Mozambique	107	47	78	57	4	30	25	300
3 Afghanistan	102	32	52	45	2x	9	9	640
4 Sierra Leone	108	35	62	48	4	77	25	450
5 Guinea-Bissau	108	48	55	44	1x	35	27	700x
6 Guinea	102	37	46	36	1x	25	25	800
7 Malawi	103	NA	82	50	7	76	45	170
8 Mali	107	59	59	44	5	9	32	2000
9 Niger	107	43	56	38	1x	44	47	700
10 Chad	107	43	44	25	1x	4	15	960
11 Ethiopia	107	NA	65	71	2	6	14	NA
12 Somalia	107	39	50	54	1	5	2	1100
13 Mauritania	107	45	70	45	4	40	20	NA
14 Burkina Faso	107	32	61	56	1	26	30	810
15 Bhutan	103	49	65	29	43	7	1310	

Contd.

TABLE 7.7 *Contd.*

1	2	3	4	5	6	7	8	9
16 Zambia	103	80	92	56	1x	68	38	150
17 Liberia	105	58	56	NA	6	20x	58	NA
18 Uganda	106	56	83	50	5	21	38	300
19 Rwanda	107	58	99	67	10	88	22	210x
20 Nigeria	107	65	82	73	6	26	37	800
21 Cambodia	106	46	NA	44	NA	22	47	500
22 Senegal	104	48	73	52	11	33	411	600
23 Yemen	101	49	30	17	NA	8	12	NA
24 Burundi	107	66	78	60	9	56	19	NA
25 Zaire	107	73	75	50	1x	29	NA	800
26 Central African Rep.	111	48	61	38	NA	87	66	600
27 Tanzania	106	95	98	80	8	40	60	340x
28 Madagascar	106	83	96	90	NA	17	62	570
29 Sudan	105	28	71x	74	9	16	69	550
30 Gabon	107	66	NA	NA	NA	86	80	190
31 Benin	107	50	51	39	9	83	45	160x
32 Lao. Peo. Dem.	106	NA	80	71	NA	3	NA	NA
33 Nepal	98	34	51	40	14	17	6	830
34 Togo	107	55	63	30	34	81	15	420
35 Iraq	105	70	84	64	18	45	50	120x
High U5MR countries	103	62	80	64	39	65	35	440
36 Lesotho	109	NA	116	148	5x	NA	40	NA
37 Haiti	106	80	94	95	10	23	20	340
38 Ghana	107	73	82	61	13	9	55	1000
39 Pakistan	100	45	55	43	12	42	40	500
40 Bangladesh	99	47	884	48	31	78	5	600

Contd.

TABLE 7.7 *Contd.*

	1	2	3	4	5	6	7	8	9
41	Cote d'ivoire	106	60	71	44	3	35	20	NA
42	**India**	**101**	**55**	**73**	**57**	**43**	**80**	**33**	**460**
43	Cameroon	106	65	86	65	16	35	45	430
44	Bolivia	1108	84	90	86	30	52	54	600
45	Namibia	105	NA	NA	NA	26	52	NA	370[x]
46	Myanmar	106	81	94	92	13	61	57	460
47	Congo	110	63	NA	38	NA	60	NA	900
48	Libyan Arab Jamahiriya	106	67	NA	NA	NA	18	76	80[x]
49	Peru	106	86	96	90	59	12	52	300
50	Guatemala	108	75	85	90	23	18	34	200
51	Morocco	106	62	68	71	36	64	26	300[x]
52	Turkey	108	79	92	62	63	20	77	150
53	Zimbabwe	106	81	97	86	43	60	60	..
54	Indonesia	106	74	96	83	48	52	32	450
55	Botswana	111	77	04	116	33	62	78	200
56	Egypt	104	54	86	78	38	71	35	320
57	Ecuador	107	95	99	104	53	5	56	170
58	Mongolia	104	..	103	109	..	..	99	140
59	Nicaragua	108	..	111	164	27	25	73	..
60	Papua New Guinea	103	58	85	63	4	3	20	900

Contd.

TABLE 7.7 *Contd.*

1	2	3	4	5	6	7	8	9
61 Dominican Rep.	107	96	101	..	50	24	92	..
62 Kenya	107	74	96	70	27	37	50	170x
63 Honduras	107	93	101	129	41	16	90	220
64 South Africa	110	..	..	..	48	..	..	83x
Middle U5MR countries	**107**	**80**	**93**	**87**	**66**	**54**	**87**	**100**
65 Brazil	109	96	..	131	66	62	95	200
66 El Salvador	110	92	101	100	47	19	50	..
67 Iran, Islamic Rep. of	102	66	88	71	23x	77	70	120
68 Algeria	103	66	85	87	36	27	15	140x
69 Paraguay	107	96	96	107	48	54	66	300
70 Tunisia	103	76	87	78	50	40	68	50
71 Viet Nam	107	91	94	93	53	14	95	120
72 Syria	106	65	89	71	52	84	61	140
73 Jordan	106	79	101	98	35	47	87	48x
74 Lebanon	106	83	90	98	55x	..	45	..
75 Philippines	106	100	99	104	36	52	55	100
76 Venezuela	109	103	100	124	49x	..	69	..
77 Saudi Arabia	105	66	86	74	..	62	90	90
78 Oman	106	..	92	73	9	97	60	..
79 Mexico	110	94	97	100	53	42	77	110
80 Romania	109	..	99	110	58x	..	100	150

Contd.

TABLE 7.7 *Contd.*

1	2	3	4	5	6	7	8	9
81 Korea, Dem Peo. Rep.	109	..	94	100	..	99	100	41
82 Thailand	108	94	99	88	66	76	71	71
83 USSR (former)	114	..	101	..	..	..	..	21
84 Albania	109	..	99	85	..	..	99	..
85 Panama	106	100	96	113	58	27	96	60
86 United Arab Emirates	016	66	99	115	..	..	99	..
87 Mauritius	110	..	102	100	75	77	85	99
88 China	105	74	90	76	72	..	94	95
89 Uruguay	109	99	99	112	..	13	96	36
90 Argentina	110	99	107	113	74	..	87	140
91 Trinidad and Tobago	107	..	103	104	53	..	98	110
92 Yugoslavia (former)	108	91	99	96	55x	..	86	8
93 Bulgaria	109	..	98	103	76x	..	100	9
94 Chile	110	99	98	108	43x	..	98	67
95 Sri Lanka	106	90	97	107	62	50	94	80
96 Colombia	109	98	102	102	66	40	94	200
Low U5MR countries	**109**	**..**	**100**	**102**	**72**	**..**	**97**	**12**
97 Malaysia	106	80	99	102	51	83	82	59
98 Jamaica	106	101	101	110	55	50	82	120
99 Costa Rica	106	100	98	102	70	68	93	36
100 Hungary	112	..	101	103	73	..	99	15
101 Poland	113	..	100	104	75x	..	100	11

Contd.

TABLE 7.7 *Contd.*

1	2	3	4	5	6	7	8	9
102 Kuwait	106	87	98	94	..	22	99	6
103 Cuba	105	98	95	112	70	88	90	39
104 Czechoslovakia	111	..	10	107	95^{x}	..	100	10
105 Israel	105	..	103	109	..	..	99	3
106 Portugal	110	92	94	119	66^{x}	..	90	10
107 USA	109	..	9	101	74	..	99	8
108 Greece	107	91	101	95	..	..	97	5
109 Ireland	108	..	101	110	..	..	..	2
110 Singapore	108	..	98	104	74	..	100	10
111 Belgium	109	..	100	101	81	..	100	3
112 Australia	109	..	99	104	67^{x}	..	99	3
113 Italy	109	98	100	100	78^{x}	..	..	4
114 New Zealand	109	..	100	102	70^{x}	..	99	13
115 Korea, Rep. of	109	95	103	97	77	..	89	26
116 Canada	109	..	100	101	73	..	99	5
117 Germany	109		99	96	..	..	99	5
118 Denmark	108		101	101	63^{x}	..	100	3
119 Switzerland	109		..	..	71	..	99	5
120 France	111		97	108	79^{x}	..	94	9
121 United Kingdom	107		101	104	72	..	100	8
122 Austria	109	..	99	102	71	..	..	8
123 Spain	108	96	98	111	59	..	96	5
124 Hong Kong	107	..	99	106	81	..	100	6
125 Netherlands	109	..	103	97	76	..	100	10
126 Norway	109	..	100	105	71^{x}	..	..	3

Contd.

TABLE 7.7 *Concld.*

1	2	3	4	5	6	7	8	9
127 Finland	111	..	100	117	80x	..	100	11
128 Japan	108	..	100	103	64	..	100	11
129 Sweden	108	..	100	104	78	..	100	5
Regional summaries								
Least developed countries	104	62	76	56	12	42	27	590
Developing countries	104	73	85	76	50	57	55	340
Developed countries	110		100	103	72	..	98	15
Sub-Saharan Africa	107	68	81	64	11	31	36	600
Middle East & North Africa	104	66	83	72	37	48	55	210
South Asia	101	54	73	56	38	73	30	490
East Asia & Pacific	106	77	92	82	66	53	81	160
Latin America & Caribbean	109	95	99	111	58	47	80	180

7.9 **Data on Less Populous Countries**

TABLE 7.8: Data on Less Populous Countries

	Under-5 mortality rate		Infant mortality rate (under 1)		Total population (thousands)	Annual no. of births (thousands)	Annual no. of under-5 deaths (thousands)	GNP per capita (US$)	Life expectancy at birth (years)	Total adult literacy rate	% of age-group enrolled in primary school (gross)	% of children immunized against measles
	1960	1991	1960	1991	1991	1991	1991	1990	1991	1985-90	1986-90	1990-91
1	2	3	4	5	6	7	8	9	10	11	12	13
1 Gambia	375	234	213	135	884	39.8	9.3	260	44	27	64	87
2 Equatorial Guinea	316	202	188	120	360	15.9	3.2	330	47	50	108^{x}	79
3 Djibouti	..	161	186	115	453	21.2	3.4	1210^{x}	48	12	47	79
4 Comoros	248	133	165	92	564	27.6	3.7	480	55	48^{x}	75	87
5 Swaziland	223	113	157	76	771	29.0	3.3	820	57	55^{x}	104	80
6 Vanuatu	..	89	..	68	153	6.2	0.6	1060	65	53^{x}	84^{x}	66
7 Sao Tome and Principe	..	89	..	68	121	4.2	0.4	420	67	57^{x}	..	68
8 Kirbati	..	85	..	56	72	2.4	0.2	760	55	96	91	63
9 Maldives	..	81	158	58	220	8.6	0.7	440	63	95	87	97
10 Guyana	126	69	100	50	801	20.7	1.4	370	65	92^{x}	106	76
11 Cape Verde	164	61	110	44	373	13.4	0.8	890	67	37^{x}	115	76
12 Samoa	..	59	..	46	158	5.7	0.3	730	66	98	91^{x}	87
13 St. Christopher-Nevis	..	43	..	36	42	0.9	0.0	3330	70	90	..	99
14 Tuvalu	..	..	..	34^{x}	12	..	..	650^{x}	..	90	..	79
15 Suriname	96	37	70	30	430	11.4	0.4	3050	70	95	124	84

Contd

TABLE 7.8 *Contd.*

1	2	3	4	5	6	7	8	9	10	11	12	13
16 Grenada	..	37	..	30	91	2.4	0.1	2120	70	96^{x}	88^{x}	96
17 Montserrat	..	35	..	29	11	0.3	0.0	3330^{x}	71	97^{x}	100^{x}	99
18 Solomon	..	..	120	28	331	12.5	..	510	70	15	65^{x}	74
19 Qatar	239	35	145	28	440	10.4	0.4	15860	70	76	73	79
20 British	..	..	..	27^{x}	17	0.2^{x}	8500^{x}	69^{x}	98^{x}	..	84	
21 Fed. States of Micronesia	..	31	..	26	107	3.7	0.1	980^{x}	71	63^{x}	101^{x}	12^{x}
22 Bahamas	..	..	51	25	260	5.1	..	11420	72	70^{x}	..	87^{x}
23 Fiji	97	30	71	25	732	18.0	0.5	1770	71	79^{x}	122	84
24 Turks and Caicos islands	..	..	..	25^{x}	12	0.2	..	780^{x}	..	98^{x}	..	99
25 Belize	..	29^{x}	..	23^{x}	194	7.0	0.2	1970	68	93	90	74
26 Marshall	..	..	..	23^{x}	47	1.3^{x}	..	..	74^{x}	76^{x}	107	25^{x}
27 Palau	..	..	..	23^{x}	15	0.5	..	790^{x}	74^{x}	75	98^{x}	100
28 St Vincent & the Grenadines	..	26	..	22	108	2.5	0.1	1610	71	82	95^{x}	99
29 Tonga	..	26	..	22	97	3.1	0.1	1010	67	78	100^{x}	63^{x}
30 Antigua	..	23	..	19	66	1.3	0.0	4600	74	95	100	89
31 Saint Lucia	..	22	..	18	135	4.0	0.1	1900	72	82^{x}	95^{x}	82
32 Seychelles	..	21	..	17	71	1.6	0.0	4670	71	88	102^{x}	89
33 Dominica	..	20	..	16	72	1.7	0.0	1940	75	94^{x}	100	98
34 Cook Islands	..	..	..	15^{x}	17	0.4^{x}	..	1550^{x}	..	75	100	100
35 Bahrain	208	18	130	14	518	13.7	0.2	6380	71	77	110	85

Contd.

TABLE 7.8 *Concld.*

	1	2	3	4	5	6	7	8	9	10	11	12	13
36	Malta	42	17	37	11	356	5.4	0.1	6610	76	88	108	80
37	Barbados	90	12	74	11	258	4.1	0.0	6540	75	98	110x	87
38	Cyprus	36	11	30	10	709	12.4	0.1	8040	77	89x	103	74
39	Brunei Darussalam	..	10	63	9	264	6.4	0.1	20760x	74	78x	..	99
40	Luxembourg	41	9	33	7	375	4.5	0.0	28730	75	..	..	80
41	Iceland	22	7	17	6	257	4.5	0.0	21400	78	..	101	99

7.10 **Data on Newly Independent Countries**

TABLE 7.9: Data on Newly Independent Countries

		Infant mortality rate (under 1) (millions)	Total population (%)	Urban population	Population under 16 (%)	Annual no. of births (thousands)	% of one-year old children fully immunized		GDP per capita (US$)	Life expectancy at birth (years)	Total fertility rate	Maternal mortality rate
		1990	1990	1989-90	1989-90	1990	Polio	measles	1989	1988-90	1989-90	1989
	1	2	3	4	5	6	7	8	9	10	11	12
	USSR (former)											
1	Turkmenistan	94	3.7	47	43	126	84	68	3170	65	4.4	55
2	Tajikistan	72	5.3	33	44	203	90	89	2060	70	5.2	39
3	Uzbekistan	64	20.5	42	41	688	61	81	2430	69	4.1	43
4	Kyrgyzstan	54	4.4	38	27	127	72	91	2950	68	3.9	43
5	Kazakhstan	44	16.7	57	33	362	86	94	3890	69	2.9	53
6	Azerbaijan	44	7.2	54	33	180	93	91	3670	70	2.8	29
7	Armenia	35	3.3	68	30	79	96	92	4750	71	2.7	35
8	Moldova	33	4.4	47	24	77	92	95	4470	68	2.5	34
9	Georgia	32	5.5	55	25	93	80	74	4270	72	2.3	55
10	Ukraine	22	51.9	67	16	659	81	88	4720	71	2.0	33
11	Russian Federation	22	148.3	74	22	1987	75	79	6200	70	2.0	49
12	Belarus	20	10.3	66	22	143	90	95	6170	72	2.1	25
13	Estonia	14	1.6	72	24	23	70	86	6200	71	2.1	NA
14	Latvia	11	2.7	71	23	39	89	96	6360	71	2.0	NA
15	Lithuania	10	3.7	69	24	57	80	86	5830	72	2.0	NA

Contd.

TABLE 7.9 *Concld.*

	1	2	3	4	5	6	7	8	9	10	11	12
	Yugoslavia (former)											
16	Bosnia & Herzegovina	15	4.4	NA	NA	64	NA	NA	2290	71	1.7	25
17	Croatia	10	4.8	58	NA	56	NA	NA	4440	71	1.7	4
18	Slovenia	8	2.0	NA	NA	24	96	90	7630	72	1.6	4

Note: 1. Within each of the two country groups, nations are listed in descending order of their 1990 infant mortality rate.
2. For countries in the USSR (former) group, GDP per capita in roubles have been converted to US dollars at the United Nations operational rate of exchange.
3. Only newly independent countries who are also members of the United Nations have been included.

8

POVERTY ALLEVIATION

8.1 Global Rural Poverty

The number of rural poor has increased to nearly one billion people today, despite more than 40 years of international development assistance. The rural poor, with the proper resources and with political power, can act as a powerful engine for the enrichment of society as a whole. In other words, they are the solution to poverty in the developing world, not the intractable problem holding back societies, which was the basis of most previous development models.

Bolivia ranks as the nation with the highest percentage of rural poor, with 97 per cent of its rural population classified as living below the poverty line. Malawi has the second highest percentage, at 90 per cent, followed by Bangladesh (86%), Zambia (80%), Peru (75%), Brazil (73%) and the Philippines (64%).

Of the four billion residents in the 114 developing nations in the survey, more than 2.5 billion live in rural areas, one billion of them below the poverty line. This represents an increase of 40 per cent over 20 years ago. Of the total number of rural poor, 633 million live in Asia, 204 million in Africa, 27 million in the Near East and North Africa, and 76 million in Latin America and the Caribbean; they constitute 36 per cent of the total rural population of the 114 nations. While urban poverty is growing, the rural poor still account for over 80 per cent of the total number of poor people in the surveyed countries. The most important groups of rural poor are made up of smallholder farmers (those who have less than 3 hectares, or 7.5 acres, of crop land) and the landless. Also included are fishermen, pastoral nomads and indigenous ethnic groups.

Three major trends that could make the situation even worse in the coming years are: (1) world population is expected to grow to 8.5 billion by the year 2025, of whom 7.1 billion will be in developing countries, a 74 per cent increase in those nations; (2) landlessness is spreading at a rate of 3-5 per cent yearly, especially in Asia and parts of Africa and Latin America; (3) the rapid increase in the incidence of rural households headed by women, which now number over 75 million.

The rural poor are poor because they have been prevented from utilising the same production resources available to other segments of the population — land, credit infrastructure, technology and social services in particular — as well as a broad range of other factors, including national policies, demographic factors, natural resource management and the environment and exploitative intermediate. One of the more injurious practices has been government policies in many countries to keep food prices down for their urban populations at the expense of rural people, who have been forced to accept artificially low prices for their goods. The report defines the basic elements of rural poverty in an approach never used before, creating four major indices to quantify each nation's position relative to the other 113 countries in the survey. The indices are:

* **Food Security Index**, which portrays the composite food security situation of each country by relating food production and consumption variables. Only 15 of the 114 nations had a high food security status (with sufficient food for their people); 44 were rated as medium and 55 as low.
* **Integrated Poverty Index**, which combines the head-count measure of poverty with the income-gap ratio, income distribution below the poverty line and the annual per capita GNP growth. Twenty-two nations had a low poverty status (low rates of poverty), 26 medium and 66 high poverty status.
* **Basic Needs Index**, which calculates such factors as adult literacy, primary school enrollment, population per physician, infant mortality rate and access to such services as health care, potable water and sanitation. Forty nations were in the low status category (insufficient basic needs for all), 50 in the medium and 24 in the high status.
* **Relative Welfare Index**, which is the arithmetic average of the other three indices.

The five nations with the worst-off rural populations on the Relative Welfare Index are Bhutan, Burkina Faso, Somalia, Mauritania and the Sudan; the five best-off rural populations live in Cyprus, Malta, South Korea, Barbados and Mauritius. Some nations have experienced sharp jumps in the percentage of their rural poor in the past 20 years: In Sri Lanka, this jumped from 13 to 46 per cent from 1965 to 1988; in Zambia, from 52 to 80 per cent; Mali, from 48 to 60 per cent; Brazil, from 66 to 73 per cent; and Kenya, from 40 to 55 per cent. IFAD's analysis is that development programmes over the past 40 years failed in large part because they were based on a number of flawed assumptions, which include:

* That growth "trickles down" from the top to the bottom of the social hierarchy.
* That a nation's overall GNP is a valid indicator of poverty (because it ignores the actual distribution of income);
* That "poverty is poverty" everywhere, and therefore efforts to reduce it can ignore local conditions and needs;
* That the rural poor are a "problem" to be overcome, and/or essentially passive recipients of development aid.

It describes how poverty forces the rural majority to mine the planet's resources without any concern for conservation, speeding up the cycle of impoverishment and environmental degradation, with one reinforcing the other in an endless chain of destruction. The world risks losing all its productive land in less than 200 years to desertification if the present annual loss of 27 million hectares (66.7 million acres) continues.

Rural Women: Rural women in the developing world are among the poorest and most vulnerable people in the world and their numbers grew to 564 million in 1988 — an increase of 47 per cent in 20 years, versus a mere 30 per cent increase for rural men.

IFAD has created another index, **Women's Status Index**, which quantifies maternal mortality, adult illiteracy and primary and secondary enrollment rate, labour force status, contraceptive usage and female/male wage ratio. The five countries on the index in which women suffer the lowest status are Afghanistan, Ethiopia, Yemen, Pakistan and Somalia. The five developing nations in which women enjoy the highest status are listed as China, Cuba, Jamaica, South Korea and Malta. Some countries have experienced a jump in the number of rural women living in poverty over the past 20 years; these include China, Egypt, Ethiopia, India, the Philippines and Zambia.

A major reason for increased rural poverty has been the increase in the number of women-headed rural households — to an estimated 76 million women with 377 million family members. Such women face a triple burden: they share all the hardships and constraints of poor rural men; as women, they face discrimination, bias and neglect; they are forced to manage homes and farms alone, unlike men. In sub-Saharan Africa, 31 per cent of all rural households are headed by women, 17 per cent in Latin American and the Caribbean, 17 per cent the Near East and North Africa and 9 per cent in Asia. In LDCs, 23 per cent of all rural households are headed by women. Bangladesh has seen the percentage of women-headed rural households increase from 6 per cent 20 years to 116 per cent today, and it doubled in Cape Verde over the same period to 40 per cent.

Help to the Rural Poor

A "new, more dynamic" development model based on three fundamental propositions: sustainable rural development starts with, rather than ends with, poverty alleviation; poverty is essentially a production problem and poverty alleviation is an investment is recommended, the poor themselves are the primary force that can produce change. The development model includes these key ingredients:

* That the rural poor must be active participants at all levels of their development;
* That the rural poor have knowledge and skills that can and must be tapped to increase production and incomes;
* That rural women are major contributors to food production and family income and thus have a key role to play in development;
* That more attention must be given to small farmers, including women, for they are the agricultural "core" in most developing countries;
* That genuine, sustainable development requires conservation and rehabilitation of the natural resource base;
* That even small investments in developing the skills and know-how of the poor and in improving their access to inputs and services can have a significant effect in raising output and incomes;
* That supporting the productivity and self-reliance of the rural poor on a micro-level can lead to macro-economic growth.

"We must bring the rural poor onto the centre stage of development, and no longer push them to the fringes," Jazairy continues. "Many factors must be involved in a close relationship, including external agencies and donors, central and local governments, non-governmental organizations, and private, and commercial entities, but above all, of course, the people themselves. In other words, the IFAD model is a 'trickle-up' rather than 'trickle down' theory."

Governments and international agencies must provide the infrastructure of roads and transport, the health and education programmes and the technological developments that are known to the wider world but have never reached the village level. Another key element is that governments must remove obstacles to rural development that have been erected over the past 40-plus years. These are chiefly bureaucratic measures, such as price controls to keep down food costs to urban dwellers, that have robbed rural populations of the incentives to produce and expand.

The smallholder farmer constitutes the most important group of all the rural poor, totalling 713 million people, or 64.3 per cent of 1,109 billion people classified as functionally vulnerable in those nations. "The smallholders contribute to relatively large share of total production of major crops, in particular of traditional crops". "The new development paradigm suggests that in these countries the smallholder farmer sector will constitute the growth factor, whose dynamic push will accelerate the overall economic growth."

Source: *The State of World Rural Poverty: An Inquiry in Its Causes and Consequences*, International Fund for Agricultural Development, reported in *Go Bulletin*, No. 38, December 1992, Special Insert.

9

WORLD POPULATION

9.1 **State of World Population, 1992**

Population Growth

Long-range population projections from the UN Population Division, the first such figures in 10 years reveal that:

* World population by mid-1992 will be 5.48 billion. It will reach six billion in 1998. Annual additions to world population in the next decade will average 97 million, the highest in history. Nearly all of this population growth will be in a Africa, Asia and Latin America. Over half will be in Africa and South Asia.
* The median, or most likely, projection of population growth implies 8.5 billion people by 2025 and a near doubling of world population to 10 billion in 2025. Growth will probably continue for another century after that, to 11.6 billion in 2150.
* On the most optimistic assumption (the "low" projection) total population could peak in mid-century at about 8.5 billion and would begin to fall thereafter.
* On the "high" projection, growth could go the other way, reaching 12.5 billion in 2050, and heading toward 20.7 billion a century later.

Much depends upon action to reduce family size during the next decade. Delay could make a difference, of up to four billion, to the size of the world's population in 2050 — equal to the whole of world population in 1975.

Migration

Unbalanced economic and population growth within and between countries is boosting migration to record levels, says the Report. Some 83% of population growth in the next decade will be in urban areas. Cities have grown faster where national populations are growing faster. Slower national population growth means slower growth of cities, and more time to provide decent accommodation and services.

As many as 70 million people, mostly from developing countries, are working (legally or illegally) in other countries. Over one million people emigrate permanently to other countries and close to that number seek asylum each year. The number of refuges rocketed from 2.8 million in 1976 to the record level of 17.3 million in 1990. During the 1980s, eight million legal immigrants settled in the United States, Canada and Australia.

The labour force in north America will not increase between now and 2025 except through immigration. In central America it will increase by 50.5 million. Western Europe's labour force will will fall by 14.5 million; north Africa's will increase by 56.6 million.

Population, Poverty and Economic Growth

Developing countries have improved living conditions for increasing proportions of their populations. But the numbers of the poor, illiterate and malnourished have continued to climb:

* 1,156 million people live in absolute poverty, 212 million more than in 1970.
* There are an extra 60 million children out of school, an extra 65 million illiterates, an extra 50 million malnourished.

However, countries which succeeded in slowing population growth saw benefits in the 1980s:

* Their average incomes per person grew 2.5% a year faster than those with more rapid population growth. Slower population growth in the 1965-80 period also helped income growth in the 1980s.
* They tended to have higher savings and investment ratios.

Developing Human Resources

Lending absolute poverty, improving health and education and raising the status of women will contribute to slower, more balanced population growth. It calls for "a sustained and concerted programme, starting immediately". The aim should be to bring future population growth towards the UN lower population projection. 1.5-2 billion less than the median and four billion less that the high projection, by the year 2050. Special attention within such a programme should be given to Africa and south Asia, where more than half of the increase in population and the majority of the world's absolute poor are found.

* Women's access to better education, health care and family planning, and work at a fair wage; raise personal incomes, speed economic development and reduce family size.
* A reduction in family size can make a direct contribution to a better education, health and nutrition: children from smaller families are healthier and better nourished, stay longer in school and do better than children from large families.
* Avoiding births to mothers under 20 could cut deaths of under-fives by 17%.
* Avoiding births spaced closer than two years apart could cut under-five mortality by the same amount.
* Eliminating both these types of poor timing could reduce maternal mortality by 40%.

Equalizing women's access to education should be a priority, says the Report. It contributes to their to their personal development, to smaller families and to better health for mothers and children.

Population and the Environment

"Fixed" or "non-renewable" resources have so far adjusted to meet demand, says the Report. New reserves and new technologies have been found. But the simultaneous explosion of population and consumption per person might overwhelm adjustment mechanisms. For example, if the world's projected population for the year 2050 consumed at US levels, world oil reserves (1987 levels) would be burned up within five years.

Paradoxically, the immediate threat might be to "renewable" or "unlimited" resources, including land, water and other species.

* Expansion of farm land has been slowing down. At current rates, the average person in developing countries will have only 0.11 hectares of land in 60 years' time — one-fifth of today's level in developed countries.
* Even to provide this modest level, plus non-farm land needs, some 4-5 million square kilometres of additional wildlife habitat will have to be converted to human uses. This is equivalent to four-fifths of the total area of nature reserves in the world in 1990.
* Water shortages due to rising populations and consumption levels will impost severe constraints on development, particularly in Africa. By 2025, one billion Africans could be facing water stress or scarcity.

Population growth is a major factor in environmental impact. In developing countries it is responsible for around 79% of deforestation, 72% of arable land expansion and 69% of growth in livestock numbers.

Environmental impact is the product of the number of people, their level of consumption and their technology. Average consumption levels in the world are bound to rise. Technology alone cannot work miracles. Slower population growth will help achieve growth with lower damage levels.

Working towards balanced population growth is part of a broad strategy to reduce environmental impact and achieve the goal of sustainability.

Source: *A World in Balance,* United Nations Population Fund, reported in *Go Between,* May 1992, Special Insert.

9.2 Estimated/Projected World Population, 1950 to 2150

TABLE 9.1: Estimated/Projected World Population, 1950-2150

Year	Estimated/Project Population
1950	2.5 billion
1990	5.3 billion
2000	6.3 billion
2020	8.5 billion
2050	10.0 billion
2150	11.6 billion

This growth is based on the assumption that developing nations can reduce their birth rate from 3.8 children per mother to 3.3 by the year 2000. If that reduced birth rate is not reached until 2010, the population will hit 12.5 billion by the middle of the next century—unless mass starvation, disease or war curbs the numbers.

Figures cited are from the medium variant of the United Nations estimates and projections as revised in 1992.

Least developed countries as defined by the United Nations General Assembly, as of 1991, include 47 countries, of which 32 are in Africa, 9 in Asia, 1 in Latin America and 5 in Oceania. They are also included in the less developed regions.

1 Including Agalesa, Rodrigues and St. Brandon.
2 Including Ascension and Tristan da Cunha.
3 Including Christmas Island, Cocos, (Keeling) Islands, and Nortolk Island.
4 Including Pitcairn, Tokelau, Johnston Island and Midway Islands.
5 Excluding Estonia, Latvia and Lithuania which are included in Northern Europe.

9.3 **World Largest Countries in 1992**

TABLE 9.2: World Largest Countries in 1992

Rank	Country	Population (millions)	Percentage of world population
1	China	1188	21.7
2	**India**	**880**	**16.1**
3	United States of America	255	4.7
4	Indonesia	191	3.5
5	Brazil	154	2.8
6	Russian Federation	149	2.7
7	Pakistan	125	2.3
8	Japan	124	2.3
9	Bangladesh	119	2.2
10	Nigeria	116	2.1

Note: More developed regions comprise all regions of Europe and Northern America, Australia-New Zealand, Japan and the former Union of Soviet Socialist Republics. Less developed regions comprise all regions of Africa, Asia (excluding Japan) and Latin America, and the regions of Melanesia, Micronesia and Polynesia.

10

WORLD TRADE : Recent Developments

10.1 Trade and Development Report, 1992

The world economy is in a danger zone in which recovery is threatened by financial fragility brought about by a combination of financial liberalization, tight monetary policies and bank deregulation. The private sector in the developed countries is too indebted to be able to provide the impetus to growth and that no single country, moreover, is in a position to act as the locomotive.It therefore advocates a return to Keynesian policies on an international scale in an effort to pull the world out of recession.

Recession Aggravated by Debt Deflation

The severity of the current recession is due to the presence of debt deflation, primarily in the United States, Japan and the United Kingdom. This is a process whereby a decline in the banks' willingness and ability to lend forces debtors to curtail operations or resort to distress sales of inventories or other assets,which in turn lowers incomes and asset prices further and thus prolongs the recession.

The origins of this process go back to the 1980s when governments, firms, households and financial institutions increased their indebtedness to record levels in the expectation that steady economic expansion and asset price inflation would persist and continue to sustain a rising burden of debt. As a result, when the expansion came to a halt in mid-1989, all sectors found themselves overcommitted. Debtors have since faced not only an erosion of real incomes but also falling values of physical and financial assets at a time of high rial interest rates. The cyclical fall-off in demand was therefore aggravated not only by the Gulf War, but also by a shift of behaviours away from accumulating debt towards repaying it.

Behind the difficulties faced by many countries was a surge in bank lending for the purchase of commercial property. In the United States and the United Kingdom this went so far as to cause a massive oversupply, followed by a sharp fall in prices. In Japan, where property is often used as collateral for stock market operations, property and stock prices were lifted in a speculative bubble. Monetary policy was then tightened, triggering steep falls in asset prices. In all three countries, banks have experienced losses on their property loans and are sharply restricting lending for this purpose.

Banks have also become much less willing to lend because of the introduction by the Bank for International Settlements (BIS) of risk-adjusted capital adequacy requirements. These will oblige many banks to hold higher ratios of capital on lending against riskier assets. Issuing equity is difficult given the erosion of bank profits, so their only option is to draw down their more risky portfolios. The reduction in bank lending has hit small and medium sized businesses most, leading to an increase in bankruptcies and to labour shedding. This has in turn obliged banks to make larger provisions for bad debts and further inhibited them from lending.

Legacy of Past Policies

The present economic situation is caused by the thrust of policy in the 1980s: deregulation of interest rates; the abandonment of fiscal tools in macroeconomic management; and the deregulation of financial transactions domestically and externally, which increased the globalization of capital markets and drew money, currency and capital markets closer together.

In the United States, the deregulation of interest rates and increased competition for deposits led to pressures to deregulate the asset side of financial institutions' balance sheets — something which encouraged excessive risk-taking and indebtedness. For instance, the Savings and Loans Associations (S&Ls) were allowed to invest in assets with higher returns and correspondingly higher risks such as "junk" bonds and mortgage-backed securities. Banks, pension funds, and insurance companies also followed the S&Ls in the acquisition of development and construction loans, and banks substituted home loans for commercial industrial loans. Consequently, they found themselves highly exposed when the sell-off by S&Ls caused property market prices to collapse.

Financial deregulation also increased mergers and acquisitions, as well as management and leveraged buyouts. The ability to repay the debt issued to finance these purchase depended on the post-takeover realization of the anticipated value of the assets. Since most mergers and acquisitions were predicated on expectations of continuing economic expansion, the impact of the recession left bondholders with devalued portfolios and firms with excessive debts — incurred, what is more, at very high interest rates.

Poor Prospects without Policy Change

In this recessionary environment the ability of some developing countries to accelerate growth or maintain relatively high growth rates has helped shore up world economic activity. However, these countries will not be able to swim against the tide for long. This is especially true in Latin America. There, a weakness in export markets and the failure, thus far, of the first positive net transfer of resources in many years to be fully reflected in new investments, risk interrupting the positive dynamics currently prevailing. The sluggishness of commodity prices, moreover, remains a serious drag on many countries of the region.

As for the rest of the developing world, recent economic performance has been generally weak, except for parts of Asia. African countries continue to face difficulties in maintaining reforms at a time of poor export earnings. Where reform efforts have been pursued rigorously and external conditions have been favourable, growth performance has improved. But commodity prices declined in 1991, and for two commodities that are important for Africa — coffee and cocoa — prices are currently at their lowest level in almost twenty years. The result has been a squeeze on the external accounts and slower growth. Besides, a number of countries are suffering from severe drought.

In West Asia, the aftermath of the Gulf War has been the determining factor. In those countries with ample financial resources, reconstruction efforts have led to dynamic expansion, whereas in those with financial constraints the pace of recovery has been much slower. In the rest of developing Asia, the quality of domestic policy has been a key factor. Economies that have pursued growth-oriented policies have continued to do well, although their very success is sometimes generating bottlenecks. Other countries have registered both weak effort in the areas of policy-making and poor growth performance.

As for the countries of Central and Eastern Europe, the difficulties inherent in introducing viable market and State mechanisms have taken a severe toll. The general picture is one of sharp declines in industrial output, shortfalls in agricultural production, disruption of trade flows, external financial strains, and, especially in the former Soviet Union, fiscal imbalances.

The global economy is at an impasse. On the one hand, most developing countries and the countries of Central and Eastern Europe cannot achieve the sustained export growth which is necessary to underpin their free-market reforms and the newly-established democratic institutions without the private sector in most major industrialized economies is unable to take the lead in generating the growth necessary for such a recovery; nor is any single country able on its own to initiate a recovery. With firms and households both engaged in reducing spending, refinancing debts and increasing earnings, debt deflation will continue unless governments in the industrialized countries intervene to support incomes and prices of real and financial assets and if interest rates remain high.

A Call for Coordination Reflation

Keynesian policies may be applied to stimulate private consumption and investment demand, and thus make fuller use of productive capacities. It recalls that counter-cyclical fiscal policies have often been used with positive results in the past. Nevertheless, because budget deficits are high, fiscal expansion is being resisted even where it is most needed, that is where the debt-deflationary undercurrent runs strongest. However, that since the cyclical component of the government deficit is larger than the structural component, the higher expenditures resulting from the promotion of income growth would probably reduce rather than increase deficits. If the ensuing recovery is to be sustained, long-term interest rates would have to be brought down and short-term rate differentials between Western Europe, on the one hand, and the United States and Japan, on the other, reduced.[1]

Following specific measures may be proposed·

1. Developed countries, particularly the United States, Japan and the United Kingdom, should raise spending on social overheads and infrastructure. This would also improve productivity and contribute to structural improvement in economic performance. Any increases in expenditure, however, should be temporary and measures should be taken to avoid upward

1. These proposals were made before the investment spending package announced by the Japanese Government and the interest rate and exchange rate changes made by other governments in September.

pressures on interest rates.

2. Developed countries should also enlarge their export markets by strengthening the flow of long-term capital to developing countries and to countries in transition, and by renewing SDR allocations. This would also accelerate growth in those countries.
3. Now that price pressures in the United States are under control, the Federal Reserve Board should return to a policy of targeting the rate of interest, i.e. the policy it pursued before changing its procedures in 1979 to counteract a virulent inflation.
4. Germany should lead the way in reducing short-term interest rates in Western Europe to provide its partners with more scope for expansionary action. Otherwise the German currency will strengthen against those of other members of the European Monetary System, forcing the latter to tighten monetary policy so as to prevent strains on the Exchange Rate Mechanism becoming intolerable.

Other Conditions for a Sustained Recovery

Despite some improvement in indicators of their external financial positions, most developing countries continue to face a difficult situation regarding their access to, and the cost of, their external financing. This is reflected in low or negative lending to them by banks, also in the form of export credits; in the large number of negotiations for the rescheduling of bank debts still underway; and in the scarcity of favourable changes in the terms on which insurance is available for the financing of their imports. Adverse perceptions of creditworthiness have also depressed bank lending to countries of Central and Eastern Europe, though this was partly offset by greater reliance on official or officially-guaranteed financing. As for Latin America, the turn-around in financial transfers in 1991 owed more to bond lending than to bank credits.

As regards official bilateral debt, recent adoption by most Paris Club creditors of the "enhanced" Toronto terms for the poorest countries are welcome but the resulting debt reduction will be significantly smaller than under the proposed Trinidad terms, and for many of the beneficiaries debt burdens will still remain unsustainable.

A sustained recovery also depends on action in the field of trade. It explains that the simultaneous adoption over the past few years of liberal trade regimes by many developing countries makes it necessary for developed economies to open up their markets as well. Otherwise, efforts by developing countries to increase exports could depress the prices of their raw materials and labour-intensive manufactures. But the trend towards greater openness in developing countries has been accompanied by more, not less, protectionism in developed ones. This shortcoming needs to be corrected in a successful, balanced conclusion to the Uruguay Round.

While reform is an urgent necessity in many developing countries, it needs to be introduced gradually and be based on practical experience. The latter shows, for example, that while protection is not necessarily inimical to export success, its removal should follow a sequence in which it is reduced substantially first on inputs used by export sectors, and on other goods only after export supply capabilities have been built up. A sudden lifting of protection, in contrast, can cause losses of capital, labour skills and technological capabilities if, as is often the case, import-competing firms are unable to adapt rapidly.

Country experiences in the 1980s also indicate that export success involves one or more of the following: management of the exchange rate and the use of export subsidies in the early stages of export growth; the establishment of export processing zones; and active industrial policies to support the learning process, especially where new products and markets are involved. However, it is very costly to protect permanently a sector which fails to become internationally competitive. Combining trade and other structural reforms with macroeconomic stabilization measures in a large package can overload policy and inflate the costs of adjustment. A phased approach whereby macroeconomic stabilization precedes the gradual introduction of structural reforms is favoured.

Public sector enterprises have often played a strategic role in industrialization in both developed and developing countries. In many instances, however, they have been made to pursue goals having little or no connection with the original rationale, and many were allowed to continue even when the reason for establishing them no longer held. Public enterprises performed especially poorly in the 1980s in most developing countries and need to be radically overhauled.

As regards various options for reform, viz., restructuring, privatization and liquidation, privatization is often desirable and feasible, but many enterprises will inevitably remain in public ownership. The question then is not how to improve their short-term financial results but how to restructure them to obtain maximum efficiency.

Relieving public enterprises of some of their non-commercial tasks is often an essential component of such restructuring. If non-commercial objectives must retained, the cost should be financed separately. In this way poor financial results would no longer be hidden behind social objectives.

Public enterprises have also been plagued by bad management, owing to a lack of effective systems of ownership, control and financing and to political pressures. Operational decisions should be left to the management and that the government should exercise control by monitoring outcomes. The autonomy granted must, however, be matched with performance-linked rewards and penalties. It adds that greater efficiency cannot be attained in the presence of clientelism and political irregularities. Thus political reform, too, can be a prerequisite for effective enterprise reform.

Source: *Trade and Development Report, 1992,* UNCTAD, reported in *UNCTAD Bulletin,* September-October, Number 16, 1992.

10.2 Trade and Tariff: Uruguay Negotiations

At their Forty-eighth Session on 2-3 December 1992, the contracting parties welcomed the recent reactivation of the Uruguay Round negotiations with the hope that this would lead quickly to balanced results. They agreed that the prompt conclusion of the Round was the most important contribution GATT members could make towards sustaining the world economic recovery, improving the international trading environment and supporting the market-economy reforms underway in many countries.

Many of the concerns raised at the Session over trade policy developments in 1993 could be addressed by a successful Round outcome, according to the Contracting Parties Chairman, Ambassador Lars Anell (Sweden), in summing up the discussions. A number of delegations had criticized recourse to bilateralism and unilateralism, anti-dumping and countervailing measures, persistence of "grey-area" measures, non-implementation of panel reports, continued protection of non-competitive sectors, and the postponement of necessary structural adjustment measures in areas such as agriculture and textiles.

Council Report

The Council during the year, according to its Chairman, Ambassador B.K. Zutshi (India), assumed a more important "management role" over a wide range of activities, in addition to day-to-day governing of the GATT on behalf of the Contracting Parties. This included overseeing activities such as the trade and environment of panel reports, and the trade policy reviews of individual GATT members.

For 1993, Ambassador Zutshi suggested that the Council take up the following specific issues:

1. ensuring regular reporting of developments in regional trade arrangements;
2. streamlining the derestriction of GATT documents to better address the information needs of the press, schools and universities, private enterprises and the general public;
3. a review of the status of observers in the GATT and their rights and obligations; and
4. the proliferation and semi-permanence of waivers requested for the implementation of the harmonized system.

The Council also would have to deal with an urgent need to remedy the serious degradation of pension and salary conditions of the GATT professional staff. This question was raised by the Director-General in mid-1992 when he said that it was very much linked to the outcome of the Uruguay Round. The Council Chairman said that since the outcome of the Round now appeared to within reach, Mr. Dunkel might be able to consult soon on this matter, and present specific proposals to the Council early in 1993.

Committee on Trade and Development Report

The Committee on Trade and Development (CTD), one of the principal standing committees of the GATT, is responsible for reviewing and negotiating issues of trade interests to developing countries. It keeps under continuous review the implementation of Part IV of the General Agreement and the operation of the "Enabling Clause", which provides for differential and more favourable treatment of developing countries in various areas of trade policy.

The CTD Chairman, Ambassador Jesus Seade (Mexico), reported that in addition to its regular work, members during the year had started thinking about its post-Round work programme. Many members believed that the Committee's work would have to be more action-oriented, particularly in identifying ways and means of increasing participation of developing countries in the multilateral trading system, which was a basic objective of the Enabling Clause.

On his consultations with delegations on the examination in GATT of MER-

COSUR (the Southern Common Market comprised of Argentina, Brazil, Paraguay and Uruguay), Ambassador Seade said no agreement had been reached although an informal paper on procedures had obtained the support of a majority of delegations. (The MERCOSUR members, supported by many developing countries, contend that as a trade arrangement among developing countries, the arrangement should be dealt with in the CTD while some GATT members, including the United States, believe that MERCOSUR should be subject to regular GATT procedures on customs unions in the Council.)

Upon Ambassador Seade's suggestion, it was agreed that further consultations on MERCOSUR would be conducted by the Chairman of the Contracting Parties.

Accession: CSFR and Albania

The flurry of political and economic developments in Eastern Europe and the former Soviet Union continued to impact on the GATT.

Representatives of the Czech and Slovak Federal Republic (CSFR) informed contracting parties that the Federation would be dissolved at the end of the year. Two new republics — the Czech Republic and the Slovak Republic — would come into existence on 1 January 1993.

The CSFR recalled that as a founding contracting party in 1948, it had participated actively in all GATT activities. After the 1989 "Velvet Revolution", it had adopted radical reforms that had liberalized its commercial and economic relations with many countries. The fact that 97 per cent of its tariff was bound, and that conventional tariffs had a weighted average of about 5.7 per cent testified to its commitment to the GATT. These provided a solid basis for the future participation of both successor States in the General Agreement.

Separately, the Czech Republic and the Slovak Republic stressed their continued commitment to GATT principles and urged an early decision on their GATT membership status based on the rights and obligations of the CSFR.

Austria welcomed the determination of these countries to assume all the GATT obligations of the CSFR, and supported their request for participation in the GATT. The United States said that new accession negotiations were not necessary for successor states provided that the defunct State had a high level of obligations under GATT with a bound tariff schedule at meaningful levels; that the new States were fully willing and able to accept an identical level of obligations and the same tariff schedule; and that the new states were not contemplating important reorientations to their basic trade and economic policies that would nullify or impair trade opportunities enjoyed by other contracting parties in their markets. It said that as far as it could tell, these conditions were satisfied in the present case.

The Contracting Parties agreed that the Czech Republic and the Slovak Republic accede to the GATT under the same terms applied by the CSFR, without carrying out any negotiations. The Secretariat would prepare draft protocols of accession for both countries as well as the corresponding draft Decisions for approval by the Council at its first meeting in the new year. Tariff schedules encompassing the concessions contained in CSFR's tariff schedule would be annexed to each Protocol of Accession. In the meantime, the GATT and other relevant instruments would be applied to both Republics as if they had already acceded to the GATT.

The Contracting Parties established a working party to examine Albania's application to join the GATT. The country was granted observer status to the GATT in June 1992.

Albania told GATT members it had broken with 15 years of total isolation and had started a process of integration into the international community. Over the past year, it had undertaken important changes to move from a centrally planned to a market economy. It was aware that the transition period would be long and that enormous problems would have to be overcome. In this context, Albania considered accession to GATT to be an essential step in its general reform. It said that since becoming an observer to the GATT, it had strengthened trade relations with some GATT members through bilateral treaties. It was already undertaking some obligations under the GATT framework, and was aiming to draft relevant laws in conformity with the General Agreement.

The Contracting Parties granted observer status to Belarus. This brought to ten the number of former states of the Soviet Union accorded such status (the Russian Federation, Estonia, Moldova, Turkmenistan, Armenia, the Ukraine, Latvia, Lithuania and Kazakhstan).

Belarus pledged it would be a reliable partner in the multilateral trading system of the GATT. It said the experience acquired in the GATT would help the country in its transition toward a market economy and in resulting problems in its integration into the world economy.

US Countervailing Action on Steel Imports

A number of steel-exporting countries expressed serious concern over the United States' recent announcement of preliminary countervailing duties on certain imports. They said they would be participating actively in renewed negotiations for a multilateral steel agreement.

The European Community said it was extremely preoccupied by the US countervailing duty on flat-rolled steel products from a number of EC member states. The US duties ranged up to 60 per cent, and affected about 2 million tonnes of EC steel exports worth nearly US$1 billion in 1991. The EC believed that the US steel industry had exploited legitimate trade policy instruments to harass foreign competitors and divert world trade flows.

Brazil charged that the US duties were threatening its privatization programme for the steel sector. Austria complained that despite its low level of steel exports to the United States, its producers were subjects to costly countervailing duty investigation. Japan contended that the US duties were unjustified because its steel products to the United States had been declining in recent years.

US and EC Export Subsidies on Wheat

Australia recalled that in September 1992, the Council Chairman had undertaken to conduct informal consultations aimed at exploring avenues for addressing problems arising from the competitive subsidization of agricultural exports, particularly wheat, between the European Community and the United States. While Australia was encouraged by the recent understanding in agriculture between the two major exporters, and the movement in the Uruguay Round negotiations, it was worried by what could happen during the gap of many months between the Round's conclusion and the implementation of results. For this reason, it would encourage the Council Chairman continue with his informal consultations on this matter.

Brazil, Chile, Mexico, Venezuela, New Zealand, the ASEAN countries, Uruguay, Canada, Hungary, Japan and Colombia expressed support for Australia's view.

The United States said its recent agreement with the Community would enable them to reach a multilateral understanding that would reduce the volume of subsidized exports by 21 per cent and the value of such subsidies by 36 per cent over a six-year period. It emphasized that in the absence of reforms, it would be forced to compete for markets with the EC, which it said afforded high levels of benefit to agricultural exporters.

US Trade Embargo on Cuba

Cuba complained that legislation signed into law by the US President in October 1992 had not only reinforced the United States' trade blockade on Cuba, but had also affected its trading partners. It said some $718 million worth of trade per year would be affected by what it said was a law that violated international obligations and GATT provisions. Cuba recalled that in November 1992, the UN General Assembly had approved a resolution that expressed the need to put an end to the US economic, trade and financial blockade on Cuba. It said it had started consultations with other affected GATT members to assess the effects of this law.

The European Community said that while it had no comments on US-Cuban trade relations, it had serious concerns over the moves to implement the trade embargo by applying legislation of an extra-territorial character. This serious development, it said, had been the subject of an EC protest in Washington.

Mexico said it firmly rejected the US legislation which it considered to be of an extra-territorial nature. Tanzania said it was concerned that a subject that should be dealt with under multilateral discipline was being dealt with a unilateral way. Brazil noted it had voted for the UN resolution cited by Cuba.

EC, US Report Resolution of Oilseeds Dispute

The European Community recalled that at the September and November Council meetings, the Community and the United states were encouraged by the contracting parties to resolve the oilseeds dispute to avoid an escalation of trade measures that could have had disastrous effects on the multilateral trading system. It reported that intensive bilateral negotiations had resulted in an agreement that enabled conclude the Article XXVIII:4 (modification of tariff schedules) negotiations with the United States. The Community said it was ready to consult and negotiate, under Article XXVIII, with the other GATT members concerned.

The United States said that it was pleased to have reached an accommodation with the EC that would enable this contentious issue to be put to rest finally. Other GATT members with trade interest on this matter — Argentina, Canada, Uruguay, Brazil, Pakistan, India, Hungary and Poland — welcomed the EC and US statements, and expressed readiness to continue their talks with the Community.

EC Imports Regime on Bananas

The Director-General, Mr. Arthur Dunkel, recalled that in September 1992, Colombia, Costa Rica, Guatemala, Nicaragua and Venezuela had requested him to lend his good offices in an ex-officio capacity, under the 1966 Decision on dispute settlement procedures, to "facilitate a satisfactory solution to a dispute over measures to restrict the import of bananas currently applied by some member States of the EC. . . . Since then, he had met with the parties several times. Recently, he had suggested to the parties involved that in order to make progress in this very complicated case, the formal good offices be suspended forthwith until 15 January 1993. He said that in the present circumstances, informal talks might lend themselves better to flexibility and innovation, the final aim being a mutually satisfactory solution.

Costa Rica, speaking on behalf of Latin American countries cited by the Director-General, said that they had accepted the suspension of good offices procedures to leave the door open for informal negotiations that would make it possible to find a solution within the Uruguay Round commitments. This was on the understanding that they retained all their rights under the 1966 Decision, which prescribed procedures for disputes involving developing countries.

Other Disputes

Argentina announced that it had resolved its dispute with Norway over a subsidy connected with a tender for a hydro-electric project in Costa Rica. It added that it might raise at a future Council meeting the whole issue of subsidies by OECD members linked to projects in developing countries. Argentina believed that when a subsidy could affect the competitive positions, there was an obligation to notify the GATT and to hold consultations with the members involved.

At the Session, the following panel reports were the subject of follow-ups:

* *US anti-dumping duties on stainless steel pipes and tubes from Sweden.* Sweden complained that this panel report, issued in mid-1990, had been on the agenda of the Committee on Anti-Dumping practices of several occasions without being adopted.
* *Section 337 of the US Tariff Act in 1930.* The European Community expressed concern that the present legislative initiatives in the US Congress did not adequately address the discrimination which the panel had condemned.
* *Anti-dumping duties on products assembled in the EC from imported parts and components.* Japan said that while it was not satisfied with developments regarding the Section 337 panel report, at least there had been some internal movement, which could not be said of the EC in the parts and components case.
* *United States' denial of m.f.n. treatment on non-rubber footwear from Brazil.* Brazil expressed concern over what it said was continued application of a measure found to be discriminatory by a panel (*note*: the panel did not issue specific recommendations on this case).
* *US restrictions on imports of tuna.* Venezuela recalled that its tuna exports had been subject to an embargo by the United States, with an estimated loss of its fishing industry of more than $60 million annually. It

said that its efforts in securing an and to the embargo through bilateral consultations and through GATT (as a third party in the panel report on US restrictions on tuna imports) had not succeeded. It noted that the tuna panel report had not been adopted, and it was concerned that the work of panel established to examine EC's complaint against US tuna measures had been suspended. Venezuela emphasized that it had been adjusting its fishing practices to those followed by Inter-American Tropical Tuna Commission, of which the United States announced that in October 1992, the US President had signed into law the International Dolphin Conservation ACt of 1992. It believed that this Act represented a balanced and effective solution to what had been difficult issue for many countries.

* *US measures on imported beer.* Canada expressed concern over possible delay at the state level of the implementation of this panel report adopted in June 1992. The United States assured Canada that it continued to consult with Congress and the state governments on bringing federal and sub-federal practices into conformity with the panel's recommendations.

Free-trade Agreements

The Contracting Parties also considered the following trade agreements:

* *Finland-Baltic States.* Finland reported that Free-Trade Agreements between itself and Estonia, Latvia and Lithuania were being provisionally applied pending their ratification in the respective countries. The Contracting Parties established a working party to examine these arrangements.
* *EFTA-Israel.* EFTA members and Israel reported that they had signed a free-trade agreement, which would enter into force on 1 January 1993. The Contracting Parties referred this matter to the Council for further action.

Source: *GATT Focus*, No. 96, January-February 1993, Geneva.

10.3 **World's Major Trade Blocks and Trading Nations**

TABLE 10.1: World's Major Trade Blocks and Trading Nations

	Population in Million/Per capita GDP in $	% share in world trade	% of Indian exports**
1	2	3	4
EC (European Community)	342 15,155	38.62	27.05
NAFTA (North American Free Trade Agreement)	368 14916	16.52	17.64
EFTA (European Free Trade Association)	33 21084*	6.22	2.61
ASEAN (Association of South East Nations)	329 5965*	4.62	5.67
GCC (Gulf Cooperation Council)	21.1 14,227*	2.3@	7.15

Contd.

Concld.

1	2	3	4
ANZCERT (Australia, New Zealand Closer Economic Relations & Trade Agreement)	21 14840*	1.47	1.26
MERCOSUR (Southern Cone Common Market)	193 2180*	1.3	0.2
SAARC (South Asian Association for Regional Cooperations)	1122 317*	0.7	3.53
Japan	124 26990	9.03	9.24
China	1156 443	2.06	0.26
East Europe and Former USSR	387 5722	5.07	10.62

Notes: All figures for 1991; * Figures for 1990; ** Figures for 1991-92; @ Excluding Qatar.

Source: *Business Today*, January 22, 1993.

10.4.1 **Exports**

TABLE 10.2: World Exports

(Billions of US Dollars)

		Year 1989	Year 1990	Year 1991											June 1992	Jul 1992
1	2	3	4	5	6	7	8	9	10	11	12	13	14	15	16	17
IFS World Total		**2908.9**	**3331.6**	**3442.9**	**814.2**	**932.5**	**850.8**	**843.7**	**824.3**	**924.3**	**878**	**NA**	**277.0**	**284.4**	**NA**	**NA**
DOTS World Total	**001**	**2909.9**	**3330.6**	**3447.7**	**808.4**	**939.1**	**866.0**	**840.6**	**825.2**	**917.2**	**888.6**	**912.3**	**276.6**	**286.0**	**316.7**	**317.5**
Industrial Countries	**110**	**2115.5**	**2436.6**	**2473.1**	**588.0**	**683.3**	**639.3**	**604.6**	**581.0**	**649.3**	**637.8**	**644.1**	**197.3**	**201.4**	**223.9**	**221.6**
United States	111	458.12	491.63	490.03	124.13	131.43	114.33	119.14	124.88	131.57	121.83	130.69	39.96	41.36	46.86	47.36
Canada	156	110.80	116.13	120.70	27.47	28.73	28.42	31.07	29.78	31.41	31.32	33.01	10.22	9.67	11.65	10.22
Australia	193	38.79	37.44	36.60	9.91	10.03	8.60	8.50	9.50	9.97	8.93	9.76	3.04	3.11	3.47	3.30
Japan	158	184.66	207.73	210.93	50.88	61.70	54.71	50.18	50.80	55.22	50.59	50.91	16.38	17.37	17.69	18.47
New Zealand	196	7.45	7.83	7.17	1.96	2.31	1.72	1.71	1.82	1.92	1.84	1.86	.62	.64	.68	.73
Austria	122	38.68	46.94	49.25	11.43	13.43	13.29	11.79	11.37	12.84	12.75	12.42	3.79	4.01	4.16	4.25
Belgium-Luxembourg	126	103.93	125.57	125.63	29.45	35.44	34.74	30.68	28.04	32.25	33.78	32.50	9.79	9.32	10.96	10.35
Denmark	128	26.16	30.79	31.75	7.38	8.67	8.26	7.75	7.45	8.27	8.29	8.07	2.53	2.25	2.70	2.48
Finland	172	22.26	23.96	20.03	5.65	6.49	5.61	4.68	4.46	5.31	5.04	5.08	1.38	1.40	1.63	1.46
France	132	188.91	227.89	229.15	53.11	65.15	61.97	55.27	50.95	61.10	60.25	58.20	18.03	18.56	19.55	18.87
Germany	134	245.82	317.69	357.78	77.41	96.84	96.39	88.60	82.17	91.26	94.36	90.48	28.31	29.98	31.50	31.94
Greece	174	16.17	19.14	20.33	4.41	5.02	5.24	4.75	4.32	6.02	5.32	5.46	1.63	1.43	1.93	1.63
Ireland	178	16.80	19.79	20.26	4.83	5.57	5.46	4.77	4.68	5.36	5.08	5.39	1.49	1.64	1.78	2.02
Italy	136	135.85	162.48	164.31	36.61	47.38	44.98	40.47	36.05	43.08	45.35	45.53	12.87	13.38	15.57	14.74
Netherlands	138	124.75	146.62	144.84	35.44	40.64	38.43	35.72	33.13	37.66	36.64	36.05	11.36	11.55	12.80	12.74
Norway	142	19.27	23.59	23.47	5.43	6.54	6.02	5.54	5.43	6.48	5.99	6.16	1.87	1.64	2.18	1.99
Portugal	182	18.17	22.74	24.94	5.35	6.61	6.68	6.35	5.29	6.61	6.86	7.21	2.15	2.02	2.52	2.51
Spain	184	66.39	81.24	87.96	17.81	22.21	22.34	21.65	19.77	24.17	25.15	25.33	7.09	7.51	8.47	8.81
Sweden	144	45.49	51.02	45.90	11.95	14.32	12.33	11.12	10.14	12.34	11.56	11.51	3.44	3.02	3.82	3.15
Switzerland	146	63.24	73.12	69.87	17.29	19.78	19.32	17.36	15.78	17.43	17.04	16.45	5.61	5.77	5.68	5.62
United Kingdom	112	182.56	201.78	190.75	49.77	54.61	50.13	47.12	44.85	48.65	49.40	51.68	15.64	15.69	18.17	18.77

Contd.

Contd.

1	2	3	4	5	6	7	8	9	10	11	12	13	14	15	16	17
Developing Countries	**200**	**746.12**	**844.16**	**932.57**	**209.57**	**241.80**	**216.71**	**226.42**	**234.17**	**255.10**	**239.71**	**257.83**	**75.74**	**80.87**	**88.68**	**91.43**
Africa	**605**	**64.61**	**74.25**	**73.81**	**17.40**	**20.41**	**18.05**	**17.92**	**17.86**	**20.16**	**18.20**	**19.52**	**6.16**	**6.45**	**6.99**	**7.40**
Algeria	612	7.97	9.33	8.11	1.98	2.61	2.20	1.95	1.81	2.14	1.71	1.95	.63	.69	.69	.70
Cameroon	622	1.18	1.31	1.09	.32	.36	.31	.26	.23	.29	.30	.29	.08	.08	.11	.11
Cote d'ivoire	662	1.84	1.66	1.74	.39	.46	.44	.44	.39	.47	.45	.42	.12	.13	.15	.17
Gabon	646	.71	.73	.83	.20	.21	.21	.22	.19	.21	.19	.21	.07	.07	.07	.07
Ghana	652	1.07	1.27	1.36	.31	.35	.32	.33	.35	.36	.33	.35	.11	.12	.13	.13
Kenya	664	2.11	2.25	2.15	.58	.58	.54	.51	.54	.56	.50	.50	.17	.19	.19	.19
Morocco	686	5.62	7.06	6.87	1.66	2.14	1.66	1.65	1.56	2.00	1.81	1.83	.55	.60	.66	.68
Nigeria	694	4.61	5.83	7.02	1.39	1.63	1.54	1.77	1.78	1.92	1.81	2.08	.65	.67	.76	.70
Senegal	722	1.08	1.24	1.18	.30	.37	.28	.29	.28	.33	.30	.29	.09	.10	.09	.10
South Africa	199	12.12	12.09	12.87	3.13	3.08	3.15	3.11	3.41	3.32	2.82	3.10	1.07	1.21	1.10	1.35
Sudan	732	1.19	1.08	1.15	.26	.31	.29	.25	.28	.33	.25	.24	.07	.09	.09	.09
Tanzania	738	.92	1.09	1.09	.24	.33	.28	.25	.25	.31	.29	.36	.08	.09	.10	.11
Tunisia	744	3.89	5.11	5.08	1.18	1.55	1.33	1.30	1.00	1.45	1.39	1.51	.51	.39	.55	.62
Zaire	636	1.36	1.76	.91	.31	.45	.27	.28	.22	.13	.15	.18	.08	.09	.07	.08
Zambia	754	.71	.91	.66	.28	.26	.16	.14	.16	.20	.14	.14	.04	.05	.05	.07
Asia	**505**	**380.22**	**433.66**	**499.09**	**109.99**	**123.99**	**117.76**	**122.18**	**126.68**	**132.20**	**127.38**	**138.03**	**41.06**	**44.11**	**47.79**	**49.50**
China, People's Rep.	924	52.04	49.29	62.28	12.35	13.78	12.11	15.26	15.81	19.52	16.48	20.36	4.96	5.55	6.57	6.52
Hong Kong	532	70.13	81.38	97.74	21.11	23.54	20.34	24.50	25.66	27.19	23.28	28.43	8.40	8.66	10.33	10.38
India	**534**	**22.05**	**22.87**	**19.77**	**5.72**	**6.46**	**6.55**	**3.81**	**4.33**	**5.00**	**6.19**	**4.59**	**1.15**	**1.38**	**1.60**	**1.46**
Indonesia	536	12.50	18.24	19.14	4.83	5.69	4.91	4.58	4.72	4.93	5.20	5.43	1.47	1.64	1.86	1.84
Korea	542	50.56	58.54	70.61	14.35	16.67	17.34	17.86	18.16	17.22	17.30	17.20	5.82	6.54	5.88	6.52
Malaysia	548	20.56	25.39	32.18	6.39	7.57	7.78	7.77	8.35	8.29	7.51	7.85	2.885	2.98	2.69	3.23
Pakistan	564	7.29	7.86	8.91	1.88	2.20	2.09	2.23	2.18	2..40	1.95	2.17	.76	.78	.78	.78
Philippines	566	11.65	13.38	12.74	3.31	3.61	3.09	3.00	3.21	3.44	3.47	3.65	1.01	1.08	1.28	1.31
Singapore	576	45.90	55.61	61.19	14.41	15.92	15.13	15.06	15.17	15.79	15.47	16.30	5.20	5.21	5.93	5.78
Thailand	578	22.42	30.33	33.48	7.56	9.10	8.31	8.54	8.41	8.20	8.43	8.88	2.80	3.17	3.00	3.61

Contd.

Contd.

1	2	3	4	5	6	7	8	9	10	11	12	13	14	15	16	17
Europe	**170**	**82.90**	**95.10**	**89.98**	**22.94**	**30.41**	**22.53**	**22.12**	**20.12**	**25.14**	**22.90**	**23.64**	**7.11**	**6.90**	**7.73**	**7.91**
Hungary	944	9.90	10.38	10.23	2.48	3.31	2.29	2.63	2.32	2.98	2.49	2.80	.89	.81	.83	.93
Poland	964	14.44	13.83	18.14	3.29	5.08	4.40	4.47	4.16	5.11	4.24	4.63	1.42	1.40	1.59	1.61
Romania	968	8.03	8.43	4.98	1.92	2.26	1.40	1.22	1.19	1.17	1.46	1.36	.39	.40	.44	.44
Turkey	186	14.60	21.47	19.99	5.23	7.12	5.25	4.66	4.72	5.33	5.17	5.17	1.56	1.57	1.83	1.74
Yugoslavia	188	15.25	19.54	16.15	4.33	6.31	4.61	4.32	3.15	4.06	3.95	3.82	1.23	1.13	1.13	1.22
Middle East	**405**	**104.12**	**111.03**	**123.83**	**26.21**	**29.18**	**26.70**	**29.53**	**31.60**	**35.99**	**32.92**	**34.07**	**9.79**	**11.02**	**11.53**	**11.64**
Bahrain	419	3.10	3.81	3.52	.96	1.16	.68	.75	1.03	1.06	.97	1.21	.24	.28	.47	.32
Egypt	469	10.44	11.99	11.99	2.99	3.17	2.95	2.81	2.85	3.38	3.03	2.89	.92	1.05	1.02	.99
Iran, I.R. of	429	9.85	14.27	19.60	3.67	4.61	4.61	4.86	4.75	5.34	5.13	5.57	1.55	1.73	1.74	1.86
Iraq	433	8.95	5.96	.35	1.03	.15	.02	.04	.12	.16	.06	.10	.02	.03	.01	.01
Israel	436	11.23	13.00	14.50	3.13	3.75	3.36	3.60	3.28	4.22	3.86	3.91	1.13	1.20	1.34	1.37
Kuwait	443	5.84	3.69	4.24	.63	.21	.30	.76	1.41	1.77	1.21	.95	.27	.38	.27	.23
Libya	672	4.87	5.12	5.49	1.28	1.43	1.34	1.34	1.30	1.56	1.36	1.28	.43	.48	.43	.49
Saudi Arabia	456	23.28	24.76	31.26	5.96	6.88	6.73	7.40	8.17	9.00	8.52	9.05	2.45	2.87	3.18	3.03
Syrian Arab Republic	463	2.01	2.34	2.70	.55	.71	.57	.61	.74	.79	.70	.77	.20	.25	.26	.29
Western Hemisphere	**205**	**114.27**	**130.13**	**145.85**	**33.83**	**37.81**	**31.67**	**34.67**	**37.91**	**41.61**	**38.31**	**41.57**	**11.62**	**12.39**	**14.63**	**14.98**
Argentina	213	4.44	4.99	7.30	1.26	1.56	1.38	1.56	2.00	2.35	2.06	2.55	.54	.66	.90	1.05
Bahamas, The	313	1.83	22.32	2.30	.64	.56	.57	.64	.45	.64	.51	.68	.21	.13	.24	.13
Brazil	223	19.40	21.49	22.10	5.87	6.80	4.36	5.04	6.36	6.34	4.64	5.30	1.79	1.93	2.04	1.90
Chile	228	6.23	6.90	7.47	1.67	1.85	1.65	1.74	1.97	2.10	1.99	2.18	.62	.67	.77	.79
Colombia	233	4.93	5.17	5.15	1.34	1.71	1.18	1.25	1.33	1.38	1.57	1.78	.35	.41	.56	.56
Ecuador	248	1.82	1.93	2.53	.50	.58	.55	.59	.71	.67	.59	.74	.18	.20	.23	.28
Jamaica	343	1.90	1.90	1.85	.49	.52	.44	.45	.50	.47	.41	.44	.15	.14	.14	.15
Mexico	273	34.21	40.08	46.94	10.24	10.92	9.99	11.61	11.81	13.48	13.65	14.56	3.93	4.01	4.99	4.91
Netherlands Antilles	353	2.22	1.53	1.64	.36	.45	.38	.44	.40	.43	.38	.43	.11	.14	.11	.15
Panama	283	6.49	7.53	8.69	2.03	2.33	2.30	1.74	2.38	2.25	2.28	2.07	.65	.79	.89	.93
Peru	293	2.15	2.39	2.96	.56	.62	.65	.74	.74	.83	.76	.75	.24	.25	.27	.29
Trinidad and Tobago	369	1.10	1.03	1.27	.23	.34	.31	.32	.28	.36	.322	.26	.09	.10	.10	.10
Venezuela	299	6.53	7.36	9.57	1.91	2.20	2.03	2.43	2.46	2.64	2.46	2.90	.82	.89	1.01	1.10

Contd.

Concld.

1	2	3	4	5	6	7	8	9	10	11	12	13	14	15	16	17
Other countries n.i.e	**910**	**86.58**	**773.38**	**56.27**	**14.66**	**17.96**	**13.27**	**12.99**	**13.46**	**16.57**	**13.30**	**14.36**	**4.40**	**4.91**	**5.01**	**5.63**
Minus adjustment for trade of other countries n.i.e	**980**	**-78.14**	**-65.36**	**-50.74**	**-13.68**	**-15.69**	**-12.80**	**-12.51**	**-12.02**	**-13.38**	**-11.76**	**-13.39**	**-3.83**	**-4.05**	**-4.39**	**-4.37**
Memorandum Items																
Oil Exporting Countries	999	102.01	113.21	126.68	27.01	30.40	28.29	30.60	32.18	35.62	35.38	35.44	10.19	11.36	12.02	12.15
Non-Oil Developing Countries	201	644.12	730.95	805.89	182.56	211.40	188.42	195.82	201.99	219.47	206.13	221.39	65.55	69.51	76.66	79.27

10.4.2 **Imports**

TABLE 10.3: World Imports

(Billions of US Dollars)

		Year 1989	Year 1990	Year 1991											June 1992	Jul 1992
IFS World Total		**2999.6**	**3430.5**	**3555.0**	**837.1**	**963.0**	**894.9**	**871.4**	**850.8**	**938.0**	**912.5**	**NA**	**279.7**	**296.1**	**NA**	**NA**
DOTS World Total	**001**	**3001.3**	**3432.4**	**3568.1**	**831.5**	**966.0**	**905.3**	**873.1**	**855.0**	**944.5**	**934.2**	**959.7**	**281.0**	**296.8**	**333.6**	**334.7**
Industrial Countries	**110**	**2159.2**	**2480.2**	**2563.4**	**592.6**	**691.7**	**651.6**	**632.2**	**601.1**	**679.2**	**670.1**	**688.4**	**202.5**	**211.1**	**239.0**	**236.8**
United States	111	369.93	400.38	442.83	95.32	104.29	106.02	114.04	107.99	114.76	116.52	120.17	36.42	36.99	41.48	37.90
Canada	156	123.01	129.32	129.10	31.24	33.13	30.49	33.71	31.46	33.46	32.55	35.48	11.00	10.21	12.06	10.50
Australia	193	40.23	42.44	42.54	10.73	11.37	10.43	10.72	10.92	10.56	10.71	11.64	3.60	3.88	3.88	3.76
Japan	158	293.52	311.13	36.94	76.61	87.14	80.44	81.47	84.03	91.44	86.74	89.17	26.83	28.74	30.88	32.03
New Zealand	196	9.81	10.35	10.39	2.56	2.53	2.61	2.66	2.60	2.64	2.54	3.04	.91	.93	1.01	.95
Austria	122	34.07	42.12	42.58	10.15	12.20	10.93	10.42	9.76	11.45	11.25	11.43	3.37	3.55	4.05	4.33
Belgium-Luxembourg	126	99.09	117.11	118.35	27.11	33.71	31.68	29.52	26.04	31.10	31.37	32.53	9.35	9.23	11.53	10.53
Denmark	128	28.30	34.39	35.46	8.28	10.10	8.94	8.57	8.26	9.66	9.29	9.93	2.83	2.55	3.82	2.87
Finland	172	24.81	27.72	24.77	6.49	7.70	6.58	5.93	5.63	6.61	6.38	6.57	1.48	1.82	2.38	1.98
France	132	178.96	217.65	225.44	50.41	62.06	58.98	54.36	50.43	61.60	61.16	62.30	17.69	18.88	21.73	22.13
Germany	134	330.40	397.15	392.53	96.67	112.02	103.91	94.30	90.38	103.96	103.89	102.05	30.09	31.62	34.59	36.35
Greece	174	8.92	9.44	9.14	2.13	2.64	2.34	2.16	2.19	2.45	2.43	2.33	.71	.81	.84	.88
Ireland	178	19.68	23.15	23.50	5.37	6.35	5.86	5.63	5.46	6.53	6.50	6.90	1.85	1.89	2.34	2.38
Italy	136	139.49	167.79	170.71	40.38	47.02	44.12	41.60	39.62	45.19	44.69	47.98	13.71	15.91	17.34	17.82
Netherlands	138	113.76	136.50	139.52	32.93	39.26	37.12	33.95	31.57	36.81	36.54	36.16	10.58	10.76	12.05	12.16
Norway	142	27.33	33.51	34.70	7.56	11.25	9.57	8.29	7.99	8.83	8.55	8.60	2.44	2.62	2.79	2.79
Portugal	182	13.27	17.22	17.27	4.25	4.78	4.78	3.98	3.94	4.58	4.78	4.38	1.25	1.52	1.39	1.78
Spain	184	43.25	53.92	59.24	11.47	15.30	16.40	14.46	12.32	16.11	16.24	16.52	4.60	5.07	6.03	6.17
Sweden	144	51.72	58.05	56.13	12.93	16.46	14.96	14.16	12.08	14.92	14.11	14.54	4.53	4.19	4.96	4.82
Switzerland	146	62.60	75.01	71.27	17.82	20.77	18.91	17.98	16.02	18.50	17.74	18.10	5.61	5.56	6.38	6.39
United Kingdom	112	145.48	174.03	179.29	41.70	51.16	46.08	43.88	41.99	47.66	45.63	47.96	13.52	14.63	17.26	18.13

Contd.

Contd.

1	2	3	4	5	6	7	8	9	10	11	12	13	14	15	16	17
Developing Countries	**200**	**831.37**	**932.80**	**980.92**	**231.48**	**268.32**	**246.87**	**234.13**	**248.52**	**260.13**	**257.89**	**264.23**	**76.83**	**84.16**	**92.49**	**96.32**
Africa	**605**	**73.90**	**85.91**	**82.75**	**19.77**	**25.65**	**22.08**	**19.86**	**19.78**	**21.11**	**20.00**	**20.56**	**6.27**	**6.86**	**7.03**	**7.60**
Algeria	612	9.85	13.42	13.04	2.93	4.68	3.78	3.07	2.85	3.34	3.18	2.82	.96	.94	.94	.97
Cameroon	622	2.05	2.33	1.89	.56	.71	.48	.46	.45	.50	.51	.50	.14	.14	.18	.20
Cote d'ivoire	662	2.84	3.30	3.30	.75	.80	.85	.90	.74	.82	.87	.87	.28	.26	.29	.28
Gabon	646	1.67	2.71	2.81	.63	.84	.75	.64	.60	.81	.62	.76	.19	.18	.25	.20
Ghana	652	1.02	1.31	1.26	.35	.33	.34	.33	.28	.31	.26	.31	.11	.10	.13	.11
Kenya	664	1.24	1.31	1.40	.31	.37	.35	.35	.34	.37	.35	.36	.11	.12	.12	.12
Morocco	686	4.28	5.49	5.69	1.38	1.43	1.64	1.30	1.28	1.48	1.68	1.36	.38	.47	.44	.54
Nigeria	694	11.36	14.40	14.00	3.04	5.06	4.12	3.08	3.36	3.46	3.05	3.37	.96	1.21	1.11	1.30
Senegal	722	.71	.74	.75	.17	.18	.22	.19	.18	.17	.17	.17	.05	.05	.05	.06
South Africa	199	14.85	14.56	14.48	3.46	3.94	3.61	3.72	3.74	3.42	3.39	3.95	1.14	1.42	1.40	1.50
Sudan	732	.60	.57	.51	.13	.15	.11	.08	.11	.21	.10	.09	.03	.04	.04	.04
Tanzania	738	.51	.44	.42	.10	.13	.12	.11	.10	.10	.12	.11	.04	.03	.04	.03
Tunisia	744	2.97	3.83	3.92	.90	1.12	.99	.94	.94	1.06	1.03	.95	.36	.37	.31	.49
Zaire	636	1.95	1.91	1.76	.49	.44	.50	.46	.45	.35	.39	.38	.15	.17	.15	.17
Zambia	754	1.43	1.43	1.28	.34	.40	.32	.36	.31	.29	.25	.40	.13	.13	.12	.09
Asia	**505**	**402.21**	**451.38**	**520.43**	**115.60**	**127.41**	**128.19**	**124.32**	**136.54**	**139.71**	**143.90**	**146.40**	**41.01**	**46.07**	**51.69**	**54.45**
China, People's Rep.	924	73.04	88.35	108.67	23.70	25.92	22.62	24.79	29.65	31.60	27.69	31.21	8.29	9.71	10.89	11.80
Hong Kong	532	46.28	49.76	57.72	13.38	13.99	12.42	13.31	15.51	17.04	16.63	19.78	4.51	5.13	8.38	8.90
India	534	18.36	20.78	21.95	5.13	5.13	7.09	5.19	5.22	5.09	7.51	5.65	1.57	1.79	1.87	2.02
Indonesia	536	23.34	26.96	29.43	6.44	8.38	7.78	6.86	7.20	7.62	7.60	7.58	2.18	2.51	2.51	2.74
Korea	542	59.06	59.42	67.19	15.47	16.04	16.06	16.98	17.87	17.06	16.70	17.98	5.52	6.02	5.98	6.21
Malaysia	548	29.36	33.95	39.91	7.97	9.91	10.31	9.03	10.19	10.40	10.27	10.83	3.19	3.47	3.95	3.97
Pakistan	564	4.74	5.44	6.44	1.26	1.43	1.61	1.65	1.66	1.57	1.76	1.98	.53	.55	.64	.61
Philippines	566	8.97	9.67	10.37	2.49	2.46	2.46	2.59	2.72	2.60	2.68	2.84	.84	.92	1.00	1.00
Singapore	576	35.61	43.21	49.22	10.92	13.32	17.77	11.96	12.35	13.12	19,15	13.18	4.06	4.20	4.60	4.53
Thailand	578	20.69	23.85	29.03	6.29	6.38	6.90	7.04	7.60	7.75	7.91	7.84	2.30	2.59	2.72	3.00

Contd.

Contd.

1	2	3	4	5	6	7	8	9	10	11	12	13	14	15	16	17
Europe	**170**	**85.21**	**83.65**	**79.83**	**19.68**	**24.02**	**20.15**	**18.64**	**18.90**	**22.21**	**20.28**	**20.36**	**5.99**	**6.68**	**6.80**	**7.36**
Hungary	944	11.26	10.93	11.04	2.59	3.34	2.46	2.60	2.60	3.39	2.65	2.82	.90	.86	.97	.93
Poland	964	15.64	18.54	17.24	4.48	5.46	4.08	4.09	4.21	4.87	4.32	4.55	1.31	1.42	1.49	1.57
Romania	968	10.44	6.31	4.54	1.48	1.57	1.19	1.03	1.07	1.25	1.17	1.12	.37	.37	.41	.41
Turkey	186	13.32	13.88	14.28	3.09	4.13	3.87	3.07	3.41	3.94	3.92	3.32	1.01	1.13	1.16	1.26
Yugoslavia	188	16.58	18.19	16.84	4.30	4.99	4.66	4.14	3.98	4.07	4.00	3.91	1.24	1.59	1.28	1.66
Middle East	**405**	**125.22**	**155.82**	**141.06**	**37.17**	**48.15**	**38.52**	**31.44**	**34.02**	**37.36**	**34.92**	**34.28**	**10.78**	**11.18**	**12.11**	**12.50**
Bahrain	419	1.76	2.03	2.33	.49	.64	.56	.56	.59	.61	.57	.53	.17	.21	.18	.20
Egypt	469	4.68	5.42	4.44	1.32	1.47	1.10	1.15	1.08	1.12	1.22	1.39	.39	.36	.43	.36
Iran, I.R. of	429	12.46	16.83	17.30	4.62	5.96	4.90	3.33	4.51	4.58	3.95	3.61	1.25	1.62	1.32	1.57
Iraq	433	13.47	11.44	.33	3.13	.20	.05	.08	.08	.11	.01	.03	.04	.03	—	—
Israel	436	9.97	11.27	11.08	2.70	2.91	2.93	2.70	2.54	2.96	2.93	2.85	.88	.98	.99	1.05
Kuwait	443	11.07	8.18	.47	2.03	.35	.03	.03	.13	.29	.25	.37	.02	.02	.12	.23
Libya	672	7.69	11.80	11.82	2.80	4.34	3.07	2.69	2.78	3.27	2.70	2.69	.83	.86	1.00	1.05
Saudi Arabia	456	35.75	50.69	55.90	11.63	19.56	15.27	12.87	13.56	14.27	14.01	13.82	4.30	4.13	4.87	4.56
Syrian Arab Republic	463	2.98	4.08	3.66	.71	.98	.76	.86	1.23	.81	.76	1.07	.45	.68	.57	.71
Western Hemisphere	**205**	**144.83**	**156.04**	**156.85**	**39.26**	**43.09**	**37.94**	**39.87**	**39.28**	**39.74**	**38.79**	**42.64**	**12.79**	**13.37**	**14.86**	**14.41**
Argentina	213	11.75	13.79	14.40	3.89	3.69	3.15	3.50	4.06	3.69	3.17	3.56	1.24	1.39	1.37	1.46
Bahamas, The	313	1.12	1.09	.96	.26	.26	.17	.23	.24	.32	.23	.38	.05	.08	.10	.06
Brazil	223	37.47	35.70	35.05	9.53	9.13	8.67	8.99	8.75	8.63	8.52	9.54	2.86	3.03	3.37	3.29
Chile	228	8.85	9.33	9.82	2.14	2.25	2.94	2.76	2.08	1.93	2.98	2.97	.74	.75	.88	.83
Colombia	233	6.01	7.03	7.09	1.69	2.16	1.70	1.64	1.75	2.02	1.81	1.75	.52	.58	.60	.59
Ecuador	248	2.84	2.87	3.51	.76	.78	.80	.96	.92	.83	.86	.96	.32	.31	.31	.36
Jamaica	343	1.28	1.46	1.51	.35	.37	.32	.41	.46	.32	.34	.39	.14	.13	.14	.13
Mexico	273	37.03	41.06	42.72	9.88	11.59	10.07	10.66	10.61	11.41	10.92	11.92	3.53	3.44	4.14	3.77
Netherlands Antilles	353	.96	1.20	1.73	.26	.43	.40	.45	.36	.52	.32	.47	.13	.12	.16	.09
Panama	283	2.80	22.55	1.68	.71	.61	.39	.48	.42	.39	.43	.56	.19	.15	.26	.19
Peru	293	3.96	3.78	3.79	1.01	.95	.79	1.02	1.03	.95	.90	1.02	.32	.35	.34	.37
Trinidad and Tobago	369	1.52	1.92	1.87	.44	.65	.48	.47	.45	.47	.44	.50	.13	.17	.17	.20
Venezuela	299	13.53	17.29	15.80	3.99	5.82	4.23	3.80	3.92	3.85	3.80	3.75	1.20	1.41	1.34	1.37

Contd.

Concld.

1	2	3	4	5	6	7	8	9	10	11	12	13	14	15	16	17
Other countries n.i.e	**910**	**78.96**	**68.81**	**55.29**	**15.18**	**17.18**	**14.04**	**13.71**	**13.15**	**14.62**	**12.96**	**14.69**	**4.21**	**4.44**	**4.84**	**4.83**
Minus adjustment for trade of other countries n.i.e	**980**	**-100.77**	**-82.97**	**-61.96**	**-15.97**	**-19.71**	**-15.49**	**-14.28**	**-14.81**	**-18.24**	**-14.63**	**-15.79**	**-4.83**	**-5.40**	**-5.50**	**-6.19**
Memorandum Items																
Oil Exporting Countries	999	160.84	201.44	189.00	47.40	65.05	52.45	42.26	45.16	49.39	46.44	45.31	13.99	14.79	15.64	16.32
Non-Oil Developing Countries	201	670.54	731.36	791.92	184.09	203.27	194.42	191.87	203.36	210.75	211.45	218.92	62.84	69.37	76.86	80.00

Notes:

1. DOTS = Direction of Trade Statistics.
2. IFS = International Financial Statistics
3. The term "Country", does not in all cases refer to a territorial entity that is a state as understood by international law and practice; the term also covers some territorial entities that are not states but for which statistical data are maintained and provided internationally on a separate and independent basis.
4. The data for Germany through June 1990 cover the former area of the Federal Republic of Germany and the data for Eastern Germany cover the area of the former German Democratic Republic. As from July 1990 the data for Germany cover the area of United Germany.
5. Republic of Yemen: On May 22, 1990, the Yemen Arab Republic and the People's Democratic Republic of Yemen became unified in a single state.
6. The data for South Africa refer to the South African Common Customs Area which includes Botswana, Lesotho, Namibia, South Africa, and Swaziland.
7. The European Economic Community (EEC) comprises Belgium, Denmark, France, Germany, Greece, Ireland, Italy, Luxembourg, Netherlands, Portugal, Spain and the United Kingdom.
8. The oil exporting countries comprise Algeria, Indonesia, The Islamic Republic of Iran, Iraq, Kuwait, Libya, Nigeria, Oman, Qatar, Saudi Arabia, the United Arab Emirates, and Venezuela.
9. The Non-oil developing Countries are all remaining developing countries, i.e. excluding those listed in footnote no. 8.

11

NEWLY INDEPENDENT STATES OF THE FORMER USSR

On December 25, 1991, ended the existence of USSR — once mighty Super Power — and several independent states came into being. Vital information on these states is provided here.

11.1 Vital Information

Armenia

Capital	:	Yerevan
Area	:	29.8 thousand square kilometres
Population	:	3.3 million
GDP	:	15.7 billion roubles
Total exports	:	6.5 billion roubles
Total imports	:	8.3 billion roubles
Natural resources	:	Agricultural land
Main industries	:	Light industry, machine-building and metallurgy, food processing, and chemical production

Azerbaijan

Capital	:	Baku
Area	:	86.6 thousand square kilometres
Population	:	7.1 million
GDP	:	22.4 billion roubles
Total exports	:	11.5 billion roubles
Total imports	:	8.8 billion roubles
Natural resources	:	Agricultural land, oil natural gas, iron ore
Main industries	:	Oil, oil production equipment, petrochemicals, food and beverages, garments, electrical equipment

Belarus

Capital	:	Minsk
Area	:	207.6 thousand square kilometres
Population	:	10.3 million
GDP	:	71.8 billion roubles
Total exports	:	38.3 billion roubles
Total imports	:	33.5 billion roubles
Natural resources	:	Agricultural land, potassium salts, peat
Main industries	:	Livestock, potatoes, flax, prefabricated construction materials, machine building, electronics, chemicals, and light industry

Estonia

Capital	:	Tallinn
Area	:	45.2 thousand square kilometres
Population	:	1.6 million
GDP	:	17.3 billion roubles
Total exports	:	5.4 billion roubles
Total imports	:	4.4 billion roubles
Natural resources	:	Timber, oil shale, limestone
Main industries	:	Fish and food products, textiles, metalworking, chemicals, plastics, furniture

Georgia

Capital	:	Tblisi
Area	:	70.0 thousand square kilometres
Population	:	5.4 million
GDP	:	23.5 billion roubles
Total exports	:	6.1 billion roubles
Total imports	:	7.3 billion roubles
Natural resources	:	Agriculture, tourism, manganese, coal, timber
Main industries	:	Light industrial products, iron, steel, tea, tobacco

Kazakhstan

Capital	:	Alma-Ata
Area	:	2.7 million square kilometres
Population	:	16.9 million
GDP	:	92.0 billion roubles
Total exports	:	15.8 billion roubles
Total imports	:	22 billion roubles
Natural resources	:	Petrol, grain, chrome, lead, wolfram, copper, zinc, coal, iron ore, wool, meat
Main industries	:	Metallurgy, heavy machinery and machine tools, petrochemicals, agro-processing, textiles

Kyrghystan

Capital	:	Bishkek
Area	:	198.5 thousand square kilometres
Population	:	4.4 million
GDP	:	15.3 billion roubles
Total exports	:	6.6 billion roubles
Total imports	:	7.4 billion roubles
Natural resources	:	Hydroelectricity, gold, mercury, uranium, coal
Main industries	:	Metallurgy, agricultural and other machinery, food and tobacco processing, electronics, textiles, sugar refineries

Latvia

Capital	:	Riga
Area	:	64.6 thousand square kilometres
Population	:	2.7 million
GDP	:	22.3 billion roubles
Total exports	:	8.8 million roubles

Total imports	:	6.5 billion roubles
Natural resources	:	Peat, dolomite, limestone, gypsum, amber, gravel, sand
Main industries	:	Machinery, food products, textiles, chemicals

Lithuania

Capital	:	Vilnius
Area	:	65.2 thousand square kilometres
Population	:	3.7 million
GDP	:	39.4 billion roubles
Total exports	:	12.3 billion roubles
Total imports	:	8.7 billion roubles
Natural resources	:	Agricultural Land, forests
Main industries	:	Machinery, metal-working, light industry, oil industry, oil, gas, food, chemicals

Moldova

Capital	:	Chisinau
Area	:	33.7 thousand square kilometres
Population	:	4.4 million (1990)
GDP	:	20.7 billion roubles
Total exports	:	8.1 billion roubles
Total imports	:	8.4 billion roubles
Natural resources	:	Agricultural land
Main industries	:	Agriculture, food processing, textiles, consumer appliances, light industry

Russian Federation

Capital	:	Moscow
Area	:	17.1 million square kilometres
Population	:	148.5 million
GDP	:	1,130.0 billion roubles
Total exports	:	210.1 billion roubles
Total imports	:	182.0 billion roubles
Natural resources	:	Grain, potatoes, livestock, coal, oil, natural gas, diamonds, phosphorites, potassium salts
Main industries	:	Oil, natural gas, machinery, chemicals

Tajikistan

Capital	:	Dushanbe
Area	:	143.1 thousand square kilometres
Population	:	5.3 million
GDP	:	13.0 billion roubles
Total exports	:	4.3 billion roubles
Total imports	:	3.8 billion roubles
Natural resources	:	Cotton, dairy production, wheat
Main industries	:	Labor-intensive industries, agricultural products processing, engineering, metalworking, power transformers

Turkmenistan

Capital	:	Ashkhabad
Area	:	488.0 thousand square kilometres
Population	:	3.8 million
GDP	:	18.6 billion roubles
Total exports	:	7.8 billion roubles
Total imports	:	6.9 billion roubles
Natural resources	:	Natural gas, oil iodine-bromine, sodium sulphate, salts
Main industries	:	Textiles, gas and oil processing, chemicals, electricity-generating industries

Ukraine

Capital	:	Kiev
Area	:	603.7 thousand square kilometres
Population	:	51.7 million
GDP	:	262.0 billion roubles
Total exports	:	61.9 billion roubles
Total imports	:	65.5 billion roubles
Natural resources	:	Agricultural land, coal, mineral deposits, natural gas, petroleum
Main industries	:	Food processing and production, heavy industry

Uzbekistan

Capital	:	Tashkent
Area	:	450 thousand square kilometres
Population	:	21.3 million
GDP	:	56.3 billion roubles
Total exports	:	19.6 billion roubles
Total imports	:	20.2 billion roubles
Natural resources	:	Cotton, natural gas, coal, gold, silver, copper, lead, zinc, wolfram, tungsten, petroleum
Main industries	:	Agriculture, cotton harvestres, textile machinery, chemicals, metallurgy, aircrafts.

Notes: 1. All data refer to 1991 unless otherwise noted.
2. See also next part, i.e., 11.2 Demographic Estimates.

Source: *Finance and Development*, September 1992.

11.2 Demographic Estimates

TABLE 11.1: Demographic Estimates

Country	Population (thousands)	Demographic indicators (average annual rate)					
		Population growth (%)	Crude birth rate (/1,000)	Crude death rate (/1,000)	Total fertility rate (/woman)	Life expectancy of birth (years)	Infant mortality rate (/1,000)
	1992	1990-92			1985-90		
Armenia	3489	2.3	23	6	2.6	71	23
Azerbaijan	7283	0.8	27	7	2.8	70	28
Belarus	10295	0.1	16	10	2.0	72	13
Estonia	1581	0.2	16	112	2.2	70	15
Georgia	5471	0.1	18	9	2.3	72	22
Kazakhstan	17048	0.8	24	8	3.0	69	28
Kyrgyzstan	4518	1.3	31	7	4.0	68	36
Latvia	2677	-0.1	15	12	2.1	70	12
Lithuania	3749	0.1	16	10	2.1	72	12
Republic of Moldova	4362	0.0	21	10	2.6	68	24
Russian Federation	149003	0.2	16	11	2.1	70	19
Tadjikistan	5587	2.5	40	7	5.4	70	46
Turkmenistan	3861	2.5	36	8	4.6	65	54
Ukraine	52158	0.2	14	12	2.0	71	14
Uzbekistan	21453	2.1	36	7	4.4	69	43

Source: *Populi*, July/August, 1992; United Nations Population Division, Department of Economic and Social Development, New York; *World Population Prospects: The 1992 Revision.*

Note: There is difference in population figures as these relate to two different periods.

11.3 Health Crisis in Commonwealth of Independent States and Baltic States

The CIS Republics and Baltic States have embarked on a process of economic transition and adjustment of unprecedented proportions. Equally unprecedented challenges are being presented by the human impact of this process on the poor and vulnerable. In similar situations in developing countries in recent years, the international community has unambiguously recognized the need for such adjustments to have "a human face". A human face needs urgently to be given to the process of transition and adjustment in the CIS and Baltic States today. The IMF, with the support of the industrial countries, already has the main international leadership role in advising on this process of adjustment and transition. The IMF, the World Bank and other partners need to bring the dimension of human concern, especially the goal of protecting children and vulnerable groups, into the adjustment process and monitor the adequacy of measures to achieve this goal. Other parts of the Unite Nations system — and donors — need to offer their full help to ensure that it is achieved.

Over the past year health systems have experienced tremendous cost escalation and as a result most essential commodities are not available. Health budgets for 1992 are reported to have risen (in terms of roubles) from 300 per cent (Central Asian Republics and Kazakhstan) to as much as 1000 per cent (Ukraine) . . . Previously self-sufficient in essential vaccines, the CIS countries have been without regular supplies for six months. The supply of measles vaccine — which never received WHO approval for stability — is exhausted; BCG and polio are in short supply, with DPT soon to follow. Even as production facilities come back on line or are replaced by new plants, cross border trade issues will have to be worked out to assure supply through the CIS and the Baltics. . .

In households, the five to seven fold increases in consumer prices over the past 12 months . . . have dramatically diminished the capacity of most families, particularly in urban areas, to purchase food and other essentials. The harshest effects initially were moderated by the use of hoarded supplies but they are running out and further price increases are still projected . . . the missions were told that some 80 per cent of the population was now below the poverty line.

With high hospitalization rates, especially for children (estimated at one admission per child per year), the missions uniformly encountered extremely high rates of drug use, particularly parenteral medicines, and witnessed procedures and practices often considered outmoded or inappropriate in western health care systems. . . . In rural and poor urban areas, polyclinics and small hospitals were housed in clean but frequently sub-standard facilities, where medical equipment was rudimentary and the most essential drugs . . . were often lacking.

Environmental problems are widely evident throughout the CIS. The most dramatic and publicized was the radiation damage caused by the Chernobyl disaster. . . . Less widely known, and as yet unverified, are the claims of chronic exposure to perhaps even greater radiation levels throughout the Urals (from nuclear wastes) and throughout much of Central Asia (as a result of atomic testing in the atmosphere through 1963 and underground until 1990). . . . Even more widespread, but largely undocumented, is the effect on human populations of extensive use of pesticides and fertilizers which have accumulated in soil and ground water in intensively cultivated areas throughout the country. More obvious is the extensive air pollution associated with industrialization and the direct threat to millions of workers in factories from on-the-job exposure to noxious fumes, dangerous machinery and other occupational hazards.

Women bear a particularly heavy burden; more than 80 per cent are employed full time and are often poorly paid and in the most menial positions. With rising food costs and the declining quality of diets their nutritional problems, especially anemia, are likely to increase. The absence of contraception exposes women to frequent abortions. . . Food shortages have forced many women to add to their normal burden of food preparation, child care and homemaking, the additional time spent in queues attempting to buy food for their families. After decades of being treated as comrades and workers, women are increasingly looking for an opportunity to assert both their equality with men and their identity as females.

This is an historic moment when a helping hand from the international community will do much to alleviate a crisis of potentially enormous proportions.

Urgent action can avert human tragedy and, at the same time, speed reform.

We, WHO and UNICEF are joining forces so that organizations of the United Nations system, and governmental and non-governmental organizations can come together to provide consolidated support. We hope that this will allow the democratic process that is under way to continue with the minimum of human suffering.

(Source: Reports of WHO and UNICEF Missions, 1992, reported in *An NGLS Briefing Paper*, UNICEF, Geneva, June 1992.)

12

WORLD OUTLOOK: Diverse Issues

12.1 AIDS

Delayed response to tackling the spread of the human immuno deficiency virus (HIV) has made India and Thailand especially vulnerable to economic crisis.

While the direct health costs for screening and treatment of AIDS worldwide have been estimated at 3.5 billion dollars a year, "the indirect social and economic costs will be much higher".

By the end of this decade, at least 40 million people — and perhaps 100 million — are expected to have been infected with HIV most of the new cases will be in Asia.

Countries such as India and Thailand with high rates of HIV infection, but as yet few cases of AIDS, face potentially very high costs in the next five to ten years.

The indirect costs include loss of productivity in industrial and farm sectors due to disability and premature death from AIDS and time taken off from work to care for the infected, possible increase in wage costs as a result of labour shortage, and damaged tourist industries.

Nearly every sector of the economy may be affected in ways not always predictable.

The impact of AIDS on India may have been reduced, had the Government taken appropriate measures in the mid-1980s. Many Indians predicted that it would remain a "foreign disease", but the reality is that it has taken root in every city.

Many development nations that do not have the technical or financial resources to contain AIDS are in danger of being overwhelmed by the indirect effect of this epidemic on families, communities, agricultural and industrial production.

Many communities will simply collapse under the strain of supporting a large proportion of ill people and bereaved dependents on very united resources.

The division of resources to the control and treatment of AIDS will also reduce the effectiveness of other health programmes.

Women's inferior economic and social status — that limits their ability to control their sex lives — increases their vulnerability to HIV. Some 15,000 women are getting infected every week.

The developing countries will be worst affected. In Thailand alone, two million children will become orphans by 2010. There will be as many as five million AIDS orphans in southern Africa by the end of the century.

Source: *Hidden Costs of AIDS*, Panos Institute, London, quoted in *Hindustan Times*, December 1992.

12.2 Afghanistan: Chronology

1978
April: Afghan government overthrown by pro-Soviet Marxist party. Armed, non-communist resistance begins.

1979
December: The Soviets launch a massive airlift of forces to save the Kabul government. Babrak Karmal installed as president.

1986
May: Karmal is replaced by Najibullah, chief of the secret service. Fighting escalates toward the end of the year when the Pakistan-based guerrillas receive U.S. weapons.

1988
April 15: Afghanistan and Pakistan sign an accord clearing the way for the Red Army's departure, but the guerrillas continue fighting.

1989
Feb. 15: The last of an estimated 115,000 Soviet soldiers departs.

1990
June: Najibullah makes sweeping constitutional reforms.

1991
April: Guerrillas capture the southern city of Khost. Najibullah's biggest military setback.

1992
March 18: Najibullah offers to transfer power to an interim government established under a U.N. peace plan. The guerrillas say they will keep fighting.

1992
April 15: Muslim rebels claim control of the country's main military base, 35 miles fro Kabul.

1992
April 16: Najibullah reportedly resigns.

12.3 Crime Prevention and Criminal Justice: A Blueprint for UN Action

The Committee on Crime Prevention and Criminal Justice concluded its inaugural session at Vienna on April 30, 1992 by approving an omnibus draft resolution which could serve as a blueprint for the future operational activities of the United Nations crime prevention and criminal justice programme.

The comprehensive draft that the Commission has recommended to the Economic and Social Council for adoption deals with all aspects of operational activities and co-ordination in the field of crime prevention and criminal justice. Approved by consensus, as orally amended, the draft covers strengthening of the operational capacity and advisory services of the programme, the establishment of sub-programme on operational activities, co-ordination of activities, funding, priorities of the programme and follow-up.

The draft was one of the three proposals approved by the Commission at two meetings on 30 April. The other two deal with preparations for the Ninth United Nations Congress on the Prevention of Crime and the Treatment of Offenders and measures against organised crime.

On preparations for the Ninth Crime Congress, scheduled for 1995, the Commission approved by consensus a draft resolution which, as orally amended, would have the Council decide that the topics to be discussed at the Ninth Congress should be international co-operation and technical assistance for strengthening the role of law; action against national and transnational economic, organised and environmental crime; management and improvement of criminal justice systems; and crime prevention strategies for urban areas, especially juvenile and violent criminality.

The Council would now with gratitude accept the offer by the Government of Iran to host the Ninth Congress in Teheran.

By the terms of the draft resolution on organised crime, approved by consensus as orally amended, the Council would reaffirm that priority must be given to the struggle against all activities of organised crime, including money laundering, infiltration legitimate business and corruption of public officers. It would request the Secretary-General to promote greater international co-operation in efforts against economic crimes and the laundering of illicit funds.

The Secretary-General would also be requested to continue analysing the impact of organised criminal activities upon society, including data on nature, extent, forms and dimensions of organised crime, on legitimate measures and international co-operation aimed at controlling organised crime and judicial practice in organised cases.

In the course of its 10-day session, which began on 21 April, 1992 the Commission adopted four other proposals. They deal with control of the proceeds of crime; strategic management of the United Nations crime prevention and criminal justice programme; the desirability of a convention on crime prevention and criminal justice; and measures to assist the Commission in carrying out its mandate.

The Commission is the newest functional body of the Economic and Social Council. Established in February with a mandate to develop, monitor and review the United Nations programme on crime prevention and criminal justice, it replaces the Committee on Crime Prevention and Control.

Operational Activities

The draft resolution on operational activities and co-ordination in the field of crime prevention and criminal justice, was approved as orally amended.

By its provisions on strengthening the operational capacity and advisory services of the United Nations crime prevention and criminal justice programme, the Economic and Social Council would request the Secretary-General to commit the necessary human and financial resources to strengthen the programme, especially designing, implementing and monitoring technical co-operation projects.

Among other things, the programme would provide technical co-operation to assist countries in the improvement of national legislation and law reform; contribute to the preservation and the reinforcement of democracy; serve as a world-wide training network for developing countries with specific requirements; strengthen the United Nations criminal justice information network; and promote policy-oriented research.

The Council would also request the Secretary-General to initiate the necessary consultations for a report setting out options and recommendations for the creation of an appropriate mechanism, such as a foundation, to mobilise resource for technical co-operation.

Ninth Crime Prevention Congress

The draft resolution on preparations for the Ninth United Nations Congress on the Prevention of Crime and the Treatment of Offenders would have the Council decide that the following topics as included in the provisional agenda for the Congress: international co-operation and practical technical assistance for strengthening the role of law; organised and environmental crime; management and improvement of criminal justice systems; crime prevention strategies for urban areas, and juvenile and violent criminality.

The Council would request the commission on Crime Prevention and criminal justice to finalise the provisional agenda for the Ninth congress taking into account that the Congress should deal with a limited number of precisely defined substantive topics, which should reflect urgent needs of the world community.

By other terms of the draft, the Council would request the Secretary-General to prepare a discussion guide for the Commission's consideration as well as draft rules of procedure for the Ninth Congress. It would invite Regional Commissions, regional and international institutes active in the field, specialised agencies and other entities in the United Nations system, intergovernmental and non-governmental organisations to become actively involved in the preparation for the Congress.

By the terms of the draft approved on organised crime, the Economic and Social Council, reaffirming that priority must be given to the struggle against all activities of organised crime, including money laundering, the infiltration of legitimate business and the corruption of public officers, would request the Secretary-General to continue analysing the impact of organised criminal activities upon society. Taken into account would be data on the nature, extent, forms and dimensions of organised crime, on legislative measures and international co-operation aimed at controlling organised crime and judicial practice on organised crime cases.

The Council would also request the Secretary-General to promote greater international co-operation in efforts against economic crimes and the laundering of illicit funds.

Other Actions

By its resolution on controlling proceeds of crime, the Commission invited Member States to make every effort to modify their national legislation to effectively prevent and control the laundering of the proceeds of crime and related offenses. It called on the Secretary-General to propose ways by which States could be assisted in revising legislation, in training financial and law enforcement personnel, and in developing regional and bilateral co-operation in a global effort to counter money laundering and related offenses.

By the resolution on strategic management of the Programme adopted as orally amended by Finland, the Commission asserted its role as the principal policy-making body in crime prevention and criminal justice and decided that it would follow a plan for strategic management as outlined in the annex to the resolution.

According to the proposals, the Commission should agree on the general goals of the Programme and the needs to be met. It should ascertain the capacity available to meet these needs and should determine the specific activities to be carried out. The mechanisms to be used for the purpose and ways of assessing implementation should also be determined.

Source: *UN Newsletter*, May 16, 1992.

12.4 **Europe in 1992**

Everything went wrong for Europe in 1992. The 'Whole and Free' continent promised by the end of the cold war appeared to be coming rapidly unstuck.

To the East, the former Communist Bloc was menaced by political instability and economic hardship; to the West, European Community's plans for union fottered on the brink of collapse; to the South, the Yugoslav war raged out of control.

The political troubles of a Europe no longer kept in balance by nuclear terror were accompanied by a harsh economic recession affecting much of the world.

Ethnic groups clashed, refugees poured frontiers, currencies seesawed, dole queues lengthened.

Europe had seen nothing like it for decades. The combination of racial intolerance, especially in Germany, and economic slump reminded some observers of the 1930s, when Nazi dictator Adolf Hitler rose to power.

As 1993 approached, there were signs that politicians were starting to address the problems, though solutions looked a long way off. It also seemed the recession could be bottoming out.

The year had begun an optimistic note. It was the first in seven decades to be rung in without the Soviet Union, which had collapsed along with the discredited Soviet Communist Party.

In its place, 15 nominally independent, nominally Democratic States were thrust blinking into the light of the day.

But all, from resource-rich Russia to remote Kyrgyzstan, soon learned that — as one Ukrainian newspaper put it — "independence is not a ready buttered piece of bread".

Decades of State control had left their economies in shambles, old problems of decrepit industries and infrastructure were compounded by rocketing, inflation and unemployment.

A Vienna institute estimated that the former Soviet Union would need annual investment of $ 465 billion a year from 1975 to 2005 to even approach western standards of prosperity.

In Russia president Boris Yeltsin, though still the most popular politician, was struggling by the year's end to defend his economic reforms and his

Government against an onslaught by Conservatives who wanted to slow the move to a market economy.

The vast ex-Soviet territories were plagued by ethnic and factional violence. The four-year-old war between Armenians and Azeris in the enclave of Nagorno-Karabakh dragged on, and there was serious fighting in Georgia, Moldova and Tajikistan.

The former Soviet Union's problems echoed those of the East European States, which had scrapped communism two years earlier. They found that industries were harder to privatise than to nationalise and that a cash-strapped west was stingy with aid.

Everywhere, living standards dropped, Governments were ridden by factionalism and ethnic problems were never far away.

The Czechs and Slovaks decided, albeit peacefully to split Czechoslovakia into two countries from Jan. 1, 1993.

But its problems dwarfed by the carnage in the former Yugoslavia, where clashes in 1991 between Serbs and Croats had already ignited Europe's worst conflict since world war two.

The war entered a new dimension of violence and horror when it spread to Bosnia-Harzegovina after that republic declared independence in March and was recognised by the EC in April.

Bosnia's minority Serbs, fearing domination by Moslems and Croats, took up arms with the backing of Serbia and the former Yugoslav Federal Army and laid siege to the capital, Sarajevo and other cities. They soon captured two-thirds of the republic.

In early December Yugoslav President Dobrica Cosic estimated that 17 months of fighting had cost 138,000 lives, while the United Nations said it had created over three million refugees.

Worse still was the widely predicted prospects of the clashes spreading southwards and touching off a general Balkan war that could drag in Albania, Bulgaria and Greece.

But Yugoslavia and other ethnic trouble spots had cast a harsh light on the weakness of the European institutions that many had hoped would deal with just such crises as these.

Neither the 52-nation conference on security and cooperation in Europe nor NATO, groping for a new role, nor the EC, which along with the United Nations set up open-ended Yugoslav peace talks in Geneva in September, were able to stop the war.

West European leaders were distracted from Yugoslavia by their struggle to rescue EC plans for economic and political union enshrined in the Maastricht Treaty, signed in February.

Denmark threw the EC into crisis when its people voted in a referendum on June 2 to reject the treaty, which envisaged a single European currency and common foreign policy.

The vote showed up widespread unease over Maastricht both in France, where just 51 per cent backed it in a later referendum, and in Britain, where Prime Minister John Major had to postpone a final parliamentary vote to ratify the treaty until May 1993.

The problem facing the community was how to win the danes round to the treaty without renegotiating it.

A spin-off from the confusion over Maastricht was a currency crisis, partly due to the strength of the German mark on the back of high interest rates.

The weaker currencies could not keep up, in September, the British pound and the Italian lira pulled out of the EC's exchange rate mechanism, and in November the Spanish peseta and Portuguese escudo were devalued by six per cent.

The currency turmoil hit a contingent already battling a long recession, EC growth was estimated at a sickly 1.1 per cent for the year, but a slight improvement was predicted in 1993.

On a more positive note, an EC-US accord on farm trade after six years of argument raised hopes for a new deal under the general agreement on tariffs and trade that could boost annual world commerce by up to $ 200 billion.

Nevertheless, unemployment in the community crept up towards 10 per cent and was expected to pass that figure in 1993. This created social strains across Europe, most dramatically in Germany where unification in 1990 had left huge inequalities.

There, discontent found its outlet from August onwards in far-right violence against East European and third world refugees by December 17 people had died in some 1,900 attacks.

Although rightist extremism also hit other European countries, 'the sight of neo-Nazis torching foreigners' hostels and desecrating Jewish cemeteries in Germany sent a shudder of alarm through a world which had not forgotten the 1930s.

Source: *Hindustan Times*, December 13, 1992.

12.5 **France : Development Policy**

Although France is the third biggest donor of Official Development Assistance (ODA), it is fundamentally different from the other two big donors, Japan and the USA, in the way it runs its development cooperation, particularly is its emphasis on French historical links.

Whereas the development policy of the USA is greatly influenced by security interests and that of Japan by foreign trade interests, the special profile of French development policy is determined by the intensive, privileged relations to the former colonies. The foundation of French development policy is acknowledgement of France's "African inheritance", to the disadvantage of a global orientation, which the French business community in particular wants. Development policy as continuation of colonial policy with different means?

In the phase of dissolution of its colonial empire after 1945 France was able successfully to adapt its policy to the new structures. French colonial policy changed into a policy of decolonisation which was followed with practically no breaks by the development and cooperation policy. But this progression has left its marks. The francophone black African states and Madagascar, which in contrast to the Maghreb and Indochina remained "loyal" to France in the transition to independence, were given preferential treatment.

The jargon word used for them is "le champ"; they receive the lion's share of French aid. A peculiarity of French development cooperation are the substantial allocations to the departments d'outer mer (DOM, overseas departments) which are regarded as part of France, and the last overseas territories (TOM). Although the TOM countries are listed in the official OECD statistics and have all the characteristics of developing countries, because of their status they are not recognised as ODA. All other developing countries are categorised as "the rest of the world" or "pays hors champ".

In this three-way division the substantial increases in official allocations have further expanded the privileged position of the countries of the "champ". At the same time, however, private inputs have dropped massively since 1987. In 1990 repayments and return-flows were a lot higher than new lending by private banks and private institutions, especially to countries south of the Sahara. Moreover, many French firms are seen to be withdrawing from Africa.

For each group of countries there are specific strategies, specific administrative structures and specific instruments. One could almost speak of separate French development policies for the three categories of countries. This is not undisputed in France. But all attempts by "Third Worldists" to establish a standard, globally oriented French development policy have failed to date. The last comprehensive attempt at reform was made by the Socialist cooperation minister, Jean Pierre Cot in 1981. The centrepiece of his reform was the dissolution of the cooperation ministry and the concentration of all development policy powers in a department of the foreign ministry which was to operate worldwide. But this upset the state presidents of the "champ" who saw the privileged status of their countries in danger and complained about Cot in the Elysee Palace. Mitterrand decided against Cot and for the acceptance of the "African inheritance". Cot's only option in November 1982 was to resign. Thereafter the old administrative division was brought back.

Although France's multilateral allocations of 23.6 per cent (1990) are below the OECD average, by volume it is a large multi-lateral donor. The distribution is similar to the German profile. French contributions to the European Development Fund (EDF) are just below the German ones; France is also strongly engaged in the Bretton Woods institutions; its contributions to the UN organisations are comparatively meagre, however. Apart from the financial contributions France has successfully pursued a policy of placing outstanding French representatives into important positions in international organisations who in turn successfully look after French interests, again to the advantage of Africa and especially the countries of the "champ".

In their core, the aims of French cooperation policy have not changed for decades. They are wrapped up with the commitment to francophonie and the countries of the "champ" to which France will continue to feel obligations but where in return the old "grande nation" will preserve its political, military, economic and cultural influence. The high proportion of free technical aid and the high grant element in French ODA are expressions of solidarity with the former colonies, many of which are among the Least Developed Countries (LDC). But although its aid may appear generous at first glance, France is trying to make it profitable again by tying it almost totally to deliveries from home.

The basic principles of this policy are also accepted by the French public. Under the umbrella of its Africa-related global concept France adjusts its strategies in the mid-term to changing conditions and international trends. Special priority is presently being given to protection of the environment and resources, development of urban zones and the role of women in the development process.

TABLE 12.1: French Official and Private Assistance to Developing Countries (Net Disbursements in mio US $)

Kind of transfer		1985	1987	1989	1990
public transfer	a	2,770	4,489 (0.5)	5,162 (0.54)	6,579 (0.55)
(ODA)	b	3,995	6,525	7,450 (0.78)	9,380 (0.79)
Other public	a	857	1,774	851	432
transfers (OOF)	b	1,143	2,106	1,254	987
private transfers	a	3,736	41	—1,471	—2,100
	b				
Total transfers	a	7,362	6,304	4,541	4,910
	b	8,873	8,671	7,232	8,266

a: without DOM-TOM; b: with DOM-TOM; ( )9 GNP share in %

Administrative Structures Match the Regional Categories

Four authorities share responsibility for development policy:

* The cooperation ministry is responsible for technical and financial aid to "champ" countries.
* The foreign ministry's general directorate for cultural and scientific-technical relations is responsible for technical co-operation with countries outside the "champ", i.e. delineates itself from the cooperation ministry not sectorally but geographically.
* The treasury in the economic and finance ministry allocates the financial aid to countries outside the "champ" (prêts du trésor). It is the most influential authority and is also responsible for multilateral development cooperation with the exception of the UN sector, which is handled by the foreign ministry.
* A state secretariat in the interior ministry administers the allocations to the DOM-TOM.

The most important implementing agency in the financial cooperation sector (for champs, hors champs and DOM-TOM) is the Caisse Centrale de coopération Economique (CCCE). Implementation of technical cooperation is further splintered; it is mainly handled by the many institutes subordinated to all French ministries.

The division of responsibilities — hard to grasp to any outsider — is compensated by informal channels, especially by persons agreements of a leadership stratum defined above all by common education at the big French elite schools.

Each authority at the centre has its own representatives in the embassies, assigned and directed by the ministries concerned: the cooperation ministry, the heads of the "missions d'aide et de coopération" (MAC), the Trésor, the "conseillers financiers" who are mostly responsible for several countries and the foreign ministry, the "conseillers culturéls". They are accountable to the ambassador but not coordinated by him. The Caisse Centrale has "agencesa" of its own, with a large measure of autonomy, in "its" countries.

Particular Cooperation Instruments for Each Region

French technical cooperation covers both cultural and scientific-cultural cooperation and accounts for more than 40 per cent of the bilateral contributions.

Source: Burghard Claus, *D & C*, June 1992.

12.6 Global Food Aid

Following a considerable fall in wheat prices during 1990/91, a sharp rise began in the second part of 1991, reflecting forecasts of increased imports. Prices continued to rise in the first months of 1992 in response to expected further imports by the former Soviet Union and a sharp draw-down of global stocks in 1991-92. Such price increases are likely to affect food aid levels, since donors generally establish their food aid budgets in monetary terms.

Cereal imports by developing countries, which declined by more than seven per cent in 1990-91, are forecast to return to the 1989-90 record level of 122 million tons. Most of the increase, however, would stem from higher wheat imports by China, while declining imports and forecast for Central America and Africa, in 1991, cereal food aid represented about 10 per cent of cereal imports by all developing countries, but a much higher share of 17 per cent by LIFDCs. Cereal food aid in 1991 was 0.7 per cent of world cereal production and seven per cent of stocks in developed countries.

Good harvests were recorded in many countries of sub-Saharan Africa in 1991, including record crops in the Sahelian countries of Western Africa and above-average harvests in several countries of eastern and central Africa. The food supply situation remains critical, however, in many countries of the region. It is particularly serious in the Horn of Africa, where deaths from starvation continue to be reported. Serious food supply difficulties remain in Ethiopia, Somalia and Sudan on account of civil war and drought. They also persist in Angola in the aftermath of a prolonged civil conflict, and in Liberia, Malawi, Mozambique and Sierra Leone following civil war and unrest leading to population displacement within and across borders. Food aid requirements for these countries will remain very high in 1992.

The outlook for much of southern Africa is far below-average crops owing to severe drought, with some countries facing the possibility of severe shortfalls in food supplies and requiring substantial increases in food aid.

Regional Perspective

In 1991 sub-Saharan Africa received the largest volume of food aid and also registered the greatest increase in deliveries. Asia and the Pacific also received a significant increase in deliveries. Asia and the Pacific also received a significant increase in deliveries as did, although to a lesser extent, North Africa and the Middle East, Latin America and the Caribbean continued to receive a declining share, but the sharpest decline was in eastern Europe, which received less than half the volume of the previous year.

Sub-Saharan Africa

The majority of LIFDCs and LDCs are in sub-Saharan Africa. Food aid flows to that region in 1991 almost returned to the peak levels reached during the serious food crises of the mid-eighties. Increased deliveries to sub-Saharan Africa resulted from emergency situations and the large numbers of refugees and people displaced by civil strife. Almost two-thirds of cereal food aid and three-quarters of non-cereal food aid to the region were for relief, the highest proportion ever. The region received 70 per cent of global relief food aid in cereals and 72 per cent of non-cereals.

Project food aid deliveries also increased by about one-quarter, reaching its highest level ever as a result of special efforts made by WFP and other project food aid donors to address the rehabilitation and longer term development needs of poor and food-insecure people.

The major food aid recipients in the region have continued to be those countries with large numbers of refugees or displaced people: Ethiopia, Sudan, Mozambique, Malawi, Liberia and Angola, which together accounted for more than two-thirds of total deliveries to the region.

North Africa and the Middle East

For the second successive year, North Africa and the Middle East has been the second largest food aid recipient region. In the aftermath of the war in the Persian Gulf, food aid deliveries in 1991 were above the average of the past ten years. More than three-quarters of deliveries continued to be on a non-project basis, the rest being almost equally divided between project and emergency food aid. Project food aid continued to decline, however, while emergency food aid more than doubled on account of increased relief assistance to refugees and displaced people.

Egypt remained the largest food aid recipient in the region, accounting for more than 60 per cent of total deliveries, followed by Tunisia, Jordan and Morocco.

Asia and the Pacific

In 1991, Asia and the Pacific received close to the average volume of food aid of the past ten years. Non-cereal food aid deliveries, however, continued to decline. Project food aid accounted for the largest share, while the share of non-project food aid continued once again to decline.

Bangladesh remained the largest food aid recipient in the region, receiving 45 per cent of total deliveries, followed by Pakistan, India and Sri Lanka.

Latin America and the Caribbean

The declining trend of the late eighties in food aid deliveries to this region continued in 1991, with a 15 per cent reduction from 1990. Non-project food aid continued to account for by far the largest share; almost all the rest was project food aid.

Peru, Jamaica, Guatemala, Bolivia and El Salvador, together received more than 60 per cent of 1991 deliveries to the region.

Eastern Europe and former Soviet Union

For the purpose of this analysis, eastern European countries and the former Soviet Union are grouped together. After emerging in 1989 as a significant recipient of food aid, this group received 1.2 million tons of food in 1991 (about eight per cent of global deliveries), less than half the volume delivered the previous year. Almost all the food aid was non-project.

In 1991, Romania, Bulgaria and Albania were the largest recipients in the region. The first food aid deliveries also were made to the former Soviet Union. It is too early to determine the extent to which other food supplied to the new countries emerging from that former entity will qualify as food aid.

A direct link between the sharp reduction in 1991 deliveries to these countries and a corresponding increase to developing countries cannot be established, especially given the unstable food aid and other concessional food flows to this group of countries. Major donor continued to reiterate that food aid to eastern Europe and the former Soviet Union is financed from additional budgetary allocations.

Food Aid Procurement in Developing Countries

Provisional delivery data for 1991 indicate that a record one million tons of cereals and 14,2000 tons of non-cereal commodities were procured in developing countries for use as food aid, representing eight per cent of total cereal and 12 per cent of non-cereal deliveries. Those amounts include both local purchases in the recipient countries themselves and triangular transactions involving the purchase or exchange of commodities by donors in one developing country for use as food aid in another developing country. To avoid double counting of food aid, however, they exclude purchases made with funds generated from the local sale of food aid commodities, even though this results in the procurement of additional local food commodities.

TABLE 12.2: Food Aid to Priority Country Groups

Commodity Type	1987	1988	1989	1990	1991
Low-income food-deficit countries					
Cereals					
Volume ('000 tons)	11756	11548	8526	8617	10584
Share of total deliveries (%)	90	88	82	67	80
Non-cereals					
Volume ('000 tons)	1175	1481	870	9226	820
Share of total deliveries (%)	86	88	88	78	72
Least developed countries					
Cereals					
Volume ('000 tons)	5042	5358	4087	3789	5200
Share of total deliveries (%)	37	41	39	29	40
Non-cereals					
Volume ('000 tons)	378	432	289	329	427
Share of total deliveries (%)	28	26	29	28	38

The largest proportion of food obtained in developing countries for use as food aid (45 per cent of cereals and 53 per cent of non-cereal commodities) was procured in sub-Saharan Africa. Most of the remainder was procured in Asia. While 60 per cent of non-cereal food aid commodities were purchased in recipient countries themselves, most of the cereals (70%) were obtained in a third country.

In 1991 WFP remained the largest purchaser of food aid in developing countries, accounting for almost half (524,000 tons) of total purchases from its own resources, followed by Japan and the Commission of the European Communities WFP also purchased 202,000 tons of commodities on behalf of bilateral donors, other United Nations organizations and NGOs, handling altogether almost two-thirds of total food aid purchases in developing countries.

Source: *Review of Global Food Aid Policies and Programmes.*

12.7 **Health**

12.7.1 *WHO Commission on Health and Environment*

The United Nations Conference on Environment and Development (UNCED), held in Rio de Janeiro from June 3 to 14, 1992, provides support for a new WHO global strategy for environmental health, which the Forth-Fifth World Health Assembly, held in Geneva in May requested the Director-General to formulate.

The framework for the future is outlined in Agenda 21, the Conference's main basis for action. Issues affecting health feature in many chapters of the Agenda and include toxic chemicals, water quality and supply, and hazardous waste disposal, among others. The introduction to Chapter 6, which is exclusively devoted to health says:

> "Health and development are intimately interconnected. Both insufficient development, leading to poverty, and inappropriate development, resulting in overconsumption, coupled with an expanding world population, can result in severe environmental health problems in both developing and developed nations.
>
> Action times under Agenda 21 must address the primary health needs of the world's population, since they are integral to the achievement of the goals of sustainable development and primary environmental care. The linkage of health, environmental and socio-economic improvements requires intersectoral efforts. Such efforts, involving education, housing, public works and community groups, including businesses, schools and universities, and religious, civic and cultural organizations, are aimed at enabling people in their communities to ensure sustainable development. Particularly relevant is the inclusion of prevention programmes rather than relying solely on remediation and treatment."

Five programme areas are specified. These are: meeting primary health care needs, particularly in rural areas; control of communicable diseases; protecting vulnerable groups; meeting the urban health challenge; and reducing health risks from environmental pollution and hazards. Each programme area has a basis for action, and sets of objectives and activities. On primary health care needs, the conference agreed on the importance of sage water supplies and sanitation, safe food supplies and proper nutrition.

Specific objectives in this programme area include incorporating appropriate environmental and health safeguards as part of national development programmes in all countries by the year 2000. Action programmes should address urban air pollution, water pollution, pesticides, waste disposal and radiation. On ultraviolet radiation, the chapter says these programmes should undertake as a matter of urgency research on the health effects as a consequence of depletion of the stratospheric ozone layer. These nationally developed programmes should if necessary have international assistance, support and coordination.

The chapter concludes with assessments of the financial costs of all the programmes for action, and says that an average annual total of between US$ 6000 million and US$7000 million will be needed from the international community over the years 1993-2000 on grant of concessional terms. These are indicative and order of magnitude estimates only, and represent about five per cent of the total estimated cost estimating Agenda 21 on these terms.

Source : *UN Newsletter*, July 18, 1992.

12.7.2 *WHO New Project on Drugs and Sports*

In recognition of this widespread problem, the World Health Organization (WHO) has implemented a preliminary cross-cultural research initiative. The primary goal of WHO project on drugs and sports is to collect data which can be used to develop substance abuse prevention and education materials. The objectives of the research project include: defining drug use patterns with respect to different sports and sport activities; identifying critical health and social problems caused by the use of drugs by athletes; and cataloguing current national and international abuse prevention policies and strategies.

No simple picture of global use has emerged but what limited research has been done suggests that the problem of drug use poses a far greater health hazard than most people have imagined. Some adverse reactions to anabolic steroids include; cholesterol increase, oedema, increased risk of coronary artery disease, liver tumours, prostate enlargement, testicular atrophy, and impotence. In addition there is evidence of an increase in aggressive and combative behaviour ("roid rage") by steroid users.

Limited surveys of athletes in Australia, Canada, Italy, the United Kingdom of Great Britain and North Ireland and the United States of America, show that between 6 per cent of 20 per cent of athletes questioned have used some form of drug, excluding alcohol and tobacco. On average approximately 6 per cent of those interviewed had used one or more diuretic, anabolic steroid or stimulant within the previous year.

One significant outcome of these surveys was to illustrate that there are numerous competitors who use a variety of drugs to aid their competitive performance. In addition it was shown that to some extent drug use affects both sexes, all ages, all sports and all levels of competition. There was also clear evidence to show that anabolic steroids have moved beyond athletic training and are now being used by non-athletes for cosmetic purposes. In a study conducted in 1988 on high school seniors in the United States 6.6 per cent of all males had taken steroids. Of this group 35 per cent did not intend to participate in school-sponsored athletic programmes and 26 per cent cited personal appearance as the primary motive for using the drugs. Furthermore the data indicated that 38 per cent had started using steroids by their 15th birthday.

With the immediacy of modern communication technology and the significance of sports and athletes as role models for children and adolescents, both in developing and industrialized countries, international concern over the prevalence and incidence of drug use in sports has grown. It has been almost four years since Canadian sprinter, Ben Johnson fell from glory in the Seoul Olympics. As the current 1992 Summer Olympics approaches, world class athletes are calling for blood testing as a means of controlling for doping in sport.

Source: *UN Newsletter*, July 18, 1992.

12.8 **International News Story**

Yugoslavia's protracted civil war was the top international news story of 1992, according to editors around the world polled by the Associated Press.

Newspaper, radio, television and news agency editors in 37 countries, excluding the United States, were asked to list what they viewed as the top ten stories of the past year.

Yugoslavia, with brutal ethnic violence that has stymied international peace efforts, received 60 first-place votes from the 105 ballots cast. Based on ten points for each first-place vote to one point for each story rated in tenth place, the ongoing war earned 938 points.

The Gulf war was the top story of 1991, followed by the hardliners' coup attempt against the then Soviet President Mikhail Gorbachev and Yugoslavia's conflict.

Mr Bill Clinton's decisive victory over Mr. George Bush, ending 12 years of Republicans in the White House, ranked as the No. two story of 1992, with 23 first-place votes and 842 points.

In third place with eight first-place votes and 598 points was the difficult transition to independence by the former Soviet republics, along with ethnic violence and Russian president Boris Yeltsin's reform attempts.

The famine that has devastated wartorn Somalia and other African countries was fifth with one first-place vote and 440 points.

In sixth place with three first-place votes and 382 points were the Neo-Nazi attacks on refugees in Germany, followed by the Earth Summit in Rio de Janeiro that focused attention on the world's environmental problems, with one first-place vote and 265 points.

South Africa's difficult moves to end apartheid, complicated by ongoing factional violence, was ranked eighth with 233 points, edging by one point the race riots that swept through Los Angeles and other US cities after four white policemen were acquitted of beating a black motorist.

Rounding out the top ten were efforts to reach a lasting peace in West Asia with 179 points.

The second ten stories, in order with points totals, were:

The continued spread of AIDS, 152.

The crash of an israeli cargo jet into an Amsterdam apartment complex, 131.

China's Communist Party Congress, 120.

European farm subsidies that threatened GATT world trade talks, 108.

Thailand's pro-Democracy crackdown, 92.

The impeachment of Brazilian President Collor de Mello, 85.

The suspension of Peru's Constitution and the arrest of the Shining Path guerilla leader, 75.

Anti-crime crusaders killed in Italy, 75.

Peace efforts in Cambodia, 72.

Muslim rebels seize Afghanistan's capita, but factional violence erupts, 65.

12.9 **Labour**

12.9.1 *World Labour Report, 1992*

The retreat of the military in Latin America, the wave of multiparty democracy sweeping over Africa, and the collapse of the Communist Party in Eastern Europe and the former Soviet Union — all have opened up new opportunities for both workers and employers. But even democratic governments can only achieve so much, trade unionists still run risks in many countries-including Colombia, Brazil, El Salvador, the Philippines, China, Sudan and in Israel's occupied territories.

Many groups of workers have to survive with no trade union protection at all. And among the most vulnerable are child labourers. There are now hundreds of millions of working children in quarries, mines, carpet factories, brothels, and countless other dangerous places-often working 12 hour days for as little as seven dollars a week, constantly exposed to physical and moral hazards. Several million of these children are literally enslaved-bonded to their "owners" as a result of their parent's debts. Child labour is sometimes considered inevitable, a product of family deprivation that will persists as long as poverty itself.

Women, too, often work without the protection of trade unions. In the industrial market economies, unemployment has reached 7 per cent as the recession continues. In Eastern Europe, unemployment has started to rise as newly privatised enterprises are to shed excess labour; in the long term it could reach 15 to 20 per cent. In Africa the position is already grim with unemployment reaching 30 per cent for urban modern sector workers. Elsewhere there are greater grounds for optimism. Several Latin American countries may now have adjusted their economies sufficiently to embark on positive growth, and in East Asia the dynamic export-oriented economies continue to thrive.

Indeed some countries in East Asia are now short labour, and, are drawing in thousands of overseas migrant workers. Japan now has 1.46 vacancies for every job seeker, and similar problems are surfacing in Hong Kong, the Republic of Korea, Singapore and Taiwan, China. This is partly because birth rates are dropping, but also because school-leavers avoid "dirty, dangerous and difficult" work in factories or construction sites. The governments of these countries are reluctant to fill the gaps with migrant workers. So thousands of workers come illegally from Pakistan, the Philippines, Bangladesh, and other neighbouring countries. There are now 300,000 workers on the move each year in the Pacific Rim, half of them illegal.

Migration of workers will also be an increasingly significant issue in Western

Europe, particularly those from Eastern Europe and the former Soviet Union. Up to 20 million people could decide to move, attracted by wages eight or ten times those they could receive at home. Germany is their favourite destination: indeed millions of ethnic Germans in the former Soviet Union have the right to live and work in Germany. Such flows need to be planned and controlled if they are not to cause disruption and distress, but there is as yet no international agreement on how this could be achieved.

Many workers will be tempted to migrate because Eastern Europe and the former Soviet Union may be unable to provide adequate unemployment benefits or other form of social security. Most countries have made a start by setting minimum income levels and establishing the basis of unemployment benefit. But tight budgets limit their options, and payments may have to be quite low. Pensions, too, will be minimal. Indeed today's workers may need to contribute not only to their own pensions, but also to those of their parents and grandparents-a considerable act of intergenerational solidarity.

Solidarity in Poland has now been joined by Podkerpa in Bulgaria, Fratia in Romania, and the new "workers movements" in the former USSR. In developing countries, although governments have traditionally dominated labour relations they have relaxed their control in some countries particularly in Africa and Latin America.

Source: *The World Labour Report, 1992,* International Labour Organisation, reported in *UN Newsletter,* August 22, 1992.

12.10 **Latin American and the Caribbean Economy, 1992**

General Overview

In 1992 the economic situation in Latin America and the Caribbean was similar to that of 1991: economic expansion that exceeded population growth, together with lower inflation. However, there is now a wider divergence among the performances of the various economies. In this regard the performance of Brazil with an economy that has a very large weight in regional averages contrasts with that of most of the other countries in the region.

This year a growing number of countries progressed in consolidating their adjustment processes. However, the persistent sluggishness of world trade and the apparent slowdown of capital inflows in the second half of the year raise some questions that were not present when the year began.

Preliminary estimates indicate that the gross domestic product of the region as a whole grew by 2.4% (compared to 3.5% in 1991). Excluding Brazil, the output of the rest of the economies of Latin America and the Caribbean increased by 4.3% (compared to nearly 5% in 1991). Accordingly, if Brazil is excluded, regional per capita GDP rose by 0.5%, or nearly 2.3% in 1992.

At the same time, the pronounced downward trend in the rate of inflation continued: only five countries experienced significant increases compared to 1991, and only one (Brazil) had inflation of over three digits. On the other hand, many countries tended to approach inflation rates that were only slightly higher than the evolution in international prices.

In view of the international backdrop of widespread recession and uncertainty,this growth, which took place in a context of increasingly stable prices, was a considerable achievement. The sluggishness of world trade in 1992 was reflected in a steady worsening of the terms of trade in goods in almost all the countries, with Argentina being the sole exception. The Central American countries were particularly affected by this deterioration. On the other hand, a considerable number of countries notably Brazil, Chile, Costa Rica and Honduras expanded the volume of their exports.

The vigorous expansion of imports observed during the preceding year continued and in some cases even accelerated in 1992, stimulated by tariff liberalization and appreciation of local currencies. This induced a negative merchandise trade balance for the first time in many years. Hence the current-account deficit of the balance of payments also widened considerably.

What sustained this trend, and at the same time contributed to stabilization efforts, was a considerable net inflow of financial resources for the second year in a row; indeed, this inflow, amounting to over US$57 billion in 1992 was perhaps the most prominent feature of the regional economic picture over the past two years.

This inflow of capital was a result, *inter alia,* of widening differentials between the real interest rates offered in Latin American markets and those prevailing in the United States, and extraordinary rates of return derived from the economic recovery and privatization processes. Another contributing factor was the expectation of more stability of permanency regarding the economic policies prevailing in the region.

The net inflow of capital was used to finance imports, investments and speculative operations; it also helped to close fiscal gaps (through the acquisition of government bonds and privatized public enterprises), spurred a non-inflationary expansion of credit to the private sector (for both investment and consumption) and shored up the region's international reserves.

As noted above, this sudden easing of external constraints contributed to economic expansion, without undermining stabilization efforts. Net capital inflows more than offset the negative effects of the deterioration of the terms of trade. On the domestic front, these resources were quickly channelled to provide a stimulus to private-sector demand. In a few countries, however, capital inflows induced an appreciation of local currencies, and occasionally made monetary policy more difficult. Moreover, when short-term capital constituted a large proportion of these inflows, a potential element of volatility was introduced into the economic situation.

The appreciation of local currencies held down the prices of tradeable goods; however, this was generally not true to the same extent for the costs of private services. Increases in public service rates, associated with fiscal adjustment or privatization, also helped to raise the relative prices of non-tradeables. Overall, the changes in relative prices acted as an incentive to allocate resources towards non-tradeable goods and away from export-oriented sectors.

The drastic fiscal adjustments of the past three years were sustained, or even tightened, in most of the countries. Naturally, these policies have contributed to stabilization processes, both directly, through their effect on monetary expansion, and indirectly, by bolstering the confidence of private agents regarding the permanence of economic policy.

In most cases, the interest burden on fiscal budgets was stabilized, although in proportions that ranged from 1% to 4% of GDP, depending on the case. Contributing factors include negotiations to regularize external debt servicing; the decline in international interest rates; and the fiscal adjustment itself, which, in the context of monetary discipline, drastically relieved the need to resort to domestic indeptedness and restricted the possibilities of doing so.

In only a few countries, however, can the fiscal accounts be said to be structurally balanced. For this to be the case, current income must be solidly backed by a stable tax base, which in turn is consistent with a level of current spending that can support the normal functioning of government administration and the provision of basic social services. The tax base must also be able to support the public investment required to revamp and develop infrastructure necessary for economic growth and enhanced social equity.

All the above-described phenomena were backed by institutional reforms aimed at reinforcing export-oriented growth and trade liberalization, deregulation of the price system, consolidation of fiscal equilibria and more prudent management of monetary policy. In most countries, however, these reforms have not yet managed to recoup the losses derived from the accumulated social setbacks of earlier years.

The apparent slowdown in capital inflows at mid-year, coupled with a continued sluggish world economy, raised some concern towards year-end. This was manifested in the more cautious expectations of economic agents, in the behaviour of stock markets and in less degrees of freedom for the region's economic management which has the objective of sustaining growing rates of economic expansion over time in a context of progressive financial stability.

After long years of efforts to diversify their export structure, it is of cardinal importance for Latin America and the Caribbean that favourable external conditions now exist or for an ordered expansion of world trade, both with respect to macroeconomic management in the major developed economies and the institutional arrangements that will govern the exchange of goods and services. At the same time, intraregional trade should be encouraged under the reciprocal agreements that have been multiplying in recent years.

That the region has become a net importer of financial resources is without doubt a positive sign, and achievements in this area should be sustained and consolidated. It is necessary that external capital flows not only maintain continuity in terms of their global dimension, but also constitute stable financing of productive investment.

This in turn requires finding a more appropriate mix of funding, with increased participation of banking capital, more flows from multilateral agencies and an enhanced proportion of institutional portfolio investment, while at the same time attempting to avoid an excess build-up of short-term capital, which could become a source of volatility. On the part of the recipient countries, it is necessary to expand emerging domestic capital markets, and strengthen the regulatory framework of financial systems. A particularly important role must also be played by fiscal policy with regard to the maintenance of an appropriate and flexible balance: on the one hand, to prevent uncertainty in the minds of private agents about the stability of domestic policy, avoiding sudden pressures on the financial system and, on the other, to allow more degrees of freedom for monetary and exchange rate policy.

The Economic Environment

Preliminary ECLAC estimates indicate that the gross domestic product of the region as a whole increased by 2.4% in 1992, thus gradually continuating the recovery already in evidence the previous year, when output expanded by 3.5%. Meanwhile, per capita GDP registered a slight increase of 0.5%.

The moderate rise in the region's level of economic activity was strongly determined by the deepening recession in Brazil. Excluding Brazil, the output of the other economies of Latin America and the Caribbean, grew by 4.3%, compared to nearly 5% the previous year and about 3% in 1990.

A significant number of countries registered notable growth rates, although their economies are at different conjunctural stages. Chile's economic growth stands put at 9.5%, in its fourth year of expansions part of a long-term growth path and in its second year after a 1990 adjustment designed to quash incipient inflationary pressures. Five countries registered growth rates of between 6% and 8%: Argentina's economy has been recovering since 1991, under the influence of stabilization inflows of external capital; Panama, in its third year of growth, has emerged from the crisis of 1988-89; despite a tight fiscal policy, Uruguay has begun growing again after its virtual stagnation of recent years, thanks in part to the recovery of neighbouring Argentina; Venezuela is still expanding rapidly, fueled by a growing fiscal deficit; and the Dominican Republic's economy has begun a strong recovery.

Another group of countries grew at rates of between 3% and 5%, in most cases higher than those of 1991, either because their growth rates have revived (Colombia, Costa Rica, El Salvador and Guatemala), or because they have consolidated their recovery (Honduras and Guyana). Bolivia and Ecuador, however, recorded a slight slowdown in their earlier rate or expansion. Mexico's economy, where output rose by 2.5%, recorded a moderate but sustained deceleration of its growth rate.

Paraguay, where output increased by only 1.5%, continued a three-year relapse from its formerly vigorous growth pattern. Jamaica's growth rate also decelerated. Nicaragua, whose output increased slightly, and Peru, whose level of economic activity fell by 2.5%, continued to undergo deep recessions for the fifth year running, despite their notable achievements in price stabilization.

Brazil's output declined by 1.5%, after a modest, temporary recovery in 1991, thus prolonging the predominantly recessive pattern registered since 1988, in a context of persistently high inflation.

Haiti's chronic recession also worsened, with a drop of 5% in its GDP. For the third year in a row, Barbados recorded a 2.5% decline in its economic activity. In Cuba, the economic recession seriously depended as a result of the complete elimination of its formerly beneficial trade relations with the countries of eastern Europe and the former Soviet Union, compounded by the lightening of the United States' economic blockade.

Price stabilization advanced and strengthened in the greater part of the region. Only Brazil, Ecuador, El Salvador, Haiti, Paraguay and Trinidad and Tobago saw a significant upsurge in their inflation rates. Excepting Brazil whose inflation rate causes the region's weighted average rate to more than double, the increase in consumer prices in the remaining countries fell from 49% in 1991 to 22% in 1992. Further, for the first time in years, most of the countries had annual inflation rates of less than 20%.

High-inflation economies that only two years ago were caught up in hyperinflationary spirals became more stable. Following a rapid deflationary process, in 1992 Argentina and Nicaragua stabilized their annual rates of growth of consumer prices at less than 18% and 2%, respectively. Peru, which had also somewhat retreated from hyperinflation in 1991, managed to limit the rate of price rises to less than 60% per year, and Uruguay also reduced its high rate of inflation to less than 60%. The situation in Brazil stands in contrast to these advances: there, inflation soared to an annual rate of almost 1,200%.

A good number of countries with moderate inflation rates kept inflationary pressures down for the second year running. Bolivia reduced its annualized price variation from 15% in December 1991 to 11% in October; Costa Rica, from 25% to 18%; Chile and Mexico, from 19% to 14% and 13%, respectively, in November; Honduras, from 21% to slightly over 5% in October. The Dominican Republic also held its annual inflation rate down, to below 6%. Jamaica managed to reduce its annualized price variation from 77% to 14% in September.

Other countries, however, have run into stumbling-blocks in their efforts to hold down inflation. In Colombia, the inflation rate was only reduced from 27% to 26% in November. In Guatemala, it rose from 10% to 12% in October. Fiscal and exchange measures taken in Ecuador in the second half of the year pushed the annual inflation rate up from 49% to 66% in October. In Paraguay, inflation also took a turn for the worse, rising from 12% to 17% annually in November. The same occurred in El Salvador, from an annualized 10% to 17% in October. In Venezuela, the annual price increase rose from 31% to 33% in October, even though the updating of public service rates was slow in taking effect.

In brief, a large number of countries of the region are registering continued growth at least for the third year in a row with relative price stability and satisfactory degrees of utilization of their productive capacity. Of those that have been in this situation for a number of years, Chile continues to grow at a high rate, boosted by its export strategy. Colombia and Costa Rica, on the other hand, are recovering after a downturn in 1991, and Paraguay is still witnessing a slowdown in its formerly vigorous rate of expansion. Other countries, which completed their recovery more recently (such as Bolivia, El Salvador, Guatemala, Mexico and Panama), also recorded continued growth with relative price stability.

Meanwhile, Ecuador, Uruguay and Venezuela are just now achieving full utilization of their productive capacity, through more rapid rates of expansion, at least in the last two cases. However, although their stabilization trends differ, they have all been operating under the regimes of controlled price instability. Ecuador has put into effect a severe adjustment and stabilization programme in recent months; Uruguay has continued to reduce its high inflation rate significantly; Venezuela, on the other hand, still has a high inflation rate, together with a widening fiscal deficit.

The economies of Argentina and Honduras have also further consolidated their recovery, while the Dominican Republic has vigorously launched its own recovery programme. In the first two cases, the process of rapid stabilization resulted in a prolonged relative price stability. In the Dominican Republic, the stabilization process has recently been completed. Nicaragua and Peru have achieved relative price stability. However, for the fifth consecutive year, these two economies are suffering from a deep recession with sizeable margins of idle capacity.

For its part, Brazil has been in a recessionary situation for five years running (within which it has had temporary, brief recoveries in its level of economic activity) and it continues to operate in a regime of high-inflation.

The year 1992 saw a new, more wide-ranging expansion of Latin America and the Caribbean's import capacity. This was due to the rise in net capital inflows, since the region's increase in the value of exports was modest and neat payments of profits and interest were reduced only marginally. This situation, coupled with in many cases appreciating local currencies and an upholding or deepening of import liberalization, made it possible to continue the general boom in imports throughout the region.

Thus, the region's formerly ample trade surplus turned into a deficit. Furthermore, only a small number of countries among which Brazil stands out due to the sheer size of its surplus have maintained a positive merchandise trade balance. Brazil's exports to Argentina under prevailing free trade agreements has been a strong factor in the increase of the former's surplus.

The terms of trade of the region underwent a new decline in 1992, this time amounting to more than 3 per cent, thus accentuating the almost steady deterioration observed since 1984, which represents 22 per cent in cumulative terms. This year the downturn affected both oil-exporting and other countries. Accordingly, the purchasing power of the region's merchandise exports expanded by only 3 per cent, despite the significant increase in their volume.

The value of merchandise exports from Latin America and the Caribbean continued to climb slowly, this time by 4 per cent, reaching US$126 billion. The sluggish growth stemmed from the slump in unit values, since export volumes rose by 6 per cent. Even so only half the countries of the region managed to augment their exports at a higher rate than that of world trade in general.

The value of exports from oil-exporting countries contracted slightly, owing to the decline in unit values, which some countries of this group were able to partially offset by increasing volumes. However, the somewhat more abundant capital inflows maintained the oil-exporting countries' capacity to import and permitted reserve accumulation.

The non-oil-exporting countries of South America raised the value of their exports: those of Brazil and Chile increased considerably in value, by about 12 per cent. Combined with the upsurge in net capital inflows to Brazil, Argentina and, to a lesser extent, Chile, this rise in export values represented a considerable expansion of the group's import capacity. Of the Central American and Caribbean countries, Costa Rica, Guatemala and Honduras significantly expanded the value of their exports, despite the slight deterioration in unit values. Conversely, lower prices resulted in lower total values in the other countries of the group.

The value of Latin America and the Caribbean's merchandise imports rose to US$132 billion, again representing an increase of 18 per cent and prolonging a sharp expansion for the third year running. This growth was even more widespread than in 1991, although the variation in the regional total was strongly influenced by the import expansion of Mexico (US$8 billion), Argentina (US$5.7 billion), Venezuela (US$2.6 billion) and Chile (US$1.8 billion).

The merchandise trade balance, which had been positive by US$10 billion in 1991, turned into a deficit of nearly US$6 billion. At the same time, net nonfactor service payments continued to expand, rising to US$4.9 billion.

Net payments of profits and interest continued to diminish, this time to US$29.6 billion. This was mainly due to the decline in international interest rates, the effect of which was partly offset by higher remittances of profits.

The balance-of-payments deficit on current account widened once again in 1992, this time to nearly US$33 billion, owing to the deterioration of the trade balance.

The bigger current-account deficit was easily financed through the net flow of US$57 billion of capital into the region, which greatly surpassed the US$39 billion inflow in 1991. Although the increase in capital inflows was fairly widespread, the net rise (of US$18 billion) in the regional total was accounted for by only a few countries. The first of these was Brazil, which registered US$10 billion in net capital inflows, compared to only a little more than US$11 billion the year before. Argentine also experienced a sizeable increase (US$4 billion) in the net inflow of capital, which totalled US$9.3 billion in 1992. Capital inflows into Mexico exceeded US$23 billion, or US$1.18 billion more than in 1991. The increase in Venezuela (US$1.5 billion) and Chile (US$1.3 billion) accounted for a good proportion of the additional capital flows into the region.

Capital entering the region in 1992 was still essentially from private, non-banking sources and consisted of various types of investments. The most import flows consisted of financial placements and short-term credits. The acquisition of stocks also represented a large proportion, mainly Argentina, Brazil and Venezuela as well. Foreign direct investment increased considerably, mainly in Mexico and, to a lesser extent, in Brazil, Argentina, Chile and Venezuela. These countries also placed abroad large amounts of either government or private sector bonds.

As the net capital inflow was far greater than the current-account deficit, the international reserves of most countries of the region continued to increase for the fourth year in a row. However, more than half the rise in the regional aggregate total corresponds to Brazil, whose reserves expanded by more than US$16 billion.

The greater amount of net capital flows, under circumstances where payments of profits and interest were on the decline, meant that the net transfer of financial resources to the region rose from US$8 billion to US$27 billion, a figure that had just become positive after a decade of negative balances in 1991. Most of this expansion was due to the fact that in 1992 Brazil, Argentina and Chile converted their formerly negative net transfers to largely positive ones.

The region's external debt registered an increase of 2 per cent, climbing to over US$450 billion. This expansion was partly due to new bond placements abroad, disbursements of official loans, an increase in short-term credit operations and an accumulation of arrears in some countries. Other factors, however, helped to shrink the debt, such as the recent recovery of the dollar against other currencies, which reduced the dollar value of the debt denominated in these other currencies, and the various debt-reduction mechanisms used in many countries of the region.

The greater amount of net capital flows, under circumstances where payments of profits and interest were on the decline, meant that the net transfer of financial resources to the region rose from US$8 billion to US$27 billion, a figure that had just become positive after a decade of negative balances in 1991. Most of this expansion was due to the fact that in 1992 Brazil, Argentina, and Chile converted their formerly negative net transfers to largely positive ones.

The region's external debt registered an increase of 2 per cent, climbing to over US$450 billion. This expansion was partly due to new bond placements abroad, disbursements of official loans, an increase in short-term credit operations and an accumulation of arrears in some countries. Other factors, however, helped to shrink the debt, such as the recent recovery of the dollar against other currencies, which reduced the dollar value of the debt denominated in these other currencies, and the various debt-reduction mechanisms used in many countries of the region.

In 1992 the indicators of the region's external debt burden continued to abate, strengthening the downward trend observed in recent years. The coefficient representing interest owed as a percentage of exports dropped for the sixth year of exports dropped for the sixth year running, this time to 20 per cent, the lowest figure since 1980. This decline was mainly due to the reduction of gross interest payments. For the region as a whole, the debt-export ratio decreased slightly, to below 290 per cent, owing to the improvement of this ratio in the non-oil-exporting countries. None the less, in 1992 only five countries had a coefficient lower than the critical threshold of 200 per cent.

Economic Activity

The level of activity in Latin America and the Caribbean grew by 2.4 per cent in 1992. Thus the recovery which had begun last year when growth was 3.5 per cent continued, albeit at a slower pace. Per capita output in 1992 again posted a slight positive increase (0.5%). Nevertheless, regional output was only 19 per cent higher than it had been in 1980, before the debt crisis erupted, while per capita output was 7 per cent below what it had been in 1980 and equivalent to a level already recorded in 1978.

The slow growth in regional output has been caused largely by the worsening recession in Brazil. Excluding Brazil, the increase in the output of the other countries was 4.3 per cent, somewhat less than this same group of countries had registered in 1991 (5%), but otherwise the highest figure since 1981.

The growth in output was a fairly general phenomenon, although there were wide divergences. In Chile, the increase was 9.5 per cent, the second highest in the past two decades, continuing its steady expansion for the ninth consecutive year, and outstripping the 1980 level by more than 50 per cent. In Argentina, the Dominican Republic, Panama, Uruguay and Venezuela, the level of activity was up between 6 per cent and 8 per cent. Also, in four countries, Costa Rica, El Salvador, Guatemala and Honduras output grew between 4 per cent and 5 per cent; in five Bolivia, Colombia, Ecuador, Guyana and Mexico it grew around 3 per cent; in three others the Bahamas, Jamaica and Paraguay between 1 per and 2 per cent. In three Nicaragua, Trinidad and Tobago and Suriname it remained unchanged and in four Barbados, Brazil, Haiti and Peru it fell. Eight countries fared better than they had in 1991, while in seven others, the growth rate remained as its 1991 level or rose somewhat more slowly; in nine others, the level of activity deteriorated or remained modest. In turn, the smaller countries of the Organization of Eastern Caribbean States (OECS) maintained their growth rate of previous years, posting an average increase of around 4 per cent, which was higher than the 1991 rate.

Despite the high rates of population growth in many countries in the region, the results in terms of per capita output were mainly positive. In six countries Argentina, Chile, the Dominican Republic, Panama, Uruguay and Venezuela this indicator of well-being went up by more than 3 per cent, while in eight others, the increase was moderate, between 1 per cent and 3 per cent.

Meanwhile, in the other 11 countries, per capita output increased slightly or fell. However, considering the poor performance of the region's economies in the past decade, per capita output was higher than the 1980 figure in only a few countries: Chile (25%), Colombia (20%), Bahamas (17%), Jamaica (7%), Uruguay (3%) and the whole group of OECS countries (72%). At the other extreme, the most severe reductions in per capita output occurred in Nicaragua (-39%), Peru (-32%), Trinidad and Tobago (-30%), Haiti (-28%), Guyana (-23%), Bolivia (-21%), Suriname, (-19%), Guatemala (-17%), Argentina (-11%) and El Salvador and Honduras (-10%).

There were few changes of any significance in unemployment rates compared to previous years, as most economies of the region experienced moderate growth. The drop in unemployment was noteworthy only in those economies where the level of activity had increased sharply, such as Chile, Panama and Venezuela. In Argentina and Uruguay, on the other hand, the jobless rate rose slightly, despite the significant increase in the level of activity. In Colombia, the unemployment rate rose by one half of a percentage point, moving to 10.5 per cent, Brazil also registered higher unemployment, for the third consecutive year, owing too the acute recession in which it has been trapped for several years.

Chile again posted a high rate of growth (9.5%), a sign that it is passing through an unprecedented period. Per capita output was thus 25 per cent higher than it had been in 1980. The vigorous expansion of 1992 was based on a 20 per cent increase in investment, a 15 per cent increase in the physical volume of exports, and a more rapid rise in consumption. The increase in expenditure occurred mainly in the private sector; whereas public expenditure rose by 5 per cent in the first half of the year, the increase in private expenditure was 14 per cent. With the acceleration of growth in the third quarter, this difference between the expansion of the public and private sectors was even more marked. The growth was attributable chiefly to the structural improvement in the balance-of-payments position. The situation in Chile was characterized by a large trade surplus, steadily rising foreign investment, a virtual return to the voluntary external credit market, net reserves equal to more than one year's imports, the maintenance of fiscal discipline and a marked decline in the relative external debt burden. This spectacular expansion, however, aroused concern about a possible overheating of the economy and growing difficulties in further developing the export strategy. In order to avoid overexpansion of domestic demand, interest rates on Central Bank financial instruments were increased three times during the year. The dynamic economic situation was also reflected itself in higher employment and a drop in open unemployment of more than two percentage points to 5 per cent, the lowest level in more than a decade.

In **Venezuela**, the rapid recovery of the level of activity continued following the 1989 recession. In fact, output rose slightly more than 8 per cent, lagging somewhat behind the 1991 figure, but still extremely high compared to past averages. This expansion was confined solely to private activities, for the petroleum sector declined by nearly 2 per cent and the public sector register modest growth. Particularly noteworthy was the boom in the trade sector, which climbed by 24 per cent, more than twice as much as it had in 1991, stimulated by increased domestic demand and by imports as a result of an appreciating local currency and trade liberalization. Construction, for its part, continued to expand significantly (18%), eventhough it trailed in 1991 rate of 31 per cent. In

1992, the sector owed its dynamism much more to the implementation of private projects than to the petroleum industry, which had been responsible for the sharp increase in 1991. The manufacturing industry also grew significantly (10%), despite the adverse effect of the foreign exchange policy. The agricultural sector continued its recovery (3.5%) begun in 1991. In response to the partial elimination of subsidies and price controls. The output of the petroleum sector declined when the international hydrocarbons market returned to normalcy after the gulf conflict and OPEC production quotas were lowered as a result. The urban unemployment rate went down from 9.6 per cent in 1991 to 7.7 per cent in the third quarter of 1992 as a result of significant growth, particularly in construction.

In **Uruguay**, gross domestic product rose by 7 per cent in 1992, the highest rate in the past five years. This lifted per capita output to an all-time high, even slightly higher than the figure for the 1980-81 biennium, mainly as a result of the demand in Argentina and the value-added earned on a huge import volume. The electricity, gas and water sector rose by 25 per cent because of increased domestic demand and, in particular, because of substantially higher sales to Argentina. business activity in the commerce, restaurants and hotels sector rose by 16 per cent, owing essentially to the selling, by middlemen, of imported goods and to tourist flows, mainly from Argentina. The agricultural sector increased its output by 9 per cent as a result of the recovery of crops from the poor weather conditions of 1991, increased cattle-raising activity and the replenishment of livestock. The other goods-producing sectors also expanded, with the sole exception of fisheries, at rates that ranged from slightly more than 2 per cent in the manufacturing industry to slightly less than 6 per cent in construction. In other services, the increase was almost 7 per cent. Despite this significant growth, the urban unemployment rate crept up, hitting 9.3 per cent.

The level of activity in **Argentina** again bounced back (6%), in a macroeconomic context that was clearly more stable than it had been in the recent past. Thus, the level of the gross domestic product was higher than it had been before the crisis of the early 1980s. Domestic demand continued to be way up, among both consumers and investors, although investment was still nowhere near its record highs. The counterpart of this increased demand was a surge in imports and a sharp increase in domestic output as well. With the exception of certain activities, such as iron and steel, which are more dependent than others on external markets, the manufacturing industry expanded considerably more than 10 per cent. This was very obvious, for example, in certain metal manufacturers sectors. In taking the average for the year, however, the effects of macroeconomic normalcy and the expansion of credit which had sparked the intense recovery seemed to lose momentum. There were signs that the growth of domestic expenditure was reaching its limit, while exports were weak, and this somewhat moderated the demand for industrial products. In any case, an overview of the whole year indicates that output stretched to meet the greater demand for manufactured goods, with only slightly higher prices. The increase in activity apparently gave rise to an increase in employment, but since the labour supply increased as well, the unemployment rate topped that of the previous year.

In 1992, growth slowed down in **Mexico** (2.5%). Although investment remained high, it was not sufficient to offset the disincentives of lower external demand, a progressively restrictive monetary policy and the intense adjustment process of the productive apparatus linked to trade liberalization. Compounding the problem were adverse weather conditions, which were responsible for the poor performance in the agricultural sector. For the fourth consecutive year, growth in output outstripped population growth. there was a major expansion of construction (8%) and of electricity, gas and water services (4%). In manufacturing activity, on the other hand, external and domestic demand fell and imports crowded out national production, compressing the rate of growth to slightly more than 2 per cent, down from nearly 4 per cent in 1991. The growth rate in services, in turn, decreased with the exception of transport, storage and communications. There were also severe job cutbacks in the manufacturing industry. On the other hand, the number of persons employed in construction, commercial activities, especially in the larger firms and the inbond assembly industry increased. Also, until September, the number of permanently employed workers contributing to the Mexican Social Security System had risen by 2.8 per cent, compared to a 7.3 per cent increase over the same period in 1991. On the other hand, employment in the informal sector of the economy continued to rise.

In **Colombia**, output grew by 3 per cent, one point higher than the year before, despite the effects of poor weather conditions in the first part of the year. The healthiest sectors were mining, which increased by more than 11 per cent, construction (10%) with housing well in the lead, and coffee threshing, which grew by 15 per cent. The growth rate was low less than 2 per cent elsewhere in the manufacturing industry. The performance of the agricultural sector was also poor because of the severe drought caused by "El Niño"; its growth was on the order of 1 per cent, whereas the average of the preceding three years had been higher than 5 per cent. The drought not only reduced harvests, but also substantially depleted the water supply in reservoirs, which made strict electrical power rationing necessary throughout the country. Services, for their part, expanded moderately, at a slower rate than total output. Domestic demand grew by 4 per cent but it was partly diverted towards imports, which grew by 20 per cent, while the volume of exports declined slightly. Private investment rose dramatically (8%), while public investment grew by over 5 per cent. Urban unemployment increased moderately, moving up to 10.5 per cent.

The gross domestic product of **Ecuador** continued to rise in 1992 (3.5%), somewhat less than its 1991 level. The main impetus came from the petroleum sector and consumption, and the rapid increase in private investment. Public-sector capital expenditure, for its part, remained unchanged, as a result of the adjustment policies implemented when the new Government took office in August. Oil drilling increased by 5.5 per cent with the exploitation of new oil-fields. As a result of this expansion, Ecuador exceeded the OPEC quota, which was doubtless one of the main reasons for its withdrawal from that organization. The agricultural, forestry, hunting and fishing sector grew by slightly more than 6 per cent overall, similar to the previous year's increase, though growth was uneven within the different subsectors. In 1992, the production of bananas, coffee and cocoa, which had been the strong players in recent years fell significantly. Fishing again showed a noteworthy rise (12%), although not as much as it had the year before. On the other hand, the increase in output was greater in sectors producing for the domestic market. The manufacturing industry continued the recovery it had begun in 1991, with growth in the vicinity of 5 per cent. Construction edged up (less than 1%) after a two-year recession. Meanwhile, the electricity, gas and water sector went down by 7 per cent, owing to weather problems at the beginning of the year.

In **Bolivia**, the growth rate (3.5%) fell only slightly and per capita output increased for the sixth consecutive year. Greater domestic demand gave rise to an expansion of activity, both because of greater consumption and the momentum gained by investment, which soared to an unprecedented rate of 24 per cent of GDP, reflecting an expansion in both public and private investment. Private investment was channelled essentially into mining and the hydrocarbons sector. There was a 5 per cent increase in industrial production, stimulated by the drop in interest rates and increased consumption. Both the mining and construction sectors rose by nearly 4 per cent. Agriculture, meanwhile, remained unchanged.

In **Paraguay**, the level of activity slowed down in 1992 for the fourth consecutive year (1.5%), and, as a result, per capita output, which had already fallen in 1991, remained on the decline. This poor performance was caused chiefly by the drop of more than 7 per cent in agricultural production, affected by the lack of rainfall at the beginning of the year and flooding in May, not to mention the lack of credit and the depressed international prices of the main export items. Harvests of the main crops were smaller: cotton (-47%), soybeans (-15%), tobacco (-32%), beans (-7%) and rice (-5%). In turn, sugarcane and cassava production held steady, while maize production increased by 9 per cent. This decline in the agricultural subsector was partly offset by higher fishery and forestry production. Industrial output grew by somewhat less than 1 per cent, while the rate of construction activity increased (3.5%), spurred by the continuation of low-income housing projects, some infrastructure works in the public sector and the construction of private homes. The services sectors, for their part, registered overall growth of nearly 2 per cent.

The economy of **Brazil** remained in a recession, with a dip of 1.5% in the level of activity amid stubborn inflation at a monthly rate of over 20% and major political changes throughout the second half of the year. Thus, per capita output fell by 3%, down 9% from its 1980 level. After a year of extreme sluggishness in 1990 and a modest, temporary upsurge in 1991, the level of activity again began to grow in the first half of 1992, bolstered by abundant harvests and the boom in the export of manufactured goods. In the second half of year, the upward trend petered out and Brazil entered another period of recession, the fourth in less than three years, largely as a consequence of the political crisis that broke out in June. The vigour of domestic demand in the first half of the year began to flag in September. It had been stimulated by the continued increase in liquidity resulting from the monthly release of frozen financial assets. When the release of assets stopped in August, so did the stimulus, and recessionary trends resurfaced, these, in turn, were aggravated by high real interest rates and the curb on external capital inflows. The manufacturing industry took a plunge (6%) owing to the sharp decline in domestic demand, which could be only partly offset by the 19% rise in the export of manufactured goods. There was also a steep decline in construction, following a turn for the worse in investment. The commerce sector followed suit, going down by 5%. The agricultural sector, on the other hand, registered an increase of 6%, as a result of the bountiful harvests in the first month of the year. The recession chiefly affected the urban sector, where the unemployment rate rose by more than a percentage point to nearly 6% of the workforce. Similarly, formal urban employment virtually held steady. In industries activity, companies reacted to the recession by cutting back so many jobs that in the State of Sao Paulo, the employment figure in October 1992 was not even 90% of what it had been in 1978.

In **Peru,** after a timid rebound in 1991, the gross domestic product again dipped (-2.5%), completing five years of severe economic recession five years of severe economic recession and representing an accumulated decline of 24% in the level of activity. Production was again hurt by tighter credit, and, beyond that, by bankruptcies in the financial system and inordinately high interest rates. Moreover, the climatic phenomenon known as "El Niño" decreased the anchovy catch and caused a drought that seriously affected agriculture and the generation of electrical power; this, in turn, affected manufacturing output. Mining, for its part, posted a decline on the order of 2 per cent

The members of the Central American Common Market registered overall growth of nearly 4%, the largest increase since the crisis of the early 1980s. Furthermore, the expansion was fairly evenly distributed, for, with the exception of Nicaragua, which remained in a deep recession, the other countries posted growth rates of around 4 per cent. **Costa Rica** registered growth of 4%, compared to a modest increment the year before, because of the turnaround in industrial activity, a very dynamic services sector and the significant expansion of the external sector. The most active areas were the service related sectors such as trade, transport, storage, communications and finance. Manufacturing, after a somewhat sluggish phase in 1991, rebounded considerably (5%). Construction, however, continued to decline, as it had in 1990 and 1991. Agricultural production rose by only 2%, compared to a nearly 6% the year before, largely as a result of the drop in international coffee prices and lower production of basic rains for domestic consumption. Banana production, for its part, continued its upward trend of recent years, owing to the yield from new plantations and the fact that international prices were still relatively high. Fishing declined, mainly because of the drought in various parts of the country.

In **El Salvador,** the increase in gross domestic product was fairly high (4.5%), although some momentum was lost at the close of the first half of the year because of serious problems with electrical power supply. Investment was the most dynamic area of aggregate demand; private investment was channelled into construction, particularly the expansion of large business. Public investment, for its part, posted a very healthy increase (40%), as a result of larger infrastructure works in social services and the restoration of electrical power generation capacity. Private consumption benefited in part from the consolidation of the economic recovery and more remittances from Salvadorans who had emigrated to other countries. In a comparative performance of what had taken place in the previous year, construction was the most dynamic sector, while the agricultural sector recovered from a poor season the year before and the manufacturing industry managed to sustain the growth rate begun in the second half of 1991. A shortage of water in the country's hydroelectric dams brought electricity production way down in the second quarter, making it necessary to reinstate a rationing programme; later, however, the situation improved markedly.

The gross domestic product of **Guatemala** rose by more than 4%, the highest rate in the past seven years, and per capita GDP again increased for the sixth straight year. Once again, investment was the most vigorous component of aggregate demand, reaching 9% as a result of private investment, in as much as the increase in public investment was moderates. The rise in consumption was the highest in the past four years, driven by the increase in both public-sector and private-sector wages. For the second consecutive year, construction registered the greatest expansion. The increase in agricultural output went down to slightly less than 3%, owing in part to the drop in the prices of export/commodities and the delayed effect of last year's drought on basic grain production. Industrial output posted a growth rate of nearly 3%, higher than the figure for 1991, as result of the recovery of real wages, the decrease in the interest rate and the dynamic growth of exports to the Central American Common Market. The inbond assembly industry, which had been a major source of foreign currency and jobs, in the past five years, remained unchanged.

Growth in output in **Honduras** (4.5%) was more than two percentage points higher than it had been the year before, and per capita GDP improved by more than 1%. The driving force behind demand was exports, whose volume swelled by 20%. Domestic demand, by contrast, after recovering in 1991, registered a slower rate of growth, for while consumption had increased, its effects was cancelled out by the sluggishness of private investment. Public investment, for its part, again increase (18%), albeit at a slower rate than in 1991. In a sectoral breakdown of output, most branches of activity demonstrated positive growth, and construction soared. Only public administration, defence and social, community and personal services continued their downward trend of the past two years. Meanwhile the agricultural sector, slowed down; although all its subsectors advanced, they did so more gradually than in 1991. Even forestry, after many years of decline, managed to reverse that trend.

The gross domestic product of **Nicaragua** rose by only 0.5%, which further pushed down per capita output by more than 3%. This means that there have been nine years of uninterrupted decline in per capita GDP, by a cumulative total of 43%. Plummeting export prices, the particularly difficult cotton situation, the series of natural disasters, outside events that had nothing to do with the economy, and the priority accorded to fiscal discipline as a key element in price stability brought on an economic slump. The agricultural sector rebounded, despite a series of setbacks, particularly in cotton, as a result of higher yields in maize, beans, rice, beef and poultry breeding, while fishing declined following the tidal wave. The manufacturing industry declined by nearly 2% after experiencing exceptional growth in 1991. Electrical power generation, on the other hand, rebounded, especially thermal energy, which minimized disruptions in service. Construction was also very vigorous (13%), owing to maintenance programmes, reconstruction projects and efforts to bring down a tremendous housing deficit. Sluggish economic activity pushed up open unemployment, from 14% to over 16%.

In **Panama,** gross domestic product rose by 7.5%, slightly trailing the rate for the previous year. The most dynamic sector continued to be construction, which, after doubling its volume in 1991, grew at a rate of over 30%. Services, the mainstay of the Panamanian economy, showed an overall trend towards recovering their levels of activity prior to the crisis of the late 1980s. Commerce in general, and in the Free Trade Zone in particular, increased as a result of bank intermediation. The Panamanian banking system was more dynamic than the international banking system in a climate of renewed competition for deposits among the various financial institutions. The manufacturing industry slightly outpaced total GDP, but there were vast discrepancies in the performance of different branches, while the agricultural sector expanded more slowly. Unemployment decreased from 20% to 18%, especially as a result of the creation of many temporary construction jobs.

In the Caribbean countries, overall performance was rather dismal. The **Dominican Republic** was an exception. There, after two years, of decline in gross domestic product, it recovered significantly (7.5%), stimulated by higher domestic demand and the export of services. Public investment grew more rapidly than private investment, while private consumption rose more quickly than government consumption. This turnaround was facilitated by a more stable macroeconomic environment, which included exchange rate stability and control of the inflationary process. Mining was the only sector in which the level of activity was lower, continuing the decline of the preceding four-year period, partly as a result of the drop in iron-nickel production in reaction to lower international prices, and partly because of the lower levels of gold and silver mining. Construction, on the other hand was a more energetic sector, principally because of increased public investment in installations preparatory to the Quincentennial. The agricultural sector expanded more rapidly, while the manufacturing industry posted a sharp increase after its poor performance in the preceding biennium, although its main activity, the sugar industry, suffered a a deep slump.

In 1992, the economic crisis in **Cuba** worsened in the wake of a renewed economic blockade by the Government of the United States and the discontinuation of its advantageous trade relations with the eastern European countries, and especially with the former Soviet Union. There was a further decline in output and in the import of goods and services. Import capacity, decreased by 73% compared to 1989, and was reflected in the scarcity of raw materials, equipment, spare parts, capital goods, and foodstuffs, but, above all, energy products. This in turn caused aggregate supply to plunge. Both domestic demand and the demand for exported goods and services decreased. Gross fixed investment also went down, despite active investments in the tourism industry. A major stride was also made in foreign investment, with the formation of nearly 80 joint ventures, mainly in tourist-related activities, basic industries, iron and steel manufactures, construction materials and agriculture.

In **Haiti,** the trade embargo declared by the Organization of American States (OAS), following the collapse of the constitutional Government and the cutoff of generally highly concessional external financing, had a severe negative impact on the level of activity, which decreased by 5%. Hardest hit was the in-bond assembly industry, which, in normal times, is a source of between 40,000 and 50,000 jobs and of nearly 50% of Haiti's total exports. The slowdown in this activity caused a loss of around 25,000 jobs in 1992. The partial incapacitation of imports also affected industries producing for the domestic market.

Source: *CEPAL Notas Sobre la Economia Y El Desarrollo*, no. 537/538, December 1992.

TABLE 12.3: Latin America and the Caribbean : Main Economic Indicators[a]

Indicators	1985	1986	1987	1988	1989	1990	1991	1992[b]
1	2	3	4	5	6	7	8	9
Gross domestic product at market prices (index, base year 1980=100)	102.6	106.4	109.9	110.8	111.7	112.0	116.0	118.8

Contd.

1	2	3	4	5	6	7	8	9
Population (millions of inhabitants)	385.2	393.3	401.4	409.5	417.6	425.7	433.7	442.0
Per capita gross domestic product (index, base year 1980=100)	91.8	93.3	94.4	93.3	92.3	90.8	92.2	92.7
Growth rates								
Gross domestic product	2.8	3.7	3.3	0.8	0.9	0.3	3.5	2.4
Per capita gross domestic product	0.6	1.6	1.2	-1.2	-1.1	-1.6	1.6	0.5
Consumer prices[c]	280.1	64.1	208.9	773.5	1205.0	1185.0	198.7	410.7
Terms of trade (goods)	-4.5	-11.0	-0.9	-0.3	1.3	-0.4	-5.6	-3.4
Purchasing power of exports of goods	-4.6	-11.9	7.8	8.1	4.5	5.3	-1.0	3.0
Current value of exports of goods	-5.8	-15.8	14.4	13.9	10.0	9.6	-0.4	4.0
Current value of imports of goods	0.0	2.6	12.5	14.0	6.5	15.7	18.1	18.4
Billion of dollars								
Exports of goods	92.0	77.5	88.7	101.0	111.1	121.8	121.3	126.1
Imports of goods	58.2	59.7	67.2	76.6	81.6	94.4	111.5	132.0
Trade balance (goods)	33.8	17.8	21.5	24.4	29.5	27.4	9.8	-5.9
Net payments of profits and interest	35.3	32.6	31.5	34.3	37.9	34.7	30.9	29.6
Balance on current account[d]	-3.6	-17.4	-11.1	-11.2	-6.8	-6.2	-19.4	-32.7
Net movement of capital[e]	3.0	9.9	15.4	5.5	9.6	20.3	39.2	57.0
Global balance[f]	-0.6	-7.5	4.3	5.7	2.8	14.1	19.8	24.3
Total gross external debt[g]	385.1	401.0	428.1	420.9	425.4	440.9	442.6	450.9
Net transfer of resources[h]	-32.2	-22.6	-16.1	-28.7	-28.0	-14.4	8.4	27.4

Source: ECLAC, on the basis of official figures.

a The data on the external sector correspond to the 19 countries listed in the table on the balance of payments of Latin America and the Caribbean.

b Preliminary estimates, subject to revision.

c Variation from December to December.

d Includes net unrequited private transfer payments.

e Includes long-and short-term capital, unrequited official transfer payments, and errors and omissions.

f Corresponds to the variation in international reserves (of opposite sign) plus counterpart items.

g See the notes to the table "Latin America and the Caribbean: total disbursed external debt".

h Corresponds to net inflow of capital, less net payments of profits and interest.

TABLE 12.4: Latin America and the Caribbean : Growth of Total Gross Domestic Product
(Percentages based on values at 1980 prices)

	Average annual rates								Cumulative variation
	1985	1986	1987	1988	1989	1990	1991	1992[a]	1981-1992[a]
1	2	3	4	5	6	7	8	9	10
Latin America and the Caribbean[b]	**2.8**	**3.7**	**3.3**	**0.8**	**0.9**	**0.3**	**3.5**	**2.4**	**18.8**
Oil-exporting countries	**2.1**	**0.3**	**2.7**	**2.0**	**0.1**	**4.0**	**4.5**	**3.4**	**24.1**
Bolivia	-1.0	-2.5	2.6	3.0	2.8	2.6	4.1	3.5	6.4
Colombia	3.8	6.9	5.6	4.2	3.5	3.7	2.2	3.0	51.1
Ecuador	3.9	2.8	-4.8	8.8	0.2	1.4	4.2	3.5	29.0
Mexico	2.6	-3.8	1.7	1.2	3.3	4.4	3.6	2.5	25.1
Peru	2.3	8.7	8.0	-8.4	-11.5	-5.1	1.9	-2.5	-11.4
Trinidad and Tobago	-4.3	-2.2	-4.6	-3.3	-0.5	2.2	1.8	0.0	-18.2
Venezuela	0.0	6.6	3.8	5.9	-7.8	6.8	10.2	7.5	23.2
Non-oil-exporting countries[b]	**3.3**	**6.3**	**3.7**	**0.0**	**1.4**	**-2.4**	**2.8**	**1.6**	**15.0**
South America	**3.6**	**6.7**	**3.7**	**0.0**	**1.2**	**-2.6**	**2.9**	**1.5**	**14.4**
Argentina	-5.1	5.2	3.1	-1.8	-6.3	0.2	7.3	6.0	4.1
Brazil	7.9	7.6	3.6	-0.1	3.3	-4.4	0.9	-1.5	15.2
Chile	2.2	5.7	5.7	7.5	9.8	2.0	5.8	9.5	53.0
Guyana	1.1	0.3	0.8	-2.6	-4.9	3.0	6.0	3.0	-18.4
Paraguay	4.0	-0.3	4.5	6.7	5.9	3.1	2.3	1.5	41.8
Suriname	2.0	0.8	-6.2	8.2	4.2	-1.7	-2.5	0.0	0.8
Uruguay	1.7	8.3	7.9	-0.2	1.5	0.7	1.6	7.0	10.2

Contd.

TABLE 12.4 *Contd.*

1	2	3	4	5	6	7	8	9	10
Central America and the Caribbean[b]	**0.5**	**2.2**	**4.4**	**0.0**	**3.3**	**0.9**	**1.4**	**2.5**	**20.9**
Bahamas	13.5	3.6	4.9	2.3	2.0	1.0	-2.0	1.0	46.9
Barbados	0.9	5.2	2.6	3.5	3.6	-3.3	-3.3	-2.5	2.8
Belize	0.3	4.5	12.9	10.0	14.2	7.6	4.8	...	...
Cuba[c]	4.6	1.2	-3.9	2.2	1.1	...	...	...	...
Haiti	0.4	0.0	-0.7	0.9	1.0	-0.2	-0.3	-5.0	-8.9
Jamaica	-5.4	2.2	6.7	1.1	6.3	3.8	1.9	1.5	23.4
Panama	4.8	3.4	2.2	-15.9	-0.2	5.2	9.1	7.5	24.7
Dominican Republic	-1.9	3.0	8.4	1.5	4.1	-5.5	-1.0	7.5	29.3
Central American Common Market		**0.1**	**1.4**	**3.3**	**1.8**	**3.32.3**	**2.3**	**3.9**	**16.8**
Costa Rica	0.7	5.3	4.5	3.2	5.4	3.5	1.2	4.0	31.7
El Salvador	1.8	0.5	2.7	1.5	1.1	3.4	3.3	4.5	6.9
Guatemala	-0.6	0.3	3.6	4.0	3.7	2.9	3.2	4.0	17.0
Honduras	2.8	2.3	4.9	4.9	4.7	-0.5	2.2	4.5	33.8
Nicaragua	-4.1	-1.0	-0.7	-12.1	-1.9	-0.7	-0.5	0.5	-13.4
OECS countries[d]	**7.1**	**6.5**	**5.0**	**8.1**	**5.0**	**4.9**	**3.1**	**4.2**	**78.0**
Antigua and Barbuda	8.7	9.7	9.1	7.7	5.2	2.7	...	...	...
Dominica	1.6	6.8	6.8	8.0	-1.2	6.6	2.1	2.0	61.4
Grenada	5.0	5.4	6.0	5.3	5.7	5.3	3.1	0.5	63.5
Saint Kitts and Nevis	5.7	6.1	7.4	9.8	6.7	3.1	6.8	...	...
Saint Lucia	9.1	5.0	0.5	9.2	5.4	5.6	1.8	...	...
Saint Vincent and the Grenadines	7.1	5.9	5.7	7.4	7.1	7.0	4.6	10.0	113.0

Source: ECLAC, on the Basis of Official Figures.

[a] Preliminary estimates, subject to revision.

[b] Does not include Cuba.

[c] Refers to total social product.

[d] OECS = Organization of Eastern Caribbean States.

TABLE 12.5: Latin America and the Caribbean : Growth of Per Capita Gross Domestic Product
(Percentages based on values at 1980 prices)

	Average annual rates								Cumulative variation
	1985	1986	1987	1988	1989	1990	1991	1992[a]	1981-1992[a]
1	2	3	4	5	6	7	8	9	10
Latin America and the Caribbean[b]	**0.6**	**1.6**	**1.2**	**-1.2**	**-1.1**	**-1.6**	**1.6**	**0.5**	**-7.3**
Oil-exporting countries	**-0.2**	**-2.0**	**0.4**	**-0.2**	**-2.0**	**1.9**	**2.4**	**1.3**	**-5.2**
Bolivia	-3.4	-4.9	0.1	0.5	0.4	0.2	1.7	1.1	-21.1
Colombia	1.7	4.9	3.7	2.3	1.7	1.9	0.5	1.4	19.9
Ecuador	1.2	0.2	-7.2	6.1	-2.3	-1.0	1.7	1.1	-5.2
Mexico	0.2	-5.9	-0.5	-1.0	1.0	2.2	1.4	0.6	-4.8
Peru	0.0	6.4	5.8	-10.3	-13.3	-7.0	-0.1	-4.5	-31.8
Trinidad and Tobago	-5.6	-3.5	-5.9	-4.5	-1.8	1.0	0.6	-1.2	-30.0
Venezuela	-2.5	4.0	1.3	3.4	-9.9	4.4	7.8	5.0	-8.3
Non-oil-exporting countries[b]	**1.3**	**4.3**	**1.7**	**-1.8**	**-0.4**	**-4.1**	**1.0**	**0.0**	**-9.0**
South America	**1.6**	**4.7**	**1.8**	**-1.7**	**-0.5**	**-4.3**	**1.3**	**-0.1**	**-8.4**
Argentina	-6.4	3.8	1.8	-3.0	-7.5	-1.0	6.0	4.8	-11.2
Brazil	5.7	5.5	1.6	-2.0	1.4	-6.1	-0.8	-3.1	-9.3
Chile	0.5	4.0	3.9	5.7	8.0	0.3	4.1	7.8	25.4
Guyana	0.5	0.0	-0.8	-2.6	-5.0	-3.4	5.3	2.1	-23.4
Paraguay	0.9	-3.3	1.4	3.6	2.9	0.2	-0.5	-1.3	-1.3
Suriname	0.0	-1.1	-8.0	6.1	2.2	-3.5	-4.3	-1.9	-19.0
Uruguay	1.0	7.7	7.3	-0.7	0.9	0.2	1.0	6.4	2.6

Contd.

TABLE 12.5 *Contd.*

1	2	3	4	5	6	7	8	9	10
Central America and the Caribbean[b]	**-1.8**	**-0.1**	**2.0**	**-2.3**	**0.9**	**-1.5**	**-1.4**	**1.7**	**-8.7**
Bahamas	11.3	1.7	3.0	0.5	0.2	-0.7	-3.7	-0.7	16.8
Barbados	0.6	4.8	2.3	3.2	3.3	-3.6	-3.6	-3.0	-1.0
Belize	-2.3	1.7	9.9	7.1	11.3	5.0	2.5	...	...
Cuba[c]	3.6	0.2	-4.8	1.1	0.0	...	...	...	...
Haiti	-1.5	-1.9	-2.6	-1.1	-1.0	-2.2	-2.3	-6.9	-27.8
Jamaica	-6.7	1.1	5.7	0.3	5.4	2.9	0.9	0.5	6.6
Panama	2.6	1.2	0.1	-17.6	-2.2	3.1	7.0	5.4	-3.0
Dominican Republic	-4.1	0.7	6.0	-0.7	1.8	-7.5	-3.1	5.5	-1.4
Central American Common Market	**-2.4**	**-1.2**	**0.7**	**-0.8**	**0.5**	**-0.5**	**-0.5**	**1.0**	**-15.0**
Costa Rica	-2.1	2.3	1.6	0.4	2.6	0.8	-1.4	1.5	-5.7
El Salvador	0.6	-1.0	1.0	-0.3	-0.8	1.4	1.2	2.4	-10.4
Guatemala	-3.4	-2.6	0.7	1.0	0.8	0.0	0.3	1.2	-16.9
Honduras	-0.7	-1.1	1.6	1.6	1.5	-3.5	-0.9	1.2	-10.3
Nicaragua	-6.7	-3.5	-3.0	-14.2	-4.5	-3.7	-4.0	-3.4	-38.6
OECS countries[d]	**6.5**	**5.9**	**4.0**	**7.4**	**4.4**	**4.3**	**2.5**	**3.9**	**71.5**
Antigua and Barbuda	7.9	9.1	8.4	7.1	4.5	2.0	...	...	...
Dominica	2.2	7.2	7.1	8.2	-0.9	6.9	2.4	2.4	69.1
Grenada	4.7	5.2	5.8	5.0	5.4	5.0	2.8	0.4	59.3
Saint Kitts and Nevis	6.2	6.6	7.9	10.3	7.2	3.6	7.3	...	...
Saint Lucia	7.5	3.5	-0.9	7.7	3.9	4.1	0.5	...	...
Saint Vincent and the Grenadines	6.3	4.9	4.7	6.4	6.1	6.0	3.6	8.9	91.5

Source: ECLAC, on the Basis of Official Figures. Population Figures have been estimated by the Latin American Demographic Centre (CELADE).

a Preliminary estimates, subject to revision.

b Does not include Cuba.

c Refers to total social product.

d OECS = Organization of Eastern Caribbean States.

TABLE 12.6: Latin America and the Caribbean: Balance of Payments

(*Millions of Dollars*)

	Net service payments[a]			Net payments of profits and interest[c]			Balance on current account[d]			Net movement of capital[c]			Global balance[f]		
	1990	1991	1992[b]	1990	1991	1992[b]	1990	1991	1992[b]	1990	1991	1992[b]	1990	1991	1992[b]
1	2	3	4	5	6	7	8	9	10	11	12	13	14	15	16
Latin America and the Caribbean	**3724**	**4546**	**4860**	**34732**	**30870**	**29590**	**-6171**	**-19401**	**-32720**	**20280**	**39204**	**57020**	**14109**	**19803**	**24300**
Oil-exporting countries	**707**	**1084**	**1740**	**13757**	**12527**	**13240**	**-1920**	**-12926**	**-27250**	**8356**	**26686**	**30825**	**6436**	**133760**	**3575**
Bolivia	169	159	175	244	242	195	-337	-422	-610	355	444	650	18	22	40
Colombia	-85	-13	420	2384	2192	1770	714	2575	1065	-102	-739	435	612	1836	1500
Ecuador	223	271	300	1053	950	840	-273	-577	-435	549	741	1060	276	164	625
Mexico	-1758	-2607	-2980	7905	7068	7400	-8413	-13469	-20750	10716	21461	23250	2303	7992	2500
Peru	848	1117	725	1406	1447	1425	-1914	-2729	-2785	2199	4105	3295	2885	1376	510
Venezuela	1310	2157	3100	765q	628	1610	8303	1696	-3735	-5361	674	2135	2942	22370	-1600
Non-oil-exporting countries	**3017**	**23480**	**3120**	**20975**	**18343**	**16350**	**-4251**	**-6475**	**-5470**	**11924**	**12518**	**26195**	**7673**	**6043**	**20725**
South America	**4477**	**5184**	**4995**	**19638**	**16996**	**14545**	**-2166**	**-4142**	**-1645**	**9597**	**8683**	**22320**	**7431**	**4541**	**20675**
Argentina	674	1634	2235	6122	5634	4200	1903	-2667	-6800	1476	5297	9300	3379	2630	2500
Brazil	3756	3891	3150	11340	9286	8300	-3509	-1006	6450	4730	1227	10090	1221	221	16540
Chile	260	-36	-105	1811	1809	1775	-744	-158	-805	3075	1404	2745	2331	1246	1940
Paraguay	-89	-68	-50	43	34	80	-44	-376	-505	263	674	50	219	298	-455
Uruguay	-124	-237	-235	322	233	190	228	65	15	53	81	135	281	146	150

Contd.

TABLE 12.6 *Contd.*

1	2	3	4	5	6	7	8	9	10	11	12	13	14	15	16
Central America and the Caribbean	**-1460**	**-1704**	**-1875**	**1337**	**1347**	**1805**	**-2085**	**-2333**	**-3825**	**22327**	**338835**	**3875**	**242**	**1502**	**50**
Costa Rica	-71	-157	-140	245	165	205	-561	-165	-450	364	513	600	-197	348	150
El Salvador	-19	6	5	124	127	110	-381	-369	-345	535	299	295	154	-70	-50
Guatemala	19	-140	-165	204	140	180	-235	-186	-540	205	740	420	-30	554	-120
Haiti	93	97	45	25	27	25	-152	-176	-90	179	154	75	27	-22	-15
Honduras	68	65	65	253	257	270	-317	-368	-340	341	434	360	224	66	20
Nicaragua	52	66	70	217	363	465	-507	-849	-1020	468	935	960	-39	86	-60
Panama	-772	-798	-830	118	51	300	133	-105	-550	163	303	615	296	198	65
Dominican Republic	-830	-843	-905	151	217	250	-65	-115	-490	72	457	550	7	342	60

Source: 1990 and 1991: ECLAC, on the basis of figures supplied by the International Monetary Fund; the 1990 and 11991 figures for Brazil are ECLAC estimates based on official figures. 1992: ECLAC, on the basis of official figures.

[a] Does not include net payments of profits and interest. [b] Preliminary ECLAC estimates. Figures have been rounded to the nearest ten or five. [c] Includes interest due. [d] Includes net unrequited private transfer payments, which were of a significant level in 1992 in the following countries: Colombia, Mexico, Brazil, El Salvador, Guatemala and the Dominican Republic. [e] Includes short- and long-term capital, unrequited official transfer payments, and errors and omissions. [f] Corresponds to the variation in international reserves (of opposite sign) plus counterpart items.

12.11 Least Developed Countries

12.11.1 *Redefining Least Developed Countries*

Reviewing the criteria for identifying the least developed among the developing countries, a group of United Nations economic experts recently recommended seven new countries to be classified as least developed countries (LDCs): Angola, Cambodia, Ghana, Madagascar, Solomon Islands, Zaire and Zambia.

They also recommended that Botswana, which enjoys a relatively high per capita GDP and meets the graduation rule, be dropped from the list of LDCs. They did not recommend Namibia for LDC status as it was judged to have a high per capita GDP and enjoys considerable natural resource endowment. The general Assembly had asked the expert group to review Namibia's application last year. If these recommendations are approved, the total number of LDCs will increase to 48, from the current 42.[1]

The definition of an LDC and the usefulness of such a classification have been a matter of controversy for some time. The original set of criteria for identifying LDCs was adopted back in 1971, and has been modified twice since then. Doubt has been expressed as to whether the criteria in fact help donors give special considerations to LDCs in allocating their development assistance.

Pending a judgement of the General Assembly on this issue, the 24-member United Nations Committee for Development Planning recently revised the LDC criteria, by taking into account the special characteristics of the least developed countries, namely "poverty combined with structural impediments which make it more difficult for them to achieve sustained development without special assistance from the international community".

The Committee now defines LDCs as "those low-income countries that are suffering from long-term handicaps to to growth, in particular low levels of human resource development and/or severe structural weaknesses". Per capita GDP (annual average for the last-three years) is still used as the most practical tool with which to measure poverty. Using the criterion the World Bank uses in defining per capita income, the expert group sets the cut-off point for including a country in the LDC list at about $600.

To measure the level of human resource development, the Committee has used an augmented physical quality of life index (APQLI) which comprises four indicators: life expectancy at birth, per capita calorie supplies, combined primary and secondary school enrolment ratio, and adult literacy rate.

Structural weaknesses is measured by two criteria: 1) natural handicaps, such as small population, geographical isolation, landlockedness, high climatic risks which may be measured by an index of instability of agricultural production or by such specific climatic risks as proneness to droughts, floods and cyclones, on a case-by-case basis; 2) low economic diversification which may be

1. Yasuhiro Veki quotes the following countries: Afghanistan, Bangladesh, Benin, Bhutan, Botswana, Burkina Faso, Burundi, Cape Verde, Central African Republic, Chad, Comoros, Djibouti, Equatorial Guinea, Ethiopia, Gambia, Guinea, Guinea-Bissau, Haiti, Kiribati, Laos, Lesotho, Liberia, Malawi, Maldives, Mali, Mauritania, Mozambique, Myanmar, Nepal, Niger, Rwanda, Samoa, So Tome and Principe, Sierra Leone, Somalia, Sudan, Togo, Tuvalu, Uganda, United Republic of Tanzania, Vanuatu and Yemen.

measured by a composite index, called EDI, comprising share of manufacturing in GDP, share of manufacturing in GDP, share of employment in industry, per capita electricity consumption, and the export concentration ratio.

Additional indices relating to natural endowment, exports and official development assistance may also be considered to measure structural weakness. Some differentials in those indices are set for those countries that are being included in or excluded from LDC status.

Even though the group of experts did not recommend Namibia for inclusion, they noted the highly skewed income distribution, particularly the very low average per capita income of the non-white population engaged in traditional activities. They recommended that the international community adopt special measures for Namibia to assist the newly independent nation in mobilizing its considerable economic potential.

Source: Yasuhiro Ueki, *Development Forum*, July-August 1991.

12.11.2 *Prospects of Least Developed Countries*

There are "grounds for hope, and perhaps even for a certain degree of optimism' concerning the prospects of the 47 least developed countries (LDCs).[2] This positive outlook is based on the relatively high growth rates in some LDCs in recent years and, above all, on the newly emerging world political and economic climate. The prospects for the settlement of many long-standing wars and conflicts are much brighter today. The peace dividend which a number of LDCs expect will come in the form of a redirection of national efforts and resources away from military pursuits, the removal of the burden of hundreds of thousands of refugees on neighbouring countries, the repatriation of flight capital and skills, and improved conditions for agricultural production. Moreover, widespread reform and democratization movements have brought hope for better economic performance in the LDCs.

Furthermore, LDCs have initiated major policy changes to establish conditions for viable long-term growth. The size, composition and quality of public investment and other expenditures have come under close scrutiny in many of them. Expenditure policies are being modified to give priority to productive investment and maintenance expenditure (for example infrastructure, storage and marketing facilities), in order to support the growth of the tradables sector and of employment-generating activities. On the revenue side, major fiscal reforms are under way to replace agricultural taxes and other fiscal disincentives to productive activities by taxes on consumption and value-added.

Differences in Long-Term Growth Patterns: The general development

2. Afghanistan, Bangladesh, Benin, Bhutan, Botswana, Burkina Faso, Burundi, Cambodia, Cape Verde, Central African Republic, Chad, Comoros, Djibouti, Equatorial Guinea, Ethiopia, Gambia, Guinea, Guinea-Bissau, Haiti, Kiribati, Lao People's Democratic Republic, Lesotho, Liberia, Madagascar, Malawi, Maldives, Mali, Mauritania, Mozambique, Myanmar, Nepal, Niger, Rwanda, Samoa, Sao Tome and Principe, Sierra Leone, Solomon Islands, Somalia, Sudan, Togo, Tuvalu, Uganda, United Republic of Tanzania, Vanuatu, Republic of Yemen, Zaire, Zambia.

The report deals with 42 countries; it does not cover the five countries (Cambodia, Madagascar, Solomon Islands, Zaire and Zambia) which joined the ranks of LDCs following a decision of the General Assembly last December.

picture of the LDCs hides large disparities in individual country performance, notwithstanding the similarity of problems faced. A steady improvement in living standards has in fact been attained by roughly one fourth of the LDCs during the 1980s. The good performers are the Maldives, Botswana, Bhutan, Burkina Faso, Burundi, Cape Verde, Yemen, Nepal, Guinea-Bissau and the Lao People's Democratic Republic, all of which registered a growth of at least one third in total real gross domestic product (GDP) and at least a 10 per cent increase in per capita GDP growth. Six others — Mali, Gambia, Bangladesh, Samoa, Lesotho and Vanuatu — also registered positive, but slower growth. Eleven — Benin, Ethiopia, Comoros, Tanzania, Kiribati, Myanmar, Malawi, Mauritania, Somalia, Central African Republic and Uganda — stagnated in terms of per capita GDP. In certain LDCs, including Afghanistan, Djibouti, Togo, Sudan, Rwanda, Sierra Leone, Haiti, Equatorial Guinea, Sao Tome and Principe, Mozambique, Guinea, Liberia and Niger, per capita GDP declined severely.

Success was generally based on: strong gains in the purchasing power of exports and a consequent ability to expand the volume of imports and maintain a high level of domestic investment, continued high levels of concessional assistance, a strong expansion of agricultural production, relatively efficient management of external debt, with debt service ratios (in half of these countries) of less than 15 per cent of exports in 1989. Other special factors which helped the relatively fast-growing countries were large emigrants' remittances, strong tourism earnings and, for the six Asian LDCs, the spill-over effects of sharply accelerated growth in neighbouring countries. The longer-standing LDCs have been performing better than the bulk of newcomers to the category, which shows the important role played by specific international support.

Effects of Slowdown in Developed Countries: The development efforts of LDCs have been affected by the economic slowdown in the developed world. This resulted in lower (mainly commodity) export earnings and an increased debt-servicing burden. The total GDP of all LDCs is estimated to have grown only slightly from 2.5 per cent in 1990 to about 2.7 per cent in 1991. Given the unabated high population growth in many LDCs, amounting to 2.7 per year on average during the past decade, per capita GDP growth rates of a large number of those countries are expected to be negative or negligible in both years, with most of the worst-off LDCs being those in Africa. After positive GDP growth rates 3.5 per cent and 5.2 per cent in 1988 and 1989 respectively, total real GDP growth of the African LDCs turned negative in 1990, to -0.3 per cent, in the wake of a sharp fall in agricultural production.

Focus on changes in per capita GDP tends to give less than full credit to the tremendous effort involved in merely keeping up with population growth. In the 1980s, the combined population of the LDCs grew by more than 26 per cent, at an annual average of 2.7 per cent, while they achieved an overall GDP growth of 29 per cent, on an average of 2.9 per year. This is not far short of the 3.2 per cent achieved by the developed market economy countries.

Effects of Natural and Man-made Disasters: Several LDCs have recently been struck by natural catastrophes. For example, damage caused by cyclone Ofa in Samoa in 1990 was estimated to be higher than the country's annual GDP and the total loss for Bangladesh of the 1991 cyclone is estimated at $2.4 billion. Several African LDCs suffered from local drought conditions or floods. No less harmful are military conflicts and civil strife, which have affected one in four LDCs since 1990. In Afghanistan, Ethiopia, Liberia and Somalia, for instance, civil strife has brought the development process to a virtual standstill. Only 13 LDCs enjoyed basic peace and stability throughout the 1980s. The crisis in the Middle East generated additional hardships for a number of LDCs. For Bangladesh alone, it resulted in an estimated total loss of $1.4 billion. It is estimated that the steep, but shortlived, oil price rise added about $140 million to the energy import bill of the African LDCs in 1990. For Djibouti, Mauritania, Somalia and the Sudan, the decline in worker's remittances, mainly originating from the Gulf region, was a major source of disruption, while the decline in international tourism affected Gambia, Nepal, Maldives and Tanzania.

Lessons of Reform Programmes: An in-depth analysis by the UNCTAD secretariat of the various aspects of reform programmes has generated a number of policy guidelines. The report shows, for example, that instances of successful privatization, often advocated in reform programmes, tend to be limited in LDCs and that the public sector must continue to play a significant, albeit lessened, role. Consequently, the design of programmes to restructure public enterprises and improve their efficiency will remain a leading task in many LDCs.

Devaluation does not necessarily boost exports, contain imports and help channel resources to the tradables sector, and that the manageability and sustainability of devaluation measures are best served by timely action and a phased approach. Another policy lesson is that efforts to promote domestic savings must attach as much, if not more, importance to the promotion of higher income as to reliance on interest rates alone. In highly commodity-dependent economies this calls for diversification, among other things.

With regard to price and marketing reforms, case studies to Mali and Malawi indicate that these need to be carefully planned, sequenced, timed and fine-tuned. Liberalization involves not only a reallocation of roles between the Government and the private sector but also a devolution of new responsibilities on Government. The report notes that "just as fiscal incentives alone cannot be a substitute for a transparent and well functioning public administration, investment codes and guarantees by themselves cannot ensure higher levels of investment".

Elements of a successful tax reform in LDCs include a broadening of the tax base and lowering of tax rates; the adoption of measures leading to the introduction of value-added tax, supplemented by selective luxury excise taxes on a few goods (petroleum, alcohol and tobacco); the continued rationalization of customs tariff structures and import taxes; reduced reliance on, and where possible elimination of, export taxes; a coordinated tax reform as opposed to isolated piecemean tinkering with the tax system; improved tax administration.

Stagnation in Assistance Flows: Total resource flows to LDCs in 1990 amounted to $13.6 billion, of which all but $34 million took the form of Official Development Assistance (ODA). While the ODA total showed an increase in nominal terms, this was largely due to valuation effects arising from the fall of the dollar. The Development Assistance Committee countries which are the main donors of ODA on average devoted 0.08 per cent of their gross national product (GNP) to LDCs in 1990, as compared to 0.10 per cent in 1980. This average masks wide country variations. Norway, Denmark, Sweden, the Netherlands and Finland continued to exceed 0.20 per cent, while France remained close to 0.15 per cent. Italy provided 0.10 per cent of its GNP. The ODA performance of some major donors in terms of percentage of their GNP was less in

1990 than 10 years ago: 0.05 per cent for Japan (as compared to 0.10 per cent in 1980), 0.04 per cent for the United States (0.05%), 0.09 per cent for Germany (0.14%), and 0.088 per cent for the United Kingdom (0.12% in 1980).

Priorities for Debt Relief: The external indebtedness of LDCs is no longer building up as rapidly as in the mid-1980s and their debt service ratio has stabilized. Even so, their outstanding external debt (of which 90% is long term) increased by about 4 per cent in 1990, to $86.3 billion, and indicators of their external debt burden have not yet shown any fundamental improvement. In over one-third of the LDCs, external debt equals or exceeds GDP. Debt service payments by the LDCs remained stable at a level of $4.2 billion annually in 1989-90, representing on average some 30 per cent of their exports of goods and services. Close to half of the LDCs are considered to be debt-distressed.

Finally, the LDCs' prospects will depend on the international trading environment, which, in turn, depends on the outcome of the Uruguay Round. LDCs should continue to enjoy preferential treatment and be shielded from negative effects of agricultural trade liberalization on the prices of basic foodstuffs. To benefit from the Single European Market, they will need additional supportive measures, such as greater participation of foreign direct investment in their export sectors and more liberal rules of origin under the Generalized System of Preferences.

Source: *Report on the Least Developed Countries*, United Nations Conference on Trade and Development, reported in *Go-Between*, February 1992, Special Issue.

12.12 **Military Expenditure Reduction in the Third World**

Military expenditures in the developing countries in 1988 approximated $170 billion, 4.3 per cent of GNP. They were only slightly less than total expenditures for health and education and they have quintupled in constant dollars between 1960 and 1988, increasing at a rate twice that of income per capita.

Such large outlays, in countries so drastically in need of capital to accelerate the rate economic and social advance of their five billion inhabitants can be reduced. A combination of following actions could lead to cuts in their military expenditures as a per cent of GNP, of more than half by the end of the decade.

* United Nations Security Council guarantees of territorial integrity;
* Continuing reductions in both conventional and nuclear arms by the Great Powers;
* Tight control of the proliferation of weapons of mass destruction and the means to deliver them;
* Substantial limitations on arms exports from arms producing nations; and
* The tying of financial aid in developing countries to reductions in military expenditures by these countries.

The end of the Cold War offers dramatic opportunities for the nations of the world to move in this direction. The international organizations, including financial institutions such as the World Bank, can catalyze the process thereby accelerating economic and social development without reducing security.

A World of Conflict

The past 45 years have seen some 125 wars and conflicts in the Third World, leading to 40 million deaths. It is often suggested that the Third World has been turned into an ideological battleground by the Cold War and the rivalries of the Great Powers. That rivalry has undeniably been a contributing factor and some of the most costly wars have directly involved one or more of the Great Powers. Others grew out of the decolonization process. Many of these conflicts, however, including some of the most costly in terms of human lives, have had their roots in historical enmities within and among developing countries. They have resulted from the desire for regional dominance on the part of some Third World governments, attempts by developing governments to alter their social order, and the persistence of substantial inequities within developing nations.

In view of the diverse reasons countries have for going to war, we must conclude that in the world of the future, conflicts within and nations will not disappear even though East and West cease to fight their proxy wars in the South. But a different world would emerge if the Great Powers and their allies agreed on and adjusted their foreign and defense policies in accordance with the conditions stipulated above.

Reducing Military Budgets

As we move to limit both nuclear and conventional forces, while providing for collective action against military aggression wherever it may occur, military budgets throughout the world — can be reduced substantially.

Over 1978-88, the Third World imported $371 billion of arms (nearly $450 billion in 1988 prices), more than three quarters of the arms traded internationally. While these figures reflect the relative lack of domestic production capability in the Third World and a legitimate concern to protect national sovereignty, there is clearly great scope for reducing Third World military expenditures by reducing arms imports.

Both supply and demand for arms must be addressed. The United States and the Soviet Union have tended to use arms transfers as a means of maintaining political support in strategically located Third World nations. For many of the Western European and some emerging Third World supplies (in particular, China and Brazil), economic considerations have been paramount. The sale of weapons and arms production technology has helped to make the domestic defense industries of these smaller producers economically viable and has opened the door to nonmilitary exports. Over the last decade or so, economic considerations have become increasingly important for the Soviet Union as well.

But the demand for weapons is strong too, and many Third World governments have actively sought to purchase arms. One of the most important demand factors is involvement in conflict — internal or external. Of the top 15 Third World arms importers during 1978-88, who together account for about three quarters of arms imported by the Third World, 13 have been party to conflicts of many years' duration. In addition, Third World governments acquire arms to protect against perceived internal and external threats, to bolster their claims to regional power status, as a symbol of unity and independence, and to reward the armed forced for support against internal opposition.

The availability of financing is an important factor in arms purchases. Seven of the top 15 arms importers have had access to petrodollars. Another five have been recipients of grants or heavily subsidized credits. Some Third World countries have received financial assistance from oil rich countries that has allowed them to acquire arms from abroad.

Not all weapons must be imported. More than 54 developing countries have some domestic arms production. Of these, 10 produce nearly all the major weapons manufactured in the Third World. The investments that have made this possible have been significant, particularly in terms of foreign exchange.

Financing Military Outlays

An important but difficult factor to assess in the financing of military expenditures is the fungibility of external resources, that is, the ability of governments to either divert such resources or free up other resources for military acquisitions. Common sense — and some evidence — suggests that general purpose balance of payments or budgetary financing from abroad enables a government to spend more on the military than would be otherwise possible. It is, therefore, bad economics and bad policy for donor nations and international financial institutions to continue to behave as if the funding of stabilization, adjustment, and development programs can be separated from financing of military expenditures.

Reducing the Demand for Arms

Wars and arms procurement (both domestic and abroad) have created a heavy military expenditure burden for a number of Third World countries. To the extent that security assistance takes the form of loans, involves barter trade, or causes additional security-related outlays, it adds to the burden. To reduce the demand for arms in the Third World, whether the arms are imported or produced locally, we should introduce into the system of Collective Security a guarantee by the Security Council and regional organizations of the territorial integrity of member states. The strengthening of regional bodies, such as the Organization of American States and the Organization of African Unity, as well as the creation of such groups for Asia and the Middle East as regional arms of the Security Council, would help this process. International organizations should agree, as well, to actively assist countries in finding negotiated solutions to conflicts.

There is, of course, the danger that reduction of tensions and military forces of the East and the West — and the effectiveness of new high-tech weapons — may lead industrial country arms producers to seek new markets for their products in the Third World. This approach would succeed only if the Third World countries have the financing for such purchases. To the extent that such financing is provided by suppliers through credits, grants, or barter arrangements, curtailment of such facilities would keep down Third World military outlays on imports.

Domestic Considerations

While external security considerations play an important role in determining military expenditures in many Third World countries, many such countries continue to allocate large proportions of their budgets to the military without any obvious external threat. Others continue to spend large amounts on security even after external threats have disappeared. The reason often is the desire of the armed forces to preserve a strong internal posture. In some countries, this is the primary objective of such expenditures.

When governments have armed themselves against their own people in an attempt to maintain themselves in power, the general public often has limited access to the policy-making process and the formal economic system. Under such conditions, elite groups fight for power and some groups are discriminated against or repressed. In such situations, international or regional conflict resolution strategies need to be matched by internal conflict resolution strategies.

In this regard, equitable development and distribution of resources play a key role. In many parts of the Third World, economic systems function primarily to benefit a relatively limited number of people, and political systems are manipulated to continue the dominance of the elites. Indeed, one of the most important effects of military expenditure, which has serious implications for political and economic development, is the degree to which it strengthens the political influence of the armed forces at the expense of civilian groups within Third World societies. The greater the political power of the security forces, the less likely it is that the requirements for democratic governance will be met. It is, therefore, necessary to strive for a political system that allows all groups to articulate their demands and is capable of producing workable compromises between competing interests. The greater the power of the security forces, the less likely the possibility of democratic governance.

When security forces claim a role in guaranteeing internal security for a society, they are not, in most cases, seeking to make all citizens equally secure. Indeed, their actions often create greater instability. All too frequently, the security forces are not protecting a majority of the population from a minority bent on pursuing its own political and economic objectives; instead, they are seeking "regime security" (which often means "military regime security").

Conditionality

The role of the military is, of course, the prerogative of each government. The international community nonetheless needs to identify ways in which it can encourage countries to reduce their security-related expenditures in favour of development.

International financial assistance should be linked to movement toward "optimal limits" of military expenditures, taking into account, of course, sources of external threat to a country. The "conditionality" inherent in such an approach could take the form of the proposal contained in *Facing One World*, the report of the "Independent Group on Financial Flows to Developing Countries", chaired by former German Chancellor Helmut Schmidt. This group, which included former Presidents or Prime Ministers of Nigeria, Peru, Canada, and the Republic of Korea, urged that in allocating foreign aid decisions, special consideration be given to countries spending less than 2 per cent of their GNP in the security sector. The huge savings that many countries could make by reducing their security expenditures to this level could be used to address pressing economic and social needs. Even though the application of conditionality may be contentious, it is an essential part of the solution to the waste represented by excessive military spending in poor countries today.

Sources of Military Aid

Reliable and detailed data on security assistance are not widely available. The United States is one of the few countries that provides such data. The three main components of US security assistance are the Military Assistance Program (MAP), which provides grants; the Economic Support Fund (ESF), which provides balance of payments help and finances commodity import programs, increasingly on a grant basis; and the Foreign Military Sales (FMS) program, which enables countries to purchase military hardware and services on credit.

In fiscal year 1989, seven countries — Greece, Honduras, Kenya, the Philippines, El Salvador, Thailand, and Turkey — received 80 per cent of the $468 million MAP funds. Nine — Egypt, Greece, Israel, Jordan, Morocco, Pakistan, Portugal, Tunisia, and Turkey — shared the $4.3 billion FMS program. Two of these — Israel and Egypt — accounted for 75 per cent of FMS credits, and all these credits were "forgiven", that is, converted into grants. Nearly 80 per cent of the 3.6 billion under the ESF went to five countries — Egypt, Israel, Pakistan, the Philippines, and El Salvador, with Israel and Egypt getting nearly 60 per cent of the total amount. In fact, these two countries received nearly two-thirds of the $8.4 billion in FMS, ESF, and MAP fund, allocated by the United States in FY 1989.

While very little is publicly known about the scale and terms of Soviet security assistance, it is clear that the Soviet economy is less and less able to support any kind of massive aid beyond its borders. For domestic political reasons, planned cuts in military aid to Cuba may not proceed in 1991, but India, for example, hitherto a major recipient of Soviet military supplies, now must pay in hard currency for weapons and arms-production technology imported from the Soviet Union.

Another source of military assistance for some Third World countries has been the oil surplus countries of the Middle East. Saudi Arabia, Algeria, Kuwait, and the United Arab Emirates have provided varying amounts of grants and credits, primarily to other Muslim countries, such as Egypt, Iraq, Pakistan, and Sudan.

Source: Robert S. McNamara, *Finance and Development*, September 1991.

12.13 **Multinational Companies/Corporations**

TABLE 12.7: R&D Expenditure of Select Countries and Their Top Companies

(*in US $ billion*)

	Canada	France	W.Germany	Japan	The Netherlands	Switzerland	USA
National R&D Expenditure for 1989, except wherein disputed	7.25	22.24	34.23	82.85	4.79	3.90	144.87
R&D Expenditure of top companies with number of companies in para brackets	2.07 (6)	7.00 (17)	14.09 (19)	27.30 (74)	4.21 (7)	4.43 (10)	37.57 (28)

Source: *World Investment Report, 1992*, U.N., 1992 reported in *Down to Earth*, December 15, 1992.

12.14 **Natural Disasters**

12.14.1 *International Decade for Natural Disaster Reduction*

Some 18 million people in southern Africa may starve to death this year as a result of drought. This, and the havoc wrecked by an increasing number of other natural disasters around the world, makes international efforts for natural disaster reduction all the more urgent.

Since 1990 alone, there have been volcanic eruptions in Japan, tne Philippines and Nicaragua; earthquakes in Iran, Guatemala, Costa Rica and Turkey. Devastating floods in China; a cyclone in Bangladesh and tidal waves in Nicaragua. The United States has recently undergone the costliest natural disaster in its history, hurricane Andrew. And such events are on the rise.

Deaths associated with disasters have increased 50 per cent each decade since the 1950s, according to the World Bank, with 3 million deaths over the past two decades and 162,000 in 1991 alone. The related losses in financial terms have increased about three times from the 1960s to the 1980s; global losses just for 1990 were estimated at 47 billion.

But the losses, both human and economic, fall disproportionately on the world's poorer countries: between 1970 and 1985, developed countries suffered only 3 per cent of the world's major disasters, but death rates in the less developed nations were about 100 times greater.

To combat the omnious effects of disasters ranging from sudden geophysical phenomena (volcanoes, earthquakes, floods, cyclones) to less sudden natural catastrophes (drought) and manmade disasters (civil strife, massive population movements and chemical/nuclear accidents), over the years the United Nations system has mobilized several of its agencies to acquire and apply the necessary scientific and technical knowledge and to assist countries in disaster preparedness and mitigation activities. In 1987, the United Nations designated the 1990s the International Decade for Natural Disaster Reduction (IDNDR). Launched on 1 January 1990, it is intended to be a period in which the international community, under United Nations auspices, builds international cooperation in order to reduce loss of life, property damage, and the social and economic disruption caused by natural disasters.

More specifically, the Decade's goals are to:

- improve each country's capacity to mitigate the effects of natural disasters;
- devise guidelines and strategies for applying existing knowledge;
- foster scientific and engineering endeavours to close critical gaps in knowledge; and
- develop and disseminate information on and evaluate the effectiveness of measures for assessing, predicting, preventing and mitigating natural disasters through programmes of technical assistance and technology transfer, demonstration projects, education and training. Governments are also asked to set up a national assessment of risks, national and/or local prevention and preparedness plans, and global, regional, national and local warning systems by the year 2000.

An international framework of action for the Decade was adopted in 1989, setting out some of the activities to be undertaken at the national level as well as within the United Nations system. The Decade secretariat, established in Geneva in 1990, now forms part of the Department of Humanitarian Affairs (DHA) of the United Nations. A Scientific and Technical Committee (STC), comprising up to 25 high-level specialists, provides guidance on substantive issues, while a special high-level council, composed of well-known personalities, assists in creating global awareness about natural disaster reduction. In addition, the second Wednesday of each October was designated the International Day for Natural Disaster Reduction, to draw attention to efforts now under way and to encourage more concerted global action. A World Conference of National Committees for the Decade is planned for spring 1994, to evaluate progress of the Decade at its mid-term.

Although the United Nations has long provided assistance to countries affected by natural and manmade disasters — the Office of the United Nations Disaster Relief Coordinator (UNDRO) was established in 1971 as the focal point for the United Nations System's Disaster Relief and Mitigation Activities — it has recently stepped up its involvement in this area. DHA, which incorporates the former UNDRO as well as other offices dealing with complex emergencies and the IDNDR secretariat, is headed by an Under-Secretary-General who also serves as the United nations Emergency Relief Coordinator. The Department, with offices in New York and Geneva (the latter being known as DHA-UNDRO), will help to improve the coordination of humanitarian assistance in the United Nations and ultimately to create a more effective and streamlined emergency management capacity for handling specific complex emergencies. Policy coordination and leadership will be exercised in New York, while the technical operational part of emergency management will continue to be carried out in Geneva.

As a result of growing needs for disaster relief, international aid increased significantly in recent years and totalled some $2.86 billion in 1990-91, with about $207 million channelled through UNDRO alone, or 15 times more than in 1986-87. It is expected that with the integration of UNDRO into DHA, an even larger amount of international assistance will be channelled through the United Nations systems in future years.

Source: *UN Newsletter*, October 10, 1992.

12.15 **Non-Aligned Movement for a New World Order**

The tenth Non-Aligned Summit concluded on September 6, 1992 after expressing concern over the adverse international economic environment that continues to impact negatively on the economies of the developing countries and giving the call for a new world order based on a collective commitment to peace and assuring a just and equitable social and economic order.

The conference was on the verge of split over its condemnation of the violation of human rights of the people of Bosnia-Herzegovina to which Yugoslavia took strong exception but managed to steer the movement on course and giving it a new programme of action to ensure fulfilment of its freshly stated objectives in the political and economic spheres.

The conference also adopted the "Jakarta Message". The Message which sums up the consensus at the Summit as also the movement's stand on international political and economic issues released here suggests coordination of

NAM efforts and strategies with the Group of 77 through the establishment of Joint Coordination Committee.

The Heads of State and Government reaffirmed that no country should have the power to dictate its concept of democracy and human rights or to impose conditionalities on others:

> "In the promotion and protection of these rights and freedoms, we emphasise the inter-relations of various categories, call for a balanced relationship between individual and community rights, uphold the competence and responsibility of national governments in their implementation."

The message reaffirms support for the Palestinian people to secure their inalienable rights to self-determination and reiterated the demand for withdrawal of Israel from all occupied Arab lands.

The collapse of the bi-polar structure of the world presents unprecedented possibilities, as well as challenges, for cooperation among nations. Interdependence, integration and globalisation of the world economy are among these new realities. Consistent with its fundamental principles and objectives of the movement, NAM had made many contributions to bringing about improvement in the present international political climate. These have also fully vindicated the validity and relevance of non-alignment and its basic approach in addressing international problems and developments.

The leaders also gave a call for a nuclear weapons free world which alone could ensure human survival and was the collective responsibility of all nations. They also urged accelerated efforts on the other priority issues including the prohibition of all weapons of mass destruction.

They also took note of the fact that deep cuts in military expenditure of developed states would release for the social and economic advance of the developing countries. At the same time, it would also promote disarmament and enhance security at lower levels of armaments.

The message expresses dismay over the failure to conclude the Uruguay Round of multilateral trade negotiations and called upon the developed countries to ensure, without delay, a balanced, equitable and satisfactory conclusions of the Round which takes into account the interests of all parties, especially the development needs and concerns of the developing countries.

The leaders condemnation of terrorism was unequivocal. They said terrorism acts endangered the very integrity and security of States, especially those which violated human rights — in particular the right of life of all citizens and which destroy the physical and economic infrastructure and attempt to destabilise legitimately constituted Governments.

At the same time the meeting denounced "brutalisation of people kept under foreign occupation the gravest form of terrorism. They condemned the use of state power for the suppression and violence against innocent civilians struggling against foreign occupation to exercise their inalienable right to self-determination." The reference is alluded to the atrocities committed in the occupied terrorists by Israel.

The Heads of State and Government also expressed concern over the recent tendency to intervene in the internal affairs of other states under the pretext of protecting human rights or preventing conflict, which would in effect erode the concept of national sovereignty. The emphasised the dangers inherent in such intervention and called for full respect for national sovereignty in all circumstances.

Before ending its six-day meeting, the Summit adopted the Final Document in three parts — global issues, political issues and economic and social issues — a draft declaration on Somalia, decisions on Africa Fund, population, strengthening international cooperation and establishment of a high-level working group for restructuring of the United Nations.

Source: M.K. Dhar, *Hindustan Times*, September 7, 1992.

12.16 **Nuclear Power**

TABLE 12.8: Nuclear Power Status around the World: Status as on December 31, 1991

	In operation		Under construction	
	No. of units	Total net MWe	No. of units	Total net MWe
Argentina	2	935	1	692
Belgium	7	5484		
Brazil	1	626	1	1245
Bulgaria	6	3538		
Canada	20	13993	2	1762
China	1	288	2	1812
Cuba			2	816
Czechoslovakia	8	3264	6	3336
Finland	4	2310		
France	56	56873	5	7005
Germany	21	22390		
Hungary	4	1645		
India	**7**	**1374**	**7**	**1540**
Iran			2	2392
Japan	42	32044	10	9192
Korea, Rep. of	9	7220	3	2550
Mexico	1	654	1	654
Netherlands	2	508		
Pakistan	1	125		
Romania			5	3125
South Africa	2	1842		
Spain	9	7067		
Sweden	12	9817		
Switzerland	5	2952		
United Kingdom	37	11710	1	1188
USA	111	99757	3	3480
USSR (former)	45	34673	25	21255
Yugoslavia	1	632		
World total*	420	3266111	76	62044

* The total includes Taiwan, China where six reactors totalling 4890 MWe are in operation. In 1991, they accounted for 37.8 per cent of the total electricity generated there. The 1991 figures for the former USSR include reactors in the newly independent States.

Source: *IAEA Bulletin*, September, 1992.

TABLE 12.9: Nuclear Share of Electricity Generation

Countries	Nuclear share in per cent
France	72.7
Belgium	59.3
Sweden	51.6
Hungary	48.4
Korea, Rep. of	47.5
Switzerland	40
Spain	35.9
Bulgaria	34
Finland	33.3
Czechoslovakia	28.7
Germany	27.6
Japan	23.8
USA	21.7
United Kingdom	20.6
Argentina	19.1
Canada	16.4
(former) USSR	12.6
Yugoslavia	6.3
South Africa	5.9
Netherlands	4.9
Mexico	3.6
India	**1.8**
Pakistan	0.8
Brazil	0.6

In 1991, five countries generated close to half or more of their total electricity using nuclear power. Some 12 countries relied upon nuclear power plants to supply at least one-fourth of their total electricity needs.

TABLE 12.10: India's Nuclear Power Program upto the Year 2000

Station	Capacity (MW)	Operating at (MW)	Location	Year of Commissioning
1	2	3	4	5
Operational Units				
Tarapur				
Unit 1	210	160	Maharashtra	1969
Unit 2	210	160	Maharashtra	1969
Rajasthan				
Unit 1	220	100	Rajasthan	1973
Unit 2	220	220	Rajasthan	1981
Madras				
Unit 1	235	235	Tamil Nadu	1983
Unit 2	235	235	Tamil Nadu	1985
Narora				
Unit 1	235	235	Uttar Pradesh	1990
Unit 2	235	220	Uttar Pradesh	1991
Under Construction				
Kakrapar				
Units 1 & 2	2 X 235	—	Gujarat	1992
Kaiga				
Units 1 & 2	2 X 235	—	Karnataka	1995-96

Contd.

TABLE 12.10 *Contd.*

1	2	3	4	5
Rajasthan Units 3 & 4	2 X 235	—	Rajasthan	1995-96
Under Sanction				
Kaiga Units 3, 4, 5, & 6	4 X 235	—	Karnataka	1996-97
Tarapur Units 3 & 4	2 X 500	—	Maharashtra	1997-98
Rajasthan Units 5, 6, 7 & 8	4 X 500	—	Rajasthan	1998-2000
Planned				
Kudankulam Units 1 & 2	2 X 1,000	—	Tamil Nadu	1998-99

Source: *Annual Report*, Department of Atomic Energy, reported in *Third Concept*, November 1992.

TABLE 12.11: Selected Programs for High-Level Waste Burial

Country	Earliest Planned Year	Status of Program
Argentina	2040	Granite site at Gastre selected.
Canada	2020	Independent commission conducting four-year study of government plan to bury irradiated fuel in granite at yet-to-be identified site.
China	none announced	Irradiated fuel to be reprocessed; Gobi desert sites under investigation.
Finland	2020	Field studies being conducted; final site selection due in 2000.
France	2010	Two sites to be selected and studied; final site not to be selected until 2006.
Germany	2008	Gorieben salt dome sole site to be studied.
India	**2010**	**Irradiated fuel to be reprocessed, waste store for twenty years, then buried in yet-to-be identified granite site.**
Italy	2040	Irradiated fuel to be reprocessed, and waste stored for 50-60 years before burial in clay or granite.
Japan	2020	Limited site studies. Cooperative program with China to build underground research facility.
Netherlands	2040	Interim storage of reprocessing waste for 50-100 years before eventual burial, possibly in another country.
Soviet Union	none announced	Eight sites being studied for deep geologic disposal.
Sweden	2020	Granite site to be selected in 1997; evaluation studies under way at Aspo site near Oskarshmn nuclear complex.
United States	2010	Yucca Mountain, Nevada, site to be studied, and if approved, will receive 70,000 metric tons of waste.
United Kingdom	2030	Fifty-year storage approved in 1982; exploring options include sub-seabed burial.

Source: Worldwatch Institute reported in *Third Concept*, November 1992.

12.17 **Prices**

The notion that 'fair prices' can be achieved through market mechanisms or laid down by administrative order has little practical validity. The very definition of what a fair price is poses problems. What can alternative trade do to secure the producer a larger share in the sales price?

Even after political independence, the former colonies have largely remained 'raw material countries'. As early as 1964, the Argentinian economist Raoul Prebisch demonstrated at the 2nd UN Conference on Trade and Development (UNCTAD) with his theory of the secular trend towards falling terms of trade (ToT) that they were gravely handicapped by this form of global division of labour. Long heavily disputed amongst economic theorists, the ToT theory has been posthumously vindicated by price trends on the international raw materials markets in recent years.

To counter the downward trend of raw material prices, producer countries at the beginning of the 70s tried to control the supply of phosphate, bauxite, mercury, copper, rubber and others (producer cartel), copper, rubber and others (producer cartel), but only OPEC, the (counter) cartel the oil-producing countries founded to safeguard their interests against the oil multis (Seven Sisters) managed to force massive price hikes. The commodity cartels were, however, quite fragile alliances. Due to divergent political systems and goals and dissimilar economic dictates, the interests of the member states, even in the partially successful OPEC, differed so much that they could not ultimately agree on common system of quotas and a common price policy. They could also be undermined by the industrial countries, for example, via technical substitution or the exploitation of new raw material deposits (North Sea oil, etc.).

In further initiatives to stabilize raw material prices, the 'raw material countries' tried to involve the 'consumer countries': the Group of 77 in UNCTAD, for example, demanded the establishment of of an Integrated Programme for Commodities for an initial 18 raw materials as a key stone of the New International Economic Order. It was, however, thwarted by the opposition of the industrial countries and financial and practical problems. The major instrument remaining was the stabilization of export earnings (STABEX) scheme as part of the ACP-EEC LomÆ Convention. as the consumer countries are involved here, the goal cannot be to raise prices, but rather to stabilize them. There have been or still are also a number of single accords between supplier and buyer countries of raw materials which have failed or are failing due to dissent amongst the raw material countries.

Source: Gerd Nickoleit and Hermann J. Wirtz, *D+C*, June, 1992.

12.18 **Sports**

12.18.1 *Barcelona Olympics, July-August, 1992*

The Olympic Games which were declared open on July 25, 1992 at Barcelona in Spain, ended on August 9, 1992.

TABLE 12.12: Medals Tally

	G	S	B		G	S	B
CIS	45	38	29	Ethiopia	1	0	2
United States	37	34	37	Algeria	1	0	1
Germany	33	21	28	Estonia	1	0	1
China	16	22	16	Lithuania	1	0	1
Cuba	14	6	11	Switzerland	1	0	0
Spain	13	7	2	Jamaica	0	3	1
S. Korea	12	5	12	Nigeria	0	3	1
Hungary	11	12	7	Latvia	0	2	1
France	8	5	16	Austria	0	2	0
Australia	7	9	11	Namibia	0	2	0
Canada	6	5	7	S. Africa	0	2	0
Italy	6	5	8	Belgium	0	1	2
Britain	5	3	12	Croatia	0	1	2
Romania	4	6	8	Yugoslavs	0	1	2
Czechoslovakia	4	2	1	Iran	0	1	2
N. Korea	4	0	5	Israel	0	1	1
Japan	3	8	11	Chinese Taipei	0	1	0
Bulgaria	3	7	6	Mexico	0	1	0
Poland	3	6	10	Peru	0	1	0
Netherlands	2	6	7	Mongolia	0	0	2
Kenya	2	4	2	Slovenia	0	0	2
Norway	2	4	1	Argentina	0	0	1
Turkey	2	2	2	Bahamas	0	0	1
Indonesia	2	2	1	Colombia	0	0	1
Brazil	2	1	0	Ghana	0	0	1
Greece	2	0	0	Malaysia	0	0	1
Sweden	1	7	4	Pakistan	0	0	1
New Zealand	1	4	5	Philippines	0	0	1
Finland	1	2	2	Puerto Rico	0	0	1
Denmark	1	1	4	Qatar	0	0	1
Morocco	1	1	1	Surinam	0	0	1
Ireland	1	1	0	Thailand	0	0	1

Source: *Hindustan Times*, August 10, 1992.

12.19.2 *World Cup, 1992 at a Glance*

TABLE 12.13: World Cup, 1992

	Runs	Wickets	Overs		Runs	Wickets	Overs
Feb 22				*Feb 26*			
India	227	*	49.2	Australia	170	9	49
England	236	9	50	S. Africa	171	1	46.5
N. Zealand	248	0	46.5	*Feb. 27*			
Australia	211	*	49	Pakistan	254	4	50
				Zimbabwe	201	7	50
Feb 23							
W. Indies	221	0	46.5	England	160	4	39.5
Pakistan	220	2	50	W. Indies	157	*	49.2
Sri Lanka	313	7	49.2	*Feb. 28*			
Zimbabwe	312	4	50	India #	Match abandoned		
				Srilanka	due to rain		
Feb 25							
N. Zealand	210	4	49.2	*Feb. 29*			
Sri Lanka	206	9	50	W. Indies	264	8	50
				Zimbabwe	189	7	70

Contd.

	Runs	Wickets	Overs
N. Zealand	191	3	35
S. Africa	190	7	50
Mar 1			
India	234	*	47
Australia	237	9	50
Mar 2			
Sri Lanka	198	7	49.5
S. Africa	195	*	50
Mar 3			
N. Zealand #	162	3	20.5
Zimbabwe	105	7	18
Mar 4			
India	216	7	49
Pakistan	173	*	48.1
Mar 5			
Australia	171	*	49
England	173	2	40.5
W. Indies	136	*	39
S. Africa	200	8	50
Mar 7			
Australia	190	3	44
Sri Lanka	189	9	50
India #	203	7	32
Zimbabwe	104	1	19
Mar 8			
Pakistan	173	8	36
S. Africa	211	7	50
N. Zealand	206	5	48.3
W. Indies	203	7	50
Mar 9			
England	280	6	50
Sri Lanka	174	*	44
Mar 10			
Zimbabwe	163	*	48.3
S. Africa	164	3	45.1
India #	197	*	49.4
W. Indies	195	5	40.3

	Runs	Wickets	Overs
Mar 11			
Australia	172	*	45.2
Pakistan	220	9	5
Mar 12			
England #	226	7	40.5
S. Africa	236	4	50
India	230	6	50
N. Zealand	231	6	47.1
Mar 13			
W. Indies	268	8	50
Sri Lanka	177	9	50
Mar 14			
Australia	265	6	46
Zimbabwe	137	*	411.4
Mar 15			
India #	180	6	30
S. Africa	181	4	29.1
Pakistan	216	6	49.1
Sri Lanka	212	6	50
N. Zealand	201	3	41
England	200	8	50
Mar 18			
Australia	216	6	50
W. Indies	159	*	42.4
England	125	*	49.1
Zimbabwe	134	*	46.1
N. Zealand	166	*	48.2
Pakistan	167	3	44.4
Mar 21	**Semi-Final**		
Pakistan	264	6	49
N. Zealand	262	7	50
Mar 22	**Semi-Final**		
England #	252	6	45
S. Africa	232	6	43
Mar 25	**Final**		
Pakistan	249	6	50
England	227	*	49.2

* All Out; # Rain Affected Match.
Source: *Times of India*, March 26, 1992.

12.19 **United Nations**

12.19.1 *Achievements and Problems*

Secretary-General Boutros-Ghali, speaking on 13 May, 1992 at the National Press Club of Washington, D.C., drew up a balance sheet of what was achieved and what was not achieved since he became Secretary-General 135 days ago.

Never before had it seemed that the United Nations was so popular with its Member States. Never before had its services been requested with such frequency, not only in its traditional role of peace-keeping and peace-making, but in a new role, that of giving assistance to democratic institutions in the countries of the Third World. And never before had the expenses incurred by the Organization in the service of peace been so great. Finally, never before had its funds been so low.

The Secretary-General had participated in the signature in Mexico of the El Salvador Peace Accord negotiated by his predecessor. In spite of certain difficulties, the operation as a whole was successful, because it was not only an operation of peace-keeping, but also one of peace-building.

Another very important event was the support given to the Secretary-General by the 15 Heads of State and Government of members of the Security Council who had mandated him to prepare a report on peace-keeping, peace-building and preventive diplomacy which should be presented in the next few weeks to the members of the Security Council.

In February, the Secretary-General had appointed a new coordinator for humanitarian assistance. This was a new approach, to try to have a better coordination, not only between the different agencies of the United Nations, but between the United Nations and non-governmental organizations. The special Coordinator was now in Geneva to try to see what ought to be done to help give humanitarian assistance to certain cities and certain parts of Yugoslavia.

Among the most important activities, being carried out by the United Nations was the operation in Cambodia, launched on 28 February. The Secretary-General was very optimistic about Cambodia because, first of all, he had been able to have a long talk with the leaders of the different factions, including the Prince Sihanouk, and he had paid a visit to the field. There was a political will among the different factions to participate in the elections next year around March/April/May. Again, a very positive thing was the new spirit of cooperation existing between the different agencies there, between the United Nations and the non-governmental organizations.

The Secretary-General had consistently stressed the importance of economic and social cooperation as was witnessed by his participation in the inaugural session of the Economic Commission for Europe, and his trip to Beijing to participate in the inaugural session of the Economic and Social Commission for Asia, and his trip to the Pacific.

As for the issues where the United Nations had been less successful, the Secretary-General said in Yugoslavia, from the beginning, they had decided to have a new approach which was based on a division of labour. The European Community would deal with the political problem and the United nations would deal only with a peace-keeping operation in Croatia. The United Nations was keen to have a division of labour and a cooperation between the United Nations on the one side and the European Community on the other. Unfortunately, they had not been able to accomplish their aims, although they did have a presence there. The Secretary-General mentioned the difficulty in carrying out any kind of operation in Bosnia-Herzegovina because peace-keeping operations had to be based on the agreement of all the parties.

Until now, they had not been able to obtain this agreement in Bosnia-Herzegovina. The Secretary-General had given instructions to remove the bulk of the officers, but not all, out of Serajevo because of situation was too dangerous.

Another area where they had not been successful was Afghanistan. Here, for months and months they had prepared a peace plan and had even discussed where the international conference would be held and who would be invited. Then the military coup or revolution happened and Najibullah lost his power, and now they had a real degradation of the situation in Kabul.

Another operation where there had been no progress was the Western Sahara. They were supposed to have a referendum at the beginning of this year. The Secretary-General was now trying to reactivate the process with the help of a new Special Representative, the former Minister of Foreign Affairs of Pakistan, Mr. Yaqub Khan. They might be able to start a new peace process towards a solution in Western Sahara.

Another region where they had a problem was in Nagorno-Karabakh. Here they had received a request from both Armenia and Azerbaijan to intervene in this dispute. The United Nations policy in this regard was the same — in other words, "Let us do this, let that be done by the CSCE." The Minister of Foreign Affairs of Czechoslovakia had been appointed to try to solve this problem. But until now they had not been successful. He had already sent Cyprus Vance on a first fact-finding mission and would send another mission to see what the possibilities were of playing a role in the dispute between Armenia and Azerbaijan.

One of the most serious problems the United Nations had to face today was the fact it was short of cash. Its resources in adequate personnel were more and more strained and stretched by the number of demands. Up to 1988, there had been 13 peace-keeping operations. During the last two or three years, they had launched 13 new operations. So in the last three years, this represented a real burden. With the support of the Member States and of international public opinion, with the new credibility of the United Nations, Boutros-Ghali.

Source: *UN Press Release*, SG/SM/1331.

12.19.2 *UN Appeal for Humanitarian Aid for Ethiopia, Eritrea, Kenya and Sudan*

On February 19, 1993 the United Nations launched four special appeals for the 1993 humanitarian assistance requirements for Ethiopia, Eritrea, Kenya and the Sudan. A total of $762 million has been identified for relief, short term rehabilitation, and refugee assistance efforts. This includes $299.9 million for Ethiopia, $80.5 million for Eritrea, $191.2 million for Kenya, and $189.8 million for Sudan.

In Ethiopia, relief assistance will be provided during 1993 to some 5 million, including refugees fleeing the conflict in Somalia and those displaced by local insecurity. Throughout the country, and especially in the north, immediate rehabilitation efforts are required to address the effects of the year of civil war and required to address the effects of the year of civil war and of the recent drought.

Eritrea is benefiting from a period of sustained peace after over 25 years of war. A better-than-average harvest following drought, however, will only meet half of the food requirements of the country. In addition to food rehabilitation assistance is urgently needed to begin to repair the devastation caused by two and a half decades of war.

In spite of recent rains in Kenya, major drought relief efforts are still needed. Continuing drought is affecting 1.5 million people. In addition, the country is hosting more than 400,00 refugees, mostly from Somalia. UNHCR is spearheading assistance not only in the camps in Kenya, but also across the border into Somalia.

In the Sudan, the conflict in the south which has resulted in 1.7 million displaced persons continues to create massive relief funds and to make access to the affected populations difficult and dangerous. Recent good rains and harvest in many parts of the Sudan have reduced the need for the emergency food aid. However, at least 1.1 million persons will need urgent food assistance. In addition, millions require immediate rehabilitation assistance in non-food sectors such as health services and the provision of seeds and tools.

The appeals identify the requirements of the UN entities carrying out emergency relief activities in these affected countries — World Food Programme, UNHCR, UNICEF, FAO, UNDP, UN Volunteers Programme, WHO, WMO, and the Department of Humanitarian Affairs.

The identified emergency humanitarian assistance requirement for 1993 are less than 1992 requirement of $970 million. This is mainly a reflection of improved harvests. At the same time, the appeals give greater attention to rehabilitation and short-term reconstruction. It is essential that the donor community respond urgently and generously to meet both the continuing emergency needs and to establish the necessary conditions for the resumption of development in these four countries.

The 1993 programme for relief and rehabilitation requirements in Somalia is being prepared and will be submitted to a conference on humanitarian assistance for Somalia to be held in Addis Ababa from 11-13 March 1993.

In the document entitled 'Eritrea Declaration of Intent' submitted and approved by the 'Conference for the Establishment of Transitional Government in Ethiopia', held in Addis Ababa from 1-5 July 1991, it was recognized inter-alia that there would be co-operation between the transitional Government in Ethiopia and the provisional Government of Eritrea.

Source: *UN Newsletter*, February 27, 1993.

12.19.3 *Membership of Principal UN Organs, 1993*

General Assembly

The General Assembly is composed of all 180 United Nations Member States. These are:

Afghanistan, Albania, Algeria, Angola, Antigua and Barbuda, Argentina, Armenia, Australia, Austria, Azerbaijan, Bahamas, Bahrain, Bangladesh, Barbados, Belarus, Belgium, Belize, Benin, Bhutan, Bolivia, Bosnia and Herzegovina, Botswana, Brazil, Brunei Darussalam, Bulgaria, Burkina Faso, Burundi, Cambodia, Cameroon, Canada, Cape Verde, Central African Republic, Chad, Chile, China, Colombia Comoros, Congo, Costa Rica, Cote d'Ivoire, Croatia, Cuba, Cyprus, Czech Republic, Democratic People's Republic of Korea, Denmark, Djibouti, Dominica, Dominican Republic, Ecuador, Egypt, El Salvador, Equatorial Guinea, Estonia, Ethiopia, Federated States of Micronesia, Fiji, Finland, France, Gabon, Gambia, Georgia, Germany, Ghana, Greece, Grenada, Guatemala, Guinea, Guinea-Bissau, Guyana, Haiti, Honduras, Hungary, Iceland, India, Indonesia, Iran, Iraq, Ireland, Israel, Italy, Jamaica, Japan, Jordan, Kazakhstan, Kenya, Kuwait, Kyrgyzstan, Lao People's Democratic Republic, Latvia, Lebanon, Lesotho, Liberia, Libya, Liechtenstein, Lithuania, Luxembourg, Madagascar, Malawi, Malaysia, Maldives, Mali, Malta, Marshall Islands, Mauritania, Mauritius, Mexico, Moldova, Mongolia, Morocco, Mozambique, Myanmar, Namibia, Nepal, Netherlands, New Zealand, Nicaragua, Niger, Nigeria, Norway, Oman, Pakistan, Panama, Papua New Guinea, Paraguay, Peru, Philippines, Poland, Portugal, Qatar, Republic of Korea, Romania, Russian Federation, Rwanda, Saint Kitts and Nevis, Saint Lucia, Saint Vincent and the Grenadines, Samoa, San Marino, Sao Tome and Principe, Saudi Arabia, Senegal, Seychelles, Sierra Leone, Singapore, Slovak Republic, Slovenia, Solomon Islands, Somalia, South Africa, Spain, Sri Lanka, Sudan Suriname, Swaziland, Sweden, Syria, Tajikistan, Thailand, Togo, Trinidad and Tobago, Tunisia, Turkey, Turkmenistan, Uganda, Ukraine, United Arab Emirates, United Kingdom, United Republic of Tanzania, United States, Uruguay, Uzbekistan, Vanuatu, Venezuela, Viet Nam, Yemen, Yugoslavia, Zaire, Zambia, Zimbabwe.

Security Council

The Security Council has 15 members. The Charter designates five States as permanent members, and the General Assembly elects 10 other members for two-year terms.

The five permanent members of the Security Council are: China, France, Russian Federation, United Kingdom and United States.

The 10 non-permanent members of the Council in 1993 are: Brazil, Cape Verde, Djibouti, Hungary, Japan, Morocco, New Zealand, Pakistan, Spain and Venezuela.

Economic and Social Council

The Economic and Social Council has 54 members, elected for three-year terms by the General Assembly. In 1993, Council is composed of the following 54 States:

Angola, Argentina, Australia, Austria, Bahamas, Bangladesh, Belarus, Belgium, Benin, Bhutan, Botswana, Brazil, Canada, Chile, China, Colombia, Cuba, Denmark, Ethiopia, France, Gabon, Germany, Guinea, India, Italy, Japan, Kuwait, Libya, Madagascar, Malaysia, Mexico, Morocco, Nigeria, Norway, Peru, Philippines, Poland, Republic of Korea, Romania, Russian Federation, Somalia, Spain, Sri Lanka, Suriname, Swaziland, Syria,

Trinidad and Tobago, Turkey, Ukraine, United Kingdom, United States, Yugoslavia, Zaire.

Trusteeship Council

The Trusteeship council has five members. One member, the United States, administers Palau, one of the remaining four entities which constituted the original Trust Territory of the Pacific Islands, the only Territory that still remained under the Trusteeship System. On 22 December 1990, the Security Council terminated the Trusteeship Agreement for three of the entities: the Federated States of Micronesia and the Marshall Islands (Now United Nations Member States), which had drawn up Compacts of Free Association with the United States; and the Northern Mariana Islands, which had agreed to a Commonwealth Convenient with the Administering Authority. Palau, However, has not yet determined the nature of its future status with the administering Authority and therefore remains under the Trusteeship Agreement.

The non-administering members of the Trusteeship Council are the other four permanent members of the Security Council (China, France, Russian Federation, United Kingdom).

International Court of Justice

The International Court of Justice has 15 members, elected by both the General Assembly and the Security Council. Judges hold nine-year terms.

As of 6 February 1992, the composition of the 15-member Court will be as follows: Roberto Ago, of Italy; Andres Aguilar Mawdsley, of Venezuela; Mohammed Bedjaoui, of Algeria; Bola Ajibola, of Nigeria; Jens Evensen, Norway; Gilbert Guillaume, of France; Sir Robert Yewdall Jennings, of the United Kingdom; Manfred Lachs, of Poland; Ni Zhengyu, of China; Shigeru Oda, of Japan; Raymond Ranjeva, of Madagascar, Stephen M. Schwebel, of the United States; Mohammed Shahabuddeen, of Guyana; Nikolai K. Tarassov, of the Russian Federation; and Christopher G. Weramantry, of Sri Lanka.

Source: *UN Newsletter*, January 23, 1993.

12.19.4 *United Nations Conference on Trade and Development*

The United Nations Conference on Trade and Development (UNCTAD) was set up by the General Assembly in 1964 as one of its permanent organs, mandated to promote international trade, particularly that of developing countries, with a view to accelerating their economic development. UNCTAD has evolved into a universal forum with a development perspective, in which member States review the interdependence of economies and of issues in trade, money and finance. UNCTAD is composed of 183 member States, including the 179 members of the United Nations; many intergovernmental and non-governmental organizations have observer status. The Conference normally meets every four yeas at ministerial level to establish policy guidelines. Between Sessions, work is carried out by the Trade and Development Board and its standing committees, working groups and other subsidiary bodies. The problems of the least developed countries and off the United National Secretariat-numbers about 400. It publishes *UNCTAD* Bulletin.

The second part of the 38th session of the Trade and Development Board (TDB) of the United Nations Conference on Trade and Development (UNCTAD), took place in Geneva from 21 April to 7 May 1992. As a permanent organ of UNCTAD, the TDB has, *inter alia*, the function of implementing and following up the recommendations, declarations, resolutions and other decisions of the general Conference. Meetings of the Conference are held every four years; the most recent, UNCTAD VIII, was held in Cartagena, Colombia from 8-25 February 1992. It took place at a time of great changes on the international scene and growing pressure for reform on UN system institutions, particularly those concerned with international trade, cooperation and development. In this new international politico-economic environment, the principal challenge to UNCTAD VIII was enormous: rigorous analysis of all components of the changed context and determination of the future role and function of the organization.

In a positive 'negotiating climate' which the delegates of the 120 countries present baptised The Spirit of Cartagena, new approaches to the world's development problems and the new structure of UNCTAD were negotiated and spelt out in an important document entitled *A New Partnership for Development: The Cartagena Commitment*. This document contains two principal texts:

* The Final Declaration of UNCTAD VIII, entitled 'The Spirit of Cartagena;
* The Cartagena Commitment.

Among the new themes which were negotiated, agreed upon and found important for the final document, the following should be cited:

* The notion of sustainable development;
* The notion of good management at national and international levels.

The most important result of Cartagena was undoubtedly the new structure and themes of UNCTAD's new work programme. In addition to the Trade and Development Board 'whose mandate has been tightened up', the new structure consists of four Standing Committees, established for a period of four years:

* Commodities;
* Poverty Alleviation;
* Economic Cooperation among Developing Countries (ECDC);
* Developing Services Sector: fostering Competitive Services Sectors in Developing Countries;

and five *ad hoc* working groups, established for a period of two years:

* Investment and Financial Flows: Non-debt creating Financing for Development; New Mechanisms for Increasing Investment and Financial Flows;
* Trade Efficiency;
* Comparative Experiences with Privatization;
* Expansion of Trading Opportunities for Developing Countries;
* Interrelationship between Investment and Technology Transfers.

Existing UNCTAD Committees have been suspended, with two exceptions: the Special Committee on Preferences and the Intergovernmental Group of Experts on Restrictive Business Practices.

The 38th session of the Trade and Development Board paid particular attention to defining the terms of reference of the Standing Committees and *ad hoc* Working Groups. Briefly, their work will consist of:

Commodities: Promotion of national and international policies; periodic and global reviews, studies and analyses of the situation of, and prospects for, commodities; definition of approaches to commodity policies, bearing in mind the particular characteristics and situation of individual commodities, including the specific problems of the LDCs; facilitation and coordination of work in the commodity field; follow-up and facilitation of intergovernmental consultations and action; analysis and encouragement of the achievement of international agreements and arrangements; study of the possibility of a "World Commodity Conference".

Poverty Alleviation: Essentially action-oriented, its objective will be to prevent, alleviate and reduce poverty, particularly where it is most acute. The mandate describes specific ways of going about this, such as exchanging and examining views, experiences and information, considering the financing and organization of social development programmes in developing countries, and identifying the links between poverty alleviation and sustainable development.

ECDC: Analyse past experiences "with a view to recommending measures to strengthen and enlarge" existing ECDC and identify "new potentials for cooperation, including with other countries interested in such cooperation" and generally aim at increasing trade liberalization and transparency.

Developing Services Sectors: Contribute through analysis and support to strengthening national services sectors (production and exports). This Committee will also deal with shipping, trade efficiency, insurance, the role of services in market-oriented development and restrictive business practices, while taking into account the work undertaken by the relevant intergovernmental Group of Experts. The work of the Committee should not overlap with that of GATT.

Investment and Financial Flows: Examine all aspects of non-debt-creating finance for development with a view of taking advantage of acquired experience in this field.

Trade Efficiency: Examine how modern organization and technology can be used to foster greater participation in international trade; contribute to fostering transparency in trade-related information flows; identify areas in which technical cooperation could be necessary; prepare the 1994 international symposium on trade efficiency.

Comparative Experiences with Privatization: Review countries' experience in this field; examine medium- and long-term objectives of the privatization process; elaborate, as possible guidelines for policy-makers, basic elements for consideration in formulating privatization programmes and plans; serve as a forum for the exchange and dissemination of relevant information.

Expansion of Trading Opportunities: Analyse prospects for, and examine ways of, expanding trade opportunities for developing countries; the group should consider trade opportunities in the light of structural adjustment

policies, trade liberalization measures (such as those adopted to implement the results of the Uruguay Round), and promotion of regional integration.
Interrelationship between Investment and Technology Transfers: Examine the interactions between investments and the transfer, absorption and generation of technology in developing countries, identify factors conducive to technology transfer through foreign investment, analyse the role of intellectual property and the role of all concerned with such transfers, examine the role of technological change, examine and encourage new initiatives and exchange of experience.

The debates and negotiations at this Spring 1992 session of the Board were deeply ingrained with the Spirit of Cartagena and sought to respect the following principles:

* concern for balance (which had often been difficult to find) between the national and international approach to the work of the Committees and Working Groups;
* particular attention to the needs of the developing countries, especially the least developed countries;
* vigilance in respect of the financial repercussions of the new terms of reference;
* concern not to duplicate the competences of UNCTAD with those of other organizations, by emphasizing increased coordination;
* provision of precise and specialised working mandates for Committees and Working Groups, while leaving macro-economic concerns, major items of global balance and multilateral negotiations (debt, the results of the Uruguay Round, etc.) to other bodies (including the Board).

However, the final phase of the negotiations was extremely tense, particularly during discussions on questions linked to financial issues (services, ECDC, investments and financial flows, among others).

The Board also adopted general principles governing meetings of its new executive sessions and decided to examine the eventual setting up of a working group on structural adjustment, in the perspective of disarmament and its consequences for development and economic growth.

The first part of the 39th session of the TDB will be held in Geneva from 28 September-9 October 1992. It will deal essentially with the substantive work of the committees and working groups, which should already be underway.

Source: *Go Between*, July 1992, Geneva.

12.19.5 *General Agreement on Tariffs and Trade*

GATT Focus

The General Agreement on Tariffs and Trade (GATT) is a binding contract between 105 governments which together account for 90 per cent of world merchandise trade. The objective of the contract is to provide a secure and predictable international trading environment for the business community and a continuing process of trade liberalization in which investment, job creation and trade can thrive. In this way, the multilateral trading system contributes to growth and development throughout the world.

TABLE 12.13: GATT Membership as on September 15, 1992
(105 Contracting Parties; dates indicate accession)

Antigua and Barbuda	30 March 1987	Lesotho	8 January 1988
Argentina	11 October 1967	Luxembourg	1 January 1948
Australia	1 January 1948	Macau	11 January 1991
Austria	19 October 1951	Madagascar	30 September 1963
Bangladesh	16 December 1972	Malawi	28 August 1964
Barbados	15 February 1967	Malaysia	24 October 1957
Belgium	1 January 1948	Maldives	19 April 1983
Belize	7 October 1983	Malta	17 November 1964
Benin	12 September 1963	Mauritania	30 September 1963
Bolivia	8 September 1990	Mauritius	2 September 1970
Botswana	28 August 1987	Mexico	24 August 1986
Brazil	30 July 1948	Morocco	17 June 1987
Burkina Faso	3 May 1963	Mozambique	27 July 1992
Burundi	13 March 1965	Myanmar	29 July 11948
Cameroon	3 May 1963	Namibia	15 September 1992
Canada	1 January 1948	Netherlands	1 January 1948
Central African Rep.	3 May 1963	New Zealand	30 July 1948
Chad	12 July 1963	Nicaragua	28 May 1950
Chile	16 March 1949	Niger	31 December 1963
Colombia	3 October 1981	Nigeria	18 November 1960
Congo	3 May 1963	Norway	10 July 1948
Costa Rica	24 November 1990	Pakistan	30 July 1948
Cote d'ivoire	31 December 1963	Peru	7 October 1951
Cuba	1 January 1948	Philippines	27 December 1979
Cyprus	15 July 1963	Poland	18 October 1967
Czech & Slovak F.R.	20 April 1948	Portugal	6 May 1962
Denmark	28 May 1950	Romania	14 November 1971
Dominican Republic	19 May 1950	Rwanda	1 January 1966
Egypt	9 May 1970	Senegal	27 September 1963
El Salvador	22 May 1991	Sierra Leone	19 May 1961
Finland	25 May 1950	Singapore	20 August 1973
France	1 January 1948	South Africa	13 June 1948
Gabon	3 May 1963	Spain	29 August 1963
Gambia	22 February 1965	Sri Lanka	29 July 1948
Germany	1 October 1951	Suriname	22 March 1978
Ghana	17 October 1957	Sweden	30 April 1950
Greece	1 March 1950	Switzerland	1 August 1966
Guatemala	10 October 1991	Tanzania	9 December 1961
Guyana	5 July 1966	Thailand	20 November 1982
Haiti	1 January 1950	Togo	20 March 1964
Hong Kong	23 April 1986	Trinidad & Tobago	23 October 1962
Hungary	9 September 1973	Tunisia	19 August 1990
Iceland	21 April 1968	Turkey	17 October 1951
India	8 July 1948	Uganda	23 October 1962
Indonesia	24 February 1950	United Kingdom	1 January 1948
Ireland	22 December 1967	United States	1 January 1948
Israel	5 July 1962	Uruguay	6 December 1953
Italy	30 May 1950	Venezuela	31 August 1990
Jamaica	31 December 1963	Yugoslavia	25 August 1966
Japan	10 September 1955	Zaire	11 September 1971
Kenya	5 February 1964	Zambia	10 February 1982
Korea Rep. of	14 April 1967	Zimbabwe	11 July 1948
Kuwait	3 May 1963		

Source: *GATT Newsletter*, No. 93, September 1992.

12.20 **United States of America: Discovery**

A Chinese Buddhist monk probably discovered the new world more than a thousand years before Christopher Columbus.

The monk and explorer Fa-Xien (337-422), reached the American west coast, probably landing somewhere between today's Los Angeles and Acapulco, in 412 A.D.

The claim is made by Lian Yunshan, 67, a retired editor of China's leading newspaper *People's Daily* and a Professor of the People's University, in his book titled *Who Came to America First?*

Fa-Xien, whose pilgrimage to India during the Eastern Jin Dynasty opened Sino-Indian relations, was blown off course to America by a storm while sailing back to China, according to Lian.

He bases his claim on travel notes written by Fa-Xien, who recorded spending 105 days at sea in a flotilla of ships after leaving Ceylon for home. Finally they sighted land and went ashore at a place he called Yepoti.

Fa-xien and his companions stayed there for 5 months before attempting to return. It took them three and a half months to arrive in East China's Shandong Province.

About 1,500 years later, when British scholar Samuel Bill translated Fa-Xien's travel notes into English, he mistakenly thought Yepoti was on the route from India to China. In trying to find a place with a similar pronunciation he inferred that Yepoti might be Java. He made an annotation that this was guesswork on his part.

Bill's views remained unchallenged for many years although there were obvious errors, according to Lian.

He points out the Ceylon is just 1,800 nautical miles from Java, which takes a mere 10 to 20 days by sailing ship, that could not be compared with the 3-month voyage from Ceylot to Yepoti which Fa-Xien recorded.

LIan notes that there are 13,700 islands in the Java Sea area, while Fa-Xien and his ship's company saw only one piece of land during the last 90 days of their stormy voyage to Yepoti.

At the time Buddhism was widespread in Southeast Asia, especially in Java, but Fa-Xien wrote in his travel notes that the people of Yepoti knew nothing of Buddhism.

Lian says that no place of Southeast Asia, India and the Gulf used the name of Yepoti and Java had been a trading partner with China since the second century. It was unreasonable for Fa-Xien and his companions to mistake Java as Yepoti.

Lian rejects the view that Yepoti was Java. He has also collected material which rebuts claims that Fa-Xien landed somewhere in Asia and did not reach America.

Lian is not the first to advance the theory that Fa-Xien reached America. At the beginning of this century, French historians and the noted Chinese scholar, Zhang Taiyun, thought it possible, but they did not have any evidence to support the claim.

Having made close studies on Fa-Xien's log book, Lian concludes that his flotilla entered the Pacific Ocean 16 days after leaving Ceylon.

Lian quotes records in Fa-Xien's travel notes to support his judgement, including the luminescence of the tide, and schools of whales and sharks sighted during the voyage.

Fa-Xien also wrote that their stone anchors could not reach the bottom and their ships, which sailed east according to the sun, ran before the wind on rainy and overcast days.

Since there was west wind drift at that tie in the North Pacific Ocean and ancient ships average 100 sea miles a day, Fa-Xien and his flotilla must have sailed east for 9,000 to 11,000 miles, Lian says.

He believes that they passed the Bashi Channel, entered the Japan current flowing to the Northeast, and at 35 to 40 degrees latitude north, shifted east until they got to the western bank of Mexico.

Lian says that what Fa-Xien wrote about Yepoti was identical with ancient Mexico and his pronunciation of Yepoti sounds like Acapulco, a coastal city in Mexico.

More importantly, Lian says, Fa-Xien recorded that his flotilla sailed at least 10,000 miles on return journey from Yepoti to China. They saw no land and in the last 13 days of the voyage they sailed northwest. This could only be done by sailing from Mexico to China.

As a result, Lian concludes that Fa-Xien landed somewhere between Acapulco and Los Angeles in 412.

However, Lian says that it does not mean Fa-Xien was the first to reach America. He says that there can be no final answer until other doubts are resolved, including those in the book *Shan Hai Jing.*

Shan Hai Jing, the book of the mountains and the seas, was an early Chinese geographical record dating from the Warring States Period (403 B.C. — 221 B.C.).

Its geographical records on the southern, northern, central and western parts of China coincide with features of the landscape. However, the record of the eastern region including notes about the coastline and 4 mountains, do not match the landscape.

To the experts' surprise, the descriptions including those of the 4 mountains and coastline correspond with North America. This was verified by an American scholar in the 1970s.

This could mean that the ancient Chinese who wrote the book had examined the geographical situation of North America?

Source: *News from China*, Vol. 5, No. 8, February 24, 1993.

12.21 World Decade for Cultural Development 1988-97

Proposed by the Member States at the World Conference on Cultural Policies (Mexico City, 1982) and approved and proclaimed by the United Nations General Assembly on 8 December 1986, the World Decade for Cultural Development, official inaugurated in 1988 will end in 1997, shortly before the beginning of the third millennium.

The two principal objectives of the World Decade for Cultural Development — greater emphasis on the cultural dimension in the development process and the stimulation of creative skills and cultural life in general — reflect an awareness of the need to respond to the major world challenges which shape the horizon of the twenty-first century. Aims of such an ambitious nature clearly imply a programme of measures for major achievements.

Plan of Action for the Decade, an intentionally open and flexible outline plan destined to trigger the imagination and to suggest various 'main axes' of new action puts forward guidelines designed to stimulate long-term activities that will produce significant results by the end of the 1990s.

This Plan of Action centres on four major objectives:

Acknowledging the cultural dimension in development.
Asserting and enhancing cultural identities.
Broadening participation in cultural life.
Promoting international cultural co-operation.

Guide to the Decade

APPENDIX I

Recommendation No. 27 of the World Conference on Cultural Policies
Mexico City, July-August 1982

World Decade for Cultural Development

The Conference,

Noting with satisfaction the achievements of the cultural policies and practices of the Member States over the last ten years,

Emphasizing the culture constitutes a fundamental part of the life of each individual and of each community and that, consequently, development — whose ultimate aim should be focused on man — must have a cultural dimension,

Noting that efforts to promote cultural development form part of the peoples' aspirations to achieve political liberation and socio-economic development,

Considering that action to promote culture should be considered in the international perspective, as an imperative of world development conducive to peace,

Recognizing the work Unesco has undertaken to promote culture and the equality of the cultures of different peoples,

Recalling Article 1 of the Charter of the United Nations,

1 *Recommends* that the General Conference of Unesco propose to the General Assembly of the United Nations the proclamation of a World Decade for Cultural Development and that it authorize the Director-General to take the appropriate measures in this connection;

2. *Requests* the General Assembly of the United Nations to study the possibility of including among its objectives for the Third Development Decade the implementation of a Plan of Action within the framework of a World Decade for Cultural Development in order to eradicate illiteracy, ensure broad participation in culture and emphasize the cultural dimension of development and the affirmation of the cultural identity of each nation.

APPENDIX 2

Resolution II.10 adopted by the General Conference of Unesco at its twenty-third session *Sofia, 8 November 1985*

World Decade for Cultural Development

The General Conference,

Recalling that the human person both acts upon and is acted upon by economic developments, and *emphasizing* that this is an essential and concrete aspect of human rights,

Emphasizing that an analysis of the imbalances characterizing the world situation clearly shows economic factors to be no longer to sole term of reference in development matters,

Considering the functions conferred on Unesco by its Constitution, especially Article I thereof, and consequently *considering* that Unesco should endeavour, in its fields of competence, to stimulate research or implement specific projects, so as to make its contribution to the models and strategies to be adopted for development,

Recalling resolution II.20 concerning the World Decade for Cultural Development adopted by consensus at its twenty-second session,

Further recalling that the proposed World Decade for Cultural Development, because it concerns all the organizations of the United Nations system, entails a procedure which should culminate in its adoption by the United Nations General Assembly at its forty-fist session (autumn 1986),

Welcoming the highly positive results of the consultations conducted by the Director-General with the organizations of the United Nations system and *taking note* of the decision adopted by the Executive Board at its 122nd session after consideration of the Director-General's report (122EX/14),

Also taking note of the declaration of the Heads of State and Government of the Organization of African Unity at their twenty-first summit (Addis Ababa, July 1985) and of the recommendation of the Eighth Regional Conference of National Commissions for Unesco of Latin America and the Caribbean (July 1985), both of which support that enterprise and emphasize its importance,

Having examined the report of the Director-General on the Draft Plan of Action for the Decade (23C/16),

1. *Approves* the main points and major proposals set forth therein;
2. *Emphasizes* that the active participation of Member States, organizations of the United Nations system and international governmental and non-governmental organizations, as well as individuals and the public in the broad sense of the word, is particularly important for the success of the proposed Decade;
3. *Invites* Member States:

   (a) to contribute in a concrete manner to the fulfilment of the objectives assigned to the decade;

   (b) to promote all forms of regional and inter-regional co-operation so as to foster, in collaboration with the competent regional and international organizations, the strengthening of international cultural cooperation and the emergence of new strategies for development;

4. *Invites* the Director-General:

   (a) to take the necessary steps, in accordance with established procedure, for the question of the proclamation of the World Decade for Cultural Development to be submitted to the United Nations General Assembly so as to enable the Decade to be launched in 1988;
   (b) to continue throughout 1986 the necessary consultations and negotiations with Member States and international governmental and non-governmental organizations, with a view to the preparation and implementation of the Plan of Action;
   (c) to take into account, when finalizing the Plan of Action for the Decade, the observations made at its twenty-third session and the consultations referred to in paragraph (b) above, and to submit a revised version of the Plan of Action to the Executive Board at its 124th session;
   (d) to include in the Draft Programme and Budget for 1988-89 (24C/5) provisions relating to the implementation of the Decade;

5. *Also invites* Member States and the Director-General to ensure, within Unesco's fields of competence, that the implementation of the Decade is linked with that of the next Medium-Term Plan and the Fourth United Nations Development Decade.

APPENDIX 3

Resolution 41/187,* adopted by the General Assembly of the United Nations Organization *New York, 8 December 1986*

Proclamation of the World Decade for Cultural Development

The General Assembly,

Considering recommendation No. 27[1] adopted by the World Conference on Cultural Policies convened by the United Nations Educational, Scientific and Cultural Organization at Mexico City in 1982, in which it recommended that the General Conference of the United Nations Educational, Scientific and Cultural Organization propose to the General Assembly of the United Nations the proclamation of a world decade for cultural development,

Considering also resolution II.20[2] and II.10[3] adopted by the General Conference of the United United Nations Educational, Scientific and Cultural Organization at its twenty-second and twenty-third sessions, respectively,

Recalling Economic and Social Council resolution 1986-69 of 23 July 1986.

Notes: * Being the subject of Item 12 of the agenda, Resolution 41/187 was adopted on 8 December 1986, at the 100th plenary meeting of the forty-first session of the Assembly General of the United Nations Organization, on the report of the Second Commission (A/41/930/Add. 2).

1. E/1984/53, p. 14.
2. Ibid., Annex. 1.
3. E/1986/116, Annex.

12.22 Yugoslavia (former): Report of the Commission of Experts on War Crimes

The Commission of Experts on war crimes in the territory of the former Yugoslavia has said that it would welcome a decision by the Security Council or another international body to establish a war crimes tribunal for crimes committed in that region. The five-member Commission was set up by the Security Council last year to investigate reports of grave breaches of the Geneva Conventions and other violations of international humanitarian law in the former Yugoslavia.

In a recent interim report to UN Secretary-General, the Commission said that a tribunal on war crimes might be established by States choosing to combine their jurisdictions under the principle of universality. Nuremberg International Military Tribunal following the Second World War was said to have derived its authority from such a combination of national jurisdictions of States.

The Commission would accept an offer from the Canadian Government to provide a team to conduct further on-site investigations of the offences in the Vukovar area. While preliminary reports showed that grave breaches and other violations of international humanitarian law had been committed in the former Yugoslavia, tangible evidence of those violations must be secured in the form of testimonies, identification of victims, forensic or pathology reports, photographs and location maps. That was why the Commission's database on human rights violations must be completed as soon as possible, "since that alone can provide the foundation for the formulation of conclusions on the evidence of war crimes in the former Yugoslavia", the Commission said.

In a letter dated 9 February which accompanied the Commission's report, the UN Secretary-General told the Security Council that he had asked the Commission to continue its work on the database and that he would take the necessary steps for the creation of a trust fund to finance the Commission's work.

(Source: *UN Newsletter*, February 20, 1993.)

13

SIGNIFICANT INTERNATIONAL EVENTS

April 1992

6 Yeltsin survives no-trust motion.

15 Muslim rebels claimed control of Afghanistan's main military base, 35 miles from Kabul.

16 Najibullah reportedly resigned.

28 Mojadidi takes over power in Kabul. Pak recognises new regime.

May

6 Cease-fire declared in Kabul.

9 Pak supplied US missiles to China.

29 Indo-US naval exercises conclude.

June

6 Monica Seles captures her third successive French Open Title.

8 Indian diplomat attacked in Karachi.

16 Bush, Yeltsin arrive at N-accord.

30 Ramos sworn in Philippines President.

July

2 Panic appointed Yugoslav P.M.

4 Graf retains Wimbledon Singles title.

9 UNESCO Peace Prize for Mother Teresa.

14 Rabin takes over as Israeli Premier.

August

23 Explosions at a depth of 1,300 metres caused by a gas build-up in an Eastern Ukraine coal mine killed 17 people.

27 US planes rule Iraqi skies.

September

1 10th NAM Summit at Djakarta.

11 45 workers died and about 29 injured due to blast in coal mine in Changshee province of China.

14 Indian stock markets open for foreigners.

20 French 'yes' to Maastricht Treaty.

27 163 killed in Nigerian air crash.

28 167 killed in PIA plane crash near Kathmandu.

October

6 Kuwaitis vote for democratic reforms.

9 Ex-German Chancellor Willy Brandt is dead.

30 India, China to open more border points.

November

4 Democrat Bill Clinton elected new US President.
12 England votes to ordain women as priests.

December

4 UN approved US-led operation in Somalia.
9 Charles, Diana to separate.
13 3000 killed in Indonesia quake.
14 Chernomyrdim elected Russian PM.
17 India sends troops to Somalia.
19 Kim Young Sam elected S. Korean President.
20 Ruling party in Taiwan defeated.
22 158 killed in Libyan plane crash.
24 Milosevik declared Serbian President.

January 1993

1 Czechoslovakia splits into two countries: Czeck Republic of the Czechs with Prague as its Capital and Slovak Republic with Bratislava as Capital.
3 Russian President Boris Yeltsin and US President George Bush sign the START-II Nuclear Arms Reduction Treaty.
4 William Jefferson Clinton sworn in as the 42nd President of the United States of America.

February

9 U.N. Office shot at Cambodia.
— Russian Privatisation Minister Anatoly Chubais officially launches Moscow's campaign to private State-owned companies. Privatisation of Russia's has been a central plan of President Boris Yeltsin plan to reform the economy.
16 US President Bill Clinton calls for bold experimentation to move the American economy forward and makes it clear that more Americans must contribute today so that all Americans can be better tomorrow.
27 US to withdraw from Somalia
— President Bill Clinton for aid to Russia.
28 New York blast caused by a bomb.

March

2 The Supreme Court of Philippine rules that citizens cannot be compelled to salute the Philippine flag, sing the national anthem or recite the oath of the allegiance if this violates their religious beliefs.
A palm-size colour television set made by Casio Computer Co. of Japan will be listed as the world's smallest in the 1994 *Guinness Book of World Records*, according to the book's publishers, reports Oana-Kyodo. The size of Casio's 'LCD colour television CV-1' will be among 17 new records carried in the book, The Liquid Crystal Display (LCD) TV is 6.0 centimetres wide, 9.1 centimetres high, 2.4 centimetres deep, and weighs 168.5 grams with a battery.
7 A ten-point accord signed by eight Afghan groups including President Burhanuddin Rubbani's Jamiat-e-Islami.

March

9 John Major's Government suffers defeat by 26 votes in the House of Commons over the Maastricht Treaty. Several members of his own Conservative Party vote against the proposal of the Government.

10 Indonesian President General Suharto was re-elected President for the sixth time for another five-year plan.

11 Russian President Boris Yeltsin stripped of most of his powers by Parliament.

12 US President Clinton unveils his four-year $19.5 billion plan for economic development.

— 78-year old Kanemaru, long-time Japanese 'fringmaker' indicted for concealing of yen 200 million.

— South Korean troops on alert to guard against provocation from Communist North Korea.

PART TWO

INDIA 1992-93

NA	NA	64	NA	NA	2290
[illegible]	[illegible]	56	NA	NA	1440
NA	NA	24	36	90	2030

[illegible] are listed in descending order of their 1990 infant mortality rate [illegible]
[illegible] GDP per capita in [illegible] have been converted to US dollars [illegible]

[illegible] members of the United Nations have been included [illegible]

14

LAND AND ITS PEOPLE

India that is Bharat covering a land area 32,87,263 sq.km is the seventh largest and the second most populous country of the world. It stretches 3,214 km from North to South between the extreme latitudes and 2,933 km from East to West between the extreme longitudes. On this 2.4 per cent of earth's surface live 15 per cent (88 crore people) of world's population.

14.1 Population

Over 160 million people are added annually to our population (President's Republic day Speech, 25th January, 1989). Since 1881, the Census in India has been taken regularly after ten years. According to 1991 Census, the total population of India (including the projected population of Assam) is 8,43,930,861. As compared to 1981 census, it showed an increase of 23.50 per cent. According to 1991 Census, the growth of urban population in the country during the decade 1981-1991, slowed down by about ten per cent as compared to the earlier decade of 1971-81. However, the number of cities and towns has been consistently increasing. The urban population at present in 25.72 per cent.

14.2 Density

The average density of population per km^2 in 1991 was 267. It varies considerably form State to State.

14.3 Sex Ratio

According to 1991 Census (Provisional) there are 43.7 crore males and 40.6 crore females; thus for every 1,000 males India has 929 females. Only Kerala has more women than men, i.e., 1,040 per 1,000 men. The lowest female ratio among the State is in Haryana, i.e., 874 for 1,000 men and the lowest female ratio among the Union Territories is in Chandigarh where it is 733 per thousand.

14.4 Literacy

According to 1991 Census, the literacy percentage is 52.11. Out of this 63.86 per cent of males and 39.42 per cent of females are literate.

14.5 **Major Religions and Persuasions, 1981**

TABLE 14.1 : Major Religions and Persuasions, 1981 (excluding Assam)

Religion Community	Population	Percentage of Total Population
Hindus	54,97,24,517	82.63
Muslims	7,55,71,514	11.36
Christians	1,61,74,498	2.43
Sikhs	1,30,78,146	1.96
Buddhists	47,19,900	0.71
Jains	31,92,572	0.48
Other persuasions	27,56,285	0.42
Religion not stated	60,217	0.01

14.6 **Languages**

The detailed data from the 1981 Census (data for 1991 not yet available) which were made available only in 1988, enumerate the main languages spoken in the household and not the mother tongue and groups related languages under a dominant language. By this count, 106 languages are separately recognised. Of these 94 are spoken by 10,000 or more people.

There were 1562 mother tongues, 10 writing system, and 76 languages as used in the school system out of 2000 codified languages.

Sixteen languages have been specifies in the Eighth Schedule of the Constitution. These are : Assamesse, Bengali, Gujarati, Hindi, Kannada, Kashmiri, Malayalam, Marathi, Nepali, Oriya, Punjabi, Sanskrit, Sindhi, Tamil, Telugu and Urdu.

14.7 **National Flag**

The National Flag is horizontally tricolour with deep saffron (*Kesari*) at the top, white in the middle and dark green at the bottom in equal proportion. The ratio of the width of the flag to its length is two to three. In the centre of the white band is a wheel, in navy blue, which represents the *Charkha*. Its design in that of the wheel (Chakra) which appears on the abacus of the sarnath Lion Capital of Ashoka. Its diameter approximates to the width of the white band and it has 24 spokes.

The design of the National flag was adopted by the Constituent Assembly of India on 22 July, 1947. Its use and display are regulated by a code.

14.8 **State Emblem**

The State Emblem of India is an adaptation from the Sarnath Lion Capital of Ashoka as preserved in the Sarnath Museum. In the original, there are four lions, standing back to back, mounted on an abacus with a frieze carrying sculptures in high relief of an elephant, a galloping horse, a bull and a lion separated by intervening wheels (*Chakras*) over a bell-shaped lotus. Carved out of a single block of polished sandstone, the capital is crowned by the Wheel of the Law (*Dharma Chakra*).

In the State emblem adopted by the Government of India on 26th January,

1950, only three lions are visible, the fourth being hidden from view. The wheel appears on relief in the centre of the abacus with a bull on the right and a horse on the left and the outlines of the other wheels in the extreme right and left. The bell-shaped lotus has been omitted. The words *Satyameva Jayate* from the *Mundaka Upanishad*, meaning 'Truth alone Triumphs', are inscribed below the abacus in Devanagri script.

14.9 **National Anthem**

The song *Jana-gana-mana,* composed by Rabindranath Tagore (1861-1941) was adopted by the Constituent Assembly as the National Anthem of India on 24th January, 1950. It was first sung on 27th December, 1911 at the Calcutta session of the Indian National Congress. The complete song consists of five stanzas. The first stanza constitutes the full version of the National Anthem. It reads :

Jana-gana-mana-adhinayaka, jaya he
Bharata-bhagya-vidhata
Punjab-Sindhu-Gujarat-Maratha-
Dravida-Utkala-Banga
Vindhya-Himachala-Yamuna-Ganga-
Uchchala-jaladhi-taranga.
Tava shubha name jage,
tava shubha asisa, mage,
gahe tava jaya-gatha,
Jana-gana-mangala-dayaka jaya he
Bharata-bhagya-vidhata.
Jaya he, jaya he, jaya he,
Jaya jaya jaya, jaya he!

Playing time of the full version of the National Anthem is approximately 52 seconds. A short version consisting of the first and last lines of the stanza (playing time approximately 20 seconds) is also played on certain occasions. The following is Tagore's English rendering of this stanza:

Thou art the ruler of the minds of all people,
dispenser of India's destiny.
Thy name rouses the hearts of Punjab, Sind, Gujarat and Maratha.
Of the Dravida and Orissa and Bengal;
it echoes in the hills of the Vindhyas and Himalayas,
mingles in the music of Jamuna and Ganges
and is chanted by the waves of the india Sea.
They pray for thy blessings and sing thy praise.
The saving of all people waits in thy hand,
thou dispenser of India's destiny.
victory, victory, victory to thee.

14.10 **National Song**

The song *Vande Mataram,* composed by Bankimchandra Chatterji (1838-1894) was a source of inspiration to the people in their struggle for freedom. It has an equal status with *Jana-gana-mana.* The first political occasion on which it was sung was the 1896 session of the Indian National Congress. The following is the text of its stanza :

Vande Mataram!
Sujalam, suphalam, malayaja shitalam,
Shasyashyamalam, Mataram!
Shubhrajyotsna pulakitayaminim,
Phullakusumita drumadala shobhinim,
Suhasinim sumadhura bhashinim,
Sukhadam, Varadam, Mataram!

The English translation of the stanza rendered by Sri Aurobindo (1872-1950) in prose[1] is:

I bow to thee, Mother,
richly-watered, richly-fruited,
cool with the winds of the south.
dark with the crops of the harvests,
the Mother!
Her nights rejoicing in the glory of the moonlight,
her lands clothed beautifully with her trees in flowering bloom,
sweet of laughter, sweet of speech,
the Mother, giver of boons, giver of bliss.

14.11 **National Calendar**

A uniform National Calendar based on the *Saka Era* with *Chaitra* as its first month and a normal year of 365 days was adopted from 22 March, 1957 (along with the Gregorian calendar) for the following official purposes in particular :

(i) *Gazette of India*
(ii) News broadcast by All India Radio,
(iii) Calendars issued by the government of India, and
(iv) Government communications addressed to members of the public.

The dates of the National Calendar have a permanent correspondence with the dates of the Gregorian calendar; *Chaitra* 1 falling on 22 March normally and on 21 March in a leap year.

Chaitra 1 of *Saka* Era is the New Year Day. *Saka* Era was established in AD 78 by Emperor Kanishka of the Saka dynasty, who ruled in the North and North-Western India in the first century of the Christian era. The day, which has been chosen to become the first day of the New Year, is *vernal equinox* when the day and the night are of equal duration throughout the world. Saka calendar is based on Solar Chaitra and not on Lunar *Chaitra*. *Chaitra Shukla Pratipada* which is celebrated as New Year Day, in many parts of the country, is called differently. It is *Gudi Padwa* in Maharashtra and *Yugadi* in Karnataka based on

1. As published in *Sri Aurobindo Birth Centenary Library*, Population edition, 1912, Vol. 8.

lunar calendar, etc. April 13, *Baishakhi* in Punjab, *Pongal* on April 14 in Tamil Nadu and *Paila Baishakh* in West Bengal are based on solar calendar. In solar calendar this discrepancy of 22 or 23 days (between March 22 and April 13/14) has been caused by an astronomical phenomenon called the precession of the equinoxes.

14.12 **National Animal**

The majestic tiger [*Panthera tigris* (Linnaeus)], the national animal of India for its rich colour, illusive design and formidable power, has always been held in high esteem in India. Among the carnivores, the tiger if very georgeous and attractive with roaring voice as symbol of power. Out of eight races of the species known the world over, the Indian race is the Bengal tiger. The Royal Bengal Tiger is found throughout the country and also in Nepal, Bhutan and Bangladesh. As shrinkage of habitat in India dwindled its population to only 1,827 in 1972, the Project Tiger was launched on 1st April, 1973. Since then there is a gradual increase in its population. The present tiger population is 4,330.

14.13 **National Bird**

The Indian peacock [*Pavo cristatus* (Linnaeus)], the national bird of India, is one of the most beautiful birds, particularly the males having the glistering blue neck, breast, fanshape crest and long magnificent tail. The courtship dance of the male by fanning up the tail before the female is most spectacular. From time immemorial, this bird has found a profound place in Indian literature, folklore and legends.

The Indian peafowl, as the peacock is called, is widely found in the country in south and east of India, Jammu and Kashmir, east Assam, south of Mizoram and the whole of Indian Peninsula. It is fully protected under the Indian Wild Life (Protection) Act, 1972.

Source : *India 1991*.

14.14 **Presidents of India**

January 26, 1950 — May 13,1962	Rajendra Prasad
May 13, 1962 — May 13, 1967	S.Radhakrishnan
May 13, 1967 — May 3, 1969	Zakir Husain
May 3, 1969 — July 20, 1969	V.V. Giri (Acting)
July 20, 1969 — August 21, 1969	M. Hidayatullah (Acting)
August 24, 1969 — August 24, 1974	V.V. Giri
August 24, 1974 — February 11, 1977	Fakhruddin Ali Ahmed
February 11, 1977 — July 25, 1977	B.D. Jatti (Acting)
July 25, 1977 — July 25, 1982	N. Sanjeeva Reddy
July 25, 1982 — July 25, 1987.	Zail Singh
July 25, 1987 — July 25, 1992	R. Venkataraman
July 25, 1992 —	S.D. Sharma

14.15 Vice Presidents of India

1952-1962	S. Radhakrishnan
1962-1967	Zakir Husain
1967-1969	V.V. Giri
1969-1974	G.S. Pathak
1974-1979	B.D. Jatti
1979-1984	M. Hidayatullah
1984-1987	R. Venkataraman
1987-1992	S.D. Sharma
1993-	K.R. Narayanan

14.16 Prime Ministers of India

August 15, 1947 — May 27, 1964	Jawaharlal Nehru
May 27, 1964 — June 9, 1964	Guljari Lal Nanda (Acting)
June 9, 1964 — January 11, 1966	Lal Bahadur Shastri
January 11, 1966 — January 24, 1966	Guljari Lal Nanda (Acting)
January 24, 1966 — March 24, 1977	Indira Gandhi
March 24, 1977 — July 28, 1979	Morarji Desai
July 28, 1979 — January 14, 1980	Charan Singh
January 14, 1980 — October 31, 1984	Indira Gandhi
October 31, 1984 — December 1, 1989	Rajiv Gandhi
December 2, 1989 — November 7, 1990	V.P. Singh
November 9, 1990 — June 20, 1991	Chandra Shekhar
June 20, 1991 —	P.V. Narasimha Rao

14.17 Speakers of the Lok Sabha

1952-1956	G.V. Mavlankar
1956-1962	Ananthasayanam Ayyangar
1962-1967	S. Hukam Singh
1967-1969	N. Sanjeeva Reddy
1969-1975	G.S. Dhillon
1975-1977	B.R. Bhagat
March 1977 — July 1977	N. Sanjeeva Reddy
1977-1979	K.S. Hegde
1980-1989	Balram Jakhar
November 19, 1989 — June 1991	Rabi Ray
July 10, 1991 —	Shivraj Patil

14.18 Important Days

National Youth Day	January 12
Army Day	January 15
Republic Day	January 26
International Customs Day	January 26
Martyrs' Day	January 30

National Science Day	February 28
International Women's Day*	March 8
World Consumers Rights Day	March 15
World Disabled Day	March (Third Sunday of March)
International Day for the Elimination of Racial Discrimination*	March 21
World Forestry Day	March 21
World Meteorological Day*	March 23
National Maritime Day	April 5
World Health Day*	April 7
May Day (Worker's Day/International Labour Day)	May 1
World Red Cross Day	May 8
World Telecommunication Day*	May 17
World Day for Cultural Development*	May 21
Commonwealth Day	May 24
World No-Tobacco Day*	May 31
World Environment Day*	June 5
International Day of Solidarity with the Struggling People of South Africa*	June 16
World Population Day*	July 11
Hiroshima Day	August 6
Quit India Day	August 9
Nagasaki Day	August 9
International Day of Solidarity with the Struggle of Women in South Africa*	August 9
Independence Day	August 15
Teacher's Day	September 5
International Literacy Day*	September 8
International Day of Peace*	September (Third Tuesday of September)
World Tourism Day	September 27
International Day for the Elderly*	October 1
University Children's Day*	October (First Monay of October
Mahatma Gandhi Birthday	October 2
World Habitat Day	October 5
Air Force Day	October 8
Universal Postal Union Day*	October 9
Day of Solidarity with South African Political Prisoners	October 11
Post Office Day	October 19
World Standard Day	October 14
World Food Day*	October 16
United Nations Day	October 24
World Development Information Day*	October 24
National Re-Dedication Day	October 31
Children's Day	November 14
National Integration Day	November 19

International Day of Solidarity with the Palestinian People*	November 29
World AIDS Day*	December 1
International Day of Disabled Persons*	December 3
Navy Day	December 4
International Volunteer Day for Economic and Social Development	December 5
Flag Day	December 7
Human Rights Day*	December 10
Kisan Day	December 23

* Proclaimed by UN System/UNESCO Associated Schools

14.19 **People of India**

14.19.1 *The Profile of a National Project, 1985-92*

The Anthropological Survey of India, established in December 1945 launched the project on People of India on 2 October 1985. The objective of the project was to generate a brief, descriptive anthropological profile of all communities of India, the impact of change and development process on them and the linkages that bring them together.

Unlike the surveys in the colonial period which covered British India and a few princely states, this project covers the whole country bringing within its ambit such parts of the country that had not been ethnographically surveyed earlier or where the survey was treated as a unit of our study. It started with the investigation of the least-known communities and then moved on to the field study of the lesser-known communities and then on the field study of the better-known ones. Ample cooperation was extended particularly by the welfare and backward classes departments of the state governments, local officers of Census of India, tribal research institutes, university departments of anthropology, other departments of local universities, etc.

The operations (October 1985-January 1992) were conducted on an enormous scale. The descriptive data are now available in about 120 volumes and 257 diskettes. As many as 500 scholars participated in this project, including 216 from 26 institutions which include university departments of anthropology, tribal research institutes, other research organizations, etc. About 100 workshops and about 100 rounds of discussions were held in all states/union territories in which about 2500 scholars participated. It was a truly participatory project. The investigators spent 26,490 days in the field which works out to six days per community studied in various states and union territories of India. The scholars interviewed a large number of people out of whom there were 26,463 key informants, which works out to about six informed informants per community. Of the informants, about 21% (i.e. 5661) were women. Interviews were conducted in connection with the study of the communities in 4513 villages, mostly multi-community ones, and in 941 towns, spread over 438 districts of India and in 89 cultural regions. On an average, a community was studied at about two places.

There is also the *Bio-Cultural Atlas of India* based on the data generated under People of India project, All India Bio-Anthropological Survey of India, All

India Physiometric Survey, etc. The second part comprises the state/union territory volumes based on a detailed write-up on each community of India, which has been contributed by scholars giving information, among other things, about place of the study of the community. A seventy-volume series will be published by the Oxford University Press and a consortium of publishers over the next four years. The first introductory volume is likely to be published by 15th April 1992. An enormous output of the descriptive material, 120 volumes and 42,000 computer sheets containing nearly 20 million words supported by 21,000 photographs and nearly 4146 maps has been generated by the project which costed approximately rupees seven crores.

The project has listed 4635 communities in all parts of India. The study reveals the strength and continuity of regional identities. The communities, no matter how they are ranked, share regional space and ethos. The states were reorganised on the basis of language. One finding of the project has been about the spread of communities across the states. Eighty-three per cent of the communities are located within the boundary of state/union territory. This shows that our states/union territories are not only linguistic and cultural but also social categories. For the first time, the communities speaking a particular language have been listed. In all, 325 languages belonging to 12 different language families are returned in the Survey. Apart from the languages, 24 different scripts also have been returned. According to the data collected in situations of culture contact, the incidence of bilingualism has been found to be as high as 65.51% in terms of the number of communities. There are a few communities which do not consider themselves migrants.

The communities have only been partly surveyed for morphological and genetic traits. 900 communities have been studied for such parameters.

Only 9.6% of the communities are pure vegetarian. There is vegetarianism of all shades and nuances practised in response to the value system, compulsions of ecology, availability of food and so on. There are vegetarians who take eggs, fertilized or non-fertilized. Males in a vast number of the communities are non-vegetarian; only in a few communities are women non-vegetarian. Alcoholic drinks are consumed by men in many communities and by women in some of them. Smoking is common.

Another important finding of the project is about the diversity of occupations. Earlier there was prevalence of a very large number of occupations like bird trapping and so on which was intimately connected with the then state of environment and of exotic occupations like acrobatics, begging, etc. A few of these have either disappeared or continue to be practised on a much smaller scale, as forests and wild life have disappeared with members of such communities having taken to occupations like labour.

The project has been able to identify 354 occupations on the basis of the data collected. There has been a sharp decline in traditional occupations like hunting and gathering, trapping of birds and animals, shifting cultivation, pastoral activities and priestly functions. There has been a rise in new and modern occupations like horticulture cultivation both settled and terrace, wage labour, animal husbandry, sericulture, business, trade industry, industrial work, service in government and private sectors and so on.

There has been a substantial rise in the number of daily wage casual labourers, agricultural, plantation, and even fishing labour. Child labour has also been reported from a large number of communities.

Anthropological Survey of India is considering the possibility to undertake an elaborate analysis of biological data in collaboration with the Department of Anthropology, Panjab University, Chandigarh, as also to analyse data in collaboration with the Centre for Ecological Sciences. The listing of the communities at the district level by incorporating the district-wise census lists of SC/ST communities, compiling the lists of the communities described in the district gazetteers and those of the communities in census village monographs (which has been computerized by the Centre) has already been.

Source: *Current Science*, 69(1) January 10, 1993.

One important feature of the study was that despite all the diversity of language and culture, there was a discernible sense common to all of "Indianness", and shared ethos, while each community sought to retain its culture, social rituals, and its own fairs and festivals. But these differences did not come as a bar to social interaction among the various communities.

(Source: *Hindustan Times*, December 26, 1992)

15

INDIA SINCE INDEPENDENCE

15.1 Achievements

Going back, India that is Bharat was the richest and the most prosperous country in the world. It was then known as the 'Golden Sparrow'. The standard of living of the common man was reasonably high. Articles of everyday needs were available in plenty. A common man could get easily things like milk, butter, ghee and foodgrains. Literally speaking 'Rivers of milk flowed'. Indian handicrafts and industrial products were known for their excellence of design and quality all over the world. From the richness of this land and from the labour and wisdom of its people had sprung great wealth, great ideas, great skills and arts. Naturally, therefore, foreigners were tempted to come to India for learning, as well as loot and plunder.

The well-knit economic organisation of the country received a serious setback with the advent of invaders and especially with the British rulers who were primarily concerned with the governance of the country, not its growth. They were greatly interested in draining out wealth from India. Industrial crafts, industries and agriculture, all suffered heavily. As a result, India became a poor country. People remained underfed, ill-housed and scantily dressed.

The statement 'A rich country inhabited by the poor people' seems paradoxical and strange. But it is still true to a considerable extent though since independence we have made a spectacular progress in different fields. The giant irrigation dams at Bhakra, Hirakud and Nagarjunasagar, the huge steel mills at Bhilai, Bokaro, Rourkela and Durgapur; the fertiliser factories at Sindri and Nangal; the 1000-tonne per day ammonia plant (said to be the largest in the world) at Tuticorin; the aircraft factories at Bangalore, Hyderabad and Nasik; the locomotive factory at Chittarajan; the atomic reactor at Trombay; the rocket launching station at Sriharikota; the ISRO's establishment like Vikram Sarabhai Space Centre, Trivandrum and Space Application Centre, Ahmedabad; launching of Indian Satellite Bhaskara and Rohini; three axis-stabilised Geostationary Communication Satellite; APPLE (Ariane Passenger Payload Experiment), establishment of Indian National Satellite System (INSAT); participation of an Indian Cosmonaut in a joint Indo-Soviet Flight; nuclear explosion at Pokaran, etc., are the prized possessions of the Indian Nation.

November 21, 1988 marked the 25th anniversary of Indian Space Programme. The Silver Jubilee Year saw the launching of three major programmes; IRS-1A, ASLV-02 and INSAT-1A (see relevant Chapter for details). Militarily we are among the first five countries in the world.

India is the sixth country to successfully detonate a nuclear device as part of its successful experiment for peace purposes.

We have the third largest reservoir of highly skilled scientific and technical manpower in the world.

India is the fifth nation to have its remote sensing satellite.

We have achieved self-sufficiency in foodgrains.

India is the third largest producer of books in English, next to the U.S.A. and U.K.

The problem of eradication of poverty of the masses became the first consideration of the government soon after we achieved independence. We decided to adopt the system of planned development for tackling our problem of poverty which was linked with rising prices, low production, unemployment and inequalities of income.

To frame a development plan for independent India, the Planning Commission was set up in March 1950, by a resolution of the Government of India. The aims of planning as defined by the resolution were, 'to promote a rapid rise in the standard of living of the people by efficient exploitation of the resources of the country, increasing production and offering opportunities to all for employment in the service of the community'.

The First Five Year Plan was initiated in April 1951. This covered the period 1951-1956. So far we have had seven Five Year Plans and three Yearly Plans. The Eighth Five-Year Plan, covers the period 1992 to 1997.

The most important achievement of planning in the post-independence period is our self-sufficiency in foodgrains. Now we need not import foodgrains for domestic requirements as we did till a few years ago. The production was about 172 million tonnes in 1991-92 as against 51 million tonnes 1950-51.

As a result of many multipurpose projects, area under irrigation increased from 226 lakh hectares in 1950 to 860 lakh hectares in 1990-91.

Our industry has many strengths: a wide range of products, a demonstrable ability to absorb and operate high technology, a large entrepreneurial capability and ample managerial and technical skills.

During the Plans, industrial production has made rapid strides, both in terms of quality and quantity. As per the index of industrial production, the growth rates achieved in the industrial sector as a whole were 8.6 per cent in 1984-85, 8.7 per cent in 1985-86, 9.1 per cent in 1986-87, 7.3 per cent in 1987-88, 8.7 in 1988-89, 8.6 in 1989 and 8.1 in 1990-91. However, there was setback in 1991-92. There was a (—)0.9 per cent decline (April-November).

In the year 1950-51, there were only two major units producing iron and steel. Now we have eleven relevant major steel plants. Steel production rose from about one million tonnes in 1950-51, to about 13.40 million tonnes in 1990-91.

Cotton textile industry holds the second place in the production of cloth in the world. At present there are about 700 textile mills in the country.

In 1951, we had 138 sugar mills in the country. This number increased to 351 in 1987. About half the mills are in the public sector.

The production of cement increased from 2.69 million tonnes in 1951 to 10.7 million tonnes in 1990-91 (provisional).

The generation of electric power registered a twenty-fold increase.

Public sector in the field of industries has witnessed a very significant rise. In 1951, we had only 5 public undertakings whereas there were 255 public undertakings in 1991, in the Central Sector.

The road network in the country has become very elaborate system of national highways, state and district roads, and rural roads totalling about 23 lakh kms. This is five and a half times the figure of 4 lakh km of roads in 1950-51.

Between 1950-51 and 1991-92, the number of trucks rose from 82,000 to 16,85,000 and busses from 34,000 to 3,70,000.

Per capita income increased from Rs. 246 in 1950-51 to about Rs. 4,254 in 1989-90 at current prices.

Prior to Independence, average life span of an Indian was 32 years. Today it has lengthened to 58 years.

Out Constitution can be described as a charter of freedom. It enshrines the supremacy of the will of the people and their resolve to secure for all citizens: justice, social economic and political; Equity of status and opportunity, and to promote among them all Fraternity assuring the dignity of the individual and the unity of the nation. The will of the people is exercised through universal adult franchise and a parliamentary democracy. Election to Parliament and State legislature are open contests for all political parties, and independent candidates also enjoy full scope to express themselves.

Notwithstanding various problems and the magnitude of the task of conducting elections, we have all general elections with significant success. Barring the period, March 1977 to July 15, 1979 and December 1989 to May 1991 when the Janata Party and National Front were in power at the Centre, the Congress had held the reigns of the Government since the first General Election in 1951-52.

Many political changes accompanied by government changes, especially in States have taken place in the country since Independence, through peaceful and constitutional means. Transfer of power from one party to another has taken place as a natural course and in an orderly manner.

Another historic step in the development of democracy in the country was the inauguration of Panchayati Raj in October 1950. The Panchayati Raj aims at giving full authority and responsibility to the village people and helping them play an active role in local development through the Panchayats. There are over 228,500 Village Panchayats in the country covering partially the entire population of India.

With the Panchayati Raj, we now have parliamentary democracy in operation from the Gram Sabha to the Lok Sabha.

We have got an established judicial system

15.2 Limitations and Tasks before the Nation

The President Dr. Shanker Dayal Sharma opened his address to the Joint Session of Parliament on February 22, 1993 by observing that the basic premise of secularism and the rule of law has been threatened.

The President called upon the various political parties, intellectuals and the people in general to "further strengthen" communal harmony in the country. The "most important task," was to restore confidence and communal amity "which have been shaken by the tragic events" of December 6.

The President also sought the cooperation of all sections of people in resolving the Ram Janmabhoomi-Babri Masjid dispute and said the construction of the temple and the mosque would be taken up in consultation and cooperation of the two communities.

The farmers in the country had made great strides in the field of agricultural production and this year the country would have the distinction of becoming the world's highest sugar producer, with a record sugar production of 133 lakh tonnes this season. The prospects for the rabi crop too have been good and a higher yield of 76 to 77 million tonnes of foodgrains was expected. The kharif production was also higher than last year's, and stood at 100 million tonnes, as against 91.42 million tonnes last time.

There has been a further consolidation of the economic stabilisation and structural reforms initiated under the new economic policy by the Government. The growth of GDP was expected to be around four per cent in 1992-93, against 1.2 per cent last year. The country enjoyed a "comfortable" foreign exchange position with a reserve of five billion US dollars. The object of controlling inflation had been achieved, as the annual rate of inflation was brought down from the "peak" of 16.7 per cent to seven per cent in January 1993.

The year also witnessed a reasonable increase of 3.8 per cent in industrial production, during April-October 1992, as compared to a decline of about one per cent in the corresponding previous year. There was a "sustained growth" rate in exports of 15 to 20 per cent in dollar terms, and there has also been a significant improvement in investments too. The total investments stood at Rs. 7,98,000 crore at the 1991-92 price level. He added that "we are moving towards indicative planning", which was in tune with the changes in the economic policy in the country.

A number of proposals for investment in private sector like petroleum and energy were also in the pipeline, and these would involve a foreign equity component of $250 million, with a total generating value of Rs. 7,500 crore. Out of this, 24 per cent would be in the energy sector, 26 per cent would be in petroleum, 12 per cent in food processing and 22 per cent in areas like communications, textiles and industrial machinery. The Government was committed to remove all impediments in exports.

In the small-scale sector also, there was a growth rate of four per cent at a time when there was a "slow-down in the industrial sector. Payments to small sector would now have to be made within 30 days — and obviate a major difficulty. The National Renewal Fund had been applied in the case of National Textile Corporation, and has benefited 22,000 workers.

A new scheme called "Rashtriya Mahila Kosh" was proposed to be set for short-term and medium-term development needs of the women. As for the backward classes, the Supreme Court order would be implemented for the reservation of jobs and steps had been initiated to "exclude" the creamy layer of the people from those benefits. The advice given by the recently appointed commission for the purpose would be ordinarily "binding" on the Government.

Talking about the relations with foreign countries, the President urged Pakistan to "eschew" its path of deliberate and provocative confrontation, and its temptation to gain unilateral advantage in its relations with India. There could be no alternative to the process of bilateral dialogue. Pakistan had been continuing support for terrorism and subversion in Punjab and Jammu and Kashmir. Despite that, the Prime Minister pursued the policy of resolving disputes through bilateral process and met his Pakistani counterpart twice. It was unfortunate that the efforts did not make much headway.

The President hoped that a strong relationship would be built with the Clinton administration in the US, and felt that a new way of "working together" with the US would be worked out.

The Indo-US ties would reflect a greater degree of understanding at the political level with growing cooperation in other areas. He also noted that in relations with China the difficulties would be overcome for good neighbourly relations. He also mentioned the recent visits by Russian President Yeltsin, British Prime Minister John Major, German Chancellor Helmut Kohl and other dignitaries and hoped that the relations with those countries would improve further.

Dr. Sharma also significantly called for a reinvigoration of the United Nations. Its effectiveness would depend on its ability to democratise and reorder its structure to accommodate and reflect the new concerns of its members.

Source: *Hindustan Times*, February 23, 1993.

15.3 **Concluding Observations**

A large part of our population still remains backward. There is a wide gulf between the rich and the poor. Unemployment is on the increase. National integration is our urgent need. Erosion in the standard of values, in fact, is the topmost blockade, which requires to be checked and a crusade for 'Clean Life, Clean Politics and Clean Administration' is to be given first priority.

India is on the move. The tasks before us are very challenging and tremendous. But there is no cause for despair. By harnessing all our resources and working unitedly and sincerely, we can usher in an era of peace, progress and prosperity.

The 21st century beckons up holding forth new hopes. We, the people of India, must march ahead as an integrated resurgent.

As Gurudev Rabindranath Tagore would advise, we must "hold the faith firm", surely "the day will dawn".

16

FIVE-YEAR PLANS

16.1 Planning Commission and Planning Process

Constituted in March 1950 by a Resolution of the Government of India, the Planning Commission works under the over-all guidance of the National Development Council which is headed by the Prime Minister and includes Ministers of the Central Cabinet, Chief Ministers of all States and Union Territories and Members of the Planning Commission. Delhi Administration is represented by the Lt. Governor and the Chief Executive Councillor, and the remaining Union Territories by their respective Administrators. The Planning Commissioning consults the Central Ministers and the State Governments while formulating Five Year Plans and Annual Plans and also oversees their implementation. The Commission also functions as an advisory body at the apex level.

The following functions have been assigned to the Planning Commission:

1. Make an assessment of the material, capital and human resources of the country, including technical personnel, and investigate the possibilities of augmenting such of these resources as are found to be deficient in relation to the nation's requirements;
2. formulate a Plan for the most effective and balanced utilisation of country's resources;
3. on a determination of priorities, define the stages in which the Plan should be carried out and propose the allocation of resources for the due completion of each stage;
4. indicate the factors which are tending to retard economic development and determine the conditions, which in view of the current social and political situation, should be established for the successful execution of the Plan;
5. determine the nature of the machinery which will be necessary for securing the successful implementation of each stage of the Plan in all its aspects;
6. appraise from time to time the progress achieved in the execution of each stage of the Plan and recommend the adjustments of policy and measures that such appraisal may show to be necessary; and
7. make such interim or ancillary recommendations as appear to it to be appropriate either for facilitating the discharge of the duties assigned to it o on a consideration of prevailing economic conditions, current policies, measures and development programmes or on an examination of such specific problems as may referred to it for advice by Central or State Governments.

Besides, the Planning Commission has been entrusted with the responsibility in respect of the following matters as per the Government of India Allocation Business Rules:

(a) Public Cooperation in National Development;
(b) Hill area Development Programme;
(c) Perspective Planning;
(d) Institute of Applied Manpower Research; and
(e) National Informatics Centre.

16.2 **Composition of the Commission**

The composition of the Planning Commission as on 31-3-1992 was as follows:

Chairman : Shri P.V. Narasimha Rao, Prime Minister
Deputy Chairman : Shri Pranab Mukherjee
Members :
1. Dr. Manmohan Singh, Minister of Finance
2. Shri Sharad Pawar, Minister of Defence
3. Shri Balram Jakhar, Minister of Agriculture
4. Dr. Chitra Naik
5. Dr. D. Swaminadhan
6. Shri V. Krishnamurthy
7. Dr. C. Rangarajan
8. Dr. S.Z. Qasim
9. Prof. J.S. Bajaj
10. Dr. Jayant Patil.

The Prime Minister, in his capacity as Chairman of the Planning Commission, participates and gives direction to the Commission on all major issues of policy.

16.3 **Five-Year Plans : A Recapitulation**

The First Five Year Plan (1951-52 to 1955-56) was 'ground preparing' exercise which gave its primary attention to the achievement of economic stability and elimination of shortages of food and basic resources. Accordingly it accorded top priority to agriculture of which irrigation and power were deemed essential ingredients. About 44.6 per cent of the total outlay was earmarked for the agricultural sector. The annual growth targeted in this Plan was 2.1 per cent of the national income.

The Plan also aimed at increasing the rate of investment from five per cent to about seven per cent of the national income.

The Second Five Year Plan (1956-57 to 1960-61) aimed, among other things, at 25 per cent increase in the national income, rapid industrialisation with particular emphasis on development of basic and heavy industries, large expansion of employment opportunities, and reduction inequalities in income and wealth and more even distribution of economic power. The Plan laid special stress on fastening industrialisation with the aim of strengthening the capital base and productive capacity.

The Plan also aimed at increasing the rate of investment from about seven per cent of the national income to eleven per cent by 1960-61.

The Third Plan (1961-62 to 1965-66) aimed at securing a marked advance towards self-sustaining growth. Its immediate-objectives were to (a) secure an increase in national income of over 5 per cent per annum and a simultaneous evolution of a pattern of investment capable of sustaining this rate of growth during subsequent Plan period; (b) achieve self-sufficiency in foodgrains (the target of foodgrains production stood at 100 million tonnes) and increased agricultural production to meet the requirement of industry and exports; (c) expand basic industries like steel, chemicals, fuel and power and establish machine building capacity; (d) utilise fully manpower resources and ensure a substantial expansion of employment opportunities; and (e) establish greater equality of opportunity and bring about reduction in disparities of income and wealth and more equitable dispersal of economic power. The Plan sought to increase the national income by about 30 per cent from Rs. 14,500 crore in 1960-61 to about Rs. 19,000 crore by 1965-66 (at 1960-61 prices) and per capita income by about 17 per cent from Rs. 300 to Rs. 385 during the same period.

The finalisation of the Fourth Plan was delayed on account of the situation created by the Indo-Pakistan War in 1965, two successful years of severe drought, devaluation of currency, general rise in prices and erosion of resources available for Plan purposes. There, three Annual Plans were formulated between 1966 and 1969.

The Fourth Five Year Plan (1969-70 to 1973-74) aimed at accelerating the tempo of development in conditions of stability and reducing the fluctuations in agricultural production as well as the impact uncertainties in foreign aid.

It sought to raise the standard of living and promote equality and social justice. The Plan laid particular emphasis on improving the conditions of the less-privilege and weaker sections of the society through gainful employment and education and on diluting the concentration through wider diffusion of wealth, income and economic power. The average annual rate of growth envisaged was 5.7 per cent.

The Fifth Plan (1974-75 to 1977-78) aimed at achieving self-reliance and adoption of measures to boom consumption standards of the people living below the poverty line. The Plan also gave high priority to bringing inflation under control and achieving stability of the economic front. The Plan targeted an annual growth rate of 5.5 per cent in national income and better capacity utilisation of industries, developing renewable sources of energy, and integration of science and technology into the main stream of development.

The Sixth Plan (1980-81 to 1984-85) assigned the highest priority to the removal of poverty. The strategy was essentially to strengthen the infrastructure for both agriculture and industry so as to create conditions for a sustained and accelerated growth in investment output and exports. It aimed at meeting the minimum basic needs of the people through special programmes and creating increased opportunities for employment, especially in the rural areas and the unorganised sector. Stress was laid on greater management efficiency and intensive monitoring in all sectors and involvement of people in formulation and speedy implementation of schemes at the local level.

The Seventh Plan (1985-86 to 1989-90) gave highest priority to food, employment and productivity. Faster movement towards the objective of self-reliance with social justice was the core idea of the Plan. The salient features of the Plan were: decentralised Planning, maximum employment generation, self-sufficiency in food at higher levels of consumption, export-import balance, modernisation and upgradation of technology. The Seventh Plan laid down an average annual growth rate target of 5 per cent. It also aimed at a 8.7 per cent annual growth rate for industries.

16.4 **Eighth Five-Year Plan** (1992-1997)

The formulation and implementation of the Eighth Five Year Plan was delayed by two years on account of rapid changes in the Central Government. It came into operation in 1992.

Salient Features of the Eighth Plan

This Plan has some features which distinguishes it from other Plans.

This Plan is indicative in nature. It concentrates on building a long-term strategic vision of the future and sets forth the priorities of the nation. While for the public sector the Plan goes into the details examining the alternatives and identifying the specific projects in various sectors, for the rest of the economy it works out sectoral targets and tends to provide promotional stimulus to the economy to grow in the desired direction.

The Plan recognises "human development" as the core of all developmental effort. It is only healthy and educated people who can contribute to economic growth and this growth in turn will contribute to human well being. The priority sectors of the Plan that contribute towards realisation of this goal are health, education, literacy and basic needs including drinking water, housing and welfare programmes for the weaker sections. In the Eighth Plan, Governments at the Centre and in the States will expand their role in this sphere.

For rapid economic development, the priority sectors identified for the growth of infrastructure are power, transport and communications. The basic assumption is that if we can provide these three essential ingredients in the urban and rural areas, it will lead to accelerated economic growth.

The Plan attempts to correct the fiscal imbalances from which the Sixth and Seventh Plans suffered.

This is an integrative Plan. If the results of our developmental activities so far have not been commensurate with the investments made, one of the main reasons for that has been our fragmented approach. Too many agencies trying to do too many things with a thin spread of resources has led to poor results. If we can integrate our developmental efforts, the results can be much more impressive even with these levels of investment.

The Eighth Plan recognises the essential need to involve people in the process of development.

The New role of the Government in the process of plan implementation devolution of power to peoples' organisations at the district, block and village levels.

This Plan is performance oriented. It concentrates not so much on its allocative role, but on how to utilise the allocations optimally. The stress is on performance improvement, quality consciousness, competitiveness, efficiency of operations and on-time completion of the projects. In order to provide incentive for good performance and bring in result orientation the formula for giving Central assistance to States has been suitably amended.

Eighth Plan pays special attention to employment in the rural areas.

This is a flexible Plan with scope for change, innovation and adjustment. In the outlays proposed for the States and some of the Central Ministries, there is a fairly large component of resources that the States and Central Ministries have to raise themselves.

Macro Dimensions

The Plan proposes a growth rate of 5.6 per cent per annum on average during the Plan period. The level of national investment is proposed at Rs. 798,000 crore and public sector outlay is proposed to be at Rs. 434,100 crore.

Source: *Yojana*, August 15, 1992.

The Sectoral pattern of investment and its financing in the Eighth Plan is presented in Table 16.1. An outlay of Rs. 434,100 crore is planned for public sector. This will have an investment component of Rs. 361,000 crore and a current component of Rs. 73,100 crore. The public sector investment then, will amount to 45.2 per cent of the total domestic investment, allowing for a much large space for the private sector than has hither to been given. The share of Centre and States in Public Sector Plan Outlay is given in Table 16.2. The share of the Public Sector in total investment during the Fifth, Seventh and Eighth Plan is shown in Table 16.3.

TABLE 16.1: Sectoral Pattern of Investment and its Financing in the Eighth Plan (1992-97)

(*Rs. crores at 1991-92 prices*)

Sector	Sources of Financing the Investment			Investment	Current Outlay	Aggregate Outlay
	Own Saving	Transfer from Household Sector's Savings	Rest of the the World			
Public Sector	68900	258400	33700	361000	73100	434100
Private Corporate Sector	68930	587770	21300	149000		
Household Sector	605170	317170	—	288000		
	743000	—	55000	798000		

TABLE 16.2 Share of Centre and States in Public Sector Plan Outlay

Item	Annual Plan 1991-92 (at current prices)	Annual Plan 1992-93 (at current prices)	Eighth Plan at 1991-92 prices
Central Deptts. Outlay	42,969	48,407	247,865
Budgetary Support	19,015	18,501	103,725
IEBR	23,954	29,906	141,140
States & UTs Outlay	28107 *	32,365	186,235
Union Territories Outlay	1,277 *	1,291	6,250
Budgetary Support	1,277 *	1,291	6,250
States Outlay+	26,830 *	31,074	179,985
Central Assistance	13,428	14,820	78,500
States own Resources	13,402	16,254	101,485
Total Plan Outlay	71,076 *	80,772	434,100

\+ Includes outlay for Area Programmes.

* Excludes Rs. 1,072 crore Plan Loans to States which were not finally agreed to by Ministry of Finance and the "Model villages" Scheme and "Equity Base for Cooperatives" which were subsequently dropped.

TABLE 16.3: Share of Public Sector in Total Investment

	Public Sector Investment (as % of total investment)	
	Projected	Realised
Fifth Plan (1974-79)	57.6	43.4
Sixth Plan (1980-85)	52.9	47.8
Seventh Plan (1985-90)	47.8	45.7
Eighth Plan (1992-97)	45.2	—

Consistent with the expected resource position, the size of the States' Plans is projected at Rs. 179,985 crore and the Central Plan at Rs. 254,115 crore (including Rs. 6,250 crore for the UTs). These are shown in Table 16.4. The share of the States in the Public Sector plan which has been declining through the Fifth, Sixth and the Seventh Plans, is sought to be raised from realised level of 39 per cent in the Seventh Plan to 41.5 per cent in the Eighth Plan. The States will be required to improve their resources, curb expenditure and improve and realise a positive contribution to the resources from their enterprises particularly in the electricity and transport sectors.

TABLE 16.4: Public Sector Plan Outlay and its Financing by Centre and States
(*Rs. Crore at 1991-92 prices*)

Items	Centre	States	Total
Balance from Current Revenue	22020	12985	35005
Public Enterprises	144140	4000	148140
Ext. Com. Borrowing & Sup. Credit (Net of repayment)	(5000)	—	(5000)
Public Bonds by Enterprises	37300	—	37300
Government Borrowings*	117755	58300	176055
Negotiated Loans	—	26200	26200
Net Capital Inflow from Abroad	28700	—	28700
Govt. Loans	24500	—	24500
Govt. Grants	4200	—	4200
Deficit Financing	20000	—	20000
Total Resources	336215	101435	434100
Central Assistance	-78500	78500	0
Resources for Plan	254115	179985	434100

* Includes market borrowings, small savings, other loans taken by Central & State Governments, State Provident Funds and net miscellaneous capital receipts.

Savings and Flow of Funds

The rate of saving is projected at an average of 21.6 per cent of GDP during the Plan period. The realised average rate of savings was 19.7 per cent of GDP during the Sixth Plan and 20.4 per cent during the Seventh Plan. The slow pace of increase in domestic savings during the eighties as compared to the rate of improvement in savings in the earlier decades is accounted for by two factors. While the savings of the household sector has shown a smaller rise than in the previous decades partly influenced by the larger availability of consumer goods, both durable and non-durable, the savings of the Government sector has shown a sharp deterioration. The rates of savings during the Sixth and the Seventh

Plans and the projected rates of savings for the Eighth Plan are shown in Table 16.5.

TABLE 16.5: Rates of Savings

(As percentage of GDPmp)

	(At Current Prices)			Projected (At 1991-92 Prices)		
	Sixth Plan	Seventh Plan	Average of 7 years (1985-86 to 1991-92)*	1991-92	1996-97	Eighth Plan (1992-97)
1. Public Sector	3.69	2.33	2.00	1.44	2.07	2.00
2. Govt. Sector	1.10	-1.36	-1.74	-2.37	-1.08	1.11
3. Public Enterprises	2.59	3.69	3.74	3.81	3.15	3.11
4. Private Corporate Sector	1.63	2.04	2.15	2.38??	2.17	2.00
5. Household Sector	14.33	16.00	16.60	17.77	17.36	17.60
6. Gross Domestic Savings	19.65	20.37	20.75	21.60	21.60	21.60

* Based on data from Quick Estimates for 1990-91 and projections for 1991-92. Abbreviation : GDPmp = Gross Domestic Product at market prices.

The savings of the household sector increased from 16 per cent of household disposable income in the Sixth Plan to 18.6 per cent in the Seventh Plan. In view of the increasing opportunities for consumption and urbanisation of the society, the increases in household savings in relation to their disposable income are not expected to be as sharp as in the previous Five Year Plans. With the increase in the proportion of financial savings in the total savings, however, the major contribution of household savings in the Eighth Plan will be towards making larger resources available for financing the investment of the private corporate sector and the Public Sector.

TABLE 16.6: Domestic Investment and Intersectoral Flow of Funds during the Eighth Plan (1992-97)

(Rs. crore at 1991-92 prices)

Item	Public sector	Private corporate sector	Household Sector	All Sector
Gross Investment	361000	149000	288000	798000
	10.50%	4.33%	8.37%	23.20%
Financed by:				
Own Savings	68900	68930	605170	743000
	2.00%	2.00%	17.60%	21.60%
Borrowings				
From Household	258400	58770	-317170	0
	7.51%	1.71%	-9.22%	0.00%
From Rest of the World	33700	21300	0	55000
	0.98%	0.62%	0.00%	1.60%

Notes : 1. Percentage are with reference to GDP at market prices during the 5 years of the Eighth Plan.

2. For the Eighth Plan financial savings of household sector as a percentage of total household savings is projected at about 52%.

Table 16.7 indicates the sectoral investment during the Eighth Plan.

Public sector outlay by major heads of development during the Eighth Plan—Centre, States and Union territories is shown in Table 16.8.

Public sector outlays by heads of development, i.e., agriculture, etc., is given in Table 16.9.

See also Annual Plan, 1992-1993.

TABLE 16.7: Sectoral Investment during the Eighth Plan (1992-93 to 1996-97)

(Rs. crore at 1991-92 prices)

Sector	Public	Private	Total	Share of sector in total investment by sectors %	Sectoral Distribution		
					6th Plan	7th Plan	8th Plan
Agriculture	52000	96800	148800	34.95	15.24	11.23	18.65
Mining & Quarrying	28500	11100	39600	71.97	6.06	6.70	4.96
Manufacturing	47100	141300	188400	25.00	23.60	26.00	23.61
Electricity, Gas & Water	92000	10120	102120	90.09	12.07	13.65	12.80
Construction	3300	17240	20540	16.07	2.73	1.86	2.57
Transport	49200	38710	87910	55.97	9.42	9.93	11.02
Communication	25000	1000	26000	96.15	1.50	2.03	3.26
Services	63900	120730	184630	34.61	29.38	28.60	23.13
Total	361000	437000	798000	45.24	100.00	100.00	100.00

Note : Sixth & Seventh Plan figures are calculated at 1980-81 prices.

TABLE 16.8: Public Sector Outlay by Major Heads of Development—Eighth Plan (1992-97) : Centre, States and Union Territories

(Rs. crore at 1991-92 prices)

Head of Development	Centre			States	U.Ts	Total	Eighth	Seventh
	Budget Support	IEBR	Total				plan % to total	plan % to total
Agriculture and Allied Activities*	12394.00	224.00	12618.00	42135.35	239.15	54992.50	12.67	14.27
Rural Development	24170.00	0.00	24170.00	10213.26	42.10	34425.36	7.93	5.01
Special Area Programmes	0.00	0.00	0.00	6750.16	0.00	6750.16	1.55	1.75
Energy**	13136.00	5359.00	66795.00	47291.58	1474.51	115561.09	26.62	30.48
Industry and Minerals	9186.00	28353.00	37539.00	9284.89	97.86	46921.75	10.81	12.48
Transport	8636.00	32341.00	40977.00	13786.58	1161.99	55925.57	12.88	12.76
Communication	715.00	24382.00	25097.00	12.50	0.48	25109.98	5.78	3.60
Science and Technology	3739.00	200.00	3939.00	188.72	3.99	41.31.71	0.95	1.13
Ecology and Environment***	1200.00	0.00	1200.00	3654.16	55.82	49.9.98	1.13	1.27
General Economic and General Services	1040.55	44.00	1084.55	5079.04	196.41	6360.00	1.47	0.94
Social Services	29508.45	4937.00	34445.45	41588.76	2977.69	79011.90	18.20	16.31
Grand Total	103725.00	144140.00	247865.00	179985.00	6250.00	434100.00	100.00	100.00

* Includes irrigation and flood control.

** Includes allocations for integrated rural energy planning programme.

*** Includes allocations for forestry and wildlife.

TABLE 16.9: Public Sector Outlay by Heads of Development—Eighth Plan (1992-97)

(Rs. crore at 1991-92 prices)

Head of Development	Centre			States	UTs	Total
	Budget	IEBR$	Total			
1	2	3	4	5	6	7
I. **Agriculture & Allied Activities**	10894.00	224.00	11118.00	11190.25	158.96	22467.21
Crop Husbandry	4681.00	0.00	4681.00	4555.88	37.93	9274.81
Soil & Water Conservation	800.00	0.00	800.00	1497.44	7.38	2304.82
Animal Husbandry	400.00	0.00	400.00	1079.95	50.86	1530.81
Dairy Development	900.00	0.00	900.00	405.71	1.80	1307.51
Fisheries	467.00	0.00	467.00	733.45	32.37	1232.82
Plantations	132.00	58.00	190.00	17.41	0.00	207.41
Food, Storage & Warehousing	320.00	166.00	486.00	58.10	0.00	544.10
Agricultural Research & Education	1300.00	0.00	1300.00	711.39	6.31	2017.70
Agricultural Financial Institutions	244.00	0.00	244.00	276.68	0.00	544.10
Cooperation	1550.00	0.00	1550.00	1485.89	21.23	3057.12
Other Agricultural Programmes	100.00	0.00	100.00	368.35	1.08	469.43
II. **Rural Development**	24170.00	0.00	24170.00	10213.26	42.10	34425.36
Special Programmes for Rural Development	4950.00	0.00	4950.00	2866.46	10.09	7817.55
Rural Employment	18400.00	0.00	18400.00	5244.88	0.00	23644.88
Land Reforms	210.00	0.00	240.00	845.54	1.88	1087.42
Other Rural Development Programmes	580.00	0.00	580.00	1256.38	39.13	1875.51
III. **Special Area Programmes**	0.00	0.00	0.00	6750.16	0.00	6750.16
Hill Area	0.00	0.00	0.00	1450.00	0.00	1450.00
North Eastern Areas	0.00	0.00	0.00	1160.00	0.00	1160.00
Other Special Area Programmes	0.00	0.00	0.00	4140.16	0.00	4140.16
(a) Backward Areas	0.00	0.00	0.00	2250.16	0.00	2250.16
(b) Tribal Areas	0.00	0.00	0.00	1250.00	0.00	1250.00
(c) Others	0.00	0.00	0.00	640.00	0.00	640.00

(Contd.)

TABLE 16.9 (*Contd.*)

1	2	3	4	5	6	7
IV. **Irrigation & Flood Control**	1508.00	0.00	1500.00	30945.10	80.19	32525.29
Major & Medium Irrigation	95.00	0.00	95.00	22310.21	9.32	22414.53
Minor Irrigation	293.00	0.00	293.00	5662.47	21.79	5977.26
Command Area Development	830.00	0.00	830.00	1679.33	0.80	2510.13
Flood Control and Drainage	282.00	0.00	282.00	1293.09	48.28	1623.37
V. **Energy**	13136.00	53659.00	66795.00	47291.58	1474.51	115561.09
Power	8902.00	22279.00	31181.00	46961.86	1445.88	79588.74
Petroleum	527.00	23473.00	24000.00			24000.00
Coal & Lignite	2600.00	7907.00	10507.00			10507.00
Non-Conventional Sources of Energy	1107.00	0.00	1107.00	329.72	28.63	1465.35
VI. **Industry & Minerals**	9186.00	28353.00	37539.00	9284.89	97.86	46921.75
Village & Small Scale Industries	2458.00	0.00	2458.00	3803.05	73.15	6334.20
Iron & Steel Industries	774.00	13805.00	14579.00			14579.00
Non-Ferrous Mining & Metallurgical Industries	352.00	1746.00	2098.00	813.74	0.00	2911.74
Cement & Non-metallic Mineral Industries	0.00	300.00	300.00			300.00
Fertilizer Industries	1018.00	4466.00	5484.00			5484.00
Petrochemical Industries	38.70	4543.50	4582.20			4582.20
Chemical & Pharmaceutical Industries	23.30	223.50	246.80			246.80
Engineering Industries	449.22	1771.61	2220.83			2220.83
Telecommunication & Electronic Industries	493.00	579.00	1072.00			1072.00
Consumer Industries	224.78	518.39	743.17			743.17
Atomic Energy Industries	800.00	400.00	1200.00			1200.00
Other Industries	80.00	0.00	80.00	4668.10	24.71	4772.81
Other Outlays on Industries & Minerals	2475.00	0.00	2475.00			2475.00
VII. **Transport**	8636.00	32341.00	40977.00	13786.58	1161.99	55925.57
Railways	5375.00	21827.00	272.00			27202.00
Ports & Lighthouses	500.00	2773.00	3273.00	260.85	79.73	3613.98

(*Contd.*)

TABLE 16.9 (*Contd.*)

1	2	3	4	5	6	7
Shipping	150.00	3250.00	3400.00		268.91	3668.91
Civil Aviation	107.00	3891.00	3998.00	45.26	40.00	4083.26
Roads & Bridges	2000.00	600.00	2600.00	9516.19	716.99	12833.18
Road Transport	264.00	0.00	264.00	3799.47	55.63	4119.10
Inland Water Transport	240.00	0.00	240.00	91.14	0.00	331.14
Other Transport Services				73.67	0.73	74.40
VIII. **Communication**	715.00	24382.00	25097.00	12.50	0.48	
Postal Services	325.00	0.00	325.00		325.00	
Telecommunication Services	264.00	23582.00	23946.00			
Other Communication Services	26.00	8.00	826.00	12.50	0.48	
IX. **Science, Technology & Environment**	4939.00	200.00	5139.00	3842.88	59.81	9041.69
Atomic Energy Research	600.00	0.00	600.00			600
Space Research	1604.00	200.00	1804.00			1804.00
Oceanographic Research	115.00	0.00	115.00			115.00
Other Scientific Research	1420.00	0.00	1420.00	188.72	3.99	1621.71
Ecology & Environment	675.00	0.00	675.00	149.00	4.11	828.11
Forestry & Wildlife	525.00	0.00	525.00	3505.16	51.71	4081.87
X. **General Economic Services**	924.00	44.00	968.00	3540.66*	40.86	4549.52*
Secretariat Economic Services	7.00	0.00	7.00	395.03	3.37	405.40
Tourism	240.00	32.00	272.00	505.18	26.92	804.10
Foreign Trade & Export Promotion	115.00	12.00	127.00			127.00
Census, Surveys & Statistics	106.00	0.00	106.00	84.72	3.15	193.87
Meteorology	130.00	0.00	130.00			130.00
Civil Supplies	30.00	0.00	123.50	123.50	5.72	159.22
General Financial & Trading Institutions	75.00	0.00	75.00			75.00
Technical & Economic Cooperation with other Countries	0.00	0.00	0.00			0.00
Other General Economic Services	221.00	0.00	221.00	1.70	2618.91	

(*Contd.*)

TABLE 16.9 (*Concld.*)

1 2	3	4	5	6	7	
XI. **Social Services**	29508.45	4937.00	34445.45	41588.76	2977.69	79011.90
General Education	6619.00	0.00	6619.00	9607.19	587.16	16813.35
Technical Education	824.00	0.00	824.00	1804.66	157.72	2786.38
Sports & Youth Services	350.00	0.00	350.00	509.06	30.54	889.60
Art & Culture	350.00	35.00	385.00	324.76	17.93	727.69
Medical & Public Health	1800.00	0.00	1800.00	5307.77	468.15	7575.92
Family Welfare	6500.00	0.00	6500.00			6500.00
Water Supply & Sanitation	5743.00	225.00	5968.00	9847.26	895.77	16711.03
Housing	831.35	860.00	1691.35	3409.08	172.59	5273.02
Urban Development	692.10	600.00	1292.10	3461.73	523.15	5276.98
Information and Publicity	184.05	15.00	199.05	215.68	6.78	421.51
Broadcasting	23295	3202.00	3434.95			3434.95
Welfare of SC, ST & Other Backward Classes	2549.42	0.00	2549.42	3050.97	35.09	5635.48
Labour & Employment	449.58	0.00	449.58	839.98	24.41	1313.97
Social Welfare	2373.00	0.00	2373.00	1467.72	14.49	3855.21
Nutrition	10.00	0.00	10.00	1742.40	43.91	1796.31
Secretariat Social Services				0.50	0.00	0.50
XII. **General Services**	116.55	0.00	116.55	1538.38*	155.55	1810.48*
Secretariat-General Services	5.00	0.00	5.00			5.00
Stationery & Printing	0.50	0.00	0.50	85.17	6.09	91.76
Police	25.00		25.00			
Public Works	36.05	0.00	36.05	1224.99	107.21	1368.25
Other Administrative Services	50.00	0.00	50.00	198.37	42.25	290.62
Grand Total	103725.00	144140.00	247865.00	179985.00	6250.00	434100.00

* Figures may not add-up to total schematic details pertaining to one State are awaited.

$ Where rules at present do not permit creation of internal resources outside the Consolidated Fund of India, IEBR has been shown in anticipation of evolution of appropriate mechanism to create such resources.

17

STATE OF INDIAN ECONOMY

17.1 Introduction

This chapter includes the findings/observations of the following: (1) World Bank Study on Indian Economy, July 1992; (2) Report of the Reserve Bank of India, September 1992; (3) National Council of Applied Economic Research, Report on GDP, October 10, 1992; (4) World Bank Study on India's Balance of Payments, October 10, 1992; (5) Report of the Central Statistical Organisation, Government of India, January 1993; (6) Asian Development Bank Study on Indian Economy, February 1993; (7) Economic Survey 1992-93, Indian Economy at a Glance Presented in Parliament, February 23, 1993.

17.2 World Bank Study on Indian Economy, July 1992

The World Bank has suggested a 10 per cent cut in the number of the Central Government employees during the next three-year period so as to make the Government's fiscal adjustment programme a success.

The Indian Government has to take measures to contain the increasing wage bill of its employees and this can be better achieved through reductions in employment rather than bringing down the real wages.

As of March 1992, the Central Government employed 4.2 million people (out of which 1.8 million were in the Railways), at a total cost of Rs. 120 billion which two per cent of the GDP. The Railways alone required Rs. 54 billion to pay wages. The total employment is estimated to increase by 1.1 per cent during 1992-93.

Given the urgent need to reduce the fiscal deficit, cuts in civil servants' real wages may be a necessity in the short-term, but in the medium term this reduction in real wages would lead to a deterioration in morale and lower standards of service and would not be sustainable. So the Government will have to take steps to reduce growth in Central Government employment to reduce total employment.

A smaller civic service would be consistent with the reorientation of the role of the Government in the economy. And it is the most efficient way of reducing the wage bill," the World Bank report says.

While in the report, the World Bank has not mentioned of the percentage of reduction, the Bank officials in the course of consultations with the Indian side have mentioned of a reduction of 10 per cent in the strength of the Central Government staff by March 31, 1995. If the Indian Government is able to convert the existing stand by loan from the International Monetary Fund (IMF to extended fund facility loan, it will be for a three-year period and this will coincide with the first three years of the Eighth Five-Year Plan period ending March 31, 1995.

The Bank in its overview of the Indian economy observes that it will be a gigantic task for the Government of India to achieve its target of bringing the fiscal deficit down to five per cent of the GDP by the end of 1992-93. A five per cent fiscal deficit implies a 0.3 per cent primary deficit. It also implies that recourse to the RBI credit could be reduced significantly from around three per cent of GDP in 1990-91 and two per cent in 1991-92 to 0.8 per cent in 1992-93.

Net RBI credit to the Central Government accounts for virtually all of RBI's net domestic assets.

Reductions in the rate of increase of such assets should limit the rate of increase of base money and, thus, help reduce broad money growth. A reduced fiscal deficit and less recourse to the RBI financing should, in turn, reduce aggregate demand and inflation. But the Bank warns that unless exports and private investments offset declines in aggregate demand, a rapid recovery will not take place.

Source : Nitya Chakravorty, *Hindustan Times*, July 26, 1992.

17.3 **Report of the Reserve Bank of India, September 1992**

The Reserve Bank of India expects the real growth of Gross Domestic Product (GDP) to be a little less than 2 per cent — the lowest since 1980-81.

This will be in contrast with 5.6 per cent during 1990-91 and the trend growth of 5.5 per cent for the decade ended 1990-91. The industrial growth rate would be a moderate 4 to 5 per cent against 8 per cent in the recent past. The severe compression in imports resorted to in 1991 had taken its toll by way of lower industrial production.

The Indian economy faced a distinct slowdown during the fiscal year 1991-92.

It expects to register a lower growth rate against the target of 183 million tonnes for 1992-93 and counselled the Government to keep part of its foreign exchange reserve for importing essential items such as cereals and pulses to maintain domestic supply.

Fiscal correction at the Centre and the States is long overdue if debt is to be kept within reasonable levels. This would essentially mean that the Governments should have their revenues to cover expenditure and where they do not, returns from investment should cover amortisation.

RBI expects rise of 3.5 per cent in the GDP against the previous year's figure of less than two per cent.

The two years of double-digit inflation and the persistently strong growth of liquidity in the economy pose a dilemma for monetary management. Further, the recent problems arising from irregularities in dealings in securities has focussed attention on the financial sector.

A satisfactory and early restoration of fuller confidence in the functioning of banks and financial institutions is vital, financial sector reforms are still the need of the hour and the recent events serve to emphasise the importance of hastening the pace of reform.

The RBI has expressed deep concern over fiscal imbalances, as a result of which indebtedness, both internal and external continues to mount. It, now, constitutes about 57 per cent of the GDP. The interest burden of the Centre alone is 4.4 per cent of GDP, which is over 20 per cent of the Government expenditure.

As regards policies and procedures which were the direct responsibility of the RBI, since July 1973, it had been allotting banks and insurance corporations an annual quota for corporations an annual quota for "switching" Government securities in their portfolios with the RBI, mainly with a view to enabling them to improve the yields on their investments.

The allotment of such quotas to banks and insurance corporations has since been dispensed within the current year as the system of switch quotas merely generated transactions in Government securities between banks/institutions and the Reserve Bank without any effect on the monetary aggregates.

A dominant factor in this low growth scenario has been the stagnation of industrial output for the first time since 1979-80 and agricultural output is also expected to register a decline of about one per cent.

While the trauma of the external liquidity crisis had been swiftly overcome, the question of the fundamental disequilibrium on the balance of payments front still remained. The reduction in the current account deficit to 1.1 per cent of GDP in 1991-92 was entirely due to the severe compression in imports, which took its toll in a reduced growth of the economy. While the management of the external sector was rendered possible as a result of the import compression, the resulting dislocation of industry and employment raises serious questions about the feasibility of the import compression route as a way out of the balance of payments disequilibrium.

Admitting that the securities scam turned out to be much larger and deeper than could be visualised, the RBI lists at length the "lessons from the securities scam". RBI is undertaking a fresh look at its (RBI) own operations and organisational structure and staffing. The avowed objective of the RBI and the Government of India is to restore confidence, both in India and abroad, in the country's financial system. RBI is confident that the financial system would become stronger.

Persistent inflationary pressure, reflecting fiscal imbalance and monetary growth in a situation of shortages in certain sectors will make the macroeconomic adjustment a more difficult task in the coming years, worrisome feature in the current situation was the slow pace in overall employment opportunities.

In this context, the central bank underlined the need to bring about a revival in industrial and agricultural growth and reduction of huge budgetary deficit by legally banning the Government borrowing from all sources beyond a certain ceiling.

The RBI pointed out that a prominent factor in this low-growth was the stagnation in industrial output for the first time since 1979-80 while the agricultural output was also expected to register a decline of about one per cent.

The macro scene concerning domestic savings and investment also remained subdued and somewhat uncertain, the gross domestic savings to GDP ratio which fell from 22.7 per cent in 1989-90 to 22.2 per cent in 1990-91 was likely to rise to 23.2 per cent in 1991-92.

Similarly, the estimated net inflow of foreign resources is estimated to decline from Rs. 14,684 crore in 1990-91 to Rs. 8,042 crore in 1991-92, representing a fall of 1.5 per cent in terms of GDP. The ratio of gross domestic investment is estimated to have fallen from 25 per cent in 1990-91 to 24.5 per cent in 1991-92.

While it was imperative to devise an effective rural credit delivery system, the report said better alignment of interest rates and mix of target and nontarget lending would need immediate attention.

Source : *Hindustan Times,* September 7, 1992.

17.4 National Council of Applied Economic Research: Report on GDP, October 1992

The prospects for a higher rate of economic growth for the current financial year have brightened following improved monsoon and industrial performance in the country.

The growth in real Gross Domestic Product (GDP) during 1992-93 is expected to be 3.5 per cent or slightly higher over the previous year. The higher GDP growth represents a modest recovery over the poor growth in 1991-92.

However, the recovery, especially in the industrial sector, will depend upon a moderate rate of inflation and availability of critical inputs especially in the infrastructure including transportation.

Underscoring that the export-trend so far raises a question mark whether the overall export target of 13 per cent in dollar terms increase over the previous year would be achieved, the report points out that the growth in exports in the general currency area during this quarter has been slightly better than the corresponding quarter of the last year.

The level of exports to the rupee trade areas has not recovered to the levels of the late eighties and this has dampened the overall export performance during the present year as well.

The NCAER visualises that the rate of inflation in terms of GDP deflator is likely to be about 11 per cent during 1992-93 over 1991-92 as compared to an estimated 13.5 per cent during the last year.

The fiscal deficit targets for 1992-93 seem to be within reach due both to improved revenue collections and better than anticipated performance in respect of GDP growth. But higher expenditures on items such as the additional dearness allowance which is now released but not provided in the budget would have an adverse affect on capital expenditure in order to keep the overall deficit in check.

The supplies to the public distribution system are likely to be improved in the coming months with improved kharif output, enhanced procurement prices and imports of wheat.

It would be difficult to contain the fertiliser subsidies to within Rs. 5,000 crore provided in the 1992-93 budget, as the kharif season was nearly over when the decision on subsidies was announced.

The Government has now announced a subsidy of Rs. 100 per tonne on potassic and phosphatic fertilisers as per the Joint Parliamentary Committee in fertiliser pricing which would again partially restore the subsidy burden on the budget.

Both in raising agricultural production and foodgrain distribution, greater attention to targetting of beneficiaries and the use of non-price policy instruments is becoming increasingly necessary now. In this regard, efforts to reverse the declining trend in investment in agriculture deserves greater attention.

The monetary scenario of April-June 1992 was characterised by an accelerated expansion of broad money supply and re-emergence of bank credit to the commercial sector as a single most important factor underlying monetary expansion.

The massive inflow of foreign exchange resources while fuelling the monetary expansion one hand has helped the Government in reducing its reliance on RBI's credit on the other hand.

Source : *Hindustan Times*, October 10, 1992.

17.5 **World Bank Study on India's Balance of Payments, October 1992**

The World Bank has warned India against the possibility of another Balance of Payments crisis (BOP) in the next few years.

BOP will remain fragile and dependent on exceptional financing over the next four to five years. The management of the capital account will continue to be difficult because of the large share of volatile Non Resident Indian (NRI) deposits ($11 billion) short-term debt ($3 billion) in India's external debt estimated at $73 billion.

New Delhi is not unaware of the tight monetary situation. An indication to this effect was given by Finance Minister Manmohan Singh during the World Bank International Monetary Fund annual meeting when he had made out a strong case for additional foreign exchange requirement of $9 billion over the next three years.

India's foreign exchange reserves are just approaching the equivalent of three months of normal imports. They are still insufficient to cope with any serious exogenous shock — such as drought related agricultural production shortfalls or adverse developments in the external environment.

Thus, considerable vulnerability to liquidity crisis remains and declines in reserves could precipitate a confidence crisis,".

Liberalising imports is central to the success of the reform process underway which however would make the management of the Balance of Payments riskier.

The drastic changes in the policy framework during the last year make it difficult to project imports with any degree of confidence and there is a risk that they may be higher than anticipated.

Even with the modest current account deficits, India's financing needs over the next five years would be substantial due to the large scheduled repayments of debt.

While a significant proportion of these external financing needs could be met through disbursements on existing and expected commitments from bilateral and multilateral sources and private creditors, the need for significant amounts of exceptional Balance of Payments support will remain for the next few years.

The World Bank visualises the success of New Delhi's Economic Reform Programme in its ability to mobilise these sizeable external resources.

This will require a substantial increase in India's reliance on foreign investment as well as a prompt and sizeable improvement in the utilisation of existing commitments of official assistance.

According to one estimate, India's sanctioned by unutilised official World Bank assistance has reached about $6.5 billion

Source: *Trends in Developing Economies, 1992*, W.H.O., reported in *Hindustan times*, October 10, 1992.

17.6 Report of the Central Statistical Organisation (CSO), Government of India, January 1993

The per capita in real terms has recorded a decline by 1.1 per cent in 1991-92 as against 1990-91. The per capita income in real terms is estimated at Rs 2174 for 1991-92 as against Rs. 2199 for 1990-91. The per capita income at current prices is estimated at Rs 5529 in 1991-92 as against Rs 4934 for the previous year.

Gross Domestic Product (GDP) at factor cost constant (1980-81) process in 1991-92 is estimated at Rs 212,316 crore as against Rs 209,791 crore in 1990-91, registering a growth of 1.2 per cent during the year as against the growth rate of 5.2 per cent achieved during the previous year. At current prices, GDP in 1991-92 is estimated at Rs 54,188 crore as against Rs 472,660 core in 1990-91, showing an increase of 14.6 per cent during the year.

At constant (1980-81) prices, the national income (i.e. net national product at factor cost) in 1991-90 is estimated at Rs 186,135 crore as against rs 184,460 crore in 1990-91 showing a rise of 0.9 per cent during the year. At current prices, the national income in 1991-92 is estimated at Rs 473,246 crore as compared to Rs 413,943 crore in 1990-91, showing rise of 14.3 per cent during the year.

The CSO data show that the growth rate during 1991-92 has not been satisfactory. Negative growth has been observed in the two most important sectors of the economy namely, agriculture and manufacturing. In the case of trade, hotels and restaurants, storage and other services the growth has come down substantially as compared to 1990-91. However, railways, transport by the other means, banking and insurance have shown improvement.

According to the All India Final Estimates of the foodgrain crops released by the Ministry of Agriculture, there was a fall of 5.3 per cent in the production of foodgrains from 176-39 million tonnes in 1990-91 to 167.06 million tonnes in 1991-92 mainly attributable to fall in rice (0-8 per cent).jowar (-28.4 per cent), bajra (-32.7 per cent), maize (10.9 percent), small millets (-20.2 per cent), and pulses (15.55 per cent)

As regards other crops, the Ministry reported an increase in the production of cotton (one per cent), jute (13.6 per cent),mesta (11 per cent), sugarcane (4.2 per cent) and fall in oilseeds (-1.8 per cent).

Private final consumption expenditure (PFCE) in the domestic market at current prices works out to Rs 389,418 crore in 1991-92 as against Rs 335,837 crore in 1990-91.

PFCE the formed 62.9 per cent of GDP at market prices. At constant (1980-81) prices PFCE work out to Rs 161963 crore in 1991-92 as against Rs 157385 crore in 1990-91. The per capita expenditure in 1991-92 works out to Rs 4549 at current prices as Rs 1891 at constant (1980-81) prices as against Rs 4003 and Rs 1876 respectively in 1900-91.

The expenditure on almost all items both at current and constant prices in creased in 1991-92 as compared to the previous year. The shares of the various groups have remained just about the same during 1991-92, expect in the case of food and transport and communication, where it has gone up while in clothing footwear, there is a slight fall.

Gross domestic saving at current prices in 1991-92 amounted to Rs 148039 crore as against Rs. 125109 crore in 1990-91, constituting 24.3 per cent of GDP at market prices as against 23.6 per cent in the previous year. This rise has been contributed by all the three institutional sectors of the economy.

The saving of the household sector went up by 15.3 per cent from Rs 105125 crore in 1990-91 to Rs 121230 crore in 1991-92 and that of the private corporate sector by 15.6 per cent from Rs. 14393 crore in 1990-91 to Rs 16633 crore in 1991-92. The saving of the public sector showed a steep rise of 82.0 per cent from Rs 5591 crore in 1990-91 to Rs 10176 crore in 1991-92. The steep rise in the public sector is due to decrease in the dissaving department from Rs (-) 14613 crore in 1990-91 to Rs(-) 12-38 crore in 1991-92 and increase in the saving of both departmental and non-departmental enterprises.

Source : *Quick Estimates of National Incomes and Related Aggregates for 1991-92*, CSO, reported in *Hindustan Times*, January 15, 1993

17.7 **Asian Development Bank Study on Indian Economy, February 1993**

The progress has not been "too bad" compared to other countries. The fiscal performance has been well. There is, however, a downtrend in investment which cannot be sustained. The other problem area is export which grew only by 6 per cent against the official target of 15 per cent, mainly because of dislocation in the former Soviet Union. There has also been some pressure on prices.

The ADB's expectation. The ADB would like to study the market, especial the proposed National Stock Exchange, to see what sort of programmes the ADB could participate in.

The Bank is "cautiously optimistic" about economic prospects in the near term which "remain mixed" While an average growth of between 5 and 6 per cent a year is "achievable over the medium term" "this would require a sustained investment effort and continuing adoption of efficiency measures."

ADB takes " a somewhat cautions view of the medium term prospects " but concedes that "there is every possibility that the transition will involve some pain and disruption in the near term" Inflation, for an example, "will remain one of the major policy issues."

The full convertibility of the rupee and decontrolling prices of key products like steel will mean that a further price increase will be" unavoidable. This can be managed through appropriate monetary and fiscal polices which the Government is now undertaking," one critical factor, in the new term, will be the time lag between reform measures and improved performance", Besides, there are still many areas where reforms are needed. While it may be desirable to move quickly in each of these areas, it is also unrealistic to expect very rapid changes.

Source : *Hindustan Times*, February, 23, 1993

17.8 **Economy Survey, 1992-93: Presented in Parliament, February 23, 1993**

17.8.1 *Indian Economy at a Glance*

Various facets of Indian economy as reflected in the Economic Survey, 1992-93, Presented in the Parliament on February 23, 1993, are presented below:

Tables 17.1 to 17.9 illustrate the following : Gross National Product, Inflation Rate, Foreign Currency Asset, Export and Imports, Subsidies, Agricultural Production, Food Grain Production, Growth Rate in Industries, and Control Government Revenues.

TABLE 17.1: Gross National Product (in percentage)

Year	GNP
1988-89	10.5
1989-90	5.6
1990-91	5.2
1991-92	1.4
1992-93	4.2 (Estimated)

TABLE 17.2: Inflation Rate (%)

Year	Wholesale Price Index	Consumer Price Index
1988-89	5.7	8.5
1989-90	6.6	9.1
1990-91	12.1	13.6
1991-92	13.6	13.9
1992-93	7.8	8.4 (Estimated)

TABLE 17.3: Foreign Currency Assets. (Rs. crore)

Year	Amount 2.5
1988-89	6,605
1989-90	5,787
1989-90	4,388
1990-91	14,578
1992-93	13,688 (Estimated)

TABLE 17.4: Exports and Import at Current Market Prices

Year	Exports	Imports
1988-89	20,233	28,235
1989-90	27,681	35,416
1990-91	32,553	43,193
1991-92	44,042	47,851
1992-93	37,329	47,480 (Estimated)

TABLE 17.5: Subsides (Rs. crore)

Year	Amount of Subsidies
1988-89	7,859
1989-90	10,826
1990-91	10,728
1991-92	10,363
1992-93	8,910 (Estimated)

TABLE 17.6: Agriculture Production

Year	Million Tonnes
1988-89	183.2
1989-90	187
1990-91	192
1991-92	186.6
1992-93	195.9 (Estimated)

TABLE 17.7: Foodgrains Production (Million tonnes)

Year	Rice	Oilseeds	Wheat	Foodgrains
1988-89	70.5	18.0	54.1	169.9
1989-90	73.6	16.9	49.8	171.0
1990-91	74.3	18.6	55.1	176.4
1991-92	73.7	18.3	55.1	167.1
1992-93	71.5	20.2	56.0	176.7 (Estimated)

TABLE 17.8: Growth Rates in Industrial Sector (%)

Year	Mining	Electricity	Manufacture	General
1988-89	7.9	9.5	8.7	8.7
1989-90	6.3	10.8	8.6	8.6
1990-91	4.5	7.8	9.0	8.3
1991-92	0.3	8.5	—1.6	—0.1
1992-93	3.9	4.2	3.7	3.8(Estimated)

TABLE 17.9: Central Government Revenues

A. Growth in Revenue, (1990-91 and 1991-92)

Year	Revenue in Rs. Crore
1940-41	09.00
1954-55	108.22
1964-65	801.51
1974-75	3230.52
1984-85	11150.84
1991-92	28382.82

B. Revenue Source of the Central Government

Item	Percentage Share of the total revenue
1. Central excise	41.90
2. Customs	32.70
3. Income tax	10.90
4. Corporate tax	10.90
5. Other taxes	3.60

C. Ten Top Revenue Yielding Commodities

	Commodity	Rs. in crore
1.	Cigarettes	2387.23
2.	Synthetic Yarn	1874.44
3.	Cement	1280.73
4.	Motor spirit	1241.73
5.	Iron & Steel	1090.6
6.	Machinery	962.07
7.	Tyres, Tubes and flaps	810.73
8.	Plastics and articles thereof	729.14
9.	Motor Vehicles	788.64
10.	Refined Diesel	702.82

D. Different Uses of Tax Revenue Collected out of Re one

	Item	Paisa Spent
1.	Central Plan and Non-Plan Expenditure	25
2.	Interest	23
3.	Defence	13
4.	Subsidies	7
5.	State's Share of Tax collected by the Centre	14
6.	Plan and Non-Plan Assistance given to States and UTs.	18

17.8.2 *Highlights of Economic Survey, 1992-93*

* The growth of the gross domestic product (GDP) is expected to exceed four per cent in 1992-93.
* Economic reforms begin to pay off.
* Inflation declines to seven per cent.
* The Kharif foodgrain harvest is likely to show a rise of as much as eight per cent.
* Agricultural output estimated to be five per cent higher than in 1991-92.
* Bumper crops of cotton, oil seeds and coarse grain expected.
* Industrial sector continues to suffer from recessionary conditions through 1992-93 though performance is better than in 1991-92.
* Industrial growth rate rise could go up to 4 per cent.
* Total bank credit to the commercial sector expanded by Rs, 21,012 crore up to Jan, 8 this year compared with only Rs 7,135 crore in the same period of 1991-92.
* The term loans sanctioned by the all India financial institutions during the period April-December 1992 show a growth of 70 per cent while disbursements show a growth of 47 per cent.
* Balance of payments position stabilise.
* The level of imports in 1992-93 as a whole is expected to be around 525 billion, which is lower than the level in 1990-91.
* Exports in 1992-93 performed far better than in 1991-92.
* Total exports in 1992-93 may not exceed $19 billion.
* The current account deficit in 1992-93 is expected to the around $7 billion.
* The annual rate of inflation as measured by the wholesale price index

declines from 13.6 per cent at the end of 1991-92 to 6.9 per cent on Jan. 30, 1993.

* Deceleration in inflation - a major achievement of economic management in the past year.
* Exports to hard currency area pick up-11.4 per cent growth in April-December 1992.
* The phase of crisis management of the economy in over. But a great deal remains to be done.
* The process of structural adjustment is expected to take at least three years.
* The current account deficit in the balance of payments is still high and needs to be reduced from 2.8 per cent in 1992-93 to less than one per cent of GDP in 1995-96.
* Other recommendation of the Raja Chelliah Committee deserve full consideration keeping in mind the Government's declared policy of moderating tax rates, widening tax base and improving compliance.
* Scope for a restructuring of the State's tax base exists.
* Reform of expenditure is needed.
* A comprehensive reform of the banking system, the capital market and their regulation is needed.
* The recent securities scam reflects systematic weaknesses in banking system and capital market, which need urgent correction.
* Survey suggests two-tier interest rates - one general and the other concessional.
* Government indicates its intention to move towards full convertibility on the trade account, including unification of the exchange rate over a period to two to three years.

17.8.3 *General Review*[1]

Although the economic crisis of mid-1991 had been contained, and a programme of structural reforms initiated, inflation was still running high, the balance of payments remained under strain and industrial production was depressed. The economic situation has improved substantially in the year under review. There has been decisive progress in overcoming inflation and the rate of inflation has declined to seven per cent. The balance of payments situation, though still difficult, shows hopeful signs with a pick-up in exports to the hard currency area. Industrial growth is picking up slowly and is better than in the previous year. The policy initiatives introduced after June 1991 have been seen to work. This gives us confidence that the direction of our reforms is right, and that if we persevere with them, we can overcome the severe constraints on our economy and assure a more prosperous future for our people.

The year (1992) has not been without setbacks. The irregularities in securities trading in some banks damaged liquidity and temporarily raised questions of confidence. The riots in December 1992 and January 1993 disrupted transport, slowed the growth of exports and industrial production, and reduced revenue. Without these setbacks there would have been faster recovery in both

1. as indicated in *Economic Survey*, 1992-93.

output and employment in 1992-93.

Growth Performance

The latest CSO (Central Statistical Organisation) estimates for 1992-92 suggest that economic growth was only 1.2 per cent, significantly lower than the growth of 2.5 per cent projected in last year's Economic Survey (Table 17.10). The prospects for the current year are distinctly better and growth of GDP is expected to exceed four per cent in 1992-93.

After a slightly delayed start, the monsoon turned out to be very good in all areas other than the middle Gangetic plain. The kharif foodgrain harvest is likely to show a rise of as much as eight per cent. The coarse grain crop, estimated at 34.7 million tonnes is almost 32 per cent higher than 26.3 million tonnes in 1991-92. The sugarcane crop lacked rain in the North at a crucial time and the total crop is likely to be 7.7 per cent lower at 230 million tonnes. But the cotton crop, at 11.7 million bales, is excellent. The kharif oilseed crop is estimated to be 10.5 million tonnes, 17.7 per cent above last year and equal to the record crop of 1988-89. With another bumper harvest of mustard expected in the coming rabi, the supplies of edible oils are likely to be very comfortable. The agricultural situation this year is broadly satisfactory and even with a modest growth in rabi crop, agricultural output could be five per cent higher than in 1991-92.

In contrast, the industrial sector has continued to suffer from recessionary conditions through 1992-93, though performance is better than in 1991-92. Production in the period April-October 1992 shows a growth of 3.8 per cent. This is better than the marginal decline recorded in the same period of 1991-92, but it is well below the normal trend growth of industry. Industrial production 1992-93 has been slow to recover for a number of reasons. Import restrictions which account for the poor performance in 1991-92 were completely removed by the end of 1991-92 when the new Liberalised Exchange Rate Management System was introduced. However, while quantitative restrictions on imports were not a constraining factor in 1992-93, the high cost of imported inputs, reflecting changes in the exchange rate, probably acted as a restraining factor in import-intensive industries. The new exchange rate will, however, help exports, and the resulting export stimulus would stimulate industrial production in more export-oriented sectors. However the export response will come only with a lag.

Credit restrictions introduced in 1991-92 needed to be continued in 1992-93 in view of continuing inflationary pressure at the start of the year. However, some relaxations were introduced during 1992-93 in light of the easing of inflationary pressure and keeping in mind the need to stimulate an industrial recovery. Interest rates wee lowered in the course of the year and the volume of credit extended to industry was expanded considerably. Total bank credit to the commercial sector expanded by Rs. 21012 crore up to January 8, 1993 compared with only Rs. 7135 crore in the same period of 1991-92.

17.8.4 *Indicators*

TABLE 17.10: Key Indicators

	Absolute values						Per cent change over previous year					
	1987-88	1988-89	1989-90	1990-91	1991-92(P)	1992-93(P)	1987-88	1988-89	1989-90	1990-91(P)	1991-92(P)	1992-93(P)
1	2	3	4	5	6	7	8	9	10	11	12	13
Gross national product@@ (Rs. thousand crore)												
At current prices	292.2	349.0	400.1	465.8	535.1@	610.0*	13.2	19.4	14.6	16.4	14.9@	14.0*
At 1980-81 prices	168.1	185.7	196.1	206.3	209.3@	218.2$	4.1	10.5	5.6	5.2	1.4@	4.2$
Gross domestic product (Rs thousand crore)												
At current prices	333.2	396.6	545.0	530.9	609.5	694.8*	13.7	19.0	14.5	16.9	14.8	14.0*
At 1980-81 prices@@	170.3	188.9	199.5	209.8	212.3@	221.2$	4.3	10.9	5.6	5.2	1.2@	4.2$
Agricultural production[1]	151.3	183.2 (P)	187.0 (P)	192.0 (P)	186.6 (P)	195.9*						
Foodgrain production (million tonnes)	140.4	169.9	171.0	176.4	167.1	176.7*	-2.1	21.0	0.6	3.2	-5.3	5.7*
Industrial production[2]	166.4	180.9	196.4	212.6	212.4	208.3[3]	7.3	8.7	8.6	8.3	-0.1	3.8[3]
Electricity Generated (TWH)	202.1	221.4	245.4	264.6	286.7	221.3[8]	7.7	9.5	10.8	7.8	8.4	4.6[8]
Wholesale price index[4]	148.5	156.9	171.1	198.8	217.8	231.0[5]	10.7	5.7	9.1	12.1	13.6	7.8[5]
Consumer price index for industrial workers[6]	153.0	166.0	177.0	201.0	229.0	244.0[7]	10.9	8.5	6.6	13.6	13.9	8.4[7]
Money supply (M3) (Rs thousand crore)	164.3	193.5	231.0	265.8	315.1	350.2[8]	16.0	17.8	19.4	15.1	18.5	11.2[8]
Imports at current prices												
(Rs. crore)	22244	18235	35416	43193	47851	47840[8]	10.7	26.9	25.4	22.0	10.8	38.7[8]
(US $million)	17156	19497	21272	24072	19411	16630[8]	9.1	13.6	9.1	13.2	-19.4	16.5[8]

Contd.

TABLE 17.10 *Contd.*

1	2	3	4	5	6	7	8	9	10	11	12	13
Foreign currency assets												
(Rs. crore)	7287	6605	5787	4388	14578	13688[9]	-4.7	-9.4	-12.4	-24.2	232.2	40.2[9]
(US $ million)	5618	4226	3368	2236	5631	5237[9]	-5.2	-24.8	-20.3	-33.6	151.8	38.8[9]
Exchange rate (Rs/US$)+	13.0	14.5	16.6	17.9	24.5	25.9[10]	1.4	10.5	13.0	7.2	26.7	6.8[10]
Market Rate (Rs/US$)#+						30.4[10]						20.3[10]

* Anticipated; (P) Provisional; @ Quick estimates; @@ At factor cost; $ Advance estimates

\+ Per cent change indicates the rate of depreciation of the Rupee.

\# Indicative exchange rate as announced by FEDAI.

1. Index of agricultural production with base triennium ending 1969-70 = 100.
2. Index of industrial production 1980-81 = 100.
3. April-October 1992.
4. Index with 1981-82 = 100.
5. As in end December, 1992.
6. Index with 1982 = 100.
7. As in November 1992.
8. April-December, 1992.
9. As on January 31, 1993 for 1992-93 and at the end of March for previous years.
10. April-January, 1993.

There is evidence that industrial growth is accelerating. The moving average annual index of industrial production was stagnant 7 months earlier and now shows a growth rate of 2.2 per cent in the year ending October 1992. The extent of disruption in December and January is not yet easily quantified but if the industrial recovery continues at the pace observed in recent months, the industrial growth rate for 1992-93 as a whole could reach four per cent.

Services account for an important proportion of GDP and have shown steady growth. In fact, the growth of 1.2 per cent in GDP in 1991-92 when both agriculture and industry showed negative growth was entirely accounted for by the growth in services. And this growth in services was real. Apart from the normal growth in services owing to the Government sector, there was a real increase in the output of important measurable services in 1991-92, as shown in Table 17.11. This growth in road and rail transport, telephone connections, cargo handled and air passengers continues in 1992-93.

TABLE 17.11: Indicators of changes in the output of services, 1990-91 to 1992-93

	April-March		April-Dec		April-March Change over 1990-91 (per cent)	April-March Previous period 1991-92 (per cent)	April-Dec 1992 (per cent)
	1990-91	1991-92	1991	1992			
1	2	3	4	5	6	7	8
Railways' revenue-earning traffic (mt)	318	337	245	254	2.7	6.0	3.9
Road transport: diesel oil consumption (mt)	21.1	22.7	10.6*	12.6*	2.1	7.33	19.1*
New telephone connections (thousand)	486	735	278	3778	16.7	51.4	36.3
Cheques cashed (Rs. thousand crore)	1183	1376	342@	387@	39.8	16.3	13.3@
Major ports: cargo handled (mt)	153	158	122	114	3.2	3.3	6.7
Air passengers (million)	17.7	18.8	14.0	14.6	-11.2	6.2	4.1
Air cargo (thousand t)	377	370	269	2295	-9.2	-1.7	9.8

* = April-September @ = April-June m = Million t = Tonnes

The Balance of Payments

By the end of 1991-92 the new Liberalised Exchange Rate Management System introduced in the Budget for 1992-93 eliminated import licensing in most capital goods, raw materials, intermediates and components and introduced a dual exchange rate system with one rate effectively floated in the market. The Budget for 1992-93 also reduced customs duties ion line with declared Government policy in order to make the Indian economy more competitive and gradually exposing Indian industry to external competitive pressure. The trade and exchange rate policy regime for 1992-93 was therefore characterised by major progress in eliminating unnecessary administrative and discretionary controls over foreign trade which were contributing to making our economy uncompetitive.

The year 1992-93 saw a revival of import to more normal levels. The total value of imports in US dollars in the period April-December 1992 increased by 16.5 per cent over the level of the corresponding period of 1991-92. The increase appears large only in comparison with a highly depressed level prevailing in 1991-92. In fact the level of imports in 1992-93 as a whole is expected to be around $25 billion which is somewhat lower than the level in 1990-91.

Exports in 1992-93 performed far better than in 1991-92. Total export growth in the period April-December was 3.4 per cent in dollar terms compared with an observed decline of 1.5 per cent in 1991-92. The performance of total exports is depressed by the decline of more than 60 per cent in exports to Russia and other States of the former Soviet Union in 1992-93. The growth of exports to the general currency area in the period April-December was 11.4 per cent. The average growth rate in April-December 1992 has been adversely affected by a decline in exports of 12.5 per cent in December, reflecting the disturbed conditions prevailing in that month. Figures for January are also likely to be depressed by the riots in Bombay. Total exports in 1992-93 may not exceed US $19 billion. But it is hoped that the export performance in subsequent months will return to the high growth rates of 15-16 per cent observed during September-November.

The current account deficit in 1992-93 is expected to be around $7 billion, reflecting the revival of imports to more normal levels. This deficit is being financed through a combination of traditional financing sources and exceptional financing.

However, there are important uncertainties in the balance of payments. The full impact of the disturbance in December 1992 and January 1993 on exports and imports is difficult to assess at this stage. Clearly, the receipts on account of tourism would be less than anticipated. The inflow of NRI deposits has in any case been small this year. The inflow of external assistance is also subject to some uncertainties consequent upon constraints that affect the rate utilisation. A step-up in commercial borrowings was, in any case, to envisaged. Finally, there is the uncertainty arising from leads and lags. Interest rates and exchange rate expectations do affect the timing of receipt of export proceeds and payment of import costs. However, while these uncertainties justify a measure of caution in assessing prospects, the balance of payment in 1992-93 has performed more or less as expected.

Inflation

The annual rate of inflation as measured by the wholesale price declined from 13.6 per cent at the end of 1991-92 to 6.9 per cent on 30 January 1993. The decline in inflationary pressure was especially marked in primary articles including foodgrains. The annual rate of inflation in foodgrains was 3 per cent on 30 January 1993 compared with 24.3 per cent at the same time in the previous year. The deceleration in inflation is a major achievement of economic management in the past year.

The moderation in inflationary pressure in 1992-93 has been partly due to the good performance of agriculture but it is in large part also due to the reduction in the Central Government's fiscal deficit, which has been a key element in the strategy for macro-economic management and control of inflation. The progress achieved in reducing the fiscal deficit in the past two years has been substantial. The Central Government's gross fiscal deficit was reduced from 8.4

per cent of GDP in 1990-91 to 6.2 per cent in 1991-92 and the 1992-93 budget envisaged a further fall to 4.9 per cent. Thus the Centre's draft on domestic savings is scheduled to come down by 3.5 percentage points of GDP in two years. This massive fiscal correction has been a major disinflationary influence in the period.

Equally important are the changes in the sources of finance for financing the fiscal deficit of 3 per cent of GDP in the gross fiscal deficit between 1989-90 and 1992-93, 1.5 per cent or almost half has been in the budget deficit; the direct impact of this fall in the budget deficit is on the growth of high-powered or reserve money. Thus the disinflationary impact of reduced Central Government dissavings has been reinforced by their reduced contribution to the growth of money supply. This is reflected in the deceleration in money supply (M3) growth in 1992-93. After growing by 15.3 per cent in 1991-92 up to 10 January 1992 M3 has slowed down in the current year with a growth of 12.3 per cent in the period up to 8 January 1993. For the year as a whole M3 growth is likely to be contained at about 13.5 per cent.

The Strategy for Economic Reform

The strategy of economic reform introduced in 1991-92 was based on a combination of measures aimed at economic stabilisation as well as structural reform. Stabilisation was inflation. The reform measures are equally important in the medium term if our economy is to grow and become competitive in the world. The results achieved thus far are satisfactory. The phase of crisis management of over. Substantial progress has been in bringing about fiscal correction and this is reflected in the deceleration in inflation in the course of the course of the year. But a great deal remains to be done. the process of structural adjustment was expected to take at least three years and only half this period is now over.

Fiscal Policy

Although considerable fiscal correction has been achieved in the past two year with a reduction in the fiscal deficit from 8.4 to five per cent, the process must continue. Inflationary pressure can be said to have been purged from the system only after inflation has been brought down to no more that five to six per cent year for two years. Besides, the current account deficit in the balance of payment is still to high and need to be reduced from around 2.8 per cent in 1992-93 to less than one per of GDP in 1995-96. This reduction in current account deficit of a little less than two per cent of GDP over a three-year period will call for further reduction in the fiscal deficit and boost in exports. The reduction in the fiscal deficit is also necessary if we want to reduce the pressure of Government borrowing on the financial system without which interest rates cannot be reduced.
(Extracts from *Economic Survey 1992-93*.)

17.8.4 *Indicators*

Selected Indicators are given in Table 17.12, Net State Domestic Product in Table 17.13 and Per Capita Net State Domestic product in Table 17.14

TABLE 17.12: Selected Indicators 1950-51 to 1991-92

	1950-51	1960-61	1970-71	1980-81	1985-86	1986-87	1987-88	1988-89	1989-90	1990-91	**1991-92**
1	2	3	4	5	6	7	8	9	10	11	**12**
Economic Indicators											
GDP at factor cost:											
(i) At current price (Rs. crore)	8978	15254	39708	122427	233799	260030	294851	353517	405827	472660	**541888 #**
(ii) At 1980.81 price (Rs. crore)	42871	62904	90426	122427	156566	163271	170332	188943	1999508	200791	**212316 #**
Per capita net national product at (1980-81) prices (Rupees)	1127	1350	1520	1630	1841	1871	1901	2065	2134	2199	**2175 #**
Index of industrial production (Base 1990-81)	18.3 @	36.2	65.3	100.0	142.1	155.1	166.4	180.9	196.4	212.6	**212.4**
Index of agricultural production (Base: Triennium ending 1969-70)	58.5	86.7	111.5	135.2	158.5	152.5	151.3	183.2 (P)	187.0 (P)	192.0 (P)	**186.6 (P)**
Gross domestic capital formation (as per cent of GDP)	10.2	15.7	16.6	22.7	21.3	21.6	23.6	25.0	27.3	26.3	**25.5 #**
Gross domestic savings (as per cent of GDP)	10.4	12.7	15.7	21.2	19.9	19.5	21.5	21.9	24.6	23.6	**24.3 #**

Contd.

TABLE 17.12 *Contd.*

1	2	3	4	5	6	7	8	9	10	11	12
Output:											
(a) Foodgrains (million tonnes)	50.8	82.0	108.4	129.6	150.4	143.4	140.4	169.9	171.0	176.4	**167.1**
(b) Finished Steel (million tonnes)	1.04	2.39	4.64	6.82	9.49	9.55	11.68	12.84	13.00	13.53	**14.33**
(c) Cement (million tonnes)	2.7	8.0	14.3	18.7	33.1	36.6	39.6	44.8	45.8	48.8	**53.7**
(d) Coal (including lignite) (million tonnes)	32.3	55.2	76.3	119.0	162.3	175.2	190.9	207.0	213.7	225.5	**243.8**
(e) Crude oil (million tonnes)	0.3	0.5	6.8	10.5	30.2	30.5	30.4	32.0	34.1	33.0	**30.3**
(f) Electricity generated (utilities only)(TWH)	5.1	16.9	55.8	110.8	170.4	187.7	202.1	221.4	245.4	264.6	**286.7**
Wholesale price index* (Base: 1981-82)	16.9	19.6	35.5	91.1	125.4	132.7	143.5	154.2	165.7	182.7	**207.8**
Consumer price index (Base : 1982=100)@@	17	21	38	81	126	137	150	163	173	193	**219.0**
Plan outlay (Rs. crore)	260$	1117	2524	15023	33421	39705	44034	48645	55630	61523	**65856 RE**
Centre's budgetary deficit (Rs. crore)	(-)33$	(-)117	285	2576	4937	8261	5816	5642	10592	11347	**7032 RE**
Foreign trade :											
(i) Exports											
Rs. crore	606	642	1535	6711	10895	12452	15674	20232	27681	32553	**44042**
US $ million	1269	1346	2031	8486	8904	9745	12089	13970	16626	18142	**17866**

Contd.

TABLE 17.12 *Contd.*

1	2	3	4	5	6	7	8	9	10	11	**12**
(ii)Imports											
Rs. crore	608	1122	1634	12549	19658	20096	22244	28235	35416	43193	**47851**
US $ million	1273	2353	2162	15869	16067	15727	17156	19497	21272	24072	**19411**
Foreign exchange reserves (excluding gold and SDRs)											
Rs. crore	911	186	438	4822	7384	7684	7287	6605	5787	4388	**14578**
US $ million	1908	390	584	5850	5972	5924	5618	4226	3368	2236	**5631**
Social Indicators											
Population											
Population (million)(1)	361.1	439.2	548.2	685.2	762.9	779.0	795,1	811.3	827.4	846.3	**860.4**
Birth rate (per 1000) (2)	39.9	41.7	33.9	36.9	32.6	32.6	31.5	30.6	30.2	29.3(P)	..
Death rate (per 1000) (2)	27.4	22.8	14.9	12.5	11.8	11.1	11.0	10.3	9.7	9.8 (P)	..
Life expectancy at birth											
(in years)(3)	31.1	41.3	45.6	50.5	..	..	..	..	..	..	..
(a) Male	32.4	41.9	46.4	54.1	..	..	..	..	..	55.9	..
(b) Female	31.7	40.6	44.7	54.7	..	..	..	..	..	59.9	..
Total persons	32.1	41.3	45.6	54.4						59.9	
Education											
Literacy rate (percentage) (4)											
(a) Male	27.16	40.40	45.95	56.37	..	..	..	..	..	64.1 (5)	..
(b) Female	8.86	15.34	21.97	29.75	..	..	..	..	..	39.3 (5)	..
Total persons	18.33	28.31	34.45	43.56	..	..	..	..	..	52.2 (5)	..

Contd.

TABLE 17.12 *Concld.*

1	2	3	4	5	6	7	8	9	10	11	**12**
Health & Family Welfare (6)											
Registered medical practitioners (RMP) (thousand)	61.8	83.7	151.1	268.7	320.3	331.8	355.6	368.6	381.9	394.0	..
RMP per 10,000 population	1.7	1.9	2.8	3.9	4.1	4.2	4.4	4.5	4.6	4.7	..
Beds (all types)** per 10,000	3.2	5.2	6.4	8.3	9.0	9.2	9.2	9.5	9.4	9.6	..

@ Relates to the calendar year 1950
$ Relates to 1951-52
# Quick estimates
* Figures for the period up to 1980-81 derived by converting the indices on earlier bases into base 1980-81=100.
** Includes beds in hospitals, dispensaries, P.H.Cs, clinics, sanatoria, etc.
@@ Figures for the period up to 1988-89 derived by covering indices on earlier bases into base 1982=100
RE Revised estiments.
.. Not available.
P Provisional

Notes:

1. As on March 1, 1951 and so on as per Census of India. figures for the period 1985 o 1990 are based on projections of the Standing Committee of Experts on Population Projections, and for 1992 based on same assumptions as adopted by the standing committee in light of 1991 Census results.
2. Data for 1950-51, 1960-61, relate to period 1941-51, 1951-61, Census estimates. Data 1970-71 onwards are S.R.R. estimates for calendar year 1971 and so on.
3. Data for 1951-51, 1960-61, relate to period 1941-51, 1951-61, census estimates. Data 1970-71 and 1981-86 respectively. Data for 1991 is based on the Age Specific Death Rates averaged over 1981-88 as estimated by Sample Registration system.
4. Data for 1950-51, 1960-61, 1970-71, 1980-91 relate to year 1951,1961,1971,1981 and 1991 respectively.
   The figures for 1950-51, 1960-61 and 1970-71 relate to population aged 5 years and above whereas those for 1980-81 and 1990-991 relation population aged 7 years and above.
5. All India literacy rate for 1991 excludes J&K.
6. Relates to calendar year i.e. 1950-51 pertains to December 1951 and soon.

TABLE 17.13: Net State Domestic Product at Current Prices (New Series)

(Rs. crore)

Sl. No.	State	1980-81	1981-82	1982-83	1983-84	1984-85	1985-86	1986-87	1987-88	1988-89	1989-90 (P)	**1990-91 (Q)**
1	2	3	4	5	6	7	8	9	10	11	12	13
1	Andhra Pradesh	7324	8974	9702	11516	11962	13412	14242	17375	21978	24912	**30112**
2	Arunachal Pradesh	97	129	148	167	196	237	267	284	335	363	**420**
3	Assam	2356	2978	3398	3766	4725	5118	5456	5993	6563	7741	**8492**
4	Bihar	6008	6998	7797	9008	110819	11765	13491	14614	17269	18710	**21789**
5	Goa	316	343	418	442	542	555	657	731	845	904	**955**
6	Gujarat	6594	8247	8745	11385	11866	12059	13299	13218	18885	21526	**244665**
7	Haryana	3032	3498	4004	4351	4747	5643	5943	6629	8698	9648	**11317**
8	Himachal Pradesh	723	846	897	1023	1031	1237	1363	1539	1873	2131	**2441**
9	Jammu & Kashmir	1050	1195	1362	1549	1747	1929	2134	2091	2619	2566	-
10	Karnataka	5964	6893	7685	9215	10392	10951	12563	14314	16974	19045	**21328**
11	Kerala	3829	4057	4720	5536	6152	6535	7384	8396	9229	10646	**11499**
12	Madhya Pradesh*	6122	6784	7732	9641	9454	10979	11564	14687	17227	18731	**23043**
13	Maharashtra	15113	16966	18277	21152	22628	26403	28120	33101	40137	48716	**55439**
14	Manipur	201	243	258	307	353	377	431	508	610	642	**694**
15	Meghalaya	180	206	227	263	302	342	386	472	513	556	**598**
16	Mizoram	62	70	78	95	122	157	194	259	260	-	-
17	Nagaland	105	132	161	194	232	261	294	338	361	382	**404**
18	Orissa	3225	3677	3765	4893	4801	5936	6206	6521	8433	9105	**9929**

Contd.

TABLE 17.13 *Concld.*

1	2	3	4	5	6	7	8	9	10	11	12	13
19	Punjab	44767	5323	5879	6491	7417	8387	9199	10863	12546	14977	**17101**
20	Rajasthan	4126	4850	5532	7043	6983	7669	8341	9437	132022	13848	**17578**
21	Sikkim	49	55	65	75	95	113	135	156	167	187	-
22	Tamil Nadu	7218	8677	8821	1022	1228	13682	15305	18195	19560	22966	**24841**
23	Tripura	268	290	352	360	442	485	512	589	765	835	-
24	Uttar Pradesh	14012	15036	17600	19533	21514	24669	27237	39347	35796	40983	**48077**
25	West Bengal	8724	9746	10658	12920	14718	15861	17636	20429	23959	27449	**31618**

P Provisional.
Q Quick estimates.
- Not available.
* Based on old (1970-71) series.

Note : Owing to differences in source material used, the figures for different States are not strictly comparable.

Source : Directorates of Economics and Statistics of respective State Governments.

TABLE 17.14: Per Capita Net State Domestic Product Current prices (New Series)

(Rupees)

Sl. No.	State	1980-81	1981-82	1982-83	1983-84	1984-85	1985-86	1986-87	1987-88(P)	1988-89(Q)	1989-90	1990-91
1	Andhra Pradesh	1380	1657	1756	2046	2986	2296	2394	2869	3566	3973	**4722**
2	Arunachal Pradesh	1561	2011	2240	2455	2793	3274	3575	3680	4212	4424	**4975**
3	Assam	1200	1474	1641	1777	2182	2313	2420	2589	2772	3196	**3427**
4	Bihar	868	988	1078	1219	1443	1527	1714	1817	2101	2228	**2539**
5	Goa	3145	3365	4003	4127	4931	4927	5702	6209	7027	7370	**7634**
6	Gujarat	1951	2391	2484	3162	3233	3224	4391	3407	4781	5368	**6060**
7	Haryana	2370	2664	2967	3133	3325	3849	3950	4312	5540	6026	**6936**
8	Himachal Pradesh	1704	1953	2032	2273	2249	2649	2870	3185	3813	4269	**4813**
9	Jammu & Kashmir	1776	1970	2190	2428	2669	2874	3099	296	3615	3453	-
10	Karnataka	623	1832	1997	2343	2588	2672	3005	3358	3908	4035	**4737**
11	Kerala	1513	1578	1803	2077	2265	2364	2625	2905	3178	3611	**3843**
12	Madhya Pradesh*	1183	1281	1432	1746	1675	1940	1963	2443	2809	2995	**3614**
13	Maharashtra	2427	2669	2813	3185	3336	3817	3992	4622	5520	6604	**7409**
14	Manipur	1429	1682	1745	2020	2270	2362	2636	3040	3568	3674	**3893**
15	Meghalaya	1361	1516	1626	1831	2047	2250	2479	2955	3118	3276	**3443**
16	Mizoram	1289	1238	1417	1724	2139	2658	3165	4077	4026	-	-
17	Nagaland	1383	1666	1941	2251	2579	2800	3034	3361	3464	3529	**3602**
18	Orissa	1231	1380	1388	1772	1707	2072	2128	2194	2793	2965	**3180**
19	Punjab	2690	3131	3384	3656	4089	4524	4857	5612	6343	7411	**8281**
20	Rajasthan	1222	1392	1544	1914	1849	1978	2095	2310	3106	3219	**3983**
21	Sikkim	1571	1701	1926	2136	2635	3023	3472	3886	4241	4755	-
22	Tamil Nadu	1498	1776	1777	2024	2341	2620	2885	3379	3581	4148	**4428**
23	Tripura	1323	1390	1641	1640	1962	2108	2171	2445	3114	3328	-
24	Uttar Pradesh	1278	1339	1534	1667	1800	2022	2187	2387	2757	3092	**3553**
25	West Bengal	1580	1730	1854	2204	2463	2604	842	3232	3724	4193	**4750**

P Provisional; Q Quick estimates; - Not available; * Based on old (1970-71) series.
Note: Owing to difference in source material used, the figures for different States are not strictly comparable.
Source : Directorates of Economic and Statistics of respective State Governments.

Source : *Economic Survey*, 1992-93, Ministry of Finance, Economic Division, Government of India, New Delhi, 1993.

TABLE 17.15: India's competitiveness in the World overall ranking slid down from 10th to 11th position in 1992 amongst the emerging nations

Over all Ranking			A	B	C	D	E	F	G	H
[1]	1	Singapore	1	1	1	1	1	1	2	1
[4]	2	Taiwan	3	3	4	7	6	3	1	3
[2]	3	Hong Kong	5	2	3	2	3	2	4	5
[5]	4	Malaysia	6	5	2	3	5	4	6	4
[3]	5	Korea	2	6	6	8	2	5	3	2
[6]	6	Thailand	4	4	5	6	12	6	7	6
[7]	7	Mexico	9	7	7	5	8	8	10	7
[-]	8	S. Africa	12	10	10	4	7	7	5	14
[-]	9	Venezuela	11	8	9	9	9	9	11	8
[8]	10	Indonesia	7	13	8	12	11	12	9	11
[10]	**11**	**India**	**8**	**14**	**11**	**11**	**13**	**11**	**12**	**9**
[9]	12	Brazil	13	12	14	10	4	10	14	12
[-]	13	Hungary	14	9	12	14	10	14	8	10
[-]	14	Pakistan	10	11	13	13	14	13	13	13

Rankings based on: A - Domestic Economic Strength, **B** - Internationalism, **C** - Government, **D** - Finance, **E** - Infrastructure, **F** - Management, **G** - Science and Technology, **H** - People

Overall Ranking in : [1991] **1992**

Source: *World Competitiveness Report* 1992, World Economic Forum reported in *Hindustan Times*, August 22, 1992.

18

POVERTY ALLEVIATION AND EMPLOYMENT

18.1 Poverty Alleviation

Alleviation of poverty continues to be a major concern of development planning. Keeping in view the goal of near-full employment by the turn of the century, in the interim period, the provision of short-term employment for the unemployed and under-employed, particularly among the poor and the vulnerable, is considered necessary. The strategy adopted is to focus not only on the creation of new jobs but also on the augmentation of the existing employment in terms of productivity and incomes through suitable technology, market and institutional interventions. As a result of the development witnessed in the various sectors of the economy during the past years, through planning and related measures, the per capita net national (NNP) at factor cost (at 1980-81 prices) has increased from Rs. 1630 in 1980-81 to Rs.2174 in 1991-92. The extent of incidence of absolute poverty has significantly declined over the years. The decline in the incidence of poverty in urban areas is greater than in rural areas (Table 18.1).

TABLE 18.1: Estimates of Incidence of Poverty

Areas	1972-73	1977-78	1983-84	1987-88
Rural	54.1	51.2	40.1	33.4
Urban	41.2	38.2	28.1	20.1
All India	51.5	48.3	37.4	29.9

Source: Planning Commission.

The Government has taken several measures for improving the quality of life of the population. The major areas/sectors which contribute to the development of the human resources are family welfare, education, health, development of women and children, welfare of weaker sections of society, housing, water supply and sanitation, labour and labour welfare, special programmes for alleviation of poverty etc. Over the years, there has been a steady improvement in important indicators of development (Table 18.2).

The progress has not been uniform and there are wide variations amongst the States. Selected indicators of development, viz estimated infant mortality rate, birth rate, death rate, literacy rate and population below poverty line for major State are given in Table 18.3.

TABLE 18.2: Selected Indicators of Development

	Life expectancy at birth (years)@			Literacy rate (Per cent) @@			Income Per capita NNP (Rs)*
	Males	Females	Total	Males	Females	Total	
1	2	3	4	5	6	7	8
1950-51	32.4	31.7	32.1	27.2	8.9	18.3	1127
1960-61	41.9	40.6	41.3	40.4	15.3	28.3	1350
1970-71	46.4	44.7	45.6	46.0	22.0	34.5	1520
1980-81	54.1	54.7	54.4	56.4	29.8	43.6	1630
1990-91	55.9	55.9	55.9	64.1	39.3	52.2	2174**

@ Data for 1950-51, 1960-61, 1970-71, 1980-81 relate to periods 1941-51,1951-61, 1961-71 and 1980 respectively. The figure for 1990-91 is based on a age specific death rates averaged over 1981-88 as estimated by the Sample Registration system (SRS) relating to 1991.

@@ Data for 1950-51, 1960-61, 1970-71, 1980-81 and 1990-91 relate to years 1951, 1961, 1971, 1981 and 1991 respectively. Figures for 1950-51, 1960-671, 197--71 relate to population aged 5 years and above whereas those for 1980-81 and 190-91 relate to population aged 7 years and above. For 1991, the literacy rate excludes J & k.

* At factor cost, at 1980-81 prices.

** Quick estimate for 1991-92.

Source: (i) Planning Commission; (ii) Central Statistical Organisation.

TABLE 18.3: Selected Indicators of Development of Major States*

State	Infant mortality rate	Birth rate	Death rate	Literacy	Population below poverty line
1	2	3	4	5	6
		(per thousand)		(per cent)	
1. Orissa	126	28.8	12.7	49.1	44.7
2. M.P	122	35.8	13.8	44.2	36.7
3. U.P	93	35.1	11.1	41.1	35.1
4. Assam	81	30.9	11.5	52.9	22.8
5. Rajasthan	77	34.3	9.8	38.6	22.4
6. Karnataka	77	26.8	9.0	56.0	32.1
7. A.P.	73	26.0	9.7	44.1	31.7
8. W.Bengal	70	26.7	8.1	57.7	27.6
9. Bihar	69	30.5	9.8	38.5	40.8
10. Gujarat	69	27.5	8.5	61.3	18.4
11. Haryana	68	33.1	8.2	55.9	11.6
12. Maharashtra	60	26.2	8.2	64.9	29.6
13. Tamil Nadu	57	20.7	8.8	62.7	32.8
14. Punjab	53	28.6	8.0	58.5	7.2
15. Kerala	17	18.1	6.0	89.8	17.0
All India	**80**	**29.3**	**9.8**	**52.2**	**29.9**

* Major States are States with population of 10 million and above as per 1991 Census.

Source: (i) Columns 2, 3 and 4 are based on Sample Registration System estimates for 1991.

(ii) Column 5 us based on final population totals of 1991 Census excluding J & K in All India.

(iii) Column 6 is based on the draft report of 43rd Round of N.S.S.O data on household consumer expenditure relating to population as on 1 March 1988.

18.2 Employment

Expansion of employment opportunities is the central objective of planning. An accelerated expansion of employment opportunities and augmentation of existing employment in terms of income and productivity are necessary both for poverty alleviation and effective utilisation of human resources for economic development. During the past two decades, employment has grown at an average rate of 2.2 per cent per annum while labour force has grown faster at about 2.5 per cent per annum and as a result the backlog of unemployment has been rising. Provisional estimates of employment in organised public and private sectors is given in Table 18.4.

TABLE 18.4: Employment in the Organised Public and Private Enterprise Sectors*

(As on 31 March)

	1990			1991		
	Males	Females	Total	Males	Females	Total
1	2	3	4	5	6	7
Public	164.88	22.41	187.29	166.22	22.43	189.65
Private	62.01	13.89	75.90	64.06	14.48	78.54
Total	226.89	36.30	263.19	230.28	37.91	268.19
			(Percent)			
Public	88.03	11.97	100.00	87.65	12.35	100.00
Private	81.70	18.30	100.00	81.56	18.44	100.00
Total	86.21	13.79	100.00	85.86	14.14	100.00

* Provisional

N.B. (i) Excludes Sikkim, Arunachal Pradesh, Dadra and Nagar Haveli & Lakshadweep which are yet to be covered by programme; (ii) Includes (a) all establishments in the public sector and (b) non-agricultural private sector.

18.3 Employment Exchanges

The National Employment Service consisted of a network of 854 employment exchanges (End of December 1991) for registration of job seekers and their placement against vacancies notified by employers. The number of applicants on the live register of employment exchanges at the end of August 1992 was 371.2 lakh (provisional) as against 358.3 lakh at the end of August 1991 i.e. an increase of 3.6 per cent. The number of job-seekers on the live register of employment exchanges increased from 178.38 lakh at the end of 1981 to 262.70 lakh at the end of 1985 and to 371.20 lakh by the end of August 1992. The number of job-seekers on the live register of employment does not, however, give a realistic estimate of unemployment and would need to be corrected for the following factors: (i) those who are employed but registered with the employment exchanges; (ii) those who are unemployed but registered with the employment exchanges, (iii) multiple registration which is common through not permitted as a matter of policy and (IV) those persons who are presently registering with employment exchanges in advance. Information regarding educated job-seekers (Matric and above) available up to the end of December 1990 shows that 61 per cent of the 346.3 lakh job-seekers on the live register of employment exchanges at the end of December 1990 were educated. The break-up of educated job seekers at the end of December, 1990 by level of education is shown in Table 18.5

TABLE 18.5: Job-Seekers (Matric and above) on the Live Register of Employment Exchanges

(As on 31 December 1990)

Educational Level	Males	Females	Total	Proportion of females
1	2	3	4	5
		(Thousand)		
1. Matriculates	9778.9	2548.8	12327.7	20.7
2. Above matriculation but below degree	4121.0	1035.4	5156.4	20.1
3. Graduates/post graduates				
(a) Arts	1114.7	452.3	1567.0	28.9
(b) Science	551.7	177.8	729.5	24.4
(c) Commerce	557.8	98.8	656.6	15.0
(d) Education	213.5	196.4	409.9	47.9
(e) Engineering	84.0	11.6	95.6	12.1
(f) Medicine	22.8	8.9	31.7	28.
(g) Others	112.6	19.9	132.5	15.0
Total (a to g)	2657.1	965.7	3622.8	26.7
Grand Total (1+2+3)	16557.0	4549.9	21106.9	21.6

Source: Ministry of Labour, DGE & T.

Matriculates and above but below graduate degree constituted 82.8 per cent of the educated job-seekers and the remaining 17.2 per cent were graduates and above. About 21.6 per cent of education job-seekers were females.

19

INFLATION, PRICES AND PUBLIC DISTRIBUTION SYSTEM

(Including Consumer Cooperatives and Consumer Protection)

19.1 Introduction

Inflation, which had reached an exceptionally high level in 1991, declined considerably in 1992-93; by January 1993 it was lower than at any time since September 1990. The cost of living indices showed as much decline in inflation as the wholesale price index. The decline was due largely to agricultural goods, both essential consumer goods and industrial inputs. The prices of many agricultural products fell. Whereas prices of agricultural goods had risen more than those of manufactures in 1991-92, this trends was partially reversed in 1992-93. Although prices of fertilizers and petroleum products were raised significantly, the increase in administered prices in 1992-93 was more moderate than in the previous two years. Minimum support prices of agricultural products were raised following cost increases. So were procurement prices, but procurement of wheat declined as market prices ruled high. With a good kharif harvest, however, rice procurement picked up in 1992. Imports of wheat and rice were contracted to replenish the depleted PDS stocks and to restrain inflationary pressure.

The inflationary spiral which began in October 1990 continued through 1991, with the rate of inflation peaking at 16.7 per cent in August 1991. Primary goods led the inflationary surge with an inflation rate of 21.6 per cent in the middle of November 1991; the pressure on foodgrain prices was even higher. The prices of manufactured goods and fuels also firmed up. The spurt in foodgrain prices pushed up consumer prices up consumer prices both in rural and urban areas. Double-digit inflation in consumer items continued throughout 1991-92; the maximum rate being 23 per cent in consumer goods used by agricultural lobourers.

The Government took several initiatives during 1991-92 and in the current fiscal year to restore price stability. At the macro-economic level the effort of the Government has been to restore fiscal stability be reducing the fiscal deficit which had reached unsustainable levels in 1990, and to moderate the growth of money supply. A good kharif harvest and eased the pressure on supply of essential goods. The improved balance of payments position and the new trade policy which ensure easy access to imports needed to sustain production have helped to remove supply constraints facing the industry. The Government has taken special care to strengthen the public distribution system.

As a result of all these measures, inflation rate began to recede from September 1991, and stabilised between 12 and 14 per cent until the middle of July 1992. Thereafter the rate of inflation declined steadily; and except for a short break in the trend on account of fertilizer decontrol and adjustments in administered prices of petroleum products, the declining trend has been maintained so far. The annual rate of inflation as measured by the WPI has came down for 13.6 per cent at the end of last financial year to 6.8 per cent in the third week of January 1993. The rate of inflation in foodgrain prices showed a especially steep decline to 1.6 per cent as on 16 January 1993 compared with 26.3 per cent at the same point last year.

Inflation in consumer prices also declined sharply during the current financial year. the decline in the rate of inflation for agricultural labourers is the steepest, from 24 per cent in May 1992 to 8.6 per cent in November 1992. (Table 19.1)

TABLE 19.1: Annual Rate of Inflation in WPI and CPI

(Per cent)

Year	Month	WPI	CPI(IW)	CPI(UNME)	CPI(AL)
1990-91	April	9.1	7.8	8.6	3.2
	May	8.7	7.7	9.3	3.3
	June	9.5	8.8	9.2	3.1
	July	9.6	9.9	9.7	4.6
	August	8.1	9.2	8.9	4.6
	September	7.5	8.5	8.2	2.6
	October	8.9	10.8	9.5	3.5
	November	10.5	12.5	11.6	8.4
	December	12.0	13.7	13.0	10.0
	January	12.9	16.1	15.0	13.9
	February	13.5	15.4	15.0	17.3
	March	12.7	13.6	13.4	16.6
1991-92	April	11.6	12.2	12.6	14.7
	May	11.8	12.1	11.8	13.7
	June	12.2	13.0	12.3	15.4
	July	13.1	13.2	13.3	15.9
	August	16.1	14.2	15.1	18.3
	September	16.3	15.7	15.7	32.1
	October	14.7	14.4	14.2	23.1
	November	14.7	13.6	14.0	21.2
	December	14.3	13.1	13.3	21.7
	January	13.6	12.9	12.4	20.4
	February	12.9	13.4	13.0	20.6
	March	13.6	13.9	13.6	21.9
1992-93	April	13.8	14.4	13.5	22.6
	May	13.8	14.7	14.0	23.9
	June	13.0	12.9	13.2	21.9
	July	11.7	13.1	12.8	20.6
	August	9.4	11.5	10.9	19.0
	September	9.6	10.0	10.9	19.0
	October	10.6	9.4	10.8	11.0
	November	8.9*	8.4	9.6	8.6
	December	8.4*	8.0	NA	NA

* Provisional; NA: Not available

19.2 **Measuring Inflation**

Inflation is measured at the wholesale level in terms of the wholesale index (WPI) and at the retail level by three consumer price indices (CPI) for (i) industrial workers, (ii) urban non-manual employees and (iii) agricultural labourers.

19.3 **Wholesale Price Index (WPI)**

The wholesale prices index, which is released with a time lag to two weeks, is provisional as it is not entirely based on actual price quotations in respect of all items covered in the index. The index is revised to yield final estimates with a time lag of eight weeks after receipt, scrutiny and processing of all quotations. the conceptual and operational issues are indicated below:

The Wholesale Price Index : Operational Issues

* The wholesale price index (WPI) with base 1981-82 reflects changes in the prices of 447 commodities (93 primary articles, 20 fuels and 334 manufactured products covering all important items transacted in the economy. Selection of items is guided by their relative important in the economy.
* The index is based on 2371 quotations (519 for primary articles, 73 for fuels and 1779 for manufactured products.
* The price quotations used represent bulk transaction usually for further sale, at the primary stage which broadly correspond to producers' prices.
* Price data collected through official as well non-official sources.
* For prescribed items or varieties, weekly price quotations as prevailing on or about each Friday are collected; prices are collected on a monthly basis for items not undergoing week-to-week price fluctuations.
* The index at the time of its initial compilation and release is provisional as some of the price quotations are received belatedly. For missing quotations the prices are either estimated or repeated from the previous week.
* The Provisional index is made final after eight weeks by which time required quotations become available.
* Whether the final index is higher or lower than the provisional index depends on whether in successive weeks the prices for missing items tend to rise of fall or remain steady. Seasonal and non-seasonal items show different patterns and affect the overall difference in these two indices.

19.4 **Consumer Price Index (CPI)**

Inflation rates in terms of consumer prices indices reflect the trend in process at the retail level. The consumer prices index for industrial workers, CPI(IW), measures changes it retail prices of commodities consumed by industrial workers' families, the consumer prices index for urban non-manual employees, CPI(UNME), measures such changes in commodities consumed by families of employees is non-manual jobs in urban areas. The consumer prices index for agricultural labourers, CPI(AL), measures changes in the retail prices of commodities consumed by agricultural labourers. Inflation rates based on the above three CPI variants are not strictly comparable as the based year, structure and coverage of these indices differ. CPI (IW) and CPI (UNME) measure changes in the prices of goods consumer in the urban areas by different sections of the working population. Their base years are close to each other and hence these two indices are, by and large, comparable.

Inflation in terms of the consumer prices index for industrial workers (CPI-IW) moved in the same direction as wholesale prices index (WPI) during the last two years. The rate of inflation (CPI-IW) decelerated from 15.7 per cent in September 1991 to 8.4 per cent in November 1992. It was higher than that of WPI when food prices increased at a higher rate that other items and vice versa on account of the higher weightage of food items in CPI-IW. The decline in the prices of food items since August 1992 has brought the annual rate of inflation in CPI(IW) sharply down. the inflation rate in other consumer price indices has also fallen sharply (Table 19.1).

Movement in the consumer prices index for urban non-manual employees, CPI (UNME), was similar to CPI(IW). The consumer prices index for agricultural labourers, CPI (AL) recorded a much higher rise that any other price index; its range of fluctuations has also been very wide (8.6 per cent to 23.9 per cent). This could be mainly due to the wide swing in the prices of essential food articles which have a higher weightage in CPI(AL) as compared to the other two CPIs. It may also be indicated of the poor impact of the public distribution system in rural India.

19.5 **Price Movements in Major Groups**

Financial Year Changes

The cumulative prices increase in wholesale prices during the current year up to 16 January 1993 is 5.6 per cent as against 12.4 per cent during the corresponding period last year. Among major groups, the rate of increase in prices this year is the lowest (3 per cent) in primary articles and the highest (10 per cent) in fuels. The prices of primary articles had recorded the highest increase of 17.4 per cent during this period in 1991-92. (Table 19.2).

The price situation was aggravated in 1991-92 when the prices of mineral oils, primary articles and manufactured products rose sharply. Subsidies on a number of products with administered were reduced to bring down the fiscal deficit. This raised their prices. Aggravations of macro-economic imbalances and the persistence of structural rigidities made the restraint of prices difficult during the year. As a result, inflation rate went up during 1991-92 despite measures taken later that year to moderate it. These measures, however, began to have an impact from the current year when disinflationary fiscal and monetary began to take effect; the rate of increase in prices in all major groups, particularly primary articles, was much lower than in the previous year.

19.6 **Annual Changes**

By November 1992 single digit inflation become a reality, and by the week ended 16 January 1993, the rate of inflation came down to 6.8 per cent, the lowest rate since the middle of September 1990; the rate at a comparable data in January 1992 was 13.3 per cent. The impact on the WPI of the 60-paise rise per kg. in the issue prices of rice and the 50-paise rise per kg. for wheat from the middle of January 1993 was offset by a decline in prices of other food articles and food products. (Table 19.3).

TABLE 19.2: Wholesale Price Movement in Major Groups

(per cent)

Group/ sub-group	April to Mid-January		Rate of Inflation	
	1991-92	1992-93	1991	(January-December) 1992
1	2	3	4	5
All commodities	12.4	5.6	14.3	7.8
I. Primary articles	17.4	3.0	20.4	2.4
Food articles	20.6	5.9	22.2	8.7
Foodgrains	25.8	-2.0	27.6	1.4
Fruits & vegetable	12.9	4.6	22.8	10.3
Condiments & spices	41.6	16.8	49.7	16.2
Non-food articles	14.9	-2.2	21.1	16.2
II. Fuel & light	11.1	10.0	11.7	13.1
III. Manufactures	9.6	6.4	11.3	10.2
Food products	10.6	6.4	13.8	7.9
Fertilizers	37.4	44.0	37.4	34.9

TABLE 19.3: Annual Rate of Inflation (WPI) during 1990-91 to 1992-93

Commodity group	1990-91	1991-92	1992-93*
All commodities	12.1	13.6	6.8
Primary articles	17.1	15.3	1.1
Food articles	18.9	20.9	6.1
Foodgrains	22.7	24.0	-1.6
Non-food articles	19.3	8.1	-7.9
Fuel & light	14.4	13.2	12.1
Mineral oils	20.6	9.2	18.0
Manufactures	8.9	12.6	9.3
Food products	13.2	10.2	6.0
Sugar, khandsari etc.	0.1	5.5	20.0
Edible oils	32.7	1.9	-8.0
Textiles	5.3	11.3	3.1
Cement	14.1	17.4	8.9
Fertilizers	0.0	28.8	34.9
Iron & steel	6.0	4.5	9.1

* As on 16 January 1993.

19.7 **Public Distribution System**

The Public Distribution System (PDS) in India has been is existence for the past for decades with the following objectives:

— Stabilisation of food prices.
— Ensuring availability of foodgrains at reasonable prices especially to the vulnerable sections of society.
— Protecting the real purchasing power of the consumers by maning steady availability of th essential commodities in fair prices.
— Supplementary to the poverty alleviation programme of the Government.
— Avoiding imbalance between demand and supply of consumer goods.
— Ensuring social justice in the distribution of basic necessities of life.

Governmental Steps

The Central Government has taken remedial measures to revamp the Public Distribution System and to strengthen its operations to avoid pilferages and malpractices that hinder the popularity of this system. The Governmental uses the PDS to counter inflation and in particular to protect the poorer sections of the population from high prices and deficit of essential commodities. The Prime Minister announced on 1st January the revamped Public Distribution System in about 1,700 of the most backward block of the country. Drought prone areas, desert areas and tribal areas are given preference. The Government is determined to ensure that foodgrains and essential commodities reach the poor and the underprivileged in adequate quantities and at affordable prices. The Central Government made a provision of Rs. 5,000 crore for fertiliser subsidy for the year 1992-93. In the year 1977-78 the fertiliser subsidy was Rs.266 crore. In the year 1991-92 it was at Rs. 4,400 crore. For the year 1992-93 it is estimated at Rs. 5,000 crore. A Parliamentary committee is also constituted to review the fertiliser prices and subsidy. The Central Government has allocated Rs. 250 crore in addition to food subsidy of Rs. 2,500 crore for revamping the Public Distribution system being implemented in 1700 backward blocks support and procurement prices for the last five years are given in Table 19.4

As on 31 March 1992, there were over four lakh such outlets in the country; 3.05 lakh in rural areas and 0.94 lakh in urban areas. On an average, one fair-price shop is envisaged to cover a population of 2000. From January 1992 a scheme to revamp the public distribution system has been launched in about 1700 block falling in the drought prone, desert, integrated tribal development project areas and certain designated hill areas. In these areas, additional commodities like tea, soap, pulses and iodised salt are also envisaged to be distributed.

Foodgrains (rice and wheat) are allocated to States and Union Territories for revamped PDS block at lower prices; Rs. 50 per quintal lower than Central issue prices (CIPs) for normal PDS blocks. The State Governments are, however, required to ensure that the retail prices of these commodities in these blocks are not higher than CIPs by more than 25 paise per kg. Sugar is also distributed at lower prices. As of today, imported oil is allocated to states at an issue prices of Rs. 20000 per tonne for bulk and Rs. 25000 per tonne in 15kg. tins. Consumer prices recommended to state are Rs.25 per kg. for bulk supply and Rs. 27.75 per kg. for supply in 15 kg. tins.

TABLE 19.4: Procurement and Minimum Support Prices

(Rs. Per quintal)

	Commodity	Type	Variety	1988-89	1989-90	1990-91	1991-92	1992-93	Increase 1992-93 (per cent)
1	Paddy	P	Common	160	185	205	230	270	17.4
			Fine	170	195	215	240	280	16.7
			SF	180	205	225	250	290	16.0
2	Coarse cereals	P	FAQ	145	165	180	205	240	17.1
3	Maize	P	FAQ	145	165	180	205	240	17.1
4	Wheat	P	FAQ	145	165	180	210	245	16.7
5	Barley	M	FAQ	183	215	225	275 @	330 @	20.0
6	Gram	M	FAQ	325	421	450	500	600	20.0
7	Arhar	M	FAQ	360	425	480	545	640	17.4
8	Moong	M	FAQ	360	425	480	545	640	17.4
9	Urd	M	FAQ	360	425	480	545	640	17.4
10	Sugarcane@@	S	FAQ	19.50	22.00	23.00	26.00	27.00	3.8
11	Cotton	M	F-414/ H-777	500	570	620	695	800	15.1
		M	H-4	600	690	750	840	950	13.1
12	Groundnut	M	FAQ	430	500	580	645	750	16.3
13	Jute	S	TD-5	-	295	320	375	400	6.7
14	Rape and mustard	M	FAQ	460	575	600	670	760	13.4
15	Sunflower	M	FAQ	450	530	600	670	800	19.4
16	Soyabean	M	Black	275	325	350	395	475	20.3
		M	Yellow	320	370	400	445	525	18.0
17	Safflower	M	FAQ	440	550	575	640	720	12.5
18	Toria	M	FAQ	430	545	570	645	752	12.4
19	Tobacco	M	VFC F-2	1175 *	1250 *	1325 *	1475 *	1600 $	8.5
		M	L-2	1200 $	1350 $	1425 $	16004	1750 $	9.4
20	Copra	M	FAQ	—	1500 #	1600 #	1700 #	—	6.3
	Copra balls	M	FAQ	—	—	1850	—	—	—

M-Minimum support price, P-Procurement, S-Statutory minimum price, FAQ-Fair average quality, @ Including a Central bonus of Rs. 25.00 per quintal, @@-These prices are linked to a basic recovery of 8.5% with a proportionate premium for every 0.1% increase above that level, *-Black soil. $-Light soil, #-For calendar years 1989, 1990 and 1991, SF- Super fine, (-)-Not fixed.

During the edible oil year 1991-92, 1.68 lakh tonnes of palmolein was imported into the country for distribution under PDS. About 47,000 tonnes of soyabean oil was also received as gift from USA under USAID programme during this year. In view of the increased production of edible oil in the country, only about 20,000 tonnes of oil has been imported as against the import authorisation of 3 lakh tonnes of edible oils in 1992-93. 29.9 lakh tonnes of wheat and 2.1 lakh tonnes or rice are being imported during the current year to improve domestic supplies of these grains

Supplies under PDS

Allocations of foodgrains in 1992-93 were restored to pre-1991 levels and additional allocations are being made for the revamped blocks. In April-December 1992, 15.44 million tonnes of foodgrains were allocated to the states for the PDS against which 13.06 million tonnes were lifted for distribution. The allocation of rice wheat in the previous year for the corresponding period was 16.52 million tonnes and the offtake was 14.62 million tonnes. (Table 19.5).

TABLE 19.5: Distribution of Foodgrains under the Public Distribution System

Commodity		1990-91	1991-92	1991	1992
Rice	Allocation	9.61	11.36	8.72	8.47
	Offtake	7.87	10.04	8.16	7.12
Wheat	Allocation	9.50	10.36	7.80	6.97
	Offtake	7.09	8.73	6.46	5.94
Total	Allocation	19.11	21.72	16.52	15.44
	Offtake	14.94	18.77	14.62	13.06

Procurement

During the 1992-93 rabi marketing season, 6.38 million tonnes of wheat was procured as compared to 7.75 million tonnes during the corresponding period in 1991-92; the shortfall was substantial. Lower procurement this year is attributed to the higher open market prices compared to the procurement prices, lower arrivals of wheat in the major wheat-producing states of Punjab, Haryana and Uttar Pradesh, and a possible holding back of the stocks be farmers in anticipation of higher open market price later in the year. Rice procurement during the marketing year 1992-93 (October-September) is better than in 1991-92 and has touched 8.3 million tonnes as on 25 January 1993 as compared to 7 million tonnes during corresponding period last year. Total procurement during the current year is likely to exceed last year's level (Table 19.6).

TABLE: 19.6: Procurement of Foodgrains

(Million tonnes)

	1990-91	1991-92	Up to January 25 1991-92	Up to January 25 1992-93
Rice	13.02	10.45	7.02	8.31
Wheat	11.07	7.75	7.75	6.38
Total foodgrains	24.26	18.25	13.61	12.57

Stocks

Stocks of foodgrains with public agencies (Central and State) as on 1 January 1993 were 13.19 million tonnes as against 14.74 million tonnes on the corresponding data last year. Actual foodgrain stocks have remained below buffer stock requirements (Table 19.7).

TABLE 19.7: Stocks of Foodgrains

(Million tonnes)

Beginning of	Wheat Minimum	Wheat Actual	Rice Minimum	Rice Actual	Total Minimum	Total Actual
1	2	3	4	5	6	7
April 1992	3.7	2.4	10.8	9.8	14.5	12.2
July	13.1	6.7	9.2	8.4	22.3	15.1
October	10.6	4.3	6.0	6.9	16.6	11.2
January 1993	7.7	3.5	7.7	9.5	15.4	13.2

On 1 April 1992, the opening stocks or rice were 1.3 million tonnes lowers and those of wheat 3.4 million tonnes lower than the corresponding stocks last year. Foodgrain stock were 2.3 million tonnes lower than the requirements of the buffer stocking policy. This rendered food management this year more difficult than before and necessitated imports of wheat and rice referred to earlier.

19.8 Consumer Cooperatives

In the successive Five Year Plans, beginning with the Second Five Year Plan, Consumer Cooperatives have been assigned an important place in the distributive trade and in the recent years they have emerged as a strong institutional framework in the distributive trade and become and integral part of the Public Distribution System, serving the Government policy by providing essential consumer articles to people, particularly to the vulnerable sections of the society.

In the 8th Five Year Plan, it is proposed to strengthen the consumer movement further and expand its coverage in distributive trade, so as to reduce regional disparities by imparting a new direction to the movement and extending its scope tc the Block and Tehsil/Taluqa Headquarters particularly in tribal and hilly areas. Super Bazar, Delhi, Apna Bazar, Bombay, TUCS, Madras, Calcutta wholesale Store, Calcutta, Janta Bazar, Kolhapur and in rural sector Warna Bazar, Kolhapur, Janta Bazar, Raigarh may be cited as leading examples.

To supplement the state resources, Government of India provides financial assistance under Central Sector and Centrally-sponsored Schemes for the development of Consumer Cooperatives. In 1991-92 the following financial outlays was provided for development of Consumer Comparative under Central and Centrally-sponsored Scheme:-

I. *Centrally-sponsored Scheme*	(Rs. in lakhs)
i). Development of Consumer Coop. in urban areas	150.00

ii).	Distribution of Essential Consumer articles through PACS and LAMPS in Rural Areas (The scheme is implemented through NCDC 10% of the assistance is assistance is earmarked for tribal areas)	200.00
II.	*Central Sector Scheme*	
i).	Strengthening of NCCF and assistance for consultancy and promotional cell	100.00
ii).	Assistance to Super Bazar, Delhi	20.00
	Total:	470.00

Structure of the Cooperative Distribution System

The Cooperative Distribution System of Consumer articles comprises Consumer Cooperatives in Urban Areas and Agriculture service and marketing Cooperatives of National Federation, Central/wholesale store at District level and primary stores at the base level has been built up in the urban Consumer Movement over the years. As on 31 March, 1991 the structure consisted of NCCF at Appex level, 30 states consumer cooperative federation/state marketing-cum-consumer Federation with 1114 branches at State level, 659 Central/wholesale consumer cooperative store with 7310 branches at District level and 22589 primary. Consumer Cooperative Stores with 10801 branches at base level. In the rural areas distribution of essential and other consumer items is provided by about 58925 Primary Agriculture Credit Societies PACS including large size multipurpose societies (LAMPS) in tribal areas and Farmers Service Societies.

Physical Progress

In the base year of 8th Five Year Plan i.e. 1991-92 total retail sales of consumer articles are estimated around Rs.6500 crores (urban articles Rs. 3200) crores and Rural Areas Rs. 3300 crores) as against the actual achievements of Rs. 5800 crores during 1990-91 (urban areas Rs. 3000 crores and rural areas Rs. 2800 crores). It is envisaged that Sales turnover of the order of Rs.124,400 crores (Rs. 6000 crores in rural areas and Rs. 6400 crores in Urban Areas) will be achieved by the terminal year of the 8th Five Year Plan. During the year 1992-93, the first year of the Eighth Plan it is expected that the retail sales are likely to reach a level of Rs, 7400 crores (Rs. 3600 crores through village coops and consumer stores in rural areas and Rs. 3800 crores through cooperatives in Urban Areas). According to a rough estimates cooperatives share is only 2% of the distributive consumer trade at present as against the long term objective of achieving 20% share in the total distribution trade of the country. In the Eighth plan coverage of tribal and hilly areas and involvement of women in cooperatives and consumer education has been given more emphasis.

Urban Consumer Cooperatives

In order the meet the day to day need of essential and other commodities of mass consumption at reasonable price in urban areas, Consumer Cooperatives have been developed over the years with modern sales technique. Bulk of the Urban Areas have been covered by the Urban Consumer Cooperatives by developing modern sales techniques and introducing Department Store, self-service counters, shopping under one roof etc.

So far 377 Department Stores, 478 Large sized Retail outlets, 1675 Small branches, 26 Mobile Van shops have been assisted under Centrally Sponsored Scheme. These outlets handles all essential commodities, viz. household goods, groceries, textiles, controlled commodities, drugs and medicines, cosmetics and toiletries etc. Some of the Departmental Stores provide round-the-clock service for sale of drugs and medicines, while other also run fruit and vegetable shops. The Consumer Cooperatives are encouraged to set up consumer industries like hosiery units, bakery, dal mills, spice units, atta-chakki, exercise note-book manufacturing units etc.

Rural Consumer Scheme

Under the Centrally-sponsored plan scheme, Government of India have been providing financial assistance to the village societies towards margin money for strengthening their share capital base in order to enable them to raise working capital finance from the financial institutions for public distribution of consumer articles in rural areas. The assistance is provided on project basis which comprises of a lead societies catering to the needs of 22-25 village societies attached to it called Linked Societies. The Lead Society is to procure goods on wholesale basis and supply the goods required by the Link Societies for distribution on retail basis. The quantum of financial assistance given to a link society under the centrally sponsored scheme is extended up Rs. 30.00 per link society and Rs. 10,000 opening new branch by village society. The Scheme is being implemented through NCDC. During the year 1991-92 a budgetary provision of Rs. 2 crore was made for the purpose.

The centrally sponsored Plan Scheme is being implemented together with the Sachems of the NCDC is providing financial assistance to lead societies by way of margin money up to Rs. 2 lakhs, and for purchase of transport vehicles up to Rs. 2 lakhs. However, the upper ceiling of financial assistance prescribed for purchase of transport vehicle has been removed since 1988-89. The NCDC also provides financial assistance for purchase of furniture and fixtures for opening of branches by lead societies at the rate of Rs. 12,00 per society besides providing similar financial assistance to the Linked Societies and their branches up to Rs. 5,000 each for purchase of furniture and fixture.

The cooperatives in rural areas are actively being involved as an integral part of the public distribution system (PDS) for supply of essential commodities namely Wheat, Rice, Sugar, Edible Oil, Soft Coke, controlled Cloth to the rural community.

NCDC is also co-ordinating with NCCF. NCDC is represented on the Board of Directors of NCCF and an amount of Rs. 2.00 lakhs has already been contributed towards its equity. During the year this Ministry has recommended that the led societies on whom indents are placed by the PACS/Consumer Cooperatives for supply of essential commodities will purchase goods worth atleast the amount of margin money sanctioned by NCDC to the primaries from

(a) The NCCR branch; or
(b) The wholesale consumer cooperatives located in the area; or
(c) A branch of the state consumers federation.

Provided the goods are supplied at competitive rates in the areas identified by NCCF NCDC has in turn, requested the lead societies as well as the State Government to ensure the said conditions.

National Cooperative Consumers Federation of India Limited (NCCF)

NCCF is the apex organisation of Consumer Cooperatives in the country. Its main functions is to render help in the development of Consumer Cooperative movement by providing adequate supply of vital consumer goods and ensuring promotional and technical guidance to consumer Cooperatives for increasing their managerial capability. It has 22 branches all over the country. It runs pulses processing unit at Bhiwani (Haryana) and Nagpur (Maharashtra), an spice processing unit at Unjha (Gujarat) and units for manufacturing exercise note-books at Hingna (Nagpur), Noida (U.P.) and Guwahati (Assam). It arranges Central procurement and supplies in bulk of several consumer goods like pulses, textiles, cereals, spices, slat, tea, edible oils, washing sop, exercise books, match boxes, etc. to the consumer cooperatives and agencies nominated by the State Government.

The working of the NCCF is being reviewed at various levels. It is envisaged that NCCF will play a leading role as the central agency in arranging supply of additional commodities like pulses, toilet soap, salt and cheaper tea in the revamped Public Distribution System. The above measures are likely to bring about an improvement in the working of the NCCF.

During the year 1991-92, the Central Government provided an amount of Rs. 15.00 lakhs also towards grant-in-aid in order to meet the expenses of its C & P Cell.

The Consultancy and Promotional Cell of NCCF, which was set up on 1972, has been providing a number of services for improving the managerial and technical skills of consumer cooperatives. Government of India extends financial assistance to NCCF to meet 75% of the expenses of the Cell under Central Sector Plan Scheme. The objectives of C & P Cell is to draw up management system, operational and business procedures, administrative and organisational guidelines to assist consumer cooperatives in implementing the CPC Management Accounting System with a view to making it an effective tool of management information an control, evolve performance indicators and business efficiency norms for different retail outlets, conduct diagnostic studies and analysis of the working of the consumer cooperatives with a view to suggesting improvement and providing plans for rehabilitations. The Cell has three Regional offices of Calcutta (Eastern Region), Hyderabad (Southern Region) and Bombay (Western Region). During the year under review, the C & P Cell of the NCCF has undertaken a number of activities, highlights of which are given as under the C & P Cell (a) Extended technical support and spot assistance to 22 societies in West Bengal, Andhra Pradesh, Assam, Maharashtra, A & N Islands and Orissa for improving display, price-making, assortment, pricing, performance etc. of their retail outlets; (b) provided guidance for opening new retail outlets, renovation of existing outlets with self-service system, project reports and shop layouts were given to 17 societies in Jammu & Kashmir, Madhya Pradesh, Andhra Pradesh, Tamil Nadu, West Bengal, Kerala & Karnataka; (c) Reviewed monthly reports, annual accounts etc. and also took follow-up action to improve management accounting system by the store. Operational report of 21 societies, trial balance of 37 societies, budget of 12 stores, standard plan of account of 15 stores and annual accounts of 85 stores were reviewed for providing feed-back and for improving implementation of management accounting system to sort out operational difficulties; (d) Conducted a 2 days training programme for the accounts personnel of U.P. State Consumer Federation and organised 5 days training programme of Management Accounting system for personnel of stores and departmental officers of Arunachal Pradesh. Reviewed rehabilitation progress of 39 stores and suggested follow up action to be taken by them.

Six days trainers training programme was organised for the lectures of Cooperation in the Northern Region in collaboration with MATCOM-ILO. Besides it also (a) Extended faculty support to cooperative training colleges at Madurai, Madras, Kalyani and Pune for their consumer training programmes. (b) Conducted a 2 days in-house training programme for show-room-cum-sales counter personnel of NCCF. (c) Participated in meetings/workshops organised by National council for Cooperative Training in Connection with the business development planning of Primary Agricultural Coop. Societies. (d) Tool follow-up action for clearance of a week's study visit of a team from Sri Lanka on the request of Sri Lanka Institute of Cooperative Management. (e) Briefed a group of trainees from Ethiopia, Zambia and Bhutan about the India Consumer Coop. movement. (f) Extended comments/suggestions to National Council for Cooperative Training for revising their scheme and syllabi for diploma course in Consumer Cooperative Management.

The Government of India is operating a credit guarantee scheme to assist the Consumer Cooperatives in securing cash credit accommodation for their working capital from the Nationalised Commercial/Cooperative Bank against hypothecation and pledging of goods on uniformly reduced margin of 10% instead of normal margin of 40% in respect of hypothecation loan and 25% in respect of pledged loans by guaranteeing their repayment. The Scheme was introduced in 1966 and is being continued in phases. It has since been decided to continue the Central Government Guarantee Scheme during the Eighth Plan period, subject to change of one per cent per annum towards guarantee fee for the amount guaranteed. The limits have also been increased to enable the consumer cooperative societies to avain increases amounts as working capital.

The Scheme will help the consumer cooperatives pick up business and gain momentum. It is hoped that they would achieve that main purpose of holding the price line and providing quality goods to the consumers at a reasonable price.

19.9 **Consumer Protection**

Consumer movement is a social movement which seeks to protect the rights of the consumer in relation to the seller. Scientific and technological development has brought perceptible changes in the economic and social life of the consumer who finds his control over the prices and quality of goods gradually diminishing.

Government has accorded a high priority to the programme of consumer protection. It has initiated a number of steps to promote a responsible and responsive consumer movement in the country. Such measures include the use of mass media for education and information of consumer involvement in increasing number of consumer organisations in taking up the cause of the consumers and coordinating the measures taken up by States/UTs and Ministries/Departments concerned with the interest of the consumers.

Keeping in view the importance given to the subject and to make the public aware of its role, the name of the Ministry of Civil Supplies and Public Distribution has been recently changed to Ministry of Civil Supplies, Consumer Affairs and Public Distribution. This has been done in view of the great demand from various sections of society particularly the voluntary consumer organisations.

Consumer Protection Movement

The consumer movement is still in its infancy in the country. Various legal and administrative measures taken by the Government need to be supplemented by a strong consumer protection movement in the country. The movement being a social one, has to be developed on a voluntary basis through greater participation of voluntary consumer organisations.

Financial Assistance to Voluntary Consumer Organisations

To strengthen the consumer organisations, Ministry has reintroduced the scheme of providing financial assistance to registered consumer organisations which are actually involved in the field of consumer protection. Under the scheme consumer organisations can be provided financial assistance to a maximum of Rs. 25,000 (on 75% grant basis).

To educate these consumer organisations various aspects of consumer protection, the Ministry has started a series of training programmes held on regional basis. One such programme was organised in Jaipur from 23-12-1991 to 27-12-1991 for the voluntary consumer organisations functioning in Northern Region. Another training programme for the voluntary consumer organisations function in Eastern and North Eastern Region is held in January, 1992 in Calcutta.

State Level Seminars

The Ministry is giving financial assistance to the State Governments and Union Territory Administrations for organising regional and State level seminars. The purpose of these seminars is to generate consumer awareness and to involve the rural people in the consumer movement.

National Awards on Consumer Protection

To involve the youth of this country in promoting a strong consumer movement particularly at grass root level, the Ministry has instituted a 'National Youth Award for Consumer Protection'. Youth including women in the age group of

15-35 years who have done outstanding work in the field of consumer protection are eligible for this award. The award comprises prize money of Rs. 20,000, Rs. 15,000 and Rs. 10,000 alogwith certificates of merit. Miss Anju D. Agarwal of Bombay and Shri P. Ramakrishna of Hyderabad was awarded I and II awards respectively for the year 1990.

To encourage voluntary consumer organisations particularly women's organisations and those functioning in rural, tribal and backward areas, the Ministry has instituted a 'National Award on Consumer Protection'. The award comprises prize money of Rs. 50,000, Rs. 40,000 and Rs 30,000 alongwith the certificates of merit. Consumer Education and Research Centre, Ahmedabad, Mumbai Grahak Panchayat, Bombay an Tricy District Consumer Council was awarded I, II and III prize for the year 1990. A special prize has also been given to Common cause, New Delhi for its outstanding contribution in the field of consumer protection.

Consumer Awareness Programme

The success of the programme of consumer protection hinges mainly on consumer awareness and development of a strong voluntary consumer movement in the country. Towards this end, the Ministry organises training programmes, exhibitions, workshops, seminars etc. and arranges for multimedia publicity on a continuous basis.

The Ministry brought out two booklets entitled *Help Prevent Adulteration* and *Salient Features of the Consumer Protection Act, 1986*. In addition, it had also brought out two brochures namely *Shopping for the Packaged Commodities* and *Rights of the Consumers*. A book on *Poisons in Our Food* was also released. The Ministry has also brought out a *Directory of Voluntary Consumer Organisations*. Ministry brought out a booklet entitled *Consumer Protection and Weights and Measures* and four post-card size material containing useful information for the consumers. The first issue of the Ministry's quarterly journal entitled *Upabhokta Jagaran* was brought out on the occasion of 'Consumer Day' on 15 the March, 1991.

Preparation of Audio Visual Material

So far, the following audio visual material in the field of consumer protection has been prepared:

(i) One film documentary entitled "Rights of Consumers" which explains the rights of consumers.
(ii) One video documentary entitled "Mubarak Kadam" which explains the salient features of the Consumer Protection Act, 1986.
(iii) Four video quickies on Rights of Consumers, Redressal Machinery under Consumer Protection Act, How to make a Purchase and Public Distribution System.

Consumer Protection Act, 1986

Enactment of the Consumer Protection, 1986 is one of the most important steps in protecting rights of consumers and promoting a strong and broad based consumer movement in the country. The salient features of the Act are as under:

(i) The Act applies to all goods and services.
(ii) It covers all sectors — private, public, cooperative etc.
(iii) In enshrines the six rights of consumers namely (1) Right to safety, (2) Right to be informed, (3) Right to choose, (4) Right to be heard, (5) Right to seek redressal and (6) Right to consumer education.
(iv) It envisages establishment of Consumer Protection Councils at the Centre and State levels whose main objects are to promote and protect the rights of consumers.
(v) It provides simple, speedy and inexpensive redressal to consumer grievances with regard to defective goods, deficient services, unfair trade practices etc., through a 3-tier quasi-judicial redressal machinery at national, state and district levels.
(vi) A complaint up to Rs. 1 lakh can be filed in the Consumer Disputes Redressal Forum (District Forum), between Rs. 1 lakh to Rs. 10 lakhs in the Consumer Disputes Redressal Commission (State Commission) and completion above Rs. 10 lakhs can be filed in the National Consumer Disputes Redressal Commission (National Commission). The National Commission and State Commissions have appellate and revisonary jurisdictions also.
(vii) The provisions of the Act are compensatory in nature.
(viii) The procedure for filing the complaint in above redressal agencies in very simple. A complaint can be field on a plain paper in writing. The assistance to lawyer is not required. There is no fee for filing a complaint.

Implementation

All the provisions of the Consumer Protection Act, 1986 have come into force w.e.f. 1.7.1987 throughout the country except the State of Jammu and Kashmir. The State of Jammu and Kashmir has enacted its own legislation in this field. All the States/UTs have constituted the state level consumer protection councils. the Central Government constituted the Central Consumer Protection Council on 1.6.1987. The council has since been reconstituted w.e.f. 23.8.1990.

The National Commission has started functioning w.e.f. 27.12.88 with Hon'ble Justice Shri V.B. Eradi as its President. As per information available, 28 State Commissions and 360 District Forums have started functioning.

On the recommendation of the Central Consumer Protection Council, Ministry constituted a high power committee under the chairmanship of the Minister for Civil Supplies, West Bengal to consider the various suggestions received to make the Consumer Protection Act and MRTP Act more effective and purposeful. The Committee has since submitted its report to the Government.

Source: *Annual Report, 1991-92*, Ministry of Civil Supplies, Consumer Affairs and Public Distribution, Government of India, New Delhi.

20

FISCAL POLICY AND BUDGET

20.1 Fiscal Policy : An Introduction

The process of fiscal reformed initiated in the financial year 1990-91 continued in 1991-92 and 1992-93. It is fully reflected in the budget speech (February 27, 1993) of the Finance Minister Manmohan Singh.

20.2 Excerpts from the Budget Speech

It is now twenty months since our Government took office; twenty eventful months in which we have worked ceaselessly to overcome the very difficult economic situation we inherited. In June 1991, the economy was in the throes of an unprecedented balance of payments crisis. A savage squeeze had been imposed on imports; international confidence had collapsed; industrial production was falling; and inflation was on the rise.

The sense of crises is now behind us. We have restored a measure of normalcy to our external payments. The annual rate of inflation has been reduced from the peak of 17 per cent in August, 1991 to below 7 per cent. International confidence has been restored. Agriculture has performed well in the current year and industrial production is beginning to recover. The growth of the economy, which had declined to 1.2 per cent in 1991-92, is expected to be around 4 per cent in 1992-93. The economic strategy we have followed, resting on the twin pillars of fiscal discipline and structural reform, has been vindicated by the decisive upturn.

Fiscal discipline was necessary because the Government had lived for too long beyond its means. The rising fiscal deficits of the Central Government were the root cause of our balance of payments problem, rising prices and high rates of interest. We have made good progress by reducing the fiscal deficit from 8.4 per cent GDP in 1990-91 to about 5 per cent in the current year.

Policies of structural reform aimed at increasing efficiency in resource use and improving our international competitiveness were crucial for providing a lasting solution to the payments crisis. It was necessary to restructure our trade and industrial policies, encourage efficiency through greater domestic competition, allow our producers to have access to imports at reasonable rates of duty, encourage foreign investment and upgradation of technology, and progressively integrate the Indian economy with the world economy. Without these reforms, India would face the certain prospect of entering the 21st century as just about the poorest country in Asia. I am convinced that the Indian people would never tolerate such an outcome. India's natural and human resources entitle us to think in terms of becoming a major powerhouse of the world economy. Our reforms are inspired precisely by this vision.

The policy initiative we have taken do not in any way reduce our commitment to take care of the poor and the disadvantaged. On the contrary, we have taken steps to minimise the burden of adjustment on the poor and working classes. We have disapproved those professional prophets of gloom who were predicting millions of people becoming unemployed.

Priorities

The priorities for economic policy, at this critical stage of our economic restructuring, are very clear:

— We must continue with the fiscal correction to ensure that inflationary expectations are effectively curbed; to this end, the fiscal deficit both at the Centre and in the States must be further reduced as a percentage of GDP.
— The room for fiscal manoeuvre gained by restraining expenditure over the past two years must be used to give a strong fillip to development expenditure in 1993-94, especially for programmes of poverty alleviation, rural development and the vital social services such as education and health.
— The hesitant industrial recovery must be converted into a strong revival in 1993-94, which can then be followed by a vigorous boom in the last three years of the Eighth Plan.
— We must make further progress with our announced strategy of tax reform, moving to a simpler tax system, with moderate rates and much greater focus on compliance.
— We must ensure that our economic strategy gives full support to agriculture on which the livelihood and well being of the majority of our people depend, and also to agroprocessing industries, which have a tremendous potential for increasing employment and income in rural areas.
— Finally, exports must be made a truly high priority national endeavour so that we can move as quickly as possible to managing the balance of payments without the need for continued exceptional financing from abroad. This is the only meaningful route to self reliance.

Adequate availability of credit at reasonable rates of interest will be critical in converting this year's weak industrial recovery into a strong revival next year. One factor behind the inadequacy of credit for the commercial sector is the preemption of a large proportion of banks' resources by the government at below-market rates of interest through the Statutory Liquidity Ratio (SLR). In 1992-93 we began the process of reducing the SLR in order to release a larger volume of resources for commercial lending. Our objective is to reduce the SLR further from an effective average level of about 36 per cent at present to about 25 per cent over the next 3 years. The precise phasing of the reduction will be announced by Reserve Bank of India, taking into account the emerging aggregate monetary and credit situation.

Interest Rate

The reduction in inflation achieved thus far justifies a reduction in interest rates. Accordingly, the Reserve Bank of India is separately notifying a reduction in the maximum interest rate on bank deposits from 21 per cent to 11 per cent. Simultaneously, the minimum lending rate of 18 per cent on commercial advances is being lowered to 17 percent. It is my expectation that the lowering of interest rates will help the economic recovery in the coming year. As inflation abates, there will be scope for further reduction in interest rates.

A major instrument for encouraging agricultural production and making it profitable is the assurance of remunerative prices to the farmers. Procurement prices for the last kharif crop and the forthcoming rabi have been handsomely raised to ensure that farmers are compensated for increases in the cost off inputs. It is also the policy of the Government not to place administrative restrictions on movements of agricultural products within the country. Out farmers must have the full benefit of prices available in the domestic market.

Agricultural credit is another critical input for agricultural and more broadly, rural development. The flow of rural credit from institutional sources is expected to jump from Rs. 13,800 crore during 1992-93 to Rs. 16,500 crore during 1993-94, an increase of 20 per cent. NABARD's investment refinance support to banks will increase by 22 per cent from Rs. 2,300 crore in the current year to Rs. 2,800 crore in 1993-94. Within this total, NABARD has evolved an innovative package of measures to ensure special attention to priority areas.

Term loans for minor irrigation will support the sinking of 3.75 lakh wells and installation of 6 lakh pumpsets. The rate of NABARD refinance of bank loans is being increased to 90 per cent in the case of North Eastern States and also of investments in 100 per cent export oriented units in agriculture and allied activities. NABARD will also take up pilot projects for intensive development of rural industries in five selected districts with an outlay of Rs. 125 crore. NABARD is setting up a Venture Capital Fund, with an initial corpus of Rs. 5 crore, to assist new and innovative investments in farm and non-farm sectors, and a Cooperative Development Fund with an initial corpus of Rs.10 crore to help improve management systems and skills in cooperative banks. In 1993-94, we shall pay special attention to revitalising the agricultural credit system so that it becomes a more effective instrument for increasing capital formation and productivity of agriculture.

Because of the new norms, however, banks will have to make large provisions amounting to over Rs. 10,000 crore for bad and doubtful advances in their portfolios. As the provisioning norms are being introduced in two stages, the first impact will be felt in the year ending March 31, 1993, with a further impact next year. The resulting losses will eat into the capital of the banks, which is already inadequate given the new capital adequacy norms. in order to protect the viability and financial health of the Indian banking system I am making provision for a large capital contribution of Rs. 5,700 crore to the nationalised banks in 1993-94 to meet the gap created by the application of the first stage of the provisioning norms.

There will be no immediate net out go from the budget, as the Government's contribution is in the form of Government bonds; but the interest payment on these bonds, and their ultimate redemption will be real burden on the budget in future. This is the price we have to pay for having long tolerated management practices in the banks and types of lending which paid inadequate attention to portfolio quality and recoveries. I may add that while undertaking such a large injection of capital into the banks, specific commitments will be required from each bank to ensure that their future management practices ensure a high level of portfolio quality so that the earlier problem does not recur.

Even this large injection of capital will only solve the immediate problem.

Additional losses will arise because of the second stage of provisioning next year. Besides, the capital adequacy requirements are also being introduced in a phased manner and there will be additional capitals needs on this account in 1994-95 and 1005-96. This burden cannot be borne entirely by the budget without eating into scarce resources which are desperately needed for development, especially in the rural areas. Government has, therefore, decided that the State Bank of India, as well as other nationalised banks which are in a position to do so, will be allowed to access the capital markets to raise fresh equity to meet their shortfall in capital requirements over the next years. The additional capital thus mobilised will help our banks to expand their lending which would otherwise be constrained by capital inadequacy. Government will continue to retain majority ownership, and therefore effective control, in the public sector banks. Necessary legislation to give effect to this decision will be introduced later in the year.

If banks are to make provisions for bad debts, they must also be able to realise the security on their bad debts. At present, the legal process for realising banks dues is tortuous, and cases take several years in the courts. Government has, therefore, decided to set up Special Tribunals to expedite legal action by the banks to enforce recoveries. Legislation to this effect will be introduced in the course of the year.

The securities scam has also revealed weaknesses in the existing system of supervision of banks. Following the recommendations of the Narasimham Committee, Reserve Bank of India has decided to strengthen its supervisory arrangements by setting up a separate Board for Financial Supervision within the Reserve Bank.

Capital Markets

Parallel with reforms in the banking system we are vigorously pursuing reforms in the capital markets. We must ensure that trading and settlement take place with speed and transparency under appropriate rules and regulations designed to ensure investor protection. The Securities and Exchange Board of India, which was given statutory status and powers twelve months ago, has been entrusted with the task of bringing about this transition. As promised in my last Budget speech, the office of the Controller of Capital Issues in the Ministry of Finance has been abolished, and almost all powers under the securities Contract (Regulations) Act have been delegated or transferred to SEBI.

Several important steps have been taken in the current year to reform the capital market. Rules and regulations have been notified to deal with insider trading, the operation of mutual funds, registration of brokers, merchant bankers and other intermediaries. The scheme for allowing foreign institutional investors to invest in the capital markets announced in my last Budget speech has been implemented and a number of approvals given. Several private sector mutual funds have recently been given clearances by SEBI. A company has been incorporated for the establishment of National Stock Exchange which is expected to operate as a model stock exchange with member brokers all over the country trading in the exchange through modern telecommunication facilities. Proposals are also being considered for the establishment of a centralised depository with a National Clearance and Settlement System.

We are determined to ensure that further reforms of the capital market are implemented in the course of 1993-94 so that the capital market can mobilise large funds for investment. On the basis of experience gained, the Government has decided to amend the Securities and Exchange Board of India Act to give SEBI additional powers in order to increase its effectiveness.

With reforms underway in the banking sector and in the capital markets, it is necessary to address the need for similar reforms in the insurance industry aimed at introducing a more competitive environment subject to suitable regulations and supervision. I propose to appoint a high powered committee to go into the these issues in depth and submit its recommendations within six months.

With reforms underway in the banking sector and in the capital markets, it is necessary to address the need for similar reforms in the insurance industry aimed at introducing a more competitive environment subject to suitable regulation and supervision. I propose to appoint a high powered committee to go into these issues in depth and submit its recommendations within six months.

In my Budget speech last year, I announced the introduction of new system of exchange rate management under which a dual exchange rate regime was introduced, and import licensing was eliminated on most items of capital goods, raw materials, intermediates and components. These items became freely importable against foreign exchange purchased in the market. The system has worked fairly well and the market exchange rate has been remarkably stable. The existence of a dual rate, however, hurts exporters and other foreign exchange earners who have to surrender 40 per cent of their earnings at the official rate, getting the benefit of the higher market rate on only 60 per cent. Many exporters have said that this amounts to a tax on exporters of goods and services whose continuation cannot be justified at a time when exports must receive our fullest support.

There is merit in this point of view, and the experience of the past year gives ground for confidence that we can unify the exchange rate and still manage the balance of payments with a reasonable degree of stability in the exchange rate. The Government has therefore decided to eliminate the dual rate arrangement. All exporters, as well as our workers abroad, will henceforth be allowed to convert 100% of their earnings at the market rate. All imports will also henceforth have to be paid for the market rate. The details of the new system are being notified separately by Reserve Bank of India. I expect that this will give a major boost to exports, and will further encourage foreign exchange flows into official channels.

Several other steps are also being taken to stimulate exports. The Commerce Ministry is reviewing the list of items whose exports are reviewing the list of items whose exports are subject to one or other restriction with a view to removing as many restrictions as possible. Reserve Bank of India is taking steps to ensure that adequate credit will be available for exports. Banks have already been asked to ensure that export credit amounts to at least 10% of their total advances. The interest rate on rupee export credit is being reduced by one percentage point. As a further measure of support for exports, the interest tax will be waived in the case of export credit from banks. I will have more to say on incentives for exporters when I come to the tax proposals in the Budget.

Foreign Investment

A new policy towards foreign investment has been an integral part of our strategy of modernising the economy, and establishing global linkages which will be of world critical importance in the emerging world economy. I have already mentioned that the initiatives taken in this area thus far have yielded encouraging results. I have no doubt that as our reforms proceed and gain momentum, we can expect to attract a substantial share of the private investment that is presently flowing to many developing countries in Asia. The Government has signed the Multilateral Investment Guarantee Agency (MIGA) convention and we expect to join MIGA formally as soon as membership procedures are completed. Several countries, including the UK, Germany and the United States, have expressed an interest in signing bilateral investment treaties. The Government has indicated a willingness to enter into bilateral negotiation on this issue.

Industrial modernisation, and especially the creation of internationally competitive industries, requires a massive expansion of and qualitative improvement in infrastructure. This is especially true of power generation, telecommunications and roads. Traditionally, these areas have been the preserve of the public sector. Substantial expansion of public investment in these areas is certainly necessary. However, the needs of the country as far beyond the capacity of the public sector to deliver in a reasonable time frame. The Government has, therefore, adopted a policy of encouraging private sector involvement and participation in these areas to supplement the efforts being made by the public sector. In order to attract such investment it will be necessary to make change in policies, procedures and the regulatory framework in these sectors. The Government proposes to make such changes as the need arises.

Revised Estimates

We have tried to maintain strict control over expenditure, but certain increases over the Budget estimates were unavoidable. An additional provision of Rs. 1,500 crore has to be made for food, fertiliser and export subsidies. The additional requirement of food subsidy is because of the delay in increasing issue prices to absorb the impact of higher procurement prices. The higher provision for export subsidy is because of settlement of claims in the pipeline for cash compensatory support and continuance of benefits for deemed exports. In respect of fertilisers the increase is due to the reduction in prices of urea and higher input costs. In addition, I have provided Rs. 340 crore as one-time assistance to farmers for purchase of fertilisers whose prices were decontrolled. Ministry of Home Affairs has to be provided additional funds for meeting security-related expenditure in the wake of disturbed conditions in certain parts of the country.

While an assessment of the actual requirements is being made, I have for the present included in the Revised Estimates an additional provision of Rs. 285 crore. If a further provision becomes inescapable, we shall come to the House for the necessary Supplementary Grants. These and other increases have been offset by a reduction of Rs. 1,300 crore in the requirements for loans to States against small savings collections. The decline in small savings collections has been a matter of concern and Government has taken measures to improve the rate of return to the investors. As a consequence, the collections have shown an uptrend in recent months. As a result of all these developments, total non-plan expenditure is higher by Rs. 3,278 crore as compared with the Budget

Estimates.

On the plan side, there is an increase in budgetary support for the Central Plan for certain sectors. An additional provision of Rs. 630 crore is being made for the National Renewal Fund, which is a key element in our strategy for economic reforms. Similarly, an additional provision of Rs. 250 crore has been made for strengthening schemes in the social sectors such as Health and family Welfare. The provision for Rural Development is being augmented by Rs. 500 crore.

Central assistance to State and Union Territory Plans is being augmented by Rs. 1,228 crore mainly for externally aided projects where the pace of implementation justifies an allocation larger than in the Budget Estimates.

Taking Plan and non-Plan expenditures together, the total provision in the Revised Estimates is Rs. 1,24,726 crore against Rs. 1,19,087 crore in the Budget Estimates.

Against these additional expenditures, revenue receipts have also been higher because of better collections and higher royalty on offshore crude oil. Capital receipts under market loans and small savings receipts are lower than in the Budget Estimates; but this is offset by the higher receipts from 364-days treasury bills, which is a new instrument designed to develop a market for Government securities.

The total receipts in the Revised Estimates are Rs. 1,17,524 crore compared to Rs. 1,13,698 crore in the Budget Estimates. The Budget deficit is estimated at Rs. 7,202 crore and the fiscal deficit for the year is now placed at Rs. 36,722 crore. These figures are somewhat higher than envisaged in the Budget Estimates but within tolerable limits for macro-economic stability.

Budget Estimates

The resource constraints facing us last year imposed a tight leash on the development programmes we could finance in 1992-93. The total size of the Central Plan in 1992-93 (BE) was only 12.6 per cent higher than in the previous year. With the improvement in the fiscal situation achieved in the course of 1992-93, and the moderation in inflation, we are now in a position to give a boost to the Plan, while ensuring continued improvement in the fiscal deficit. Accordingly, the Central Plan outlay for 1993-94 has been fixe at Rs. 63,936 crore which is almost 32 per cent higher than the figure of Rs. 48,047 crore in 1992-93.

The Certain Plan will be financed to the extent of Rs. 23,241 crore from budget support which is almost 26 per cent higher than the budget support of Rs. 18,501 crore in 1992-93. The balance of the Central Plan outlay of Rs. 40,695 crore will be met from internal and extra-budgetary resources compared with Rs. 29,906 crore in 1992-93 representing a step-up of 30 per cent. I am providing Rs. 18,010 crore for Central assistance for States and UT Plans in 1993-94 compared to Rs. 16,111 crore in 192-93. The total budgetary support from the Central Government Budget to the Central and State Plans increases by almost 19 per cent from Rs. 34,612 crore in 1992-93 to Rs. 41,251 crore in 1993-94.

The development of human resources is given high priority in the Eighth Plan. Hon'ble Members are also aware that education is an area which is very close to my heart. I am, therefore, particularly happy to announce that the outlay for education is being increased from Rs. 952 crore to Rs. 1,310 crore, which is a step up of 37.6 per cent. Universal provision of primary education and adult literacy of satisfactory quality, particularly for girls and women, is a pre-requisite for the modernisation of the economy and the society. I am happy to inform Honourable Members that our total literacy campaigns are breaking new grounds, and are now being implemented in 182 districts covering approximately 430 lakh adult learners.

A new scheme is being launched for the improvement of primary education in educationally backward districts and in districts where the total literacy campaigns have been successful, leading to an enhanced demand for primary education. In these districts, districts specific and population specific plans for achieving universalisation of elementary education are being prepared. Twenty to twenty-five districts out of about 200 educationally backward districts where female literacy is below national average, will be taken up for preparation of districts plans in 1993-94. In the sphere of higher and technical education, modernisation and upgradation would receive high priority. Keeping in view the aspirations of the North-Eastern region, the government has decided to set-up a university in Nagaland and an Indian Institute of Technology in Assam.

For Health, the provision is Rs 438 crore, which is 60 per cent higher than the level of Rs 302 crore in the current year's Budget. A major part of the provision will be for national programmes for control of communicable and other diseases. The Family Welfare Programme is of overriding national importance; the provision under this head is being stepped up from Rs. 1,000 crore for the current year to Rs. 1,270 crore for the next year. A programme to improve the quality of family planning services in Uttar Pradesh is being launched at a cost of US $325 million, with assistance from USAID. In addition, with the aim of reducing maternal mortality, under the Social Safety Net Scheme, assistance will be provided for improvement of infrastructure at Primary Health Centres in 90 demographically backward districts.

The National Commission for Women set up last year is looking into various important issues relating to women. For the integrated child development services the provision is Rs. 474 crore compared to Rs. 360 crore in the current year. This will enable us to strengthen the infrastructure set up of the scheme. The provision for the Ministry of Welfare has been increased from Rs. 530 crore to Rs. 630 crore. This includes Rs. 73 crore for the liberation and rehabilitation of Safai Karmcharis. A provision of Rs. 247 crore has been made for special Central assistance for Scheduled Castes component plan. The operations of the National Scheduled Castes Finance and Development Corporation and the National Backward Classes Finance and Development Corporation will be further expanded.

Non-Plan Expenditure

Turning to non-Plan expenditure, I would like to draw the attention of the House of the tremendous burden of interest payments. The provision for 1993-94 is Rs. 38,000 crore compared with Rs. 32,500 crore in the current year. The high interest burden is due to the rising volume of government debt, which itself reflects the large fiscal deficits, incurred year after year. However, with the reduction in the fiscal deficit and hence in the Government's borrowings, the growth of this item is expected to decelerate sharply by 1995-96.

For Defence expenditure the provision has been increased from Rs. 17,500 crore in the current year to Rs. 19,180 crore next year. The requirements on account of fertilisers and export subsidies will be significantly lower reflecting the impact of the measures already taken to rationalise these subsidies. The expenditure on the Farm Loan Waiver scheme will be Rs. 500 crore; with this, the Government's commitment for payment under the scheme will be fulfilled. I am providing Rs. 3,000 crore for food subsidy as against Rs. 2,800 crore in the burden of food subsidy at a reasonable level and to ensure at the same time that the vulnerable sections of society are fully protected. Excluding the expenditure on interest, the provision for other non-plan expenditure in 1993-94 is about Rs. 3,180 crore lower than the Revised Estimates for the current year. As in previous years, no separate provision is being made for additional dearness allowance which may become payable next year. The additional expenditure on this account will have to be absorbed by all Ministries within the approved budget provision.

Coming to receipts, gross tax revenues at the existing level of taxation are estimated at Rs. 89,389 crore compared to Rs. 78,782 crore in the current year. States' share of taxes next year is estimated at Rs. 22,590 crore as against Rs. 20,525 crore in the current year's Revised Estimates. I am taking a credit of Rs. 3,700 crore for market borrowings as against the current year's level of Rs. 3,670 crore. External assistance, net of repayments, is estimated at Rs. 6,819 crore as against Rs. 5,374 crore in the current year. Net small savings collections next year are estimated to reach the current year's level of Rs. 5,500 crore despite heavy maturities falling due next yea. As in the current year's Revised Estimates, I am taking credit of Rs. 3,500 crore for receipts from disinvestment of equity in public enterprises. Total receipts at the existing levels of taxation are estimated at Rs. 130,990 crore and total expenditure at Rs. 131,323 crore leaving a gap of Rs. 333 crore.

20.3 **Union Budget at a Glance**

TABLE 20.1: Union Budget 1993-94

(Rs. Crores)

	1991-92 Actuals	1992-93 Budget Estimates	1992-93 Revised Estimates	1993-94 Budget Estimates
1	2	3	4	5
Revenue receipts	66047	75688	78279	84209
Tax revenue (net to Centre)	50070	56456	58179	62739
Non-tax revenue	15977	19232	20100	21470
Capital receipts	38528	38010	39245	42800
Recoveries of Loans	6020	6491	6225	6655
Other receipts	3038	2500	3500	3500
Borrowings & Liabilities	29470	29019	29520	32645
Total receipts (1+4)	104575	113698	117524	127009
Non-plan expenditure	80469 *	84475	87753	90072
On revenue account	67234 *	71233	74461	77654
On capital account	13235	13242	13292	12418
Plan expenditure	30961	34612	36973	41251
On revenue account	15074	18337	20518	24185
On capital account	15887	16275	16455	17066

Contd.

TABLE 20.1 *Contd.*

1	2	3	4	5
Total expenditure (9+13)	111430	119087	124726	131323
Revenue expenditure (10+14)	82308	89570	94979	101839
Capital expenditure (11+15)	29122	29517	29747	29484
Revenue deficit (1-17)	16261	13882	16700	17630
Budgetary deficit (8-16)	6855	5389	7202	4314
Fiscal deficit {(1+5+6)-16=7+20)}	36325	34408	36722	36959
Primary Deficit (21-11)	9762	2408	4222	-1041
Increase in net RBI credit to Central Government #	5508	5389	5400	4314 **

*Includes grants under article 275(1) of the Constitution for meeting Plan Expenditure, # Including other variations in RBI credit to Central Govt., ** Not independently estimated.

20.4 Highlights of the Budget

The Union Budget for 1993-94 presented to Parliament on May 27, 1993 by Finance Minister Manmohan Singh, had the following highlights:

Direct Taxes

Standard deduction raised from Rs. 12,000 to Rs. 15,000 and from Rs. 15,000 to Rs. 18,000 for working women with income upto to Rs. 75,000.

Wealth tax exemption in respect of one house or part of a house belonging to an individual or a Hindu undivided family.

Basic exemption limit for gift tax raised from Rs. 20,000 to Rs. 30,000.

Exemption for gifts to dependent relatives at marriage time raised from Rs. 10,000 to Rs. 30,000.

Tax rebate raised from 10 to 20 for persons aged 65 and above.

Qualifying limits of gross total incomes for them raised from Rs.50,000 to Rs. 75,000.

Deductions on medical treatment etc. of handicapped dependents raised from Rs. 12,000 to Rs. 15,000.

Reliefs up to Rs. 20,000 for parents of handicapped minors.

Complete tax holiday for new undertakings in power sector for five years.

Indirect Taxes

Excise duty reduced on following items:

Total exemption for coffee, tea and instant tea.

On vanaspati reduced from Rs. 1,900 to Rs. 1,500 per tonne.

On electric fans from 17.25 to 10 per cent.

On coolers from 23 to 10 per cent.

On specified domestic electrical appliances from 23 to 15 per cent.

On radio sets from 23 to 10 per cent.

On plastic moulded luggage from 34.5 to 25 per cent.

On mattresses and bedding articles of cellular rubber from 69 to 30 per cent.

On cars from 55 to 40 per cent.

On colour TV sets ranging from Rs. 1,250 to Rs. 2,200 per set.

On refrigerators ranging from Rs. 400 to Rs. 3,500 per piece.

On air-conditioners ranging from Rs. 7,000 to Rs. 17,000 per unit.

Personal computers, typewriters, fax machines of value not exceeding Rs. 60,000 exempted for accredited journalists.

20.5 Where the Rupee Comes from and Where It Goes

TABLE 20.2: Where the Rupee Comes from

Source	Paise
Excise	22
Internal borrowings	18
Customs	18
Non-tax revenue	14
Non-debt capital receipts	7
Corporation tax	7
Income tax	6
External borrowings	3
Borrowings from RBI	3
Other taxes	2

TABLE 20.3: Where the Rupee Goes

Source	Paise
Interest Payments	25
Central Plan	15
States' share taxes and duties	14
Defence	13
State plan assistance	12
Non-plan expenditure	12
Subsidies	5
State non-plan assistance	4

20.6 Text of Part B of Budget Speech

50. I now turn to the tax proposals for 1993-94.

Chelliah Committee's Recommendations

51. In framing these proposals I have been acutely conscious of the conflicting requirements of comprehensive reform of the tax structure on the one hand, and the need to protect revenues to finance the large increase in the Plan, on the other. Last year significant reforms were made in personal income taxation based on the recommendations of the Chelliah Committee. Reform of corporate taxation was deferred until the detailed recommendations of the Chelliah Committee were received. These have since been received. The Committee has also recently submitted its final report on indirect taxes, recommending significant reduction in customs duties as well as rationalisation and simplification of excise duties.

52. I accept the broad thrust of the Chelliah Committee's recommendations on both direct and indirect taxes. We must move as rapidly as possible to a regime of moderate tax rates in direct taxation, which will encourage better compliance especially if supplemented by efforts at broadening of the tax base. We must also move to regime of low to moderate customs duties which is essential for efficient and competitive industrialisation. Our excise duties should also be simplified with fewer rates and our long term aim should be to move to a Value Added Tax System. However, a nationwide value added tax system cannot be introduced overnight. There has to be a broad agreement among the Centre and the States on the design of such a system. In order to prompt informed discussion and debate, I am requesting the National Institute of Public Finance and Policy to prepare the design of a possible value added tax system.

Notes 1. Para numbers relate to para numbers of Budget Speech.
2. Captions added.

53. Although all the major recommendations of the Chelliah Committee are important, they cannot be implemented immediately for the simple reason that tax reform, which typically involves lower tax rates collected on a broader base often involves a loss of revenue in the short run. Fiscal experts tell us that the loss of revenue will be made up in the medium term, but there is no guarantee that this will happen immediately, and Finance Ministers have to look after the short term if they want to survive in the medium term. I hope the House will agree with me that a phased transition is needed.

Priorities to Critical Areas

54. A key issue in phasing the transition is whether to do a little on all fronts or to make decisive changes in certain areas, with a clear declaration of progress to be made in other areas in future. I have thought over this matter carefully and I feel that decisive action in critical areas is more important than marginal improvements on all fronts. The most critical area for action at present is customs duties. Despite the adjustments in customs duties in the last two budgets, our duties are still much higher than in most of our competitor countries, especially on capital goods. With these duties, and the resulting high capital costs, our producers will never be able to compete in world markets. Nor can we expect new investment, both domestic and foreign, to flow into areas with export markets in view, if high customs duties make them uncompetitive. Yet it is such investments that we need most at present if we want to reduce our dependence on external assistance. We cannot and must not continue with the approach of setting up industries aimed solely at the domestic market in the belief that replacing imports ipso facto contributes to self reliance, without considering at what cost we are effecting the replacement. In fact, replacement at unduly high cost contributes to inefficient industrialisation, an inability to export and a permanent dependence on external assistance. We must take a bold initiative in this area while taking due care to protect the legitimate concerns of our industry. Normally, the revenue loss from customs duty reduction could have been made up through higher excise duties. However, there are compelling reasons for rationalising and reducing excise duties over a wide range of industries because many of our duties are too high and parts of industry are also suffering from recessionary conditions.

Direct Taxation Proposals

55. In these circumstances. Hon'ble Members will appreciate that I have limited room for manoeuvre in the area of direct taxes. Major reform of the corporate tax structure, along the lines recommended by the Chelliah Committee is undoubtedly desirable. However, for the reasons indicated, it will have to be postponed to the next year.

56. I would like, however, to give a stimulus to new investment in those States in which all the districts are industrially backward. Accordingly, I propose to give a five-year tax holiday, commencing from the year of production, for new industrial undertakings located in all the North-Eastern States, Jammu & Kashmir, Himachal Pradesh, Sikkim, Goa and Union Territories of the Andaman and Nicobar Islands, Dadra and Nagar Haveli, Daman and Diu, Lakshadweep and Pondicherry.

57. Electricity is critical input for the future growth of our economy. I, therefore, propose to introduce a five-year tax holiday in respect of profits and gains of new industrial undertakings set up anywhere in India for either generation or generation and distribution of power. The five-year tax holiday will begin from the year of generation of power.

58. The five-year tax holiday, in both these cases, will be part of section 80-IA of the Income-tax Act. At the end of the five-year period, these units will be entitled to the existing deduction under section 80-IA for the remaining period.

59. The promote a cleaner and healthier environment, I propose to allow depreciation admissible on plant and machinery relating to environment protection and pollution control at 100 per cent, instead of the existing 40 per cent, of capital cost under the Income-tax Rules.

60. Hitherto, our institutions of higher learning have been almost entirely dependent on Government funds. As government funds are limited, we must find ways of funding these institutions from industry. This will also bring them closer to industry and more responsive to its needs. I, therefore, propose to raise the income tax deduction given to contributions to approved universities, institutes of technology, institutes of management and equivalent institutions from 50 per cent at present to 100 per cent.

61. A strong science and technology base is an essential prerequisite for a modern, progressive economy. Indian scientists and technologists have proved, time and again, that they are second to none in the world, given the right work atmosphere, proper motivation and adequate facilities. Indian industry needs to spend a lot more on research and development. In doing so, I would encourage industry to make use of the facilities offered by our national laboratories and research institutes. To that end, I propose to introduce a weighted deduction of 125 per cent, of the contribution out of income from business or profession for research programmes in approved national laboratories and institutions carrying out research and development in natural and applied sciences. This weighted deduction will be available only for research programmes determined by the users and the producers of research, and approved by the prescribed authority.

62. I propose to extend the five-year tax holiday under section 10A of the Income-tax Act, at present available to units set up in the Free Trade Zones, to units set up in Software Technology Parks and Electronic Hardware Technology Parks. In July, 1991, I had introduced a 100 per cent, deduction for three years in respect of income derived from export of software. Software exports have done well and I propose to extend the concession for one more year i.e. for assessment year 1994-95.

63. Under the scheme for permitting Foreign Institutional Investors in our capital market, we had indicated that such investors would be liable to tax at 20 per cent, on investment income and 10 per cent, on long term capital gains. I also propose to extend a concessional rate of tax of 30 per cent, in respect of short term capital gains for such investors.

64. As I have already mentioned, a substantial reform of personal taxation was carried out last year based on the recommendations of the Chelliah Committee. I propose to leave the rate structure and exemption limit unchanged and make only a few modifications.

65. Last year, because of severe resource constraints, I was compelled to retain the surcharge on personal income above Rs. 1 lakh at 12 per cent. I had hoped to be able to remove the surcharge in the current year but I am constrained to

continue with it for one more year. However, I propose to raise the standard deduction from salary income from Rs. 12,000 to Rs. 15,000 and the standard deduction for working women with incomes upto Rs. 75,000 from Rs. 15,000 to Rs. 18,000.

66. In recognition of the hardship to old people in these days of inflation, I had given a tax rate of 10 per cent last year to senior citizens whose gross total income is below Rs. 50,000. I propose to raise the tax rebate to 20 per cent and further increase the income limit from Rs. 50,000 to Rs. 75,000.

67. Last year, I had announced that a scheme for giving Advance Rulings in respect of transactions involving non-residents would be worked out. The scheme has been drawn up and I am bringing forward legislative proposals for the creation of a statutory authority, headed by a retired judge of the Supreme Court. I do hope that the scheme will be welcomed by non-residents.

68. I propose to extend the simplified scheme of presumptive taxation introduced last year to small road transport operators operating, hiring or leasing on transport vehicle.

69. Payments made under Voluntary Retirement Schemes to public sector employees were fully exempt from income tax, last year I extended this exemption to private sector employees. I propose now to extend this facility to employees of statutory authorities and local authorities.

70. Recognising the trauma of bringing up a handicapped child, I had, last year increased the deduction permissible for guardians of handicapped dependents under the income-tax law from Rs. 6000 to Rs. 12000. I now propose to further raise this deduction to Rs. 15000. I also propose to allow a deduction in respect of income of handicapped minors clubbed with the income of their parent to the full extent of the child's income upto a maximum of Rs. 20,000.

71. In my first Budget Speech in July, 1991, I had proposed the setting up of the National Foundation for Communal Harmony to provide assistance to the children of families affected by communal riots. The Foundation has since been established under the aegis of the Home Ministry. I now propose to extend the benefit of 100 per cent deduction under section 80G of the Income-tax Act in respect of donations made to the Foundation. I also propose to exempt the income of the National Foundation for Communal Harmony fully from income tax.

72. At present, charitable trusts and institutions have to seek approval every three years from the Commissioner of Income-tax in order that donations to them are eligible for tax exemption. To reduce paper work and simplify the procedure, I propose to increase the maximum period of approval by the Commissioner to five assessment years.

73. I would like to see India gain prominence, not only in the global economy, but also in the world of sports. There are provisions in the Income-tax Act to allow exemption in respect of income of approved sports associations or institutions and to grant 50 per cent, deduction in respect of donations made in them. I propose to amend the Rules relating to eligible projects or schemes under section 35AC of the Act to include promotion of sports in such activities. This would provide 100 per cent deduction in respect of spending on approved sports projects and schemes.

74. Last year, I had proposed the setting up of a National Court of Direct Taxes for expeditious settlement of litigation in direct tax matters. The proposal has been examined in detail and I hope soon to bring forward legislation in this regard. In regard to a Direct Taxes Code, the Government will take a final view,

taking into account the recommendations of the Chelliah Committee on the subject.

75. The Wealth-tax Act was considerably recast last year and the basis of taxation was shifted from wealth to unproductive assets. There has been persistent demand that a residential dwelling is a universal necessity and should not be subjected to wealth-tax. Hence, I propose to exempt the value of one residential house or part thereof from the levy of wealth-tax.

76. Last year, I had exempted residential houses, motor cars, etc. held as stock-in-trade. However,to discourage speculation in the guise of stock-holding, I propose to restrict the exemption to three years beginning from the year in which the land is acquired.

77. The exemption limit for purposes of gift-tax was fixed at Rs. 20,000 some years ago. I agree with the recommendations of the Tax Reforms Committee that this limit needs to be revised and, therefore, propose to raise it to Rs. 30,000.

78. Gifts made by a person to any dependent relative in respect of marriage of the relative is exempt from gift-tax only up to rs. 10,000, whereas vast expenditures on ostentatious marriages go scot-free. In order to encourage savings and productive investment, I propose to raise the exemption limit at the time of the marriage of a dependent relative from Rs. 10,000 to Rs. 30,000.

79. As an incentive to the export drive which has to be kept up at all costs, I propose to exempt all banking companies from the levy of Interest-tax on export credit provided by them.

80. The various changes that I have proposed would result in a loss of Rs. 300 crore of which the States' share would be Rs. 194 crore. The amount involved is very small-less than 2 per cent of the gross direct tax collections. I am ignoring it in the expectation the better tax collection would cover this loss.

81. I now turn to the proposals relating to indirect taxes.

Custom Duties

82. Since 1973, we have been levy a separate auxiliary duty in addition to the basic customs duty. In order to simplify the tariff structure and the assessment process, I propose to do away with the basic duty.

83. Our first priority in restructuring customs duty should be in the area of capital goods and project imports since these duties affect the incentives for new investment. Last year the duty on projects and general machinery was brought down from 80% to 55%. This is still too high compared with rates in competitor countries and a further reduction is necessary. I, therefore propose to lower the import duty on projects and general machinery to 35%. Projects in certain priority sectors such as, power, coal mining and petroleum refining currently attract a duty rate of 30%. I propose to reduce the rate of 25% in the case of coal mining and petroleum refining. In view of the special importance of the power sector the duty on power projects is being reduced to 20% and this rate is also being extended to machinery required for modernisation and renovation of power plants.

84. The House can rest assured that in restructuring duties on capital goods, I have made every effort to protect the legitimate interests of domestic capital goods industry. We have had extensive discussions with various Ministries as well as representatives of concerned industries. In order to ensure that lower

duties on imported machinery do not hurt the domestic capital goods industry, it is necessary to lower the import duty on components, to enable our manufactures to compete effectively. I therefore, propose to reduce to 25% the duty on components of general machinery which presently is either 40% or 35%. In order, however, to ensure that domestic industries producing such components are not adversely affected. I propose to impose countervailing duty on such components at 10% with full facility of set-off under MODVAT.

85. At present there are a number of other capital goods, including various types of machine tools, which attract different rates of duty in the range of 60% to 110%. There are also instruments which attract duties varying from 40% to 110%. I propose to rationalise this structure into three duty rate slots viz., 40%, 60% and 80%. The rationalisation involves generally a duty reduction between 20 to 30 percentage points. Consequential reduction is being made in the rates of duty on specified parts and components.

86. Hand-operated tools are capital goods for artisans and skilled workers and currently attract duties varying from 40% to 110%. I propose to prescribe a uniform rate of 40% for all these tools.

87. The logic of reducing duties on capital goods requires lowering of duties on metals and metal goods as well, as these are the basic raw materials of the domestic capital goods industry. Accordingly, to help domestic producers, I propose to lower the customs duty rates on ferrous metals by 10 to 20 per centage points in most cases. In line with the these changes the import duty on steel scrap is being refixed at 15%. The import duty on specified refractory raw material is being reduced to 30%. Turning to non-ferrous metals, I propose to reduce the duty rates by 10 to 55 percentage points in most cases. The resulting rates on unwrought and unalloyed forms will vary from 25% to 50% and on wrought forms from 70% to 80%.

88. The duty structure for chemicals is characterised by a multiplicity of rates and many irrationalities. Input duties are often out of line with duties on finished products. I, therefore, propose to restructure the duty rates on chemicals with a view to significantly lowering duty rates at the upper end and also ensuring that the duty rates on inputs are not generally higher than the duty on end products. The present duty rates on basic feed-stock such as, ethylene, propylene, butadiene, benzene, styrene and ethylene dichioride vary between 25% and 80%. These rates are being replaced by a uniform low duty rate of 15%. The duties on xylenes, paraxylene, toulene, acrylonitrile and cumene are being reduced to 40%. The duties on DMT, PTA and MEG which represent a higher stage of production, are being reduced and unified at 70%. In the case of caprolactum, however, the duty is being increased from 50% to 60%, in order to adequately protect the interests of the domestic units.

89. The electronics industry has the potential of becoming a world class industry contributing to our export effort and to employment generation. I propose to take up this challenge. The rates of duty on project imports and on specified capital goods for electronics attract duty at either 30% or 50% at present. I propose to reduce these rates to a uniform rate of 25%. The import duties on raw materials, pieces-parts and components at present are levied at 40%, 60% and 80%. These rates are being reduced to 20%, 35% and 50%, respectively. The import duty on specified raw materials for the manufacture of optical fibre cables is being drastically reduced from 90% to 20% in recognition of the urgency to expending and modernising th telecom sector.

Import Duties

90. In order to strengthen our export capability in existing export-thrust areas such as textiles, leather, marine products, gems and jewellery, etc. where we have a comparative advantage, I propose to reduce the import duty on specified capital goods for these sectors from 40% to 25%. In addition, certain recommendations have been made by the Groups on Extreme Focus items for export for augmenting the export potential of certain sectors such as food processing, horticulture and floricultural industries. Accordingly, the import duty on specified items for these sectors is being reduced to 25%.

91. The ship-breaking industry is employment intensive and an important source of raw materials for the secondary sector of our steel industry. In order to encourage the growth of this industry, I propose to prescribe a lower merged duty of customs at 5% ad valorem. The ferrous materials obtained from breaking up of such ships etc. which are presently subject to excise duty are being fully exempted.

92. Our film industry is one of the largest in the world in terms of footage of films produced. Although it has achieved this status without much need for incentives, it is now facing greater competition from the electronic media, and deserves some special encouragement. I therefore, propose to reduce the duties on jumbo rolls of cine positive films from 55% to 25% and on finished cine film rolls from about 65% to 40%. I also propose to reduce the duty on negative cine films from about 35% to 25%.

93. In order to encourage the development of non-conventional energy sources, especially solar energy, the import duty on specified raw materials and items of this industry is being reduced by 15 to 20 percentage points. In respect of wind-operated electricity generators I propose to reduce the import duty from 40% to 25%.

94. As a gesture of goodwill towards Bangladesh, I propose to fully exempt the famous Jamdanee saris from payment of import duties. Small-scale units, eligible for excise duty exemption for clearances to domestic area are at present required to pay excise duty on goods exported by them to Nepal and Bhutan. I propose to exempt these from this levy. I hope these steps will make a contribution towards improving trade with SAARC countries.

95. At present, accredited press cameramen have the facility of importing photographic equipment free of duty upto a limit of Rs. 60,000 but no such facility is available to other journals to import specialised equipment such as, laptop computers, personal computers, fax machines and typewriters. I have often wondered whether this explains why my photographs in the Press are better than the editorial comments! As a measure of my commitment to encourage modern technology in Indian journalism, and in recognition of the sterling role played by our Pressmen in creating a wider appreciation of issues of economic reform in the country, I propose to allow accredited journals also a one time facility to import such equipment duty free upto a value of Rs. 60,000.

96. The duty rate on certain specified items of baggage was recently reduced from 255% to 150%. As a measure of simplification, I propose to reduce the general baggage rate itself from 255% to 150%.

97. In line with these reductions in import duties for individual sectors, and keeping in mind the present exchange rate, there is scope for reduction in the maximum rate of duty on all goods. Accordingly I propose to reduce the maxi-

mum rate from 110% to 85% except for a few items including passenger baggage and alcoholic beverages.

98. I am aware that Honourable Members will be concerned that lowering of import duties and import liberalisation may put too much pressure on our industry and make it vulnerable to unfair competition and dumping. I would like to assure Honourable Members that these issues have been carefully considered and the proposed changes will not put undue pressure on industry. The change in the exchange rate over the past two years has created considerable room for duty reduction without hurting domestic industry. Besides, I am also reducing duties on raw materials and inputs which will help to reduce cost for our producers, enabling them to compete more effectively. Even with these changes, duties on finished products will be well above the long term structure recommended by the Chelliah Committee. We can move to that goal in phases over the next few years. As for unfair competition through dumping, our anti-dumping laws are already operational and action under these laws will be taken expeditiously whenever it is needed. I may mention that provisional action has recently been taken in one case.

99. In last year's Budget export duties had been imposed on iron ore and unpolished granite. Certain difficulties faced by these sectors have since been brought to my notice. I, therefore, propose to withdraw the export duty on iron ore and unpolished granite.

Excise Duties

100. I turn now to my proposals relating to excise duties. These are guided by the need to simplify the rate structure, to give some relief on articles of mass consumption, help the domestic capital goods industry so as to increase its competitiveness and also reduce capital costs, assist industries suffering from depressed demand conditions, and to provide relief to small-scale industry.

101. A surcharge by way of special excise duty has been levied since 1988, and the rate is currently 15% of the basic excise duty. As a measure of simplification, I propose to merge the special excise duty with the basic excise duty rates while also rationalising the resulting duty rates.

102. I propose to give some relief from taxation on a large number of articles of mass consumption as a measure of protection to the common people, who have been hard hit by inflation. Coffee, tea and instant tea are being fully exempted from excise duty. I also propose to reduce excise duty on vanaspati from Rs. 1900 to Rs. 1500 per metric ton. I propose to fully exempt footwear made by units under KVIC as well as those run with cash assistance received under the integrated Rural Development Programme, irrespective of the value limit. In respect of footwear manufactured by other units, I propose to enhance the present value limit for the purpose of exemption from Rs. 75 to Rs. 125 per pair. I also propose to reduce the excise duty

— on evaporative coolers from 23% to 10%;
— on electric fans from 17.25% to 10%;
— on specified domestic electrical appliances from 23% to 15%;
— on dry cell batteries from 34.5% to 25%;
— on printing and writing ink from 17.25% to 10%;
— on radio sets from 23% to 10%;

— on tooth powder from 17.25% to 10%;
— on noodles and roasted cereals from 17.25% to 10%;
— on biscuits from 11.5% to 7.5%;
— on plastic moulded luggage from 34.5% to 25%;
— on mattresses and bedding articles of cellular rubber from 69% to 30%.

103. At present the excise duty on capital goods and instruments varies from 11.5% to 23%. In order to lower capital costs and stimulate investment, I propose to reduce the excise duty on a large number of capital goods and instruments to a uniform rate of 10%. For the power sector, I am proposing an even lower rate of 5%.

104. Revival of industrial growth is a key element in the strategy for 1993-94. Sectors such as the automotive sector, television and the refrigeration and air-conditioning industries are currently suffering from recession. Workers employed in these industries face an uncertain future. Revenue prospects will also suffer if the present trend is not reversed. I, therefore, propose to provide a significant relief to these industries by way of reduced incidence of excise duties. I expect them to respond positively to this stimulus.

105. In order to encourage the public transport sector, I propose to reduce excise duty from 23% to 15% on non-petrol driven commercial vehicles for carrying goods and passengers. Correspondingly, the excise duty on the chassis of such vehicles will also stand reduce to 15%. I also propose to fully exempt excise duty on body-building on chassis of buses and similar passenger vehicles. The excise duty on three-wheelers is being reduced from 23% to 15%. I also propose to reduce the excise duty on motor cars from 55% to 40%.

106. I propose to reduce the specific excise duty on colour television sets from rates at present varying from Rs. 1925 to Rs. 4785 per set to rates varying from Rs. 1250 to Rs. 2200 per set.

107. The rats of excise duty on refrigerators presently vary from Rs. 575 to Rs. 5750 per refrigerator depending on their capacity. I propose to reduce the rates to Rs. 400 to Rs. 3500 per refrigerator. Other refrigerating appliances, including those used for cold storage in the agriculture sector currently attract an ad valorem duty of 69%. This is far too high as it affects the growth of food processing and preservation industries. I, therefore, propose to reduce the duty to 20%. I propose to reduce excise duty on air-conditioners from rates varying from Rs. 13800 to Rs. 85100 per unit at present to rates varying from Rs. 7000 to Rs. 70000 per unit depending on its capacity. In respect of compressors for air-conditioner of capacity not exceeding 7.5 tonnes, I propose to reduce the excise duty from Rs. 6900 to Rs. 5500 per compressor.

108. I propose to reduce the excise duty on bulk plastic resins such as low and high density polyethylene, polyvinyl chloride, polystyrene, etc. from 46% to 35%. This measure will benefit small-scale units manufacturing plastic products.

109. Metals are the basic raw materials of industry and the Tax Reforms Committee has suggested reduction of excise duty in this category. I, therefore, propose to rationalise the existing duty structure on metals. On ferrous metals, the ad valorem rates generally vary between 11.5% to 23%. I propose to rationalise the structure into two slabs, 12.5% and 15%. Aluminium has duty rates ranging from 23% to 40.25%. I propose to replace these rates by a uniform rate of 25%. Other non ferrous metals like copper, zinc, lead etc. attract duty rates varying from 11.5% to 34.5%. I am proposing a uniform duty of

15% for these. Certain ferrous materials are still subjected to specific rats of duty. I have proposed some upward adjustment in these rates taking into account the price increase since last year.

110. As a measure of environment protection, and in order to save wood, I propose to reduce the excise duty on plywood from 34.5% to 20%. I also propose to include pulp made from rice and wheat straws in the scheme of full excise duty exemption for production of writing and printing paper and uncoated kraft paper containing not less than 75% of pulp made from bagasse, jute, etc. This will widen the scope for using non-conventional raw materials in the manufacture of paper.

111. Currently, excise duty is being levied on mechanised, semimechanised, non-mechanised and cottage sectors of the match industry at Rs. 3.15, Rs. 2.10, Rs. 175 and Rs. 0.75 per hundred boxes respectively. The Government of Tamil Nadu has brought to my notice certain difficulties faced by this industry and also certain anomalies in the structure. Accepting this suggestion, I propose to reduce the rates to Rs. 2.40, Rs. 1.25, Re. 1.00 and Re. 0.50 respectively and also to restrict the existing concessions in the cottage sector only to units which are registered co-operative societies or recognised by KVIC or the State KVIB.

112. The excise duty on cosmetics and everyday toilet preparations such as, talcum powder, shampoos, face creams, shaving creams, etc. is very high at 120.75%. These items are now being increasingly used by a wide section of the people for personal care. I have received several representations from the trade, consumers and women's organisations for reduction of excise duty, I have also received complaints regarding the growth of spurious products and other abuses related to the evasion of this very high duty. I, therefore, propose to reduce the excise duty on cosmetics and toilet preparations from 120.75% to 70%.

113. I propose a marginal upward revision in the specific rates of excise duties levied on tyres, tubes and flaps.

114. I also propose to revise upwards the specific rates of excise duty on molasses from Rs. 172.50 to Rs. 200 per tonne.

Small Scale Sector

115. The small-scale sector has been a source of strength of Indian industry and a nursery for new entrepreneurship. The central excise duty exemption scheme for this sector has contributed significantly to its development along with other measures taken by the Central and State Governments. I propose to simplify the scheme and restructure it to give additional incentives to the smaller units and at the same time respond to certain recommendations of the Estimates Committee and the Public Accounts Committee.

116. I propose to enhance the limit for exemption from registration from Rs. 7.5 lakh at present to Rs. 10 lakh at present to Rs. 10 lakh. This will free a large number of the smaller units from the necessity of registration, and at the same time enable the tax authorities to devote greater attention to the comparatively larger units. At present, excise duty is completely exempted from the first 20 lakh of turnover for units producing goods under one chapter of the excise tariff, and the limit is Rs. 30 lakh if the goods produced are under more than one chapter of the tariff. I propose to enhance the duty exemption limit to Rs. 30

lakh for all units. This should benefit a large number of units in the lower segment of the small-scale sector.

117. As part of the restructuring, I feel that the larger units in this sector can contribute a little more to the exchequer. At present, the excise duty payable above the zero duty limit and upto Rs. 75 lakh is normal duty minus 10 percentage points, subject to a minimum of 5% ad valorem.

118. At present, buyers of goods from small-scale manufacturers, get a notional credit under MODVAT which is 5 percentage points more than the central excise duty actually paid by the latter. The Public Accounts Committee has found certain irregularities in the operation of this facility. The Tax Reform Committee has also not favoured continuance of this special dispensation, which essentially helps the large scale user industry. I, therefore, propose to withdraw the higher notional credit which the buyers of goods produced by the small scale units are getting at present. They will receive MODVAT credit only on the basis of duty actually paid.

119. In respect of cosmetics and refrigerators and air-conditioning appliances, I propose to liberalise the excise duty concessions for the small-scale sector having regard to price escalation over the years. I propose to extend full exemption in respect of clearances from Rs. 5 lakh at present to Rs. 15 lakh. Thereafter, clearances upto Rs. 30 lakh in a financial year would attract 50% of the normal duty. Clearances above Rs. 30 lakh in a financial year will attract normal duty. The liberalised scheme of exemption will be available only to those units whose value of clearances does not exceed Rs. 50 lakh in a financial year.

120. All the proposed changes in the small-scale sector will take effect from 1st April, 1993.

121. *Custom and Excise Duties on Agriculture, Textile and Health Section*

I now turn to certain proposals relating to agriculture, textiles and health sectors, covering both customs and excise duties.

122. Agriculture is the key to our economic growth, and deserves special fiscal incentives aimed at modernisation and diversification of this sector. I propose to reduce the import duty on various items of machinery used for agriculture, horticulture, forestry, poultry-keeping, etc. from 55% to 25%. I propose to reduce the import duty on rice transplanters from 40% to 15%. I also propose to reduce the import duty on grand parent poultry stocks from 105% to 40%. The import duty on certain amino acids is proposed to be reduced from 65% to 15%.

123. In respect of out-board motors used for fishing, I propose to reduce the import duty from 40% to 15%.

124. I propose to reduce the import duty on specified pesticides from 110% to 75%. The import duty on certain pesticide intermediates is being reduced from rates ranging between 65% and 110% to 50%.

125. I propose to reduce the import duty on specified goods for horticulture and green houses to 25%.

126. At present, tractors of engine capacity above 1800cc and trailers attract a total excise duty of 17.25% and 23% respectively. I propose to reduce the excise duty on them to 10% and 15% respectively.

127. I have a package of excise duty concessions for the textile industry. Next to agriculture, it is the largest employer in the country. The present excise duty rates on polyester and nylon filament yarn are higher as compared to other

types of yarn. Substantial capacities have been set up in the synthetic sector of fibre and yarn. As part of a long term policy of bringing synthetic fabrics within the reach of the common man, I feel there is a need to reduce the excise duty rates in this sector. Hence, I propose to reduce the excise duty on polyester filament yarn from Rs. 80.60 to Rs. 69 per kg and on nylone filament yarn from Rs. 71.50 to Rs. 57.50 per kg. I also propose to reduce excise duty on polyester staple fibre from Rs. 13.65 to Rs. 12.65 per kg and on viscose staple fibre from Rs. 15.60 to Rs. 14.95 per kg. On polypropylene filament yarn, I propose to reduce the excise duty from Rs. 32.50 to Rs. 28.75 per kg. I further propose to reduce excise duty on acrylic staple fibre from Rs. 15.60 to Rs. 14.95 per kg.

128. Health-care deserves special treatment. I propose to reduce import duty on specified bulk drugs at 110% or 80% to 25%. I also propose to fix a uniform rate of 50% on specified drug intermediates which currently attract import duties varying from 60% to 110%. In respect of homoeopathic medicines, I propose to reduce import duty from 40% to 25%.

129. Indigenous manufacture of medical equipment deserves all encouragement. At present, full exemption from import duty is available to certain parts of specified life saving electronic medical equipments. To help in accelerating the indivenisation process. I propose to extend full exemption to such parts for the manufacture of specified non-electronic life-saving medical equipments also. In respect of components for the manufacture of certain other medical equipments, I propose to reduce import duty from 45% and 25% at present to 15%. Further, for the same reason, I propose to fully exempt specified sight-saving equipments from excise duty and to lower excise duty on some medical equipments to 10%.

130. I propose to reduce the import duty on aseptic form-fill-seal machines for packing intravenous fluids by the pharmaceutical industry from 40 to 15%.

131. I have also proposed certain amendments in the Finance Bill seeking to effect changes in the excise and customs tariffs which are generally in the nature f enabling provisions and have no revenue significance. Besides, there are proposals for amendments of some of the existing notifications. In order to save the time of House. I do not propose to recount them.

132. The proposals in regard to changes in the excise duties outlined above are likely to result in a revenue loss of Rs. 2249 crore as conventionally calculated. However, I expect that as a result of the many steps that the Government is taking, including the duty reductions, the production of excisable goods will go up, and the loss will therefore be partially offset by a gain of about Rs. 1000 crore on this account. Out of the net loss of revenue in excise duties the Centre's share will be Rs. 708 crore and that of States Rs. 541 crore.

133. The proposed restructuring of customs duties results in a net loss of Rs. 3273 crore. This revenue loss will be entirely borne by the Centre.

Net Impact of Proposals

134. The net impact of my proposals on customs and excise duties taken together amount to a revenue loss of Rs. 4522 crore on indirect taxes. The impact on the Centre's revenue is a loss of Rs. 3981 crore and that on State's is Rs. 541 crore. I believe this is a temporary loss and is necessary to impart a new dynamism to India's economy. In the medium term, this loss will be more than made up by increased efficiency, competitiveness and faster growth of the

economy.

135. Copies of notifications giving effect to the changes in customs and excise duties effective from the 28th February, 1993 will be laid on the Table of the House in due course.

136. Taking into account the revenue loss arising from my proposals relating to indirect taxes the budget deficit for 1993-94 is estimated at Rs. 4314 crore and the fiscal deficit at Rs. 36,959 crore.

Meeting Challenges

137. Mr Speaker, Sir, the world around us is changing very rapidly, becoming more integrated as a marketplace and also more competitive. Other developing countries are successfully transforming themselves to meet these challenges. We cannot afford to stay out of this process, appearing to be absorbed with abscurantist preoccupations and sectarian divisions. The solution lies precisely in harnessing the considerable energies of our people, especially the young, to the exciting task of economic rejuvenation. I have used this Budget as an opportunity to put economic and social development firmly back on the national agenda. This is the only way to show the world that India is a nation on the move and is determined to succeed.

138. It is India's destiny to be a major player on the global economic and political scene. For that we need a vibrant and rapidly expanding economy with deep and abiding concern for the poor and the under-privileged. Politics has to be a purposeful instrument for realising our cherished goals. There is no scope for confrontation or cold war tactics when it comes to dealing with the nation's social and economic objectives. We need wisdom, sobriety, firmness of purpose and above all national unity.

139. As, Swami Vivekananda used to say there is an element of divinity in each human being. We have to create an environment in which this divine potentiality can be mobilised for building a strong economy and a just society. This is the challenge that our political system must face squarely. I venture to think that this budget focusses the nation's attention on this imperative task.

140. Sir, I commend the Budget to this august House.

20.7 **Some Vital Facts on Fiscal Policy and Budget (1989-90 to 1993-1994)**

TABLE 20.4: Deficit Trend

(Rs. crore)

Year	Fiscal	Revenue	Budgetary
1989-90	35,632	11,914	10,592
1990-91	44,632	18,562	11,347
1991-92	36,325	16,261	6,855
1992-93	36,722	16,700	7202
1993-94	36,959	17,630	4,314

TABLE 20.5: Subsidies

(Rs. crore)

Year	Major subsidies	Food	Indigenous fertilizers	Export promotion & market development
1989-90	9,032	2,476	3,771	2,014
1990-91	9,581	2,450	3,730	2,742
1992-92	9,809	2,850	3,500	1,754
1992-93	9,480	2,800	4800	800
1993-94	7,000	3,000	3000	500

TABLE 20.6: Tax Revenue

(Rs. crore)

Year	Customs	Income Tax	Corporation Tax	Union Excise Duties
1989-90	18,036	5,010	4,729	22,406
1990-91	20,644	5,371	5,335	24,514
1991-92	22,257	6,724	7,853	28,110
1992-93	25,500	8,300	9,200	32,500
1993-94	31,000	9500	10,500	35,000

21

BALANCE OF PAYMENTS, FOREIGN TRADE AND EXTERNAL DEBT

21.1 Introduction

The unprecedented payment crisis which emerged in the first quarter of 1991-92 was overcome by the concerted policy reforms initiated by the Government in July 1991. As a result of these policy reforms and successful mobilisation of exceptional financing, there was marked improvement in the external payment situation. This was reflected in build-up of foreign exchange reserves by an additional amount of US$ 3.57 billion during 1992-92. The increase in reserves combined with stabilisation and structural reforms restored international confidence and also provided the basis for further liberalisation of trade, tariff, export credit and foreign investment policies during 1992-93. The 1992-93 Budget saw the introduction of LERMS (Liberalised Exchange Rate Market System) which constituted a dual exchange rte mechanism.

As a result of these measures, foreign currency assets which had plummeted to US$ 1.1 billion in June 1991 rose to US$ 6.9 billion in the middle of July 1992 and were US$ 5.0 billion on 12 February 1993. net inflows to the FCNR (Foreign Currency Non-Resident) accounts have again become positive and there has been an acceleration in direct foreign investment proposals and approvals in the current financial year.

Exports have increased at 3.4 per cent during the first nine months of 1992-93 compared to decline of 3.7 per cent in 1991. This disguises a faster rate of growth at 11.4 per cent to the general currency area because exports to the Rupee payment area declined by 64.4 per cent in dollar terms. Given the expected lag in pushing up export growth and the immediate import needs of the economy, the current account deficit may continue to be around 2 per cent of GDP (Gross Domestic Product) in the medium term. This could be met to some extent by an improvement in utilisation of committed external funding. However, there will continue to be a need for exceptional financing in the medium term.

The balance of payments continued to be under pressure in 1992-93; but there was a distinct improvement compared to the crisis situation prevailing in the middle of 1991. The foreign exchange position, which had deteriorated rapidly after the Gulf was in the second half of 1990 and reached a crisis in June 1991, eased considerably by the end of 1991-92. The server import restrictions introduced in 1990-91, which had produced a highly disruptive import squeeze, were relaxed in the second half of 1991-92 as the foreign exchange situation improved and international confidence was gradually restored. By the end of 1991-92, foreign exchange reserves had been built up to a a respectable level of $ 5.63 billion from a low of $ 1.29 billion at the end of July 1991.

The trade policy regime was substantially liberalised in March 1992 when the LERMS was introduced. Under LERMS, forty per cent of foreign exchange earnings of exports of goods and services are required to be surrendered at the official exchange rate; this supply of foreign exchange finances import of essential items such as petroleum, fertilisers or life-saving drugs. The remaining sixty per cent is to be sold in the market and finance all other imports. Along with this change in the exchange rate regime, the import licensing mechanism was virtually abolished, almost all capital goods, raw materials, intimidates an components being made freely importable, subject only to tariff protection. The peak tariff was also lowered in the Budget 1992-93 with the objective of gradually reducing protection to levels comparable with those in other developing countries.

An essential element in the strategy for managing the balance of payments was the mobilisation of external assistance from the IMF (International Monetary Fund), the World Bank, the ADB (Asian Development Bank) and bilateral donors to support the balance of payments until the new economic policy generated a substantially higher level of exports. The package was designed to eliminate bureaucratic delays and arbitrariness in import licensing and to give exporters a more realistic exchange rate.

The results obtained in the first year have been encouraging. Imports have increased significantly but this was necessary and desirable given the artificially depressed level of imports in 1991-92. The growth of exports to the General Currency Area (GCA) has been very encouraging through overall export performance has suffered form the collapse of trade with the former Soviet Union and other Rupee Payment Area (RPA) countries. Despite the increase in imports to more normal levels during 1992-93, it has been possible to manager the balance payments with a stable exchange rate and comfortable foreign exchange reserves throughout the year.

21.2 **Recent Development in the Balance of Payments**

The main components of the balance of payments from 1988-89 onwards are summarised in Table 21.1. It is evident that the balance of payment was under pressured since 1988-89, when the current account deficit was almost $ 8 billion and there was a significant draw down of reserves. The situation improved in 1989-90 but then deteriorated again in 1990-91.

The worsening in the current account deficit in 1990-91 was partly on account of the Gulf war and the higher price of POL (Petroleum, Oil and Lubricants) imports. However, as pointed out in last year's Economic Survey, this was only one factor in the crisis of 1990-91. The higher prices of POL imports was in part offset by lower level in other imports; the trade balance in 1990-91 was only marginally worse than in the previous year. However, the trade deficit was exacerbated by a deterioration in the invisibles account because of lower remittances and higher interest payments; the current account deficit was thus $ 7727 million in 1990-91 compared with $6837 million in the previous years.

TABLE 21.1: Balance of Payments: Key Indicators

		1988-89	1989-90	1990-91*	1991-92**	(Apr.-Sept.)** 1991	1992
1		2	3	4	5	6	7
				(US$ million)			
1	Exports.f.o.d	14257	16955	184491	18135	8275	8720
2	Imports c.i.f.	23618	24411	26241	21213	10535	13003
	Oil	3009	3768	6028	5365	2308	3074
	-Non-oil(DGCI&S)	16488	17504	18045	14031	6827	8097
	-Non-DGCIL&S	4121	3139	2168	1817	1400	1832
3	Trade balance (1-2)	-9361	-7456	-7750	-3078	-2260	-4283
4	Non-monetary gold movement	0	4	0	191	0	0
5	Invisible (net)	1364	615	23	52	-378	287
6	Current account (3+4+5)	-7997	-6387	-7727	-2835	-2638	-3996
7	External assistance (net)	2217	1856	2268	2803	1353	227
8	Commercial borrowings (net)	1894	1777	729	1805@	45	-88
9	Non-resident deposits (net)	2511	2403	1259	-747	-818	44
10	Other capital	1442	938	979	1767	1000	3045
11	Capital account (7 to 10)	8064	6974	5235	5628	1580	3228
12	Overall balance (6+11)	67	137	-2492	2793	-1058	-768
13	IMF borrowings (net)	-1068	-877	1214	781	626	472

Contd.

TABLE 21.1 *Concld.*

	1	2	3	4	5	6	7
14	Official reserves (-increase, + decrease)	1001	740	1278	-3574	432	296
	Memo			(per cent of GDP)			
	Exports	5.2	6.3	6.2	7.3		
	Imports	8.7	9.0	8.9	8.6		
	Trade balance	-3.4	-2.8	-2.6	-1.2		
	Invisible balance	0.5	0.2	0.0	0.0		
	Current account	-2.9	-2.5	-2.6	-1.1		

* Provisional estimates

** Quick estimates

@ Includes India Development Bonds of US$ 1627 million.

Note Official grant receipts are taken as current account receipts on invisibles account. Interest payments forming part of withdrawals under FCNRA deposits have been put under invisible payments. Similarly, interest accused during the year and credited to NRI deposits has been treated as notional outflow under invisible payment and added as re-investment in NRI deposits in capital account. Therefore, invisibles (net), current account, and inflow under NRI deposits may not tally with those elsewhere in the Survey.

The worsening in the current account deficit in 1990-91 came at a time when the ability to finance the deficit had weakened massively. Political uncertainty at home, coupled with rising inflation and widening fiscal deficits, led to a loss of international confidence. External commercial borrowing dried up an there was on outflow from NRI (Non-Resident Indian) deposits. This forced substantial recourse to the IMF with net borrowings of $ 1.2 billion (gross borrowing of $ 1.8 billion) and a large reserve drawdown ($ 1.3 billion).

The situation continued to deteriorate in first quarter of 1991-92. By the time the new Government took over in June 1991, it had reached crisis proportions. Foreign exchange reserves had declined to $ 1.1 billion and a default in payments appeared imminent. The new Government took a series of measures to restore viability in external payments. The exchange rate was adjusted downwards. Steps were take to restore macro-economic stability by reducing the fiscal deficit from 8.4 per cent of GDP in 1990-91 to 6.2 per cent of GDP in 1991-92. These efforts at macro-economic stabilisation were accompanied by far-reaching reforms in the area of trade and industrial policy. Simultaneously, the Government negotiated access to external finance from multilateral agencies and bilateral donors to support the balance of payments over the next two to three years. The new economic policies can be expected to generate substantially faster export growth which is the only lasting solution to the balance-of-payments problem.

21.3 Merchandise Trade

Export in dollar terms increased by 3.4 per cent during April-December 1992 compared with a decline of 3.7 per cent during April-December 1991. Imports in April-December 1992 increased by 16.5 per cent compared with a decline of 22.5 per cent during April-December 1991 (Table 21.2). Hence the trade deficit rose from $1.6 billion in 1991 to $3.5 billion this year. Although the levels of month-wise imports during current year indicate substantial recovery from the depressed levels during 1991-92 the total imports in dollar terms during 1992-93 are unlikely to reach the 1990-91 level.

21.4 Imports

Table 21.3 shows imports by major categories and commodities for 1991-92 and for the first half of 1992-93. The share of bulk imports, consisting food products, raw per cent in 1991-92; while the share on non-buck imports increased increased from 47.1 per cent to 47.9 per cent over the same period. The decline in the levels of bulk imports in 1991-92 was contributed, besides POL, by pulses, edible oils, non-ferrous metals, iron and steel, ores and metal scrap and paper & paperboard. The declaration in growth on non-bulk imports in 1991-92 was largely on account of a fall in the import of capital goods, textile fabrics and yarn, chemicals, non-metallic minerals and professional instruments. Imports have picked up significantly during April-September 1992 with substantial increase in the imports of POL, cereals, edible oils, fertilisers, non-ferrous metals, coal, ores and metal scrap, chemicals, professional instruments and export-related imports as a consequence of partly a decline in domestic production of petroleum products and partly the liberalised import policy. the share of bulk imports in total imports has increased to 48.5 per cent during April-September 1992 compared with 45.1 per cent during April-September 1991, while that of non-bulk imports has declined to 46 per cent in April-September 1992 compared with 49 per cent during April-September 1991.

TABLE 21.2: Trends in Foreign Trade

Year	Imports	Exports	Trade Balance	Changes in Imports	Changes in Exports	Trade Balance as % of exports
		(Rs. hundred crore)		(Per cent)		
1986-87	201.0	124.5	-76.51	2.2	14.3	61.4
1987-88	222.4	156.7	-65.7	10.7	25.9	41.9
1988-89	282.4	202.3	-80.0	26.9	29.1	39.6
1989-90	354.2	276.8	-77.3	25.4	36.8	27.9
1990-91	431.9	325.5	-106.4	21.9	17.6	32.7
1991-92	478.5	440.4	-38.1	10.8	35.3	8.7
April-Dec 1992	474.8	373.3	-101.5	38.7	23.1	27.2
April-Dec 1991	342.4	303.3	-39.1	7.9	30.8	12.9
		(US$ billion)		(Per cent)		
1986-87	15.7	9.7	-6.0	-2.1	9.4	61.4
1987-88	17.2	12.1	-5.1	9.1	24.0	41.9
1988-89	19.5	14.0	-5.5	13.6	15.6	39.6
1989-90	21.3	16.6	-4.6	9.1	19.0	27.9
1990-91	24.1	18.1	-5.9	13.2	9.1	32.7
1991-92	19.4	17.8	-1.6	-19.4	-1.5	8.7
April-Dec 1992	16.6	13.1	-3.5	16.5	3.4	27.2
April-Dec 1991	14.2	12.6	-1.6	-22.5	-3.7	12.9

Note: Data for April-December 1992 are provisional.
Source: DGCI & S for trade data and RBI for exchange rate.

TABLE 21.3: Imports by Major Commodity Groups

Items	1990-91	1991-92	1991-92 Apr-Sep	1992-93 Apr-Sep (P)	1990-91	1991-92	1991-92 Apr-Sept	1992-93 Apr-Sep (P)	1990-91	Compositor($ terms) 1991-92	1991-92 Apr-Sep	1992-93 Apr-Sep	Growth rate($terms) 1991-92 1990-91	Apr-Sep92 Apr-Sep 91
1	2	3	4	5	6	7	8	9	10	11	12	13	14	15
	(Rs. hundred crore)				(US$ million)					(Per cent)			(Per cent)	
I Bulk imports	200.2	219.7	94.8	146.3	1158	8951	4111	5421	46.4	46.1	45.1	48.5	-19.8	31.9
(a) Food & Allied Products	9.9	6.8	2.7	4.9	552	275	117	173	2.3	1.4	1.3	1.5	-50.2	47.9
1 Cereals etc.	1.8	1.7	0.7	2.1	100	69	30	74	0.4	0.4	0.3	0.7	-31.3	142.4
2 Edible oils	3.3	2.5	0.6	1.1	184	101	26	39	0.8	0.5	0.3	0.3	-44.9	48.1
3 Pulses	4.8	2.6	1.4	1.7	268	105	61	60	1.1	0.5	0.7	0.5	-60.6	-1.9
(b)Fuel	116.1	141.7	58.0	90.1	6470	5787	2515	3451	26.9	29.8	27.6	30.9	-10.6	37.2
1 POL	108.2	131.3	53.8	82.1	6030	5365	2333	3171	25.1	27.6	25.6	28.4	-11.0	35.9
2 Coal	7.9	10.4	4.2	8.0	440	422	182	280	1.8	2.2	2.0	2.5	-4.2	53.9
(c) Ores & metals	47.4	39.8	18.3	29.5	2642	1615	793	1033	10.9	8.3	8.8	9.3	-38.9	30.3
1 Iron and steel	21.1	19.7	9.6	13.1	1176	799	416	459	4.9	4.1	4.6	4.1	-32.0	10.2
2 Non-ferrous metals	11.0	8.4	3.3	5.6	6.13	341	143	196	2.5	1.8	1.6	1.8	-44.4	37.1
3 Ores & metal scrap	15.3	11.7	5.4	10.8	853	475	234	378	3.5	2.4	2.6	3.4	-44.3	61.6
(d) Fertilisers	17.7	23.5	11.7	17.5	986	953	507	613	4.1	4.9	5.6	5.5	-3.4	20.8
(e) Paper, board & pulp	9.1	7.9	4.1	4.3	507	320	178	151	2.1	1.7	1.9	1.3	-36.8	-15.3

Contd.

TABLE 21.3 *Concld.*

1	2	3	4	5	6	7	8	9	10	11	12	13	14	15
II **Non-bulk imports**	203.5	229.4	103.1	146.6	11341	9306	4470	5136	47.1	47.9	49.0	46.0	-18.0	14.9
(a) Capital goods	107.7	104.4	48.6	62.2	5835	4235	2107	2179	24.2	21.8	23.1	19.5	-27.4	3.4
(b) Mainly export-related imports	66.0	88.3	38.2	61.5	3678	3582	1656	2154	15.3	18.5	18.2	19.3	-2.6	30.1
1 Pearls and precious stones	37.4	48.2	21.7	33.0	2084	1955	941	1156	8.7	10.1	10.3	10.3	-6.2	22.9
2 Chemicals	22.9	34.0	13.9	24.4	1276	1379	603	855	5.3	7.1	6.6	7.7	8.1	41.8
3 Textile yarn, fabrics etc.	4.4	3.4	1.8	2.3	245	138	78	81	1.0	0.7	0.9	0.7	-43.8	3.2
4 Cashewnuts	1.3	2.7	0.8	1.8	72	110	35	63	0.3	0.6	0.4	0.6	51.2	81.8
(c) Other non-bulk items	32.8	36.7	16.3	22.9	1828	1489	7.7	802	7.6	7.7	7.8	7.2	-18.6	13.5
1 Professional instruments etc.	10.6	10.0	4.5	7.4	591	406	195	259	2.5	2.1	2.1	2.3	-31.3	32.9
2 Chemicals	9.2	10.5	4.2	6.8	513	426	182	238	2.1	2.2	2.0	2.1	-16.9	30.8
3 Plastics & resins	10.9	14.0	6.6	7.3	607	568	286	256	2.5	2.9	3.1	2.3	-6.5	-10.6
4 Non-metallic minerals	2.0	2.2	1.0	1.4	111	89	43	49	0.5	0.5	0.5	0.4	-19.9	13.1
III. **Unclassified**	28.3	29.4	12.4	26.0	1573	1154	538	614	6.5	5.9	5.9	5.5	-26.6	14.2
IV. **Total**	431.9	478.5	210.3	318.9	24072	19411	9119	11171	100.0	100.0	100.0	100.0	-19.4	22.5

(P) Provisional.

Notes: 1. Item I(d) includes fertiliser crude, manufactured & fertiliser material.

2. Item II (b)2 includes organic and inorganic chemicals.

3. Item II(c)2 relates to materials and products including pharmaceuticals and dyeing and colouring material.

21.5 **Exports**

The slow-down in export growth during 1990-91 continued during 1991-92. In the previous four years 1986-87 to 1989-90, exports grew at 17 per cent per annum in dollar terms. By contrast in 1990-91, export growth was modest at 9.1 per cent in dollar terms and during 1991-92, dollar exports actually declined by 1.5 per cent. This deceleration was caused by a number of factors, such as slow-down in the expansion of world trade, recession in the major industrial economies, loss of markets in The Middle East consequent to the Gulf crisis, and a virtual collapse of exports to the erstwhile Soviet Union.

Composition of exports by major commodities and groups for 1991-92 and April-September 1992 along with the respective growth rates are given in Table 21.4. The data reveal that while exports of manufactured goods increased by 0.2 per cent in 1991.92, exports of agricultural and allied products declined by 5.2 per cent. Consequently, the share of manufactured goods in total exports increased from 72.9 per cent in 1990-91 to 74.2 per cent in 1991-92 while the share of agricultural commodities slipped from 19.4 per cent 18.7 per cent. Among agricultural and allied products, while there was significant improvement in export of marine products, oilcake, spices, cashew kernels, rice and sugar some of the traditional export commodities such as tea, coffee and raw cotton either stagnated or declined. Among manufactured goods, while there was a modest growth in exports of chemicals and textiles, exports of most other items particularly readymade garments and gems and jewellery declined. During April-September 1992, exports of oilcakes, rice engineering goods, readymade garments and jute manufactures picked up. While export of agriculture and allied products as a whole declined by 11 per cent during April-September 1992, exports of manufactured products increased by 11.1 per cent during the same period.

21.6 **Principal Elements of Balance of Payments Strategy**

Fiscal and Monetary Discipline

* Strict fiscal an monetary discipline to control aggregate demand. The Central fiscal deficit reduced from 8.4 per cent of GDP in 1990-91 to 6.2 per cent of GDP in 1991-9 and to be further reduced to 5 per cent of GDP in 1992-93. Monetary policy aimed at sowing down the growth of money supply from 18.5 per cent in 1991-92 to 10.5 per cent in the current year. As a result, inflation brought under control.

Liberalised Exchange Rate Management System (LERMS)

* LERMS, a dual exchange rate system, introduced in the Budget for 1992-93. Under this system, 40 per cent of foreign exchange earnings to be surrendered at the official exchange rate. Remaining 60 per cent to be converted at a market-determined rate. The foreign exchange surrendered at official exchange rate is utilised to import essential items. the foreign exchange converted at the market rate is available to finance all other imports. Represents a transitional stage to full convertibility on current account.

TABLE 21.4: Exports by Major commodity Groups

Items	1990-91	1991-92	1991-92 Apr-Sep	1992-93 Apr-Sep (P)	1990-91	1991-92	1991-92 Apr-Sept	1992-93 Apr-Sep (P)	Composition ($ terms) 1990-91	1991-92	1991-92 Apr-Sep	1992-93 Apr-Sep	Growth rate($terms) 1991-92 1990-91	Apr-Sep92/ Apr-Sep 91
1	2	3	4	5	6	7	8	9	10	11	12	13	14	15
	(Rs. hundred crore)				(US$ million)				(Per cent)				(Per cent)	
I. **Agriculture & allied products**	63.2	82.3	36.5	40.2	3522	3338	1583	1408	19.4	18.7	19.5	16.5	-5.2	-11.0
1. Cashew kernels	4.5	6.8	3.5	3.5	251	276	152	123	1.4	1.5	1.9	1.4	10.0	-19.2
2. Coffee	2.5	3.3	1.3	1.6	139	134	56	56	0.8	0.7	0.7	0.7	-3.9	-0.6
3. Marine products	9.6	14.4	6.0	7.1	535	584	260	249	2.9	3.3	3.2	2.9	9.2	-4.4
4. Oil meals	6.1	9.2	3.4	5.4	340	373	147	189	1.9	2.1	1.8	2.2	9.88	28.3
5. Raw cotton	8.5	3.0	2.8	0.3	474	122	121	11	2.6	0.7	1.5	0.1	-74.3	-91.3
6. Rice	4.6	7.6	2.5	4.8	256	308	108	168	1.4	1.7	1.3	2.0	20.3	55.1
7. Spices	2.3	3.7	1.7	1.8	128	150	74	63	0.7	0.8	0.9	0.7	17.1	-14.5
8. Sugar	0.4	1.6	0.6	0.6	22	65	26	21	0.1	0.4	0.3	0.2	191.1	-19.2
9. Tea & mate	10.7	12.1	4.8	4.5	596	491	208	158	3.3	2.7	22.6	1.8	-17.7	-24.3
10. Tobacco	2.6	3.8	2.4	2.6	145	154	104	91	0.8	0.9	1.3	1.1	6.4	-12.5
II. **Ores and minerals**	15.0	20.3	8.7	7.5	836	823	377	263	4.6	4.6	4.7	3.1	-1.5	-30.4
11. Iron ore	10.5	14.4	5.9	4.4	585	584	256	154	3.2	3.3	3.2	1.8	-0.2	-39.7

Contd

TABLE 21.4 *Concld.*

1	2	3	4	5	6	7	8	9	10	11	12	13	14	15
III. **Manufactured goods**	237.4	326.9	137.7	189.3	13231	13261	5971	6631	72.9	74.2	73.7	77.6	0.2	11.1
12. Engineering goods	38.8	55.1	21.5	33.2	2162	2235	932	1163	11.9	12.5	11.5	13.6	3.4	24.8
13. Chemicals	25.4	39.2	16.0	19.1	1416	1590	694	669	7.8	8.9	8.6	7.8	12.3	-3.6
14. Textiles	21.0	32.0	14.1	18.3	1170	1298	611	641	6.5	7.3	7.5	7.5	10.9	4.9
15. Jute manufactures	3.0	4.0	1.4	2.0	167	162	61	70	0.9	0.9	0.7	0.8	-3.0	15.4
16. Leather & mfrs.	26.0	31.3	13.7	17.6	1449	1270	594	6117	8.0	7.1	7.3	7.2	-12.4	3.8
17. Readymade garments	40.1	54.2	21.5	32.5	2235	2199	932	1139	12.3	12.3	11.5	13.3	-1.6	22.1
18. Handicrafts	61.7	883.5	38.11	48.6	3439	3387	1652	1703	19.0	19.0	20.4	19.9	-1.5	0.0
of which: Gems & Jewellery	52.5	67.5	31.6	39.1	2926	2738	1370	1370	16.1	15.3	16.9	16.0	-6.4	0.0
IV. **Minerals fuels and lubricants**	9.5	10.4	3.7	7.0	529	422	160	245	2.9	2.4	2.0	2.9	-20.3	52.8
19. POL	9.4	10.2	3.6	6.8	524	414	156	238	2.9	2.3	1.9	2.8	-21.0	52.6
V. **Others**	0.6	0.5	0.3	0.0	34	21	13	0	0.2	0.1	0.2	0.0	-38.2	-100.0
VI. **Total**	325.5	440.4	186.9	244.0	18142	17866	8104	8548	100.0	100.0	100.0	100.0	-1.5	5.5

(P) Provisional.

Notes:
1. Item 12 includes machinery, transport equipment, metal manufactures (including iron and steel), electronic goods and computer software.
2. Group IV includes coal.
3. Item 13 excludes rubber, glass, paints and other products.
4. Item 14 includes cotton yarn, fabrics, made up etc.
5. Item 18 includes handicrafts, carpets (handmade) & gems and jewellery.

* Import restrictions on capital goods, raw materials and components virtually eliminated. Thus, excess import demand will be reflected in a higher market exchange rate and self-correcting mechanism will operate to keep trade deficit in check. Considerable reductions in peak tariffs, tariffs on capital goods. Cash margins an interest surcharge on import credit abolished. Harmonised system of customs classification introduced.

Structural Reforms

* Substantial deregulation of industry and trade. Many industries delincensed. Competition promoted by the opening up of many areas previously reserved for the public sector to private and foreign investment. Policies put in place to attract foreign direct and portfolio investment. Amendment of SICA (Safe Industrial Company's Act).

Mobilisation of Exceptional Financing

* Mobilisation of exceptional financing form multilateral agencies and bilateral donors. Standby arrangement with the IMF. Structural adjustment and social safety net loans from World Bank. Financial Sector loan negotiated with ADB.

21.7 **Foreign Investment Policy**

Policy towards foreign investment was liberalised in 1991 to permit automatic approval for foreign investment up to 51 per cent equity in 34 industries. The Foreign Investment Promotion Board (FIPB) was also set up to process applications in cases not covered by automatic approval, During 1992-93 several additional measures were taken to encourage investment flows: direct foreign investment, portfolio investment, NRI (Non-Resident Indian) investment and deposits and investment in global depository receipts. they are given below:

(i) The dividend-balancing condition earlier applicable to foreign investment up to 51 per cent equity is no longer applied except for consumer goods industries.
(ii) Existing companies with foreign equity can raise it to 51 per cent subject to certain prescribed guidelines. Foreign direct investment has also been allowed in exploration, production and refining of oil and marketing of gas. Captive coal mines can also be owned and run by private investors in power.
(iii) NRIs and overseas corporate bodies (OCBs) predominantly owned by them are also permitted to invest up to 100 per cent equity in high-priority industries with repatribility of capital and income. NRI investment up 100 per cent of equity is also allowed in export houses, trading houses, star trading houses, hospitals, EOUs (Export Oriented Unit) sick industries, hotels and tourism-related industries and without the right of repatriation in the previously excluded areas of real estate, housing and infrastructure. Foreign citizens of Indian origin are now permitted to acquire house property without the permission of the Reserve Bank of India.
(iv) Disinvestment of equity by foreign investors on longer needs to be at

prices determined by the Reserved Bank. It has been allowed at market rates on stock exchanges from 15 September, 1992 with permission to repatriate the proceeds of such disinvestment.

(v) India has signed the Multilateral Investment Guarantee Agency Protocol for the protection of foreign investments on 13 April 1992.

(vi) Provisions of the Foreign Exchange Regulation Act (FERA) have been liberalised through an Ordinance dated 9 January, 1993 as a result of which companies with more than 40 per cent of foreign equity are also now treated on par with fully Indian-owned companies.

(vii) Foreign companies have been allowed to use their trade marks on domestic sales from 14 May, 1992.

The government has allowed reputed Foreign Institutional Investors (FIIs) including pension funds, mutual funds, asset management companies, investment trusts, nominee companies and incorporated or institutional portfolio managers to invest in the Indian capital market subject to the condition that they registered with the Securities and Exchanges Board of India (SEBI) and obtain RBI approval under FERA. Portfolio investment by the FIIs in the primary and secondary markets are subject to an overall ceiling of 24 per cent of the issued share capital in any company and the FIIs are required to allocate their total investment between equities and debentures in the ratio of 70:30. FIIs investing under the scheme enjoy a concessional tax rate of 20 per cent on dividend and interest and 10 per cent on long-term capital gains. Countrywise Breakup of Foreign Investment Approved is Table 21.5

21.8 External Assistance and Borrowings

The strategy for balance of payments management includes substantial support in the form of external financial flows including external assistance and external borrowings including fast-disbursing assistance from official multilateral and bilateral sources and also through new schemes to attract funds from non-residents, their corporate bodies and foreign banks.

External Assistance

The gross inflows under external assistance from both multilateral and bilateral sources increased substantially from $ 3.74 billion in 1990-91 to US$ 4.69 billion in 1991-92, i.e., by 25 per cent (Table 21.6). Of the total external assistance, US$ 1.11 billion - about a quarter - was fast-disbursing not linked to projects. This included the first tranche of the Structural Adjustment Loan (SAL) of US$ 300 million, and the Oil & Gas Sector Programme Loan of US$ 150 million from the World Bank; US$ 150 million for Special Assistance Projects and US$ 125 million as the first tranche of the Hydrocarbon Sector Loan from the Asian Development Bank; and about US$ 380 million from Japan, Germany, and the U.K.

The Aid-India Consortium, which met in Paris in June 1992, pledged to provide US$ 7.2 billion of assistance in 1992-93; this represents an increase of US$ 500 million or about 7.5 per cent more over the pledges of the previous year. The quick-disbursing component of this assistance is US$ 1.79 billion, i.e., 25 per cent of the total, US$ 1.13 billion from multilateral sources and the rest from bilateral sources.

TABLE 21.5: Countrywise Breakup of Foreign Investment Approved, 1990-1992

		Total Approvals			Shares		
		1990	1991	1992	1990	1991	1992
	1	2	3	4	5	6	7
			(Rs million)			(per cent)	
1	U.S.A	344.8	1858.5	12315.0	26.91	34.8	31.7
2	Switzerland	135.0	355.0	6897.6	10.5	6.6	17.7
3	Japan	50.0	527.1	6102.3	3.9	9.9	15.7
4	U.K.	90.6	321.0	1176.7	7.1	6.0	3.0
5	Netherlands	37.6	559.2	967.9	2.9	10.5	2.5
6	Germany	195.1	418.0	862.7	15.2	7.8	2.2
7	Italy	68.2	178.1	893.9	5.3	3.3	2.3
8	Australia	6.3	26.1	776.2	0.5	0.5	2.0
9	Hong Kong	11.5	211.5	570.8	0.9	4.0	1.5
10	Malaysia	1.2	1.8	744.3	0.1	0.0	1.9
11	Singapore		13.7	602.1	0.0	0.3	1.5
12	France	88.8	193.3	296.4	6.9	3.6	0.8
13	Sweden	3.3	69.8	484.1	0.3	1.3	1.2
14	Korea(Rep. of)	70.6	61.5	394.0	5.5	1.2	1.0
15	Denmark	27.2	111.7	252.3	2.1	2.1	0.6
16	Russia	71.8	86.1	115.9	5.6	1.6	0.3
17	Belgium		16.1	237.0	0.0	0.3	0.6
18	Taiwan	8.4	4.5	237.0	0.7	0.1	0.6
19	Finland	5.6	25.3	105.0	0.4	0.5	0.3
20	NRIs	52.4	197.0	4391.3	4.1	3.7	11.3
21	Others	14.8	105.8	452.9	1.2	2.0	1.2
	Total	1283.2	5341.1	38875.4	100.0	100.0	100.0

A worrying aspect of India's balance of payments in 1992-93 has been the low utilization of external assistance. In spite of the larger pledges from the Aid-India Consortium donors this year, the disbursements have been running at a much lower level than last year. Up to December 1992, the gross disbursements have amounted to only US$ 2 billion against US$ 3.16 billion during the same period last year - 36.7 per cent lower. As a result, for the first three quarters of 1992-93, net capital transfer under external assistance has been zero. This is in spite of the drawal of about US$ 625 million fast-disbursing funds during April-December 1992 - US$ 200 million as the last tranche of World Bank's SAL, about US$ 100 million from World Bank under Social Safety Net Loan, US$ 125 million from Japan under Hydrocarbon Sector Loan, and about US$ 50 million from Germany during 1992-93 up to December 1992. The recent decision to pass on to the States the entire external assistance as additional central assistance in respect of all sectors (not just in respect of only social sectors as before) and to release advance central assistance to meet the initial liquidity requirements of State Governments are important steps in the direction of speeding up aid utilization.

External Commercial Borrowings

The Gulf crisis and the consequent downgrading of India's credit rating below the investment grade effectively prevented India from accessing international capital markets. This resulted in net outflows on ECB account both in 1990-91 and 1991-92 (Table 21.7). The successful handling of the BOP crisis and the series of structural reforms introduced since July 1991 restored external investors' confidence to some extent. It would, however, be imprudent to conclude that the markets have opened up on a normal basis for Indian borrowers to take resource to such borrowings on a significant scale. Moreover, the Government has decided to reduce the share of short-term borrowings in total debt. Consequently, a major portion of the commercial borrowings raised during the last two years have been by way of export credits supported by official export credit agencies such as the US Exim Bank, the Japanese Exim Bank, the ECGC of U.K, etc. Overall, the improvement in outlook in 1992-93 is evident from the fact that authorizations have amounted to US$ 1.6 billion during April-September compared to US$ 680 million in the corresponding period of 1991-92.

21.9 Non-Resident Deposits

As with external commercial borrowings, dependence on NRI deposits, which are on commercial terms as well as of relatively short maturity, was significant from 1985-86 to 1989-90. The outflow from non-resident deposits, which started in October 1990 following the erosion of international confidence, had assumed alarming proportions in the second quarter of 1991. From over US$ 300 million a month then, the outflow slowed with the introduction of the package of new policy measures to about US$ 75 million a month in the remaining part of the year. It further declined to less than US$ 50 million a month in 1992-93 up to September; inflows have begun in Foreign Currency Non-Resident (FCNR) accounts since October 1992.

TABLE 21.6: External Assistance

	1985-86	1986-87	1987-88	1988-89	1989-90	1990-91	1991-92	April-December 1991	April-December 1992
1	2	3	4	5	6	7	8	9	10
				(Rs. hundred crore)					
1. Authorisations	56.50	61.60	92.65	130.70	108.26	81.23	127.07	67.24*	33.62*
2. Gross disbursements	29.36	36.05	50.52	53.04	58.02	67.04	116.15	75.82	60.77
3. Debt service payments	13.67	20.29	26.24	29.46	36.86	42.82	66.56	39.92	60.79
(a) Amortisation	7.76	11.76	15.81	16.46	19.87	23.29	36.50	21.51	32.47
(b) Interest payments	5.91	8.53	10.43	13.00	16.99	19.53	30.06	18.41	28.32
4. Net capital inflow (2-3a)	21.60	24.29	34.71	36.58	38.15	43.75	79.65	54.32	28.30
5. Net capital transfer(2-3)	15.69	17.76	24.28	23.58	21.16	24.22	49.59	35.90	-0.02
				(US $ billion)					
1. Authorisations	4.62	4.82	7.15	9.03	6.50	4.53	5.51	2.29*	1.11*
2. Gross disbursements	2.40	2.82	3.90	3.66	3.48	3.74	4.69	3.16	2.00
3. Debt service payments	1.12	1.59	2.02	2.03	2.21	2.39	2.69	1.66	2.00
(a) Amortisation	0.63	0.92	1.22	1.14	1.19	1.30	1.47	0.90	1.07
(b) Interest payments	0.48	0.67	0.80	0.90	1.02	1.09	1.21	0.77	0.93
4. Net capital inflow (2-3a)	1.77	1.90	2.68	2.53	2.29	2.44	3.22	2.26	0.93
5. Net capital transfer (2-3a)	1.28	1.23	1.87	1.63	1.27	1.35	2.00	1.50	-

* For the the period April-Sept only.

Note: The data include Government and non-Government loans and grants (including food assistance but excluding other commodity grant assistance). These figures do not include suppliers' credits, commercial borrowings and IMF credits other than Trust Fund loan.

TABLE 21.7: External Commercial Borrowings*

		1985-86	1986-87	1987-88	1988-89	1989-90	1990-91	1991-92	April-December 1991	April-December 1992
	1	2	3	4	5	6	7	8	9	10
	(Rs. hundred crore)									
1	Authorisations	17.00	13.96	26.54	43.14	54.79	34.14	52.76	15.59	48.06
2	Gross disbursements	17.99	24.74	22.52	40.69	41.96	30.50	27.14	14.06	16.68
3	Debt service payment	11.75	15.65	17.36	22.24	30.41	40.06	53.93	21.69	30.65
	(a) Amortisation	5.65	7.96	8.71	11.03	14.55	21.37	28.98	11.12	18.25
	(b) Interest payments	6.10	7.69	8.65	11.21	15.86	18.69	24.95	10.57	12.40
4	Net capital inflow (2-3a)	12.34	16.78	13.81	29.66	27.41	9.13	-1.84	2.94	-1.57
5	Net transfer (2-3)	6.25	9.09	5.16	18.45	11.55	-9.56	-26.79	-7.63	-13.97
	(US $ billion)									
1	Authorisations	1.39	1.09	2.05	2.98	3.29	1.90	2.13	0.68	1.59
2	Gross disbursements	1.47	1.94	1.74	2.81	2.52	1.70	1.10	0.61	0.55
3	Debt service payment	0.96	1.22	1.34	1.54	1.83	2.23	2.18	0.94	1.01
	(a) Amortisation	0.46	0.62	0.67	0.76	0.87	1.19	1.17	0.48	0.60
	(b) Interest payments	0.50	0.60	0.67	0.77	0.95	1.04	1.01	0.46	0.41
4	Net capital inflow(2-3a)	1.01	1.31	1.07	2.05	1.65	0.51	-0.07	0.13	-0.05
5	Net transfer (2-3)	0.51	0.71	0.40	1.27	0.69	0.53	-1.08	-0.33	-0.46

* Excludes borrowings up to 1 year maturity. The estimates are based on data of EECB Division of the Department of Economic Affairs. Ministry of Finance. External commercial borrowing includes loans from commercial bank and other financial institutions, bonds & FRNs, suppliers' credit, buyers' credits and credits from export credit agencies of concerned government, IFC(W), private sector borrowings from ADB, etc. The data in this table does not tally with that given the Table 5.1 which also include external assistance on non-Government account, suppliers' credits form East-European countries repayable in rupees, and also the funds raised through India Development Bonds in 1991-92. US$ 1.63 billion was raised through India Development Bonds in 1991-92.

As the external finance crisis unfolded, Reserve Bank of India introduced a new scheme in November 1990 similar to the FCNRA scheme to mobilize foreign funds. This scheme was called the Foreign Currency (Bank and Others) Deposit [FC(B&O)D] scheme; it is also open to foreign citizens or banks and other institutions, but, withdrawals are not allowed before maturity unlike in the case of NRI deposits. It attracted relatively small amounts of US$ 262 million in 1990-91 and US$ 304 million in 1991-92. IN the current year. it attracted large net inflows of about US$# 1.62 billion up to July 1992. As reserves mounted the scheme was suspended from end-july 1992. There have been since outflows from, these deposits as they were repaid.

Interest rates on NR(E)R deposits have been aligned with domestic deposit rates from 9 October 1992. Term deposits under NR(E)RA for all maturities would be subject only to the stipulation that they must not exceed 13 per cent annum (one per cent above the maximum domestic deposit rate). Similarly, the interest rate on saving deposits under NR(E)RA has been raised from 5 per cent to 6 per cent 6 per cent annum.

Drawals from the IMF

Substantial drawals have been made from the IMF from 1990-91 onwards under one or other facility. Besides the Reserve tranche drawings of SDR 487 million (US$ 666 million), India drew SDR 1269 million (US$ 1240 million). Indian made a 20 month standby arrangement with the Fund on October 1991 for total loan of SDR 1656 million (US$ 2262 million); two instalments worth SDR 270 million (US$ 382 million) were drawn in 1991-92. In April-December 1992 SDR 942 million) has been availed of, leaving a balance of SDR 462 million (US$ 650 million) to be drawn till May 1993 (Table 21.8).

TABLE 21.8 Drawals from International Monetary Fund, 1990-1992

	Facility (million)	SDR (million)	US$ (crore)	Rs.
1	2	3	4	5
July-Sept 1990	RT	487	666	1168
23-01-1991	FCI	552	789	1450
23-01-1991	CCFF	717	1025	1884
22-07-1991	CCFF	166	221	570
16-09-1991	UCT	469	637	1647
15-11-1991	UCT	85	117	305
02-01-1992	UCT	185	265	683
02-01-1992	UCT	462	663	1771
09-12-1992	UCT	462	643	1685
Expected in Feb'93	UCT	231	325	845
Expected in May'93	UCT	231	325	845

RT Reserve tranche
FCT First credit tranche
CCFF Compensatory and contingency financing facility
UCT Upper credit tranche.

21.10 Foreign Exchange Reserves

Movements in the country's foreign exchange reserves given in Table 21.9 reflect the net result of external transactions. The new balance of payments adjustment strategy adopted since July 1991 has resulted in a considerable improvement in reserves during 1991-92 and 1992-93. Foreign exchange reserves stood at US$ 9220 million at the end of March 1992, an increase of US$ 3386 million over the end-March 1991 level. Among the three components of the foreign exchange reserves, foreign currency assets stood at US$ 5631 million at the end of March 1992, an increase of US$ 3395 million in 1991-92 as against a decline of US$ 1132 million 1990-91. Foreign currency assets reached US$ 6.9 billion in the middle of July 1992 and stood at US$ 5096 million as on 5 February 1993 showing a decline of US$ 535 million over the end-March level. The decline of foreign currency assets during 1992-93, in spite of recourse to IMF resources as discussed earlier, was mainly due to a substantial increase in imports as industry recovered and replenished its inventories.

21.11 External Debt

The growing payment deficits and external borrowings after the mid-eighties coincided with a deterioration in the quality of external financing. Maturities shortened and the average rate of interest increased. This is reflected in an increase in the total debt. Table 21.10 provides a picture of India's external debt since 1980-81. The development have necessitated a close monitoring of the size, composition and growth of external debt in the future.

TABLE 21.9 Movements in Foreign Exchange Reserves

Year	Foreign currency assets at the end of the year		Reserves at the end of the year @		Movements in reserves		Net drawals on IMF	
1	2	3	4	5	6	7	8	9
	Rs.Crore	$ million	Rs.crore	$ million	Rs.crore	$ million	Rs.crore	$million
1980-81	4822	5850	5544	6823	-390	-538	814 *	1029 *
1981-82	3355	3582	4024	4390	-1520	-2433	637	639
1982-83	4265	4281	4782	4896	758	758	1893	1958
1983-84	5498	5990	5972	5649	1190	1190	1342	1298
1984-85	6817	5482	7243	5949	1271	1217	63	53
1985-86	7384	5972	7820	6520	577	577	-327 *	-267 *
1986-87	7645	5924	8151	6574	331	331	-840	-690 *
1987-88	7287	5618	7687	6223	-464	-464	-1388 *	-1123 *
1988-89	6605	4226	7040	4802	-647	-647	-1749 *	1175 *
1989-90	5787	3368	6251	3962	-789	-789	-1688 *	-1035 *
1990-91	4388	2236	11416 #	5834	5165 #	5165 #	2043 *	1106
1991-92	14578	5631	23850 #+	9220 #+	12434 #+	12434 #+	2078	780
1992-93 (upto end Jan 1993)	13688	5237	22720	8693	-1130	-1130	2625	1006

@ Includes foreign currency assets of RBI, gold holdings of RBI and SDR holdings of Government.
* Includes Trust Fund loan drawals and repayment.
\# Effective october 17, 1990 gold is revalued close to international market price at the end of every month. For earlier periods gold is valued at official rate of Rs. 84.39, per 10 grammes.
\+ Includes purchase of gold of Rs. 494 crore (US $ 191 million) from Government of India.

TABLE 21.10: External Debt and Debt Servicing : Key Indicators

	1980-81	1985-86	1988-89	1989-90	1990-91	1991-92	Sep.92
1	2	3	4	5	6	7	8
Year-end external debt							
US$ billion	23.50	37.35	53.90	58.63	63.40	67.58	71.11
Rs. hundred crore	194.70	459.61	844.92	1003.76	1229.50	1989.67	2029.72
Debt service payments							
US$ billion	1.41	2.61	5.65	6.02	6.43	6.44	
Rs. hundred crore	11.16	31.89	81.77	100.22	115.41	159.28	
Total Debt as per cent of GDP	13.7	17.4	19.7	21.5	21.4	27.3	
Debt service as per cent of current receipts	9.3	16.7	26.5	25.2	24.7	24.6	

Note: Data on short-term debt and estimated interest payments on NRI deposits are not available prior to 1988-89, hence the series from 1988-89 onwards in not strictly comparable with that prior to 1988-89. The external debt data conform to the reclassification suggested by the Report of the Task Force and the Policy Group on External Debt Statistics of India, 1992 from 1988-89.

22

MONETARY TRENDS

22.1 Monetary and Credit Policy in 1992-93

Monetary policy in 1992-93 was guided by the objectives of moderating the growth in Money Supply (M3) and implementing the recommendations of the Narasimham Committee on financial sector reforms. In the second half of the year, in recognition of the noticeable slowing down of inflation and the need to stimulate production, monetary policy in 1992-93 relaxed the restrictions, placed in 1991-92.

22.2 Credit Policy Measures in 1992-93

* Lending rate structure simplified into four slabs instead of six.
* The floor interest rate for bank credit (other than export) of over Rs. 2 lakh reduced in two stages to 18 per cent.
* Interest rate on pre-shipment and post-shipment export credit reduced across the board by one percentage point.
* Banks free to fix interest rates on term deposits subject to a cap of 13 per cent (reduced later to 12 per cent).
* Banks free to set interest rates on Non-Resident External (Rupee) Accounts subject to a cap of 13 per cent.
* Interest rate on saving deposits raised to 6 per cent.
* Interest rate for export credit denominated in US Dollars reduced to 6.5 per cent and for refinance from RBI on this credit to 5.5 per cent.
* Forty-five per cent ceiling on the ratio of incremental credit (minus export credit) to deposits removed.
* Target for export credit set at 10 per cent of net bank credit to be attained by banks by June 1993.
* Restrictions on loans for consumer durables and on other non-priority sector personal loans removed.
* Selective credit controls on bank advances against stocks of oilseeds and vegetable oils, cotton and kapas relaxed.
* RBI's limits to NABARD enhanced by Rs. 400 crore.
* RBI's refinance limits to IDBI for discounting bills relating to purchase of machinery, commercial vehicles etc. increased by Rs. 400 crore, linked to IDBI providing Rs. 200 crore from its own resources.
* Threshold limit for term loans by the banks raised to Rs. 10 crore.
* Relaxations in the method of computing maximum permissible bank finance for individual borrowers in order to increase effective credit availability.

22.3 Scheduled Commercial Banks

The remarkable shift from demand to time deposits was induced by (a) high interest rate of 11 per cent offered on short-term time deposits (i.e. deposits from 46 days up to one year) and (b) removal of tax deduction at sources (TDS) on interest income (Table 22.1). Another factor which boosted time deposit growth, particularly up to July 1992, was the large inflow of foreign currency deposits under Foreign Currency (Banks and Others) Deposit (FC(BO)D) scheme to invite deposits from foreign citizens (not just from NRIs), banks and corporations. Under the scheme, which was in effect up to 31 July 1992, there wa 1 1inflow of US$ 1615 million in 1992-93 as against US$ 302 million in 1991-92 as a whole. Since August 1992 this scheme has been closed and repayments have started, which was somewhat moderated time deposit growth.

The lending capacity of the banks has been substantially augmented in the current financial year because of the removal of the incremental CRR (Cash Reserve Ratio) and reduction in SLR (Statutory Liquid Ratio) and the refund of one-third of incremental CRR cash balances held by RBI. This is reflected in the sharp increase in scheduled commercial bank credit in the period up to 8 January 1993. Total bank credit increased by Rs.19934 crore in this period compared with Rs. 5013 crore in the previous year. If food procurement credit is excluded, the increase is even more dramatic — from Rs. 4984 crore in 1991-92 to Rs. 19110 crore in 1992-93. Demand for bank credit by the commercial sector got a boost from the reduction in interest rates on bank advances, availability of attractive refinance facilities for export credit and removal of the ceiling on incremental non-food (excluding export) credit-deposit ratio.

Tables 22.2 and 22.3 reflect the working results of Scheduled Commercial Banks and Public Sector Banks respectively.

22.4 Securities Trading

In April 1992 investigations conducted by RBI into certain aspects of securities trading by some banks led to the exposure of serious irregularities and frauds in the securities transactions of several banks. Unscrupulous brokers; colluding with some bank officials, were found to be violating established rules and guidelines in a manner designed to siphon off bank funds to brokers for speculative transactions in shares. These irregularities and frauds, popularly termed the "securities scam", revealed serious weaknesses of internal control and supervision in banks which need to be urgently corrected.

A high-level enquiry committee known as the Janakiraman Committee was set up by RBI. It has submitted three reports in May, July and August 1992. It identified several types of irregularities in securities transactions which were used to siphon funds out of the banking system:

(i) Purchases were made by banks and their subsidiaries of securities and other instruments where the counter-party was ostensibly another bank but when in reality the proceeds were directly or indirectly credited to brokers' accounts;

(ii) Ready-forward (sale and repurchase) transactions were entered into either on their own or on clients' accounts by banks with brokers who used these funds for speculative activity;

(iii) Brokers were directly financed by banks by discounting bills not supported by genuine transactions;

(iv) Banks and other institutions showed large payments as call money with other banks. However, in the books of the receiving banks thee was no record of call money acceptances but instead the amounts were credited to the accounts of individual brokers. On the due date, these alleged call loans were rapid by payment out of the brokers' accounts in the name of other banks;

(v) Banks and institutions rediscounted bills of exchange held by other banks and institutions but the proceed and repayments were routed through brokers' accounts; and

(vi) Sums received as inter-corporate deposits and under portfolio management schemes (PMS) and similar schemes by merchant banking subsidiaries of public sector and other banks were passed on to broker through ready-forward deals.

TABLE 22.1: Scheduled Commercial Banks — Selected Indicators

		Variations during			
		1990-91 March 23 1990 to March 22 1991	1991-92 March 22 1991 to March 20 1992	1991-92 March 22 1991 to Jan. 10 1992*	1992-93 March 20 1992 to Jan. 8 1993*
			(Rs. crore)		
1	Aggregate deposits (a+b)	25583	38217	28290	31256
	a) Demand deposits	4337	11896	8704	-1446
	b) Time deposits	21246	26321	19586	32702
2	Borrowings from R.B.I.	1069	-2891	-1346	2536
3	Cash in hand and balances with R.B.I.	554	10522	10977	2036
	a) Cash in hand	156	204	104	180
	b) Balances with R.B.I.	398	10318	10873	1856
4	Net Balances with R.B.I. (3(b)-2)	-671	13209	12219	-680
5	Money at call and short notice	-489	904	965	1328
6	Bank Credit (a+b)	14848	9291	5013	19934
	(a) Public food procurement credit	2500	164	29	824
	(b) Non-food bank credit	12348	9127	4984	19110
	Of which to Priority Sector	2532	2554	633@	853@
7	Investment in Government and other approved securities	10696	15131	12144	10957
	(a) Government securities	7706	12729	10713	8741
	(b) Other approved securities	2990	2402	1431	2216
8	Balances with other banks in current account	276	621	574	200
			(per cent)		
9	Credit-deposit ratio	60.4	54.4	54.9	55.5
10	Non-food credit-deposit ratio	58.1	52.4	52.9	53.4
11	Investment-deposit ratio	39.0	39.9	39.5	38.6

* Provisional

@ Data available up to June of respective years.

TABLE 22.2: Working Results of Scheduled Commercial Banks for 1990-91 and 1991-92

	SBI group		Other public sector banks		Private sector banks		Foreign banks		All Banks	
	1990-91	1991-92	1990-91	1991-92	1990-91	1991-92	1990-91	1991-92	1990-91	1991-92
A Rupees crore										
A. Income	10019	13428	17134	21018	1151	1528	2278	3674	37361	39659
(i) Interest	9061	11775	15695	18975	1056	1380	1880	2829	34250	34979
(ii) Other income	958	1653	1439	2043	94	147	398	845	3111	4689
B. Expenditure	9869	13184	16808	20458	1114	1446	2046	3354	36605	38452
(i) Interest	5673	7392	11436	13630	632	810	1307	1845	22944	23684
(ii) Other operating expenses	2556	2864	4327	5020	358	424	395	570	10509	8881
(iii) Provisions and contingencies	1640	2928	1045	1809	124	212	344	939	3152	5888
C. Profit	150	246	315	499	38	81	348	495	1058	1320
D. Working Funds	93012	115081	166296	186636	10552	14069	15985	25103	36565	340984
B Percent of working funds										
A. Income	10.77	11.67	10.30	11.26	10.91	10.86	14.25	14.64	10.33	11.63
(i) interest income	9.74	10.23	9.44	10.17	10.01	9.81	11.76	11.27	9.47	10.26
(ii) other income	1.03	1.44	0.87	1.09	0.89	1.04	2.49	3.37	0.86	6.94
B. Expenditure	10.61	11.46	10.11	10.96	10.56	10.28	12.80	13.36	10.12	11.28
(i) other operating expenses	2.75	2.49	2.60	2.69	3.39	3.01	2.47	2.27	2.91	2.60
(iii) provisions and contingencies	1.76	2.54	0.63	0.97	1.18	1.51	2.15	3.74	0.87	1.73
C. Profit	0.16	0.21	0.19	0.27	0.36	0.58	2.18	1.97	0.29	3.03

TABLE 22.3: Published Profits of Public Sector Banks

(Rs. crore)

		Year ended March 31	
		1991	1992
A	**State Bank of India Group**		
1	State Bank of India	107.01	175.05
2	State Bank of Bikaner & Jaipur	5.50	9.50
3	State Bank of Hyderabad	8.51	12.75
4	State Bank of Indore	2.94	3.23
5	State Bank of Mysore	2.87	3.85
6	State Bank of Patiala	14.59	29.78
7	State Bank of Saurashtra	4.50	6.00
8	State Bank of Travancore	4.00	5.09
B	**Nationalised Banks**		
1	Allahabad Bank	19.84	28.11
2	Bank of Baroda	56.66	95.10
3	Bank of India	19.49	56.63
4	Bank of Maharashtra	3.10	4.04
5	Canara Bank	136.04	156.59
6	Central Bank of India	9.48	30.49
7	Dena Bank	7.26	9.10
8	Indian Bank	31.84	36.50
9	Indian Overseas Bank	6.74	9.05
10	Punjab National Bank	73.69	112.44
11	Syndicate Bank	2.84	4.46
12	United Bank of India	5.78	6.68
13	Union Bank of India	10.05	29.45
14	UCO Bank	-42.96	-20.99
15	Andhra Bank	8.21	8.42
16	Corporation Bank	4.65	5.20
17	New Bank of India	-45.00	-41.52
18	Oriental Bank of Commerce	22.83	26.78
19	Punjab & Sind Bank	-5.45	0.68
20	Vijaya Bank	0.25	1.84

The extent of unreconciled amounts as estimated by the detailed investigation made by the Janakiraman Committee has been estimated at Rs. 3543 crore. These irregularities have been detected in some banks in each of the three segments of the banking industry, viz. public sector banks, private sector banks and foreign banks.

The government took early action to identify and punish those responsible for the fraudulent transactions and to recover the money lost by the banks. A special court was appointed to try all matters relating to the scheme and legislation has been passed providing powers to attach the assets of notified persons involved in the scam. A special judge of the Bombay High Court has been appointed for trial of scam-related cases. The government has appointed a custodian for prompt disposal of the attached assets. The Central Bureau of Investigation (CBI) has been asked to take over investigation of all the frauds and underhand dealings exposed by RBI's investigations. Finally, in recognition of the seriousness of the fraudulent transactions exposed and of the need for thorough examination of all aspects of the matter, a Joint Parliament Committee (JPC) was set up to enquire into all aspects of the scam, to fix responsibility to make suggestions about future reform of the system. The JPC has examined a number of persons including bank and government officials and brokers. Its enquiry is in progress.

The scam has brought into focus serious weaknesses in the country's financial system which need to be corrected. At one level the scam reflects deliberate and criminal violation of rules and procedures with intent of defrauding the banks. This was done through criminal collusion between brokers and some bank officials. However, there are also systemic weaknesses which made it possible. These are:

(i) Weaknesses in the internal control mechanism within the commercial banks themselves. More effective internal control mechanism could have ensured that such manipulations even if they did occur would have been detected much earlier;

(ii) There have also been weaknesses in the supervisory mechanism which need to be removed. The proposed new Board of Financial Supervision to be set up under the aegis of RBI will rectify this;

(iii) The prevalence of a very high level of pre-emption of bank resources at low rates of interest has also put pressure on banks to find various mechanisms for earning higher rates of return to supplement their income from non-fund-based activities;

(iv) It is also important to recognise that these irregularities to some extent reflect the difficulty in running an overregulated financial system in which administered interest rates in one part of the system co-exist with market-determined rates of return in the capital market. Rigid control over interest rates which takes them too far away from market-determined rates of interest is not workable and only leads to attempts to by-pass regulations in search of available high rates of interest.

The Government has been successful in minimising the adverse effects of the scam on the economy and on the working of the financial sector. Steps are being taken to improve internal control mechanisms in the banks and to strengthen the supervisory system so that such problems will not recur in future. Structural reforms envisaged in the banking sector (outlined in the next section) will also overcome some of the systemic pressures on the system which led to the evolution of practices which were deliberately misused by unscrupulous persons. The confidence in the country's banking system remains strong. The expansion in commercial credit, increase in the volume of stocks traded in the market and continued interest on the part of foreign investors bear testimony to this. It is, however, also true that such irregularities badly affect the small investor and create uncertainties in the investment environment. Therefore, it is necessary to prevent the recurrence of such irregularities in future.

22.5 **Financial Sector Reforms**

The current year witnessed the initiation of major financial sector reforms based on the report of the Narasimham Committee which was submitted in November 1991. The report was placed before Parliament in December 1991 and its recommendations have been extensively discussed in the Consultative Committee of Parliament for the Finance Ministry. Following are the main reforms in sector.

22.6 **Banking Sector Reforms**

* Statutory Liquidity Ratio (SLR) on increment in net demand and time liabilities (DTL) over 3 April 1992 level reduced to 30 per cent from 38.5 per cent.
* Phased reduction in SLR on net DTL as on 3 April 1992 to 37.75 per cent by 6 March 1993.
* Incremental Cash Reserve Ratio (ICRR) of 10 per cent on increase in net DTL over 3 May 1991 level removed from 17 April 1992.
* Number of lending and deposit interest rates reduced.
* New prudential norms relating to income recognition, classification of assets and provisioning for bad debts introduced.
* Time schedule for capital adequacy norms announced — (a) 8 per cent to be attained by foreign banks operating in India by 31 March 1993,, (b) 8 per cent to be attained by Indian banks with branches abroad, by 31 March 1994 and (c) 4 per cent to be attained by other banks by 31 March 1993 and 8 per cent by 31 March 1996.
* Revised format for balance sheet and profit and loss account reflecting actual financial health of the scheduled commercial banks introduced from the bank accounting year 1991-92 and the accounts for 1990-91 to be reformatted.
* Banks attaining capital adequacy norms and prudential accounting standards given freedom to open new branches and upgrade branches or extension counters; other banks given freedom to rationalise existing branch network.
* Guidelines finalised for objective selection procedures for non-official directors of the banks.
* New Board of Financial Supervision to be set up in Reserve Bank of India.
* New RBI guidelines to govern entry of new private sector banks.

22.7 **Capital Market Reforms**

The Capital Issues (Control) Act, 1947 was released in May 1992, and the office of the Controller of Capital Issues (CCI), was subsequently abolished. With the abolition of CCI, prior government permission was no longer needed by companies to access the capital markets. Companies were free to approach the capital .markets without prior government permission subject to getting offer documents cleared by SEBI. Control over price and premium fixation has also been removed and most issuing companies are free to fix the price of their securities for public as well as rights issues.

Indian companies have been permitted to access international capital markets through Euro-equity issues aimed at mobilising capital for modernisation and import requirements. Several companies have been given such permission. Up to the end of January 1993, two companies have raised around $ 250 million from the Euro-market.

A number of steps have been taken in the course of 1991-92 and 1992-93 by the Government and SEBI (Securities and Exchange Board of Indian) to introduce improved practices and greater transparency in the capital markets in the interest of healthy capital market development.

(i) SEBI was authorised to conduct inspections of various mutual funds. These inspections have been conducted and SEBI has submitted a report on each inspection which brings out various deficiencies of individual mutual funds. Corrective steps are being taken to set right these deficiencies.

(ii) SEBI has also drawn up a programmes of inspecting stock exchanges. Eight stock exchanges have been inspected. Reports of SEBI in each case, and the recommendations therein, are under the consideration of the stock exchanges.

(iii) The process of registration of intermediaries such as stockbrokers and subbrokers has been provided under the provisions of the Securities and Exchange Board of India Act, 1992. The registration is on the basis of certain eligibility norms such as capital adequacy, infrastructure etc.

(iv) Companies issuing capital in the primary market are now required to disclose all material facts and specific risk factors associated with their projects. Proposals are under consideration to improve the disclosure of information regarding the basis of calculation of premium while leaving companies free to fix the premium.

(v) Merchant banking has been statutorily brought under the regulatory framework of SEBI. The merchant bankers are now to be authorised by SEBI. They will have to adhere to stipulated capital adequacy norms. Merchant bankers have to abide by a code of conduct which specifies a high degree of responsibility towards investors in respect of the pricing and premium fixation of issues, and disclosures in the prospectus or offer letter for issues.

(vi) The Government has given formal approval for the setting up of the National Stock Exchange of India (NSEI) by financial institutions and banks with IDBI as the nodal agency. The NSEI is expected to serve as a model exchange integrating the stock markets all over the country by providing nation-wide stock trading facilities and electronic clearing and settlements.

(vii) In order to induce companies to exercise greater care and diligence for timely action in matters relating to the public issue of capital, SEBI has advised the stock exchanges to collect from companies making public issues, a deposit of one per cent of the issue amount which could be forfeited in case of non-compliance with the provisions of the listing agreement and, non-despatch of refund orders and share certificates by registered post within the prescribed time.

(viii) Regulations on insider trading under the provisions of the SEBI Act have been notified. Such regulations will help in protecting and preserving the market's integrity,.and in the long run help inspire investor confidence in the market.

(ix) RBI has liberalised the investment norms evolved for NRIs by allowing companies to accept capital contributions and issue shares or debentures to NRIs or overseas corporate bodies without prior permission.

(x) The Government has allowed foreign institutional investors (FIIs) such as pension funds, mutual funds, investment trusts, asset or portfolio management companies etc. to invest in the Indian capital market provided they register with SEBI.

(xi) To make the governing body of a stock exchange more broad based SEBI has issued guidelines for its composition. According to these guidelines the governing body of the stock exchanges should have five elected members, not more than four members nominated by the Government or SEBI and three or fewer members nominated as public representatives, besides its executives director.

(xii) The trading in stock exchanges is now for three hours instead of two-and-a-half hours.

(xiii) SEBI has set up an advisory committee for primary and secondary capital markets to provide wider consultation with the investors etc.

23

PUBLIC FINANCE AND ANNUAL PLAN

23.1 Introduction

Despite financial constraints, the outlay for Central Plan has been kept up at reasonable levels. The Central Annual Plan outlay for 1992-93 was stepped up by 20.5 per cent to Rs. 48407 crore. The budgetary support for the Central Plan was, however, reduced from 44 per cent in RE 1991-92 to 38.2 per cent in BE 1992-93.

The importance of reducing the fiscal deficit and bringing inflation under control has been evident for some time. Decisive action to limit the fiscal deficit was initiated in the Budget of July 1991-92, which reduced the Central Government's fiscal deficit from 8.4 per cent of GDP in 1990-91 to 6.2 per cent in 1991-92. This represented a reduction in the primary deficit from 4.4 per cent to 1.7 per cent of GDP. The Budget of 1992-93 continued the process of restoring fiscal discipline and targeted a further reduction in fiscal deficit to 5.0 per cent of GDP.

The process of fiscal consolidation initiated in the Union Budget for 1991-92 was continued in 1992-93. All three deficit indicators included in the Budget namely, revenue deficit, budget deficit and fiscal deficit show a significant reduction in BE 1992-93 compared to RE 1991-92. This is sought to be achieved by substantially higher tax and non-tax receipts and by measures to contain expenditure.

On the expenditure side, the estimates show a degree of restraint. The total increase in BE 1992-93 over BE 1991-92 is Rs. 5665 crore, of which interest payments alone account for Rs. 4750 crore. Interest payments continue to show high growth due to Government moving gradually to market related rates of borrowing and high interest payments falling due on small savings instruments maturing after a lock-in-period of 5 to 5.5 years. Expenditure compression of this magnitude was made possible by keeping budget support for the Central Plan at more or less the same level in nominal terms as in BE 1991-92. The Plan outlay was however higher by Rs. 5438 crore over BE 1991-92 due to higher estimates of internal resources and borrowings. Non-plan establishment expenditure continued to be tightly controlled. The decontrol of phosphatic and potassic fertilisers in August 1992 was a major measure to control the outgo on fertiliser subsidy. The increase in petroleum product prices announced in September 1992 is expected to generate a surplus in the OC (Open Cost) pool account and will, therefore, avoid pressure on the Government Budget.

As part of expenditure control strategy, and in order to regulate the level of borrowing from the Reserve Bank, fiscal deficit ceilings were prescribed for the quarters ending June, September and December 1992.

Throughout the 1980s, all important indicators of fiscal imbalance were on the rise. The trend in the various indicators of fiscal imbalance since 1975-76 is given in Table 23.1. The fiscal deficit of the Central Government was around 8 per cent of GDP from 1985-86 onwards, as compared with 6 per cent at the beginning of 1980s and 4 per cent in the mid 1970s. During the year 1990-91, the fiscal deficit rose to 8.4 per cent of GDP. The fiscal deficit can be decomposed into primary deficit and interest payments by the Government. The primary deficit was 2.5 per cent of GDP in 1975-76, increased to 4.3 per cent of GDP in 1980-81, and rose further to 5.5 per cent of GDP in 1985-86. It remained around 4.5 per cent of GDP till 1990-91.

TABLE 23.1: Central Government Deficit

(per cent of GDP at current market prices)

	Budget deficit	Revenue deficit	Monetised deficit	Fiscal deficit	Primary deficit
1	2	3	4	5	6
1975-76	0.5	1.1	0.0	4.1	2.5
1980-81	1.8	1.5	2.6	6.2	4.3
1981-82	0.9	0.2	2.0	5.4	3.4
1982-83	0.9	0.7	1.9	6.0	3.8
1983-84	0.7	1.2	1.9	6.3	4.0
1984-85	1.6	1.8	2.6	7.5	5.0
Average Sixth Plan	1.2	1.1	2.2	6.3	4.1
1985-86	2.0	2.2	2.4	8.3	5.5
1986-87	2.	2.7	2.4	9.0	5.8
1988-89	1.4	2.7	2.0	8.1	4.7
1989-90	2.3	2.6	3.0	7.8	3.9
Average Seventh Plan	2.1	2.6	2.3	8.2	4.8
1990-91	2.1	3.5	2.8	8.4	4.4
1991-92(R.E.)	1.2	2.8	0.9	6.2	1.7
1992-93(B.E.)	0.8	2.0	0.8	5.0	0.3

Note: GDP at current market prices is estimated to grow at 14 per cent in 1992-93.

The budget deficit is the difference between all receipts and expenditure, both revenue and capital. The revenue deficit denotes the difference between revenue receipts and revenue expenditure. The monetised deficit is the increase in net RBI credit to the Central Government, which is the sum of the net increase in the holdings of Treasury Bills of the RBI and its contribution to the market borrowing of the Government. The fiscal deficit is the excess of total expenditure including loans net of lending over revenue receipts, grants and non-debt capital receipts. The primary deficit is the fiscal deficit less interest payments.

23.2 Savings and Capital Formation

The Economic and Functional classification of the Central Government BUdget reveals a steady decline in the proportion of expenditure on capital formation (Table 23.2). Gross capital formation of the Central Government which was over 40 per cent of the total expenditure in the first half of the 1980s started declining from 1986-87 onwards. This trend continued in 1991-92. The growth of gross capital formation shows a similar pattern. It averaged 18.8 per cent per annum from 1982-83 to 1985-86 and 11.4 per cent from 1986-87 to 1989-90. It fell further to an average of only 4.1 per cent in 1990-91 to 1991-92 (RE) (Table 23.3).

TABLE 23.2 Economic Classification of Total Expenditure of Central Government

	1980-81	1984-85	1985-86	1986-87	1987-88	1988-89	1989-90	1990-91	1991-92 (R.E.)	1992-93 (B.E.)
				(Rs. crore)						
1. Consumption expenditure	5174	9428	11210	14665	16551	18763	20784	22359	24731	27130
(a) Defence	3571	6647	7962	10439	11875	13237	14298	15319	16256	17405
(b) Other Government administration	1603	2781	3248	4226	4676	5526	6486	7040	8475	9725
2. Transfer payments (Current)	6912	14938	18347	21243	25380	31399	37877	45134	52674	55905
(a) Interest payments	2253	5646	7090	8648	10702	13347	16525	19949	25682	29646
(b) Subsidies	1912	4484	5070	5542	5976	7859	10862	10728	10363	8910
(c) Grants to States & UTs (including local bodies)	1810	2863	3922	4205	4962	5831	5725	7664	9102	9239
(d) Others	937	1945	2265	2848	3740	4362	4765	6793	7527	8110
3. Gross capital formation out of budgetary resources	9012	17551	21477	24320	25770	28977	33012	35058	35746	3859
(a) Physical assets	1907	4123	4558	5905	5961	7056	8136	8602	9520	11787
(b) Financial assets	7105	13428	16919	18415	19809	21921	24876	26456	26226	26806
4. Others	1397	1962	2078	3795	2603	2263	3376	2422	1613	1250
5. Total expenditure	22495	43879	53112	64023	70304	81402	95049	104973	114764	122878
As per cent of total expenditure				(per cent)						
1. Consumption expenditure	23.0	21.5	21.1	22.9	23.5	23.0	21.9	21.3	21.5	22.1
(a) Defence	15.9	15.1	15.0	16.3	16.9	16.3	15.0	14.6	14.2	14.2
(b) Other Government administration	7.1	6.3	6.1	6.6	6.7	6.8	6.8	6.7	7.4	7.9
2. Transfer payments (Current)	30.7	34.0	34.5	33.2	36.1	38.6	39.8	43.0	45.9	45.5
(a) Interest payments	10.0	12.9	13.3	13.5	15.2	16.4	17.4	19.0	22.4	24.1
(b) Subsidies	8.5	10.2	9.5	8.7	8.5	9.7	11.4	10.2	9.0	7.3
(c) Grants to States & UTs (including local bodies)	8.0	6.5	7.4	6.6	7.1	7.2	6.0	7.3	7.9	7.5
(d) Others	4.2	4.4	4.3	4.4	5.3	5.4	5.0	6.5	6.6	6.6
3. Gross capital formation out of budgetary resources	40.1	40.0	40.4	38.0	36.7	35.6	34.7	33.4	31.1	31.4
(a) Physical assets	8.5	9.4	8.6	9.2	8.5	8.7	8.6	8.2	8.3	9.6
(b) Financial assets	31.6	30.6	31.9	28.8	28.2	26.9	26.2	25.2	22.9	21.8
4. Others	6.2	4.5	3.9	5.9	3.7	2.8	3.6	2.3	1.4	1.0

TABLE 23.3: Capital Formation by the Central Government and its Financing

	1980-81	1984-85	1985-86	1986-87	1987-88	1988-89	1989-90	1990-91	1991-92 (R.E.)	1992-93 (B.E.)
1	2	3	4	5	6	7	8	9	10	11
				(Rs. crore)						
I. Gross capital formation out of budgetary resources of the Central Government	9012	17551	21477	24320	25770	28977	33012	35058	35746	38593
(i) Gross capital formation by the Central Government	1907	4123	4558	5905	5961	7056	81136	8602	9520	11787
(ii) Financial assistance for capital formation in the rest of the economy	7105	13428	16919	18415	19809	21921	24876	26456	26226	26806
II. Gross savings of the Central Government	3	-963	-1441	-2852	-4294	-5722	-5142	-10502	-8288	-4039
III. Gap (I-II)	9009	18514	22918	27172	30064	34699	38154	45560	44034	42632
Financed by										
a. Draft on other sectors of the domestic economy	7339	16657	21068	24794	26299	31639	34831	41794	39083	37703
(i) Domestic capital receipts	4762	12912	16131	16533	20483	25997	24239	30447	32051	32314
(ii) Budgetary deficit	2577	3745	4937	8261	5816	5642	10592	11347	7032	5389
b. Draft on foreign savings	1670	1857	1850	2378	3765	3060	3323	3766	4951	4929

Contd.

TABLE 23.3 *Concld.*

1	2	3	4	5	6	7	8	9	10	11
AS per cent of GDP				(per cent)						
I. Gross capital formation out of budgetary resources of the Central Government	6.6	7.6	8.2	8.3	7.7	7.3	7.3	6.6	5.9	5.6
(i) Gross capital formation by the Central Government	1.4	1.8	1.7	2.0	1.8	1.8	1.8	1.6	1.6	1.7
(ii) Financial assistance for capital formation in the rest of the economy	5.2	5.8	6.5	6.3	5.9	5.5	5.5	5.0	4.3	3.9
II. Gross savings of the Central Government	0.0	-0.4	-0.5	-1.0	-1.3	-1.4	-1.1	-2.0	-1.4	-0.6
III. Gap (I-II)	6.6	8.0	8.7	9.3	9.0	8.7	8.4	8.6	7.2	6.1
Financed by										
a. Draft on other sectors of the domestic economy	5.4	7.2	8.0	8.5	7.9	8.0	7.7	7.9	6.4	5.4
(i) Domestic capital receipts	3.5	5.6	6.2	5.6	6.1	6.6	5.3	5.7	5.3	4.7
(ii) Budgetary deficit	1.9	1.6	1.9	2.8	1.7	1.4	2.3	2.1	1.2	0.8
b. Draft on foreign savings	1.2	0.8	0.7	0.8	1.1	0.8	0.7	0.7	0.8	0.7
I. Increase in gross capital formation out of budgetary resources of the Central Government	24.7	19.4	22.4	13.2	6.0	12.4	13.9	6.2	2.0	8.0

Notes: (i) Gross capital formation in this table includes loans given for capital formation on a gross basis. Consequently, domestic capital receipts includes loan repayments to the Central Government.

(ii) Because of revisions in the series of GDP, the ratios given here may differ from those given in the earlier issues of Economic Survey.

23.3 Government Debt

Increasing resort to borrowings over the years has led to a continuous growth in the total outstanding debt. Internal liabilities registered a sharp increase in the 1980s, from 35.6 per cent of GDP in 1980-81 to 53.3 per cent in 1990-91. This was due to a combination of revenue deficits and poor returns on assets financed by capital receipts, a summary measure of which is the fiscal deficit. Liabilities did decline marginally, however, to 52.1 per cent in 1991-92 (RE) (Table 23.4). Other liabilities (small savings, provident funds etc.) have risen much more than market borrowings. Their share in total internal liabilities increased from 36.3 per cent in 1980-81 to 46.5 per cent in 1991-92 (RE).

External liabilities are shown in the budget converted at the exchange rate prevailing in March of the year in which they are incurred. The ratio of these liabilities to GDP has come down from 8.3 per cent in 1980-81 to 5.8 per cent in 1991-92 (RE). However, it is more appropriate to convert them at current end-of the year exchange rates, to reflect the burden of the debt fully. When this is done, external liabilities of the Central Government at the end of 1990-91 and to 18 per cent at the end of 1991-92 (RE).

The increasing fiscal deficits and consequent borrowings from the domestic private sector have also put upward pressure on interest rates. This is reflected in the increasing trend in average rates. The average rate of interest on internal liabilities rose from 7.2 per cent in 1985-86 to 8.2 per cent in 1990-91 (Table 23.5), and further to 8.7 per cent in 1991-92 (RE), because of the continued replacement of old lower-interest debt by new higher-interest debt. The rate of interest on external liabilities similarly increased from 3.2 per cent in 1985-86 to 8.4 per cent in 1991-92 (RE). This was due to the reduction in the proportion of soft loans provided by multilateral lending institutions (IDA etc.), and the hardening of international interest rates in the 1980s.

The growth in internal and external liabilities and the increasing rate of interest have resulted in a mounting burden of interest payments. While gross interest payments as a ratio of total expenditure more than doubled between 1980-81 and 1991-92 (RE), from 11.66 per cent to 23.7 per cent, interest payments net of interest received increased by nearly four times 3.6 per cent to 13.9 per cent. The fiscal correction measures introduced in the 1991-92 budgets marginally reduced the total (internal and external) liabilities-to-GDP ratio from 59.3 per cent in 1990-91 to 57.9 per cent in 1991-92. However, this has not helped in reducing the net interest liability. It would take a few years before the reduced level of borrowings has a perceptible impact on the heavy interest burden of the Government. It is imperative that the Government continue the policy of fiscal correction in the coming years.

At the beginning of 1980s, book value of assets and liabilities of the Central Government were both at 44 per cent of GDP (Table 23.4). Since then, there has been a growing divergence between the two, with liabilities overtaking assets. Liabilities exceeded assets by 15.2 per cent of GDP in 1991-92.

23.4 Finances of States and Union Territories, 1991-92

There was a sharp deterioration in the finances of the States and Union Territories in 1991-92 with the combined budgetary deficit touching Rs. 1896 crore

TABLE 23.4: Outstanding Liabilities of the Central Government

	1980-81	1985-86	1986-87	1987-88	1988-89	1989-90	1990-91	1991-92 (RE)	1992-93 (BE)
1	2	3	4	5	6	7	8	9	10
				(Rs. crore)					
1. Internal liabilities	48451	119331	146247	172338	204025	239849	283194	317680	356291
(a) Internal debt	30864	71039	86312	98646	114498	133193	154004	170104	188536
(a) Marketing borrowing	15676	35352	40880	46743	55161	62565	70565	78066	83066
(b) Others	15188	35687	45432	51903	59337	70628	83439	92038	105470
(b) Other internal liabilities	17587	48292	59935	73692	89527	106656	129190	147576	167755
2. External debt (outstanding)*	11298	18153	20299	23223	25476	28343	31525	35501	39565
3. Total outstanding liabilities (1+2)	59749	127484	166546	195561	229771	268192	314719	353181	395856
4. Amount due from Pakistan on account of share of pre-partition debt	300	300	300	300	300	300	300	300	300
5. Net liabilities (3-4)	59449	137184	166246	195261	229471	267892	314419	352881	395556
6. Total assets	58999	123966	143776	162810	184303	209623	236970	260186	288979
7. Excess of liabilities over assets (5-6)	450	13218	22470	32451	45168	58269	77449	92695	106577
As per cent of GDP at current prices				(Per cent)					
1. Internal liabilities	35.6	45.5	49.9	51.7	51.4	52.8	53.3	52.1	51.3
(a) Internal debt	22.7	27.1	29.5	29.6	28.9	29.3	29.0	27.9	27.1
(b) Other internal liabilities	12.9	18.4	20.5	22.1	22.6	23.5	24.3	24.2	24.1

Contd.

TABLE 23.4 *Concld.*

1	2	3	4	5	6	7	8	9	10
2. External debt (outstanding)*	8.3	6.9	6.9	7.0	6.5	6.2	5.9	5.8	5.7
3. Total outstanding liabilities (1+2)	43.9	52.4	56.9	58.7	57.9	59.1	59.3	57.9	57.0
6, Total assets	43.4	47.3	49.1	48.9	46.5	46.2	44.6	42.7	41.6
7. Excess of liabilities over assets (5-6)	0.3	5.0	7.7	9.7	11.4	12.8	14.6	15.2	15.3
Memorandum items									
External Debt (Rs. crore)	13479	26638	32312	36578	468388	54100	66314	109675	112022
(Converted at year-end exchange rates) @ (as per cent of GDP)	9.9	10.2	11.0	11.0	11.8	11.9	12.5	18.0	16.1

* External debt figures represent borrowings by Central Government from external resources and are based upon historical rates of exchange.

@ End-March rates. For 1980-81, the rates prevailing at the end of March, 1981; for 1985-86, the rates prevailing at the end of March, 1986 and so on. However, for 1992-93 the information pertains to end-September 1992.

Note: GDP (at current prices) for 1992-93 is estimated to grow by 14 per cent.

as compared with only Rs. 139 crore in 1990-91. However, the gap between current revenue and total outlay (including Public Sector Units) declined to 3.8 per cent of GDP in 1991-92 (RE) from 4.1 per cent in 1990-91. The current revenue of the States and Union Territories increased by 23 per cent from Rs. 60381 crore to Rs. 74379 crore in 1991-92 (RE). The increase was almost entirely due to an increase in grants from the Centre, and State's share of income-tax and Union excise duties, collected by the Centre. There was a decline in receipts from land revenue by 6.8 per cent. The dissavings of State Public Undertakings amounted to Rs. 1699 crore in 1991-92 (RE), almost the same as in 1990-91. While non-development expenditure increased by 21.5 per cent in 1991-92, developmental expenditure increased by only 17.3 per cent. The fiscal deficit of the State Governments and Union Territories came down from 3.5 per cent of GDP in 1990-91 to 3.3 per cent as per the revised estimates of 1991-92.

23.5 Budgetary Transactions of Centre, States and Union Territories, 1991-92

The combined budgetary transactions of the Centre and the State Governments in 1991-92 (RE) mark a departure from the pattern of deteriorating fiscal imbalance. As a proportion of GDP the gap between total outlay and current revenue came down from 12.4 per cent in 1990-91 to 10.9 per cent in 1991-92 (RE) (Table 23.6). This was due both to a slower growth of total expenditures and increased revenues. Within these expenditure levels there was also a relative shift from non-development to development expenditure. The current revenue-GDP ratio increased from 20.8 per cent in 1990-91 to 21.7 per cent in 1991-92 (RE). Both direct and indirect taxes increased as a proportion of GDP.

The dependence on deficit financing which had increased dramatically over the years showed a decline in 1991-92. The budget deficit in 1991-92 accounted for 13 per cent of the gap between current revenue and total outlay against over 17 per cent in 1990-91 and 19 per cent in 1989-90.

The rising gap between total expenditure and current revenues over the past decade set in motion a vicious cycle of increased borrowings, higher debt and increased interest payments. Interest payments, as a percentage of total expenditure of the Centre and the States increased from 7.6 per cent in 1984-85 to nearly 16 per cent in 1991-92 (RE). The burden of interest payments comes out more clearly when seen in relation to non-developmental expenditure. As a proportion of non-developmental expenditure, interest payments amounted to over 39 per cent in 1991-92 (RE). This is the major factor which has led to an increase in the proportion of non-developmental expenditure in total expenditure to nearly 41 per cent in 1991-92 (RE) (Table 23.6). In principle, a reduction of debt through either a primary surplus or from the proceeds of asset sales would reduce long-term debt liabilities. The effectiveness of the latter can be increased by retiring high-interest debt or disinvestment of the equity of selected PSUs which were making losses.

23.6 Central Government Fiscal and Budgetary Developments, 1992-93

The Budget of 1991-92 succeeded in reversing the increasing trend in fiscal deficit. The Budget of 1992-93 continued the process by putting the fiscal deficit on a firm downtrend. The objective of reducing the deficit from 6.2 per cent to

TABLE 23.5: Interest on Outstanding Liabilities of Central Government

	1980-81	1985-86	1986-87	1987-88	1988-89	1989-90	1990-91	1991-92 (R.E.)	1992-93 (B.E.)
1	2	3	4	5	6	7	8	9	10
				(Rs. crore)					
1. Interest on internal liabilities	2373	6974	8480	10275	13036	16241	19637	24615	29084
a) Internal debt	1369	3919	4763	5514	6913	8273	9814	11191	13264
i) Market borrowings	808	2465	3098	3681	4506	5368	6366	7215	8250
ii) Others	561	1454	1665	1833	2407	2905	3448	3976	5014
b) Other internal liabilities	1004	3055	3717	4761	61223	7968	98223	13424	15820
2. Interest on external debt	231	538	766	977	1242	1494	1834	2635	2916
3. Gross interest payments	2604	7512	9246	11252	14278	17735	21471	27250	32000
4. Net interest payments	809	2917	3893	5497	7297	9269	12687	15953	18536
Average rate of interest				(per cent)					
1. Internal liabilities	N.A.	7.2	7.1	7.0	7.6	8.0	8.2	8.7	9.2
(a) Internal debt	N.A.	6.7	6.7	6.4	7.0	7.2	7.4	7.3	7.8
(i) Market borrowings	N.A.	8.1	8.8	9.0	9.6	9.7	10.2	10.2	10.6
(ii) Others	N.A.	5.22	4.7	4.0	4.6	4.9	4.9	4.8	5.4
(b) Other internal liabilities	N.A.	8.0	7.7	7.9	8.3	8.9	9.2	10.4	10.7
2. External debt	N.A.	3.2	4.2	4.8	5.3	5.8	6.5	8.4	8.2
3. Total liabilities	N.A.	6.6	6.7	6.8	7.3	7.7	8.0	8.7	9.1

Note: The interest liabilities indicated above are on cash basis and not on accrual basis.

TABLE 23.6: Budgetary Transactions of the Central and State Governments and Union Territories (Including extra-budgetary resources of public sector undertakings for financing their Plans)

	1980-81	1985-86	1986-87	1987-88	1988-89	1989-90	1990-91	1991-92 (BE)	1991-92 (RE)	1992-93 (BE)
1	2	3	4	5	6	7	8	9	10	11
					(Rs. crore)					
I. Total outlay	36845	83961	100790	112169	130048	158107	176548	198158	198922	220275
(a) Developmental	24426	53397	63778	68801	79548	98501	105922	116724	117391	129161
(b) Non-developmental	12419	30564	37012	43368	50500	59606	70626	81434	81531	91114
II. Current revenue	24563	56773	64823	73485	85714	103115	110607	132411	132452	150289
(a) Tax revenue	19844	43267	49540	56976	66925	77693	87723	102896	102475	115331
(i) Direct taxes	3268	6252	6890	7483	9757	11165	12259	15338	16233	18066
(ii) Indirect taxes	16576	37015	42650	49493	57168	66528	75464	87558	86242	97265
(b) Non-tax revenue	4719	13506	15283	16509	18789	25422	22884	29515	29977	34958
III. GAP (I-II)	12282	27188	35967	38684	44334	54992	65941	65747	66470	69986
Financed by:										
(i) Domestic capital receipts	7161	21899	24439	29415	36172	40812	50192	50424	51504	57528
(ii) Net external assistance	1670	1850	2378	3765	3060	3567	4263	4377	6038	5375
(iii) Budgetary deficit	3451	3439	9150	5504	5102	10613	11486	10946	8928	7083
As per cent of GDP						(per cent)				
I. Total outlay	27.1	32.0	34.4	33.7	32.8	34.8	33.3	32.5	32.6	31.7
(a) Developmental	18.0	20.4	21.8	20.6	20.1	21.7	20.0	19.2	19.3	18.6
(b) Non-developmental	9.1	11.7	12.6	13.0	12.7	13.1	13.3	13.4	13.4	13.1

Contd.

TABLE 23.6 *Concld*

1	2	3	4	5	6	7	8	9	10	11
II. Current revenue	18.1	21.6	22.1	22.1	21.6	22.7	20.8	21.7	21.7	21.6
(a) Tax revenue	14.6	16.5	16.9	17.1	16.9	17.1	16.5	16.9	16.8	16.6
(i) Direct taxes	2.4	2.4	2.4	2.2	2.5	2.5	2.3	2.5	2.7	2.6
(ii) Indirect taxes	12.2	14.1	14.6	14.9	14.4	14.7	14.2	14.4	14.1	14.0
(b) Non-tax revenue	3.5	5.2	5.2	5.0	4.7	5.6	4.3	4.8	4.9	5.0
III. GAP (I-II)	9.0	10.4	12.3	11.6	11.2	12.1	12.4	10.8	10.9	10.1
Financed by:										
(i) Domestic capital receipts	5.3	8.4	8.3	8.8	9.1	9.0	9.5	8.3	8.5	8.3
(ii) Net external assistance	1.2	0.7	0.8	1.1	0.8	0.8	0.8	0.7	1.0	0.8
(iii) Budgetary deficit	2.5	1.3	3.1	1.7	1.3	2.3	2.2	1.8	1.5	1.0

5 per cent of GDP was designed to bring inflation pressured under control and bring down the current account deficit to a sustainable level. In addition to expenditure controls the Budget initiated the process of comprehensive tax reform designed to remove distortions and increase the income elasticity of revenue. Over a medium-term horizon, this would put revenue on a rising path as well as stimulate growth.

The growth of non-plan expenditure as per the budget estimates is estimated to be 5.5 per cent in 1992-93. If interest payments are excluded, this represents a marginal reduction from the previous year. An important element of expenditure are various subsidies, such as on fertilisers, which had risen over the years. On receipt of the Report of the Parliamentary Committee, prices of urea were reduced by 10 per cent, and the prices, distribution and movement of phosphatic and potassic fertilisers decontrolled. The Retention Price Scheme related to low analysis nitrogenous fertilisers, which were decontrolled in July 1991, was reintroduced. Another important decision was to increase the ex-storage point prices of all petroleum products except for kerosene for domestic use which is used by the weaker and more vulnerable sections of the society. This has reduced the increasing deficits of Oil Industry.

The budgetary deficit is sought to be reduced from Rs. 7032 crore in 1991-92 (RE) to Rs. 5389 crore in 1992-93, and the fiscal deficit from Rs. 37792 crore (RE) to Rs. 34408 crore (BE). During the last few weeks, the level of deficit has been lower than the level prevailing during the corresponding weeks of the last two years. The fiscal deficit has been kept within target. The fiscal deficit targeted for the quarter ending June 1992 was Rs. 12000 crore. Against this, the actual deficit was Rs. 12163 crore. The fiscal deficit at the end of September 1992 at Rs. 14976 crore was substantially lower than the target of Rs. 18500 crore. Similarly, the deficit at the end of December was Rs. 22692 crore, close to the target of Rs. 25300 crore.

Aggregate resources of the Centre (including PSUs) in 1992-93 are estimated at Rs. 145882 crore, 11.6 per cent higher than in 1991-92 (RE). Aggregate disbursements are estimated at Rs. 151271 crore, 9.8 per cent higher than in 1991-92 (RE). The containment of disbursements through a series of policy measures is expected to lower the budgetary and fiscal deficits to Rs. 7032 crore and Rs. 37792 crore respectively. A noteworthy feature of the Budget is the higher rate of growth of developmental expenditure at 9.6 per cent as compared with 4.7 per cent in 1991-92 (RE). The overall gap in the resources of the Centre and its PSUs is estimated at Rs. 58061 crore. While tax revenue is estimated to grow by 12.8 per cent, non-tax revenue is estimated to grow by 19.8 per cent.

The Central Plan Outlay for 1992-93 (BE) was stepped up by 20.5 per cent, to Rs. 48407 crore, over 1991-92 (RE). The budgetary support for the Central Plan Outlay has been reduced to 38.2 per cent from 44 per cent in 1991-92 (RE). Over the years, there has been a gradual reduction in the budgetary support. This is in keeping with the policy of the Government to bring about greater accountability and self-reliance in the working PSUs, so that funds are raised from the market as far as possible. In terms of sectoral allocations, the emphasis remains on the development of infrastructure services for industry, agriculture and energy sectors. The outlay on transport and on communications was stepped up by 23.1 per cent and 34.7 per cent respectively, in 1992-93 (RE).

Additional Resource Mobilisation

The net effect of the various fiscal measures in the 1992-93 Budget was an expected additional revenue of Rs. 983 crore. Whilst direct taxes were to raise an additional Rs. 795 crore, a loss of Rs. 2023 crore on customs was to be offset by a gain of Rs. 2211 crore on excise. There was likely to be a net gain of Rs. 1500 crore to the States, and a loss to the Centre of Rs. 517 crore (Table 23.7). The Railway Budget for 1992-93 increased passenger fares and freight rates and rationalised parcel rates. These measures were estimated to yield an additional revenue of Rs. 1366 crore. The total additional revenue to the Centre through a revision in tax rates and in fares and freights was thus estimated at Rs. 2349 crore in 1992-93, of which it would retain Rs. 849 crore.

Savings and Capital Formation

The decline trend in the proportion of expenditure going to capital formation is likely to be halted, and the decline in the rate of growth of gross capital formation to the reversed, during the current year. Gross capital formation is expected to grow by 8 per cent this year (Table 23.3). Investment in physical assets is estimated to increase to 9.6 per cent of the total expenditure. Consumption expenditure is estimated to be 22.1 per cent of total in 1992-93, only 0.6 per cent more than in 1991-92 (RE). The ratio of defence expenditure to total expenditure will remain unchanged at 14.2 per cent (Table 23.2). Gross dissavings are expected are expected to be reduced by Rs. 4249 crore to Rs. 4039 crore (Table 23.3).

TABLE 23.7: Additional Resource Mobilisation in the Central and Railway Budgets for 1992-93

(*Rs. crore*)

1	Centre's share 2	States' share 3	Total 4
I. Taxes	—517	1500	983
(a) Direct taxes	360	435	795
(i) Corporation tax	325		325
(ii) Income tax	135	435	570
(iii) Expenditure tax	—100		—100
(b) Indirect taxes	—877	1065	188
(i) Custom duties	—2023		—2023
(ii) Excise duties	1146	1065	2211
II. Posts & Telecommunications tariffs, Railway fares and freight rates	1366		1366
(a) Railways	1366		1366
(b) Post & Telecommunications	0		0
III. Total (I+II)	849	1500	2349

Government Debt

The decline in the ratio of internal liabilities to GDP is likely to continue in 1992-93, with this ratio being reduced to 51.5 per cent. This is primarily due to a reduction in the share of other liabilities to 47.1 per cent of total internal liabilities. The gap between book value of liabilities and assets will, therefore, increase marginally to 15.3 per cent of book value of liabilities and assets will, therefore, increase marginally to 15.3 per cent of GDP from 15.2 per cent. The average rate of interest on internal liabilities is, however, expected to increase to 9.2 per cent from 8.7 per cent in the previous year.

23.7 Tax Structure Reforms

The Government set up a Tax Reforms Committee* under the Chairmanship of Dr. Raja J. Chelliah in August 1991 to recommend a comprehensive reform of both the direct and indirect tax system. The Committee submitted its Interim Report in February 1992 in which it stressed the importance of lower rates of taxation, a narrower spread between the entry rate and the maximum marginal rate, and the fewest special exemptions and deductions. In the field of indirect taxes, the Committee recommended a reduction in the general level of tariffs and in the dispersion of tariff rates and the abolition of end-use exemptions and concessions. The basic philosophy underlying these recommendations, with which the Government is in consonance, is to cut through the welter of detailed changes which have been made over the past 40 years to serve narrow objectives, and restore the tax system to its primary function of generating revenues in an efficient and equitable manner. Some of the recommendations of the Committee were embodied in the Budget proposals, while others are under the Government's consideration.

Direct Taxes

On the basis of international experience, the Chelliah Committee recommended that moderate taxes combined with fewer deductions and exemptions and effective enforcement would encourage voluntary tax compliance and increase revenue. Accordingly, personal income tax was restructured, with lower taxes, fewer slabs and a higher exemption limit. As the saving-linked tax exemptions available under Sections 80CCA and 80CCB of the Income-Tax Act conferred larger tax benefits on higher income groups, these were merged with Section 88 which provides for a tax rebate on savings. Similarly, deduction available under Section 80L was reduced. Deductions available in respect of income from housing were rationalised by clubbing deductions for repairs and collection charges and disallowing setting off of losses from houses property against other income.

There had been a long standing demand to end the double taxation of partnership firms. The Budget revamped the system of taxation of firms by eliminating the distinction between registered and unregistered firms and prescribed a flat rate of tax of 40 per cent on all partnerships. Reforms in the area of corporate taxes were postponed till the final recommendations of the Chelliah Committee were received and examined. To widen the tax base, a scheme of presumptive taxation was introduced for small traders and retailers on an optional basis. For a long time, it had been felt that the existing provisions for clubbing of minors' income from gifts with their parents' were not effective in checking tax avoidance. To plug the possible loopholes and leakage of revenue,

* *See also* Section 23.11 in this chapter.

minors' income except their professional income was clubbed with that of their parents. The expenditure tax on airconditioned restaurants was abolished, and the room charge limit for purpose of its levy was raised from Rs. 400 to Rs. 1200.

Changes in Personal Income Tax in 1992-93

* Exemption limit of personal income tax raised from Rs. 22000 to Rs. 28000.
* Income tax slabs reduced from four to three: new tax rates — 20 per cent up to Rs. 50000, 30 per cent up to Rs. 1 lakh and 40 per cent above Rs. 1 Lakh. Surcharge on income tax remains on last slab.
* Sections 80CCA and 80CCB providing for 100 per cent deduction from taxable income on netting principle in respect of deposit under National Saving Scheme, Equity Linked Saving Schemes and Annuity Schemes of LIC abolished.
* Deduction under Section 80L in respect of income from dividends; interest on securities, deposits, debentures; and units of the Unit Trust of India reduced from Rs. 13000 to Rs. 7000.
* Maximum limit of 20 per cent tax rebate under Section 88 in respect of specified savings increased from Rs. 10000 to Rs. 12000. Section 88 to include schemes covered earlier 80CCA and 80CCB.
* Scope of Section 88 widened to include contributions to Pension Funds set up by the National Housing Bank and Mutual Funds.
* Higher standard deduction of Rs. 15000 for women employees, 10 per cent additional tax rebate for senior citizens and enhanced deduction of Rs. 12000 for handicapped dependents.
* Deduction for medical insurance for self-employed persons raised from Rs. 3000 to Rs. 6000.
* Presumptive income tax of Rs. 1400 for shopkeepers and retail traders with an annual turnover of Rs. 5 lakh and below.
* Income of minors' other than income from profession to be clubbed with that of parents.

The taxation of capital gains was reformed in several directions. Taxation of capital gains was completely restructured, so that only capital gains net of price increases would be taxed. Long-term capital gains will now be taxed at flat rates after allowing the cost of assets to be adjusted for inflation. The standard deductions in computing taxable capital gains and also other exemptions available under sections 53 and 54E were withdrawn. This new scheme will favour long-term capital gains. In order to stimulate investment on productive assets, wealth tax on these assets were abolished. Specified assets like farmhouses, residential houses, motor cars, jewellery, bullion, yatch, aircrafts and boats would, however, continue to be subject to wealth tax. To prevent tax avoidance the wealth of a minor was to be clubbed with that of his or her parents. The cooperative banking sector was exempted from the levy of the interest tax.

As part of the reform of the financial system, an announcement was made that companies with good track records would be permitted to issue bonds or equity in foreign exchange to investors abroad in order to tap investible funds available in international market. These issues would be subject to the same tax treatment as is available to offshore mutual funds. Simultaneously, it was proposed to allow reputable foreign investors to invest in the Indian stock market subject to equity share limits, reporting requirements and mechanisms to ensure that this does not result in the loss of management control. Under the scheme, portfolio investments in primary or secondary markets will be subject to equity share limits, reporting requirements and mechanisms to ensure that this does not result in the loss of management control. Under the scheme, portfolio investments in primary or secondary markets will be subject to a ceiling of 24 per cent of issued share capital for the total holdings of all registered Foreign Institutional Investors (FII), in any one company. The holding of a single FII in any company would also be subject to a ceiling of 5 per cent of total issued capital.

Changes in Capital Gains and Wealth Tax in 1992-93

* Long term capital gains to be taxed at flat rates of 20 per cent for individuals and HUFs, 30 per cent for firms and 40 per cent for companies.
* Capital gains to be adjusted for inflation. Cost inflation Index with 1981-82 = 100 notified.
* Exemption up to Rs. 2 lakh under Section 53 on transfer of residential property and exemption under Section 54E on investment of capital gains in specified modes withdrawn.
* Public and private mutual funds to granted same tax treatment.
* Wealth tax abolished on shares, securities, bonds, bank deposits etc.
* Wealth tax to be levied on non-productive assets such as farmhouse, urban land, jewellery, bullion, cash, motor cars, planes, boats etc.
* Wealth tax exemption limit raised from Rs. 5 lakh to Rs. 15 lakh. Wealth tax to be levied at 1 per cent.

Indirect Taxes

The measures proposed in the area of indirect taxes were a first step towards promoting competitiveness in the Indian industry. This requires a reduction in tariffs to the levels comparable with those in similar developing countries, a reduction in the dispersion of tariff rates and a drastic pruning of end-use exemptions. Similarly, the excise duty structure has to be progressively converted from a MODVAT to a VAT. This will allow simplification in administration through a reduction in rates and a switch to accounting methods of enforcing tax compliance.

23.8 **Import Duties**

On the basis of the recommendations of the Chelliah Committee the Budged lowered the peak tariff level of import duties to 110 per cent with the exception of passenger baggage and alcoholic beverages. to reduce the cost of new investment, the duty on project imports was lowered from 80 per cent to 55 per cent and in the case of electronic industry to 50 per cent. A deeper reduction to 30 per cent was proposed for capital goods for projects of coal mining and crude petroleum refining. In the case of power projects a uniform duty of 30 per cent was fixed.

The Budget announced reductions in import duty on specified pesticides, pesticide intermediates and full exemption on oilseeds and seeds of vegetables, flowers and ornamental plants, cuttings or saplings of flower plants, seeds of fruit plants and pulses for the purposes of sowing and planting. As a measure of relief to the asbestos cement industry which serves the housing, water supply irrigation sectors, the Budget reduced the import duty on asbestos fibres from 90 per cent to 70 per cent. The import duty incidence on rags and synthetic waste was equalised at 110 per cent.

Changes in Import Duties in 1992-93

* Peak tariff level lowered to 110 per cent.
* Duty rate on project imports and general machinery reduced to 55 per cent, and in the case of electronic industry to 50 per cent.
* Uniform import duty rate of 30 per cent for capital goods for coal mining, petroleum refining and power projects.
* Import duty on other capital goods reduced by 10 percentage points.
* Extension of concessional import duty of 80 per cent to specified electronic components.
* Import duty on 15 specified pesticides reduced from 110 per cent to 75 per cent and on two pesticide intermediates from 120 per cent to 65 per cent.
* Full exemption from duty for oilseeds, seeds of vegetables, flowers, ornamental plants for the purpose of sowing and planting.
* Full exemption for glazed newsprint, specified formulation of certain life-saving drugs and medicines.
* Import duty on propylene reduced from 120 per cent to 80 per cent, on butadiene from 55 per cent to 40 per cent, on benzene from 40 per cent to 25 per cent and a uniform duty of 40 per cent of ethyl benzene and styrene.
* Reduction in import duty on asbestos fibre, colour negatives of cinematographic films and raw silk.
* Returning Indians allowed to import gold up to 5 kg. at a duty of Rs. 220 per 10 grams (approximately 3 per cent).
* Import duty on computers and computer peripherals raised to 110 per cent.

23.9 **Excise Duties**

In the area of excise duties, full exemption was provided for bricks and tiles with a minimum content of 25 per cent of red mud, light-weight concrete building blocks, doors and windows made of plastic, iron and steel. So also complete exemption was given to panel doors. Besides concessional duty rates were announced on prefabricated buildings.

A number of measures were directed towards simplification and additional revenue generation. The multiplicity of slabs for cotton yarn was reduced to five and for cellulosic spun yarn to three. The number of excise duty slabs on two wheelers was reduced from five to two, with the first slab of 15 per cent up to an engine capacity of 75cc and 25 per cent on those exceeding 75cc. The Budget proposed a switchover from specific rates to ad valorem rates wherever feasible. In the case of metals namely, copper, lead, zinc and its products, iron forgings and certain steel products a uniform ad valorem levy of 10 per cent was fixed in place of existing specific rates of duty.

To augment revenue, excise duties were raised on cigarettes, cocoa, cocoa preparations, certain plastic resins, watches, wires and cables, tyres, tubes and flaps, cement, paints, organic surface active agents, ingots and certain rolled products like bars, rods of ferrous metals other than stainless steel etc. Excise duties were also raised on viscose fibre, viscose filament yarn and acrylic fibre. The duty on light commercial products which were attracting a 10 per cent rate of duty, to 15 per cent. This increase did not apply to petroleum products, motor cars and TVs.

Changes in Excise Duties in 1992-93

* Switchover from specific rates a uniform 10 per cent ad valorem duty on copper, lead, zinc, iron and products thereof.
* Number of rates for cotton yarn reduced to five slabs.
* Full exemption from excise duty on bricks and tiles with a minimum content of 25 per cent of red mud; lightweight concrete building blocks; doors and windows made of plastic; iron and steel; and jute yard in hanks and jute products manufactured in rural areas by registered cooperative societies.
* Full exemption from excise duty on insulated thermoware, vacuum flasks, specified soya products and candles for water filters.
* Full exemption of duty on specified pesticide intermediates.
* Excise duty on nylon filament yarn and polyester filament yarn reduced.
* Special excise duty raised from 10 per cent to 15 per cent on all goods except motor cars, TVs and petroleum products.
* Excise duties increased on cigarettes, cement, steel, tyres, two wheelers, viscose fibre, acrylic fibre, filament yarn, cocoa, plastic resins, paints and watches.
* Increase in excise duty on pig iron, iron forgings, steel ingots.

A number of suggestions contained in the recommendations were implemented in the 1992 Budget. Some other changes remained to be implemented. These relate to ad valorum rates of duties in place of specific duties for certain products: such as sugar, vegetable products, refined oils, pan masala, inorganic chemicals, tyres and tubes, paper and paper products, air conditioners, compressors, refrigerators etc. The Committee submitted its final report in two parts, Part I in August 1992 and Part-II in January 1993. Part I of the Report contains recommendations for comprehensive reforms in the areas of corporate tax, tax administration and enforcement machinery. The Committee has suggested measures to tackle problems relating to auditing, appeal procedures, search and seizures. Part II gives Committee's final recommendations regarding the restructuring and rationalisation of import duties for specific groups of industries and their phasing. The final Report also deals with the restructuring of excise duties and review of exemption notifications in the import tariffs.

23.10 **Post-Budget Developments in 1992-93**

* Concessional tax regime for Foreign Institutional Investors such as Pen-

sion Funds, Mutual Funds, Investment Trusts etc. investing in the capital market.

* Duty exemption for gold imported under the scheme for export of gold jewellery by domestic units and the MMTC.
* Import duty exemption for raw materials and components for the goods to be supplied to offshore oil exploration.
* Concessional customs duty of 35 per cent for specified drug intermediates.
* Reduction by 10 per cent in customs duty on components for fuel efficient vehicles.
* Exemption from customs duty for import of wood pulp, used in manufacture of newsprint.
* Value limit of duty-free import of tags, labels, printed bags and stickers by exporters raised from Rs. 1000 to Rs. 10,000 in each case.
* Full import duty exemption for goods for renovation and modernisation of fertiliser plants.
* Exemption from basic duty in excess of 50 per cent and the whole of auxiliary and additional duties for import air conditioned cars and coaches for State Tourism Corporations, classified hotels and travel agencies.
* Duty free allowance under baggage rules raised from 2400 to Rs. 3000.
* Customs duty reduced from 255 per cent to 150 per cent on 35 articles on personal or household effects such as FAX machine, video camera, cordless and cellular telephone, personal computer, airconditioner, refrigerator, washing machine, microover, TV, VCR, music system etc.
* Total value of articles imported as baggage not to exceed Rs. 1.5 lakh.
* Silver import up to 100 kg per passenger at a concessional rate of Rs. 500 per kg. allowed.
* Excise duty on colour TVs, VCRs, VCPs, motor vehicles and chassis reduced.

23.11 Chelliah Committee on Tax Reforms

Tax Reforms Committee's Recommendations on Customs and Excise

* Tariffs on finished goods should be higher than on basic raw materials and those on components and machinery should be in between.
* Agricultural imports should be subject to some import duty.
* The import duty structure for 1997-98 (excluding CVD) should be a zero rate for essential agricultural goods; 10 per cent for other agricultural goods (e.g. oilseeds); 15 per cent for tin, pig iron, aluminium, and nickel; 20 per cent for medical equipment, organic and inorganic chemicals, lead, zinc, and machinery; 25 per cent for polymers, textiles, fibres and yarns; 30 per cent for articles of nonferrous metals and of iron & steel; and 50 per cent for non-essential agricultural goods such as almonds and cashewnuts.
* Central excise duties be restructured in the light of the recommendations made in the Interim Report; three-rate MODVAT regime at the manufacturing level at 10, 15 and 20 per cent and selective excise on non-essential commodities at 30, 40 and 50 per cent.
* Examination of the feasibility of collection of excise duty on cigarettes

through banderoles.

* Extension of MODVAT to textiles and petroleum products.
* Excise duty on selected products at present exempted from excise.
* Corporate tax rate for domestic companies be lowered to 45 per cent in 1993-94 from the present level of 51.75 per cent by abolition of surcharge and further to 40 per cent in 1994-95.
* Tax rates for foreign companies be lowered and the differential between the rates on domestic and foreign companies should be around 7.5 percentage points. Differential not to exceed 10 percentage points.
* Agricultural income in excess of 25000 accruing to the non-agriculturists be taxed by aggregating it with non-agricultural income.
* Retention of the general rate of depreciation on plant and machinery at 25 per cent.
* Abolition of interest tax.
* Exemption limit for the gift tax be raised to Rs. 30,000 from the present level of Rs. 20,000.
* Taxation of perquisites and fringe benefits.

23.12 **Budgetary Deficit: Centre, States and Union Territories, 1992-93**

The overall budgetary deficit of the States and Union Territories for 1992-93 is estimated at Rs. 1694 crore. This gap between the total expenditure and receipts narrows down to Rs. 194 crore on receipt of the States' share of Rs. 1500 crore in the additional resource mobilisation by the Centre. However, the fiscal deficit of the States does not show any marked decline. During the current year, the fiscal deficit of all the States is estimated at 3.2 per cent of GDP.

Current revenue of the States, including internal resource generation by their enterprises, is estimated to increase by 10.7 per cent, to Rs. 82363 crore, in 1992-93. Aggregate disbursements are to rise by 10.1 per cent to Rs. 107315 crore. The resource gap is thus estimated at Rs. 24952 crore. Of this gap, 48.5 per cent is to be financed by loans from the Centre, 16.8 per cent from market loans, 8.6 per cent from provident funds and the remaining from other capital receipts.

The budgeted non-developmental expenditure of the States is expected to increase by 16.2 per cent in 1992-93 against a 7.1 per cent increase in development expenditure over 1991-92 (RE). The ratio of development expenditure to total expenditure has declined from 74.4 per cent in 1983-84 to 65.5 per cent in 1992-93.

The overall budgetary deficit of the Centre, States and Union Territories in 1992-93 (BE) is placed at Rs. 7083 crore, 20.7 per cent lower than in 1991-92 (RE). Aggregate receipts including borrowings are budgeted to increase by 12.2 per cent to Rs. 213192 crore while aggregate expenditure is estimated to increase by 10.7 per cent to Rs. 220275 crore. Developmental expenditure is projected to rise by 10 per cent and non-developmental expenditure by 11.8 per cent (Table 23.8). The current revenue was estimated to increase by 13.5 per cent to Rs. 150289 crore. The gap between current revenue and disbursement which denotes the total gap in the resources of the States and the Centre, is estimated at Rs. 69986 crore, or 10.1 per cent of the GDP.

TABLE 23.8: Annual Plan Outlay: Centre, States and Union Territories

Heads of development	1991-92 (RE)	1992-93 (BE)	1991-92 (RE)	1992-93 (BE)
	(Rs. crore)		(per cent)	
1	2	3	4	5
1. Agricultural and allied activities	3944	4710	6.0	5.8
2. Rural development	4113	4536	6.2	5.6
3. Special area programme	1101	1180	1.7	1.5
4. Irrigation and flood control	3956	4935	6.0	6.1
5. Energy	18843	23574	28.6	29.2
6. Industry and minerals	8026	9884	12.2	12.2
7. Transport	9512	11756	14.4	14.6
8. Communications	3632	4890	5.5	6.1
9. Science, technology and environment	888	992	1.3	1.2
10. General economic services	861	1105	1.3	1.4
11. Social services	10732	12847	16.3	15.9
12. General Services	247	363	0.4	0.4
Total	65855	80772	100	100

23.13 **Annual Plan**

The Annual Plan for 1992-93 provides for a total outlay of Rs. 80772 crore for the Centre, States and Union Territories, 22.7 per cent higher than in 1991-92 (RE) (Table 23.8). The allocation for the Central Plan is Rs. 48407 crore, 20.5 above 1991-92 (RE). The allocation for the States and Union Territories' plans at Rs. 32365 crore works out to 40.1 per cent of the total outlay.

In the pattern of financing of the Annual Plan 1992-93, it is envisaged that domestic resources would finance 79.3 per cent of the outlay and the net inflow from abroad would contribute another 14 per cent. The remaining 6.7 per cent is estimated to be met by the budget deficit. The contribution of the balance from current revenue at current rates of taxation is estimated to be Rs. 351 crore. The generation of internal resources and issue of bonds by public enterprises is estimated at Rs. 22027 crore.

24

AGRICULTURE (Including Animal Husbandry and Dairy Development)

24.1 Introduction

On account of the erratic behaviour of south-west monsoon, foodgrains production in 1991-92 fell by 5.3 per cent to 167.1 million tonnes from a record level of 176.4 million tonnes in 1990-91. Production of rice and wheat was 73.7 million tonnes and 55.1 million tonnes respectively. There was a substantial decline in the production of coarse cereals and pulses. Production of oilseeds at 18.3 million tonnes in 1991-92 was 1.6 per cent less than previous year's production of 18.6 million tonnes. Sugarcane attained a record production of 249.3 million tonnes. Production of cotton at 9.8 million bales was same as that of the previous year whereas jute and mesta recorded production of 10.2 million bales which was 10.9 per cent higher than that of 9.2 million bales of the previous year.

Production of foodgrains during 1992-93 is expected to be of the order of 176.7 million tonnes — 98.7 million tonnes of kharif and 78.0 million tonnes of rabi. Production of oilseeds is expected to be around 20 million tonnes. The acreage under sugarcane is reported to have gone down resulting in a decrease in cane production from 249.3 million tonnes in 1991092 to 230 million tonnes in 1992-93. Production of cotton is expected to be of the order of 11.7 million billion bales and that of jute and mesta 7.6 million bales.

Monsoon during 1992 was 92 per cent of the long-term average. Though it was a little delayed and sluggish up to middle of July, its temporal and partial spread was more even than in the previous year. The cumulative irrigation potential likely to be created and utilised by the end of 1992-93 would be 83.9 million hectares and 75.7 million hectares respectively.

Fertiliser consumption during 1992-93 is expected to be around 12.7 million tonnes of nutrients. In August 1992, prices of urea were reduced by 10 per cent, and control over price and movement of phosphatics and potassic fertilisers as withdrawn. Import of naphtha and di-ammonium phosphate (DAP) has been decanalised.

24.2 Agricultural Production

Performance of agricultural production during the past four years and the prospects during 1992-93 are shown in Table 24.1

TABLE 24.1: Performance of Agricultural Production

Items	1988-89	1989-90	1990-91 Revised	1991-92 Target	1991-92 Final	1992-93 Target	1992-93 Likely
1	2	3	4	5	6	7	8
			(Million tonnes)				
Rice	70.5	73.6	74.3	76.5	73.7	77.3	71.5
Wheat	54.1	49.8	55.1	56.5	55.1	57.0	56.0
Coarse cereals	31.5	34.8	32.7	34.0	26.3	34.2	34.7
Pulses	13.8	12.8	14.3	15.5	12.0	14.5	14.5
Total foodgrains	169.9	171.0	176.4	182.5	167.1	183.0	176.7
Kharif	95.6	101.0	99.4	103.2	91.4	103.3	98.7
Rabi	74.3	70.0	77.0	79.3	75.7	79.7	78.0
Oilseeds	18.0	16.9	18.6	18.5	18.3	19.0	20.0
Sugarcane	203.0	225.6	241.0	230.0	249.3	243.0	230.0
Cotton @	8.7	11.4	9.8	12.0	9.8	12.0	11.7
Jute & mesta $	7.9	8.3	9.2	9.1	10.2	9.2	7.6
			(Percentage variation in production over the previous year)				
Rice	24.1	4.4	1.0		-0.8	-3.0	
Wheat	17.1	-7.9	10.6		Negligible	1.6	
Coarse Cereals	19.3	10.5	-6.0		19.6	31.9	
Pulses	25.5	-7.2	11.7		-16.1	20.8	
Total foodgrains	21.0	0.6	3.2		-5.3	5.7	
Kharif	28.2	5.6	-1.6		-8.0	8.0	
Rabi	12.9	-5.8	10.0		-1.7	3.0	
Oilseeds	41.7	-6.1	10.1		-1.6	9.3	
Sugarcane	3.2	11.1	6.8		3.4	-7.7	
Cotton	35.9	31.0	-14.0		0.0	19.4	
Jute & mesta	16.2	5.1	10.8		10.9	-25.5	

@ Bales of 170 kg each.
$ Bales of 180 kg each.

Rice

The area under rice was 42.3 million hectares in 1991-92, about one per cent less than the previous year. With only 45 per cent of the total area under irrigation, there is heavy dependence on rains during he south-west monsoon. The total production of rice in 1991-92 was 73.7 million tonnes, against previous year's record production level of 74.3 million tonnes. The decrease in production can mainly be attributed to a decline in area since yield remained almost at the same level (1741 kg per hectare) as in the previous year. Decreases in production of kharif rice were reported by Bihar, Uttar Pradesh, Tamil Nadu, Madhya Pradesh and Maharashtra due to a decline in area, a result of unfavourable weather conditions at the time of sowing. Orissa, West Bengal and Karnataka have, however, reported increases in production of rice.

During kharif 1992 the area under rice is expected to have gone down because of late arrival of monsoon. The yield may also have been adversely affected in Bihar, east Uttar Pradesh, parts of east Madhya Pradesh and Andhra Pradesh because of deficient rains. The net result would be lower production during kharif 1992 as compared to the previous year. The total production of rice (kharif and rabi) during 1992-93 is expected to be about 71.5 million tonnes.

Wheat

During 1992, the production of wheat was 55.1 million tonnes, roughly at the same level as in the previous year. The area under wheat declined by 4.9 per cent from 24.2 million hectares in 1991 to 23.0 million hectares in 1992. The decline in the area under wheat was offset by an improvement in yield, which reached a record level of 2397 kg per hectare. Uttar Pradesh, Rajasthan, Punjab and Haryana reported increased production whereas Madhya Pradesh, Gujarat and Maharashtra reported lower production during over 1991.

The moisture content in the soil at the time of the sowing of rabi crops for 1993 was quite good. Wheat production during 1993 is anticipated to be around 56 million tonnes.

Coarse Cereals

Jowar, bajra, maize, ragi, small millets and barley constitute coarse cereals. The area under total coarse cereals was 33.75 million hectares in 1991-92, 7.1 per cent less than in the previous year. This can partly be attributed to inadequate rains during the south-west monsoon of 1991 in the major producing states of Rajasthan, Gujarat, Maharashtra, Madhya Pradesh, Uttar Pradesh and Bihar. As a result of decline both in area and yield, the production of coarse cereals during 1991-92 was 26.3 million tonnes, registering a fall of 19.6 per cent over the previous year.

Because of fairly good rainfall in the major producing states, the production of coarse cereals is expected to be around 34.7 million tonnes during 1992-93, 31.9 per cent more than in 1991-92.

Pulses

The production of pulses also suffered a setback during 1991-92 as these are grown mainly under rainfed conditions and the weather was not very conducive for their cultivation. It was 12.0 million tonnes in 1991-92, 16.1 per cent less than in the previous year. All the pulses i.e. tur, gram and other pulses showed a decline in production. Production of gram, the major pulse crop, declined substantially.

With fairly good rainfall in the major pulses growing States, production of pulses during 1992-93 is expected to be about 14.5 million tonnes.

Oilseeds

The production of nine oilseeds (groundnut, repeseed and mustard, soyabean, sunflower, sesamum, castorseed, nigerseed, linseed and safflower) was estimated at 18.3 million tonnes during 1991-92 against previous year's production of 18.6 million tonnes. Kharif oilseeds, particularly groundnut in Gujarat, parts of Andhra Pradesh and Maharashtra and soyabean in Madhya Pradesh and Rajasthan, suffered a setback during 1991-92 because of adverse weather conditions prevailing at the critical stage of crop growth. However, production of sunflower and rapeseed and mustard recorded impressive increases during 1991-92, owing to higher acreage in the major producing States of Rajasthan, Uttar Pradesh and Haryana. Production prospects during 1992-93 of groundnut (kharif), soyabean and rapeseed and mustard are reported to be excellent. The total production of oilseeds during 1992-93 is expected to reach a record level of 20 million tonnes.

Sugarcane

Production of sugarcane touched 249.3 million tonnes in 1991-92, registering an increase of 3.4 per cent over the previous year. There has been a rising trend in the production of sugarcane during the past few years. Uttar Pradesh, Andhra Pradesh, Karnataka, Haryana, Punjab, Madhya Pradesh, Orissa and Rajasthan have reported increases both in area and production during 1991-92. Maharashtra, Bihar and Gujarat have, however, reported a decrease in cane production.

During 1992-93, the acreage under sugarcane is expected to decline owing to heavy cane overdues and the inability of the sugar mills to accept cane from farmers during the previous year specially in the northern States. The production of sugarcane during 1992-93 is expected to be lower at about 230 million tonnes.

Cotton

Cotton, basically a rainfed crop (irrigated area being only 33.6 per cent), is grown over an area of 7.7 million hectares. During 1991-92, the production of cotton was estimated at 9.8 million bales (of 170 kg), almost the same as in the previous year, Maharashtra, Gujarat, Madhya Pradesh and Rajasthan have reported a decrease both in production and yield, primarily owing to unfavourable weather conditions prevailing during the south-west monsoon of 1991. This was, however, offset by higher production in Punjab, Andhra Pradesh, Karnataka, Haryana and Tamil Nadu.

The production prospects of cotton during 1992-93 may reach a record level of 11.7 million during 1992-93.

Jute and Mesta

The production of jute and mesta was 10.2 million bales (of 180 kg) in 1991-92, showing a substantial increase of 10.9 per cent over the previous year's production of 9.2 million bales.

The acreage under jute a expected to have decline in 1992 due to scanty pre-monsoon (March to May 1992) rains in the eastern States, particularly in West Bengal. The production of jute and mesta together may be around 7.6 million bales during 1992-93.

Plantation Crops

Tea

Tea production during 1991-92 reached 727 million kg compared to 719 million kg in 1990-91. The increase in production was mainly through increase in yield which rose from 1707 kg per hectare in 1990-91 to 1761 kg per hectare in 1991-92. Domestic demand constitutes about two-thirds of the tea output. Exports during 1991-92 has been estimated to be 210.4 million kg. valued at Rs. 1157.14 crore. An export target of 210 million kg. valued at Rs. 1200 crore has been fixed for 1992-93.

Coffee

Coffee production varied from about 195000 tonnes in 1984-85 to 170000 tonnes in 1990-91. In 1991-92, the production is estimated to be around 180000 tonnes. Most of the coffee produced in the country is exported; domestic consumption is stable around 55000 tonnes.

Rubber

Natural rubber is grown in about 466 thousand hectares. Production of natural rubber is anticipated to be 392000 tonnes in 1992-93 registering an increase of 7 per cent over the previous year. The increase in production was due to an increase both in area and yield. Consumption of rubber is expected to increase from 390000 tonnes in 1991-92 to around 410000 tonnes in 1992-93. The gap between domestic demand and supply is normally met through canalised imports. No imports of natural rubber were made in 1991-92.

24.3 **Irrigation**

By the end of 1991-92, the cumulative irrigation potential created was 81.2 million hectares comprising of 30.9 m.ha. under major and medium and 50.3 m.ha. under minor irrigation projects. The target for the year 1992-93 is an additional 2.7 m.ha. (0.7 m.ha. under major and medium projects and 2.0 m.ha under minor irrigation projects). Thus the total potential likely to be created by the end of the year 1992-93 would be 83.9 m.ha. The development of irrigation potential and their utilisation are given in Table 24.2.

TABLE 24.2: Development of Irrigation Potential and its Utilisation

(Million hectares)

	Seventh Plan end	1990-91	At the end of 1990-91	1991-92 (Likely)	1992-93 (Target)
1	2	3	4	5	6
1 Major and medium irrigation					
Potential	29.9	0.4	30.3	0.6	0.7
Utilisation	25.5	0.5	26.0	0.6	0.7
2 Minor irrigation					
Potential	46.6	1.8	48.4	1.9	2.0
Utilisation	43.1	1.7	44.8	1.7	1.9
3 Total					
Potential	76.5	2.2	78.7	2.5	2.7
Utilisation	68.6	2.2	70.8	2.3	2.6

Note: Irrigation projects with a Cumulative Command Area (CCA) of more than 10000 hectares are classified as major projects and projects with CCA of more than 2000 hectares and up to 10000 hectares as medium projects.

There has been a lag in utilisation of created potential, particularly in major and medium irrigation projects. At the end of 1991-92, utilisation was 73.1 m.ha. against a created potential of 81.2 m.ha. This leaves a gap of 8.1 m.ha (4.3 m.ha in major and medium and 3.8 m.ha in minor irrigation). The main reasons for the gap are delays involved in the development of on-farm works like construction of field channels, land levelling and adoption of the warabandi system and finally the time taken by farmers in switching over to the new cropping patterns, i.e. from dry farming to irrigated farming.

A Centrally sponsored Command Area Development Scheme was initiated in 1974-75 with the basic objective of bridging the gap between potential created and potential utilised and increasing agricultural production from the irrigated commands. The programme *inter alia* envisaged execution of on-farm development works like construction of field channels, land levelling and shaping, implementation of warabandi (network of distributories and minors over the command area) for rotational supply of water and construction of field drains. In addition, the programme also encompasses adaptive trials, demonstration and training of farmers and introduction of suitable cropping patterns. Up to March 1992, Rs. 3214 crore was spent on the programme, of which the Central assistance amounted to Rs. 1081 crore.

Minor irrigation schemes include groundwater and surface water projects. While groundwater schemes include dugwells, shallow tubewells and pumpsets, the surface water includes tanks and reservoirs diversion schemes, lift irrigation from rivers and streams etc. These schemes have been accorded special attention under the Special Foodgrains Production Programme. For 1992-93, the targets for irrigation potential created and utilisation are 2.0 m.ha and 1.9 m.ha respectively. Emphasis is being laid on creation of minor irrigation schemes to cover both surface and ground water. Because of advantageous watertable levels, the eastern sector will receive special attention for exploration of minor irrigation during the Eighth Plan.

Strengthening the infrastructure for irrigation is one of the major objectives of the Eighth Plan. The major elements of the strategy envisaged for meeting this objective include giving priority attention to the completion of on-going projects, ensuring speedy transit to irrigated agriculture and optimum use of water through Command Area Development (CAD) programme, installation of sprinkler and drip irrigation systems in water scarce and drought-prone areas and encouragement to minor surface water and lift irrigation schemes.

24.4 **Seeds**

The distribution of certified quality seeds was 5.75 million quintals in 1991-92, roughly the same level as that of the previous year. Expansion of area under location specific High Yielding Varieties (HYV) is a major component of the strategy to increase foodgrains production in the country. The HYV programmes is supported by minikits demonstration programme for rice, wheat and coarse cereals for popularising newly identified/released varieties suitable for different agro-climatic zones. Though there has been a considerable increase both in the quantum of quality certified seeds and the area under HYV over the last few yeas, there has not been a commensurate increase in productivity. To augment the infrastructural facilities for seeds development, a project has been launched with World Bank assistance for varietal development, strengthening of seeds certification agencies and seeds testing laboratories, training and consultancy services and investment credit facility to seed companies. The area under HYV seeds under different crops and their share in the total area are given in Table 24.3.

TABLE 24.3: Area under High-Yielding Varieties of Seeds

Crop	1985-86	1986-87	1987-88	1988-89	1989-90	1990-91	1991-92	1992-93*
1	2	3	4	5	6	7	8	9
				(Million hectares)				
Paddy	23.5	24.0	22.1	25.4	26.2	28.1	27.2	30.5
Wheat	19.1	19.2	19.7	20.2	20.3	20.4	21.4	22.2
Jowar	6.1	5.5	6.1	6.1	6.9	6.7	8.0	8.3
Bajra	5.0	5.3	4.0	5.9	5.6	5.1	6.0	6.3
Maize	1.8	2.2	2.2	2.5	2.3	2.6	3.0	3.2
Ragi	-	-	-	-	-	1.0	1.0	1.1
Total	55.4	56.2	54.1	60.1	61.2	63.9	66.6	71.6
			(Percentage of HYV area to Total Area under the crop)					
Paddy	57.2	58.4	57.0	60.9	62.1	65.8	64.3	
Wheat	83.0	83.1	85.3	83.8	86.4	84.3	93.0	
Jowar	37.9	34.6	38.1	41.8	46.6	46.5	63.5	
Bajra	46.7	46.9	46.0	49.2	51.4	48.6	60.0	
Maize	31.0	37.3	39.3	42.4	39.0	44.1	51.7	
Ragi	-	-	-	-	-	45.5	45.5	

* Provisional

24.5 **Fertilisers**

Consumption of fertilisers has gone up marginally to 12.7 million tonnes in 1991-92. The unsatisfactory off-take of fertilisers during 1991-92 was due to erratic monsoon during 1991 and to some extent an increase in fertiliser prices. Trend in fertiliser consumption from 1985-86 onwards is given in Table 24.4.

TABLE 24.4: Consumption of Chemical Fertilisers

Year	Nitrogenous	(Million tonnes of nutrients) Phosphatic	Potassic	Total NPK
1	2	3	4	5
1985-86	5.7	2.0	0.8	8.5
1986-87	5.7	2.1	0.9	8.7
1987-88	5.7	2.2	0.9	8.8
1988-89	7.3	2.7	1.1	11.1
1989-90	7.4	3.0	1.2	11.6
1990-91	8.0	3.2	1.3	12.5
1991-92	8.0	3.3	1.4	12.7
1992-93*	8.4	3.2	1.1	12.7

* Anticipated.

Production of nitrogenous and phosphatic fertilizers during 1991-92 stood at about 9.9 million tonnes registering about ten per cent increase over the previous year. The gap in domestic demand was met through imports. Details of fertilizer production, imports and subsidies are given in Table 24.5.

TABLE 24.5: Fertilisers: Production, Imports and Subsidies

Year	Production (N+P)	Imports (N+P+K)	Subsidies on imported fertilisers	Subsidies on domestic fertilisers	Total
1	2	3	4	5	6
	(Thousand tonnes)			(Rs. crore)	
1985-86	5756	3399	324	1600	1924
1986-87	7070	2310	97	1700	1897
1987-88	7131	984	114	2050	2164
1988-89	8964	1608	201	3000	3201
1989-90	8543	3114	771	3771	4542
1990-91	9045	2758	659	3730	4389
1991-92	9863	2769	1300	3500	4800
1992-93*	10000	2915	1009	5568	6577

* Likely.

On the recommendations of the Joint Parliamentary Committee on Fertiliser Pricing the Government announced a package of measures in August and September 1992 relating to pricing and production of fertilizers. With effect from 25 August 1992 the prices of urea have been reduced by ten per cent. Simultaneously, price and movement control in respect of all phosphatic and potassic fertilisers were withdrawn. To maintain relative price parity among all the nitrogenous fertilisers, low-analysis nitrogeneous fertilisers, namely calcium ammonium nitrate, ammonium chloride and ammonium sulphate were brought back under price and movement control. In order to enable the indigenous manufacturers of di-ammonium phosphate (DAP) and complex fertiliser to compete with the imported DAP, the import duty on phosphoric acid has been abolished.

In order to cushion the impact of increase in the prices of decontrolled fertilisers on farmers during rabi 1993 season, the Government has announced a special subsidy of Rs. 1000 per tonne for DAP and muriate of potash (MOP) and corresponding relief in the case of complex fertilisers. This scheme will be administered by the State Governments. However, in spite of decontrol of phosphatic and potassic fertilisers, the subsidy liability is expected to be of the order of about Rs. 6577 crore during the current year.

24.6 **Pesticides**

The concept of Integrated Pest Management (IPM) has been adopted through need-based and judicious application of pesticides. It aims at better cost-effective plant protection measures by adopting environmentally safe practices. Indiscriminate use of pesticides is discouraged. This technology harmonises with other segments of crop husbandry for achieving greater productivity. During 1991-92, 26 Central Integrated Pest Management Centres have been set up by the Central Directorate of Plant Protection in 22 states and one union territory. Major activities of these centres include crop pest monitoring, promoting biological control, organising demonstrations and training on IPM both for extension workers and farmers.

The consumption of pesticides in 1991-92 is estimated to be 78400 tonnes. Most of the requirements of pesticides were met through indigenous production. A limited quantity of pesticides is imported.

24.7 **Agricultural Credit**

Co-operatives, commercial banks and Regional Rural Banks (RRBs) are providing both long-term and short-term credit to farmers to help them adopt modern technology and improved agricultural practices so as to increase crop productivity and production. The total quantum of agricultural loans has increased from Rs. 7005 crore in 1985-86 to Rs. 11199 crore in 1991-92. The target for 1992-93 has been fixed at Rs. 17438 crore. Agency-wise disbursement of agricultural credit from 1985-86 to 1991-92 and the target for 1992-93 are given in Table 24.6.

TABLE 24.6: Disbursement of Agricultural Credit

(Rs. crore)

Item	1985-86	1986-87	1987-88	1988-89	1989-90	1990-91	1991-92	1992-93*
1	2	3	4	5	6	7	8	9
Cooperatives								
Short term	2787	3007	3120	3594	3689	2306	3843	5096
Medium term	505	585	567	602	709	317	387	441
Long term	582	615	733	655	684	785	1008	1133
Total	3874	4207	4420	4851	5082	3408	5238	6670
Commercial and Regional Rural Banks	3131	3809	4009	4233	4719	5438	5961	10768
Grand Total	7005	8016	8429	9084	9801	8846	11199	17438

* Target

Despite phenomenal increase in overall agricultural credit, there is a serious problems of overdues which has been inhibiting credit expansion on one hand and economic viability of the lending institutions, specially the cooperatives and the RRBs. on the other. The waiver of agricultural loans in 1990 has further accentuated the problem of recovery. For strengthening the cooperative credit structure, the National Bank for Agriculture and Rural Development (NABARD) is contemplating an institutional strengthening programme. The Government has also initiated certain measures to revitalise the cooperatives on the recommendations of the Agricultural Credit Review Committee. These measures include amendment to State Cooperative Laws, augmenting the reserve base of the Primary Agricultural Credit Societies (PACS), holding elections of cooperative bodies, revitalising PACS by business development planning and formulating Deposit Insurance Guarantee Schemes for PACS.

Considering the increase in prices of agricultural inputs and with a view to enabling the NABARD to extend adequate credit support for the rabi crop operations, Reserve Bank of India has announced additional lines of credit for short-term agricultural operations in January 1993.

24.8 Comprehensive Crop Insurance Scheme

The Comprehensive Crop Insurance Scheme (CCIS) was introduced in April 1985 and at present covers wheat, paddy, millets, oilseeds and pulses. Half of the premium payable by small and marginal farmers is subsidised equally by the Central and State Governments. Indemnity claims are shared between the Government of India and State Government in the ratio of 2:1.

Under the scheme 317 lakh farmers have been covered by the end of rabi 1992, insuring a sum of Rs. 7071.3 crore. The total amount of claims paid and payable up to rabi 1992 was Rs. 951.1 crore.

With a view to broadbasing the CCIs and implementing it on a self-supporting basis, it has been decided that while the existing CCIS would continue, a pilot scheme would be implemented in one district of every State covering all farmers and all crops against all risks, preferably at lower unit areas and charging actuarial rates of premia. Suitable changes would be made to the existing system depending on the results of the pilot scheme.

24.9 Animal Husbandry and Dairy Development

Animal husbandry is one of the important and rapidly growing sectors of the agricultural economy. It plays a vital role in supplying essential nutrients of animal origin to the vast multitude of rural and urban people, besides providing gainful employment to large sections of people who are small/marginal farmers and agricultural labourers. This sector also provides wool, hides and skins and a variety of by-products like blood, bones, fats and casing. Farm-yard manure is one of the useful and income generating products of activity in the sector. Animal power for transportation particularly in the rural, hilly and desert areas also makes a significant contribution to the economy.

According to the estimates prepared by the Central Statistical Organisation, the gross value of output from livestock sector alone at current pries was about Rs. 382 billion in 1989-90, which is about 25% of the value of total agricultural output. This excludes the contribution of animal draft power. Thus, animal husbandry's role in diversifying agriculture, increasing employment opportunities especially for the weaker sections and providing subsistence to ecologically delicate areas has been vital.

India is endowed with livestock resources of considerable genetic diversity within species with fair traits of adaptability to withstand environmental stress and inadequate levels of nutrition and management. According to the provisional results of the latest livestock census, the country has about 192.8 million cattle, 79.1 million buffaloes, 44.9 million sheep, 100.0 million goats, 10.7 million pigs and 253.7 million poultry birds. Besides these we have about 3 million pack animals. With its large livestock population, Indian has vast potential for meeting the growing needs of the rapidly increasing human population in respect of animal protein and raw-material for industry. To improve this potential, special emphasis is laid on projects and programmes for enhancing the production of various species of livestock through genetic improvement and effective health cover.

Objectives, Approach and Strategy

The basis objectives, approach and strategy followed for the development of the livestock and dairy sector are as follows :

— to improve the productivity of livestock breeds by cross-breeding of low producing non-descript stock, and also selective breeding in well recognised indigenous breeds of animals;
— to strengthen the infrastructure of the existing farms to make available quality breeding material to meet the requirements of various livestock development programmes;
— to provide facilities for animal health care at the door steps of the farmers to safeguard their livestock and to increase the production of quality vaccines for livestock and poultry;
— to increase the production of quality fodder seeds and the adoption of mixed farming systems with suitable crop rotation, to increase the use of waste lands and establish pasture lands;
— to provide more job opportunities and supplement the income of the rural poor;
— to bring sheep breeders/poultry farmers and milk producers within the cooperative fold and prevent their exploitation by middle-men;
— to establish linkages between rural milk producers and urban consumers by replicating the 'Anand' pattern of dairy cooperatives in the country;
— to lessen the adverse impact of regional and seasonal imbalances in milk procurement and marketing; and
— to improve the data base in respect of livestock and livestock products.

The gross value of output at current prices from this sector is estimated at Rs. 44500 crore which accounted for 25.5 per cent of the total output of agricultural and livestock sectors during 1990-91.

The importance of milk and milk products in our daily life cannot be over emphasized. With rapid urbanisation, the requirement of liquid milk has assumed daunting proportions specially in those regions where milk production has been traditionally low. Development of cattle and increase in the production of milk is crucial for managing liquid milk supplies in the urban areas on the one hand and for providing increased employment opportunities in the rural areas on the other.

Unlike the distribution of agricultural land, the distribution of livestock is less uneven. The vast majority of landless rural people also own some head of cattle. Organised and sustained dairy development provides an opportunity to s such landless families to increase their income on a regular basis, reduce unemployment and improve their social and economic status within the rural community.

Operation Flood

Operation Flood (OF) Project, the world's largest integrated dairy development programmes designed to link the rural milk producers with urban consumers was started in 1970 by the National Dairy Development Board. The project as approved by the World Bank and the (EEC) European Economic Community with a total outlay of Rs. 915.00 crores envisages the coverage of 80 lakh farm families in 190 milk sheds of the country. Since the beginning of Operation Flood over 64700 dairy cooperative societies have been organised in 170 milksheds involving nearly 81 lakh farmer members these cooperatives procured on an average 88.3 lakh kg. of milk per day and marketed over 83 lakh litres per day. The provisional estimate of milk is 36.4 million tonnes in 1991-92. A technology mission for Dairy Development has been launched in order to systematise and coordinate dairy development with various field level developmental programmes. The Government has issued the milk and milk product order in June 1992 under the essential commodities Act 1955, which seeks to regularise the production, supply and distribution of milk and milk products throughout the country.

The cumulative progress in respect of key components of Operation Flood Programme upto December, 1991 and the proposed targets for 1992-93 are given in the Table 24.7.

TABLE 24.7 Operation Flood-III—Physical Progress

Sl. No.	Components	Achievements upto December, 1991	Proposed targets 1992-93
1.	Societies organised ('000)	64.2	67.9
2.	Farmer members (Lakh)	79.0	79.4
3.	Average rural milk procurement (lakh kg. per day)	88.3	105.0
4.	Rural Milk Processing capacity (lakh litres per day)	152.0	159.4
5.	Urban milk marketing (lakh litres per day)	83.3	87.1

The Operation Flood Programme which is currently in its third phase would extend into Eighth Plan period (i.e. 1992-97). The primary objective of Operation Flood-III as in earlier phases is to replicate "Anand Pattern" of dairy cooperatives by organising milk procurement at remunerative prices, providing efficient marketing of rurally produced milk and dairy products; introducing productivity enhancement measures; organising training programmes for meeting manpower requirement, developing National Milk Grid and undertaking applied research and development programmes for the benefit of milk producers. The programme envisages to organise 70,000 DCS covering 80 lakh farmer members. It is proposed to procure on an average 137 lakh kg. of milk per day and establish a milk processing capacity of 200 lakh litres of milk per day by the end OF-III Period.

Technical Inputs

By December, 1991 over 34,930 societies were covered under the Animal Health Programme, 22,230 had first aid, while 14,120 village societies were providing artificial insemination (AI) services, nearly 22,700 societies were marketing balanced cattlefeed. The by pass protein feed which is being sold through 8780 societies has now been increasingly adopted by farmers as this reduces the requirement of cattlefeed by about 40%, increased protein conversion by 33%, dry matter conversion by 30% and minimises dry matter requirement by 24%. In addition 9 urea-molasses block plants with a total capacity of 72 MT/day have been established.

Milk Procurement and Marketing

Milk procurement by the cooperatives which had touched all time high during 1989-90 has shown a declining trend during 1990-91. During the period under review the average milk procurement was 88.3 LKPD. which was 6.6% lower than the procurement during the corresponding period in the previous year. Procurement during December 1991 reached a level of 110.4 LKPD against 110.6 LKPD during December 1990. The total milk processing capacity under Operation Flood Programme has reached 152 llpd. with powder production capacity of 727 MT a day. A continually rising trend in ghee production due to high prevalent prices, sharp rise in the price of feed ingredients and unfavourable climatic conditions are the major factors which have contributed to a declining trend in milk procurement.

National Milk Grid

The National Milk Grid under Operation Flood Programme has played an effective role to lessen the adverse impact of regional and seasonal imbalances in milk procurement and marketing. A fleet of 1197 road/rail milk tankers for long distance transportation of liquid milk have been provided.

Manpower Development

Training programmes in areas of dairy development were organised in different functional areas at Anand and other NDDB training centres and were attended by 1,025 union/federation officials. A need-based programmes on 'Personal Management and Industrial Relation' was attended by 16 managers/officers from 15 organisation. Officers from Dairy Unions/Federations were sponsored for management courses at IRMA (27 officers for a 4 month General Management Programme and 23 Officers for the 1 year Diploma in Rural Management). Human Resource Development and Organisational Development activities were taken up for 3 cooperative organisations. Manpower studies were conducted in 6 milk unions to rationalise manpower use. Under the Technology Mission 214 officers from various state Governments took part in the orientation programmes on Anand Pattern Dairy Cooperatives.

Cooperative Development Activities

Cooperative Development programmes are now taking place in 60 milk unions. A series of training programmes were organised for the cooperative development core staff of milk unions and 116 officers/staff including 51 women instructors were trained. To bring about an understanding of the role and responsibility of the Board of Directors of Milk Unions and the role of professional management, 3 day workshops conducted at Anand were attended by 49 elected Board of Director. At village level 664 Women Education and 693 Member Education programmes were conducted in which 49,585 Women and 47,317 other members participated. Besides 113 Management Committees Member's seminars were conducted in which 2,674 elected committee members of village cooperatives participated.

Source: *Annual Report, 1991-92*, Department of Annual Husbandry and Dairy Development, Ministry of Agriculture, New Delhi.

24.10 Poultry

Poultry farming is becoming an important activity of the rural economy as it provides additional income and job opportunities to a large segment of the population particularly the weaker sections of the society. New strains of both eggs and meat type of birds have been developed in the country. As a result, dependence on import and grand parent stock from outside the country has, by and large, been eliminated. The provisional estimate of production of eggs during 1991-92 is 22 billion, about 4.5 per cent higher that the previous year's production.

24.11 Fisheries

Production of fish has recorded an all-time high of 4.2 million tonnes during 1991-92, an increase of 10.5 per cent over previous year. This comprised 2.5 million tonnes of arine fish and 1.7 million tonnes of inland fish. Special efforts have been made to promote extensive and intensive fish farming activity in the inland sector through modernisation of coastal fisheries, encouragement to deep sea fishing through joint ventures etc. The share of inland fish production in total fish production in total fish production increased from 36 per cent in 1980-81 to 41 per cent in 1991-92. In the case of marine fish a quantum jump in production in recent years was possible through measures like banning of bulk trawler by chartered foreign fishing vessels, speedy motorisation of traditional fishing craft and incentives provided for reimbursement of central excise duty on high speed diesel oil used by the modernised boats. Production of fish is expected to be 4.3 million tonnes during 1992-93. Exports of marine products have registered a substantial increase to the level of Rs. 1375 crore in 1991-92 from Rs. 893 crore in the previous year. Export earnings are anticipated to be Rs. 1675 crore during 1992-93.

24.12 Agricultural Marketing

Agricultural trade is mainly carried out by the private enterprises. The Government intervention is limited to protecting the interests of producers and consumers and also promoting organised marketing of agricultural commodities in the country. Most of the Governments of the States and Union Territories have enacted necessary legislation with a view to safeguarding the interest of both the producer-seller and the consumer. The number of regulated markets in the country by March 1992 was 6738. The Central Government is providing assistance for the creation of infrastructural facilities in the markets and also for setting up of rural godowns. These schemes have been transferred to the States and Union Territories with effect from April 1992. To facilitate grading, standards have been laid down for 143 agricultural and allied commodities under the

Agricultural Produce (Grading and Marking) Act, 1937. To promote the setting up of cold storages under cooperative sector, the National Cooperative Development Corporation has provided a sum of Rs. 70 crore for installation of 241 cold storages having an installed capacity of 7 lakh tonnes till the end of March 1992.

A number of organisations, namely the Commission for Agricultural Costs and Prices, the Food Corporation of India, the Cotton Corporation of India, the Jute Corporation of India etc., have been established in order to help the Government in the implementation of the various development programmes. Agricultural marketing is also being attended to by a network of cooperatives at primary level, state level and at the national level. This network comprises both general marketing societies as well as commodity marketing societies. The marketing of agricultural produce through cooperatives has registered a remarkable growth from Rs. 1950 crore in 1980-81 to Rs. 6274 crore in 1990-91.

24.13 **Farming Policy (Draft)**

The policy lists 17 major challenges before agriculture. Some of these are: increasing the involvement of Non-Government Organisations in agricultural development and village uplift programmes, reviving and strengthening the local institutions of the farming community, and decentralised planning with full participation of the farming community.

Another major challenge, according to the draft policy is developing areas of untapped potential thereby correcting imbalances in growth in eastern, hilly, rainfed and drought-prone areas. Addressing technological and input needs of farm women and other disadvantaged sections of rural society with a view to remove the drudgery and burdens of their lives and augmenting income is yet another challenge.

The draft paper also mentions the challenge of value addition in agriculture to be achieved by a concerned thrust in increasing processing, marketing and storage facilities. Exports of agricultural produce need to be accelerated, feels the paper.

According to the draft paper another vital issue is water conservation. One of the measures proposed for this is to increase the use of plastics for this is to increase the use of plastics in micro-irrigation systems.

Source: *Hindustan Times,* March 6, 1993.

24.14 **Allocation for Agriculture**

Agricultural activities received an allocation of Rs. 2,515.60 crore under Plan and non-Plan expenditure in the 1993-94 budget proposals.

The Department of Agricultural Research and Education will have an outlay of Rs. 430 crore.

The Department of Animal Husbandry and Dairying has Rs. 369.81 crore earmarked for its operations.

This relates mainly to expenditure on central cattle breeding farms established at Suratgarh, Chiplima, Hesserghatta, Koraput, Dharnord, Alamadhi and Andesh Nagar, for bringing herds for milk production.

The provision for agriculture alone is Rs. 1,255 crore, for crop husbandry, foodgrain crops, manures and fertilisers, commercial crops, crop insurance, agricultural economics and statistics.

Other services of Department of Agriculture and Cooperation have an allocation of Rs. 460.74 crore. The outlay is intended for soil and water conservation, inland and marine fisheries, fishing harbours and fish landing facilities, processing and marketing.

Source: *Hindustan Times*, February 28, 1993

24.15 Unemployment among the Agricultural Workers

A very high degree of unemployment or underemployment prevails among the 160 million people engaged in agriculture either as cultivators or labourers in the country.

These people were not getting even the minimum work opportunity of 270 days in a year.

On an average, the work opportunity for an agricultural worker in the country was only 180 days, leading to the conclusion that only 100 million people were sufficient to carry out the entire agricultural operations including those of animal husbandry. Thus as many as sixty million people were left with virtually no work in agriculture and allied activities.

Inter-state variation in agricultural labour absorption capacity exists there.

Only Punjab, Haryana, Himachal Pradesh and Kerala were the four states where agriculture provided full work opportunities of 270 days of eight hour duration to every worker.

On the other hand, in states like Andhra Pradesh, Bihar and Tamil Nadu, employment in agriculture was available to less than 50 per cent of the work force.

Agriculture in Karnataka, Maharashtra and Uttar Pradesh also had quite inadequate labour absorption capacity in the rural areas.

The agriculture sector would be able to absorb only 120 million of the available 180 million people by the end of the current century, provided the rate of labour replacement by mechanisation was not accelerated.

Most of these unemployed or underemployed people would be concentrated in the states of Uttar Pradesh (104 lakh), Bihar (104 lakh), Andhra Pradesh (80 lakh) and Tamil Nadu (66 lakh).

With a view to remedying the situation several measures for taking up labour intensive land based programmes could be followed.

These included diversification of crop production programme which placed high priority on needs of poor people and transforming the crop production pattern from the present low valued to high valued and labour intensive programmes.

Quantum jump in the production of milk and eggs, making best use of water and land resources and improving the degraded land to the tune of 175 million hectares, which was about half of the total geographical area, mainly through afforestation is advisable.

As far as improving of the degraded land was concerned, the next five or ten years, at least an area of 20 to 25 million hectares should be improved mainly through afforestation which would require an investment of Rs. 40,000 to Rs. 50,000 crore. For this private investment has to be attracted.

This might require modification in the present law of land ceiling, which had even otherwise, become counter-productive, the report said.

Source: *Hindustan Times*, September 8, 1992

24.16 Agricultural Research

The Department of Agricultural Research and Education (DARE) provides the necessary governmental linkage to the Indian Council of Agricultural Research (ICAR), the national organization is responsible for co-ordinating and promoting research in agriculture and related disciplines. The ICAR undertakes research directly through 42 institutes, 4 bureaux, 20 national research centres and 9 project directorates. In addition, it also operates 71 multilocation, multidisciplinary all-India co-ordinated research projects on important commodities and research areas through 26 agricultural universities and a few selected public and private institutions.

A large number of improved crop varieties have been developed and appropriate technologies were evolved for controlling biotic and abiotic stresses. This has resulted in an all-time record foodgrain production of 176.23 million tonnes (74.6 million tonnes of rice and 54.5 million tonnes of wheat).

The overall productivity of foodgrains increased by about 35 kg/ha. Oilseeds production has reached about 18.5 million tonnes—1.5 million tonnes higher than the previous year. The major setback to *kharif* groundnut was balanced by increased productivity of rapeseed-mustard and increase in the area under sunflower.

In horticulture, several promising varieties have been developed in mango, guava, pomegranate, potato, hybrids and several selection in vegetables, coconut, cashew, black-pepper, arecanut, cassava, sweet-potato and colocasia. For the first time, a black-pepper variety tolerant to root-knot nematode has become available. Potato and cassava raised from true seed have shown promise. Coconut-based mixed farming model has proved very remunerative. In post-harvest technology, zero-energy evaporative cool chamber enhanced the shelf-life of fresh as well as processed fruits, vegetables and their products under rural conditions.

Sero-surveillance against equine influenza and equine infectious anaemia revealed a downward trend of incidence due to vaccination and rigid control policy.

Simple and reliable diagnostic tests like DOT-ELISA against rinderpest, theileriosis, babesiosis, anaplasmosis have been developed for field use.

FORV *Sagar Sampada* made 15 research cruises, spending 260 days in seas off south-west and north-west coats of India and in Lakshadweep waters. A new portable hatching-cum-rearing unit for hilsa has been designed and installed at Farakka to revitalize the depleting hilsa resources of the Ganga. The nature and the intensity of EUS was studied in Bihar, Haryana, Karnataka, Madhya Pradesh, Tamil Nadu and Uttar Pradesh where it caused large scale fish mortality. Technologies for breeding and culture of commercially important freshwater, blackishwater and marine finfish and shellfish, mariculture and sea-ranching, feed formulation, cryopreservation of spermatozoa were standardized and demonstrated. methods were worked out for improving the keeping quality of different fish and fishery products and for development of speciality products.

24.17 Agricultural Education

The activities of the DARE and the ICAR relating to agricultural education are carried out through several schemes and programmes relating to : (i) infrastructural development of educational institutions, (ii) manpower development, and (iii) quality improvement in collaboration with the state agricultural universities and deemed-to-be universities.

Infrastructural Development

By the end of Seventh Plan about 2,000 million were invested towards the establishment and development of agricultural university system. During the Eighth Plan it has been decided not to establish additional agricultural universities. The Central Agricultural University proposed for the North-Eastern Hills Region will have 7 constituent colleges : (i) College of Agriculture at Imphal, Manipur; (ii) College of Horticulture and Forestry in Arunachal Pradesh; (iii) College of Fisheries in Tripura; (iv) College of Veterinary Science and Animal Husbandry in Mizoram; (v) College of Agricultural Engineering in Sikkim; (vi) Post-graduate College at Barapani, Meghalaya; and (vii) College of Home Science at Tura, Meghalaya. The headquarters of the university will be at Imphal, for which the Manipur Government has allocated 112 hectares. The bill for the establishment of the university is proposed to be submitted to Parliament for approval during the forthcoming Budget Session.

Review of Infrastructure

During 1990-91 visiting teams of experts were constituted for each of the agricultural universities, deemed-to-be universities and colleges of the institutes of Agricultural Sciences, Banaras Hindu University, Varanasi, Vishwa Bharti, Shantiniketan, and Pali Shiksha Sadan, to assess their programmes and requirements of funds for the Eighth Plan. Some centres of excellence and advanced studies have been proposed for re-training of teachers, researchers and extension workers.

Manpower Development

The ICAR gives scholarships and fellowships for promoting agricultural education. Provision has been made to assist students belonging to the weaker sections of the society.

To support outstanding students belonging to the economically weaker sections of the society, about 600 merit-cum-means scholarships have been awarded during the year in addition to the 2,000 continuing ones. The rate of the scholarship is Rs. 170 a month.

A competitive examination to select candidates for the award of ICAR junior fellowships was held on 14 April, 1991. In 38 disciplines of agriculture and allied sciences, 350 fellowships were awarded.

In 31 disciplines of agriculture and allied sciences, 40 senior fellowships are reserved for the teachers and students of agricultural universities and the ICAR. Selection of candidates for 1991-92 programmes will be complete by March 1992.

Post-doctoral fellowships are offered to enable outstanding students to continue research after completion of their doctoral programmes. The proposal to revise the rate of this fellowship is under consideration.

On the recommendations of the Agricultural Universities Review Committee, the agricultural universities have introduced internship training as a compulsory requirement for the veterinary graduates. The contribution of the ICAR towards internship allowance is Rs. 400 per month per student for 6 months.

Quality Improvement

During the Seventh Plan, an outlay of Rs. 40 million was approved for the scheme of Professors of Eminence and National Fellows. At present 3 Professors of Eminence and 11 National Fellows working in the agricultural universities and ICAR institutes are completing their terms. They are in the revised pay-scale of Rs. 7,600 (fixed) and Rs. 4,500-7,300 respectively. The scheme has been modified for continuation during the Eighth Plan period with a proposal to establish 10 chairs of ICAR National Professors (including Dr. Pal's Chair at IARI, New Delhi) with a fixed pay of Rs. 7,600 along with 50 chairs of National Fellows in the scale of Rs. 4,500-7,300.

Centres for Post-Graduate Agricultural Education and Research

During the year, 3 on-going projects continued as Centres for Post-graduate Agricultural Education and Research under UNDP-ICAR projects. IND/83/020 covers 5 centres with a contribution of US $ 4.438 million by the UNDP and Rs. 25 million by the ICAR. IND/85/020 covers 11 centres at a cost of US $ 12 million and Rs. 66.31 million.

IND/83/020 utilized 99% of the resources provided. During the year 9 consultants utilized 10.25 man-months and 14 fellows utilized 62 man-months. The implementation of the project has been graded as very good by the FAO. This project was phased out in December 1991.

Under IND/85/020 project, 48 consultants have utilized 40 man-months and 60 fellows utilized 224 man-months. Equipment worth US $ 4,712,650 (out of total allocation of US $ 6,007,000) has been delivered and Us $ 647,502 is in the pipeline. The progress of the project has been adjudged as very good by the Evaluation Mission to the FAO/UNDP.

Under IND/86/012 project, 3 consultants utilized .25 man-months, and 7 fellows have utilized 23 man-months. Equipment worth US $ 373,925 has been procured and US $ 11,283 is in the pipeline.

Summer Institutes

About 570 persons engaged in research, teaching and extension have updated their knowledge at 19 summer institutes and short courses organized at agricultural universities and ICAR institutes.

Admission of Students under ICAR Quota

During 1991-92, the ICAR allocated 570 seats to under-graduate programme of students of different states and union territories. Seats were also allocated to about 150 students from international organizations and foreign countries selected under various programmes of the Government of India.

Best Teacher Award

The Best Teacher Award is given for agriculture and allied sciences at (i) faculty level (Rs. 3,000), (ii) university level (Rs. 5,000), and (iii) national level (Rs. 10,000). Four universities have already instituted faculty and university level awards and the remaining will be awarded by March 1992. The scheme will cost around Rs. 4 million during the Eighth Plan.

University-Level Books

The ICAR is implementing the university-level book production scheme, and 12 titles have been approved. The authors have taken up assignments following the curriculum recommended by the Deans' Committee.

The expenditure envisaged during the Eighth Plan will be around Rs. 11.5 million.

Emeritus Scientists

The ICAR provides opportunities to the retired scientists to continue research for a reasonable period after retirement. It provides for honorarium to the scientist @ Rs. 2,500 per month, a research fellow @ Rs. 1,500 per month and a contingent grant of Rs. 12,000 per year. At present 32 Emeritus Scientists are in position.

25

CULTURE

25.1 **Pream**

The Department of Culture set up in 1985 is one of the constituents of the Ministry of Human Resources Development. The Department of Arts which was one of the Departments of the Ministry has been merged for all practical purposes with the Department of Culture.

The Department has two attached offices, namely, Archaeological Survey of India and National Archives of India. It has six Subordinate Offices and 22 Autonomous Organisations which are fully or partially financed by the Government of India. The Subordinate Offices and Autonomous Organisations are as under :

Subordinate Offices

1. Anthropological Survey, of India, Calcutta.
2. National Museum, New Delhi.
3. National Gallery of Modern Art, New Delhi.
4. National Library, Calcutta.
5. National Research Laboratory for Conservation of Cultural Property, Lucknow.
6. Central Reference Library, Calcutta.

Autonomous Organisations

1. Rashtriya Manav Sangrahalaya, Bhopal.
2. National Council of Science Museum, Calcutta.
3. Nehru Memorial Museum and Library, New Delhi.
4. Sangeet Natak Akademi, New Delhi.
5. Sahitya Akademi, New Delhi.
6. Lalit Kala Akademi, New Delhi.
7. National School of Drama, New Delhi.
8. Centre for Culture Resources and Training, New Delhi.
9. Gandhi Smriti and Darshan Samiti, New Delhi.
10. Allahabad Museum, Allahabad.
11. Delhi Public library, Delhi.
12. Raja Ram Mohan Roy Library Foundation, Calcutta.
13. Central Institute of Higher Tibetan Studies, Varanasi.
14. Central Institute of Buddhist Studies, Leh (Ladakh).
15. Victoria Memorial Hall, Calcutta.
16. Indian Museum, Calcutta.
17. The Asiatic Society, Calcutta.
18. Salar Jung Museum, Hyderabad.
19. Khuda Baksh Oriental Public Library, Patna.
20. Rampur Raza Library, Rampur.
21. Jallianwala Bagh National Memorial Trust, Amristar.
22. T.M.S.S.M. Library, Thanjavur.

The Department of Culture is also looking after the Indira Gandhi National Centre for Arts which was being looked after formerly by the Department of Arts.

The Department of Culture plays a vital role in the promotion and dissemination of art and culture. It directly operates several schemes for promotion of specific performing literary and visual arts. It provides assistance for development of voluntary action in these fields through grants and training programmes etc. it also endeavours to promote and develop traditional crafts and skills, especially folk art and crafts.

The Department also looks after the preservation, conservation and exploration in the field of man-made heritage, namely, archaeology, anthropology, museums etc. It also promotes activities relating to these fields including buddhists, tribal and rural traditions, crafts and societies through specialised agencies like the Archaeological Survey of India, Anthropological Survey of India, Rashtriya Manav Sangrahalaya etc. It administers a number of museums and galleries of national importance.

The Department is concerned with the formulation of Archival Policy of the Government of India, development and protection of archives both at the Centre and at the States, a responsibility which it is implementing through the National Archives. It is also concerned with the development of public libraries and administrators National Library at Calcutta and a number of other libraries of national importance.

A number of scholarships, fellowships and grants are given by the Department of Culture to promote excellence in the various fields of art and culture. Anniversaries and centenaries of importance personalities are organised, memorials commemorating certain important persons or a particular period of history are maintained.

The Department coordinates all matters relating to the International Cultural Relations. It acts as the nodal agency for executing cultural exchange programmes with different countries, organises incoming and outgoing exhibitions, holds exhibition both in India and abroad and undertakes programmes envisaged in the field of activities of UNESCO in the field of art and culture.

25.2 Archaeology

The Archaeological Survey of India (A.S.I.) conducted many successful excavations in 1991 in Bihar, Gujarat, Haryana, Karnataka, Madhya Pradesh, Maharashtra, Manipur and Tamil Nadu. The excavations carried out at Kolhua in District Muzaffarpur (Bihar) brought to light a number of votive stupas, part of monastic complex and brick temple with a square *garbhagriha* entered through a *mondapa* on the front and *antarala* behind datable to late Gupta period. Excavation at Dhadavira in Kutch district of Gujarat was resumed during the year with a view to confirm the general lay-out of different divisions of the city and to obtain a cultural sequence. Among the notable antiquities found during excavations were seals and sealings, copper objects, gold pieces and a variety of semi-precious beads and bead-making tools. The excavation have indeed added new dimensions to the Harppan civilization in areas of urban planning, architecture and water structures. As a result of excavations at Karkabhat, district Drug, Madhya Pradesh, different types of menhirs were exposed and a large number iron tools, copper bangles, pieces of silver and a gold were encountered form excavated graves. A unique find was a profile of a man chiselled on a 4m high rock menhir erected over one of the graves.

A large number of sites ranging from pre-historic to medieval periods were discovered by the A.S.I during the course of village-to-village survey in different parts of the country, including (a) extensive lower palaeolithic site of Anangpur, late-Harappan, painted grey ware, early historic, historic and medieval site at Kharakhari Nahar, Sarai Pipal Thala Banher, Majnu-ka-Tila, etc., within the U.T. of Delhi, (b) Buddhist monasteries and stupas in Nubra valley of Ladakh region in J & K, and (c) painted grey ware sites in district Bijnore of Uttar Pradesh.

A large number of stones inscription, copper plates and brick inscription were copied by the Epigraphy Branch of the A.S.I. form various districts of Andhra Pradesh, Gujarat, Karnataka, Madhya Pradesh, Maharashtra, Tamil Nadu and Uttar Pradesh.

During the year, the A.S.I. continued with its activity of conservation. As many as 490 monuments were taken up for major structural repairs besides annual maintenance of other monuments. The open joints of the facade of main masoleum of the Taj Mahal were strengthened, missing inlay bars of black marble of the railing around the platform were replaced and entrance gateways at the Taj Mahal were replastered. In the Agra Fort, the decayed stones of veneering dab and cue etc. of the fortification wall were replaced and walls of Diwan-i-Khas and Dewan-i-am replastered. The joints, cracks and crevices at the *Vimana* of Bimla temple located within the compound of Lord Jagnnatha temple Puri were filled, matching with the originals. In Delhi, at Qutab Minar, decayed and cracked veneering stones were replaced with new ones. In the Red Fort complex, plastering of ceiling in Hammam, replacement of wornout veneering stones and filling-in of cracks in the fortification wall, and replacement of weathered and damaged stones in Mumtaz Mahal were taken up. The work on necessary conservation of Tawang Monastery in ARunachal Pradesh was also attended to during the year.

25.3 **Museums**

The National Museum, New Delhi continued with its activities of acquisition, exhibitions, conservation and education. It acquired 916 art object including some outstanding ones like a bronze silva of Chila period, 10th Century, A.D.; one miniature painting showing the portrait of Maharaja Ranjit Singh; and a Buddha image in ivory screen, 20th Century A.D., skull trident, Tibet 19th Century A.D.

Under the cultural exchange programme, negotiations were on with different countries like egypt, Australia, Japan and China for exchange of exhibition of cultural heritage on reciprocal basis.

In organisation international exhibitions, the National Museum sent an exhibition to Germany as a part of Festival of India in the country. An exhibition of "Indian Miniature Paintings" was also sent to Algeria under the Indo Algerian cultural exchange programme.

Under its educational activities, the National Museum organized special training programme in Museology for university students, an educational programme for the physically handicapped students of the Spastic Society of India and a summer course on Indian and European Art for 149 schools students.

The National Gallery of Modern Art, as a premier institution representing various changing visual art forms continued to extend its activities. It acquired 154 art objects during the year including the works of Harkrishnalal, A.P. Santhanaraj, Laxman Pai, Sanat Kar, Sarbari Roy Chowdhury and Ajit Chakravorty to name a few. Apart from this, the Gallery organized an exhibition of Carlo Carra, a futurist painter of Italy beside an exhibition of its new acquisitions. The Gallery also carried forward its activities relating to educational programmes, art sketch club and film shows etc.

The Indian Museum, Calcutta organised a day long seminar in July 1991 and exhibition was opened on Raja Rajendralal Mitra, a great orientalist and pioneer of popular studies in science. An exhibition was also organised to present a visual profile of the indologist. On the occasion of the 301st anniversary of the city of Calcutta, the Museum arranged its annual lecture series with the theme "Historic Theatre Architecture of Calcutta". An exhibition on "Calcutta, the city and its Stage" also opened to the public displaying the drawings and paintings of Sri Rathin Mitra and Kausik Sanyal. As a part of its activities of organising inter-state exhibitions, the Indian Museum Launched a photographic exhibition on "Women in Indian art" at Kohima, exhibiting 102 exhibition size photographs and eight fibreglass replicas of the specimens oriented with women in Indian Art and Culture.

The Allahabad Museum organised an impressive exhibition of the works of the late Shri Asit Kumar Haldar, the renowned exponent of the Bengal of Paintings. The museum also organized a short terms course on "Appreciation of Indian Art" for student of undergraduate level. The Museum also organised an exhibition of paintings drawn by students of a local school, which was a big draw for school children and their parents.

The Victoria Memorial Calcutta participated in the National Portrait Gallery (London) exhibition entitled "The Raj: India and the British 1600-1947". It also organised an exhibition "From Kalighaṭ to Gopal Ghosh", an exhibition of paintings by some of the stalwarts of the Bengal School marking the Tagore Birth anniversary. A series of illustrated lectured on Indian history, art, architecture and culture were also organized by the Memorial on various topics.

The National Council of Science Museums stressed on planning of new exhibits for exhibition in permanent galleries of its Museums/Centres. Completion of the projects of establishment of the National science Centre at Delhi, Raman Science Centre at Nagpur and Regional Science centre at Guwahati were the major achievements of the museum during the year. Twelve new Mobile Science Exhibition Units were also developed to augment science awareness activities in the rural areas of the country. During the period April November, 1991 more than 14 lakhs people visited its various Museums/Centres.

25.4 **Anthropology**

The Anthropological survey of India, was honoured with "Best Industrial and commercial profile trophy" awarded by EDICOIN, an international organisation based in Madrid, Spain for its outstanding professional contribution. The Survey took up the analysis and consolidation of information generated through the "People of India" project. Six volumes containing analysed data on socio cultural variables like marriage, kinship religion and language were also released during the year. Beside other plant projects viz. "Ethnicity Politics and Political System in Tribal Areas", "Tribal India: Structure Pattern and Transformation", "Tribal Arts Oral Tradition" were also completed.

The Rashtriya Manav Sangrahalaya, dedicated to depiction of the story of human kind in time and space, completed the first phase of open air exhibition "Rockart Heritage", besides further developing another permanent open-air-exhibition "Tribal Habitat". It also organized a craft demonstration programme 'Padav' featuring traditional rural art and craft by about 45 art design from different parts of the country. The Sangrahalaya also collected about 2000 specimens covering different facets of material culture from tribal and folk population.

25.5 **Archives**

National Archives of India (NAI) continued to accession public records, private papers of national importance and microfilm copies of records of Indian interest from abroad. Of the private papers received by the NAI one diary (1935) of Kumari Manibehn consisting of 166 pages was received for keeping its microfilm copy for the use of scholars. A set of 59 photocopies of Subhas Chandra Bose papers (1938-1941) were also received by the NAI during the year as gift from the U.S.S.R. Among the microfilms, 3 rolls comprising historical manuscripts of Indian interest viz. Akbar-i-Jahangir, Labbul Tawarikh-i-Hind and the Tarikh-i-Aurangzeb Ya Alamgir were received from the Afghanistan under the cultural exchange programme. An exhibition of original documents and photographs entitled "Archives and Social Change" was organized by the NAI as part of its centenary celebration. A very significant achievement of the year was fabrication of a portable fumigation vault by the NAI for use of Archives and Libraries.

25.6 **Buddhist and Tibetan Studies**

The Central Institute of Buddhist Studies, Leh continued with its activities of preparing students for classes Purv Madhyama, Sashtri, Acharya and Ph.D. as also publishing the rare and valuable buddhist texts to preserve and promote the buddhist art and culture besides translation of buddhist books from Tibetan to Hindi.

The Central Institute of Higher Tibetan Studies, Sarnath, Varanasi successfully conducted its various activities to preserve the cultural heritage of both India and Tibet through its academic programmes, research projects etc. During the year, the Institute's library acquired a total 5847 new books in Buddhology, tibetology and Himalayan studies for the use of scholars.

Under the scheme of financial assistance to Buddhist/Tibetan organisation for propagation/development and research in buddhist/tibetan culture, 107 institutions were selected for grant of financial assistance.

25.7 **Libraries**

The National Library, Calcutta, the biggest library in the country having a collection of more that 23 lakh volumes, issued about 74,000 books to the readers and lent out about 32,000 books to the borrowers. Under the scheme of arranging exhibitions of books and illustrations to mark national and international events, the library organised an exhibition on Dr. Bhimrao Ramji Ambedkar, a great national scholar, freedom fighter and chief architect of the constitution of India on the occasion of his birth centenary. The library received the manuscripts of late Kabisekhar Kalidas Roy. In order to keep it self abreast of latest Developments in the fields of preservation/conservation etc. the staff and officers of the library attended various seminars and workshops abroad.

The Central Secretariat Library, New Delhi which provides facilities for research and reference to Government organisations and researchers enrolled/ renewed 2619 members during the year 1991-92 and received around 1700 books in Hindi and English. A bibliographic database (CATALOG) for the books added to the Library with imprint initiated date 1989 onwards has been created with UNIMARC specification in HP 3000/376 system. The Library work on creating a database on *Mahabharata* and 5000 *slokas* were put into computer.

Raja Rammohan Roy Library Foundation, Calcutta is engaged in the promotion of library services all over the country, in cooperation with State Governments and Union Territory Administrations. During the year, the Foundation brought out four issues of its quarterly newsletter giving information on its activities. It also brought out a bi-annual journal Granthana: Indian journal of Library Studies, containing important articles on library and information science and allied subjects. The Foundation also initiated a number of promotional activities with a view to promoting library movement in the country.

Khuda Bakhsh Oriental Public Library, Patna having a rich collection of over 18000 manuscripts, 1,48,000 printed books and over 2000 original paintings of Mughal, Rajput, Iranian and Turkish school, continued with its activity of acquisition of manuscripts through purchase, exchange, gift etc. Under the scheme recording the preserving data on eminent people of composite culture of India, the Library continued during the year to collect audio and video tapes of those persons.

25.8 **Academies**

The Sangeet Natak Akademi (SNA) organised four Zonal Theatre Festivals at Jodhpur, Lucknow, Guwahati and Mysore during the year in collaboration with respective State Akademies or State Departments of Culture. The Lok Utsav, 1991 which featured traditional music, dance and theatre was presented by the Akademi in New Delhi. The Nrityostava at Bangalore and Nritya Mahotsava at Bombay featuring almost all forms of Dances of India was another important programme of SNA. About 1840 photographs and 155 hours of audio/video recordings were added to the archives of the Akademi.

The Sahitya Akademi, the organisation setup for working towards development of Indian letters and to set high literacy standards participated in 8 book exhibitions, organised 5 seminars, 6 "Meet the Author" functions, besides one "Men and Books" programme. The Akademi also published fourth volume of Encyclopaedia of Indian Literature.

The Lalit Kala Akademi, set up for promotion of visual and plastic arts in India, organised an exhibition on the works of Late Shri Asit Kumar Haldar, as a part of Birth Centenary Celebrations. An exhibition of the photographs of the paintings of Vincent Vangogh was also organised in Guwahati during the year. It also organised "Colours of the Earth", an exhibition of ceramics form Britain alongwith a parallel section of Indian ceramics in the Rabindra Bhavan Galleries at New Delhi. The Akademi also sent an exhibition of contemporary Indian art to Seychelles. An exhibition of the photographs of the paintings of Rabindra Nath Tagore was arranged at Rabindra Bhavan on the occasion of the 50th death anniversary of the painter-poet.

The National School of Drama, established for promoting theatre in India through high standards of theatre education, conducted four theatre workshops at Manipur, Faridabad, Shimla and Chandigarh under its extension programme. The Repertory company of the school organised an exhibition "Rang Yatra", based on photographs, models, etc. of the company production during the past 25 years the Repertory Company stage shows of different plays in Delhi and other places in the country. During the year the school enrolled 20 fresh students to its 3 years diploma course in Dramatics.

25.9 **Promotion and Dissemination of Culture**

During the year 1991-92, the Centre for Cultural Resources and Training (CCRT) organised seven orientation courses at New Delhi where a total of about 600 teachers from almost all the States and UTs participated. It also organised workshops on (i) socially useful productive works, (ii) Creative activities of teaching science and maths, (iii) crafts in education and other useful themes during the year. The centre also organised two seminars: "Indian Art and Culture" and "Indian Society-Dynamics of Change" for 12 college teachers and 17 school teachers from USA during the year. In order to motivate and give incentive to teachers, the Centre selected 57 teachers during the year for CCRT award for their outstanding contribution in the field of art and culture.

The seven Zonal Cultural Centres established so far have become the premier field institutions for encouraging and disseminating fold and tribal arts and culture. These centres organised/participated in a large number festivals, crafts meals, drama festivals, workshops anniversaries etc. all over the country.

25.10 **Memorials**

The Gandhi Smriti and Darshan Samiti setup to propagate the life, mission and thoughts of Mahatma Gandhi through socio-educational and cultural programmes, organised a "Taking Gandhi to School" programmes, Shanti Sena training programme, Kavi Sammelan, Seminars, Workshops etc. for promotion of ideals and causes identified with Gandhiji. It also observed a communal harmony month and held *Sarva Dharma Prathanas* on communal harmony.

25.11 **Indira Gandhi National Centre for the Arts, New Delhi**

The Indira Gandhi National Centre for the Arts (IGNCA) set up in November 1985 has become a major Centre for collection of multi-media primary and secondary source materials, exploration of fundamental concepts, identification of number of forms and elucidation of technological terminologies at the level of theory and text and intellectual tasks and interpretation under its programmes of Kal Nidhi and Kala Kosha. Similarly the programme Janapada Sampada and Kala Darshana are focusing on manifestation, process life-function and life-style and oral tradition. During the year, the IGNCA organised an exhibition on Buddhist Cave Paintings form China, two international workshops on the development and a application of experts systems in life style studies and on conceptual structure and models for preparing a multi-volume encyclopaedia. A pupetary workshop on the presentation of Gandhiji's messages and episodes from his life was also held.

26

DEFENCE

26.1 Defence Expenditure

Table 26.1 indicates the defence expenditure since 1977-78 to 1993-94 (BE).

TABLE 26.1: India's Defence Expenditure

Year	Defence Exp. '000 crores	GDP at factor cost '000 crores	Defence Exp. as percentage of GDP
(1)	(2)	(3)	(4)
1977-78	2,813	87,118	3.23
1978-79	3,060	93,724	3.26
1979-80	3,550	102,595	3.46
1980-81	4,091	122,427	3.34
1981-82	4,651.80	142,916	3.25
1982-83	5,408.30	158,851	3.40
1983-84	6,309.17	185,991	3.39
1984-85	6,660.51	208,577	3.19
1985-86	7,987.49	233,476	3.42
1986-87	10,477.45	259,055	4.04
1987-88	11,967.49	294,266	4.06
1988-89	13,341.02	351,724	3.79
1989-90	14,146	395,143	3.78
1990-91	15,426	461,512*	3.78
1991-92	16,347		
1992-93	17,500		3.54
1993-94 (BE)	19180		

*Estimated

Source: 1. Defence Expenditure Data from Government of India; Defence Services Estimates for relevant years.
2. GDP data from *Economic Survey* (Government of India) for 1989-90 and 1990-91.
3. Finance Minister's Statement, Feb 27, 1993.

26.2 Allocation for Defence, 1993-94

For 1993-94 Defence Budget, there is a marginal increase in real terms.

The Defence outlay has been increased by Rs. 1,680 crore for 1993-94. The increase from Rs. 17,500 crore in the current year to Rs. 19,180 crore reflects a 9.6 per cent rise.

In real terms, it makes an increase of just 2 per cent to cover for rise in inflation.

The components of the 1993-94 defence outlay are: Army (Rs. 9,425.46

crore), Navy (Rs. 1,125.42 crore), Air Force (Rs. 3,064.49 crore), Ordinance factories (Rs. 65.10 crore) and capital outlay on all these services (Rs. 5,499.53 crore).

In the next year's Budget, 13 paise of each rupee spent will go to defence sector.

Interestingly, while there has been a decline of Rs. 209 crore in Defence capital expenditure for 1992-93, the revenue expenditure of defence has gone up by the same amount, thus the Budget estimates and the revised estimates for defence in 1992-93 remains perfectly matched.

If one takes into account the current rate of inflation as 7 per cent, the increase in Defence expenditure for 1993-94 in real terms would be just above 2 per cent. But if one takes into account annual average double-digit inflation rate, the Defence allocation in real terms would have marginally come down, instead of going up.

The Army always gets major share of the Defence budget in view of the bulk of manpower compared to the Navy and Air Force. For the next year, the Budget for the Army has been raised by 7 per cent from Rs. 8,772.97 crores to Rs. 9,425.46 crore, an increase of Rs. 653 crore.

For the first time, the Air Force gets a major rise of about 20 per cent, with the Budget being raised to Rs. 3,064.49 crore from the current year's revised budgetary estimates of Rs. 2,532.99 crore — an increase of about Rs. 531.50 crore.

Such a big increase in the Air Force share is because of the higher costs of equipment in this technology intensive force. A major expenditure lies ahead for the Air Force as it plans to induct an advance trainer jet. The Air Force has been allocated an additional Rs. 1,615.77 crore for capital outlay on aircraft and aero-engines.

The Navy has been given a 13 per cent rise in its budgetary allocation of Rs. 1,125.92 crore as compared to the current year's revised estimates of Rs. 994.34 crore — an increase of Rs. 131.7 crore.

In view of the modernisation of communication, electronic warfare and acquisition of self-propelled 155 mm guns, the Army has been allocated an additional allocation of Rs. 1,261.35 crore for purchase of equipment under the capital outlay head.

An outlay of Rs. 65.10 crore has been earmarked under the expenditure head and Rs. 231 crore for capital outlay for the Defence ordnance factories.

Another major expenditure head under the defence budget is the outlay of Rs. 2,379 crore for defence pensions. A major factor for rise in Defence pension's money is one-time increase to pre-January 1, 1986, Defence pensioners.

26.3 Test-Firing of Prithvi Surface-to-Surface Missile

"Prithvi", India's indigenously-produced surface-to-surface missile, streaked majestically into the sunny blue skies over the Interim Test Range sharp at 9.30 a.m. on August 18, 1992, marking its 10th successful launch.

The missile with a range of 150 km to 250 km with a maximum payload of one tonne, has the latest onboard computers and a very advanced inertial navigation system, comparable to those of advanced countries.

The Balasore district administration shifted 61 families consisting of 600 villagers from three villages along the periphery of the launch pad to nearby Kusumali.

The first test firing of Prithvi was conducted on Feb. 22, 1988 from the rocket launching centre at Sriharikotta in Andhra Pradesh.

The last time that Prithvi was test fired from here was on May 5 this year. Prithvi's launching was deferred by a day this time also because of inclement weather at the launching site.

Defence Minister who watched the lift off of Prithvi said, "the launch has shown our capability and preparedness to the world."

The technology of executing the Prithvi mission with two mobile vehicles — one for the launcher and one for the computerised launched control — was also validated.

President Shankar Dayal Sharma congratulated Indian scientists and the institutions involved in the successful launch of Prithvi.

Among the mission objectives was meeting the peak performance capability of about 250 km with accurate delivery of the payload. The technology of executing a Prithvi mission with two mobile vehicles — was also validated.

Like other missiles being developed and productionised under the IGMDP, Prithvi, is characterised by the "consortium approach". Engineers and scientists drawn from Bharat Dynamics Ltd. the productionisation agency; PSUs like HAL and BEML; a host of DRDO labs; private industry; and from the academic community are active participants in the Prithvi project.

26.4 **Arjun Battle Tank**

After two decades of labour, India's own battle tank is ready. It is ranked among the three main battle tanks of the world.

'Arjun' is a multi-laboratories programme, involving defence and other Government public undertakings. The team behind Arjun claims that this tanks has been designed to meet the Army's stringent specifications, it represents the translation of advanced design into a reliable and effective weapon system to meet the varied threats of 90's and beyond. Adopting most advanced technologies. MBT Arjun offers the troops in the battlefield, a state-of-the-art tank with superior fire power, high mobility and excellent protection.

In mobility and fire power, it is claimed, Arjun measures up to advanced tanks in production today, in the other parts of the world. At present, only five military powers manufacture MBTs. They are : America's Abrams M1A1, Germany's Leopard-2; France's Le Clere, UK's Challenger and Israel's Merkava. MBT Arjun is more or less like Germany's Leopard, as the Indian tank carries the German engine. It an also be compared with Abrams M1A1 in performance.

To conceive Arjun, the beginning was made far back in 1974, with a modest fund of Rs. 15.5 crore. The defence scientists and others got breakthrough in 1988 with the making of some pieces of prototype Arjuns. So far, Rs. 240 crore have been spent on the Arjun project. The Government had sanctioned Rs. 280 crore. In the first decade, valuable time was wasted in efforts to make the MBT's engine in the country itself. Foreign companies had also offered their engines.

Realising that technologies were changing too fast, the idea was dropped, and the German tank's engine was adopted. So far, only a few prototypes of Arjun have been made, and a decision will be taken in coming months to start the manufacturing plant. The prototypes contain only 35 per cent foreign components, which include the engine and its electronic systems. But so much foreign component in a pre-production big weapon system is acceptable in the development phased due to the limited volume of manufacture, the MBT Arjun team maintain, claiming that in the production phase, this will be reduced to about 20 per cent.

The prototype evaluation of Arjun have been carried out over a period of four years. Some further improvements are likely to be made in consultation with the user — the Army. For example, the MBT Arjun team is not happy with its wireless set, and plan to go for a better one which has less possibility of being jammed. So far, Arjun has gone over different types of terrain — to a cumulative run of about 2,000 kms. The weapons system, comprising a dense packaging sophisticated up to electronic circuits, has gone through over 1,000 rounds evaluation.

27

EDUCATION

27.1 Constitutional Provisions

The 42nd amendment to the Constitution effected in 1976 made education a concurrent subject, thereby empowering the Central Government to legislate on education. However, the Centre, continues to play the role of a co-ordinator and monitor of educational programme and an initiator of innovative programmes. The approach, thus has been to evolve a meaningful partnership between the Central and the State Governments. The Government of India, Ministry of Human Resource Development (Department of Education) appoints Committees and Commissions to examine the state of education in the country and to suggest measures for improvement. It also serves as a clearing house of ideas.

Educational planning in the country is essentially the joint endeavour of the Central and State Governments. At the Central level, planning and monitoring division in the Ministry of Human Resource Development works in close liaison with the education division of the Planning Commission at the Centre and the State Planning Departments.

Actions related to education at the national level including planning and policy-making are guided and coordinated by the Central Advisory Board of Education and a few national level institutions specialising in particular aspects of education.

27.2 Department of Education, Ministry of Human Resource Development, Government of India

The Department of Education, one of the constituents of the Minister of Human Resource Development, is under the overall charge of Minister of Human Resource Development. The Secretariat of the Department is headed by the Secretary who is assisted by Additional Secretary and Educational Adviser. The Department is organised into Bureaux, Divisions, Branches, Desks, Sections and Units. Each Bureau is under the charge of a Joint Secretary/Joint Educational Adviser assisted by the Divisional Heads.

Important functions of the Department of Education are to evolve educational policy in all aspects and to coordinate and determine the standards of higher education and technical education; to develop and coordinate research in social sciences; to coordinate, in partnership with the States, activities aimed at achieving national goals such as universal Elementary Education (UEE), adult literacy, making education relevant to the world of work, development of scientific temper amongst students, removal of sex bias, provision of access to education for the deprived and disadvantaged etc to foster and develop study of languages—Hindi, Modern Indian and Classical languages including

Sanskrit; to deal with intellectual property; to improve quality of textbooks and develop book industry; to administer scholarship for the deprived and the talented; andoto coordinated UNESCO programmes.

Autonomous Organisations, Attached and Subordinate Offices and Allied Organisations connected with Department of Education

1. All India Council for Technical Education (AICTE) New Delhi for coordinating and setting standards in the area of technical education.
2. Central Advisory Board of Education (CABE) Department of Education, Shastri Bhawan, New Delhi.
3. Central Board of Secondary Education (CBSE), Preet Vihar, Delhi; for affiliating schools and conducting examinations.
4. Central Institute of Indian Languages (CIIL).
5. The Kendriya Hindi Sansthan (KHS), Agra, for the promotion of Hindi in India and abroad.
6. Kendriya Vidyalaya Sanghathan (KVS), New Delhi for running schools for the benefit of transferable Central Government employees.
7. Indian Institute of Advanced Study (IIAS), Shimla, for Research in Higher Education.
8. Indian Council of Historical Research (ICHR), New Delhi, for research in History.
9. Indian Council of Philosophical Research (ICPR), New Delhi, for research in Philosophy.
10. Indian Council of Social Science Research (ICSSR), New Delhi, for research in Social Sciences.
11. National Council of Educational Research and Training (NCERT), New Delhi, a National level resource institution operating in the school sector.
12. The National Institute of Educational Planning and Administration (NIEPA), New Delhi, also a national level resource institution, specialising in problems of Educational Management.
13. Navodaya Vidyalaya Samiti (NSU), New Delhi, for running schools for the benefit of talented rural children.
14. Rashtriya Sanskrit Sansthan, New Delhi, for promotion and development of and Research (from school to higher education level) in Sanskrit; it conducts examinations also.
15. University Grants Commission (UGC), New Delhi, which coordinates and sets standards in the area of higher education

Organisation for the Promotion of Books and Languages are :

16. Bureau for Promotion of Urdu (BPU), New Delhi.
17. Central Hindi Directorate (CHD), New Delhi.
18. Commission for Scientific and Technical Technology (CSTT), New Delhi.
19. The National Book Trust (NBT), New Delhi.

In the field of Adult Education, following organisations work :

20. Directorate of Adult Education (DAE) New Delhi.
21. National Literacy Mission (NLM).
22. National Institute of Adult Education (NIAE).

In higher education, the following organisation acts as a bureau of information:

23. Association of Indian University, (AIU), New Delhi.

In the area of Technical Education, the organisations are —

24. Administrative Staff College of India (ASCI), Hyderabad
25. Indian Institute(s) of Management (IIM) at Ahmedabad, Bangalore, Calcutta and Lucknow.
26. Indian Institute of Science (IIS), Bangalore.
27. Indian Institute(s) of Technology (IIT) at Bombay, Delhi, Kanpur, Kharagpur and Madras.
28. Indian School of Mines (ISM), Dhanbad.
29. National Institute of Training in Industrial Engineering (NITIE), Bombay.
30. National Institute of Foundry and Forge Technology (NIFFT), Ranchi.
31. Regional Engineering College(s) (REC) (17 in number)
32. School of Planning and Architecture (SPA), New Delhi.
33. Technical Teacher Training Institute(s) at Bhopal, Calcutta, Chandigarh and Madras.

While, UGC, Central Universities and Institutes like IITs, were set up by Acts of Parliament, the other autonomous organisations were registered under Societies Registration Act.

27.3 National Policy on Education (NPE)

The NPE was adopted by Parliament in 1966 and its implementation commended soon thereafter.

Universalisation of elementary education, equalisation of educational opportunities, women's education and development, vocationalisation of school education, consolidation of higher education, modernisation of technical education, improvement of quality content and process of education at all levels are themes of national endeavour in the field of education as envisaged in NPE. The NPE was slightly modified in 1992 but the essence and the programmes remain the same.

Table 27.1 shows the growth of recognised educational institutions in India.

27.4 Elementary Education

In elementary education, the focus shifted from enrolment, *per se*, to retention and achievement—a shift which reflects the renewed concern for improving efficiency of investment and for monitoring programmes in terms of outcomes rather than in terms shifted from exclusive concern with schooling to a holistic perception which stressed the need for providing alternative system of education of comparable quality to working children and girls whom the schools cannot reach.

27.4.1 Universalisation of Elementary Education (UEE)

Universalisation of Elementary Education (UEE) is a constitutional mandate. Article 45 of the Constitution stipulates, as a Directive Principle of State Policy, that 'the State shall endeavour to provide, within a period of ten years from the commencement of this Constitution for free and compulsory education for all

TABLE 27.1: Growth of Recognised Educational Institutions Since 1951

(As on 31 March)

	1951	1961	1971	1981	1991
Primary	209671	330399	408378	494503	558392
Upper primary	13596	49663	90621	118335	146636
Secondary schools/ pre-degree colleges	7416	17329	37051	51624	78619
Colleges for general education	370	967	2285	3421	4862
Colleges for professional education	208	852	992	1156	886*
Universities	27	45	82	110	146

* Includes only engineering, medical and teacher training institutions whereas the data for previous decades include physical education, nursery, mid-wifery, agriculture, veterinary, music, etc.

children until they complete the age of fourteen years.' Indeed, over the years, the Centre and the States have made considerable investments in promoting elementary education. Facilities in elementary education have grown from about 2.22 lakh to 7.05 lakh schools, enrolment from 22.28 million to 132.4 million children and outreach of primary education facilities to over 94 per cent of the rural population within 1 km walking distance of their houses. Over the last five years in pursuant of the NPE, effort has been made to focus attention on the quality of education being provided by this vast and possibly the largest, educational network of the world. Several schemes have been launched to improve retentions and reduce disparities; provide basic minimum facilities to schools; open non-formal education centres for part-time education of school dropouts and working children; improve teacher training facilities and teacher effectiveness; lay down Minimum Levels of Learning (MLLs); decentralise educational management and involve the community in the running of schools. Most of these schemes are ambitious in target and scope, and require sustained efforts and considerable resource support to make an impact. The progress of enrolment and teachers in primary and upper primary schools is given in Table 27.2.

TABLE 27.2: Enrolment and Teachers in Primary and Upper Primary Schools

(Lakh, as on 31 March)

Year	Primary				Upper Primary			
	Boys	Girls	Total	Teachers	Boys	Girls	Total	Teachers
1951	138	54	192	5.38	26	5	31	0.86
1961	236	114	350	7.42	51	16	67	3.45
1971	357	213	570	10.60	94	39	133	6.38
1981	453	285	738	13.63	139	68	207	8.51
1991	581	410	991	16.37	209	124	333	10.59

Source: Ministry of Human Resource Development.

The infrastructure facilities in terms of primary and upper primary schools increased more than threefold between 1951 and 1991. The gross enrolment ratio (GER) in 1990-91 in the primary stage (classes I-V) and upper primary stage (classes VI-VIII) was 101 and 60 per cent respectively. The droupout rate in 1987-88 was 47.0 per cent at the primary stage and 62.3 per cent for the elementary stage as a whole.

28

ENERGY

28.1 Performance

There has been a 40-fold increase in power generating capacity in India between 1950-51 and 1991-92. Alongwith this, there was six-fold increase in production of coal and a 130-fold increase in production of crude oil. Yet, energy shortages persist. In power sector, there is an energy deficiency of almost 8 per cent and a peak time shortage of almost 20 per cent. We are required to import about 30-33 million tonnes of crude oil and petroleum products annually, and this year even 5 million tonnes of coking coal is having to be imported. At the rate at which our economy is growing, it is estimated that by the year 2005 the country would require 450 million tonnes of coal (as compared to about 250 million tonnes at present), 94 million tonnes of oil (as compared to 55 million tonnes at present) and 645 billion units of electricity (present consumption being 284 billion units). Even in the best scenario that can be envisaged, resources that would be required to generate such energy would not be available. Reducing the demand for energy, therefore, becomes the only available alternative.

Energy conservation does not, however, imply only reduction of demand. It calls for optimum use of energy without affecting economic and social development. It encompasses a wide range of activities ranging from improving the efficiency of energy extraction, conversion, transmission and distribution, increasing the productivity of energy used, to inter-fuel substitution. It also entails changing the energy use habits of consumers. Its results are cost-effective, being much less than what is required to generate additional energy and also have much shorter gestation periods. And it would result in reducing the burden of country's precarious balance of payments.

Almost 5 to 10 per cent of potential savings in energy can be realised by adopting virtually no cost house keeping measures. A substantial additional savings can be realised with retrofitting or minor process/technology improvement measures, the pay back-up periods for which range from a few months to less than three to four years. It is estimated that the overall potential for energy conservation in transport, industrial and agricultural sectors ranges from 20 to 30 per cent.

Energy conservation programmes in our country were initiated during the VII Five Year Plan and a review of the activities has brought out into focus the needs for providing higher financial outlays for implementing programmes and other measures identified for effecting savings in energy consumption. In the Eighth Plan, an outlay of Rs. 1000 crores for energy conservation has been made and a National Energy Efficiency Programme is being launched to coordinate and monitor the efforts of all the relevant agencies. An Action Plan, which could result in effecting savings in energy consumption equivalent to 5000 MW of electricity and 6 million tonnes of petroleum products.

The performance of coal and power has been below target. Domestic production of crude oil has continued to decline since 1989-90.

Productivity levels in coal need to be improved. Washing capacity is inadequate to meed demand. The private sector has been invited to put up captive coal washing capacity. Government has also decided to allow the private power-generating companies to develop captive coal mines.

The average plant load factor of the State Electricity Boards has been below expected levels. Transmission and distribution (T & D) losses continue to be high. The government has increased investment outlays in the power sector during the Eighth Plan and permitted private sector investment with a view to improve the demand-supply balance in the medium term.

There has been a decline in the production of crude oil despite rising domestic demand. To help the oil companies generate internal resources, the prices of petroleum products were increased by an average 18 per cent in September, 1992.

Trends in performance of energy are given in Table 28.1

28.2 **Coal**

Coal production increased by 2.9 per cent during April-December 1992 over the corresponding period in 1991. The output of 158.22 million tonnes reached by December 1992 was, however, three per cent below target. The shortfall was due almost entirely to a 12.7 per cent slippage in output of Singareni Collieries Company Limited (SCCL) owing to disturbed law-and-order condition (Table 28.2).

28.3 **Power**

In 1991-92, total power generation at 286.7 billion kWh increased by 8.5 per cent over 1990-91 (Table 28.3). While thermal and hydro generation went up by 11.8 per cent and 1.4 per cent respectively; nuclear generation declined by 9.7 per cent.

Total generation of power in April-December, 1992 was 221.28 billion kWh compared to 211.47 billion kWh during the same period last year, showing a growth of 4.6 per cent. Thermal generation went up by 7.7 per cent and nuclear power by 20.2 per cent. However, hydel generation at 54.25 billion kWh was lower by 4.5 per cent. This shortfall may be made up during the remaining months as the monsoon has been bountiful in the southern region where the shortfall was concentrated.

The PLF (Plant Load Factor) provides a powerful indicator of operational efficiency in conditions of excess demand. As Table 28.4 reveals, the PLF in 1991-92 in central sector was appreciably higher than achieved by the SEBs (State Electricity Boards). The overall PLF of 55.3 per cent in thermal plants achieved in 1991-92 can be substantially improved because, under the same conditions, the central sector and private thermal plants achieved PLF of 64.7 per cent and 56.7 per cent respectively. Every one per cent improvement in PLF makes available an additional 500 MW of power. Improvement in the PLF will increase power availability as well as generate greater financial resources for the SEBs.

TABLE 28.1: Trends in the Performance in Energy

				April-December*			Change over previous year		
	Unit	1989-90	1990-91	1991-92*	1991	1992	1990-91	1991-92	1992-1993@
1	2	3	4	5	6	7	8	9	10
Energy									
1. Coal									
(a) Production	Mn. tonnes	200.89	211.73	229.28	153.8	158.22	5.40	8.29	2.87
(b) Pit-head stocks (year-end)	Mn. tonnes	37.43	42.56	48.73	34.49	37.72	13.71	14.50	9.37
(c) Despatches	Mn. tonnes	191.93	201.07	218.85	158.34	166.36	4.76	8.84	5.07
2. Electricity generated (Utilities only)	Bn. kWh	245.4	264.3	286.7	211.47	221.28	7.70	8.48	4.64
(a) Hydel	Bn. kWh	62.1	71.53	72.55	56.83	54.24	15.19	1.43	-4.56
(b) Thermal (incl. nuclear)	Bn. kWh	183.3	192.7	214.15	154.64	167.04	5.13	11.13	8.02
3. Petroleum									
(a) Crude oil production	Mn. tonnes	34.09	33.02	30.34	22.92	20.44	-3.14	-8.12	-10.82
(b) Refinery throughput	Mn. tonnes	51.94	51.77	51.42	37.54	40.36	-0.33	-0.68	7.51

* Provisional
@ April-December.

TABLE 28.2: Trends in the Coal Sector

				April-December*		Change over previous year		
	1989-90	1990-91	1991-92*	1991	1992	1990-91	1991-92	1992-93@
1	2	3	4	5	6	7	8	9
		(Million tonnes)					(per cent)	
1. Petroleum								
(i) CIL								
(a) Opencast	119.92	133.80	147.52	95.78	99.49	11.57	10.25	3.87
(b) Underground	58.70	55.84	56.62	40.28	40.44	-4.87	1.40	0.40
(ii) SCCL								
(a) Opencast	5.77	6.59	8.28	5.10	5.34	14.21	25.64	4.71
(b) Underground	12.03	11.12	12.30	9.24	9.54	-7.56	10.61	3.25
(iii) Others								
(a) Opencast	—	—	—	—	—	—	—	—
(b) Underground	4.47	211.73	229.28	153.80	158.22	5.40	8.29	2.87
2. Production (By coal grades)								
(a) Coking coal	44.43	45.30	46.28	30.07	29.87	1.96	2.16	-0.67
(b) Non-coking coal	156.46	166.43	183.00	123.73	128.35	6.37	9.96	3.73
(c) Washed coal	11.12	11.19	12.88	8.67	8.78	0.63	15.10	1.27
(d) Middlings	4.61	4.40	4.94	3.44	3.66	-4.56	12.27	6.40
3. Pithead stocks (year-end)	37.43	42.56	48.73	34.49	377.72	13.71	14.50	9.37
4. Despatches	191.93	201.07	218.85	158.34	166.36	4.76	8.84	5.07
5. Lignite production$	12.60	11.76	12.50	9.01	9.28	-6.67	6.29	3.00
6. Output per man-shift (OMS)								
(i) CIL	1.21	1.31	1.40	1.26	1.33	8.26	6.87	5.56
(ii) SCCL	0.99	0.96	0.98	0.91	0.94	-3.03	2.08	3.30

* Provisional.
@ April-December.
$ By NLC Only.

TABLE 28.3: Trends in the Power Sector (utilities only)

				April-December*		Change over previous year		
	1989-90	1990-91	1991-92*	1991-92	1992-93	1990-91	1991-92	1992-93@
1	2	3	4	5	6	7	8	9
		(Billion kWh)					(per cent)	
1. Power generation	245.10	264.20	286.70	211.47	221.78	7.79	8.552	4.64
(i) Hydro-electric	62.00	71.50	72.50	56.83	54.25	15.32	1.40	-4.55
(ii) Thermal	178.50	186.50	208.60	150.67	162.26	4.48	11.85	7.69
(iii) Nuclear	4.60	6.20	5.60	3.98	4.78	34.78	-9.68	20.15
		(per cent)						
2. Plant load factor of thermal plants	56.50	53.80	55.30	53.40	54.80	—	—	—

* Provisional.
@ April-December.

TABLE 28.4: Plant Load Factors : Achievements during 1990-91, 1991-92 and April-December, 1992

(*per cent*)

Board/Undertaking/Sector	Plant Load Factor			
	1990-91 Actual	1991-92 Actual	April-December 1992 Target	April-December 1992 Actual
PLF above 50%				
1. West Bengal Power Development Corporation	57.30	61.40	61.50	58.70
2. Rajasthan State Electricity Board	42.80	52.60	67.00	72.80
3. Maharashtra State Electricity Board	58.20	61.30	56.20	58.30
4. Andhra Pradesh State Electricity Board	65.80	62.10	64.00	60.30
5. Gujarat State Electricity Board	57.70	57.00	58.10	59.60
6. Punjab State Electricity Board	53.00	52.80	60.60	58.20
7. Delhi Electricity Supply Undertaking	50.90	57.20	53.40	53.80
8. Tamil Nadu State Electricity Board	58.30	55.70	58.80	62.20
PLF 40% to 50%				
1. Madhya Pradesh State Electricity Board	52.70	49.20	53.70	48.80
2. Uttar Pradesh State Electricity Board	52.10	44.30	47.00	48.60
3. Haryana State Electricity Board	34.60	45.80	48.20	48.90
4. Karnataka Power Corporation	76.30	59.10	59.90	45.40
PLF below 40%				
1. West Bengal State Electricity Board	30.90	30.80	35.80	28.70
2. Orissa State Electricity Board	34.00	30.00	31.80	31.70
3. Assam State Electricity Board	27.70	24.60	33.70	23.50
4. Durgapur Projects Ltd.	24.50	17.80	25.80	25.30
5. Bihar State Electricity Board	24.00	21.30	33.20	24.00
PLF of Central Sector (Total)	58.10	64.70	61.60	59.50
PLF of individual units:				
1. Neyveli Lignite Corporation	69.60	66.30	57.30	54.60
2. National Thermal Power Corporation	60.90	69.20	66.20	65.20
3. Damodar Valley Corporation	33.30	33.60	38.00	30.10
PLF of private utilities	58.40	56.70	53.00	60.10

28.4 **Petroleum**

Crude oil production during 1991-92 was 30.34 million tonnes, 4.6 per cent below target and 12.4 per cent lower than the peak of 34.09 million tonnes achieved in 1989-90. Oil and Natural Gas Commission's (ONGC) off-shore structures contributed 62 per cent of the total. Oil India Limited's (OIL) on-shore output accounted for eight per cent.

Targeted crude production during 1992-93 is 28.46 million tonnes, 6.6 per cent lower than 1991-92 output. This decline is evident in the output of April-December 1992 which at 20.44 million tonnes was 10.8 per cent below the previous year's level (Table 28.5).

Consequently, domestic production, which accounted for 70 per cent of total consumption in 1984-85, saw its share decline to 56 per cent in 1990-91 and further to 50 per cent in 1991-92. It will go down further during 1992-93 and put pressure on the balance of payments.

TABLE 28.5: Trends in the Petroleum Sector

				April-December*		Change over previous year		
	1989-90	1990-91	1991-92*	1991-92	1992-93	1990-91	1991-92	1992-93@
1	2	3	4	5	6	7	8	9
	(Million tonnes)					(per cent)		
1. Crude oil production	34.09	33.02	30.34	22.92	20.44	-3.14	-8.12	-10.82
(i) Onshore	12.37	11.83	11.38	8.57	8.44	-4.37	-3.80	-1.52
(a) ONGC	9.67	9.18	8.85	6.63	6.55	-5.07	-3.59	-1.21
(b) OIL	2.7	2.65	2.53	1.94	1.89	-1.85	-4.53	-2.58
(ii) Offshore	21.72	21.19	18.96	14.35	12	-2.44	-10.52	-16.38
2. Refinery throughput	51.94	51.77	51.42	37.54	40.36	-0.33	-0.68	7.51
3. Production of petroleum products	48.69	48.56	48.35	35.17	37.71	-0.27	-0.43	7.22
	(Billion cubic metres)							
4. Natural gas production	16.98	18.00	18.65	13.87	13.61	6.01	3.61	-1.87

* Provisional.

@ April-December.

TABLE 28.6: Consumption of Petroleum Products**

				April-December*		Change over previous year		
	1989-90	1990-91	1991-92*	1991-92	1992-93	1990-91	1991-92	1992-93@
1	2	3	4	5	6	7	8	9
	(Million tonnes)					(per cent)		
1. Light distillates	9.41	9.8	10.13	7.47	7.65	4.14	3.37	2.41
(a) Naphtha	3.35	3.45	3.43	2.53	2.48	2.99	-0.58	-1.98
(b) LPG	2.27	2.42	2.65	1.91	2.1	6.61	9.50	9.95
(c) Petrol	3.49	3.55	3.57	2.69	2.7	1.72	0.56	0.37
2. Middle distillates	32.48	33.11	34.35	25.17	26.74	1.94	3.75	6.24
(a) Kerosene	8.24	8.42	8.35	6.19	6.29	2.18	-0.83	1.62
(b) Diesel oil	20.71	21.14	22.68	16.49	18.09	2.08	7.28	9.70
3. Heavy ends	12.2	12.13	12.36	9.08	9.13	-0.57	1.90	0.55
(a) Fuel oil	8.82	8.99	9.13	6.82	6.86	1.93	1.56	0.59
Total	54.09	55.04	56.84	41.72	43.52	1.76	3.27	4.31

* Provisional.
@ April-December.
** Excluding Refinery Boiler Fuel (RBF).

28.5 **Natural Gas**

The output of natural gas grew at 24 per cent a year in the 1980s. However, it was 18.7 billion cubic metres in 1991-92; only 3.6 per cent higher than in the previous year. It was 13.61 billion cubic metres in April-December 1992; a shortfall of 1.9 per cent over the same period last year. This indicates a considerable slowdown in the production of natural gas in the face of the excess demand for gas as a source of energy and chemical feedstock. The utilisation of natural gas during April-December 1992 was 89 per cent of total production during the period.

28.6 **Renewable Sources of Energy**

Major programmes launched for the development and utilisation of new and renewable sources of energy include programmes for development of biogas, solar photovoltaic, wind power and micro-hydel. Over 15.75 lakh biogas plants had been set up in the country till end of March 1992 under the National Project on Biogas Development. An estimated biogas generation capacity equivalent to over 49.1 lakh tonnes of fuelwood per year valued at Rs. 245.5 crore and 2236.6 lakh tonnes of manure a year has been created. The target for 1992-93 is fixed at 1.35 lakh plants of which 82800 were installed during April-December 1992.

After a relatively low rise in 1991-92, consumption of petroleum products during April-December 1992 rose by 4.3 per cent over the same period last year. The rate of growth was highest in the case of LPG (9.9 per cent) and HSD (9.7 per cent) (Table 28.6). Thus this year is likely to witness a significant acceleration in the growth of demand.

While the household sector consumes around 80 per cent of LPG (Liquefied Petroleum Gas), the transport sector consumes around 90 per cent of HSD (High Speed Diesel). The other products are, by and large, consumed by industry. Since the household and infrastructure sectors are still deficient in energy consumption and per capita energy consumption levels are low, there is every likelihood that demand for these petroleum products would continue to increase rapidly. Unless domestic production of crude and petroleum products increases faster, an increasing amount of imports of these commodities will be required to meet the demand.

28.7 **Solar Energy**

Solar energy is perennial and non-polluting source of energy and is available in all parts of the country. It can be directly converted into heat energy through Solar Thermal Devices and Systems. Heat energy, thus produced, can be used for variety of applications in industries, dairies, hospitals, hotels, hostels etc. It can also be used for generation of electric power, using steam cycle and conventional turbines. Solar thermal systems are broadly categorised as:

a) Low Temperature Systems (Upto 100 degree C)	Solar water heaters, Solar air heaters, solar driers, solar timber kilns, solar desalination systems and solar cookers, solar Green House, Solar Passive build-

	ings etc.
b) Medium Temperature Systems (Above 100 and up to 250 degree C)	Solar refrigeration, Solar air-conditioning, Solar pumping, solar industrial heating etc.
c) High Temperature Systems (Above 250 degree C)	Solar power generation.

Potential

India is blessed with plenty of sun-shine. The daily average solar energy incident in the country varies from 5 to 7 kWhr per square metre. Approximately 5 x 10^{15} kWhr of energy per annum from the sun is received in India.

Achievements at a Glance (Table 28.7)

— Low Temperature systems have been installed in all the States of the country under 'SOLAR THERMAL EXTENSION PROGRAMME'.
— Target for 1992-93 for various: 60,000 m^2 low grade solar thermal devices: collector area
— Target for 1992-93 for Solar Cookers: 40,000 Nos.

TABLE 28.7: Status of Installation as on 31-3-92

Sl. No.	System	Number	Capacity (Litres per day)	Collector Area (M^2)
1.	Industrial/Commercial Water Heating Systems	4,829	91,38,000	1,86,172
2.	Domestic Solar Water Heating Systems	10,127	13,47,700	26,905
3.	Solar Cookers	2,27,483		—
4.	Solar/Driers/Solar Air Heaters	61		—
5.	Solar Timber Kilns	71		—
6.	Solar Stills (Water Distillation Systems)	9,651		—
7.	Green House	7		—
8.	Solar Huts	200		—
9.	Passive Buildings	6		—
10.	Experimental Solar Thermal Power Plant	2		—

Programme Incentives by Central Government

i) Financial Assistance/Subsidy to Users

— Solar Water Heaters : Rs. 1,000 per m^2 of Collector Area
— Solar Air Heaters : Rs. 800 per m^2 of Collector Area
— Solar Stills : Rs. 500 per m^2 of Basin Area
— Solar Cookers : Rs. 150 per Solar Cooker
— In addition, some of the State Governments also give their own subsidy on various systems.

ii) Service charges to State/Implementing Agencies: 10 per cent of Central Subsidy
iii) Medium temperature and high temperature solar thermal systems are being developed and installed for field evaluation under research and development programmes.
iv) For carrying out R&D, prototype development and testing of solar systems; the Ministry has set up Solar Energy Centre at Gwalpahari, Gurgaon (Haryana).
v) R&D is also being carried out at various institutions in the country.
vi) Over 100 numbers of manufacturers have been promoted and registered for manufacturing of low temperature solar thermal systems.
vii) In association with MNES, BIS has brought out Indian standards on solar flat plate collectors and solar cookers.
viii) Six Regional Test Centres/Technical Back-up Units have been set up to facilitate testing for BIS certification.

Energy Saving

— Installed collector area : 2.22 lakh sq. metre
— Thermal Energy Equivalent : 150.00 million kWh.

Achievement in States is given in Table 28.8.

TABLE 28.8: Achievements : States

Sl. No.	State/Union Territory	Solar Photovoltaic Systems 31.3.92			
		SLS (Nos.)	WPS (Nos.)		SPP* (kWp)
1.	Andhra Pradesh	6515	61	20.00	(4)
2.	Bihar	164	94	—	
3.	Goa	28	2	7.00	(2)
4.	Gujarat	1818	98	8.00	(2)
5.	Karnataka	252	8	—	
6.	Kerala	393	6	—	
7.	Madhya Pradesh	3793	93	—	
8.	Maharashtra	7078	92	6.64	(3)
9.	Orissa	1308	65	29.00	(4)
10.	Rajasthan	6082	86	10.00	(1)
11.	Sikkim	83	2	—	
12.	Tamil Nadu	912	31	—	
13.	Uttar Pradesh	2546	174	60.00	(15)
14.	West Bengal	1000	39	—	
15.	North-east States	1559	245	26.00	(14)
16.	Haryana, Himachal Pradesh J&K and Punjab	711	26	20.00	(1)
17.	Union Territories	590	49	45.00	(4)
	Total	34832	1171	244.64	(5)

SLS—Street Lighting Systems
WPS—Water Pumping Systems
SPP—Small Power Plants
*—Figure in parenthesis indicates the number of power plants.

Non-Conventional Sources of Energy

Improving the quality of life through Renewable Energy because of their reliability, cost-effectiveness, and flexibility of scale, renewable energy technologies are ideal for use in developing economies. The economic benefits and environmental sustainability of renewables lead to a realistic long-term energy approach for improving social and economic growth. Achievements are given in Table 28.9.

TABLE 28.9: Achievements at a Glance

Sl. No.	Programme	Cumulative Achievements upto 31.3.92 (Numbers)
1.	Family size biogas plants (in lakh)	15.75
2.	Community/Institutional Biogas Plants	819.00
3.	Improved Chulhas (in lakh)	125.00
4.	Domestic Solar Water Heating Systems	10,127.00
5.	Industrial Solar Water Heating Systems	4,829.00
6.	Solar Stills	9,651.00
7.	Solar Timber Kilns	71.00
8.	Solar Air Heaters	61.00
9.	Solar Cookers (in lakh)	2.27
10.	Villages provided with Photovoltaic street lights	8100.00
11.	Photovoltaic Water Pumps	1171.00
12.	Photovoltaic Power Units (KWP)	750.00
13.	Photovoltaic Community lights/TV and Community facilities	968.00
14.	Photovoltaic Domestic lighting units	9050.00
15.	Photovoltaic lanterns	
16.	Wind pumps	2916.00
17.	Wind Farms (MW)	2916.00
18.	Mini-micro Hidro (MW)	86.53
19.	Urjagram Energy Surveys	1557.00
20.	Urjagram Projects	155.00
21.	Biomass Energy Plantations (Hectares)	17110.00
22.	Biomass Gasifiers/Stirling Engines	1000.00

Improved Chulha Programme

Energy is a vital input for economic and social development. In most of the developing countries, wood and other biomass fuel are still the primary source of energy for the majority of people, particularly the poor. In the fast few decades, however, there has been a rapid depletion of the forest resources, requiring people in the rural areas, specially women and children, to spend a considerable part of their time and energy covering long distances to obtain the supply of fuelwood. Deforestation has also led to grave ecological consequences.

The National Project on Demonstration of Improved Chulha was designed and launched in 1983 by the Department of Non-Conventional Energy Sources with the following objectives:

— to conserve and optimise the use of fuel wood specially in the rural and semi-urban areas;
— to help in preventing deforestation;

— to reduce women's drudgery and health hazards by eliminating smoke from the kitchen; and
— to help in improvement of domestic environment.

The project was subsequently converted into a National Programme with effect from April 1985. In view of the overwhelming response from the beneficiaries. It now forms part of the Twenty Point and the Minimum Needs Programmes of the Government of India.

Nearly 12.5 million improved chulhas have been installed in domestic households from the inception of the programme till March 31, 1992. A target of an additional 18 million chulhas has been envisaged during the 8th Five Year Plan period, 1992-97, striving to achieve nearly 25 per cent coverage of the potential households.

The traditional wood chulha has very low efficiency ranging from 2 to 10 per cent. The result is long hours spent on cooking in smoke filled kitchens and in collecting cooking fuel, especially for the rural poor who cannot afford to buy fuel. The slow deterioration in the health of most of the rural women caused due to respiratory diseases and deterioration in eye sight are direct results of the hours they spend in poorly ventilated smoky kitchens.

The improved chulha incorporates an optimum size of combustion chamber, air inlet, grate, baffles, dampers. It is with or without a chimney. The improved models of chulha are of thermal efficiency ranging from 20 per cent onwards.

New Thrust

The new strategy for implementation envisages large scale extension of the programme from a level of nearly 10 per cent coverage as at present to about 25 per cent coverage of potential households by the end of the 8th Plan. It focuses on greater association of beneficiaries in selection of models, their financial participation, education and awareness through wide publicity over the electronic and print media.

The programme thrust during 8th Plan also attempts liberalised marketing and easy availability of various models of chulhas, including ISI marked portable chulhas for quality satisfaction.

Source: Ministry of Non-Conventional Energy reported in *Hindustan Times*, October 28, 1992.

29

ENVIRONMENT AND FORESTS

The Ministry of Environment and Forests serves as the Focal Point in the administrative structure of the Central Government for planning, promotion and coordination of environmental and forestry programmes. The main activities include: (1) protection of environment; (2) prevention and control of pollution; (3) conservation and survey of flora, fauna, forests and wildlife and (4) afforestation and regeneration of degraded areas. These tasks are being fulfilled through environmental impact assessment; eco-regeneration; assistance to organisations implementing environmental and forestry programmes; promotion of environmental and forestry research, extension, education and training to augment the requisite manpower: dissemination of environmental information; international co-operation and creation of environmental awareness at national level.

29.1 **Control of Pollution**

Control of Water, Air and Noise Pollution

- To augment the resources of the Pollution Control Boards, the Water (Prevention and Control of Pollution) Cess (Amendment) Bill, 1991, has been passed in both the Houses of Parliament.
- Seventeen problem areas have been identified on the basis of the survey and reports of the Central and State Pollution Control Boards and time targeted Action Plans for controlling pollution in nine of these areas have been finalised.
- A scheme for setting up of common effluent treatment plants in all clusters of small scale industries/industrial estates with a central subsidy of 25 per cent of the capital cost has been launched.
- In order to assess the pollution load and various other activities responsible for it, studies on Narmada, Tapti and Brahmaputra rivers have been completed.
- Thirty new inland water quality monitoring stations have been identified for establishment under 'Assessment of Pollution by Monitoring' scheme.
- Under Indo-Dutch bilateral programme, two automatic water quality monitoring stations have been installed on the river Yamuna at Delhi.
- Thirty new stations have been identified for establishment, in phases, for monitoring of ambient air quality under 'National Ambient Air Quality Monitoring Programme'.
- Pollution control status of 17 categories of industries in 23 States/UTs including all major industrial estates has been prepared. Defaulting units have been identified and actions are being initiated against these units.
- Noise limits have been prescribed for automobiles, domestic appliances and construction equipments to be adopted at the manufacturing stage.
- Codes of practice for controlling noise from sources other than industries

and automobiles like public address system, aircraft operation, railway operation, bursting of crackers etc. have been evolved.

— Standards for effluents and air emissions for the industries like Natural Rubber and Processing, Dairy, Ceramic, Bagasse-fired Boilers and Tannery have been finalised.
— The Central Pollution Control Board (CPCB) has been empowered to enter any place or inspect any equipment, industrial plant, record, register etc., and to take samples of air, water, soil or any other substance for the purpose of analysis from any factory premises or other places under the rules of Environment (Protection) Act, 1986.
— Environmental Audit has been proposed to be made compulsory in the companies sc that brief particulars of compliance with environmental law are reported in the reports of their Board of Directors.
— The Scheme of "Labelling of Environment Friendly Products" has been notified.
— Out of identified 16 consumer product categories, criteria for two product categories viz. toilet soaps and detergents have been notified.

29.2 **Research**

Environmental Research

— During the year two research projects under Environmental Research Scheme and Man and Biosphere Programme were sanctioned while 26, sanctioned earlier were completed.
— An All India Coordinated Programme for studies on 'Sea Level Rise' continued at 10 different institutions of the country and a new project on 'National Methane Campaign' for actual methane measurement has been initiated.
— Under the Integrated Action Oriented Research, Demonstration and Extension Programme on Eco-Development, 21 projects under 'Himalayan Region', 19 under 'Western Ghats' and 12 under 'Eastern Ghats' remained operational while six projects sanctioned earlier in 'Himalayan Region' and nine in 'Western Ghats' were completed.
— Salient findings of the programme on river Cauvery in respect of bio-monitoring and physio-chemical profiles of the river water, pollution status of the tributaries and different species of fauna in the river basin have been recorded.
— During the year, monitoring of the progress of 57 research projects under Environmental Research Scheme, Man and Biosphere Programme, Western Ghats and Eastern Ghats has been conducted.
— The G.B. Pant Institute on Himalayan Environment and Development, an autonomous organisation of the Ministry was provided 35,844 ha. of land, free-of-cost, at Kosi-Kaatarmal, Almora, by Government of U.P. for the construction of the building 'Genebank' and 'Arboretum'.
— The research and development activities of the Institute were extended on major themes of land and water resource management, sustainable development and rural eco-system, conservation of biological diversity and ecological economics and environmental impact analysis. The Institute also continued eight research projects, sanctioned earlier.

29.3 **Survey of Natural Resources**

Flora

- Intensive floral surveys in the priority areas of Andaman and Nicobar Islands, Manipur, Assam, Nagaland, South Western Ghats and Western Himalayas were undertaken by the Botanical Survey of India and about 2500 plant specimens were collected during the surveys. A critical study of description of about 1285 species collected from the States of Himachal Pradesh, Jammu and Kashmir, Mizoram, Nagaland, Manipur and Assam are completed.
- Editing and scrutiny of 225 Red Data Sheets on rare, vulnerable and endangered species have been completed and being processed for publication.
- Manuscripts of the taxonomic revision of the families consisting of Tamaricaceae, Hypericaceae, Sonneraticeae and Goodeniaceae are being scrutinised for publication of "Fascicle 21" of the Flora of India.
- State Flora of Kerala, Rajasthan (Vol. II & III), Manipur (Vol. I) and Mizoram (Vol. I) are being published.
- District flora of Silent Valley in Palghat District of Kerala and that of Nasik District of Maharashtra have been published.
- Ethno-botanical studies on plants used by the tribals in Tamil Nadu, Karnataka and plains of Uttar Pradesh have been initiated under the All India Coordinated Research Project on Ethno-biology.
- Collection and compilation of data in respect of five less known economic plants of India were completed.
- Multiplication through tissue culture technique of some selected endangered orchid species has been undertaken and a tissue laboratory has been set up.

Fauna

- A total of 80 surveys covering 65 districts falling under different ecosystem all over the country were conducted by the Zoological Survey of India.
- Faunal studies in the States of Meghalaya, Tripura, Uttar Pradesh, Tamil Nadu and those of Himalayan Eco-system, Bio-sphere Reserves and National Parks Were undertaken.
- Status survey of Capped Langur and Hoolock Gibbon was conducted in Meghalaya.
- The National Zoological collections were enriched by the addition of 56,243 identified specimens pertaining to 2889 species. In addition 879 zoological specimens pertaining to 290 species were identified.

Forest Survey

- Forest-Survey of India completed 3rd assessment of forest cover in India and the draft report 1991 has been prepared.
- Thematic maps of 213 sheets covering the States of Bihar, Madhya Pradesh, Maharashtra, Rajasthan, Haryana, Punjab, Uttar Pradesh and

West Bengal have been completed.

— The inventory of forest resources of Nagaland, Manipur, Meghalaya, Assam and Mizoram has been completed and the inventory report of Nagaland has been published.

29.4 Conservation of Natural Resources

Forest Conservation

— Guidelines have been framed under the Forest (Conservation Act), 1980, to facilitate speedier clearance of the proposals received from the State Governments and the project authorities.

— The Regional Chief Conservator of Forests have been delegated with powers to clear proposals involving forest land less than 1 ha.

— Out of 4661 proposals received under Forest (Conservation) Act, 1980, 2348 proposals have been approved.

— Regional Offices of the Ministry located at Bangalore, Bhopal, Bhubaneshwar, Chandigarh, Lucknow, Shillong have been delegated powers to process proposals for diversion of forest land for non-forest uses up to 1 ha.

— A new scheme has been formulated providing 100 per cent central assistance to the State Governments for protection and regeneration of degraded forests through tribal people and other poor people living near forests who in turn will receive more than half of the share of the forest produce thereby creating sustainable economic base to these people through forestry.

— A set of six guidelines have been issued to the State Governments to provide benefits to the tribal people at the forest-tribal interface.

— In view of the new National Forest Policy, 1988, the on-going forestry practices and programmes have been reoriented to meet the objectives.

— In order to reduce the illegal felling and to strengthen the efforts of the State Governments, a scheme on "Development of Infrastructure for Protection of Forests from Biotic Interferences" has been initiated on 50:50 sharing basis.

Wildlife Conservation

— The Wildlife (Protection) Amendment Bill, vetted by Parliament has been promulgated as an Act No. 44 of 19911 after it has received the ascent of the President w.e.f. 2nd October 1991.

— Financial assistance was provided to 28 National Parks and 123 Sanctuaries for conservation programme.

— Eighteen Tiger Reserves in 13 States covering over 28600 sq kms. forest area have been established so far in the country. During the year, an amount of Rs. 6 crores has been provided as central assistance for the maintenance and development of these Tiger Reserves.

— A Nature Interpretation Centre at Melghat Tiger Reserve has been completed. Setting up of such Centres at Buxa, Nagarjunasagar and Corbett Tiger Reserve have been taken up with the Central assistance.

— The Project Elephant is being launched with the objective on ensuring long term survival of identified viable population and to tackle the problematic elephant population that are causing serious depredation.

— The National Zoological Park presently displaying 1143 animals comprising of 71 species of mammals, 88 species of birds and 5 species of reptiles continued its captive breeding programmes of rare and endangered species of wild animals.
— Six States have so far notified the formation of State Advisory Boards for their Animal Welfare Activities under the Prevention of Cruelty of Animals Act, 1960.

National Conservation Strategy and Policy Statement on Environment and Development

— A document entitled 'National Conservation and Policy Statement on Environment and Development' covering various environmental problems and its regulatory and promotional measures, development of policies from environmental perspectives, international cooperation, policy and instrumental support for the implementation of the strategy etc. has been prepared.

Assistance to Botanic Gardens and Field Centres

— A scheme has been initiated to augment the activities for conservation and protection of plant genetic resources in different regions of the country through a net work of botanic gardens and field centres.

29.5 **Wasteland Development**

— The National Wastelands Development Board (NWDB) has adopted a mission approach for enlisting peoples' participation, harnessing inputs of science and technology and achieving interdisciplinary coordination in the planning and implementation of the wastelands development programmes.
— Various Centrally Sponsored and Central Sector Schemes to promote afforestation and wastelands development, to check land degradation, to raise minor forest produce, to regenerate inaccessible areas and develop people's nursery etc. were continued.
— Apart from continuing the greening programme, the concept of 'Smritivans' has been introduced with the twin purpose of planting trees as life memorial in perpetuating the memory of departed ones and greening the lands for maintenance of ecological balance. During the year 'Rajiv Smriti Van' was inaugurated.
— A pilot project of the tree growers' cooperative has been taken up in five states in collaboration with the National Dairy Development Board and 102 Cooperatives have so far been registered with a total membership of 11,046.
— Realising the role of communications in sensitising people to social development NWDB prepared a paper on 'Communications Strategy' and circulated to all concerned.
— A National Fund for Afforestation and Wastelands Development has been

set up to regenerate degraded areas/wastelands. Donations towards this fund are 100 per cent exempted from income tax under the relevant provisions.

— Nine pilot projects are being implemented in different agro-climatic zones with a view to promote the use of Geographical Information System (GIS) technology for landuse management and the wastelands development.
— Seven Regional Centres, set up by the NWDB in different Universities and National level institutions of the country, continued to provide technical and extension support to State Forest Departments in preparing projects for wastelands development and afforestation with people's participation.

29.6 Education and Information

Forestry Education and Training

— The Indian Council of Forestry Research and Education (ICFRE), an autonomous organisation of the Ministry, continued to provide financial assistance to various Universities in improving their courses both at Graduate and Post graduate levels. Forest Research Institute, Dehradun, a research institutions under the Council, has been notified as a deemed University by the Department of Education.
— The Indian Institute of Forest Management, Bhopal organised two one-week course for IFS Officers and conducted Management Development Programmes on issues related to social forestry, rehabilitation of degraded eco-systems, forestry administration, etc.
— The Indian Plywood Industries Research Institute, Bangalore, an autonomous organisation of the Ministry, organised 17 short-term courses in the areas of Saw Doctoring, Saw Milling, Plywood manufacturing, Low-grading etc., during the year. The institute also conducted a one-week course for IFS Officers on 'Wood Panel Technology'.
— Forth seven IFS probationers and two foreign trainees from Bhutan were provided in-service training by Indira Gandhi National Forest Academy (IGNFA) Dehradun.
— Three State Forest Service Colleges located at Dehradun (U.P.), Burnihat (Assam), and Coimbatore (T.N.), continued to impart initial two-year in-service training to the officers of the State Forest Services (SFS).
— Eastern Forest Rangers' College, Kurseong organised a two-year training course for 93 Ranger Trainees.
— About 1200 IFS officers attended the compulsory training orientation programme organised by the Ministry.

Wildlife Education and Training

— The Wildlife Institute of India (WII), Dehradun organised nine-month Post-Graduate Diploma and three month Certificate courses on Wildlife for Protected Area Managers at the professional and field technician's level. Nineteen Officer Trainees including one from Lao, PDR graduated in XII Diploma Course, conducted by the Institute.
— A Zoo Management Course for the middle-level managers and technicians and a four-week course for 16 trainees from Zoos and Wildlife Or-

ganisations from different States were organised by the Institute.

- The IUCN recognised WII as a Regional Centre for Wildlife Training and provided fellowships for Diploma and Post Graduate Students.
- Under the Indo-US Project, the Institute conducted a 10-day training workshop on 'Chemical Restraint Techniques' for Capture of Wild Animals.

29.7 Environmental Information System (ENVIS)

- The Environmental Information System (ENVIS) continued its activities of collection, collation, storage, retrieval and dissemination of environmental information to all concerned.
- Three new ENVIS Centres in the field of 'Desert Ecology', "Estuary, Mangroves, Corals and Lagoons" and "Environmental Education" have been set up during the year, thus increasing the number of ENVIS network partners from 10 to 13.
- ENVIS enriched the existing documentation base by procuring several documents on environment and its related areas for dissemination of environmental information to the user groups.
- During the year, ENVIS network both as National Focal Point (NFP) and Regional Service Centre (RSC) of INFOTERRA/UNEP responded to more than 4100 National and International queries and provided substantive information to the users. Out of these queries, the ENVIS focal point in the Ministry alone responded to 1554 queries of which 1493 were National and 61 were International.
- The quarterly abstracting journal entitled "Paryavaran Abstracts" continued to be published. During the year, four issues of the journal containing about 1000 abstracts were published.

29.8 International Cooperation

- The Ministry continued to function as the nodal agency for participation in various international agreements and participated in several intergovernmental negotiating committees for 'Convention of Climate Change' and 'Bio-diversity' during the year.
- The Asian Development Bank (ADB), under the Indo-ADB collaboration programme provided assistance for a project on 'Review of Environmental Laws in India'.
- One ambient air quality monitoring station in Delhi has been installed under the Indo-EEC collaboration programme.
- Under Indo-Dutch bilateral programme, basic training on sampling and analysis was provided under the project "Monitority of the River Yamuna".
- Two seminars on administrative development in forestry sector have been held under the Indo-Sweden Collaborative Programme.
- An agreement was signed with the World Bank for a major project on Industrial Pollution Control. Three Sewage Treatment Plants in U.P. and 12 Pumping Stations Schemes in West Bengal are being executed with World Bank assistance under the Ganga Action Plan.
- The Ministry has set up an Inter-Ministerial Group (IMG) to consider various issues related to United Nations Conference on Environment and

Development (UNCED) being held in Brazil in June 1992. The IMG held a number of meetings during the year. The Ministry also held consultations with selected NGOs and Experts to coordinate the preparation for the UNCED Conference.

— Two Publications one on "Environment and Development: Traditions, Concerns and Efforts in India" and the other on "An Overview of India's Approach to Environment andDevelopment" are also being prepared by the Centre for Environment Education, Ahmedabad, a Grants-in-Aid institution of the Ministry for the UNCED conference.
— With a view to obtain expert advice on impact of global changes on earth's environment, and to promote and coordinate various multi-institutional andmulti-disciplinary studies and research projects in these areas the Ministry constituted an Expert Advisory Committee (EAC) on Global Environmental Issues. On the recommendations of EAC, an All India co-ordinated programme on Sea level rise along the Indian coast and a National Methane Campaign have been launched by the Ministry.
— The Ministry participated in the on-going negotiations under the aegis of UNEP in the Global Convention on Conservation of Bio-diversity.
— The Ministry actively participated in the Vienna Convention and other meetings related to various aspects of the Montreal Protocol. Drafting of a strategy for reduction and eventual phase out of ozone depleting substances has also been initiated.
— A Global Environment Facility (GEF) has been jointly established by the World Bank, UNDP and UNEP and the Ministry has co-ordinated within the Government in dealing with the GEF.

30

HEALTH

30.1 **Medical Infrastructure**

There has been considerable expansion of institutional facilities for treatment of sick and health care (Table 30.1). The doctor-nurse ratio works out to be 1:0.67 in 1991 against the ideal ratio considered to be 1:3. The number of registered medical practitioners per 10000 population was 1.7 in 1951; it increased to 4.7 in 1991. Hospital beds of all categories were 3.2 per 10000 population in 1951 and increased to 9.6 in 1991. There has been a considerable increase in the number of primary health centres and sub-centres. However, there is shortage of nurses, pharmacists, laboratory technicians, radiographers and dental surgeons in addition to a shortage of buildings.

TABLE 30.1: Expansion of Health Services

	Items	1951	1961	1971	1981	1991
1.	Medical colleges@	28*	60	98	106	128
2.	Hospitals**	2694	3054	3862	6804	11571
3.	Dispensaries**	6515	9406	12180	15968	27994
4.	Community health centres@	0	0	0	217	1925
5.	Pri. Health Cent.@	725	2565	51112	5568	22243
6.	Sub-centres@	0	0	28489	51192	129999
7.	Hospital beds**	117178	230000	348655	569495	806409
8.	Doctors**	61840	83756	151129	268712	394068
9.	Dentists**	3290	3582	5512	8648	11011
10.	Nurses**	16550	35584	80620	154230	264504

* Pertains to 1950. @ As on 31 March.
** As on 31 December. Source: Ministry of Health and Family Welfare.

30.2 **Primary Health Care**

Primary health care has been accepted as the main instrument for achieving the target of Health for All by 2000 A.D. Accordingly, a three-tier system comprising of community health centres (CHCs), primary centres (PHCs) and sub-centres has been established. These institutions are providing an integrated primary health care and family welfare service to people at their doorstep. There were about 2067 CHCs, 22495 PHCs and 130474 sub-centres at the end of June 1992. The target of setting up of one sub-centre for every 5000 people in ordinary areas and for 3000 in hilly and tribal areas and one PHC for population of 30000 in general and 20000 for hilly and tribal areas have almost been achieved. However, 58.6 per cent of sub-centres, 42.6 per cent of PHCs and 39.4 per cent of CHCs as in June 1992 did not have buildings of their own. The lack of buildings, shortage of manpower and inadequate provision of drugs, equipment etc. constituted major impediments to full utilisation of these units.

30.3 Control of Communicable Diseases

Acquired Immuno-Deficiency Syndrome (AIDS) has emerged as a new public health problem in the country. The AIDS Control Programme was launched in 1986 as a Central Sector Scheme. Establishment of surveillance centres, testing of cases for infection, training of personnel and mass health education formed the main activities of the programme. But the incidence of the disease has shown an increase from 1137 seropositives among 141 tested up to May 1987 to 11071 seropositives among 15.55 lakh persons tested up to November 1992. The measures undertaken include establishment of 62 surveillance centres in 335 cities for tracking the spread of infection amongst group practising high risk behaviour, ensuring blood safety by surveillance and undertaking a phased programme of development of blood banks, establishment of 118 zonal blood testing facilities for testing HIV infected blood collected at the blood banks, strengthening of 13 regional hospitals for management of HIV infected persons and AIDS cases and health education. Inadequate surveillance system, absence of facilities for examination of blood and blood products and growing menace of intravenous drug abuse contributed to an upsurge in infection. A new centrally sponsored scheme, viz. National AIDS Control Programme, is being launched during the Eighth Plan with assistance from International Development Agencies.

Leprosy continues to be a major health and social problem. About 2 million persons are estimated to be suffering from this disease at the end of March 1992 as against 4 million in 1981. A National Leprosy Eradication Programme was re-launched in 1982. It is proposed to arrest the disease in all known leprosy areas by 2000 A.D. The introduction of Multi-Drug Therapy (MDT) has shown encouraging results. For containing the transmission of the disease, the strategy adopted is the introduction of MDT in the districts in a phased manner. All 201 endemic and 41 low endemic districts have been covered under MDT.

The incidence of malaria has come down from about 6.47 million cases in 1976 to 2.11 million cases in 1991, i.e., a reduction of 67.4 per cent. This is the result of several measures taken like the implementation of the Modified Plan of Operation from 1976 onwards under the National Malaria Eradication Programme (NMEP). The Annual Parasite Index (API) has come down from 11.24 per cent in 1976 to 2.57 per cent in 1990. The problem of drug resistance in several States is a cause for concern. Irrigation projects without management of water resources, floating labour population in the cities and major project sites contribute to the increase in incidence of malaria. Appropriate measures to tackle these problems have already been initiated.

Kala-azar and Japanese Encephalities (JE) have emerged as major public health problems in recent years. It is highly endemic in about 30 district in Bihar and 9 districts in West Bengal covering a population of about 75 million. Since 1990-91, separate funds are provided for control of the disease. The indigenously produced vaccine for JE has proved to be effective, safe and required standard. The reported cases and deaths due to JE in the affected States of Andhra Pradesh, West Bengal, U.P., Tamil Nadu and Assam have shown a considerable decline.

Tuberculosis (TB) is another major public health problem in India. About 1.5 per cent of the total population is estimated to be suffering from tuberculosis of the lungs. Under the National Tuberculosis Control Programme, 390 districts out of 440 districts as in December 1992 have been provided with District TB Centres equipped with equipments and trained staff for undertaking districtiwise TB Programme in association with general health and medical institutions. In addition, there about 330 TB clinics mostly located in big towns and cities for catering to the needs of the local population. More than 16 lakh new cases are tested and treated each year. About 47000 beds are available for treatment of seriously sick patients. Short-course treatment through chemotherapy drug regimens have been introduced in 235 districts to reduce the duration of treatment.

30.4 **Allocation for Health Sector, 1993-94**

Finance Minister Dr. Manmohan Singh announced an enhanced outlay for health sector. A provision of Rs. 483 crore has been made for the health sector, which is 60 per cent higher than the level of Rs. 302 crore in the current year's budget.

A major part of the provision would be for national programme for control of communicable and other diseases. The Family Welfare Programme being of overriding national importance and the provision under this head has been stepped up from Rs. 1000 crore for the current year to Rs. 1,270 crore for the next year.

A programme to improve the quality of family planning services in Uttar Pradesh is to be launched at a cost of US$ 325 million with assistance from USAID.

31

HOUSING

The total backlog of housing is estimated to be 31 million comprising 2006 million in rural areas and 10.4 million in urban areas. It is estimated that about 48.8 million persons were living in slums in 1990. The service deficiency in terms of access to proper sanitation and safe water within reasonable distance is equally alarming. Land, provision of basic services, finance, availability of adequate building materials, low cost technology and trained construction workers are critical inputs for housing. Several constraints are encountered in each of these critical areas. Housing has been primarily set-help activity for the majority of the households. The role of the government would include creating an enabling environment and removing constraints in housing activity among various sections of the society, promoting the supply of housing and related services and supporting the extension of appropriate technology and materials and upgradation of the housing stock.

The National Housing Policy (NHP) was prepared and placed before both Houses of Parliament in 1992. The main elements of the Housing Policy include evolution of suitable housing norms with due regard to location, life style of the people etc. for promoting cost-effective standardised housing designs, supply and management of land, expansion of infrastructural facilities like public transport, potable water supply and sanitation as well as housing finance facilities, stimulating production and availability of building materials like cement, steel, bricks, etc. incorporating low-cost technology and materials in the standards and specifications wherever the scope exists and special programmes for disadvantaged sections especially SCs/STs and women in disadvantaged circumstances.

31.1 National Housing Policy

Objectives

* To assist all people in securing affordable shelter, in particular the houseless, inadequately housed and vulnerable sections.
* To create an enabling environment for housing activity.
* To expand provision of infrastructure facilities.
* To improve the housing of the poorest by direct initiative and financial support.
* To help mobilise resources and facilitate expansion of investment in housing.
* To promote vernacular architecture and preserve the nation's rich heritage in the field of housing settlements.

A package of excise concessions was provided in the budget for 1992-93 for boosting housing activity. These include full exemption from excise duty on bricks and tiles having a minimum content of 25 per cent of the red mud, lightweight concrete building blocks, doors and windows made of plastic, iron and steel and panel doors. A reduction in excise duty from 15 per cent to 5 per cent has also been given on pre-fabricated buildings. Housing has also been dovetailed with other Central and Centrally Sponsored Schemes. Under Jawahar Rozgar Yojana, 6 per cent of the resources are earmarked for Indira Awaas Yojana (IAY). AY aims at construction of dwelling units for the poorest belonging to SCs/STs and freed bonded labourers in rural areas. Under IAY, houses are to be built in clusters as far as possible as per micro-habitat approach so as to achieve economy in the provision of common facilities. During 1991-92 about 2.07 lakh houses were built under Indira Awaas Yojana.

The Scheme of Environmental Improvement of Urban Slums (EIUS) forms a part of the Minimum Needs Programme as well as the 20-Point Programme. It aims at ameliorating the living conditions of urban slum dwellers by provision of basic amenities. During 1991-92, 16.21 lakh slum dwellers were covered under th scheme as against the target of 12.96 lakh. The Urban basic Services for the Poor (UBSP) seeks to integrate the provisions of social services under UBSP and that of physical amenities envisaged under the scheme of EIUS in the State sector. Under NRY, the scheme for Housing and Shelter upgradation (SHASU) seeks to provide assistance for housing and shelter upgradation to the urban poor in settlements having a population between one lakh and 20 lakh with a relaxation in the lower population limit of one lakh in the case of certain specified areas.

31.2 **National Housing Bank (NHB)**

The National Housing Bank (NHB) was established in July 1988 to promote a healthy housing finance system by setting up housing finance institutions both at local and regional levels for providing adequate finance to the housing sector. It is a wholly owned subsidiary of the Reserve Bank of India (RBI) with paid-up capital of Rs. 250 crore. The resources of the National Housing Bank have been augmented by RBI's National Housing Credit (LTO) fund, issue of 11.5-12 per cent 20-year Government guaranteed bonds, the LIC and UTI. Besides raising Rs. 185.6 crore through its Home Loan Account Scheme from 6.17 lakh account holders up to September 1992, NHB also collected about Rs. 155 crore up to the end of June 1992 from 9 per cent capital gains bonds (the scheme was discontinued on September 30, 1992) and 40 per cent of Rs. 152.1 crore mobilised by NHB under Voluntary Deposit Scheme from October 1 1991 to January 21 1992 was transferred to NHB's Special Fund. Total external borrowings of NHB under the USAID Government Housing Guarantee Programme and the Housing Programme of Overseas Economic Cooperation Fund of Japan amount to Rs. 90.84 crore.

The NHB is providing assistance for housing through a number of schemes. These include, Home Loan Account Scheme, refinance for direct loans for housing given by scheduled banks (commercial and cooperative) and non-banking institutions (housing finance companies and apex cooperative housing finance societies) and refinance for Land Development and Shelter Projects (LDSP). till the end of September 1992, the NHB recognised 18 housing finance companies in public and private sectors (including HUDCO) having a network of 246 branches as eligible to draw refinance from it. The NHB has cleared equity participation in four building material projects. This will go a long way in promoting the use of alternative building materials produced from agricultural and industrial wastes. The cumulative refinance assistance provided by NHB to eligible primary lenders by way of housing loans for acquisition or construction of new dwelling units including upgradation of existing units for land development and shelter projects amounted to Rs. 1367.50 crore till the end of November 1992. About one million dwelling units, of which 60 per cent were located in rural areas, have been provided assistance by NHB. Till November 1992 NHB has approved 102 detailed project reports involving a total outlay of Rs. 669.41 crore for development of 22310 plots and construction of 73532 dwelling units.

31.3 National Cooperative Housing Federation (NCHF)

The NCHF, set up in 1969, is a national level organisation spearheading the entire cooperative housing movement in India. Its aims are to coordinate the Apex Cooperative Housing Finance Societies and to promote and develop cooperative housing societies in the country. Out of 25 State level Apex Societies/Federations as on March 1991, 23 have become members of the NCHF. The State level Apex Societies have advanced loans of Rs. 2154.29 crore to the Primary Cooperatives for the construction of about 12.21 lakh houses up to the year ending March 31, 1991. The State level Apex Societies are entitled to get refinance from NHB and loans from HUDCO for enlarged operations. About 60 per cent of the house finance disbursed by Apex co-operative has gone to Economically Weaker Sections (EWSs) and Low Income Groups (LIGs). Central and State Governments give preference in land allotment to cooperatives.

31.4 Housing and Urban Development Corporation (HUDCO)

Since 1970, the HUDCO is playing an important role for meeting the housing needs of the poorer sections and vulnerable groups through various States and local agencies. HUDCO finance is available to institutions like State Housing Boards, Developmental Authorities, Improvement Trusts, Cooperative Societies etc. It is earmarking 55 per cent of its sanctions for housing projects for the benefit of Economically Weaker Sections (EWSs) and Low-Income Groups (LIGs). Fifteen per cent of its resources are reserved for rural (EWS) housing schemes. Up to end of September 1992, it has financed over 52 lakh dwelling units including 23.86 lakh units in rural areas. HUDCO plans to expand its lending for various forms of housing activities and infrastructure during the Eighth Plan. It is also operating a network of building centres for extension of appropriate housing technology and skills promotion.

31.5 Water Supply and Sanitation

Provision of safe drinking water to all, especially the underserved villages, is considered to be crucial for the health and better quality of life of our population. The drinking water supply and sanitation schemes are implemented under the State Sector Minimum Needs Programme as well as under centrally sponsored schemes. It had been envisaged during the Seventh Plan that all the 161722 identified problem villages would be covered with the facility of safe drinking water. However, by the end of the Seventh Plan, 153357 villages could be provided with at least one source of drinking water supply, leaving a balance of 8365 hard core, no-source problem villages. Out of these, 3032 villages were covered during 1990-91. A special allocation of Rs. 250 crore was approved during the year 1991-92 for coverage of the residual 5333 no-source villages by 31 March 1993. Out of these, 2365 villages were covered during 1991-92 and the remaining 2968 are targeted to be covered during 1992-93. Out of this, 708 problem villages have been covered up to October 1992. Besides, about 1.5 lakh partially covered villages and habitations also require augmentation for achieving full coverage during the Eighth Plan. However, as per latest information about 500 no-source villages are likely to spill over for coverage during 1993-94. A survey is in progress to ascertain the actual number of partially covered villages. it is also expected that a sizeable number of new no-source villages are likely to emerge due to recurring droughts and depletion of water table. The achievements in the Sixth and Seventh Plans are shown in Table 31.1.

TABLE 31.1: Population with Drinking Water and Sanitation Facilities

		(Per cent as on 31 March)	
	1985	1990	1992*
Rural water supply	56.3	73.9	78.4
Rural sanitation	0.7	2.4	2.7
Urban water supply	72.9	83.3	84.9
Urban sanitation	28.4	45.9	47.9

* Provisional.
Source: Eighth Plan, Vol. II.

The problems in sanitation, particularly in rural areas, are formidable. Only 2.7 per cent of the population in rural areas and 47.9 per cent in urban areas are estimated to have been covered with sanitation facilities by the end of March 1992. During the past seven years, i.e. April 1985 to March 1992, the coverage of rural population with rural water supply increased from 56.3 per cent to 78.4 per cent and in urban areas from 72.9 per cent to 84.9 per cent mainly due to efforts made during International Drinking Water Supply and Sanitation Decade (1981-1991).

The highest priority in the Eighth Plan is to ensure that the remaining no-source hard-core problem villages are provided with sustainable supply of drinking water by March 1993. Augmenting supply of water in all the partially covered villages is also considered to be equally important. Special attention would be given for coverage of SC/ST population and other poor/weaker sections. Priority will also be accorded to solve problems of quality of drinking water to achieve zero incidence of guineaworm disease by 1993 and total eradication by 1 April 1995 besides progressively finding solutions for other bacteriological and chemical problems like excess fluorides, salinity and iron in water sources. In the case of rural sanitation, the concept of 'Total Environmental Sanitation' would be followed. Information, Education and Communication (IEC) should form an integral part of rural sanitation programme. In all these efforts, emphasis would be on decentralisation of functions, particularly operation and maintenance, with greater involvement of the community and the NGOs.

The Eighth Plan lays emphasis on elimination of manual scavenging as it is the most undignified work offered to the weakest section of the society. Its elimination will require (i) making provision of pour flush water-seal latrines mandatory in every house in urban areas and (ii) provision of alternative work opportunities to those engaged in it.

31.6 **Indira Awaas Yojana (IAY)**

With a view to ameliorating the lot of rural poor, scheme for allotment of house-sites to landless agricultural labourers was initiated in October 1971. Around 77 lakh families had been covered prior to the Sixth Five Year Plan. A target of 68 lakh families was envisaged during the Sixth Plan based on the eligible landless families estimated at 145 lakh by 1985. During the Sixth and Seventh Plans and 1990-91, house-sites have been provided to 105 lakh rural landless families.

The Indira Awaas Yojana (IAY) was started as a specific programmes in 1985-86 as part of Rural Landless Employment Guarantee Programme (RLEGP). IAY aims at construction of dwelling units free of cost for the poorest of the poor belonging to Scheduled Castes Scheduled Tribes and freed bonded labourers and is now being implemented under the Jawahar Rozgar Yojana. Houses under IAY, as far as possible, are built in clusters as per microhabitat approach so that common facilities can be provided for the clusters. The plinth area of the house should be 17-20 sq.m. The design may be specific to the areas keeping in view the climatic conditions. The house should have a kitchen, smokeless chulha and a sanitary latrine unit.

Permissible Expenditure

The permissible expenditure for each house under IAY is as under.

(i)	Construction of house	Rs. 8,000.00
(ii)	Construction of sanitary latrine and smokeless chulha	Rs. 1,400.00
(iii)	Cost of providing infrastructure and common facilities	Rs. 3,300.00
	TOTAL :	Rs. 12,700.00

TABLE 31.2: Number of Houses Built (1985-91)

Year	Expenditure incurred (Rs. in lakhs)	No. of houses built
1985-86	5,768.95	51,406
1986-87	14,797.22	1,51,812
1987-88	16,730.26	1,64,055
1988-89	15,075.60	1,37,435
1989-90	17,586.36	1,82,242
1990-91	18,796.37	1,70,805

In difficult areas like hills, the cost of construction may be upto Rs. 9,800. Where houses are not built in clusters, the amount of Rs. 3,300 provided for common facilities and expenditure may be used for construction of the house.

A total of over 8.57 lakh houses have been constructed since the inception of the programme upto 1990-91. The table shows the year-wise details of the number of houses built under the IAY during the period 1985-91.

During the year 1991-92, 2,03,434 houses were been constructed. Construction of 1,30,473 houses was under progress. The expenditure incurred was Rs. 22,707.32 lakhs. An allocation of Rs. 122.76 crore has been made for the current year.

Source: *Yojana,* July 15, 1992.

32

INDUSTRY

32.1 Introduction

Many of the fiscal and monetary restraints which had a dampening effect on industrial production in 1991-92 were removed or relaxed in 1992-93. The downtrend in industrial production was reversed. Industrial growth of 4-4.5 per cent is expected in the current financial year.

Industrial policy reforms were carried further in 1992-93. The capital market was freed from Government control and the office of the Controller of Capital Issues was abolished. Foreign Regulation Act was amended and investment restrictions on FERA companies were substantially removed. Foreign investment was further liberalised by removing the conditionality of dividend balancing for the non-consumer goods. Private investment in exploration and refining was allowed in the hydrocarbon sector. The Textile Control Order was repealed. Investment activity has picked up as evidenced by the substantial increase in investment proposals from both domestic and foreign investors. There was a quantum jump in new capital issues after the decontrol of the capital market.

The recent policy measures including the substantial deregulation of the industrial sector and liberalisation of trade policies will take time to yield results. There are, however, already some signs of a turnaround with industrial production showing a modest recovery in the first seven months of 1992-93. In April-October 1992, the IIP registered an increase of 3.8 per cent over the same period of 1991. It can be expected that this recovery will be further strengthened during the remaining months of 1992-93 in view of an exceptionally good kharif harvest. The increase in exports to the General Currency Area (CA) as also the resurgence of domestic demand both for investment goods and consumer products may be expected to contribute to sustaining the rate of growth in industrial production in the second half of 1992-93.

32.2 Industrial Policy Reforms

Industrial Licensing

* Manufacture of industrial alcohol was delicensed and veneers were brought under the compulsory licensing list.

De-regulation

* Most of the conditions stipulated in the letters of intent and industrial licences issued earlier to firms in industries now delicensed were waived.
* The system of endorsement of capacity expansion under modernisation/renovation was discontinued except in the case of industries which are still under compulsory licensing or are located in restricted areas.
* Small-scale industries engaged in the manufacture of delicensed items were exempted from obtaining Carry On Business (cob) licences on their graduation to medium-scale industries.

* The private sector has been invited to invest in oil exploration and refining which is otherwise reserved for the public sector.
* The power sector is now open to both domestic and foreign private investment.

Procedural Reforms

* The Chief Inspector of Factories has been designated as the Appropriate Government Authority under the stipulations regarding conversion of letters of intent to industrial licences in the case of hazardous industries.
* An Investment Promotion and Project Monitoring Cell has been set up in the Department of Industrial Development to provide information and guidance to entrepreneurs regarding licensing policy, tariffs, corporate laws, current status of applications pending with the Department, infrastructure facilities and incentives available at State levels for setting up industries etc.

With the announcement of the New Industrial Policy in July 1991, a large number of Government-induced entry restrictions, licensing requirements and controls on corporate behaviour were eliminated. The thrust of the policy measures undertaken in 1992-93 has been to deepen these reforms and extend them to other sectors of industry. Further, the industrial and trade policy changes introduced since the presentation of the previous Economic Survey have made imported inputs cheaper and more accessible for industry and have, at the same time, exposed a larger segment of the Indian industry to international competition. Fiscal policy initiatives have sought to improve the incentives for investment in the industrial sector and encourage a shift towards exports and away from domestic markets.

The process of industrial de-regulation and structural reforms has been carried further during 1992-93, and the direction for future policy action has been firmly established. As experience is gained and the economy begins to respond to the policy changes, the reforms will be extended to other sectors. Consolidation of these reforms by way of ensuring their implementation and removing anomalies will be focussed upon. The role of state governments is critical in this regard.

32.3 **Fiscal and Monetary Policy Measures**

A number of measures were initiated in the Budget and the monetary policies to revive industrial growth.

(i) The Budget for 1992-93 announced LERMS (Liberalised Exchange Management System) under which 60 per cent of foreign exchange earnings are allowed to be converted at market rate of exchange. Consequent to this, import of all raw materials, components and capital goods for use in the manufacturing sector, barring a few in a small restricted list, would be freely allowed as long as the importer obtained the required foreign exchange from and raw materials. Trade policy was liberalised and the restricted list of imports pruned substantially. All intermediate goods, industrial raw materials, components and spare parts are now on the Open General Licence (i.e., importable without licence).

(ii) The peak import tariff was brought down from a maximum of 150 per cent to 110 per cent, thereby reducing costs of imported industrial inputs. Rates of import duties on project imports, capital goods and general machinery were substantially reduced. The Export Promotion Capital Goods (EPCG) Scheme made capital goods importable at 25 per cent and 15 per cent duty as long as the importers agreed to fulfil a stipulated export commitment.

(iii) The floor level of interest rate on commercial bank advances was reduced by 2 percentage points in two stages in March and October 1992.

(iv) The Capital market was liberalised and Government control over capital issues withdrawn. The office of the Controller of Capital Issues was abolished. The Securities and Exchange Board of India (SEBI) has been converted into a statutorily empowered Board to regulate the functioning of capital market and stock exchanges. Companies are now free to price their equity issues at their own risk and at self-determined premia, within the guidelines laid down by SEBI for investor protection.

(v) Taxation of capital gains was restructured to allow for inflation accounting. Double taxation of partnership firms was abolished and financial assets such as equities and debentures were exempted from wealth tax. These fiscal measures have improved the incentives for industrial investment and encouraged flow of resources towards industry.

32.4 Foreign Investment

A number of measures have been put in place to attract foreign investment.

(i) Under the new Industrial Policy, approvals for foreign direct investment up to 51 per cent of equity in specified high-priority industries were to be given automatically subject to the condition that the dividend payments should be balanced by export earnings over a specified period of time. This conditions of dividend balancing was withdrawn in respect of all foreign investment approvals except for some notified consumer goods industries. The list of high-priority (Annex III) industries where foreign investments up to 51 per cent were allowed automatically was revised, rationalising the earlier grouping and adding new items. The software industry is now included in the list.

(ii) Automatic approval of RBI for raising foreign equity up to 51 per cent will be available to : (i) companies wishing to raise foreign equity as part of an expansion programme in the high-priority (Annex III) industries and (ii) companies predominantly engaged in high-priority industries to raise the equity base without an expansion programme. Such companies can issue equity abroad at prices determined by the shareholders by a special resolution.

(iii) Approvals for foreign investment and foreign technology agreements had a condition earlier prohibiting the use of foreign brand name or trade mark in goods sold in the domestic market. This restriction has since been withdrawn.

(iv) Foreign Exchange Regulation Act 1973 (FERA) was substantially liberalised through on Ordinance promulgated by the President on 8 January, 1993. All restrictions on FERA companies in the matter of borrowing funds or raising deposits in India as well as taking over or creating any interest in business in Indian companies have been removed. Indian companies and Indian nationals are now allowed to start joint ventures abroad and accept directorship in overseas companies. FERA companies are also exempted from restrictions on the establishment of branches liaison offices and acquisition of the whole or a part of any undertaking or company in India carrying on business in trade, commerce or industry excepting agriculture and plantations.

(v) Non-Resident Indians (NRI) and Overseas Corporate Bodies (OCB) predominantly owned by them are allowed to invest up to 100 per cent foreign equity in high priority and other industries with full benefits of repatriation of capital invested and income accruing thereon. Investment by NRIs up to 100 per cent on full repatriation basis is also allowed in export houses, trading houses, hotels and tourism-related industries.

32.5 National Renewal Fund

The National Renewal Fund (NRF) has been operationalised. A sum of Rs. 200 crore had been earmarked for the fund in the 1991-92 budget. This has been supplemented by a substantial input of IDA resources, at concessional interest rates to the tune of Rs. 500 crore in 1992-93. The first tranche of these resources has been received. Another Rs. 500 crore will be available from IDA during 1993-94. The objectives of the NRF are:

(i) to provide assistance to firms to cover the costs of retraining and redeployment of employees arising as a result of modernisation and technological upgradation of existing capacities and from industrial restructuring.

(ii) to provide funds for compensation to employees affected by restructuring or closure of industrial units, both in the public and private sectors.

(iii) to provide funds for employment generation schemes in the organised and unorganised sectors in order to provide a social safety net for labour. The Department of Industrial Development, which administers NRF, has now taken up the first set of cases relating to the National Textile Corporation units.

32.6 Industrial Production, 1992-93

Index for Industrial Production (IIP) for the first seven months of the year 1992-93 (April-October) showed continued improvement compared with the situation in 1991-92. Industrial output has increased by 3.8 per cent over 1991-92 and the manufacturing sector has recorded a growth of 3.7 per cent. These positive growth rates are with reference to the depressed conditions of 1991-92 but it is important to note that when compared to the output levels during the first seven months of 1990-91, the overall industrial production and manufacturing production in the first seven months of 1992-93 show positive growth of 3.2 and 1.1 per cent respectively.

An examination of 172 industries by use-based classification for the period April September 1992 reveals that during this period intermediate goods, capital goods, consumer durables and basic industries recorded positive growth rates (Table 32.1). The only industry segment to record a negative growth rate was consumer non-durables where also the growth rate has declined only marginally. The slowdown in industrial and manufacturing sector growth rates during July and August 1992 had generated apprehensions of Indian industry being in the grip of strong recessionary conditions. These apprehensions have been somewhat allayed as a result of industrial growth having registered a substantial increase during September. Industrial growth as yet is far from robust but the higher growth rate during September could mark the beginning of an upturn which could be sustained during the remaining part of the year on account of better demand and supply conditions. The year 1992-93 may record a 4 per cent rate of growth in the manufacturing sector and a similar growth for the industry as a whole.

TABLE 32.1: Growth Rates of 172 Manufacturing Industries (Use-based classification)

Industry groups	Weight in IIP	(per cent) Change over previous year 1991-92	April 1991	September 1992
Basic industries	36.36	6.2	6.2	2.2
Consumer durables	2.30	-12.5	-10.6	2.4
Consumer non-durables	20.09	1.2	2.7	-1.5
Capital goods	12.02	-12.8	-16.9	8.8
International goods	17.34	-0.7	-0.6	7.2
All manufacturing industries	88.11	-0.5	-0.9	4.1

Note: The growth rate for 1991-92 (full year) relates to 155 industries with a total weight of 85.54 per cent in the IIP.

32.7 Performance of Selected Industries

Chemicals, Petrochemicals and Allied Industry

Drugs and Pharmaceuticals

The production of drugs and pharmaceuticals as well as the range of production continued to show an upward trend. As against production levels of Rs. 355 crores of bulk drugs and Rs. 1760 crores of formulations in 1983-84, their production in 1991-92 of the order of Rs. 790 crores and Rs. 4200 crores, respectively. The increased production of drugs has facilitated our aim of ensuring the national goal of abundant and easy availability of life saving and essential drugs at reasonable prices for the common man.

In the field of drugs and pharmaceuticals there are five public sector undertakings, namely, Indian Drugs and Pharmaceuticals Limited (IDPL), Hindustan Aeronautics Limited (HAL), Bengal Chemicals and Pharmaceuticals Limited (BCPL), Bengal Immunity Limited (BIL) and Smith Stanistreet Pharmaceuticals Limited (SSPL). The value of production and sales of IDPL in 1990-91 was of the order of Rs. 155 crores and Rs. 170 crores respectively. HAL had achieved production of the value of Rs. 107.16 crores as compared to Rs. 100.93 crores for the year 1989-90. The sales turnover of the company during 1990-91 was Rs. 109 crores as against Rs. 86.59 crore for the previous year. The company has entered into a Memorandum of Understanding (MOU) with the Government in 1991-92. The net profit earned by the company was Rs. 0.79 crores in 1990-91. There was a marginal reduction in production and sales of BCPL in 1990-91 mainly because of shortage of raw materials and other constraints. BIL's overall performance showed encouraging improvement in 1990-91. The company's production and sales were of the value of Rs. 14.39 crores and Rs. 13.90 crores, respectively.

Pharmaceuticals industry in India has the capability of producing a wide range of bulk drugs, covering a large spectrum of technologies and almost all formulations. In fact, the country is almost fully self-reliant in terms of formulation technology. In the case of bulk drugs, the technologies include those for Sulpha drugs, Vitamins, Hormones and a number of other New drugs like Cefachlor, Omeprazole, Nefopam, Butalex, Etoposide, Ketotifen, Roxatidine, Felodipine, Terfenadine, Ramipril etc.

Among the bulk drugs which are critical to the country's health needs, the two most important ones are penicillin and Rifampicin. Penicillin is being manufactured in the country mainly by the two PSUs — Indian Drugs and Pharmaceuticals Ltd. and Hindustan Antibiotics Ltd. However, taking into consideration the growing need for this drug, it was decreased from the public sector and seven private sector companies were given industrial approvals for its manufacture. Some of them have made progress in implementing these projects. The two PSUs have also progressively enhanced their production to meet up to 50% of the country's demand. The country has for a number of years been on the look out for the technology for the manufacture of Rifampicin from the basic stage of fermentation. The indigenous need for this drug was being met through manufacture from penultimates and intermediates. However, by 1992-93, there are very good prospects of two companies manufacturing this bulk drug from the stage of fermentation.

1991-92 witnessed changes in the Industrial sector with the announcement of the new Industrial Policy. The new measures of economic liberalisation like the amendment of the MRTP Act, FERA regulations, etc. will have an impact on the Pharmaceuticals sector also. This sector had been almost totally delicensed under the various Delicensed Registration Schemes. The New Industrial Policy has abolished these schemes whereby the pharmaceuticals sector has temporarily come under the ambit of Industrial Licensing. A significant feature of the exports of pharmaceuticals products is that basic drugs were mainly exported to developed countries.

The pharmaceuticals sector has been performing well in the field of exports over the last few years. In the last three years it has been a net exporter. Therefore, the sector has been identified by Government as a thrust area for boosting exports. India has earned repute as a dependable bulk drug manufacturer in the international market and a fair share of such exports have been to the sophisticated markets in the Western countries. In the current year the political changes which have taken place in the USSR have had some impact on the export performance of this sector.

Drug Pricing

With a view to encouraging indigenous production at competitive costs the process of rationalisation of duties was continued. Customs duty on 61 bulk drugs used for essential and life saving formulations was reduced to zero. Customs duty on 41 drug intermediates used for the production of 32 bulk drugs was also reduced.

To encourage indigenous research and development in the field of drugs, an incentive scheme exempting bulk drugs and formulations based thereupon, from price control is available to a manufacturer who has indigenously developed/improved the process to manufacture a drug from its basic stage.

So far the following bulk drugs and their formulations have been granted exemption from price control under Drugs (Price Control) Order, 1987 (DPCO) for a period of 5 years from the data of commencement of their commercial production on the grounds of indigenous Research and Development.

TABLE 32.2: Bulk Drugs and Formulation Granted Exemption from Price Control for Five Years

Sl. No.	Name of the Bulk Drug	Name of the Company
1.	Ranitidine	M/s Ranbaxy Laboratories Ltd.
2.	Metoclopramide	M/s IPCA Laboratories
3.	Dextropropoxyphene	M/s Wockhardt Limited
4.	Salbutamol	M/s Cipla Limited
5.	Ephedrine	M/s Malladi Drugs
6.	Ranitidine	M/s Globe Organics
7.	Amoxycillin Sodium	M/s Duphar Interfran
8.	Verapamil Hcl	M/s Associated Drug C. (P) Ltd.
9.	Metoclopramide Hcl	M/s Infar (I) Limited
10.	Naladixic Acid	M/s Ranbaxy Laboratories Ltd.
11.	Naproxen	M/s Rallis India Limited.

Another incentives scheme to encourage indigenous research and development in th field of drugs and formulations is to grant exemption from the DPCO to manufacturing units for formulations having New Delivery schemes developed by them indigenously and certified by the Drug Controller (India). The following formulations have so far been allowed exemption from price control under DPCO for a period of 3 years from the date of approval by the Government.

TABLE 32.3: Formulation Granted Exemptions from Price Control for Three Years

Sl. No.	Name of the Formulation	Name of the Company
1.	Diclonac Sustained Release Tablets	M/s Lupin Laboratories Limited, Bombay
2.	Terramycin L/A	M/s Pfizer Ltd., Bombay
3.	Norswal 600 Mg. Sustained Release Tabs.	M/s Cadila Labs. Ltd., Ahmedabad
4.	Fefol-Spansule Sustained Release Caps.	M/s Eskayef Limited, Bangalore
5.	Isoptin 240 Mg. Sustained Release Tabs.	M/s Boehringer Knoll Ltd., Bombay
6.	Theo PA controlled Release Tabs.	M/s Nucron Pharmaceutical Private Limited, Pune

Chemicals, Pesticides and Allied Industries

The Chemicals industry has recorded a rapid growth during the last few yeas. Some of the major industries which recorded rapid growth in production were caustic soda, soda ash, DDT, Azo Dyes, Carbon Black, Phenol and Methanol. The production and availability of chemicals are by and large satisfactory; there is sufficient capacity and imports have been curtailed.

The main thrust in the Chemicals sector is modernisation as to improve efficiency by operating costs since technology obsolescence is one of the prominent features of this sector. There are a few exceptions where capacity is not sufficient to meet the demand, e.g. Titanium Dioxide, Citric Acid, Oxalic Acid, MDI/TDI.

Iron and Steel

Consequent to the removal of price and distribution controls on iron and steel on

16 January 1992, the integrated steel plants increased their prices by an average of 15 per cent on 18/19 May 1992 to offset the increase in input costs. After some increase in market prices following the price revision by integrated steel plants, the prices of various items of steel have established throughout the country. The import of all items of steel is now freely allowed. Along with the deregulation of iron and steel, import of all items of steel is no freely allowed. Along with the deregulation of iron and steel, import duty on steel melting scrap was reduced from 35 per cent to 10 per cent, on pig iron from 55 per cent to 35 per cent and on billet and HR coils from 65 per cent to 45 per cent.

Production of saleable steel by the integrated steel plants (main producers) in 1991-92 at 10.57 million tonnes recorded a growth of 13.3 per cent over 9.33 million tonnes in 1990-91. Output of finished steel in the secondary sector declined by 1.6 per cent in 1991-92 both because of the inadequate availability of imported melting steel scrap and a fall in demand. There was also a deceleration in the growth of production of saleable pig iron by the main plants from 12.1 per cent in 1990-91 to 6.5 per cent in 1991-92 which reflected the slowdown in forging and casting industry.

Production of saleable steel in April-December 1992 went up by 8 per cent over the corresponding period of 1991. Production of finished steel increased by 5.2 per cent and that of saleable pig iron by the main plants, by 13.9 per cent. Production of finished steel in 1992-93 is expected to be 16.1 million tonnes as against 14.2 million tonnes in 1991-92.

Sponge Iron

Sponge iron is a metallic product produced by direct reduction of high grade iron ore or pellets into the solid state. Also known as direct reduced iron (DRI) or Hot Briquetted Iron (HBI), it contains a large percentage of metallic iron. This is a partial substitute for steel melting scrap used by the secondary steel sector. The indigenous availability of metal scrap is very low. Steel scrap abroad is becoming scarce on account of technological advancement in steel production as a result of which imports are becoming more and more costly. Moreover, most of the imported steel scrap has to be brought in hard currency. Production of sponge iron is, therefore, being encouraged by the Government in order to conserve free foreign exchange.

It is expected that production will be 50 to 60 lakh tonnes by the end of 1996-97. The installed capacity of sponge iron units till 1988-89 was only 3.3 lakh tonnes.

Pig Iron

(i) The Engineering Industry is a major consumer of pig iron. Production has, however, not been increasing appreciably to cater to the internal demand. The major producers of pig iron have been the Integrated Steel Plants, which can divert only part of their hot metal production as pig iron for sale. The demand for pig iron is expected to increase substantially in the coming years. Government is, therefore, keen to increase its production in the secondary sector. Though pig iron production had been delicensed earlier, it is only now that some private entrepreneurs have indicated interest in establishing production facilities. Financial Institutions are now extending assistance to such units and have sanctioned assistance to six units with a total capacity of 6.85 lakh TPA.

(ii) Production of pig iron requires coke as a raw material. Availability of indigenous coke has however, also been limited. Government is therefore, keen to develop merchant coke oven batteries in the secondary sector to overcome the shortage.

Steel

Steel is perhaps the most basic material required for industrialisation and plays a crucial role in the Country's economic development. In India, Steel production began more than a century ago. Our country is well endowed with natural resources required for a healthy and vigorous iron and steel industry. Apart from recoverable iron ore reserves of almost 12 billion tonnes, we also have vast reserves of coking coal, manganese ore, limestone and dolomite.

Some of the major steel plants in the country, Tata Iron and Steel Company Ltd. (TISCO), Indian Iron and Steel Co. (IISCO) and Visvesvarya Iron and Steel Co. Ltd. (now a subsidiary of SAIL) were set up in the pre-Independence period. Immediately after Independence investment in the steel sector was prioritised by the setting up of three 1 MT steel plants, at Bhilai, Rourkela and Durgapur. The Indian Steel Industry made rapid strides in the 2nd and 3rd five year plans when capacity for crude steel increased from 1.5 MT to 8.9 MT. However, the pace slowed down in the 70s and 80s during which there was long period of stagnation in investment for plant upgradation and modernisation. In the last decade, production of steel has been falling short of the domestic demand necessitating imports to fill the gap. As a result, the per capita consumption is as low as 20 Kgs. per person while in neighbouring China it is 64 kg per person. In some of the developed countries it various from 600 kgs to 700 kg per person.

India has most of the raw materials and technical expertise for steel production. In our efforts to augment steel production we have tried to match production to met domestic demand. The estimation of future demand unfortunately has been based on historical consumption figures to basic industrial raw materials which do not reflect the actual or potential demand but a constrained demand which is the consequence of low domestic production and controlled imports. Our national economy has reached a stage of diversification and sophisticate and the demand for steel, provided it is made available at reasonable prices and is of an acceptable quality, is likely to grow at a much faster rate than before.

Another significant feature has been the almost total absence of public investment in steel for export purposes. Like many developing countries, our exports wee directed in favour of primary products and mineral resources. A perusal of global statistics revealed that about 100 million tonnes of steel is internationally traded and steel manufacturing countries have exported around 25% of their production even during recessionary periods. This shows that there is considerable potential for India to export iron and steel provided we are com petitive in cost and quality.

Demand and Production

The 8th Five Year Plan has been extended by two years, i.e. terminating in

1996-97. The revised demand and domestic availability of finished steel and pig iron is as follows :

TABLE 32.4: Demand and Production of Steel and Pig Iron

(in million tonnes)

Financial Year	Total Projected demand	Main Producers	Estimated production: Secondary Producers	Total
I. Finished Steel:				
1991-92 (Est.)	16.35	8.28	6.27	14.55
1996-97	25.00	13.06	11.03	24.09
II. Pig Iron:				
1991-92 (Est.)	1.92	1.34	0.10	1.44
1996-97 (Projected)	3.03	2.13	1.00	3.13

Sources of Finished Steel

Plant-wise break up of the above production levels are as follows:

TABLE 32.5: Plant-wise Breakup Production

(in '000 tonnes)

	Finished		Pig Iron	
SAIL Plants	1991-92	1996-97	1991-92	1996-97
BSP	2190	2535	140	470
DSP	547	743	86	211
RSP	1058	1562	40	66
Bokaro	2559	3532	140	551
IISCO	317	354	384	357
TOTAL:	6671	8726	790	1655
VSP	395	2165	550	475
TISCO	1214	2167	—	—
Main Producers	8280	13058	1340	2130
Secondary Producers	6267	11034	100	1000
Total:	14547	24092	1440	3130

The modernisation and expansion programme of the main producers, coupled with the delicensing and deregulation measures taken by the Government would result in improved efficiency, product quality and international competitiveness. It will also provide the requisite environment for the creation of new capacities in the private sector for meeting the increasing requirements of the future.

Source: *Annual Report*, 1991-92 Ministry of Steel, New Delhi.

Fertilizers

The Government of India announced major changes in the fertilizer pricing policy in August 1992. All price and distribution controls on phosphatic and potassic fertilizers were removed and the consumer price of urea was reduced by 10 per cent from Rs. 3060/tonne to Rs. 2760/tonne. Low-analysis nitrozenous fertilizers were brought back under the retention price scheme.

Production of fertilizers increased by 9.1 per cent in 1991-92. During April-December, 1992 fertilizer output showed a marginal growth of 0.3 per cent. Production of nitrogenous fertilizers increased by 2.4 per cent and that of phosphatic fertilizers declined by 7.6 per cent compared to the corresponding period of the preceding year. The targets set for indigeneous production of fertilizers for the current financial year are 7.7 million tonnes of nitrogen and 2.75 tonnes of phosphate. Production of fertilizers, particularly that of phosphates, is likely to fall short of the targets set for the year. Capacity utilisation which had improved from about 86 per cent to 88 per cent for N and from 75 per cent to 93 per cent for P2O5 during 1991-92 slipped back to around 86 per cent both for N and P2O5 during April-December 1992. Consumption of fertilizers in the current year has been projected at 14.3 million tonnes (including 1.5 million tonnes of potassic fertilizers). A shortfall in domestic production is, however, not likely to create any supply shortages in fertilizers in view of the liberalisation of imports.

Leather

The leather industry, with its substantial contribution to the employment and export growth, occupies a pre-eminent place in the Indian economy. Total employment in the industry is estimated to be about 1.4 million. Since the 1970s there has been a steady structural change taking place in leather industry. On the export front, there was a gradual switchover from semi-finished hides and skins to finished leather and leather manufactures which account for over 70 per cent of leather exports now.

Small-scale units engaged in manufacture in all areas of leather industry still dominate the production base of leather industry. The cottage sector, with its traditional rural artisans, dominates in leather finishing. The India leather industry is characterised by several inherent advantages. A large raw material base of about 166 million pieces of hides and skins available annually is the main strength of the industry. This will go up to 185 million pieces in 1994-95 and 218 million pieces in 2000 A.D. Some of the goat/calf/sheep-skin of India are regarded as speciality products commanding a good market. Abundance of traditional skills in tanning, finishing and manufacturing downstream products and relatively low wage rates are the two other factors of comparative advantage for India.

Exports of leather in value terms at current prices increased from Rs. 278 crore in 1990-91 to Rs. 3076 crore in 1991-92 recording an increase of about 19 per cent. In dollar terms, there was a decline of 13 per cent. India is still a small player with a meagre 3 per cent share in the global exports of leather and leather products. Germany (32 per cent), USA (20 per cent), USSR (17 per cent) UK (17 per cent) and Italy (14 per cent) were the five leading buyers of our leather and leather goods in 1991-92. Leather industry has been identified as one of the thrust areas of export and an export target of Rs.4253 crore has been set for 1992-93.

Sugar

The sugar industry has maintained a high growth in the past three years. Production in the sugar year (October-September) 1991-92 is provisionally estimated at 13.28 million tonnes, 10.2 per cent more than the previous production of 12.05 million tonnes. Average annual growth in sugarcane output during the past 3 years was 7.1 per cent: that of sugarcane crushed by sugar factories, 16.7 per cent; and that of sugar production, 15.1 per cent. The share of sugarcane going into sugar production has also been increasing. Domestic consumption has lagged behind the increase in production and thus leading to rising stocks of sugar. These stocks at the close of the sugar year 1991-92 was over 4.8 million tonnes.

Electronics

The foreign exchange crisis and the consequent import compression hit the electronics industry particularly hard, largely due to the import-intensive nature of its production. The upheavals in the erstwhile USSR and East Europe, which accounted for over 60 per cent of Indian electronics hardware exports, also had strong negative effects on the demand for Indian electronics products. As a result, the growth rate of the industry has slipped sharply from the annual 32 per cent level of the previous decade to about 5.7 per cent.

On the positive side, exports to the General Currency Area (GCA) have increased quite substantially. In particular, exports of software and consumer electronics have shown very encouraging trends. The liberalisation of the Indian economy has also led to considerable interest being shown by major international companies for investing in the electronics sector. It is hoped that this industry will prove to be a prime attraction for direct foreign investments and will again attain the highly dynamic growth part of the previous decade.

In order to consolidate the existing industry and to take advantage of the new policy environment for future growth, the Department of Electronics took a number of initiatives in 1991-92, some of which are described below.

Promotional Policy Measures

- The electronic industry was freed from locational constraints in view of its non-polluting nature.
- The Exim Scrip entitlement on exports of electronics items was increased to 40 per cent.
- Import of items like populated PCBs and video mechanisms has been allowed under Exim Scrips earned against export of selected electronic items like TV sets, audio systems, colour picture tubes etc.
- Exim Scrip entitlement for export of computer software was also enhanced to 30 per cent of net foreign exchange earnings.
- Income tax waiver on computer software under Section 80-HHE of the Income Tax Act.

The Exim Scrip Scheme was later replaced by partial convertibility of Rupee in the Union Budget for 1992-93.

Software Development

To give boost to software export, the Department of Electronics has set-up an autonomous society 'Software Technology Park of India' with the objective of establishing infrastructural facilities such as data communication, core computer and built in accommodation. The society has so far set up 7 Software Technology Parks (STPs) at Bangalore, Pune, Bhubaneshwar, Thiruvananthapuram, Hyderabad, Gandhinagar and NOIDA. Orders for satellite earth station facility for data communication have been placed for 4 STPs.

The Department is also setting up another society for providing high speed data communication facility from 3 centres namely Delhi, Bombay and Bangalore with French financial assistance.

Consumer Electronics

Consumer electronics contributes about one-third of the total electronic production in the country. On account of continued recession in the TV market, the growth of this sector has been restricted to 21 per cent. In this sector, electronic watches, audio cassettes and radio cassette recorders witnessed growth.

In order to create healthy competition, licensing policy has been liberalised and now no licence is required to manufacture consumer electronic products except compact disk players, tape recorders, VCRs/VCPs, colour TV receivers and microwave ovens. The private sector units are now allowed to manufacture modules for electronic wrist watches. This would create healthy competition, reduce dependence on import and check smuggling.

The electronics industry has maintained a high growth rate for almost three decades. Starting from a mere Rs. 15 crore in 1960, the production of this sector today stands at over Rs. 10,000 crore (Table 32.2). In the 1960s, the annual growth rate averaged about 25 per cent, which dropped to 17 per cent in the 1970s, and then picked up to over 30 per cent in the 1980s.

TABLE 32.6: Production of Electronics (Sectoral Breakup) : 1988-89 to 1991-92

(Rs. crore)

Item/sector	1988-89	1989-90	1990-91	1991-92
1 Consumer electronics	2650	2850	3000	3100
2 Industrial electronics	1000	1360	1370	1500
3 Computer systems (including microprocessor systems)	560	835	820	870
4 Communication & broadcasting equipment	1010	1560	1710	2130
5 Strategic electronics	410	505	635	430
6 Components	1125	1520	1510	1900
7 Free trade zones (hardware)	160	215	275	275
8 Software for exports (including EPZ, 100% EOU)	115	165	220	385
TOTAL	7030	9010	9540	10590

The electronics industry stands substantially deregulated under the new industrial policy. No licence is now required for establishing production capacities except for consumer durables and defence equipment. There are no locational restrictions other than environmental clearance and local zoning and land-use regulations. Automatic approval up to 51 per cent foreign equity and 100 per cent NRI equity is given for a wide range of electronic products. Approval for foreign technology agreements is also automatic for all electronic products except aerospace and defence equipment.

Exports of the electronics sector have risen steadily over the past five years from 6.5 per cent of production in 1987-88 to 10.2 per cent in 1991-92. Aggregate exports have risen from Rs. 910 crore in 1990-91 to Rs. 1090 crore in 1991-92 (i.e. by 19.8 per cent). About 77 per cent of the electronics exports in 1991-92 went to the General Currency Areas as against 53 per cent in 1990-91.

Textiles

The textile industry was one of the industries delicensed in August 1991 under the new industrial policy. The Textile Control Order, 1986 was repealed in December, 1992 and replaced by the Textile (Development and Regulation) Order, 1992. Under the new policy no prior approval of the Government is required to set up textile units, including powerlooms, except locational clearance as laid down in the Industries (Development and Regulation) Act, 1951 in the case of non-SSI units. New textile units have only to file an Information Memorandum with the Textile Commissioner, Government of India.

The textile industry is extremely complex and varied with hand-spun and hand-woven sector at one end and sophisticated, capital intensive and high speed operations of the mill sector at the other. In between, falls the decentralised small scale powerloom sector. The problems facing the industry are complex and inter-related and expectedly different in both magnitude and nature from those obtaining in relatively homogeneous system.

With a view to providing a policy frame-work for an integrated and balanced development and harmonious existence of the three sectors of the industry viz. organised mill sector, the powerloom sector and the handloom sector, Government announced Textile Policy Statement in June, 1985. This Policy aims at production of cloth of acceptable quality at reasonable prices to meet the clothing requirements of the growing population, keeping in view the employment and export potential of the country. This Policy makes a major departure from the earlier Policies in that it views textile industry in terms of the stages of manufacturing processes and allows full fibre flexibility.

Having regard to the fact that the Textile Policy of June, 1985 had been in operation for three years, Government set up in May, 1988 a Committee headed by Shri Abid Hussain to assess the impact of the policy on different sectors of the textile industry, especially its effectiveness in protecting the handloom sector and in maintaining the pre-eminent role of cotton as the main raw material. The Committee submitted its report in February, 1990. The Committee felt that the 1985 Policy was anchored on the right principles, although no policy is immutable. The Committee, however, concluded that the Policy did not address itself adequately to the institutional, financial and other aspects required to achieve the objectives it had set for itself. The Committee made far-reaching recommendations in respect of raw materials (cotton and synthetic fibre/yarn) the spinning sector, the weaving sector (handloom, powerloom and mills), exports, fiscal levies and modernisation. The Government have discussed the Report of the Committee with State Governments, industry representatives and other organisations concerned and also with the concerned Ministries/Deptts. A conference chaired by the Minister of Textiles was also held with State Textiles Ministers. In the light of these discussions, Government are in the process of formulating a new textile policy. The new Textile Policy is expected to aim at strengthening infrastructural support to handlooms and powerlooms, augmenting raw materials supply and exports, a fair return to cotton farmers, acceleration of modernisation etc.

The spindleage has gone up from 11 million in 1951 to 27.27 million in 1992, while the weaving capacity declined from the level of 1,95,000 looms in 1951 to 1,78,000 looms in 1992. The decrease in weaving capacity is attributable to structural transformation taking place, leading to delinking of weaving units from spinning units. It is significant to note that while yarn production takes place almost entirely in the organised mill sector, about 85% of the total cloth production takes place in he decentralised handloom, powerloom sectors and hosiery sector. The organised mill sector contributes only 15% of the total cloth production.

Per Capita Consumption

The per capita consumption of textiles as revealed by households surveys has been steadily going up. It rose from a level of 13.84 linear metres in 1984 to 16.35 linear metres in 1987. The pattern of consumption has also undergone a significant change. While cotton cloth accounted for around 72 per cent of the total consumption in 1984, its share fell to 60 per cent in 1987. The share of non-cotton cloth went up marginally from 13 per cent to 15 per cent in the same period. Blends on the other hand, showed the largest increase from around 15 per cent in 1984 to nearly 20 per cent in 1987.

A study of the wholesale price index of textile items shows that the prices of VFY increased by 45.8% during 1991-92 as against the increase in the percentage of the price index of commodities by 12.4%. The main reason for such steep rise in the prices of viscose filament yarn and nylon yarn are increase in the prices of raw materials, their inputs, including wages and salaries, some upward revision in excise duty, restrictions on imports and better demand.

The Nodal Agency came into being as a sequel to the textile policy of 1985. The Nodal Agency evolves rehabilitation packages for potentially viable sick mills. The Nodal Agency has so far examined 177 sick and closed textile units in different States and has determined viability as follows :

Mills examined	177
Declared viable	51
Declared non-viable	51
Mills whose viability is yet to be decided	75

The Board of Industrial and Financial Reconstruction has come into its existence to tackle the problem of sickness of mills in all types of industries. The textile industry being the oldest and largest industry in the country, many cases have been registered with BIFR for determining the future course of action.

The Textile Modernisation Fund Scheme was set up in August, 1986 as a sequel to th textile policy of 1985 with a view to accelerating the pace of modernisation in the textile industry.

The Textile Workers' Rehabilitation Fund Scheme was introduced with effect from 15-9-1986, as a corollary to the textile policy of 1985 with a view to safeguarding the interests of the workers affected by permanent closure of the mills.

The bulk of world trade in textile and clothing is regulated under the Multi Fibre Arrangements (MFA), an instrument under the GATT. The MFA which has presently been extended upto 31-12-1992 is proposed to be phased out over a period of 10 years beginning from 1-1-1993, in accordance with the deliberations of the Uruguay Round of Negotiations at Geneva.

The textile industry is the largest industry in the country, accounting for about 20 per cent of the total industrial output, providing employment to about 15 million people and contributing nearly 25 per cent of the total value of exports. The structure of the industry is extremely complex with the hand-spinning and hand-weaving (handloom) sectors at the one end and the modern, sophisticated and highly mechanised mill sector at the other. In between falls the decentralised small-scale powerloom sector. The present policy regime will result in more rapid and harmonious growth of the three segments (mill, powerloom and handloom) and also give a thrust to exports.

India's textile industry continues to be predominantly cotton based, 73 per cent of fabric consumption in the country being accounted for by cotton. Total fabric production in 1991-92 at 22588 million square metres was marginally lower than the production in 1990-91. The shares of the mill, powerlooms and the handloom sectors in this output were 10.5 , 71.2 and 18.3 per cent respectively in 1991-92. Production during April-December, 1992-93 increased by 2.2 per cent over April-December 1991-92. The powerloom sector increased its share marginally to 72.8 per cent at the expense of both the mill and the handloom sectors whose shares have declined. Production of yarn is available in Table 32.3.

TABLE 32.7 Production of Spun Yarn

(Million kg.)

	Cotton yarn	Blended yarn	Non-cotton yarn	Total
1987-88	1321	152	82	1555
1988-89	1310	185	92	1587
1989-90	1372	173	107	1652
1990-91	1510	207	107	1824
1991-92	1450	234	122	1806
(April-December)				
1991-92	1072	175	89	1336
1992-93	1086	186	99	1371

Textile exports (yarn, fabrics, made-ups and ready-made garments; excluding jute goods and handicrafts) accounted for about 23 per cent of India's total exports in 1991-92. It is also the largest net foreign exchange earner as the import content in textile goods is very low. During 1991-92 textile exports amounted to Rs. 10106 crore, an increase of 46 per cent over the previous year. In Dollar terms, the increase was 6.2 per cent. Exports of textiles in the first six months (April-September) of the current fiscal year are estimated at Rs. 5080 crore, an increase of 43 per cent (15.3 per cent in Dollar terms) over 1991-92. Most of the exports go to the General Currency Area. This sharp increase in export growth in textiles is one of the highlights of the industrial performance during 1992-93.

Output of textile machinery and spare parts has witnessed a substantial growth during the last 5 years. Total value of production of textile machinery and spares increased from Rs. 447 crore in 1987-88, to Rs. 1009 crore during 1991-92, recording a growth of about 126 per cent. During the same period, exports of textile machinery have gone up by about 280 per cent, from Rs. 41 crore during 1987-88 to rs. 156 crore in 1991-92. The target of production of textile machinery, fixed at Rs. 1210 crore for the year 1992-93, is likely to be achieved.

Several policy measures have been adopted to improve the health of the textile industry. These include:

(i) The Textile Modernisation Fund set up in 1986 with a corpus of Rs. 750 crore has received an overwhelming response from the mills. Till the end of September 1992 financial institutions had sanctioned loans amounting to Rs. 1368 crore for 357 cases while disbursements aggregated to Rs. 858 crore.

(ii) A turnaround strategy for the sick mills of NTC and BIC has been evolved by the Government. The package includes providing working capital finance to tide over the liquidity problems, capacity modernisation and shedding of surplus labour through a voluntary retirement scheme which will be handled through the recently established NRF.

(iii) In the jute sector, which has been in the grip of a recession since 1991-92, a new package of revitalisation programme is being implemented with the help of UNDP to cater to the needs of the sector from production to export stage. Major thrust of the programmes is on diversification of product range and involvement of entrepreneurs.

(iv) Other programmes relate to the technological upgradation of ginning and pressing operations and also of the handloom sector. Powerloom co-operative societies are being encouraged to upgrade capacities in this sector. It is expected that these policy measures will further encourage upgradation of capacities and a higher export orientation to the industry.

Small-Scale and Village Industries

The number of small-scale units is provisionally estimated to have gone up from 19.48 lakh in 1990-91 to 20.80 lakh in 1991-92 — 14.96 lakh registered units on the rolls of the State Industries Departments and 5.84 lakh unregistered units — registered units on the rolls of the State Industries Departments and 5.84 lakh unregistered units — registering an increase of about 6.8 per cent. However, if the results of the census of SSI (Small Scale Industries) units 1987-88 are any guide, about 30 to 40 per cent of these registered units might be non-functional. The value of output of the SSI sector in 1991-92 at current prices, is estimated at Rs. 178700 crore, about 15 per cent higher than the output of Rs. 155340 crore in 1990-91. Adjusted for inflation, the real growth of output of the sector in 1991-92 might be less than 2 per cent. Estimated employment in the sector has also increased from 125.3 lakh in 1990-91 to 128.8 lakh in 1991-92, an increase of about 3 per cent. The growth of the sector in 1991-92 was in spite of a number of constraints like import restrictions affecting the availability of requisite raw materials and credit squeeze and a rise in the interest rates leading to severe erosion of the liquidity position of the SSI units.

Government have taken a number of steps for the promotion of small-scale industries pursuant to the policy measures announced on 6 August 1991.

(i) There were restrictions on registering new SSI units for the manufacture of certain products although the products are reserved for the small scale sector. The list of such restricted products was disbanded.
(ii) Industry-related service and business enterprises with investment up to Rs. 5 lakh in fixed assets (excluding land and building) irrespective of their location are now treated on par with small-scale industries.
(iii) Steps have been taken to alleviate the credit bottlenecks of this sector. The eligibility limit of projects under the National Equity Fund Scheme has been doubled from Rs. 5 lakh to Rs. 10 lakh.
(iv) The Single Window Scheme was extended to be operated by scheduled banks also in addition to State Financial Institutions.
(v) An Ordinance was promulgated on 23 September 1992 making payment of interest obligatory on delayed payments to small scale and ancillary industrial undertakings. It has been re-promulgated in January 1993.

Khadi and Village Industries Commission

The Khadi and Village Industries Commission (KVIC) covers about 2.1 lakh villages throughout the country through 30 State KVI Boards, 2320 registered institutions, 29813 cooperatives and over 5 lakh individuals. Over the years, the main thrust of KVIC activities has been to provide a larger share of employment to SC/STs and women. At present SC/ST comprise nearly 30 per cent of workers and women nearly 46 per cent.

It is provisionally estimated that during 1991-92 the KVI sector produced goods worth Rs. 2458 crore and provided employment to 49.7 lakh persons. During 1992-93 the production level is expected to go up to Rs. 2670 crore and employment to 51.05 lakh persons.

32.8 **Impact of New Industrial Policy**

So far, Industrial Policy focused attention on the need for promoting competition in the domestic market. The policy laid the foundation for increasingly competitive export base and for encouraging foreign investment in high technology areas. A climate for rapid industrial growth in the country was also created. Thus, a broad-based infrastructure had been built up; basic industries had been established. A high degree of self-reliance in the large number of items-raw materials intermediates, finished goods had been achieved. New growth centres of industrial activity had emerged, as also a new generation of entrepreneurs. A large number of engineers, technicians and skilled workers had also been trained. The accent was on opening the domestic market to increased competition and readying our industry to stand on its own in the face of international competition.

Industrial licensing has been done away with for all industries except a short list of hazardous chemicals. Entrepreneurs are, therefore, now free to set up chemical industries by intimating Government through the Industrial Entrepreneurs' Memorandum. The New Policy envisages an automatic clearance of capital goods import, if foreign exchange cost is met by foreign equity or through exim scrips.

Foreign investment limit of 40% has been relaxed. This relaxation would enable inflow of improved state of threat technology for chemicals, agro-chemicals in particular, and pharmaceuticals into India.

Pesticides

Pesticides including insecticides, fungicides, weedicides etc. are used extensively in Indian agriculture and public health. During the last three decades, the Pesticides industry has made good progress and today more than 57 technical grade Pesticides are being manufactured in the country. Approximately 125 units are currently engaged in the manufacture of technical grade Pesticides and over 500 units are making formulations. As a result of the increased production of Pesticides in the country, import of technical grade Pesticides has come down considerably. The current installed capacity of technical grade Pesticides is about 1,25,000 tonnes.

Pesticides manufacturing industry generally employs relatively high technology. Many of the units in India have obtained foreign technology. Now technology development as made rapid strides particularly in the field of Agrochemicals. Newer Pesticides are developed by the National Laboratories as well as private sector units with their in house R&D. Some of the newer generation of synthetic Pyrethroids like Fenvalerate, Cypermethrin etc. have been successfully developed and are cheaper and safer. Today manufacture of Pesticides are almost totally based on domestic technology. Thus India has achieved near self-sufficiency in Pesticides production and supply and only about 2% of technical grade material is imported.

Petrochemicals

Petrochemicals can be broadly categorised as follows :

1. Plastics (such as low density and high density polyethylene, commonly known as LDPE and HDPE; Polypropylene and Polyvinyl chloride, which are commonly known as PP and PVC).
2. Synthetic Rubbers (such as styrene butadiene rubber and polybutadiene rubber, which are commonly known in the abbreviated form of SBR and pbr).
3. Synthetic fibres (such as nylon, polyester and acrylic fibre).
4. Intermediates (such as ethylene, propylene, benzene, dimethyl terephthalate (DMT), Caprolectum etc.) which, in turn, are used in the manufacture of various petrochemical items.

Petrochemicals are manufactured from petroleum feedstocks like naphtha and gas and also from alcohol and calcium carbide. At present naphtha is the dominant feedstock in our country. With the commissioning of IPCL's Maharashtra Gas Cracker Complex at Nagothane, natural gas made available by ONGC from its Uran Terminal is also now being put to use. The cyclic availability of alcohol, combined with periodical changes in the levy of excise duty, renders reliable the alcohol route for petrochemicals. Similarly the use of calcium carbide for the manufacture of petrochemicals products such as PVC is constrained by the fact that the route is energy intensive.

Production of basic petrochemicals in India made a beginning at a comparatively late stage during the 1960s. A small capacity naphtha cracker of 20,000 TPA ethylene capacity was set up in 1966 by Union Carbide. In 1968 a slightly larger capacity naphtha cracker of 60,000 TPA ethylene capacity was set up by National Organic Chemicals Limited. Both the plants were set up in the private sector in the vicinity of Bombay area. Prior to that, small quantities of petrochemicals (mainly plastics resins and intermediates) were being produced in alcohol, coal tar intermediates, calcium carbide stc. as feedstock.

A major thrust in this field was made when IPCL's naphtha cracker of 130,000 TPA ethylene capacity was set up at Baroda in 1978. The present range of production of petrochemical items in India is quite large.

The trend of growth in consumption of plastics, synthetic rubbers and synthetic fibres has indicated the need for setting up of such industries, so that in the coming years, dependence on imports is reduced/eliminated. To cover the gaps between projected demand and already approved capacity in respect of some of the petrochemicals products, the following projects were completed and commissioned during the 7th Plan and commercial production has started in IPCL:

1. Polypropylene compoylmer project
2. Acrylic fibre expansion
3. Xylene expansion project
4. Linear Alkyl Benzene expansion/kerosene pre-fractionation project.

32.9 Steel Authority of India Limited (SAIL)

Production of saleable steel in the five integrated steel plants of SAIL for 1991-92 (upto January, 1992) was 6.55 million tonnes and that of crude steel was 7.96 million tonnes.

Major Construction Projects

(a) *SAIL Projects*

(i) Construction work on the modernisation of Durgapur Steel Plant is in full swing and the project is expected to be completed by March, 1993.

(ii) The modernisation scheme for the Rourkela Steel Plant was approved in December 1989 and is presently under progress. This project is scheduled to be completed by April, 1995.

(b) *Visakhapatnam Steel Project*

The project management continued its efforts to achieve new milestones in the completion and commissioning of the units under Stage-I. The notable achievement was the actual fulfillment of the projected commencing schedules of major units of State-I and State-II. During the year under report Coke Oven Battery

No. 2 and Bar Mill of the Light a Medium Merchant Mill — the two last units of Stage-I — were commissioned during October, 1991. With the commissioning of Coke Oven Battery No. 2 full coking coal requirements of Blast Furance No. 1 are assured. Sinter Plant No. 2, a unit of Stage-II, was commissioned in December, 1991. On March 28, 1992 Coke Over Battery 3 was lighted while Blast Furance 2 and MMSM were commissioned. Availability of water for VSP was causing concern because of delay in completion of the Yeleru Canal Scheme. This scheme was completed on 30.6.91 and water reached VSP reservoir on 9-7-91.

32.10 Exports

32.10.1 Iron Ore

A major portion of the exports was from the two undertakings of the Ministry of Steel, namely National Mineral Development Corporation Ltd. (NMDC) and Kudremukh Iron Ore Company Ltd. (KIOCL).

32.10.2 Other Minerals

In respect of other minerals the Government policy has been in the direction of substituting value added products like ferro alloys in place of raw ores and promoting greater utilisation of the lower grade ores through beneficiation and other means. In keeping with this policy ceilings were fixed on exports of manganese and other ores.

32.11 Steel Consumers Council

The Steel Consumers Council was established in January, 1986 under the Chairmanship of Minister for Steel and Mines (now Minister for Steel) to provide a forum for international between Government and various sections of steel consumers. The Council has been reconstituted on 31st October, 1991 with a fresh tenure of two years.

32.12 Management Information System (MIS)

The computerised MIS introduced in the Ministry of Steel with the assistance of National Informatics Centre (NIC) is functional in the areas of Personnel Management, Project Monitoring, Data Bank for Secondary Producers and Financial Accounting and Budgeting. The Computer Centre in the Ministry is re-equipped with the latest hardware with appropriate linkages with the NIC Super Computer and its Electronic Mail Package. Terminals have been provided to senior officers and also to some Sections requiring the facility for interactive usage with the MIS. Training Programmes for the staff for computer usage are also organised by NIC from time to time.

32.13 Standardisation

The year 1992 will witness greater market consolidation in Europe. Also the influx of foreign investment would bring alongwith it greater challenge in the standardisation and quality assurance. ISO-9000 qualification is a major thrust area in this field. For the manufactures of the electronic components, the IECQ certification includes ISO-9001 or ISO-9002 qualification automatically.

Recognising the strong potential for software development and export, software also has to be certified as per ISO-9000 Part III. The Department is fully geared through their STQC Directorate to provide this service for the industry.

The major achievements made during the year are:

- Standards issued by "International Electrotechnical Commission (IEC)" viz., IEC-801 series have been adopted for EMI/EMC testing. Four STQC laboratories have been equipped to carry out this testing.
- Test facility for opto-electronics components and devices has been created at ERTL, Calcutta.
- Test facilities for safety testing of consumer electronics, information technology and business equipment as per international standards like VDE, IEC etc., have been installed at STQC laboratories at Delhi, Bombay and Calcutta. Laboratory at Bombay has been authorised by Underwriters Laboratory (UL), USA, to carry out testing as per UL standards for consumer electronic (UL-1950), cathode ray tubes and high voltage deflection components (UL-1413).
- Facilities recognised by Director General of Mine Safety (DGMS) for safety testing of mining electronic products have been installed at ERTL, Calcutta.
- Fourteen standards developed at STQC have been adopted by BIS as IS standards.

32.14 **Technology Application/Development**

- Delivery of 256 nodes PARAM parallel super computer of computing power exceeding 1G flops/7500 MIPs. It has brought India at par with European development in the super computer arena.
- The national HVDC link of 100 MW/100 kV between lower Sileru in Andhra Pradesh and Barsoor in Madhya Pradesh went into continuous operation on full rated capacity from October 20, 1991.
- ERNET, the education and research network, gained wide popularity among the academicians and research community. The number of institutions connected to ERNET grew to over seventy, servicing over four thousand users. Technology spin-offs in terms of OSI, inter-networking etc., also moved out of laboratories to the user community.
- Rapid technology changes in modern automation and control technology call for a planned approach to integrated automation in industries. AAPP with its network is providing adoption and assimilation of advanced technologies by the core sectors. DOE as launched retrofit programmes to achieve optimal capacity utilization and productivity in Textile industry. Indian Railways, Tea industry, Cement Industry, Paper and Pulp, Fertilizers, Sugar Industry etc.

32.15 **Manpower Development**

- To enhance the quality of computer manpower training initiated by the private institutions, Department of Electronics has announced a scheme under which institutes meeting the defined quality and service standards would be given accreditation for conducting certain specified computer courses viz., 'O' (foundation), 'A' (advanced diploma), 'B' (graduate) and 'C' (post-graduate) level.

— A project, namely, Electronics Industry Development Project (IMPACT), assisted by World Bank and Swiss Development Corporation, involving 32 institutions and 5 resource centres for quality improvement of education at engineering colleges, polytechnics, etc., and to provide in-service training to professional was initiated in June 1991.A Memorandum of Understanding has been signed with Resource Centres and the participating institutions.

32.16 International Co-operation

A significant development in international cooperation was the finalisation of the Indo-French Project for setting up a Value Added High Speed Data Communication Network to facilitate and increase software export from the country. The Project is expected to be commissioned next year. The Project involves Fr. Franc 17 million financial assistance from the French Government.

Projects taken up under the Indo-EEC Memorandum on Technical Co-operation also progressed satisfactorily. A significant feature of this co-operation will be the setting up of two centres in key high-tech areas, namely, Software Engineering and Surface Mounted Technology (SMT). In addition, several workshops were organised in India to disseminate technical information on European standards and certification procedures, so as to help the Indian electronics industry to attain global standards and thereby enhance competitiveness. A series of workshops to promote the export of India's computer software to Europe have also been finalised. Several proposals for cooperation with various countries such as Sweden, Germany, USA, Turkey, Canada, Saudi Arabia, Egypt, South Korea etc., were made by this Department for the consideration of the respective Joint Commissions. These proposals are aimed at enhancing our technological capabilities, modernisation and development of exports.

32.17 Annual Plan for 1992-93

For the year 1992-93, budgetary support of Rs. 750 million for various projects have been provided. The budgetary allocations have been reformulated to reflected the changed priorities of the Government. Export efforts, particularly of Software, have been given equal priority with research and development, which has been the traditional focus of the Department. Considerable emphasis has also been placed on Manpower Development.

In line with the current trends, no budgetary provision has been provided for the public sector undertakings under the administrative control of the Department. These are expected to raise their own resources. Problems in this regard are expected only in the case of Semiconductor Complex Ltd., and steps have been initiated to raise the necessary funds for completing its rebuilding.

32.18 Eighth Five Year Plan

An extensive exercise to reformulate the 8th Five Year Plan proposals for the period of 1992-1997 was undertaken bearing in mind the emphasis laid down in the Approach Paper of the 8th Five Year Plan. These were to maximise employment generation, exports, backward area development, decentralisation wherever possible and finding linkages between various programmes of the Government to maximise benefits to the beneficiaries/end-users. The textile industry, both in the organised mill and jute sectors as well as in the decentralised sectors like the handlooms, powerlooms, handicrafts and sericulture have high employment potential both in urban and rural areas. The proposals formulated in the Ministry and submitted to the Planning Commission emphasised taking up of schemes towards achieving these ends.

The Planning Commission have approved an outlay of Rs. 217.00 crores including IEBR of Rs. 11.00 crore for the first year of the Eighth Plan. The size of the Plan for the subsequent years of the Plan period will be intimated by the Planning Commission at a later stage.

Source: *Annual Report*, 1991-92, Ministry of Textiles, New Delhi.

The total public sector outlay on industry and minerals at 1991-92 prices is Rs. 44,337 crores of which Rs. 34,842 crores will be by the Central Sector (as against RS. 17,268 crores during the Seventh Plan) and Rs. 9,495 crore by the States and Union Territories. Within the industry and mineral sector, the outlay on the village and small industries will be Rs. 4,778 crores which will be shared between centre to the extent of Rs. 2,458 crores and States and Union Territories to the extent of Rs. 2,320 crores. The outlay on large and medium industries will be Rs. 26,900 crores by the Centre and Rs. 7,175 crores by the States and Union Territories. The entire public sector outlay on fertilizers of the order of Rs. 5,484 crores will be incurred by the Centre.

The significant departure in the Eighth Plan is in respect of the distribution of investment in between the public and private sectors. In view of the shift in economic policy placing greater reliance on the market, the private sector is expected to shoulder a greater responsibility for investment in electricity, communication, mining and quarrying, oil and coal, petro-chemicals, metals, fertilizers, heavy capital goods and the organised segment of commercial services.

In consequence, the proportion of public investment going to manufacturing which was 26% during the Seventh Plan has been reduced to 23.61% for the Eighth Plan. In mining and quarrying too, it is 4.96% as against 6.70% of the Seventh Plan.

32.19 **Industrial Sickness**

As at the end of March 1991, there were 2.24 lakh sick or weak industrial units on the rolls of commercial banks. A little over 2.21 lakh (99 per cent) of them were in the small scale sector. Outstanding bank credit of Rs. 10768 crore, which constituted about 17.5 per cent of total industrial credit, was locked in these 2.24 lakh sick of weak industrial units (excluding 127575 non-existent and non-traceable SSI units with an outstanding bank credit of Rs. 284 crore). A slight abatement in the increasing incidence of sickness due to early detection and preventive measures taken by the banking system is in evidence. Total outstanding bank credit locked in sick or weak industrial units which had increased by 23.2 per cent between December 1987 and December 1988 and by 21.4 per cent between December 1988 and March 1990 (17.1 per cent on an annualised basis) showed a much lower increase of 15.1 per cent during the year ended March 1991.

33

INFORMATION AND BROADCASTING

The objective of the Ministry of Information and Broadcasting is to inform, educate and entertain the people. The media units of the Ministry seek to create a climate of awareness of the directions of development and ensure people's participation in the implementation of Government's policies, plans and programmes.

The aforesaid objectives of the Ministry are achieved through its media units viz., Akashvani (All India Radio), Doordarshan, Press Information Bureau, Publications Division, Research and Reference Division, Directorate of Advertising and Visual Publicity, Photo Division, Song and Drama Division, Directorate of Film Festivals and the Films Division. The Ministry is also associated with the National Film Development Corporation. Children's Film Society of India, Film and Television Institute of India, Indian Institute of Mass Communication, Press Council of India and Central Board of Film Certification.The activities of the media units during 1991-92 are indicated in the succeeding paragraphs. They are followed by detailed chapters on each of the media units. Appendices at the end of the Report contain information in statistical and tabular formats.

Akashvani (All India Radio)

The network of All India Radio stations has expanded from 104 to 125 stations. Eighteen local radio stations and three non-local radio stations started their regular broadcast during this period.

The Central Education Planning Unit of All India Radio has embarked on a massive serial, entitled "Human Evolution" in collaboration with the National Council for Science and Technology Communication. The programme started on 2 June, 1991 from 88 stations of AIR in 18 languages. There will be a total of 130 episodes. One lakh children in the age group of 10 to 14 years have been registered as the target audience. In addition, ten thousand schools have also been taken as listening points.

Two News Magazines in Hindi and English were introduced from 16 August, 1991 in place of the usual English and Hindi news bulletins in the morning. The magazines include a news bulletin, a commentary and news headlines from details. With the introduction of hourly bulletins from 0100 hours to 0500 hours, All India Radio now has hourly bulletins round the clock.

All India Radio provided analytical coverage of the election to the Lok Sabha and some state assemblies in a comprehensive manner. Round the clock, hourly and mid-hourly bulletins, a series of commentaries, discussions and interviews with leaders of political parties and political analysts in different parts of the country were arranged in connection with the coverage of election results.

Special programmes were mounted at the national and regional level to highlight the extent of damage caused by the earthquake in the hill district of Uttar Pradesh in October 1991 and the massive efforts of relief and rehabilitation undertaken by the administration and other agencies.

Doordarshan

Doordarshan with its present network of 21 programme production centres, including Central Production Centre (CPC) and 531 transmitters of varying power reaching 81.17 per cent of the country's population, has become one of the premier TV organisations in the world.

On 3 December 1991, Doordarshan commenced the experimental telecast of the recorded version of Question Hour in both the Houses of Parliament.

The Railway Budget Speech of the Railway Minister and the Budget Speech of the Finance Minister were telecast live for the first time in the history of Doordarshan.

Doordarshan also commenced telecast of educational programmes produced by the Indira Gandhi National Open University. These programmes are telecast for half-an-hour in the mornings, three times a week.

During the year 1991-92, Doordarshan undertook with CCTV, the co-production of a two hour telefilm entitled "Bodhi Dharma", the first patriarch of Zen and an Indian Prince who embraced Buddhism. Shooting was done in India and China.

Guidelines were issued for accepting, processing and approval of proposals received from outside producers for telecast under Doordarshan's "Commissioned Programme Scheme".

Film Division

The Films Division produced 21 News Magazines as well as 39 documentaries, short films and featurette films from April to December 1991. Out of these, 35 films were produced departmentally and four films through independent producers. Among them, 15 documentary films were on family welfare.

One hour documentary on Dr. Ambedkar was completed and telecast during his birth centenary year.

During the year, eight films produced by the Films Division have won national and international awards, and seven others, have been selected for Indian Panorama section of the International Film Festival of India 1992.

The second Festival for Documentary and Short Films was organised at Bombay, from 1-5 February 1992.

The Films Division continued to produced and release films on India's struggle for Independence. Six films, on the role of different states in the freedom struggle are in different stages of production.

A film on various tribal development programmes undertaken by the different state governments in India has been completed under the title *"Utthan"*.

Directorate of Film Festivals

The Directorate organised a number of film weeks in India under the Cultural Exchange Programme. These were Egyptian, Chinese, French, Turkish and Hungarian film weeks. The Directorate achieved its objective of making Indian films popular abroad by organising Indian Film Weeks in Switzerland and Mogolia. Besides this, under the Cultural Exchange Programme, packages of Indian films were sent abroad to Spain, Ghana, France, Algeria, Burkino Faso and Hungary. This year's Dada Saheb Phalke Award was conferred on the noted actor Shri Akkineni Nageshwara Rao. The 23rd International Film Festival of India was successfully organised in Bangalore from 10-20 January 1992. More than 200 films from 14 countries including India were screened during the festival. More than 40 foreign delegates participated in the festival.

Children's Film Society of India

Children's Film Society of India has its main objective as production, distribution and exhibition of films for children. The Society completed production of one feature film and three short films and dubbing of seven feature films. The Seventh International Children Film Festival of India was held in Thiruvananthapuram from 14-23 November 1991, in collaboration with the Government of Kerala.

National Film Archive of India

The National Film Archive of India since its inception in 1964, is making steady progress in preserving the country's film heritage, building up representative collection of contemporary world cinema for permanent record, reference and research and diffusion of film culture in the country.

By 31 December 1991, the archival collection consisted of 12,570 films, 1,957 micro films, 696 video cassettes, 1,822 disc-records, 21,075 scripts, 20,235 books, 1,18,273 press clippings, 94,821 stills, 5,851 song booklets, 7,133 pamphlets, 5,984 wall posters, 152 periodicals, 150 audio tapes and 42 microfiche.

During the year 1991 the Archive in collaboration with the West Bengal Government organised New Theatre Film Festival and Short Film Festival at Calcutta. Screenings, were also held at Bangalore, Bhopal, Bombay, Hyderabad, Vijayawada, Pondicherry, Puthukottai.

The new building complex is commissioned to meet the requirements of full-fledged expansion of the organisation. The centrally air-conditioned building complex has three basement film storage vaults with capacity to store about 60,000 reels, a 330 seat auditorium and a small preview theatre of 30 seats capacity along with provision for other facilities required by the research workers.

Film and Television Institute of India

The Film and Television Institute of India provides technical training in a systematic manner in the art and craft of film-making. It also provides in-service television training to officers and staff of Doordarshan. The Institute conducted the 34th and the 35th in-service training courses in basic TV production and technical operations for the Doordarshan staff during the year. It also organised a short duration course on television production orientation for Indian Information Service probationers.

National Film Development Corporation (NFDC)

The NFDC handles a wide range of film-related activities like production, export and import, distribution of good films, marketing of video cassettes and providing finance for the construction of theatres.

Under the agreement signed between National Film Development Corporation and Doordarshan, good feature films and tele-films are being produced jointly. Till 30 November, 1991, 21 such films have been approved and eight have already been completed.

Out of 25 films approved, 24 were completed under the NFDC's scheme to undertaken production of films based on good scripts and to be directed by well known directors.

The Corporation presently imports about 35 to 45 films a year. Keeping in view its limited resources,greater stress is being laid on the import of good quality commercial family entertainers.

With a view to fighting the menace of video piracy, NFDC started marketing good quality video cassettes to video libraries through their distributors. Two hundred and thirty titles have been released on video till November 1991.

Central Board of Film Certification

Films can be exhibited to the public in Indian only after they have been certified by the Central Board of Film Certification set up under the Cinematography Act, 1952. The Board has a Chairman and 25 other members. Its headquarters is at Bombay and regional offices at Bangalore, Bombay, Calcutta, Cuttack, Delhi, Hyderabad, Madras and Thiruvananthapuram.

During the year 1991 the office at Cuttack was set up. The Board and its advisory panels at various centres were reconstituted with eminent persons from a cross section of society. The overall representation of women on the Board and its advisory panels is about thirty-five per cent. Government also issued on 6 December 1991 revised "Guidelines" for certification of films.

Out of 910 Indian feature films (celluloid) certified by the Board in 1991, 615 were granted "U" certificates, 94 "UA" certificates and 201 "A" certificates. Of the 124 foreign feature films (celluloid) certified, 40 were given "U" certificates, 10 "UA" certificates and 74 "A" certificates.

Press Information Bureau (PIB)

During the year 1991, the Bureau arranged publicity for the steps taken by the Government to cope with the situation in Assam, Kashmir and Punjab. A special computerised analysis of the election results was prepared and released to the Press soon after the elections. Publicity was also provided for the New Industrial Policy and New Trade Policy. The Bureau also arranged publicity for the drastic measures taken by the Government to overcome unprecedented economic crisis.

The Bureau has been going ahead with the plan schemes.for computerisation. The basic thrust of computerisation is to speed up the transmission of documents of News value. The computerisation of activities of the Bureau is being taken up in two phases.

Registrar of Newspapers for India (RNI)

During April to December 1991, RNI cleared 9,349 titles for newspapers/periodicals against the target of 9,000 titles for the whole year 1991-92. The title verification work was computerised in the RNI Office to facilitate speedy clearance of titles. During the same period, 1,252 newspapers were issued certificates of registration. Circulation claims of 773 newspapers were verified till December 1991. The Newsprint Allocation Policy for 1991-92 was announced on 4 October 1991.

Publications Division

The Division under its publications has brought out volumes on "Speeches of R. Venkataraman" (as Vice-President), the fifth and last volume of former Prime Minister late Shri Rajiv Gandhi's speeches and writings and a booklet titled, "Selected Thoughts of Rajiv Gandhi". It also completed Supplementary Volume in English and Volume 82 in Hindi under its multi-volume project "Collected Works of Mahatma Gandhi". Besides, the usual publications, the Division also brought out low priced titles under its pocket book series.

"The Employment News" added this year two new features "India This Week — World This Week", and "Apni Hindi Sudharein". Concerted efforts were made during the year to increase the circulation of Employment News and the print run increased from about 4.02 lakh copies during 1990-91 to an average of 4.25 lakh copies in 1992.

As part of its sales promotion drive, the Division participated in over 50 book exhibitions/fairs all over the country and abroad.

Directorate of Advertising and Visual Publicity (DAVP)

Through different media of mass communication, the DAVP advertises the policies, programmes and achievements of the Government of India. During April-December 1991, the Directorate organised 187 exhibition spread over 1,244 exhibition days. The major themes covered by the exhibitions were "national integration and communal harmony", "family welfare", "upliftment of scheduled castes and scheduled tribes", "welfare of women and children and campaign against illicit trafficking in drugs".

Printed publicity material brought out by DAVP during April-December 1991 included book-lets/folders titled "Secularism and National Unity", "Factshetts on Assam", "Swift Actions to Surge Ahead", "No compromise on Secularism" and Concerted Action needed to curb atrocities on Scheduled Castes and Scheduled Tribes".

To equip the Field Exhibition Officers of the North and the North-East region with the latest technology of organising the exhibitions, the Directorate organised a four-day workshop in November 1991.

Research and Reference Division (R & RD)

The Research and Reference Division functions as an information servicing agency to the Ministry of Information and Broadcasting, its media units and their field offices. It serves s an information bank as well as an information feeder service to the media units to help in their programming and publicity campaigning work. The Division also studies trends in mass communication media and maintains reference and carries out documentation service on current affairs and mass communication.

These functions are discharged by the Division by issuing material in different formats like, Background to the News and Reference Papers on issues of public importance, Biographical Sketches of eminent Indians, Dairy of Events covering important national events, compilation of two annual reference publications entitled, *India* and *Mass Media in India* and issuing updated documentation and reference services on mass media. The documentation services are carried on by the National Documentation Centre on Mass Communication, which forms an integral part of this organisation. In addition to the issue of backgrounder and reference papers on current topics, this year, the Division issued seven background papers on various subjects relevant to the promotion of national integration during the *Quami Ekta Week.*

Photo Division

The main function of the Photo Division is to photographically document the growth and special changes in the country and providing visual support required in communication. During April-December 1991, the Division covered over 2,280 assignments of various functions/events. The Division also undertook photo coverages of foreign VVIPs/dignitaries who visited India during the year 1991.

under the "Pricing Scheme" the Division earned a revenue of Rs. 4.40 lakhs during the period April-December 1991. Under this scheme, black and white and colour photographs are supplied to non-publicity organisations and general public on payment basis.

The Division organises Annual National Photo Contest and Exhibition on a particular selected theme. The amateur photographers from all over the country are invited to participate in the competition. The Third National Photo Contest on the theme of "Literacy for All" was held in New Delhi in March 1991.

Under the "Pricing Scheme" the Division earned a revenue of Rs. 4.40 lakhs during the period April-December 1991. Under this scheme, black and white and colour photographs are supplied to non-publicity organisations and general public on payment basis.

The Division organises Annual National Photo Contest and Exhibition on a particular selected theme. The amateur photographers from all over the country are invited to participated in the competition. The Third National Photo Contest on the theme of "Literacy for All" was held in New Delhi in March 1991.

Directorate of Field Publicity

Throughout the year, the Field Publicity units of the Directorate of Field Publicity continued highlighting important themes like commitment to democracy, secularism, national integration and communal harmony, family welfare and eradication of social evils such as drug abuse, alcoholism, dowry, child marriage etc., through film shows, song and drama programmes, oral communication programmes, special competitions and contests.

During April-September 1991, DFP arranged over 30,712 film shows, 3,757 song and drama programmes, 20,168 photo exhibitions and 32,383 oral communications catering to a total of three crore people belonging to different sections of the society.

In order to promote national integration and communal harmony and to create awareness of national achievements in various fields among the people of remote and tribal areas, the Directorate organised 13 conducted tours of opinion leaders of these regions, to other parts of the country.

Song and Drama Division

The Song and Drama Division utilises live media specially the folk and traditional media to create awareness among the masses regarding various programmes of socio-economic significance. The Division presented 34,120 performances from January to December 1991.

This year, the Song and Drama Division is celebrating Silver Jubilee year of its two main schemes, i.e., Armed Forces Entertainment Wing and Border Publicity Scheme. The year was observed as "Year of Non-violence", wherein several special programmes and festivals were organised in various States.

The Division presented new Sound and Light Programme "Aur Qadam Badhte Rahe" highlighting the cultural heritage, freedom struggle and development process of the country till date. Another Sound and Light Programme "Onnkazcha" in Malayalam highlighting the spirit of Onam, conveying the message of social justice, equality and communal harmony has been prepared and is being presented at Quilon in Kerala.

The departmental artists produced and presented a play titled "Angoori" on Giri Child. The Division also conducted a training-cum-orientation camp in collaboration with UNICEF on the theme of "Girl Child" wherein all the Programme officers of the Division participated.

A new play on life and works of Dr. Bhim Rao Ambedkar was presented in Tamil Nadu and several other programme activities were carried out in various parts of the country to mark the birth centenary celebrations of Baba Bhim Rao Ambedkar.

Indian Institute of Mass Communication (IIMC)

The Indian Institute of Mass Communication conducted two training programmes and four diploma courses. In addition, the Institute organised a number of refresher courses for the personnel of Indian Information Service. In all, the Institute imparted training to 203 candidates during the year.

Non-Aligned News Agencies Pool (NANAP)

Non-Aligned News Agencies Pool (NANAP) is a system of News exchange based on professional co-operation and co-ordination among the News Agencies of the Non-Aligned countries. To co-ordinate the activities of the Pool, there is an elected body known as the Co-ordinating Committee of the Pool. For a close review and monitoring of the Pool operations, there is a smaller group known as the Monitoring Group. Ever since the inception of the Pool in 1976, India is a member of NANAP. India News Pool Desk (INPD) is being operated by the Press Trust of India on behalf of the Government of India.

PTI continued to run the INDP at a high professional level during the year, handling daily an average of 45,000 words of incoming news traffic and contributing over 10,000 words (or 50 items) a day in the Pool's outgoing life. PTI maintained an average of 250 placements of items per month in leading Indian newspapers.

During the Gulf War, PTI had special arrangements with IRNA, a leading Pool participant, and at a time when authentic sources of information about the war dried up because of restrictions on mediamen imposed by the warring parties, there were 175 placements of IRNA items in leading Indian newspapers in February 1991.

Miscellaneous (Films, Doordarshan, etc.)

The High Powered Committee set up under the chairmanship of Secretary (I & B) to study the problems of Film Industry, submitted its report in January 1990. In all, the Committee has made 59 recommendations, recommending a number of concessions/reliefs for the industry in the matter relating to entertainment tax, excise duty, customs duty on cine equipment/cine raw stock, concessional institutional finance, increased royalty for telecast/broadcasting of film/songs, licensing and regulation of video exhibition for combating video piracy etc. Seven recommendations have already been implemented. Twenty-two recommendations fall within the jurisdiction of state governments/union territory administrations. On 18 recommendations, action is being taken by various central ministries like Ministry of Industry, Department of Education, Ministry of Finance, Ministry of Communications, action is to be taken by the film industry or further information is to be supplied by the film industry. Seven recommendations on reconsideration have been rejected.

A total number of 11 units were registered during the period from January to December 1991 under the scheme of registration units.

In the Budget Estimates for 1991-92, the budget provision of Rs. 3.00 lakhs for extending financial assistance to the Federation of Film Societies, which is the apex body of about 240 film societies in the country, has been made. For the next year also, a provision of Rs. 300 lakhs has been made, however, no amount released so far.

In June 1989, the Government constituted an Inter-Departmental Committee in this Ministry to study various aspects of the establishment of Cable TV Network and Dish Antennae systems in the country and to make suitable recommendations for consideration of the Government. The Committee gave its Report to the Government on 21 February 1991. The recommendations of the Committee are under active consideration of the Government.

Source: *Annual Report*, 1991-92. Ministry of Information and Broadcasting, New Delhi.

34

LAW AND JUSTICE

Following were the most important judgments :

1. *Justice Ramaswami Case :* Supreme Court Judgment—August 27, 1992 (Chapter 34).
2. *Mandal Commission — Reservation for Backward Classes*: Supreme Court Judgment — August 27, 1992 (Chapter 35).
3. *Capitation Fee :* Andhra Pradesh High Court Judgment—September 18, 1992 (See Chapter 27).
4. *Capitation Fee :* Supreme Court Judgment—February 4, 1993 (Chapter 27).

Supreme Court Judgment on the Case of Mr. Justice Ramaswami

Mr. Justice V. Ramaswami is not entitled to challenge findings of an inquiry committee before its report is placed before Parliament, the Supreme Court ruled today while laying down the law governing removal of a judge.

A five-judge Constitution bench headed by Mr. Justice J.S. Verma held that Mr. Justice Ramaswami could only seek judicial review if the President of India passed an order of removal against him. The judgment was passed by a four-to-one verdict.

Mr. Justice Verma, who delivered the majority judgment, said the judge should be given an opportunity when Parliament takes up the motion for his removal for consideration along with the committee's report and other relevant material.

Mr. Justice Verma, in his 121-page judgment, observed: "It is the obligation of the Speaker/Chairman to supply a copy of the report to the concerned judge while laying it before Parliament under Section 4(3) of the Judges of Inquiry Act as a part of this opportunity to be given to the learned judge".

"The precise details of the manner in which such an opportunity is to be given to the concerned judge may be for the Speaker/Chairman and the Parliament to decide, but it does appear to us to be the clear mandate in our constitutional scheme that the procedure adopted for this purpose should be such as would ensure availability to each House of Parliament of the concerned judge's point of view and comments, if any, on the finding of guilty made in the committee's report when it takes up for consideration the motion for removal of the judge," Mr. Justice Verma said, adding that such a procedure must ensure fairness to the concerned judge and should be in keeping with the dignity of the high office held by the judge.

Mr. Justice Verma read out the judgment for himself and on behalf of Mr. Justice K. Jayachandra Reddy and Mr. Justice S.C. Agrawal, Mr. Justice N.M. Kasliwal delivered a concurring but separate judgment. Mr. Justice K. Ramaswamy gave the dissenting judgment on the petition field by Mrs. Sarojini Ramaswami, wife of the aggrieved judge.

Mr. Justice Verma observed that "the remedy of judicial reviews to the concerned judge is available only when his misbehaviour is 'deemed to be proved' in law and not against the inchoate finding of 'guilty' made by the inquiry committee, which may or may not be acted upon by the Parliament."

Another reason to support this view appears to be that the proceedings for removal of a judge are required to be concluded at the earliest in the public interest and, therefore, no interdiction of the process is contemplated at the stage of an inchoate finding of "guilty" by the inquiry committee, he said.

Mr. Justice Verma said an opportunity to the concerned judge at that stage also to show cause against that inchoate finding of "guilty" fully safeguards his interest without the need for judicial review at that stage, the scope for Parliament's scrutiny of the committee's findings of guilty being very wide.

He said even though judicial review of the finding of "guilty" made by the inquiry committee may be permissible on limited grounds pertaining only to legality, yet the power of Parliament would not be so limited while considering the motion in spite of the finding of "guilty" made by the committee on a consideration of the entire material before it which enables it to go even into the probative value of the material on which the finding is based and to decide the desirability of adopting the motion in a given case.

The Parliament decides by voting on the motion and is not required to give any reasons for its decision if it chooses not to adopt the motion, the judge said.

The judges made it clear that the finding recorded by the committee where it finds the judge guilty of any misbehaviour being subject to acceptance by the Parliament is not final and is, therefore, not conclusive.

No action is to be taken on the motion in case the committee finds that the judge is not guilty of any misbehaviour, the judges said.

The court rejected the contention of Mrs. Ramaswami's counsel, Mr. Kapil Sibal, that the committee was a tribunal. The judges observed that "the report of the committee cannot be treated as 'tribunal' for the purpose of Article 136 of the Constitution. For this reason, no provision is made in the law enacted under Article 124(5) of the Constitution for supply of a copy of the report by the committee to the concerned judge before submitting it to the Speaker."

Referring to the scheme of judicial review, Mr. Justice Verma said the scheme adequately protects the right of the concerned judge, ensures expeditious conclusion of the process once it is commenced in the manner prescribed and accords with the view that the scheme is "a judicious blend of the political and judicial processes for the removal of judges". It ensures preservation of the right, interest and dignity of the learned judge and is commensurate with the dignity of all the institutions and functionaries involved in the process.

It also excludes the meddling in the process by busybodies confining the participation in it to members of Parliament, the Speaker/Chairman and the inquiry committee comprising the high judicial functionaries apart from the concerned judge, if the allegations permitted to be made only in the prescribed manner justify an inquiry into the conduct of the judge, Mr. Justice Verma said.

Referring to the procedure governing removal of a judge, Mr. Justice Verma said that the law provides that any accusation made against a sitting judge to enable initiation of the process of his removal from office has to be only by not less than the minimum number of members of Parliament specified in the Judges Inquiry Act, all other methods being excluded.

On initiation of the process in the prescribed manner, the Speaker/Chairman is to decide whether the accusation requires investigation. If the chooses not to act on the accusation made in the form of motion by the specified minimum number of MPs, the matter ends there, Mr. Justice Verma said.

On the other hand, if the Speaker/Chairman, on a consideration of material available and after consulting such persons as he thinks fit, forms the opinion that a *prima facie* case for investigation into the accusation against the judge is made out, the constitutes a committee of judicial functionaries.

If the inquiry committee at the conclusion of the investigation made by it records a finding that the judge is "not guilty", the process ends with no one, not even the Parliament, being empowered to consider much less question the finding of "not guilty" recorded by the inquiry committee. If the finding made by the inquiry committee is that the judge is "guilty", then the Parliament considers the motion for removal of the judge along with the committee's report and other available materials, including the cause, if any, shown by the concerned judge against his removal for which he has to be given an opportunity after submission of the report to the Speaker.

To be effective, this opportunity must include supply of a copy of the report to the concerned judge by the Speaker while causing it to be laid before the Parliament. If the Parliament does not adopt the motion for removal of the judge, the process ends there with no challenge to any one. If the motion for removal of the judge is adopted by the requisite majority by the Parliament culminating in the order of removal by the President of India under Article 124(4) of the Constitution, then only the concerned judge would have the remedy of judicial review available on the permissible grounds against the order of removal, the judges said.

In his dissenting judgment, Mr. Justice Ramaswamy expressed the view that the judge is entitled for a copy of the report of the committee.

By a majority decision of four-to-one the court also dismissed a petition by Congress member of Parliament Krishna Swami and an another petitioner challenging the constitution of the committee and the procedure followed by it on the ground that the petitioner has no locus standi. However, Mr. Justice K. Ramaswamy gave the dissenting judgment.

Highlights of Judgment

The following are highlights of the judgment in the Ramaswami case:

* Every Judge of the Supreme Court and the High Courts is irremovable from officer except by process of impeachment.
* Findings of the Inquiry Committee are not subject to judicial review unless the Judge is removed.
* While appointing the Inquiry Committee, the Speaker should consult the Chief Justice of India.
* The Inquiry Committee is the sole and final arbiter on the question of removal of the concerned Judge. If the majority view makes a findings that the Judge is 'not guilty' no further scrutiny is allowed.
* The Inquiry Committee is not a tribunal.

* A copy of the evidence received by the Inquiry Committee along with its report has to be laid before Parliament.
* Despite finding of 'guilty', Parliament may choose not to adopt the motion for removal. It cannot be challenged in any court of law.
* The Speaker is under an obligation to supply the Judge a copy of the Inquiry Committee report after it is placed before Parliament.
* Opportunity should be given to the Judge to express his point of view or comments before Parliament.

Source: *Hindustan Times*, August 28, 1992.

35

MANDAL COMMISSION :

Supreme Court Judgment and Follow Up

35.1 Supreme Court Judgment on Reservation for Backward Classes

A nine-member bench of the Supreme Court of India gave its judgment on reservation of jobs on November 16, 1992.

In a 5:3:1 majority judgment the nine-judge Constitution bench presided over by the Chief Justice, Mr. Justice M.H. Kania, partially upheld the two impugned notifications dated August 13, 1990 and September 25, 1991—issued by the V.P. Singh and Narasimha Rao Governments respectively — providing job quotas to the backward classes in the wake of the Mandal Commission report.

The Supreme Court directed that the Union Government, within four months from today, shall specify the bases, applying the relevant and requisite socio-economic criteria to exclude socially advanced persons, by setting up a Commission, to "siphon off the Creamy Layer."

The Court, however, struck down the Narasimha Rao Government's decision to reserve 10 per cent of the vacancies in Government civil posts and services for other economically backward sections of the people who are not covered by any of the existing schemes of reservation.

Another significant aspect of the majority judgment, delivered by Mr. Justice B.P. Jeevan Reddy, was that the reservation should not exceed 50 per cent. "While 50 per cent shall be the rule, it is necessary not to put out of consideration certain extraordinary situations inherent in the great diversity of this country and people. In such a situation, some relaxation to this strict rule may become imperative," Mr. Justice Reddy observed.

The majority judgment written by Mr. Justice Reddy, Chief Justice M.H. Kania, Mr. Justice M.N. Venkatachalliah and Mr. Justice A.M. Ahmadi directed the Union Government, each of the State Governments and the Administrations of Union Territories to constitute a permanent body for entertaining, examining and recommending upon requests for inclusion and complaints of over-inclusion and under-inclusion in the lists of other backward classes of citizens. The advice tendered by such body shall ordinarily be binding upon the Government.

Referring to socio-economic criteria which is aimed to exclude socially advanced persons from other backward classes, the judges made it clear that this direction shall not, however, apply to States where the reservations in favour of backward classes are already in operation. They can continue to operate them.

Such States shall, however, evolve the said criteria within six months from today and apply the same to exclude the socially advanced persons from the designated "other backward classes".

designated "other backward classes".

The Court directed that any dispute regarding new criteria to be evolved by the Union Government or the State Government shall be preferred only before the Apex Court and not before any other High Court or Tribunal. Similarly, any petition challenging the validity, operation or implementation of the two impugned office memoranda shall be filed only before the Supreme Court and not before any other Court.

The majority judgment said that the office memoranda dated August 13, 1990 issued by the V.P. Singh Government is accordingly held valid and enforceable subject to the exclusion of the socially advanced members/sections from the notified "other backward classes".

Similarly, clause I of the office memorandum dated September 25, 1991, issued by the Narasimha Rao Government — to uphold its validity, to be read, interpreted and understood as intending a distinction between backward and more backward classes on the basis of degrees of social backwardness and rational and reputable distribution of the benefits of the reservation amongst them.

Referring to the method to be adopted for identification of the backward classes, Mr. Justice Reddy said that neither the Constitution nor the law prescribes the procedure or method of identification of backward classes. Nor is it possible or advisable for the Court to lay down any such procedure or method.

Mr. Justice Reddy observed that "it must be left to the authority appointed to identify. It can adopt such method as it thinks convenient and so long as its survey covers the entire populace no objection can be taken to it. Identification of the backward classes can certainly be done with reference to castes among, and along with, other occupation groups, classes and sections of people. Once can start the process either with the occupation groups or with castes or with some other groups."

The judge said that "it is not necessary for a class to be designated as a backward class that it is situated similarly to the Scheduled Castes/Scheduled Tribes. Creamy Layer can be, and must be, excluded."

Mr. Justice Reddy in his judgment said that the rule of 50 per cent should be applied to each year. It cannot be related to the total strength of the class, category, service or cadre, as the case may be.

He said that Article 16(4) does not permit provision for reservations in the matter of promotion. This rule shall, however, have only prospective operation and shall not affect the promotions already made, whether on regular basis or any other basis.

The majority judgment directed the Government that "our decision on this question shall operate only prospectively and shall not affect promotions already made, whether on temporary, officiating or regular/permanent basis.

The Court further directed that wherever reservations are already provided in the matter of promotion, be it Central services or State services, or for that matter services under any corporation or authority, such reservations may continue in operation for a period of five years from this day.

Within the period of five years, the Judges said it would be open to the appropriate authorities to revise, modify or re-issue the relevant rules to ensure the achievement of the objective of Article 16(4) of the Constitution.

The Judges observed that "if any authority thinks that for ensuring adequate representation of backward class of citizens in any service, class or category, it is necessary to provide for direct recruitment therein, it shall be open to it to do so. It would not be impermissible for the State to extend concessions and relations to the members of reserved categories in matter of promotion without compromising the efficiency of the administration.

The majority judgment said that while the role of reservation cannot be called anti-meritian, there are certain services and posts to which it may not be advisable to apply the rule of reservation.

The judgment said that it may not be advisable to provide for reservations, for example, technical posts in research and development organisation, departments/institutions, in specialities and super-specialities in medicine, engineering and other such courses in physical sciences and mathematics, in defence services and in the establishments connected therewith.

Similarly, in the case of posts at the higher echelons e.g., professors in education, pilots in Indian Airlines and Air-India, scientists and technicians in nuclear and space application, provision for reservation would not be advisable, the Judges said.

The Judges observed that "in view of the directions given by us, it is not necessary to express any opinion on the correctness and adequacy of the exercise done by the Mandal Commission. It is equally unnecessary to send the matter back to the Constitution of five Judges."

While agreeing with the majority view, Mr. Justice P.B. Sawant in his separate but concurring judgment said that "it is impermissible to keep a common quota of reservation for all the backward classes together and make available posts for the backward classes if they are left over after requirements of the more or most backward classes."

In his order, Mr. Justice Sawant said that the benefit of reservation cannot be given to advanced sections of the socially and educationally backward classes because they no longer belong to the socially and educationally backward classes although they may be members of the caste, occupational groups or social groups.

Mr. Justice Sawant said that the Government may evolve the necessary socio-economic criteria to define the advanced sections of the backward classes to give effect to the order.

"When the backward classes are classified into backward and more or most backward classes on the basis of the degrees of social backwardness (and not on the basis of economic criteria alone), exclusive quotas of reservations will have to be kept separately for the backward and the more or most backward classes," Mr. Justice Sawant said in his judgment.

He said that economic criteria by itself cannot identify a class as a backward unless the economic backwardness of the class is on account of its social backwardness. No restrictions of posts can be kept in services under the State based services exclusively on economic criteria either under Article 16(4) or Article 16(1) of the Constitution.

Mr. Justice Sawant said that ordinarily, the reservation kept both under Article 16(1) Article 16(4) together should not exceed 50 per cent of the appointments in a grade, cadre or service in any particular year. It is only for extraordinary reasons that the percentage may exceed. However, every excess of 50 per cent will have to be justified on valid grounds.

Only one Judge, Mr. Justice S. Ratnavel Pandian, in a separate judgment, fully upheld the validity of the August 13, 1990 notification issued by the V.P. Singh Government, reserving 27 per cent posts in Government services for backward classes on the basis of Mandal Commission report.

Agreeing with Mr. Justice Sawant, Mr. Pandian held that no maximum ceiling on reservation can be fixed under Article 16(4) of the Constitution for reservation of appointments or posts in favour of any backward class of citizens "in the service under the State". The decision of reservation only up to maximum of 50 per cent is unsustainable, he observed.

As regards the reservation in the matter of promotion under Article 16(4) of the Constitution, Mr. Justice Pandian said that he was in agreement with the majority view.

Mr. Justice Pandian also agreed with the majority view that there are certain services and posts to which it may not be advisable to apply the rule of reservation. He also struck down the reservation of 10 per cent of the vacancies in civil posts and services in favour of economically backward section of the people who are not covered by any other scheme of the reservation.

He said that no section of the SEBCs can be excluded on the ground of Creamy layer till the Government—Central and State—takes a decision in this regard on a review of the recommendations of a Commission or a Committee to be appointed by the appropriate Government. Therefore, Mr. Justice Pandian struck down the Narasimha Rao Government decision to provide reservation to the backward classes by adding the economic criteria. The judge declared valid the notification issued by the V.P. Singh Government in this regard.

However, the dissenting judgment was delivered by Dr. Justice T.K. Thommen, Mr. Justice Kuldip Singh and Mr. Justice R.M. Sahai declaring both the notifications issued by the Union Government were unenforceable for want of valid identification of the backward classes of citizens qualified for reservation under Article 16 of the Constitution.

The dissenting judges directed the Union Government to re-examine the question of identification of the backward classes of citizens in accordance with the principles and directives constrained in their judgments.

Highlights of Judgment

* Reservation for the backward classes is permissible provided the 'creamy layer's excluded.
* A backward class cannot be identified only and exclusively with reference to economic criteria.
* Backward classes of citizens can be identified into backward and more backward categories.
* The total reservation in government jobs shall not exceed more than 50 per cent.
* Reservation in certain technical posts like scientific departments, superspecialities in medicine, engineering, defence research, professors in education, pilots in Indian Airlines and Air India etc. not advisable.
* There can be no reservations in promotions.
* Reservation purely on economic criteria for poor struck down.
* Permanent Commission to be set up within four months by the Union and State Government to examine complaints of over-inclusion and under-inclusion and requests for inclusion in the list of backward classes.
* The Union government shall specify within four months the socio-economic criteria to exclude socially advanced persons among the backward classes.

* All disputes in this regard shall be preferred before the Supreme Court and not before any other Court or Tribunal.

Dissenting Verdict by 3 Judges

The three judges of the nine-member Constitution bench of the Supreme Court in their dissenting judgment declared as unconstitutional the V.P. Singh and Narasimha Rao Governments' decision for providing 27 per cent reservation in Government jobs to backward classes and 10 per cent to other weaker sections of the people who are not covered by any of the existing scheme of reservation.

Dr. Justice T.K. Thommen, Mr. Justice Kuldip Singh and Mr. Justice R.M. Sahai in their separate but concurring judgments held that the two impugned notifications dated August 13, 1990 and September 25, 1991, issued by the V.P. Singh and Narasimha rao Governments, respectively, were unenforceable for want of valid identification of backward classes of citizens qualified for reservation under Article 16 of the Constitution.

The judges directed the Union Government to re-examine the question of identification of the backward classes of citizens in accordance with the principles and directives contained in their respective judgments and pass appropriate orders providing for reservation under Article 16(4) of the Constitution.

In his 84-page judgment, Dr. Justice Thommen said that it was open for the State to adopt valid classification and make special provisions for the protection of classes of citizens whose comparative backwardness the State has a mandate to redress by affirmative action programmes.

Any such programme must be strictly tailored to the Constitutional requirement that no citizens shall be excluded from being considered on the basis of merits for any public employment except to the extent that a valid reservation has been made in the favour of backward classes of citizens.

He said once a class of citizens is identified on correct principles as backward for the purpose of reservation, the "means test" must be strictly and uniformly applied to exclude all those persons in that class reaching above the predetermined economic level.

Dr. Justice Thommen said that reservation in all cases must be confined to a minority of available posts or seats so as not to unduly sacrifice merits. The number of seats or posts reserved Constitution at all times remain well below 50 per cent of the total number of seats or posts.

He further said that reservation has no application to promotion. It is confined to initial appointment, whichever be the level of grade a at which such appointment is made in the administrative hierarchy, and whether or not the post in question is borne on the cadre of the service.

Dr. Justice Thommen observed that "once reservation is strictly confined to the constitutionally intended beneficiaries, there will probably be no need to disappoint any deserving candidate legitimately seeking the benefit of reservation. In that event, questions such as caste or religion will become merely academic and the competing maddening rush for 'backward' label will vanish."

He suggested a periodic administrative review of all affirmative action programmes, including reservation of seats and posts, must be conducted by a specially constituted permanent authority with a view to adjustment and readjustment of such programmes in proportion to the nature, degree and extent of backwardness. All such programmes must stand the test of judicial review whenever challenged.

Dr. Thommen said that whenever and wherever poverty and backwardness are identified, it is the Constitutional responsibility of the state to initiate economic and other measures to ameliorate the conditions of the people residing in those regions.

The Judge said that poverty which is the ultimate result of inequities and which is the immediate cause and effect of backwardness has to be eradicated not merely by reservation, but by free medical aid, free elementary education, scholarships for higher education and other financial support, free housing, self-employment and settlement schemes, effective implementation of land reforms and strict and impartial operation of the law enforcing machinery.

Similar views were expressed by Mr. Justice Kuldip Singh and Mr. Justice R. M. Sahai.

35.2 **Expert Committee Report on Identification of Creamy Layer**

Union Welfare Minister Sitaram Kesari announced on March 16, 1993 in both Houses of Parliament the Government's acceptance of the Justice Ram Nandan Prasad committee report which dealt with the identification of the "creamy layer" among the socially and educationally backward classes (SEBC).

The report identifies the creamy layer among the SEBC for excluding it from the list of Mandal beneficiaries, following the Supreme Court verdict on the controversial Mandal report last year.

The Justice Prasad Committee report states that only when the creamy layer is substantial and stable, formed after crossing the rubicon of social backwardness, then and then alone can it be made the basis for disentitlement.

However, it says certain constitutional posts qualify for the rule of exclusion. Listed among them are the posts of President, Vice-President, judges of the Supreme Court and High Courts, chairmen and members of the UPSC and state public service commission, chief election commissioner, comptroller and auditor general of India, governors, ministers, and membership of legislatures, the last three being temporary ones.

The rule of exclusion, it says, covers class one officers of Central and State services (direct recruits), public sector undertakings, armed forces and paramilitary forces, professional class including trade, business, and industry, and property owners.

It excludes from the list of reservation beneficiaries those having gross annual income of Rs. one lakh and above.

In the service category, the rule of exclusion will apply if either the husband or wife is a class one officer. Where both are class one officers and if one of them dies, the rule or exclusion is still applicable. But if both die, then the rule of exclusion becomes invalid. Permanent incapacitation is treated as death by the Committee and it follows the above logic in the application of the rule exclusion.

Thus, the Committee says that if before the unfortunate event of death of either of or both such spouses occurs, either of the spouses has had the benefit of employment in any international bodies like the United Nations, IMF, World Bank for a period of not less than five years, then exclusion from the benefits or reservation would continue to apply to the offspring.

Stating that if sometimes a lady who has got marries to a class I officer might herself like to apply for a job, it says if she belong to the SEBC category, she would not be disentitled by the rule of exclusion.

Referring to group B class II—Central Services and State Services (direct recruitment), it says that if both spouses are class II officers then rule of exclusion would apply to their offspring. If one one of the spouses is a class II officer, it would not apply, but if a male officer from class II category gets into class I category at the age of 40 or earlier, then the rule of exclusion would apply to this offspring.

Where both spouses are class II officers and one of them dies, it is better to let be children have the benefit of reservation which means rule of exclusion would not apply.

Where the husband is a class I officer (direct recruit of pre-40 promoted) and the wife is a class II officer and the husband dies, the rule of exclusion would not apply. Also when the wife is a class I officer and the husband is a class II officer and the wife dies the rule or exclusion would not apply but if the husband dies the rule of exclusion would apply on the principle that one of the parents, namely, the mother continues to be a class I officer.

The service category criteria for exclusion enumerate above also applies to officers holding equivalent or comparable posts in public sector undertakings, banks, insurance organisations, universities and also to equivalent or comparable posts and positions under private investment, the report says.

Referring to armed forces including paramilitary forces (not including persons holdings civil posts), the Committee says the exclusion rule would apply at the level of colonel and above in the Army and to equivalent post in the Navy and Air Force and paramilitary forces.

If the wife of an armed forces officer is herself in the armed forces, the rule of exclusion would apply only when she herself has reached the rank of colonel, the service ranks below colonel of husband and wife shall not be clubbed together.

Even if the wife of an officer in the armed forces is in civil employment, this would not be taken into account for applying the rule of exclusion, unless she falls in the service category.

Even if the wife of an officer in the armed forces is in civil employment, this would not be taken into account for applying the rule of exclusion, unless she falls in the service category.

Referring to professional class and those engaged in trade, business and industry, the committee says for the purpose of determining whether they would fall in the disentitlement category or not would be governed by the income/wealth criterion.

For property owners, the Committee says that if a person belongs to a family (father, mother and minor children) which owns irrigated land, and the extent of irrigated land is equal to or more than 65 per cent of the statutory ceiling area, then the disentitlement would occur. The rule of exclusion would not disentitle persons belonging to families owning only unirrigated land irrespective of the area of such land.

In the case of members of a family owning both irrigated and unirrigated land, the exclusion rule would apply where the pre-condition exists that the irrigated area is 40 per cent or more of the statutory ceiling limits for irrigated land.

However, the exclusion rule on the basis of land holdings will not apply on the States of Nagaland, Mizoram, Meghalaya, Arunachal Pradesh and Goa and in the Union Territory of Andaman and Nicobar Islands, Lakshadweep, Daman and Diu where there is no ceiling law.

Referring to residuary category, the committee says that persons having gross annual income of one lakh of rupees of above or possessing wealth above the exemption limit as prescribed in the wealth tax Act would be excluded from the benefit of reservation.

Source: *Hindustan Times,* March 17, 1993.

35.3 **Backward Classes Bill**

Minister for Welfare Sitaram Kesari introduced the Backward Classes Bill on March 17, 1993.

Minister for Welfare Sitaram Kesari said in the Rajya Sabha that a beginning in the implementation of the new socio-economic criteria for job reservations, eliminating the creamy layer, for the backward classes under the Mandal Commission scheme would be done in "less than three months' time".

He made this observation in response to a point raised by Mr. Ram Jethmalani, who wanted to know from the Minister if the "application" of the new criteria in the light of the report of the expert committee (Justice Prasad Panel) could be done within three months. M. Kesari responded by saying "before that".

He felt that the Bill should incorporate one assurance, that if the Government disagreed on any occasion with the report of the commission, it would record its reasons for such disagreement in writing. He said such a provision in the law would safeguard the interests of the backward classes and it would not be possible for the bureaucrats and others opposed to the scheme to defeat the purpose of the Bill.

Mr. Kesari said in his opening remarks that the recommendations of the commission shall "ordinarily" be binding on the Government. He added that whenever the Government disagreed with the report, it would record its reasons for such dissent.

He claimed that it was a historic day and a day of fulfilment and achievement for him to move the Bill which would mark the beginning of the implementation of the job quotas for the OBCs. The Bill, he added, also showed that the demand for job quotas for the OBCs had become a "reality" now, and that there would be no misuse of reservations, in the light of the Prasad Committee report, which the Government had accepted.

Source: *Hindustan Times,* March 18, 1993.

36

PARLIAMENTARY AFFAIRS

Consultative Committees

The present Consultative Committees of Members of Parliament in their broad features, owe their origin of the suggestions set out by Prime Minister Shri Jawaharlal Nehru in 1954 in a note circulated to the Members of Cabinet. Shri Nehru wanted some kind of standing Advisory Consultative Committees of Parliament to provide opportunity to Members to have some glimpse into the working of the Government which would also have the effect of reducing the number of questions asked by Members. Accordingly, informal Consultative Committees were constituted for the various Ministries/Departments of the Government of India.

In 1969 discussions were held with Leaders of opposition Parties/Groups in Parliament and detailed guidelines were drawn up for constitution and functioning of these Committees. It was also then decided that these Committees would be known as "Consultative Committees", retaining, however, the informal nature of deliberations in these Committees. These Committees have since then been functioning under these guidelines.

Distinctive Features

It may be rightly claimed that the institution of Consultative Committees is a unique innovation of the Indian Parliamentary system. The Consultative Committees have distinctive features that mark them out from the Parliamentary Committees which function under the rules of procedures of the respective House of Parliament. The Members of the Parliament or nominated by the Speaker/Chairman who also appoint the Chairman of the Committee. The meetings of Parliamentary Committees are held in private. They can examine witnesses on oath or affirmation, a verbatim record of the proceedings of the Committee is kept. There is a quorum required for each sitting of the Committee. A Member of the Committee may be discharged from its membership if he is absent from two or more consecutive sittings of the Committee. The Committee can take decisions. Every report of a Parliamentary Committee is laid on the Table of the House.

In contrast to the above features of a Parliamentary Committee, the Consultative Committees function in a less formal setting. There are certain guidelines that govern the constitution and functioning of Consultative Committees. These guidelines were agreed upon by all parties/groups in Parliament. the membership of a Consultative Committee is voluntary and broadly left to the choice of the member concerned and the leader of his party in the House. The Minister incharge of the Ministry is the Chairman of the respective Committee. The meetings of Committee are open to the senior officers of the Ministry, who, when called upon, explain matters to the members at the meetings. Agenda items are called from the members or the Ministry themselves suggest subjects for discussion at the meeting of the Committee. No decisions are taken by the Consultative Committees. They may make recommendations which, if passed unanimously by the Committee may be accepted by the Government subject to certain conditions laid down in the guidelines. No verbatim record is kept of the deliberations of the Consultative Committee.

The above characteristics of the Consultative Committees are meant to make them a forum for free and frank discussions between the Members and Ministers and Senior Officers of the Government on the policies and problems of Government and the working of Administrative departments in a way not practicable on the floor of Parliament or in Parliamentary Committees. Notes and other material on the subject for discussion are supplied to the members in advance. Minutes are prepared and circulated in the case of meetings of all Committees (exception gin the case of Committees for Defence, External Affairs and Atomic Energy). Action taken Report on the minutes are also supplied to Members regularly.

During the time of the Ninth Lok Sabha there were 28 Consultative Committees. But after the constitution of the Tenth Lok Sabha the number has risen to 32 with the creation of more Ministries. The Membership of these Committees being voluntary, it was not found feasible to constitute Consultative Committees for the Ministries of Law and Justice and Company Affairs and Personnel, Public Grievances and Pensions, as sufficient number of Members have not opted for these Committees.

A Consultative Committee may appoint a Sub-Committee or a Study Group for the purpose of going into any particular subject and reporting to the Committee. During the year under report two Sub-Committees one on Handloom and the other on Cotton of the Consultative Committee for the Ministry of Textiles were set up, but their term lapsed with the dissolution of 9th Lok Sabha on 13.3.1991. Another Sub-Committee of the Consultative Committee for the Ministry of Coal was constituted on 29.1.1992 to go into matters relating to demolition of private houses etc. of Ghugus Colliery site in Chandrapur District of Maharashtra.

Committees for Railways

There are at present 9 Informal Consultative Committees for the 9 Railway Zones of the Country. It is noteworthy that these Committees continue to be called "Informal Consultative Committees". Members are nominated on these Committees according to the geographical jurisdiction of their State/Constituency/permanent address. Meetings of these Committees are held only during the Session Periods. For this reason no meeting of the main Consultative Committee for the Ministry of Railways is held during the Session periods. At these Informal Consultative Committees, Members are free to ventilate grievances or give suggestions for improvement regarding the working of the Railways in the Zones.

Committees and Delegations

Committees are appointed to deal with specific items of business requiring expert of detailed consideration. These are two types of Committees Official Committees i.e. those appointed by Government and Parliamentary Committee i.e. those appointed by Lok Sabha and Rajya Sabha or by the Presiding Officers of the two Houses of Parliament. While Parliamentary Committees consist of Members of Parliament. Government Committees are composed of experts, officials and non-officials. Among the non-officials, some time, members of Parliament are also made members of such bodies.

Nomination of Members of Parliament on Government Bodies

A convention has been established whereby various Ministries/Departments of the Governments of India consult the Ministry of Parliamentary Affairs before appointing Members of Parliament on Committees/Councils/Boards or on other temporary assignments by the Government, including deputation of members to various International Seminars, Conferences etc. so as to ensure that the representation of M.P.s is evenly and widely distributed and that Members are placed on various Bodies with due regard to their membership of other Bodies, their qualification, background, experience and aptitudes. Members of Parliament are nominated by the Minister of Parliamentary Affairs on Committees, Councils, Commissions and other Bodies set up by various Ministries of the Government. these are different from the Bodies on which Members are nominated by the Speaker, Lok Sabha Chairman, Rajya Sabha or elected by the Members of either House or both Houses. During the year 1991, 162 Members of Lok Sabha and 119 Members of Rajya Sabha were nominated on Government Bodies by the Minister of Parliamentary Affairs, as shown below :

Nomination

List showing the names of various Committees/Councils/Boards, etc., and the number of Lok/Rajya Sabha Members Nominated thereon during January, 1991 to January, 1992.

Names of the Ministry	Name of the Committee/ Board/Council	Numbers of MPs Nominated	
1	2	3	4
		LS	RS
Agriculture	- Hindi Salahakar Samiti for the Department of Agriculture and Cooperation	-	2
	- Indian Tobacco Development Council	2	1
	- Indian Sugarcane Development Council	1	2
	- Indian jute Development Corporation	1	2
Commerce	- Hindi Salahakar Samiti	2	2
Civil Supplies & Public Distribution	- Bureau of indian Standards	3	2
	- Central Consumer Protection Council		
	- During the term of 9th Lok Sabha	1	-
	- During the term of 10th Sabha	5	3
Defence	- Central Advisory Committee for Territorial Army	1	-

Contd.

Contd.

1	2	3	4
	- Kendriya Sainik Board	2	1
	- Committee to go into the problems being faced by the cantonment Boards and use of unutilized lands in the Cantonment areas.	5	3
	- High level Committee to look into the problems of Defence Pensioners	5	1
	- Hindi Salahakar Samiti	2	2
	- Hindi Salahakar Samiti for the Deptts. of Defence production and Supplies and Defence Research and Development.	2	2
Energy	- Hindi Salahakar Samiti		1
Food & Civil Supplies	- Hindi Salahakar Samiti During the term of 9th Lok Sabha	1	1
	- Hindi Salahakar Samiti for the Ministry of Food (During the term of 10th Lok Sabha)	2	
Civil Aviation and Tourism	- Nagar Vimanan Hindi Salahakar Samiti	2	2
	- Hindi Salahakar Samiti for the Deptt. of Tourism	2	2
Communications	- Philatelic Advisory Committee	2	2
	- Postal Advisory Committee	34	18
	- Hindi Salahakar Samiti for the Department of Posts.	2	2
	- Hindi Salahakar Samiti for the Deptt. of Telecom.	2	2
Environment and Forests	- Award Scheme for Books written Originally in Hindi	1	-
	- National Wasteland Development Board	-	1
	- Hindi Salahakar Samiti	2	2
	- Central Board of Forestry	2	1
	- Society for G.B. Pant Institute for Himalayan Environment and Development. Almora.	1	1
External Affairs	- Hindi Salahkar Samiti	2	2
Finance	- Hindi Salahakar Samiti for the Deptt. of Revenue & Expenditure	2	2
	- Customs & Central Excise Advisory Committee	1	1
	- Regional Direct Taxes Advisory Committee. Nagpur.	-	1
Health and Family Welfare	- C.G.H.S. Advisory Committee	1	1
	- Governing Body of Central Research Institute for yoga.	1	1
	- Hindi Salahakar Samiti	2	2
	- Central Council of Health and Family Welfare	2	2
Home Affairs	- Kendriya Hindi Samiti	2	2
	- Hindi Salahakar Samiti	2	2
Human Resource Development	- Indo-US-Sub-Commission on Education and Culture		
	- During the term of 9th Lok Sabha	1	-
	- During the term of 10th Lok Sabha	-	1
	- National Literacy Mission Authority	2	1
	- Governing body of the Nehru Yuva Kendra Sangathan	2	1

Contd.

Contd.

1	2	3	4
	- Office of Chairman, UNESCO Appeals Boards.	-	1
	- Indian Institute of Management Ahmedabad.	1	-
	- National Advisory Committee for the Festival of India-in Germany.	1	-
	- Hindi Salahakar Samiti for the Department of Culture	2	2
	- Central Advisory Board of Museum	2	1
	- Hindi Salahakar Samiti for the Department of Education	2	2
Information & Broadcasting	- Newsprint Advisory Committee	3	2
	- Hindi Salahakar Samiti	2	2
Labour	- Central Advisory Committee set up under the Equal Remuneration Act, 1976	1	-
	- General Council of National Labour Institute	3	2
	- Hindi Salahakar Samiti	2	2
Law and Justice	- Hindi Salahakar Samiti	2	-
Mines	- Hindi Salahakar Samiti	2	2
Planning and Programme	- Hindi Salahakar Samiti	-	2
Implementation	- Hindi Salahakar Samiti Planning & Programmes Implementation	2	2
power and Non-Conventional Energy Sources	- Hindi Salahakar Samiti for the Department of Power	2	2
	- Hindi Salahakar Samiti for the Deptt. of Non-Conventional Energy Sources	2	2
Railways	- Divisional Railway Users Consultative Committee (DRUCC)	2	2
	- Zonal Railway Users Consultative Committee (ZRUCC)	2	-
	- Hindi Salahakar Samiti	2	2
Surface Transport	- Review Committee for Merchant Shipping Act	1	1
	Central Advisory Committee for Light-Houses		
	- During 9th Lok Sabha	1	1
	- During 10th Lok Sabha	1	1
	- Advisory Council of DTC	2	-
	- Hindi Salahakar Samiti	2	2
Textiles	- Hindi Salahakar Samiti	2	2
Urban Development	- Hindi Salahakar Samiti	2	2
Water Resources	- Hindi Salahakar Samiti	2	2
Science & Technology and Other Scientific Deptts.	- Joint Hindi Salahakar Samiti for the Ministry of Science & Technology and Deptt. of Ocean Development	2	2
Welfare	- Hindi Salahakar Samiti	2	2
Delhi Administration	- Planning Board of Delhi	5	-

Parliamentary Committees

A Parliamentary Committee is appointed or elected by Rajya Sabha or Lok Sabha or nominated by the Chairman, Rajya Sabha or nominated by the Chairman, Rajya Sabha or by the Speaker, Lok Sabha. These Committees work under the directions of the Presiding Officers and present their report to the House(s) or to the concerned Presiding Officer. The Secretarial assistance to such Committees is provided by the concerned Secretariat of Parliament. While nomination of Members of Parliament on Joint Committee on any Bill is finalised by the Minister of Parliamentary Affairs, in other cases the suggestions of the various parties/groups are taken into account by the two Presiding Officers before nominating members on them. In some cases the composition is decided by moving appropriate motions in the two Houses and going through the normal election procedure whereby dates of filing nominations, withdrawal and of election by respective Houses are notified and results are announced through Parliamentary Bulletins.

Recommendations of General Application by Parliamentary Committees

The Ministry of Parliamentary Affairs is concerned with processing of action by Ministries on the recommendations of general application made by Parliamentary Committees :

Action on the recommendations of general nature contained in the following reports was initiated by the Ministry :

(i) Third and Fourth Reports of the Committee on Papers Laid on the Table of Ninth Lok Sabha.
(ii) Thirty-ninth, Fortieth and Forty-first Reports of the Committee on Papers Laid on the Table of Rajya Sabha.
(iii) Second and Third Reports of the Committee on Subordinate Legislation of the Ninth Lok Sabha.
(iv) Eighty-third to Ninetieth Reports of the Committee on Subordinate Legislation of the Rajya Sabha.

Parliamentary Delegations from Abroad

During the year 1991, 6 Parliamentary Delegations visiting India from various countries called on the Minister of Parliamentary Affairs for exchange of views regarding the system of Parliaments and Governments in India and in those countries. The details of each foreign delegation that met the Minister during the year are given below:

1. H.E. Mr. Rasool Montajob Niya, Deputy Speaker of the National Assembly of Iran alongwith 2 MPs of Iran Parliament called on the Minister of Parliamentary Affairs on 13.2.1991.
2. H.E. Mr. Kaya Erdem, President of the Turkish Grand National Assembly alongwith 13 MPs Delegates of Turkey Parliament called on the Minister of Parliamentary Affairs on 21.2.1991.
3. H.E. Mr. Chong Ken Kim, MP and Leader of the Delegation of Republic of Korea alongwith 3 other MPs of Korean Parliament called on the Minister of Parliamentary Affairs on 5.8.1991.
4. H.E. Mr. George Stevenson, Leader of the European Parliamentary Delegation and Chairman of the Delegation for relations with the countries of Sough Asia and SAARC alongwith 12 other members of the delegation called on the Minister of Parliamentary Affairs on 7-11-1991.

5. H.E. Mr. Ahmed Zaki, Speaker of the Citizens' Majlis Leader of the Delegation alongwith 4 MPs of Maldives Parliament called on the Minister of Parliamentary Affairs on 19.11.1991.
6. H.E. Dr. Sa'ad Bottross Haddaddin, Deputy and Leader of the Delegation alongwith 5 MPs of Jordan Parliament called on the Minister of Parliamentary Affairs on 6.12.1991.

Visit of Members of Parliament to Foreign Countries

According to the procedure, the names of Members of Parliament for inclusion in the Government delegations sent abroad are to the approved by the Minister of Parliamentary Affairs. Members of Parliament also inform the Ministry of Parliamentary Affairs about their foreign visits. The Ministry of Parliamentary Affairs received intimation in 20 such cases (6 Members of Lok Sabha and 14 Members of Rajya Sabha) during the year. This Ministry in turn referred all these cases to the Ministry of Home Affairs and the Ministry of External Affairs for clearance.

Permission Under Foreign Contribution (Regulation) Act, 1976

Under the Foreign Contribution (Regulation) Act, 1976 it is incumbent on the Members of Parliament, among others, to obtain prior permission of the Ministry of Home Affairs, where such visits involve receipt of hospitality from a foreign Government or organisation. With a view to help Members of follow this statutory requirement, the Minister of Parliamentary Affairs communicated detailed information about the procedure involved to all Members of Parliament through a letter dated the 8th July, 1991.

Source: *Annual Report, 1991-92*, Ministry of Parliamentary Affairs, Government of India, New Delhi.

37

POPULATION AND FAMILY WELFARE

The Census of 1991 estimated the population of India at 846.3 million. In the decade of 1981-1991, 163 million persons were added to the population. Population increased at an annual exponential growth rate of 2.1 per cent during the decade which is marginally lower than the 2.2 per cent growth rate in the previous decade of 1971-1981.

The National Family Planning Programme was launched in 1951 which gradually expanded into a community-oriented service network. Its progress is outlined in Table 37.1. While the targets set for Seventh Plan in the case of couple protection rate, crude death rate and infant mortality rate have been achieved, that for crude birth rate has not been achieved (Table 37.2). The cumulative performance since inception of the family planning programme reached about 80.79 million sterilisations and 46.37 million IUD (Intra-uterine Device) insertions by 31 March, 1992. Besides, there were around 14 million conventional contraceptive users and over 3 million oral pill users during 1991-92. It is estimated that out of 148 million couples in the country, 43.5 per cent were effectively protected by various methods of family planning as on 31 March 1992. Table 37.3 presents targets and achievements for the years 1991-92 and 1992-93 (up to November 1992).

TABLE 37.1 Birth Rate, Death Rate and Infant Mortality Rate (IMR)

(per thousand)

Year	Crude birth rate			Crude death rate			I.M.R.		
	C	R	U	C	R	U	C	R	U
1971	36.9	38.9	30.1	14.9	16.4	9.7	129	138	82
1975	35.2	36.7	28.5	15.9	17.3	10.2	140	151	84
1980	33.7	35.1	27.8	12.6	13.7	7.9	114	124	65
1985	32.9	34.3	28.1	11.8	13.0	7.8	97	107	59
1990	30.2	31.7	24.7	9.7	10.5	6.8	80	86	50

Note: C-Combined, R-Rural, U-Urban, IMR - Infant Mortality Rate
Source: *Sample Registration System Bulletin*, June 1992.

According to the provisional SRS (Sample Registration System) estimates of Registrar General of India, birth rate and death rate at the national level were 29.3 and 9.8 per thousand respectively for the year 1991. The infant mortality rate for the year 1991 was 80 per thousand live births. However, there are wide inter-State variations. In 1981, 90 districts had a crude birth rate of 39 per thousand population and above. Of these, 83 districts were located in the States of Bihar, Madhya Pradesh, Rajasthan and Uttar Pradesh. The main thrust of the intervention strategies has, therefore, to be increasingly focused on areas in States and districts with poor performance.

TABLE 37.2: Performance of the Family Welfare Programme

		Seventh Plan Target (1985-90)	Achievement (1990)
1	2	3	4
(i) Couple protection rate	(per cent)	42.0	42.0
(ii) Crude death rate	(per thousand)	10.4	9.7
(iii) Infant mortality rate	(per thousand)	90.0	80.0
(iv) Crude birth rate	(per thousand)	29.1	30.2

Source: *Sample Registration System Bulletin*, June 1992.

TABLE 37.3: Couple Protection under the Family Planning Programme

(Thousand)

Family planning methods	1991-92		April-November 1992	
	Target	Achievement	Target	Achievement
1	2	3	4	5
Sterilisations	5434	4055	2901	2061
Intra-uterine devices	5956	4321	3511	2491
Conventional contraceptives	16151	13980	16037	11029
Oral pills	2650	3325	4354	2079

Source: Ministry of Health & Family Welfare.

Several interventions have been included under the Child Survival and Safe Motherhood Programme to reduce infant, child and maternal morbidity and mortality rates. Besides reducing the disease burden, and infant and maternal mortality rates, it is essential to create a positive environment for the promotion of a small family norm. The Immunisation Programme achieved high levels of immunization coverage in large parts of the country and control of vaccine preventable diseases has also established an outreach network of services and contacts with communities. Neo-natal tetanus and poliomyelitis have been brought down to negligible levels in large parts of the country. The incidence of poliomyelitis declined from over 28000 reported cases in 1987 to around 8000 cases in 1991; the decline in the incidence was particularly evident in the ten States and Union territories (with a total population of 250 million) which had high levels of immunisation coverage and an efficient surveillance system. In 1991, 1663 cases were reported in these States, a reduction of more than 80 pr cent as compared to 8819 cases in 1987. Over two lakh cases of neo-natal tetanus were estimated to have been presented in 1991 as a result of the immunization programme. The fall in the infant mortality rate from 97 per thousand live births in 1985 to 80 in 1990 is estimated to have led to the saving of about 4 lakh lives in 1991. The access to women and children established under the Immunization Programme is now being utilized to further extend and intensify the reach of other services related to maternal and child health and to accelerate the declining trend of IMR and maternal mortality rates. The package of services for children includes newborn care, immunization services, administration of Vitamin A, pneumonia therapy and appropriate case management of diarrhoeal diseases to prevent deaths. In addition, pregnant women would be provided ante-natal care, TT (Titurus Toxide) immunization, anaemia control, screening and referral of high risk cases, promotion of clean and safe delivery practices and birth spacing.

The containment of population growth is one of the priority objectives of the Eighth Plan. The Plan aims at reducing birth rate from 30.2 per thousand in 1990 (estimated at 29.3 in 1991) to 26 per thousand by 1997. The infant mortality rate (IMR) is also to be brought down from 80 per thousand live births in 1990 (estimated at 80 in 1990) to 70 by 1997. The National Health Policy (1983) aimed at achieving a net reproduction rate of unity (NRR=1) by the turn of the century with a crude birth rate of 21 per 1000 population crude death rate of 9 pr 1000 population and an annual natural growth rate of 1.2 per cent. The Seventh Five Year Plan envisaged the attainment of this goal in the period 2006-2011 AD. It has now been shifted to 2011-2016 A.D.

Growth rate in population is given in Table 37.4.

TABLE 37.4: Growth Rate in Population during 1901-1991

Year	Population	Decadal Growth		Average annual exponential growth rate (per cent)	Progressive growth rate over 1901 (per cent)
		Absolute	Per cent		
1	2	3	4	5	6
1901	238,396,327	—	—	—	—
1911	252,093,390	+ 13,697,063	+ 5.75	0.56	+ 5.75
1921	251,321,213	- 772,177	- 0.31	- 0.03	+ 5.42
1931	278,977,238	+ 27,656,025	+ 11.00	1.04	+ 17.02
1941	318,660,580	+ 39,683,342	+ 14.22	1.33	+ 33.67
1951	361,088,090	+ 42,420,485	+ 13.31	1.25	+ 51.47
1961	439,234,771	+ 77,682,873	+ 21.51	1.96	+ 84.25
1971	548,159,652	+108,924,881	+ 24.80	2.20	+ 129.94
1981	683,329,097	+135,169,445	+ 24.66	2.22	+ 186.64
1991	843,930,861	+160,601,764	+ 23.50	2.11	+ 254.00

Notes: 1. In 1981, census was not conducted in Assam. Based on the 1971 Census and the provisional results of the 1991 Census the population of Assam as on March 1, 1981 has been interpolated.

2. As a consequence of the revised estimate for Assam for the year 1981, the total population of India as of 1981 has been estimated as 683,329,097 as against the earlier published figure of 685,184,692.

3. The 1991 Census was not conducted in Jammu and Kashmir. The provisional population figures for India include the population figure for Jammu and Kashmir projected by the Standing Committee of Experts on Population Projections.

4. The 1971 Census was conducted with April 1, 1971 as the reference date. In both the 1961 and 1981 Census the reference date was March 1. The average annual exponential growth rate presented in the statement takes into account this difference. No such adjustment has been made while calculating decadal growth rate.

5. In working out 'decade variation' and 'percentage decade variation' for India for 1941-51 and 1951-61, the 1951 population of Tuensang district of Nagaland i.e. 7,025 and 1961 population of Tuensang (83,501) and Mon (5,774) districts have not been taken into account as these areas were censused for the first time in 1951 and these figures are not comparable.

6. In Arunachal Pradesh the Census was conducted for the first time in 1961. While working out the decadal growth, both absolute as well as per cent, for 1951-61, 1961 Census population of Arunachal Pradesh has been excluded.

38

POSTS AND TELECOMMUNICATION

The Postal Service

Indian postal services have grown rapidly over the years. The country has the largest network of post offices in the world. By the end of March, 1992 the national postal network had 150346 post offices in the country. A post office covered on an average an area of 21.9 sq. km. and a population of 5827. The long-term objective is to locate a post office within three km. of every village. During the Eighth Five Year Plan (1992-97), the Postal Department will open 500 Departmental sub-offices and 3000 extra-departmental branch offices.

The main thrust areas in the Eighth Plan are computerisation and associated networks for electronic mail, money transfer, mechanical sorting, quality stamps and seals.

The major projects initiated for introduction of computers for customer services have started functioning in the areas of Savings Bank, Postal Life Insurance, Counter Computerisation through Front Post Office Machines, and development of integrated Management Information System (MIS).

The number of speed post centres under the National Network has increased from six at inception in 1 August 1986 to 62 on 31 October 1992. In addition, point-to-point speed post service has been extended to 666 pairs of stations. Contractual Speed Post service is now available for any place in the country. Speed Post carried 1.2 million packets and earned Rs. 3.17 crore in 1987-88; in 1991-92 it carried 5.2 million packets and earned Rs. 22 crore. During April-September 1992 the traffic and revenue figures were 3.55 million and Rs. 13.5 crore respectively. A manual track-and-trace system has been introduced in speed post to answer the various questions raised by the customers and to intimate to them the status of their articles whenever desired.

The Post Office Savings Bank operates through a network of 146251 Post Offices out of which about 88.7 per cent are located in rural areas. The gross collections during 1991-92 through Post Office Savings Bank were Rs. 17365 crore; net collections were Rs. 574 crore. The outstanding deposit balances as on 31 March 1992 were Rs. 56064 crore.

The Post Office Savings Bank has been identified as an important area for computerisation. Computers have been commissioned in seven Head Post Offices in Delhi.

The maximum limit of insurance for which an individual can take Postal Life Insurance (PLI) or policies was raised from Rs. one lakh to Rs. two lakh. The minimum condition of three years' service for certain categories of employees of local bodies has been removed and brought at par with other categories of employees. Extra-Departmental Agents' Group Insurance Scheme 1992 has been introduced from 1 April, 1992 at a low coast and on a wholly contributory basis. Three lakh Extra-Department employees of the Department of Posts will be covered. An almost threefold increase in the sum assured under postal life insurances and twofold increase in the number of policies has been registered as compared to 1983-84.

The gross receipts of the Department of Posts increased from Rs. 841 crore in 1990-91 to Rs. 948 crore in 1991-92. There was a revision of rates of foreign traffic on 1 November, 1990. With working expenses of Rs. 1162 crore, there was a net deficit of Rs. 214 crore, Rs. 41 crore less in 1991-92 (RE). The mounting deficit in the postal system has to be addressed to. Since 80 per cent of the total expenditure is accounted by establishment expenses, measures to improve staff productivity and further rationalisation of the rate structure are called for to eliminate this deficit.

Telecommunications

The main functions of the Department of Telecommunications include planning, engineering, installation, maintenance, management and operations of voice and non-voice telecommunication services all over the country as well as the neighbouring countries of SAARC regions. In addition, the Department is also responsible for frequency management in the field of radio connection in close coordination with the international bodies. It also enforces wireless regulatory measures by monitoring wireless transmission of all users in the country.

The telecom services continued to make progress. 241 new telephone exchanges were added till December, 1991 bringing the total to 15,332 exchanges. The switching capacity and direct exchange lines have been increased by 3.26 lakh lines and 2.77 lakh lines respectively. The total of optical fibre system went up to 4432 route kilometres. The satellite services are being maintained now through INSAT-ID Satellite and leased transponders of ARABSAT. Under the scheme for providing Remote Area Business Message Network, Master Earth Station has been commissioned at Sikandrabad (Uttar Pradesh) on July 20, 1991. This scheme provides packet switched data services for low speed data between subscribers-owned Very Small Aperture Terminals located at far flung places. The telephone facility to Panchayat villages has been increased by more than 16000 during the current. The new services proposed to be introduced are voice mail to be introduced in Delhi and Bombay, electronic mail expected to be operational, Video TAX for Delhi and Video Conferencing expected to be implemented during this year.

Efforts are being made for achieving the target of connecting all the Grampanchayats totalling about 2,28,000 in the country by March 31, 1995 at the target rate of 100 panchayats per day in the current year. Up to February, 1992 about 61,330 Grampanchayats have been connected. In the major urban areas the Department aimed to wipe out the waiting list for the connections within a reasonable time. Under the liberalised industrial policy several well-known companies have come forward to set up units to manufacture switching equipment and with this the constraints of availability of equipment are likely to disappear. The network service will be further improved when the remaining districts of the countries are provided with the STD facilities during the current year. The work of providing telephone facilities on National Highways has also made progress.

Action has also been initiated towards introduction of value-added services in the near future. In the first phase, a beginning will be made in the field of cellular mobile radio telephone service. In subsequent phases, other value-added services such as electronic mail, voice conferencing, radio paging, etc. will be covered.

A Committee has also been appointed to review the provisions of the Indian Telegraph Act 1885 to make recommendations for suitable amendments. The Government is also considering the recommendations made by a High Level Committee for restructuring of the Department of Telecommunications.

Source: *Annual Report, 1991-92*, Department of Telecommunications, Government of India, New Delhi.

India has a network comprising of over 15000 exchanges with a capacity of 70 lakh lines and 60 lakh working telephones. The network is growing at the rate of 15 per cent per annum. Additional switching capacity of 9.58 lakh lines was commissioned during 1991-92 — 72 per cent more than in 1990-91. About 25 per cent of this capacity expansion was in Delhi, Bombay, Calcutta and Madras.

Between 1979 and 1989 the number of telephone connections grew at 8.4 per cent annually. The number of new telephone connections provided in 1991-92 was 7.35 lakh direct exchange lines (DELs), 51.4 per cent more than in 1990-91 Table 38.1). The four metros accounted for around 27.8 per cent. The number of people waiting for new connections on 31 March 1992 was 22.87 lakh, 16.6 per cent higher than a year earlier. The demand for telecommunication services has far outstripped the availability. The Eighth Plan endeavours at reducing the waiting period by installing additional switching capacity of 93 lakh lines in order to provide 75 lakh new telephone connections.

An excess capacity has been built up in tele-instruments production, which is roughly three times the actual demand. There is an urgent need to augment the production of the switching equipment so as to eliminate the mismatch. The total production of switching equipment (strowger, crossbar and electronic switches) by the Indian Telephone Industries (ITI) during 1991-92 was 10.96 lakh lines, 16.1 per cent higher than in 1990-91. The Government has opened these sectors to private investment. Companies which are joint-ventures of leading foreign companies and domestic companies have been permitted to manufacture electronic switches. With this initiative, it may be possible to meet the Eighth Plan demand for additional switching capacity through domestic production.

The increase in telex switching capacity during 1991-92 was 2206 lines, 7.6 per cent higher than in 1990-91; 17795 telex connections were added, 16.7 per cent less than in 1990-91. Demand for Telex connections has declined because of increased use of FAX.

The old strowger and crossbar exchanges will be phased out of production and replaced by digital switching equipment. During the Eighth Plan the ITI will expand into the manufacture of cordless telephones and transmission equipment including fibre optic systems. Production of switching capacity so far has been an ITI monopoly, but is not being opened to the private sector. During 1991-92 and 1992-93 (April-December), licences were issued for switching capacity of over 1.5 million lines.

During 1991-92, 91.29 lakh conductor kilometres (lckms) of cables were laid, 28.8 per cent more than in the 1990-91. Cables laid in four metro cities accounted for 25.5 per cent of the total. In the manufacture of teiecom cables, private sector investment has been allowed.

TABLE 38.1: Performance of the Telecommunications Sector

	1989-90	1990-91	1991-92*	April-December* 1991-92	April-December* 1992-93	Change over previous year 1990-91	Change over previous year 1991-92	Change over previous year 1991-93@
1	2	3	4	5	6	7	8	9
							(per cent)	
I Net additional switching capacity (lakh lines)	4.78	5.57	9.58	3.26	3.84	16.53	71.99	17.79
(i) Metro districts	1.45	1.44	2.41	1.25	0.7	-0.69	67.36	-44.00
(ii) Others	3.33	4.13	7.17	2.01	3.14	24.02	73.61	56.22
II Net telephone connections provided (DELs) (thousand)	416.22	485.76	735.41	277.62	378.3	16.71	51.39	36.27
(i) Metro districts	122.45	133.09	204.56	91.52	92.85	8.69	53.70	1.45
(ii) Others	293.77	352.67	530.85	186.1	285.45	20.05	50.52	53.39
III Telex service:								
(i) Telex capacity (lines)	1020	2051	2206	1744	2589	101.08	7.56	48.45
(ii) Telex connections	3080	2156	1795	1167	232	-30.00	-16.74	-80.12
IV Production of switching equipment (thousand lines)	974.4	944	1095.7	573.1	796.9	-3.12	16.07	39.05
(i) Strowger	175.8	85.8	39.2	39.2	0.0	-51.19	-54.31	0.0
(ii) Crossbar	63.5	57.9	55.2	37.3	23.3	-8.82	-4.66	-37.53
(iii) Electronic	735.1	800.3	1001.3	496.6	773.7	8.87	25.12	55.78
V Laying of telephone cables (lakh conductor-km)	64.7	70.85	91.29	55.9	64.1	9.51	28.85	14.67
(i) Metro districts	22.37	19.48	23.25	13.6	16.25	-12.92	19.35	19.49
(ii) Others	42.33	51.37	68.04	42.3	47.85	21.36	32.45	13.12
VI Rural communications:								
(i) New exchanges	484	2727	4779	1122	1891	463.43	75.25	68.54
(ii) New long distance public telephones (LDPTs)	1633	1742	21752	7663	13309	6.67	1148.68	73.68

* Provisional
@ April-December.

The Telecom Department has embarked upon a programme of providing public telephones in village panchayats. During 1991-92, 21800 thousand villages were provided with telephone facilities as compared to 1700 villages during 1990-91.

While retaining the objective of providing telephones against registered demand, the expansion of value-added services in urban areas and increasing access to the telephone network in the rural areas the two other objectives in the telecommunication sector. It has been decided to expand the supply of the value-added services (telematics) with a participation of the private sector. Accordingly, these services are being given to the private sector on a franchise or licence basis, consisting of cellular mobile services, voice and electronic mail services, audio and video conferencing services, radio paging and videotex. This will relieve the Department of Telecommunications (DOT) of the financial costs of providing these services, and will give it additional revenue from licence fees and additional tariffs. Network operations may also be opened to the private sector participation. The Government will shortly come out with a National Telecom policy which will provide directions for the future expansion of the system and for structural reforms required to achieve it.

Increase in Telecom Tariff

The Department of Telecommunications increased in tariff in respect of leased telecom lines services with effect from Nov. 1, 1992, casting additional burden on subscribers including newspapers and news agencies.

In the case of telegraph circuits for subscribers other than Press, the rate for 50 baud lines have gone up from Rs. 125 per kilometre to Rs. 200 per annum and for 75 baud lines from Rs. 200 to Rs. 300. For Newspapers and news agencies the revised rates are Rs. 67 (old rate Rs. 42) for 50 baud lines and Rs. 100 (Rs. 67) for 75 baud circuits.

Hiring of local leads is also more costly now with a uniform rate of Rs. 1,200 per annum per pair up to five km for full time use of the circuit and Rs. 1,500 for distances beyond five km. The slab system has been given up.

For ticket connections the new rate is Rs. 2200 per km per annum against Rs. 125.

The old and revised rates for different services are:

Leased services Telephone voice circuit	Old rates Rs. 400 per km p.a.	New Rates point to point upto 1000 kms Rs. 600 per km —beyond 1000 kms Rs. 300 per km p.a. subject to a maximum as for 1500 kms. single party network mode —upto 1000 km Rs. 750 per km p.a. —beyond 1000 km Rs. 375 per km p.m. subject to a maximum as for 1500 kms.
Local leads of voice circuits	upto 5 kms chargeable distance as for respective circuits (full time use) beyond 5 kms CD Rs. 1500 per km p.a.	point to point Rs. 1200 per km p.a. per pair single party network mode network mode Rs. 1500 per km p.a.

Source: *Hindustan Times*, February 5, 1993.

39

PRESIDENTIAL AND VICE PRESIDENTIAL ELECTIONS, 1992

Presidential Election

Dr. Shanker Dayal Sharma was sworn in as the ninth President of Indian Republic, on July 25, 1992. The election was held on July 16. A total of 4,748 elected Members of Parliament and State Assemblies constituted the electoral college (or votes). Of this 543 members belonged to the Lok Sabha, 233 to the Rajya Sabha and 3,972 to the State Assemblies. The members of the Assemblies in the Union Territories were not entitled to participate in the election of the President.

The value of each vote for the election of the President is not the same. It varies from State to State, according the total population of the State and the number of elected MPs and MLAs, as per the formula laid down in the Constitution. The voting will be on the basis of proportional representatives by means of a secret ballot. Under the 42nd amendment to the Constitution, the population figures of the 1971 census would form the basis for this purpose, according to a Press Note of the Election Commission.

Under the formula of determining the value of each vote in a State (both of the MP and MLA), the total value of votes of each member of the assembly is worked out by multiplying the number of elective seats by the number of votes for each member. Then, the total value of votes of all the States added together is divided by the total number of elected members of Parliament (Lok Sabha and Rajya Sabha) to get the value of votes for MPs.

According to this intricate formula, the value of a vote of an MLA in Andhra Pradesh, for example, works out to 148, and seven for Sikkim, 51 for Himachal Pradesh, 174 for Bihar, and 208 for Uttar Pradesh (which is the highest). For Haryana it is 112. The total value of votes of MLAs will be 5,44,971. Added to this will be the value of 5,44,752 of the MPs, which would make a grand total of 10,89,723.

Vice-President Election

Shri K.R. Narayanan was elected Vice-President on August 10, 1992. He polled 700 votes out of a total of 711 votes cast in the election held in the Parliament House. It was the fifth occasion when contest took place for the office of the Vice-President since the country became Republic in 1952. The first contest was when Dr. Zakir Husain was the Congress nominee.

TABLE 39.1: 4,7488 Voters in Presidential Election

State	No. of Assembly seats (elective)		Value of a member of legislative assembly	Total votes for the State
Andhra Pradesh	294	X	148 =	43,512
Arunachal Pradesh	60	X	8 =	480
Assam	126	X	116 =	14,616
Bihar	324	X	174 =	56,276
Goa	40	X	20 =	800
Gujarat	182	X	147 =	26,754
Haryana	90	X	112 =	10,080
Himachal Pradesh	68	X	51 =	3,468
Jammu and Kashmir	87	X	72 =	6,264
Karnataka	224	X	131 =	29,344
Kerala	140	X	151 =	21,280
Madhya Pradesh	320	X	130 =	41,600
Maharashtra	288	X	175 =	50,400
Manipur	60	X	18 =	1,080
Meghalaya	60	X	17 =	1,020
Mizoram	40	X	8 =	320
Nagaland	60	X	9 =	540
Orissa	147	X	117 =	21,903
Punjab	117	X	116 =	13,572
Rajasthan	200	X	129 =	25,800
Sikkim	32	X	7 =	224
Tamil Nadu	234	X	176 =	41,184
Tripura	60	X	26 =	1,560
Uttar Pradesh	425	X	208 =	88,400
West Bengal	294	X	151 =	44,394
Total	3,972		Total value =	544,971

(a) Vote value per MP = 544,971/776 = 702.282 or 702 (rounded)
(543+223 = 776)

(b) Total vote value for MPs = 702 X 776 = 544,752.
Grand total = 544,971 + 544,752 = 1,089,723

TABLE 39.2: Presidential Election Results — 1992

State/ Parliament	No. of MPs/ MLAs	Value of each Vote	Votes Polled								Invalid		Total		Valid votes (Value)
			S.D. Sharma		G.G. Swell		Dhartipakad		R. Jethmalani						
			Votes	Value	Votes	Value	Votes	Value	Votes	Value	Votes	Value	Votes	Value	
Andhra Pradesh	294	148	204	30192	73	10804					8	1184	285	42180	40996
Arunachal Pradesh	60	8	60	480									60	480	480
Assam	126	116	99	11484	19	2204			1	116	5	580	124	14384	13804
Bihar	324	174	126	21924	172	29928	1	174			1	174	300	52200	52026
Goa	49	29	27	540	11	220			1	20	1	20	40	80	780
Gujarat	182	147	105	15435	66	9702			1	147	3	331	175	25725	25284
Haryana	90	112	72	8064	1	1904			1	112			90	10080	10080
Himachal Pradesh	68	51	19	969	46	2346					2	102	67	3417	3315
Karnataka	224	131	197	25807	22	2882					5	655	224	29344	28689
Kerala	140	152	132	20064	2	304			2	304			136	20672	29672
Madhya Pradesh	320	130	65	8450	235	30550	1	130	1	130	7	910	309	40170	29260
Maharashtra	288	175	223	39025	53	9275					1	175	277	48475	48300
Manipur	60	18	56	1008	3	54			1	18			60	1080	1080
Meghalaya	60	17	36	612	23	391							59	1003	1003
Mizoram	40	8	26	208	13	104							39	312	312
Orissa	147	149	23	3427	119	17731					2	298	144	21456	21158
Punjab	177	116	97	11252	15	1740			1	116	3	348	166	13456	13108
Rajasthan	200	129	84	10836	110	14190	1	129	1	129	3	387	199	25671	25284
Sikkim	32	6	32	224									32	224	224
Tamil Nadu	234	176	228	40128	5	880							233	41008	41008
Tripura	60	26	52	1378									53	1378	1378
Uttar Pradesh	425	208	128	26624	280	58240			1	208	5	1040	414	86112	85072
West Bengal	2294	151	263	39713							7	1057	270	40770	39713
Parliament	776	702	510	358020	218	153036	11	702	2	1404	14	9828	745	522990	513162
Grand Total	4601		2865	675864	1502	346485	4	1135	13	2704	67	17199	4451	1043387	1026188
Percentage			64.78%		33.21%		0.11%		0.26%		1.65%				
Lead			329379												

TABLE 39.3: Margin of Victory in Presidential Elections

	Votes Value	Percentage
1. Dr Rajendra Prasad (May 3, 1952)	507,400	83.8
2. Dr. Rajendra Prasad (May 6, 1957)	459,698	99.3
3. Dr. S. Radhakrishnan (May 7, 1962)	553,067	98.3
4. Dr. Zakir Husain (May 6, 1967)	471,244	56.2
5. V.V. Giri (August 16, 1969)	420,077	50.2
6. Fakhruddin Ali Ahmed (August 17, 1974)	765,587	80.2
7. Neelam Sanjiva Reddy (August 6, 1977)	Unopposed	
8. Zail Singh (July 12, 1982)	754,113	72.7
9. Ramaswamy Venkataraman (Sept. 1987)	740,198	72.3
10. Dr. S.D. Sharma (July 16, 1992)	675,864	64.78

TABLE 39.4: Vice-Presidential Elections (1952 to 1992)

	Runner-up	Winner	Runner-up
1. S. Radhakrishnan, May 12, 1952	—	Unopposed	—
2. S. Radhakrishnan, May 11, 1957	—	Unopposed	—
3. Zakir Husain, May 7, 1962	N.C. Samantsinhar	568	14
4. V.V. Giri, May 6, 1967	Prof. Habib	486	192
5. G.S. Pathak, August 30, 1969	H.V. Kamath	400	156
6. B.D. Jatti, August 27, 1974	N.E. Horo	521	141
7. M. Hidayatullah, August 27, 1979	—	Unopposed	—
8. R. Venkataraman, August 23, 1984	B.C. Kamble	508	207
9. S.D. Sharma, September 7, 1987	—	Unopposed	—
10. K.R. Narayanan, August 19, 1992	Kaka Joginder Singh	700	1

40

PUBLIC SECTOR ENTERPRISES

Public enterprises constitute a major national capability in terms of their scale of operations, coverage of the national economy, technological capabilities and stock of human capital. There are over a thousand public enterprises, about 700 of which are owned by the States. The rest are in the Central Sector. These include department undertakings (e.g., railways, posts and telecommunications), financial institutions (e.g. the State Bank of India, the Industrial Financial Corporation of India, the Unit Trust of India and the Industrial Development Bank of India), and non-departmental enterprises or Government companies or corporations which are either incorporated under the Company Law (e.g., the Steel Authority of India and the Indian Petrochemical Corporation Ltd.)) or statutorily created by Acts of Parliament (e.g., Coal India, Air India, Indian Airlines and the National Thermal Power Corporation). Non-departmental enterprises account for 75 per cent of value addition, more than 50 per cent of gross investment and about a third of the total employment in PSEs. PSEs contribute the entire output in the case of petroleum, lignite, copper and primary lead; about 98 per cent of zinc; well over 90 per cent of coal; more than half of steel and aluminium and about one-third of fertilizers.

Non-departmental PSEs have thus been an important sector of our economy and have dominated infrastructure and basic industries. Over the decades their production activity has become perhaps over-diversified and extends from steel-making and oil refining to manufacture of bread and footwear. This has been a result of a number of circumstances and has diluted the original strategic and commanding heights objectives of PSE activity. Infrastructural or producer services are dominated by public sector corporations in transport, energy and communications. PSEs also operate in diverse service sectors such as international trade, consultancy, contract and construction services, hotels and tourist facilities etc. Since the beginning of 1950s, a phenomenal growth in investment in such enterprises has taken place (Table 40.1).

As on 31 March 1992, there were 246 central public sector enterprises (excluding 8 companies with Central Government investment but without direct responsibility for management, 6 insurance companies and 3 financial institutions). Of these, 9 were in the construction sector, 72 in services and 165 were engaged in manufacture.

Performance of Central Public Sector Enterprises

The financial performance of the public enterprises has been a matter of wide interest and concern. As may be seen from Table 40.1, profits of profit-making enterprises went up from 1293 crore in 1981-82 to Rs. 6149 crore in 1991-92; but the losses of loss-making enterprises also increased from Rs. 848 crore to Rs. 3674 crore over the same period. Thus, PSEs earned a rate of return of 2.23 per cent on capital employed in 1990-91, which declined to 2.09 per cent in

1991-92. During 1991-92, nine PSEs have shown improvement in their performance over 1990-91. The gross margin (i.e. before depreciation, interest and taxes) of PSEs as per cent of capital employed improved from 10.88 in 1990-91 to 11.69 in 1991-92. The heavy capital investment in the past combined with a massive interest burden eats into the gross margins of PSEs and results in an unsatisfactory financial performance overall.

TABLE 40.1: Profitability Profile of Central PSEs

	1981-82	1990-91	1991-92
1. Operating enterprises	188	236	237
(i) Profitable enterprises	104	124	134
(ii) Loss-making enterprises	83	109	102
		Rs. Crore	
2. Capital employed	21935	102083	118492
3. Gross margin	4012	18312	22435
4. Gross Profit	2654	11102	13857
5. Net Profit	445	2272	2475
6. Profits of profit-making enterprises	1293	5432	6149
7. Losses of loss-making enterprises	848	3064	3674
		Per cent	
8. Ratio of gross margin to capital employed	18.29	17.94	18.93
9. Percentage of gross profit to capital employed	12.10	10.88	11.69
10. Ratio of net profit to capital employed	2.03	2.23	2.09

The profitability of PSEs in 1991-92 in terms of ratios of gross margins, gross profits and net profits to capital employed at 18.93 per cent, 11.69 per cent and 2.09 per cent, respectively, has not improved over the last ten years and was, indeed, depressed in 1990-91 and only slightly improved in 1991-92 as compared to past several years.

In view of the overall resource constraints and in the face of very large revenue, budgetary and fiscal deficits being experienced since 1979-80, accumulation of substantial losses by a large number of public enterprises cannot be allowed to continue. Hence, the serious concern with the loss-making enterprises which numbered 102 in 1991-92 and incurred a total net loss of 3674 crore.

The loss-making public enterprises also represent a variety of product or industry groups and market structures. There are 15 large enterprises which are monopolies and operate in the core sector, while the remaining ones function in a competitive environment producing a variety of goods and services. As between these categories, the monopolies account for about three-fourths of the capital employed and one-fourth of the accumulated losses; the competitive enterprises employing a quarter of the capital, make three-quarters of the losses. The share of monopolies and competitive PSEs in employment is nearly equal.

The loss-making monopolies mentioned above include Food Corporation of India, Indian Airlines Corporation, Delhi Transport Corporation, Coal India Ltd., Vayudoot, Bharat Gold Mines, National Film Development Corporation and North Eastern Regional Agricultural Marketing Corporation. In view of their large

TABLE 40.2: Production Performance of Public Sector Undertakings Under the Department of Heavy Industry

(Rs. Lakhs)

Sl. No.	PSUs	1988-89 (Actuals)	1989-90 (Actuals)	1991-91 (Actuals)	1991-92 Target	1991-92 Anticipated	1992-93 Target (Tentative)
	1	2	3	4	5	6	7
1.	AY & Co.	10864	14483	15338	20572	19096	22611
2.	BHEL	261995	292150	315358	319605	321000	335000
3.	BHPV	13601	15152	20046	20900	20900	21600
4.	BPME	475	464	542	660	670	690
5.	WIL	97	100	81	135	128	160
6.	BPCL	3973	3707	5949	5400	7000	7875
7.	BWEL	4081	4348	5347	4850	7637	7959
8.	Braithwaite	7690	8380	9154	10600	10555	14566
9.	BSCL	14257	22049	23902	26668	24226	30494
10.	BBVL	559	657	672	750	750	850
11.	RBL	156	115	158	563	237	400
12.	BBJ	1592	1650	2686	2000	2500	2750
13.	CCIL	582	589	553	740	578	765
14.	NBCIL	243	201	84	495	35	100
15.	HEC	35267	36862	26380	43044	26000	41300
16.	HCL	44330	33969	27104	46701	35505	51929
17.	HMT	53460	62145	75913	85000	84610	94782
18.	HMT (B)	2345	2516	2575	3203	32033	3668
19.	ILK	10084	10256	12401	15400	13600	15400
20.	REIL	835	631	742	1300	1309	1350
21.	JESSOP	11000	12100	13700	13500	12500	13700
22.	Lagan Jute	397	512	544	562	670	727
23.	MUL	89815	113419	147725	183805	178928	132059
24.	MAMC	8688	19835	8864	12500	9000	12500
25.	NIL	889	1010	851	1535	1125	1305
26.	PTL	4054	4488	4504	5672	5440	6250
27.	R&C	6027	7035	7680	8400	7050	7500
28.	SIL	840	771	998	2775	1880	3375
29.	TSL	4104	3701	3674	5000	4200	5100
30.	TSPL	18840	2003	2810	3000	3160	3500
31.	CCI	26115	32980	40891	47016	52080	56490
32.	HPC	10474	16522	19022	25046	21347	24194
33.	HNL	7983	11285	12941	13388	13915	14025
34.	MNPM	1207	2367	2353	2607	2904	3546
35.	NPPC	231	118	350	950	461	524
36.	NEPA	6408	6204	9747	110569	11868	11993
37.	BOGL	174	254	256	425	65	75
38.	HPF	15439	19347	21408	27422	27146	31268
39.	HSL	1101	325	479	547	555	585
40.	SSL	183	266	414	647	590	645
41.	TAFCO	643	690	487	1094	968	1326
42.	TCIL	3652	3617	3811	4226	4227	9881
43.	RIC	1129	915	480	3187	2000	2700
44.	BLC	325	316	275	342	335	363
45.	EPI	8754	11267	11222	15240	15240	19240
46.	NIDC	303	444	605	650	650	725
47.	HOOGHLY	66	84	8885	8737	9050	10500
48.	B&R	6199	7384	8885	8737	9050	10500
49.	HMT(I)	2316	4688	4717	5875	5875	8000
	Total	685842	7853711	874786	1013536	972909	1036497

size and significance of operations, a case-by-case approach may be needed to resolve their problems.

The remaining loss-making enterprises, of which about half constitute sick units taken over by the Government from the private sector, account for the bulk (about three-fourths) of the losses of public enterprises. The loss per employee in these enterprises exceeds the average wage rate. The Government has also been borrowing at a high cost from the market to support them. They, therefore, deserve special attention in economic restructuring. Most of the (about 18) of the State Electricity Boards have incurred losses.

TABLE 40.3: Profit(+)/Loss(-) of Public Sector Undertakings Under the Department of Heavy Industry

(Rs. Lakhs)

Sl. No.	PSUs	1988-89 (Actuals)	1989-90 (Actuals)	1991-91 (Actuals)	1991-92 Target	1991-92 Anticipated	1992-93 Target (Tentative)
1		2	3	4	5	6	7
1.	AY & Co.	513	1008	1100	1595	1512	1843
2.	BHEL	19256	21319	20146	20100	16500	17000
3.	BHPV	263	251	304	450	450	650
4.	BPME	-679	-692	-837	-733	-810	-780
5.	WIL	-103	-100	-137	-184	-117	-102
6.	BPCL	-1692	-809	-296	-350	-50	25
7.	BWEL	-172	3	79	2	160	186
8.	Braithwaite	-629	-567	-539	-490	-401	-358
9.	BSCL	-430	-598	-344	-100	-185	1
10.	BBVL	-211	-226	-195	-150	-146	-118
11.	RBL	-115	-128	-119	11	-89	-64
12.	CCIL	-1646	-3071	-3016	-2787	-2499	-2874
13.	NBCIL	-829	-1011	-1820	-1105	-1170	-1252
14.	HEC	1253	-3362	-9951	533	-12823	-7412
15.	HCL	2422	791	232	1658	589	2526
16.	HMT	615	581	1558	1317	1317	1510
17.	HMT (B)	-109	21	158	150	150	239
18.	ILK	263	211	14	270	50	90
19.	REIL	70	64	68	100	106	115
20.	JESSOP	122	135	-138	130	-70	20
21.	Lagan Jute	30	20	28	35	83	96
22.	MUL	3142	5005	4812	8000	2867	-1907
23.	MAMC	-1131	-1529	-3769	-2123	-3737	-1772
24.	NIL	-517	-535	-818	-77	-722	-715
25.	PTL	134	83	-170	225	43	234
26.	R&C	-818	-777	-864	-70	-985	-890
27.	SIL	-3721	-4289	-4825	-5250	-5250	-5900
28.	TSL	-282	-442	-361	-165	-678	-455
29.	TSPL	72	21	47	99	99	150
30.	CCI	-4662	-6288	-2933	-5041	-572	123
31.	HPC	-8629	-5584	-6137	-2247	-5324	-4012
32.	HNL	200	2036	3102	2556	3731	3572
33.	MNPM	-1033	-648	-571	-717	-658	-419
34.	NPPC	-2394	-2333	-2024	-2666	-2547	-2322
35.	NEPA	-510	-426	-618	130	172	-219
36.	BOGL	-720	-864	-1040	-988	-1142	-1099
37.	HPF	756	797	198	1020	250	250
38.	HSL	8	-18	-10	21	26	40

Contd.

TABLE 40.3 *Concld.*

1	2	3	4	5	6	7
39. SSL	-28	5	71	68	50	53
40. TAFCO	-1405	-1616	-1870	-1824	-1803	-1765
41. TCIL	-991	-1195	-1418	-1683	-1571	-1780
42. RIC	-1453	-1942	-2712	-1888	-2629	-3156
43. BLC	-50	-77	-129	-87	-87	-124
44. EPI	-3829	-10432	-5387	-5990	-6190	-7005
45. NIDC	-69	7	16	12	16	17
46. HOOGHLY	-13	-16	-7	-3	-3	1
47. BBJ	-7	-13	72	-21	64	68
48. B&R	78	722	79	181	162	210
49. HMT(I)	118	281	349	106	106	150
Total	-9563	-16851	-19386	1400	-23755	-17331

TABLE 40.4: Salary/Wage Bill and Social Overheads as Percentage of Turnover of Public Sector Undertakings under the Department of Heavy Industry

Sl. No.	Unit Name	Wages & Salaries as %age of turnover				Social overheads as %age of turnover			
		1988-89 (Actuals)	1989-90 (Actuals)	1990-91 (Actuals)	1991-92 (Anti.)	1988-89 (Actuals)	1989-90 (Actuals)	1990-91 (Actuals)	1991-92 (Anti.)
1		2	3	4	5	6	7	8	9
1.	AY & Co.	17.65	16.19	15.90	13.69	2.82	2.49	3.25	2.72
2.	Hooghly Printing (Subs. AY & Co.)	40.07	335.46	23.31	22.70	2.46	2.12	1.18	1.00
3.	BHEL	14.35	14.04	15.60	14.90	1.98	2.12	2.25	2.50
	BBUNL-holding Co. Subsidiaries								
4.	BSCL	24.90	29.30	30.81	225.33	2.22	2.65	2.77	2.39
5.	BBVL (Subs. BSCL)	37.00	36.00	37.00	35.00	13.00	13.00	12.00	11.00
6.	RBL (Subs. BSCL)	57.05	73.91	55.06	31.39	12.82	15.65	11.39	6.57
7.	Jessop	29.62	21.26	23.61	27.75	1.47	0.80	0.90	1.08
8.	Braithwaite	30.51	32.08	39.21	31.55	2.65	2.77	3.39	2.89
9.	BWEL	39.00	36.00	36.00	36.00	6.00	4.00	3.00	4.00
10.	BPME	68.26	84.53	71.23	45.03	0.19	0.23	0.19	0.30
11.	WIL (Subs. BPME)	93.13	99.05	128.40	87.86	9.80	9.43	12.50	7.86
12.	Lagan Jute	31.73	31.06	31.91	28.81	1.60	2.06	2.20	1.99
	BYNL-Holding Co. Subsidiaries								
13.	BHPV	13.37	15.37	11.51	12.14	1.60	1.59	1.51	1.11
14.	BPCL	17.80	19.90	15.30	13.70	1.20	1.10	0.90	0.90
15.	R&C	29.28	25.01	23.82	30.00	1.95	1.75	1.64	2.29
16.	TSL	20.92	255.42	24.99	31.55	4.31	4.19	5.28	5.95

Contd.

TABLE 40.4 *Contd.*

1	2	3	4	5	6	7	8	9
17. TSP	25.55	20.33	24.46	15.92	5.27	3.57	1.71	1.14
18. CCIL	160.00	179.00	209.00	165.00	12.00	14.00	16.00	12.00
19. HCL	4.51	6.00	7.85	6.44	1.40	2.03	2.94	1.95
20. HEC	22.38	28.40	38.17	27.91	4.44	5.48	7.96	5.67
21. HMT	23.80	24.27	23.14	20.76	3.63	3.70	3.77	3.86
22. PTL (Subs. HMT)	20.38	20.95	24.42	18.11	1.89	2.47	2.74	2.24
23. HMT Bearings (Subs. HMT)	0.23	0.23	0.19	0.16	0.03	0.02	0.02	0.03
24. HMT(I)	6.86	3.58	4.19	3.55	0.77	0.25	0.27	0.25
25. ILK	17.70	17.82	19.03	18.28	1.84	2.05	1.76	1.62
26. REIL (Subs. ILK)	5.72	5.78	8.95	5.00	1.30	1.63	1.53	0.94
27. MAMC	32.00	27.00	37.00	35.00	5.00	4.00	5.00	6.00
28. MUL	1.70	2.02	1.89	1.71	0.66	0.85	0.40	0.38
29. NBCIL	140.30	152.30	305.90	757.10	30.10	30.20	47.50	128.60
30. NIL	37.70	36.011	39.56	32.61	0.21	0.18	0.19	0.15
31. SIL	84.14	105.59	91.04	53.85	24.54	32.50	28.77	17.95
32. BOGL	82.59	145.46	138.83	65.00	7.16	14.07	14.16	7.69
33. CCI	7.98	6.74	6.57	5.40	0.63	0.49	0.50	0.32
34. HPC	6.10	7.28	8.83	9.44	7.37	5.46	4.54	4.96
35. MNPM (Subs. HPC)	2.43	2.73	2.79	2.96	10.25	5.80	5.38	5.65
36. NPPC (Subs. HPC)	3.10	3.44	4.02	4.38	56.65	136.61	59.32	43.79
37. HNL (Subs. HPC)	4.30	4.70	5.113	5.69	2.86	2.88	3.03	3.06
38. HPF	7.36	5.70	6.89	6.91	0.25	0.26	0.29	0.25
39. HSL	64.15	54.18	41.33	39.73	12.74	9.29	6.22	6.78

Contd.

TABLE 40.4 *Concld.*

1	2	3	4	5	6	7	8	9
40. SSL (Subs. HSL)	57.82	54.77	53.35	44.53	14.22	11.31	9.33	7.42
41. NEPA	15.00	17.00	11.00	10.00	0.03	0.04	0.03	0.03
42. RIC	43.00	75.00	115.00	40.00	(Merged with wages' salaries)			
43. TAFCO	68.00	57.00	91.00	55.00	2.30	1.80	2.80	1.70
44. TCIL	21.00	20.00	19.00	20.00	10.00	1.00	2.00	1.00
45. BLC	26.00	29.00	37.00	29.00	6%	9%	7%	10%
46. EPI	6.87	8.16	7.43	5.67	1.38	1.00	1.06	0.70
47. NIDC	50.00	53.47	52.20	43.02	8.24	9.05	8.50	10.79
48. BBJ (Subs. BBUNL)	14.00	12.00	7.50	8.40	0.70	0.50	0.30	0.30
49. B&R (Subs. BYNL)	11.29	10.65	11.05	11.93	1.11	0.97	1.06	1.22

TABLE 40.5: Order Book Position of PSUs under the Department of Heavy Industry

(Rs. Crores)

Sl. No.	Unit Name	1987-88 As on 1.10.87	1988-89 As on 1.10.88	1989-90 As on 1.10.89	1990-91 As on 1.10.90	1991-92 As on 1.10.91
1.	Andrew Yule	39.23	40.07	51.52	56.55	53.07
2.	Hoog. Printing (Subs. AY & CO)	0.20	0.30	0.40	0.15	0.19
3.	BHEL	700.00	6900.00	7379.00	7146.00	6754.00
	BBUNL-Holding Co. Subsidiaries					
4.	BSCL	163.84	147.18	146.31	194.14	168.88
5.	BBVL (Subs. BSCL)	7.14	9.30	7.09	4.05	7.53
6.	RBL (Subs. BSCL)	2.69	2.48	4.27	3.64	2.89
7.	Jessop	144.00	133.00	153.00	184.63	217.24
8.	Braithwaite	58.72	72.48	65.31	60.07	72.37
9.	BWEL	11.17	26.58	34.52	29.29	43.50
10.	BPME	9.95	3.40	5.91	5.52	0.93
11.	WIL (Subs. BPME)	0.57	0.62	0.57	0.76	0.77
12.	Lagan Jute	2.39	4.24	4.37	5.97	6.54
	BYNL-Holding Co. Subsidiaries					
13.	BHPV	247.00	172.00	339.00	341.00	293.00
14.	BPCL	59.00	53.33	75.52	75.11	62.74
15.	R&C	51.04	59.19	76.24	50.18	62.35
16.	TSL	54.04	65.31	56.00	51.00	52.00
17.	TSP	14.25	31.89	57.31	33.19	40.00
18.	CCIL	0.17	0.10	0.13	0.12	0.14
19.	HCL	183.57	152.12	61.16	254.94	380.09
20.	HEC	359.50	353.90	506.90	418.20	689.00
21.	HMT	88.40	131.70	149.90	162.10	173.50
22.	Praga Tools (Subs. HMT)	24.07	27.35	15.99	17.56	16.34
23.	HMTB (Subs. HMT)	9.92	13.79	13.11	15.82	28.15
24.	HMT (I) (Subs. HMT)	22.14	50.84	52.28	47.05	50.67
25.	IL	90.00	111.95	119.69	133.92	132.19
26.	REIL (Subs. ILK)	—	1.42	1.56	3.39	4.36
27.	MAMC	134.00	181.62	183.53	175.18	258.45
28.	MUL	1802.32	1170.49	890.23	—	—
29.	NBCIL	1.00	0.50	0.70	0.35	0.25
30.	NIL	4.11	6.37	10.06	7.47	—
31.	SIL	—	—	—	—	—
32.	BOGL	1.37	1.28	1.05	0.14	0.54
33.	CCI	38.85	56.25	54.15	91.50	22.22
34.	HPC	22.78	51.52	82.57	29.81	30.00
35.	MNPM (Subs. HPC)	—	—	—	—	—
36.	NPPC (Subs. HPC)	—	—	—	—	—
37.	HNL (Subs. HPC)	—	—	—	—	—
38.	HPF	137.35	148.43	185.94	92.11	95.23
39.	HSL	0.92	0.45	0.89	0.74	1.21
40.	SSL (Subs. HSL)	1.51	0.25	0.42	0.14	2.61
41.	NEPA	10.94	1.22	18.84	12.97	9.81
42.	RIC	14.74	10.32	48.15	64.78	61.41
43.	TAFCO	5.56	4.41	2.88	22.15	1.81
44.	TCIL	2.85	9.53	7.04	12.73	4.87
45.	BLC	1.08	1.18	0.96	0.79	0.84
46.	EPIL	190.00	216.00	217.00	531.00	640.16
47.	NIDC	10.56	4.92	5.40	6.98	8.72
48.	BBJ (Subs. BBUNL)	—	—	—	93.05	79.14
49.	B&R (Subs. BYNL)	56.69	113.60	121.14	138.93	151.80
	Total	11328.5711	11338.02	12028.24	111322.79	11434.73

TABLE 40.6: Export Performance of Public Sector Undertakings under the Department of Heavy Industry

(Rs. crores)

Sl. No.	Unit Name	1989-90 (Actual)			1990-91 (Actual)			1991-92 (Anticipated)			1992-93 (Target)		
		Physical	Deemed	Total	Physical	Deemed	Total	Physical	Deemed	Total	Physical	Deemed	Total
	1	2	3	4	5	6	7	8	9	10	11	12	13
1.	Andrew Yule	1.43	—	1.43	0.80	—	0.80	3.23	—	3.23	3.78	—	3.78
2.	Hooghly (Subs. AY & CO)	—	—	—	—	—	—	—	—	—	—	—	—
3.	BHEL	23.00	358.00	381.00	68.00	422.00	490.00	130.00	464.00	594.00	130.00	605.00	735.00
	BBUNL-Holding Co. Subsidiaries												
4.	BSCL	21.33	0.15	21.48	21.32	—	21.32	21.58	—	21.58	9.06	—	9.06
5.	BBVL (Subs. BSCL)	—	1.01	1.01	—	—	—	—	—	—	—	—	—
6.	RBL (Subs. BSCL)	—	—	—	—	—	—	—	—	—	—	—	—
7.	Jessop	0.26	—	0.26	2.75	—	2.75	0.70	—	0.70	4.50	—	4.50
8.	Braithwaite	—	2.81	2.81	—	10.63	10.63	—	10.25	10.25	—	8.12	8.12
9.	BWEL	—	—	—	—	—	—	—	—	—	—	—	—
10.	BPME	—	0.48	0.48	—	—	—	—	—	—	—	0.40	0.40
11.	WIL (Subs. BPME)	—	—	—	—	—	—	—	—	—	—	—	—
12.	Lagan Jute	0.60	—	0.60	0.03	0.42	0.45	0.02	—	0.02	—	0.72	0.72
	BYNL-Holding Co. Subsidiaries												
13.	BHPV	0.37	8.00	8.37	—	4.27	4.27	—	0.32	0.32	1.75	55.00	56.75
14.	BPCL	—	5.24	5.24	—	4.00	4.00	—	3.44	3.44	8.30	10.00	18.30
15.	R&C	0.28	2.56	2.84	0.05	2.12	2.17	0.50	1.50	2.00	0.50	1.00	1.50
16.	TSL	—	3.12	3.12	—	6.37	6.37	—	10.09	10.09	—	2.00	2.00
17.	TSP	2.00	3.36	5.36	—	4.10	4.10	—	1.20	1.20	—	2.00	2.00
18.	CCIL	—	—	—	—	—	—	—	—	—	—	—	—
19.	HCL	0.75	3.06	3.81	2.53	9.08	11.61	—	7.60	7.60	—	34.91	34.91
20.	HEC	3.70	26.39	30.09	1.69	18.85	20.54	1.66	—	1.66	2.00	—	2.00
21.	HMT	45.44	0.53	45.97	46.73	0.91	47.64	57.72	—	57.722	80.25	—	80.25
22.	PTL (Subs. HMT)	1.78	—	1.78	5.18	—	5.18	4.00	—	4.00	5.00	—	5.00
23.	HMT(B) (Subs. HMT)	—	—	—	—	—	—	—	—	—	—	—	—

Contd.

TABLE 40.6 *Concld.*

1	2	3	4	5	6	7	8	9	10	11	12	13
24. HMT (I) (Subs. HMT)	44.8	0.34	45.22	45.95	0.80	46.75	54.54	2.05	56.59	77.50	2.50	80.00
25. IL	7.94	—	7.94	7.85	—	7.85	1.00	—	1.00	3.00	—	3.00
26. REIL (Subs. ILK)	—	11.10	1.10	—	2.85	2.85	0.02	2.85	2.87	—	—	—
27. MAMC	10.10	6.30	16.40	12.05	6.54	18.59	2.07	12.11	14.18	5.00	—	5.00
28. MUL	30.08	0.49	30.57	31.19	1.06	32.25	194.37	1.75	196.12	165.79	1.00	166.79
29. NBCIL	0.47	—	0.47	0.38	—	0.38	0.20	—	0.20	0.50	—	0.50
30. NIL	0.07	—	0.07	0.03	—	0.03	0.06	—	0.06	0.10	—	0.10
31. SIL	0.27	—	0.27	—	1.29	1.29	—	3.00	3.00	—	5.00	5.00
32. BOGL	—	—	—	—	—	—	—	—	—	—	—	—
33. CCI	—	—	—	—	0.33	0.33	—	39.98	39.98	—	50.00	50.00
34. HPC	—	—	—	—	—	—	—	—	—	—	—	—
35. MNPM (Subs. HPC)	—	—	—	—	—	—	—	—	—	—	—	—
36. NPPC (Subs. HPC)	—	—	—	—	—	—	—	—	—	—	—	—
37. HNL (Subs. HPC)	—	—	—	—	—	—	—	—	—	—	—	—
38. HPF	0.58	—	0.58	—	1.00	1.00	1.00	—	1.00	—	—	—
39. HSL	0.83	—	-.83	1.64	—	1.64	1.56	—	1.56	11.43	—	1.43
40. SSL (Subs. HSL)	0.229	—	0.29	—	0.74	0.74	1.06	—	1.06	0.87	—	0.87
41. NEPA	—	—	—	—	—	—	—	—	—	—	—	—
42. RIC	—	—	—	—	—	—	—	—	—	—	—	—
43. TAFCO	0.24	—	0.24	0.30	—	0.30	2.25	—	2.25	2.86	—	2.86
44. TCIL	0.64	—	0.64	0.36	—	0.36	0.52	—	0.52	0.57	—	0.57
45. BLC	—	0.34	0.34	—	—	—	—	—	—	—	—	—
46. EPIL	—	21.79	21.79	—	4.00	4.00	—	2.43.	2.43	—	1.14	1.14
47. NIDC	0.12	0.01	0.13	0.05	0.03	0.08	0.10	—	0.10	0.20	—	0.20
48. BBJ (Subs. BBUNL)	—	—	—	—	—	—	—	—	—	—	—	—
49. B&R (Subs. BYNL)	6.18	—	6.18	9.78	—	9.78	0.95	—	0.95	3.00	—	3.00
Total	203.63	444.08	647.71	258.66	501.39	760.05	479.11	743.57	1041.68	505.96	778.75	1284.75

41

RAM JANAM BHOOMI-BABRI MASJID CONTROVERSY

41.1 Ordinance on Ayodhya, January 1993

The following is the text of the Ordinance promulgated by the President:

An Ordinance to provide for the acquisition of certain area at Ayodhya and for matters connected therewith and incidental thereto.

Whereas there has been a long-standing dispute relating the the structure (including the premises of the inner and outer courtyards of such structure), commonly known as the Ram Janam Bhoomi-Babri Masjid, situated in village Kot Ramchandra in Ayodhya in Pargana Haveli Avadh, in tehsil Faizabad Sadar, in the district of Faizabad of the State of Uttar Pradesh;

And whereas the said dispute has affected the maintenance of public order and harmony between different communities in the country;

And whereas it is necessary to maintain public order and promote communal harmony and the spirit of common brotherhood amongst the people of India;

And whereas with a view to achieving the aforesaid objectives, it is necessary to acquire certain areas of Ayodhya;

And whereas Parliament is not in session and the President is satisfied that circumstances exist which render it necessary for him to take immediate action;

Now, therefore, in exercise of the powers conferred by Clause (1) of Article 123 of the Constitution, the President is pleased to promulgate the following Ordinance:

CHAPTER I

Preliminary

1. (I) This Ordinance may be called the Acquisition of Certain Area at Ayodhya Ordinance, 1993.
   (II) It shall come into force at once.
2. In this Ordinance, unless the context otherwise requires, —
   (a) "area" means the area (including all the buildings, structures or other properties comprised therein) specified in the Schedule;
   (b) "authorised person" means a person or body of persons or trustees of any trust authorised by the Central Government under Section 7;
   (c) "Claims Commissions"; means the Claims Commissioner appointed under sub-Section (2) of Section 8;
   (d) "prescribed" means prescribed by rules made under this Ordinance.

CHAPTER II

Acquisition of the area in Ayodhya

3. On and from the commencement of this Ordinance, the right, title and interest in relation of the area shall, by virtue of this Ordinance, stand transferred to, and vest in, the Central Government.

4. (I) the area shall be deemed to include all assets, rights, leaseholds, powers, authority and privileges and all property, movable and immovable, including lands, buildings, structures, shops of whatever nature or other properties and all other rights and interests arising out of such properties as were immediately before the commencement of this Ordinance in the ownership, possession, power or control of any person or the State Government of Uttar Pradesh, as the case may be, and all registers, maps, plans, drawings and other documents of whatever nature relating thereto.

(II) All properties aforesaid which have vested in the Central government under Section 3 shall by the force of such vesting be freed and discharged from any trust, obligation, mortgage, charge, lien and all other encumbrances affecting them and any attachment, injunction, decree or order of any Court or Tribunal or other authority restricting the use of such properties in respect of the whole or any part of such properties shall cease to have any effect.

(III) If, on the commencement of this Ordinance, any suit, appeal or other proceeding in respect of the right, title and interest relating to any property which has vested in the Central Government under Section 3 is pending before any Court, Tribunal or other authority, the same shall abate.

5. (I) The Central Government may take all necessary steps to secure possession of the area which is vested in that Government under Section 3. This pertains to the duty of the person or State Government in charge of the management of the area to deliver all assets.

(II) On vesting of the area in the Central Government under Section, the person or State Governments of Uttar Pradesh as the case may be, in charge of the management of the area immediately before such vesting shall be bound to deliver to the Central Government or the authorised person all assets, registers and other documents in their custody relating to such vesting or where it is not practicable to deliver such registers or documents, the copies of such registers or documents, authenticated in the prescribed manner.

6. (I) Notwithstanding any thing contained in sections 3, 4, 5 and 7, the Central Government may, if it is satisfied that, any authority or other body or trustees of any trust, set up on or after the commencement of this Ordinance, is or are willing to comply with such terms and conditions, as that Government may think fit to impose, direct by notification in the Official Gazette, that the right, title and interest or any part thereof, instead of continuing to vest in the Central Government, vest in that authority or body or trust either on the date of the notification or on such later date as may be specified in the notification.

(II) When any right, title and interest in relation to the area or part thereof vest in the authority or body or trust referred to in sub-section (1), such rights of the Central Government in relation to such area or part thereof, shall, on and from the date of such vesting, be deemed to have become the rights of that authority or body or trust.

(III) The provisions of sections 4, 5, 7 and 11 shall, so far as may be, apply in relation to such authority or body or trust as they apply in relation to the Central Government and for this purpose references therein to the "Central Government" shall be construed as references to such authority or body or trust.

CHAPTER III

Management and Administration of Property by Government

7. (I) Notwithstanding anything contained in any contract or instrument or order of any court, tribunal or other authority to the contrary, on and from the commencement of this Ordinance, the property vested in the Central government under Section 3 shall be managed by the Central Government or by a person or a body of persons or trustee or any trust authorised by that Government in this behalf.

(II) In management the property vested in the Central Government under Section 3, the Central Government or the authorised person shall ensure that the position existing before the commencement of this ordinance in the area on which the structure (including the premises of the inner and outer courtyards of such structure), commonly known as Ram Janma Bhoomi-Babri Masjid stood in village Kot Ramchandra in Ayodhya, in Pargana Haveli Avadh, Tehsil Faizabad Sadar in the district of Faizabad of the State of Uttar Pradesh is maintained.

CHAPTER IV

Miscellaneous — Payment of Amount

8. (I) The owner of any land, building, structure or other property comprised in the area shall be given by the Central Government, for the transfer to and vesting the Government under section 3 of that land, building, structure or other property, in case an amount equivalent to the market value of the land, building, structure or other property.

(II) The Central Government shall, for the purpose of deciding the claim of the owner or any person having a claim against the owner under sub-section (1), by notification, appoint a Claims Commissioner.

(III) The Claims Commissioner shall regulate his own procedure for receiving and deciding the claims.

(IV) The owner or any person having a claim against the owner may make a claim to the Claims Commissioner within a period of ninety days from the date of commencement of this Ordinance.

Provided if the Claims Commissioner is satisfied that the claimant was prevented by sufficient cause from preferring the claim within the said period of ninety days, the Claims Commissioner may entertain the claim within a further period of ninety days and not thereafter.

9. The provisions of this Ordinance shall have effect notwithstanding anything inconsistent therewith contained in any other law for time being in force or any instrument having effect by virtue of any law other than this Ordinance or any decree or order of any court, tribunal or other authority.
10. Any person who is in charge of the management of the area and fails to deliver to the Central Government or the authorised person any asset, register or other document in his custody relating to such area or, as the case may be, authenticated copies of such register or document, shall be punishable with imprisonment for a term which may extend to three years or with fine which may extend to ten thousand rupees, or with both.
11. No suit, prosecution or other legal proceeding shall lie against the Central Government or the authorised person for anything which is in good faith done or intended to be done under this Ordinance.
12. (I) The Central Government, may, by notification in the Official Gazette, make rules to carry out the provisions of this Ordinance.
    (II) Every rule made by the Central Government under this Ordinance shall be laid, as soon as may be after it is made, before each House of Parliament, while it is in session, for a total period of thirty days which may be comprised in one session or in two or more successive sessions, and if, before the expiry of the session immediately following the session or the successive sessions aforesaid, both Houses agree in making modification in the rule or both Houses agree that the rule should not be made, the rule shall thereafter have effect only in such modified form or be of no effect, as the case may be; so, however, that any such modification or annulment shall be without prejudice to the validity of anything previously done under that rule.

Source: *Hindustan Times*, January 8, 1993.

41.2 White Paper on Ayodhya, February 24, 1993

On February 24, 1993 the Government of India released a 35-page document which traces the history of the structure in dispute and various attempts made to resolve Mandir-Masjid issue.

The erstwhile BJP Government in Uttar Pradesh has been "condemned" by the Centre for events leading to demolition of Babri Masjid at Ayodhya on Dec. 6, 1992. The White Paper charged that while the criminal activities were going on, the local authorities and the police appeared to be standing as mute as spectators, ostensibly under the instruction of the Chief Minister.

It has laid the blame squarely on the State Government and more so on the Chief Minister Kalyan Singh who had instructed police not to open fire under any circumstances. The White Paper alleges that the entire episode was a dismal picture of inaction and the State Government's dereliction of duty because of the orders of the Chief Minister.

The Paper points out that even the small contingent of Central Reserve Police on duty was rendered inactive and powerless by express directions given to them by the local magistrates and higher State Government authorities. A worse example of irresponsibility and abdication of power by those who had taken oath to defend the Constitution and uphold the rule of the law cannot be imagined, it adds.

The White Paper which gives a chronological account of what happened in Ayodhya on Dec. 6, 1992 leading to demolition and building of another structure on the same site tries to show how the Centre was in constant touch with the State Government and para-military forces deployed in the area, but was unable to do anything because the local officers and the magistrates on duty refused to act in the absence of instructions from the State authorities.

It also points out that the Central Government had maintained constant pressure on the State Government to make use of the Central forces for the protection of the structure but the State Government at no stage explicitly stated that it would not make use of these forces. On more than one occasion during the day the forces were actually requisitioned but there movement was delayed due to non-availability of magistrates.

When eventually a magistrate accompanied the force comprising two companies, he sent the force back after going part of the way only. Thus the State Government kept up a pretence without actually using the Central forces effectively. The White Paper points that in the beginning there were only about 70,000 persons assembled at Ram Katha Kunj and about 500 sadhus, collected there for performing puja. Everything seemed to be going according to the plan announced by the organisers of performing symbolic kar sewa only.

But suddenly about 150 persons broke through the cordon and started pelting stones on the police. Within few minutes just before noon they were joined by 1,000 persons who broke into the protected Ram Janmabhoomi-Babri Masjid structure. The actual damage to the structure started around 12.20 p.m. when the crowd was about 25,000 inside the complex and about 75,000 outside.

The White Paper points out that no action had been taken by the State police to check about 150 kar sevaks who had stormed the disputed complex, even though senior officers were present on the site. This information was received in Delhi and the Home Secretary tried to establish contact with the Government of UP and urged the Director-General of Police to use the Central forces located near Ayodhya.

He also spoke to the other senior officials like Principal Secretary of UP Government asking him to persuade the Chief Minister to requisition Central forces, but the only reply was that they would get back after consulting the Chief Minister.

The Union Home Minister also spoke to the Chief Minister of UP and urged him to protect the structure, but the Chief Minister maintained that he had received conflicting reports and would verify and deal with the matter, but he, however, did not call back the Home Minister as promised. The White Paper also points out that according to the information received two battalions of Rapid Action Force at the Dogra Regimental Centre at Faizabad were ready to move.

The Director General in-charge also informed the Centre that damage to the structure was continuing and no action was being taken by the senior officers of the State Government who were present in the police control room. The Director General Indo-Tibetan Border Police also conveyed to the DIG, CRPF to request the district magistrate, Faizabad, to send magistrates to accompany the troops but go no response. Around 1 p.m. the Home Minister also spoke to the UP Governor seeking early action to protect the mosque.

Around 1.45 p.m. report came in that considerable damage has been caused to the structure. In view of the absence of any action, the Home Minister again spoke to the UP Chief Minister asking him about the action taken for protection of the structure. The UP Government told the Centre that they have instructed that the firing should not be resorted to, but the other kind of force could be used.

In the meantime, the Home Secretary spoke to Defence Secretary to keep the helicopters ready to enable them to move force by air. The anxiety was growing as between 3.30 and 4.30 p.m. communal incidents started occurring in Ayodhya. The DGP, UP, agreed that the situation was fast deteriorating and it cannot be controlled without firing for which the permission of Chief Minister was sought. At this stage the Home Ministry also informed the Chief of Army Staff to provide help wherever necessary in case of communal situation deteriorating in other parts of the country. The officials in the States were also informed about the developing situation.

The Home Minister again spoke to the UP Governor at 5 p.m. but no order was received, to use force nor magistrates were provided to accompany the forces. Meanwhile idols were placed back at the disputed site and the construction of temporary structure had started.

The Union Cabinet which met at 6 p.m. recommended the issue of proclamation under Article 356 of the Constitution to impose President's rule in the State and to dissolve the State Assembly. This proclamation was issued at 9.10 p.m. and immediately two senior officers were posted as advisors to the Governor. They also decided to take action to take over the Ayodhya complex.

In the first instance, the evacuation of kar sewaks had been started and by Dec. 7, 70,000 persons had been evacuated. The Central forces moved in to secure the area with the minimum use of force. This task was accomplished with minimum use of force and without resorting to firing on Dec. 7-8 night.

The White Paper also gives details of the action taken after the imposition of President's rule in UP. It included action against communal organisation including ban, action against those responsible for the demolition and fixing the responsibility of various authorities in the lapses that occurred on Dec. 6.It also gives details which led to action against the BJP Governments in Himachal Pradesh, Madhya Pradesh and Rajasthan. The paper also mentions the decision to hold an inquiry by a sitting judge into the events on Dec. 6 and cases of assault on Press persons and photographers at Ayodhya.

The paper also gives details about how the Centre had relied on the assurances held out by the UP Government and the efforts made to resolve the dispute. It also gives details about the changing stand of the UP Government, particularly, with regard to court cases pending in various courts. It also gives details of the assurances given by the Chief Minister in the National Integration Council and the Supreme Court. The paper concludes with a review of communal situation in the country in the wake of Ayodhya incidents which led to rioting in a large scale in most of the States and the relief provided by the Centre to riot victims.

Source: *Hindustan Times*, February, 25, 1993.

41.3 **Ayodhya Bill, 1993**

On March 24, 1993 the Lok Sabha approved the controversial Bill providing for acquisition of a certain area at Ayodhya including the disputed structure relating to the Ramjanmabhoomi-Babri Masjid after walkouts by the BJP, Janata Dal and Left members.

While the BJP staged a walkout after the leader of Opposition L.K. Advani had expressed his dissatisfaction with the Bill and sought a assurance from the Home Minister that the temple will be built on the disputed structure only was refused by Mr. Chavan. The Home Minister clarified that the issue will be decided in accordance with the advice of the Supreme Court whose opinion had been sought.

The Janata Dal and Left party members walked out later when their amendments which stood in the name of Syed Shahabuddin of Janata Dal were rejected by the House through a voice vote. The amendments sought to exclude the area of disputed structure and also wanted that reference be made to the Supreme Court under Article 138(b) which was not acceptable to the Government. It has sought advisory opinion in terms of Article 143. The Home Minister, however, assured the House that the Government would implement the Supreme Court advice.

The Home Minister in his reply to the discussion requested the members to not attribute motives to the Government and said that they were serious in bringing about communal amity in the country. It may suit some other parties to go in different directions but not us, he added.

He also reiterated charge against the BJP that the Union Government was betrayed on the Ayodhya issue. He asked were they not justified in coming to this conclusion because they could not consider what was stated by the leader of the Opposition in the House or to regard the affidavit filed in the Supreme Court by Chief Minister of UP and the BJP leaders as "frivolous".

He said that even the BJP leaders immediately after the demolition of the mosque admitted that this was not the part of the game. At this stage Ms Uma Bharti of BJP intervened to ask if the Prime Minister also had not gone back on the promises made by him to the leaders of the Vishwa Hindu Parishad and religious saints.

The Minister said that he would not like to comment on the talks between the Prime Minister and other leaders but said that even the leaders of Janata Dal and Left would have objected if the Centre had chosen to intervene after the assurances held out by BJP leaders regarding the protection of the mosque.

He said that they were facing a difficult situation as the State Government was not cooperating and had even denied to provide some basic facilities for the parliamentary forces moved into the area. He justified the acquisition of the land and said that the same had been done after consulting legal experts.

He also justified the reference to the Supreme Court under Article 143 and said that for any reference under Article 138(b) consent of the State Government was necessary, which the BJP Government had refused. They did not want to subsequently take the advantage of the fact that Uttar Pradesh had been placed under President's Rule by getting the consent of the Governor. More so, it was felt that reference under Article 138 will lead to delays.

He ridiculed the claims made by the BJP about the Congress trying to take advantage by announcing the construction of a temple at Ayodhya while the

BJP had done all the initial work. He said that he knew that the BJP wanted to exploit it fully for the elections and were not interested in construction of the temple. In case they are serious they would contribute the money collected for the temple purposes to the Government funds. He accused the BJP of raising non-issues and said that they were destroying the country in the name of temple and mosque.

The leader of Opposition L.K. Advani who spoke after the Home Minister said that the biggest problem with the Government is that it cannot take a strong stand on the Ayodhya issue. It decides it on the basis of political convenience. The issue is not of building temple or mosque, but of where the temple will be built. He said that they would not be satisfied unless it was built at the original site. He said that immediately after the destruction of the mosque, the Government had announced that it would rebuild the mosque, but has been trying to get of the commitment subsequently. After this, the BJP members walked out of the House as a protest.

The Janata Dal and Left members staged a walk out later when their amendments were rejected, by the House. Janata Dal member Syed Shahabuddin criticised the Government in the Lok Sabha for seeking to acquire certain area at Ayodhya saying that the measure was a "grand design" to facilitate the construction of a Ram temple at the site of the demolished disputed structure.

Participating in the discussion on the acquisition of certain area at Ayodhya Bill, he said the measure was an "act of deception" and "an act of hostility" against the Muslim community in the country.

Opposing the Bill, he said the motive of the Government behind bringing it was that it did not want to give credit for the construction of Ram temple to the BJP leaders. While Mr. Sudhir Roy (CPI-M) wanted the reference to be made to the Supreme Court under Article 138(2) of the Constitution, Mr. Kartikeshwar Patra (Cong) alleged that the sangh parivar wanted to grab power through the mandir issue.

Mr. Sudhir Roy (CPM) wanted a reference to be made to the Supreme Court on the issue under Article 138(2) instead of 143. Dr. Kartikeshwar Patra (Cong.) accused political parties of indulging in power games.

Intervening in the debate, Minister of State for Parliamentary Affairs P. R. Kumaramangalam lashed out at the BJP, the Vishwa Hindu Parishad and their allied organisations for the demolition of the disputed structure at Ayodhya. The VHP unilaterally announced on Dec. 6, 1992, as the date for the Kar Seva when the talks between its representatives and the All India Babri Masjid Action Committee were progressing for a solution, he said.

The Government had also made every effort to find an amicable solution to the dispute and it was committed to maintain communal harmony in the multi-religious and multi-lingual country, he said.

Mr. Kumaramangalam, who had mediated in the talks between the VHP and the AIBMAC said the Government had referred the issue to the Supreme Court under Article 143 for the immediate disposal of the case.

Mr. S.C. Dixit (BJP) said the construction of a temple and a mosque side by side at the site of the demolished disputed structure would turn out to be a "a bone of contention".

This, he said, would not promote communal harmony but generate hatred between the two communities. Referring to the repeated assertion of the Government that it would like to reach a negotiated settlement on the issue, Mr

Dixit said his party was not responsible for the break in the negotiations.

"We are even now ready for negotiations", the BJP member said.

Mr. Vishwanath Shastri, CPI, held both the Congress and the BJP responsible for the developments in Ayodhya and said it was under the Congress rule in Uttar Pradesh when the doors of the disputed structure were unlocked and demolished when the BJP was in power.

He said there was some secret understanding between the Congress and the BJP. The present Bill was no solution to the main problem and was brought forward with the vote banks as the major consideration, he said.

Questioning the real intention of the Government behind the Bill, Mr. Satyapal Singh Yadav, JD-A, said the provisions would not help maintain communal harmony.

He was also of the opinion that the real intention behind the provision was to keep the vote banks intact.

Source: *Hindustan Times*, March 25, 1993.

42

RURAL DEVELOPMENT

42.1 Highlights of Rural Development

The major objective of rural development has been the alleviation of poverty in the rural areas. With 77 per cent of the population in India living in rural areas and a large majority of them living below power line, this is a necessary and logical direction in the course of rural development.

The vast human resource that constitutes the rural poor is in fact an asset, but has been a cause of concern owing to low productivity and poverty. The programmes in rural, development thus aim at improving productivity by improving the rural infrastructure in terms of roads, irrigation, drinking water, housing and access to skill development, credit and markets which, in turn, should increase incomes.

The experience gained in implementing a variety of Community Development Programmes in the first three Five Year Plans and specific employment oriented programmes in the Fourth, Fifth, Sixth and Seventh Plans have lent great strength to the national capabilities. Detailed analysis of the strength and weaknesses of these programmes, and evaluation of their performance has helped the determination of the new courses in which they need to be directed.

The new directions have been incorporated in the implementation of the Jawahar Rozgar Yojana (JRY) which requires a wage component of 60 per cent; preference for employment to SC/ST and 30 per cent for women. In order to improve the quality of life of the most deprived, 6 per cent of JRY funds are earmarked for the Indira Awas Yojana (IAY) which is for provision of housing for SC/ST and freed bonded labour. Rural housing is being given special emphasis and in the Eighth Plan there would be more investment for upgrading existing dwelling units and assistance for new units. 20 per cent of the JRY funds are earmarked for the Million Wells Schemes which is to benefit small and marginal farmers amongst the SC/ST and freed bonded labour, creating productive assets and leading to sustained employment.

In the context of the on-going economic reforms, JRY has an added significance. It is recognized as an ideal fast disbursing programme to help the poor to overcome the transitional social costs of the adjustment process.

The other instrument for income generation has been the Integrated Rural Development Programme (IRDP) for generating self-employment. The quality of implementation of the programme has significantly improved, ensuring sustained incomes for the beneficiaries by assisting them with a second dose of assistance, should that intervention be necessary in selected cases. In order to ensure assistance to the poorest, 50 per cent of the beneficiaries are to be from SC/ST and 40 per cent have to be women, 3 per cent have been reserved for the disabled. The subsidy element has also been made uniform for SC/ST beneficiaries and physically handicapped at 50 per cent.

With the Eighth Plan emphasis on generation of opportunities through rural Industrialization, the upgradation of skills and technology is highly essential. The role of Training of Rural Youth for Self Employment (TRYSEM) which is a component of IRDP, and its training contents are being re-oriented. In the overall effort of poverty alleviation, TRYSEM functions as a facilitating component of IRDP. The target of beneficiaries has been raised to over 4 lakh during the year.

The programme of Development of Women & Children in Rural Areas (DWCRA), a component of IRDP, aims at special facilities for the rural women. The basic objective of DWCRA is to improve their socio-economic status through creation of opportunities in income generation activities on a self sustained basis. Group formation is the strategy adopted under the scheme. The scheme has been implemented selectively in 240 districts. In order that all districts may be covered under DWCRA during the Eighth Plan, it is proposed to add 50 additional districts every year during the Plan period. It is now proposed to encourage the promotion of thrift and credit groups by women with matching contribution from Government of India, from the budget provision under DWCRA. The programme will also arm women against gender and other socio-economic discrimination, through a conscientisation process.

The subject of Rural Water Supply and Rural Sanitation was transferred from the Ministry of Urban Development in August 1985 to the Ministry of Rural Development to accelerate the progress of rural drinking water projects and their integration with other rural development programmes. The National Drinking Water Mission was launched in 1986. Provision of safe drinking water in rural areas and maintenance of hygienic standards of sanitation are the important objectives of the Accelerated Rural Water Supply Programme (ARWSP) and also the Central Rural Sanitation Programme (CRSP).

With about 11 per cent of the total population remaining to be covered and more than 35 per cent of the Scheduled Castes and 25 per cent of Scheduled Tribes population, living mostly in difficult and inaccessible areas, yet to be adequately covered, the strategy and approach to be adopted in the Eighth Plan is being oriented towards reaching this population at the earliest. Sizeable Plan outlay will be earmarked for Operation and Maintenance also and for replacing the defunct installations and rejuvenating old installations which can still be repaired. An appropriate strategy for upkeep of the assets created so far will also be adopted. A detailed survey of all habitations has also been undertaken to identify specific issues and find appropriate solutions to them.

It is well recognized that restructuring of agrarian relationship is an important pre-condition for rural transformation. The achievements in this regard, however, have not been satisfactory. Various possibilities of restructuring the laws and ensuring effective implementation are under consideration. In order to modernize the land records system, the computerization of land records and a scheme for strengthening revenue administration and updating of land records, have been undertaken.

The Desert Development Programme (DDP) aims at controlling the process of desertification, restoration of ecological balance and improvement of economic conditions of people through raising and stabilising the productivity of land, water, livestock and human resources in these areas. Likewise, the Drought Prone Area Programme (DPAP) provides for integrated area development on watershed basis and optimum utilization of land, water, livestock and human resources and for restoration of ecological balance to mitigate the effects of drought.

The programmes under agricultural marketing have underscored the importance of market research, market survey and market development. State master plans and Tribal master plans have been prepared to arrive at a scientific approach to agricultural marketing. Training in agricultural marketing, seminars and workshops have been held by the Directorate of Marketing and Inspection (DMI) and the Centre for Agricultural Marketing (CAM). Quality Control of agricultural commodities and quality assurances for the consumers have been intensified by enlarging the coverage of quality marking.

The upgradation of the delivery system for rural development has received special attention through the strengthening of the trained institutions at the national, state and regional levels in terms of infrastructure as well as training content.

The process of decentralized administration continued to receive attention. The Constitution (Seventy Second Amendment) Bill for strengthening the Panchayati Raj Institutions has been introduced and referred to a Joint Committee of Parliament.

TABLE 42.1: Schemes of the Ministry of Rural Development and Financial Outlays

(Rs. in Crores)

Sl. No.	Name of the Plan Scheme	Approved outlay 1990-91	1991-92	1992-93
(1)	(2)	(3)	(4)	(5)
1.	Rural Water Supply Programme	423.00	758.00	460.00
2.	Rural Sanitation	20.00	37.59	20.00
3.	I.R.D.P.	390.00	390.40	390.20
4.	T.R.Y.S.E.M.	8.00	8.00	8.00
5.	Drought Prone Area Prog.	51.26	56.00	51.26
6.	Desert Development Prog.	50.00	55.00	50.00
7.	Jawahar Rozgar Yojana	2100.00	2100.00	2046.00
8.	Land Reforms	25.33	34.61	25.02
9.	D.W.R.C.A.	11.48	13.00	13.00
10.	Grants to N.I.R.D.	2.20	3.60	2.00
11.	Assistance to CAPART	5.50	6.00	5.00
12.	Organisation of Trg. Courses, Seminars & Workshops	0.35	0.50	0.25
13.	Strengthening of Extension Training Centres	3.00	3.50	1.00
14.	Strengthening of State Training Centres	5.00	6.00	1.50
15.	Communication Cell	0.25	0.30	0.25
16.	Promotion of Voluntary Scheme	2.00	5.00	5.00
17.	Organisation of Beneficiaries	4.00	4.00	1.00
18.	Panchayat Development & Training	2.00	2.00	1.00
19.	Rural Godowns	4.00	5.00	0.01
20.	Agricultural Marketing			
	(a) Rural marketing	5.00	6.00	0.01
	(b) Centre for Agricultural Marketing	0.30	1.00	4.00
	(c) Estt. Expdr. D.M.I.	1.70	2.00	3.00
21.	Building for AARRO	0.30	0.50	0.50
22.	Roads in Special Problem Areas	14.40	10.00	2.00
23	Rural Housing (New)	14.40	10.00	2.00
	Total	3129.08	3508.00	3100.00

TABLE 42.2: Minimum Wages/Manday

1.	Andhra Pradesh	17.00
		(Zone-1 = 15.00, Zone-2 = 16.80, Zone-3 = 19.25)
2.	Arunachal Pradesh	16.00
		(Area-1, 15.00, Area-2, 16.00, Area-3, 18.00)
3.	Assam	25.00
4.	Bihar	24.00
5.	Goa	25.00
6.	Gujarat	15.00
		(PWD-20.00)
7.	Haryana	33.45
		(including Rs. 2.70 adjusted due to rise in price)
8.	Himachal Pradesh	22.32
		(Tribal area 27.50 Non-Tribal area 22.00)
9.	Jammu & Kashmir	15.00
10.	Karnataka	16.00
11.	Kerala	23.00
12.	Madhya Pradesh	20.27
13.	Maharashtra	14.25
		(Zone-1 = 20.00, Zone-2 = 16.00, Zone-3 = 14.00, Zone-4 = 12.00)
14.	Manipur	25.20
15.	Meghalaya	25.00
16.	Mizoram	28.00
17.	Nagaland	15.00
18.	Orissa	25.00
19.	Punjab	37.00
		(unskilled workers 36.00 other agri. lab. 38.00)
20.	Rajasthan	22.00
21.	Sikkim	17.00
22.	Tamil Nadu	15.00
		(14.00-16.00)
23.	Tripura	16.00
24.	Uttar Pradesh	18.53
		(Eastern part 18.00, Western part 20.00)
25.	West Bengal	22.88
26.	A&N Islands	20.50
		(Andaman 20.00, Nicobar 21.00)
27.	Chandigarh	33.30
28.	D&N Haveli	14.00
29.	Daman & Diu	18.00
30.	Delhi	28.85
31.	Lakshadweep	18.00
32.	Pondicherry	27.00
	All India	

Source: *Annual Report 1991-92*, Ministry of Rural Development, New Delhi.

43

SCAM

43.1 Text of Prime Minister's Statement

The events that have unfolded in the last few months in the financial sector of the country have caused grave anxiety to me and the country at large.

The ramifications of this matter have to be thoroughly probed and effective measures taken so hat the basic integrity of the financial institutions of the country is not jeopardised and the new economic initiatives taken by the Government to strengthen and accelerate the economic growth are in no way inhibited.

"My Government has been taking concrete and effective steps at every stage in the last few months as required in the circumstances. The inquiry by the CBI and action by the Special Court will be pursued and whatever is required to be done as a consequence thereof, shall be done.

"While this aspect is being fully attended to, I feel that there is need for a comprehensive inquiry through the instrument of Parliament which not only fully establishes parliamentary supremacy but also provide an effective safeguard to protect the country's interests.

"We have had consultations with all political parties in Parliament and there is consensus on the desirability of setting up a Joint Parliamentary Committee in this regard.

"I am, therefore, requesting the Hon'ble Speaker to proceed with the formation of a Joint Parliamentary Committee and entrust it with the task I have mentioned which may be completed within a reasonable time.

"I would like to assure this august House that my desire and purpose remain, as they have been so far to unravel the truth, and ensure the smooth transformation to a vibrant economy in the larger interests of the nation".

Source: *Hindustan Times*, July 10, 1992.

43.2 SCAM Chronology

Feb. 29, 1992 : The income-tax department raids Harshad Mehta's offices and seizes incriminating documents involving banking receipts and funds from abroad.

Feb. 29: Finance Minister Dr Manmohan Singh presents his second budget. The stock markets turn bullish.

April 2: The BSE index touches 4378 from the level of 1209 on April 2, 1991. The share market fever grips the middle class and poorer section. Lakhs join the fray for the first time.

April, second half: Harshad Mehta's dealings with the SBI come out. The irregularity is estimated at Rs. 622 crore. The reconciliation of BRs starts and many more defaults come to light.

April 30: Dr Manmohan Singh announces in Parliament that the RBI committee will probe the securities scam. Mr. R. Janakiraman, Deputy Governor, to head the body.

May 11: Dr Manmohan Singh announces the setting up of another enquiry committee headed by CBI Joint Director K. Madhavan.

May 14: The CBI issues orders to seize Harshad Mehta's and his associates properties bank accounts are frozen and so are all deals transacted by Mehta in stock markets.

May 15: The Governing Board of Bombay Stock Exchange suspends the membership of Mehta, his wife Jyoti and brother Ashwin.

May 20: Harshad meets CBI team and extends his cooperation to its investigations but claims that banks won't suffer. The RBI's two-day meeting with the banks on reconciliation of BRs ended with nine banks reporting wide-spread irregularities in securities transactions.

May 26: The Bombay Court accepts an agreement reached between BSE, Harshad and CBI to release funds totalling Rs. 12 crore for settlement in BSE.

May 27: Bank of Karad to be liquidated. Metropolitan Cooperative Bank Board replaced.

June 2: First interim report to the Janakriaman Committee submitted. Rs. 3,079 crore involved in scam, Banker-Broker collusion revealed.

June 3: Harshad Mehta among eight held after CBI raids.

June 6: Ordinance promulgated for attaching properties: special court to try scam cases.

June 7: Bank scam guilty won't be spared: says PM in an interview to HT Editor H.K. Dua.

June 14: UCO Bank chief admits fraud.

June 29: Executive vice president of Canfina, Canara Bank subsidiary Ashok Kumar arrested by CBI in Bombay.

June 30: Any minister involved in scam won't be spared says PM at his first press conference in Delhi.

July 6: Second interim report of Janakriaman committee released. gross irregularities by four foreign banks and Fairgrowth Financial Services Ltd. revealed.

July 8: Bureau on frauds to deal with scam, says finance minister Dr. Manmohan Singh in Lok Sabha.

July 9: PM orders joint parliamentary committee to probe scam, commerce minister P. Chidambaram's resignation accepted by PM.

July 14: RBI governor not involved in scam, says Dr Manmohan Singh in Rajya Sabha.

July 21: Planning commission member V. Krishnamurthi resigns for his Fairgrowth connections.

July 30: Mr K. Madhavan, joint director of CBI probing the scam seeks premature retirement-confirms official sources.

August 7: 30-member joint parliamentary committee set up to inquire into the scam.

August 8: CBI files a case of corruption against V. Krishnamurthi, Harshad Mehta and M/S K.J. Investment (P) Ltd. V. Krishnamurthi and son arrested.

Source: *Hindustan Times*, August 9, 1992.

43.3 Jankiraman Committee's Fourth Report, March 1993

The fourth report of the Janakiraman Committee set-up to enquire into the securities transactions of banks and financial institutions has revised its estimates and pegged the "problem exposure" at Rs. 4024.45 crore from the earlier Rs. 3192.79 crore. The report which was released on March 6, 1993, has dealt extensively on broker-bank nexus as also new violations unearthed by the panel.

The panel has, in its foreword, however observed that the new figure of "problem exposure" does not include depreciation in the values of assets held by banks and financial institutions. While the panel has not arrived at any figure on the depreciation factor, market observers aver that the depreciation in the value of assets in current market conditions — where there are no quotations and no sales in several or most securities — could range from between 15 to 20 per cent.

Continuing on the saga of broker-bank nexus and large-scale violations of both RBI and prudential norms, the panel has:

* unearthed questionable transactions in the books of the hitherto untouched ANZ Grindlays Bank;
* exposed the nexus between Andhra Bank Financial Services and Fairgrowth Financial Services Ltd. as also broker Hiten P. Dalal;
* questioned the figures that Standard Chartered Bank has claimed as its losses;
* severely indicated the methods and the manner in which Canara Bank subsidiary, Canfina has conducted its business — both in securities and equity;
* bust open the nefarious deals that Vijaya Bank has put through ostensibly on behalf of its portfolio clients and questioned the placing of funds by the bank with Kotak Mahindra;
* and lastly made scathing observations on the functioning of the treasury operations of State Bank of Patiala.

The Committee has made a shocking discovery that ANZ Grindlays Bank was involved in "badla" financing which is expressly prohibited by the Reserve Bank of India guidelines. On November 14, 1991, Essanda Finanz and Leasing Ltd. (ESANDA), an associate of the bank, is reported to have pledged Rs. 2 crore with the bank for being deployed "on their behalf prudently that is, some form of secured investment without price risks."

This amount, the panel reveals, was passed on to N.K. Aggarwala through a ready forward (RF) transaction involving eight scrips. The initial RF covering two scrips for a period of 12 days, was rolled over for subsequent settlement days and also by exchanging one set of scrips for another. The rates quoted for the ready forward transactions for the equity had no relevance to the prevailing market rates of the respected scrips. The rates appear to have been fixed with the agreed rate of return of about 32 per cent to 34 per cent.

The bank received back Rs. 2,27,26,700 on April 7, 1992 which included a net return of Rs. 27,19,321. In fact the bank had to return the funds deployed by Esanda on March 27, 1992 that is, prior to the due date at the latter's request "thereby taking the remaining 11 days of RF through PMS books." In other words ANZ has apparently undertaken "badla" financing for broker N.K. Aggarwala camouflaging it in RF transactions to give it an air of legitimacy.

Further, it has observed that the bank's securities transactions were often conditioned by the special relationship it shared with brokers, Hiten P. Dalal and Harshad S. Mehta. This relationship enabled HSM to "route his securities transactions through Grindlays", to ask Grindlays to undertake "put through transactions" for his benefit and to enjoy unauthorised overdraft facilities.

Grindlays has entered into a number of transactions in PSU bonds ostensibly with NHB through several brokers but there are no corresponding entries for these transactions in NHB's books. Grindlays has also entered into several purchase and sales transactions with Esanda on a buy-back basis in contravention of RBI guidelines. These transactions, the panel reports, appear to be in the form of book entries with no physicals being exchanged.

The most scathing indictment made by the fourth report of the Janakiraman Committee deals with the portfolio operations of the ANZ. It states, "Grindlays has violated or circumvented most of the RBI guidelines on the operations of PMS."

The panel has reserved its most severe indictment of any financial outfit for Andhra Bank Financial Services Limited (ABFSL). According to its findings, ABFSL has clearly acted as a conduit for the transfer of large sums mainly from public sector enterprises to the stock market by diverting these funds mainly to Fairgrowth Financial Services Limited (FGFSL)/(who in turn presumably deployed the funds with brokers) and to Hiten P. Dalal.

This diversion was done on a pre-determined basis as proved by FFSL's letter to Andhra Bank dated, February 4, 1991, and contrary to the purpose for which the bank was given permission by RBI to float a subsidiary. The report states, "This de-basement of the true role of ABFSL appears to have been done with the full knowledge of and under the direction of Bank's top management."

The report has backed its criticism of ABFSL with full details of transactions, correspondence between brokers, bankers and financial companies and documents thereof, to drive its point home on the can of worms that ABSFL has been discovered to be.

As regards the sordid saga of Standard Chartered Bank, the panel has not minced words. It states that, "Stanchart has been carrying out its securities transactions in total contravention of RBI guidelines and violations of norms and prudent banking."

The large volume of its transactions have been with or through broker Hiten P. Dalal. Interestingly, these transactions were mostly entered to obtain a guaranteed rate of return on its investments. In fact, the bank had appeared to have nominated Hiten Dalal as its treasury chief and allowed him to operate and direct the bank's operations. In fact, it has used its own funds to carry the broker's position in forward contracts. And startlingly enough, the panel observes: "There is sufficient evidence to show that the senior management was in fact aware of this situation". Indeed, the committee states that there was a close nexus between Stanchart's dealers and Hiten Dalal.

The dealers had "totally surrendered their independence" and looked upon Hiten Dalal to bail them out for huge losses which they incurred in their dealings in t he Bank's own account. As a consequence of this loss of independence the safeguards customarily used in securities transactions were abandoned. Payments were made in advance of receipt of securities and SGL transfer forms or

BRs. Discharged receipts were returned without receipt of securities and delivery was accepted for securities other than those contracted for and of BRs issued in favour of other banks.

Inevitably, this led to an ever-expanding "hole" in Stanchart's investment portfolio. To cover this hole the dealers entered into wholly fictitious transactions mainly involving Bank of Karad, and the Metropolitan Co-operative Bank. These transactions were not backed by securities or backed by BRs of doubtful value.

Stancharts investment and account records have been manipulated to camaflouge the real arrangement with H.P. Dalal and later to record the fictitious transactions undertaken to cover the "hole" in its investment portfolio. This explains the dummy transactions, transactions recorded at rates different from the rates at which the transactions have actually taken place and most significantly, those recorded to hold back or book profits, which have later been reversed.

Stanchart has also collected huge amounts under the Corporate Cash Deposits Scheme (CCDS) in total violation of RBI guidelines. The scheme appears to have been devised to get around RBI regulations, both on interest rates on deposits and on PMs.

The panel has also been very critical of Canara Bank's subsidiary, Canfina. Like other subsidiaries of banks, Canfina was required to confine itself to the business of merchant banking, leasing, hire purchase and portfolio management and not to do normal banking business. However, it transpires, Canfina obtained substantial sums of money under PMs and its specialised "Corporate Investment Advisory Services" (CIAS) and transferred these funds to brokers under RF deals. Indeed in many cases there is no evidence to show that there were underlying securities for these transactions.

In fact, Canfina on a number of occasions short-sold securities (sold securities that they did not possess) and thus raised money on a clean basis. Canfina also did not deal with Canara Bank or Can Bank Mutual Fund at "arm's length". Large sums collected under PMS and CIAS scheme were placed on deposits with Canara Bank and incredibly funds collected were also used to boost collections for schemes floated by CanMutual, Canfina also routed loans to brokers through CanMutual.

Significantly, for the first time, the RBI has admitted (through the panel's report) the magnitude of the problem at Canfina. Report states, "the manner in which securities transactions of Canfina have been undertaken has not only been in violation of RBI guidelines but also exposed it to an aggregate net exposure which is far in excess of its capital and reserves and has left it in a position where its assets will probably be inadequate to meets liabilities.

The panel has come down heavily on Vijaya Bank, particularly for its violations of RBI guidelines and the manner in which it operated its portfolio schemes. It observes that the bank did not conduct PMS in a nature of investment management for a fee at the customer's risk; but conducted it with an assured, predetermined rate of the client.

Although the bank was maintaining a client-wise record of PMS funds accepted and invested, particulars of credit and debit relating to the account were not reflected in the client's account and periodical statements were not furnished to the clients. Further, transactions between the bank's investment account and PMS clients' account were not put through at market rates.

The panel has also observed that most of the PMS transactions were through the Kotak group and the exposure was to the tune of 66 per cent of the total PMS funds. Scrutiny of the bank's books and those of Kotak Mahendra Finance Limited reveal that funds accepted under PMS were diverted into badla financing.

In its observations on the State Bank of Patiala, the panel has criticised the functioning of the bank's treasury operations. According to the report, the manner in which deals were conducted exposed the bank to a high risk. This was true particularly with regard to deals concerning National Housing Bank, ANZ Grindlays and big bull Harshad Mehta.

Source: *Indian Express*, March 7, 1993.

44

SPACE, SCIENCE AND TECHNOLOGY

44.1 SPACE

Primary Objective of Indian Space Programme

In a short span of about four decades, the exploration and uses of outer space have made a deep impact on the technological progress in many countries. This new frontier of human enterprise has not only witnessed spectacular achievements beyond the boundaries of our planet but also demonstrated its relevance for accelerating the process of cultural and socio-economic development.

In India, the space programme was formally organised in 1972 with the setting up of Space Commission and the Department of Space. The primary objective of the Indian space programme is to provide space-based services in the areas of communication, meteorology and resources survey and management and, as integral to it, develop satellites, launch vehicles and associated ground systems. The past two decades have already seen the Indian space programme making a remarkable progress through a well integrated, self-reliant programme. Space communications has not only enhanced the communication capabilities in the country but also it is now being widely deployed for providing advanced disaster warning, search and rescue measures and distance education to remote areas. Likewise, space remote sensing is providing vital inputs on agriculture, soil, forestry, land and water resources, environment, minerals, ocean development and in the management of drought and flood disasters, thus touching every facet of national development. Integrated sustainable development at microlevel for substantially improving agricultural productivity without causing any environmental degradation has now become possible with inputs from space.

Highlights

A significant event was the launch of the second state-of-the-art Indian Remote Sensing Satellite, IRS-1B, on August 29, 1991 and its successful commissioning on September 16, 1991 after a series of intricate postlaunch operations. The success of IRS-1B is an unequivocal demonstration of not only the maturity India has achieved in satellite technology, but also the commitment of the space programme to provide remote sensing services on a continuous and assured basis. The first satellite in the IRS series, IRS-1A, launched in March 1988 has successfully completed the design life of three years and it still continues to provide operational services to the users. IRS-1A and IRS-1B together provide a repetivity of 11 days thus covering the country more frequently, enhancing the scope for monitoring dynamic features associated with natural resources and environment.

The development of second generation, highly advanced IRS satellites, namely IRS satellites, namely, IRS-1C and IRS-1D, with much better spectral and spatial resolutions, more frequent re-visits, stereo viewing and on-board recording capabilities, has made further progress. IRS-1C and IRS-1C are planned to be launched during 1993-94 and 1996-97 respectively.

The Indian National Satellite (INSAT) system, established in 1983 with the successful commissioning of INSAT-1D, continues to provide vital operational services to the nation. There are 126 telecommunication terminals now operating in the INSAT Network providing about 4,500 two-way speech circuits over 140 routes.

INSAT-2A, the first satellite in the indigenously built second generation INSAT-2 series to replace the first generation satellites procured from abroad, is now ready for transportation to French Guyana for its launch on board the European launch vehicle, Ariane. INSAT-2 series of satellites are more advanced and have one a half times the capacity of INSAT-1 satellites. They are expected to lead to a substantial enhancement in the space segment capacity and consequently for communication, TV broadcasting, meteorology and other new areas.

Innovative uses of INSAT system have already extended to the establishment of rural telegraphy in the north-eastern part of the country and National Informatics Centres to provide nationwide data communication links between district and state capitals. Library networking on a large scale has been initiated.

The meteorological date gathering with VHRR instrument on board INSAT and its dissemination, along with the collection of remote area meteorological data from unattended platforms, has made a quantum difference in weather forecasting in the country. Satellite-based locale specific disaster warning receivers installed in the cyclone-prone eastern coast, has been able to facilitate dramatic saving of human lives and livestock during flood and cyclones.

The most spectacular impact of INSAT has been in the rapid expansion of Television (TV) which 520 TV transmitters and direct reception sets, now provides access to over 75 per cent of India's population. Rapid increase in the regional services, use of transportable earth stations and satellite news regional services, use of transportable earth stations and satellite news gathering vehicles, utilisation of satellite media for university education and nationwide radio networking has enabled even remote areas to become part of the main stream of the nation.

Special inexpensive hardware have been developed to promote and effective interactive educational system through satellites. The system has been successfully experimented in Gujarat where Village sarpanchs, preraks and voluntary teachers in Rupal, a remote village of Gandhinagar district, were able to interactively communicate with teachers located at the Space Applications Centre and Gujarat Vidyapeeth at Ahmedabad. The successful conduct of ISRO-UGC experiment enabling students in a number of Universities to interact, in real-time, with the experts through specially developed talk-back facility has again demonstrated the efficacy of the system. The continuing education experiment for industrial workers conducted from Bangalore in February 1992 is another example of satellite capability demonstration.

Considering that eradication of illiteracy in the rural areas is of utmost importance for the nation to achieve all-round development though ushering a new green revolution and assimilation of scientific ideas and attitudes into the cultural fabric of the Indian society, evolution of a new concept of dedicated GRAMSAT satellites, specially tailored to meet the basic requirements of rural areas, has emerged. The GRAMSET will also help in providing continuing education for special groups to ensure that their technical skills are periodically updated to overcome technological obsolescence. The design of GRAMSET incorporating six to eight high power C-band transponders has been already taken up.

Remote sensing applications in the country under the umbrella of the National Natural Resources Management System (NNRMS) for which the Department of Space is the nodal agency, now cover diverse fields such as crop acreage and yield estimation, drought warning and assessment, flood control and damage assessment, landuse/land cover information, water resources management, underground water exploration, prediction of snow-melt run-off, management of watersheds and command areas, fisheries development, urban development, mineral prospecting, forest resources survey, etc. Active involvement of the user Ministries/Departments has ensured the effective harnessing of this powerful technology.

Integrated sustainable development programme, which involves an understanding of the mutual interdependencies of various resources, integration of land and water resources, characterisation of coherent zones of agricultural identities and identification of the constraints/ecological problems at the microlevel, through use of satellite and other conventional data for evolving effective locale specific prescriptions has been taken up in the country. The strategy will provide solutions for optimal exploitation of resources with proper enriching mechanisms wile taking the needs of various sectors of economy into consideration. A pilot project to implement the programme has been initiated covering 18 districts, representing diverse terrains, agroclimatic zones and social practices for which site-specific solutions are being evolved according to the land capability assessment made through integrated resource surveys.

In the area of launch vehicle technology development, from a modest launch capability of SLV-3, the nation is on the threshold of realising large, cost effective operational launch vehicles required for IRS and INSAT classes of satellites. The third development flight of Augmented Satellite Launch Vehicle, PSLV, capable of launching 1,000 kg class of satellites into a polar sun-synchronous orbit has reached and advanced stage. The first development launch of PSLV, carrying irs-1c on board, is scheduled by the end of 1992. the development of Geosynchating Satellite Launch Vehicle, GSLV, incorporating cryo engine technology, capable of placing 2,500 kg INSAT class of satellites in geosynchronous transfer orbit, is making rapid progress and its first launch is expected by 1995-96

The Indian industry continues to be a major partner in the space programme. ISRO has also made a beginning in the export of highly sophisticated space products. Interaction with the academic institutions in the country has also continued through the Sponsored Research Programme.

Indian space programme continues to have cooperation with different countries.India and China have signed a Memorandum of Understanding for cooperation and space applications. India hosted for the benefit of developing in April/May, 1991.

A programme on Geosphere-Biosphere research comprising carefully planned balloon, rocket and satellite-based experiments to study the effects of anthropogenic activities on the earth environment has also continued. The programme will be one of the many initiatives taken in the light of the year 1992 being designated as International Space Year by the United Nations.

The successful launch of IRS-1B during the year and the realisation of the complex INSAT-2A flight model testifies to India's capability in building state-of-the-art operational remote sensing and communication satellites. Withe the planned launches of ASLV and PSLV during 1992-93 and the initiation of GSLV project, India is on the threshold of achieving self-reliance in the launch vehicle technology as well. Emerging from the dire needs for sustainable development and rural the education, innovative applications of space technology through satellites such as GRAMSAT have been evolved which will place the country in a unique position to have achieved excellence in adopting the frontier space technology for rapid development of the society. The space programme is now set to meet not only the growing demands of the country for space-based services but also to exploit the potential of the competitive international market for advanced space products and services.

Space-Industry Partnership

The Indian space programme has a close interaction with Indian industries. As a policy, DOS has been imparting an impetus to forge the symbiotic relationship with the industry for mutual benefit and growth. The space-industry partnership involves transfer of programme to industry on the one hand and utilisation of industry's technological potential and expertise for the space programme on the other. The objectives of technology transfer programme caters:

* the requirement of space programme through buy-back of products manufactured by industry as a result of technology transfer
* the market generated by the space programme such as satellite communication, TV and radio broadcasting, meteorological observations and management
* market generated by spin-off applications of the space programme..

Technology Transfer

Technology for 12 new products/processes have been transferred during the year. They include air-slide, audio video combiner and separator, three extended C-band earth station equipment, two subsystems for satellite-based rural telegraphy network, composite CxC feed, oven controlled crystal oscillator, ADPCM transputer TR-version of FEAST software with pre- and post-processor packages.

Additional licences have been given for seven technologies to industries to meet the growing market demand. About 100 products and application software packages are currently in advanced stages of development has been initiated. Some of them include specialised gold plating on aluminium alloys, black plating on stainless steel, anodising on titanium alloys, (CCD)Charge coupled Disk?? camera (Mark-II), Standard-C ship terminal, multi-lingual electronic subititler, epoxy encapsulant, CAPFLOINK and texturemeter. The involvement of industry during the development stage of a product/process has helped in early productionisation and availability of the products in the market.

There has been a large demand for additional licensing of many technologies developed by DOS. The technology transfer process is in advanced stage for a number of items including technology for PC version of FEAST software with the pre- and post-processor packages, 402.7MHz planar antenna, extended C-band high power amplifier, precision pressure transducers, etc. As application specific system for medical imaging has been developed and installed at Gujarat Cancer Research Institute, Ahmedabad, where it is extensively used for generating large X-ray data and analysis.

Market Survey and System Studies

Preliminary market survey and feasibility reports for a number of items for which technologies have been developed by DOS have been undertaken during the year.The market demand assessment for telemetry system in oil sector and anaerobic adhesive systems has been made. Market survey of integral black anodising on magnesium alloys and electroless nickel and gold plating on titanium alloy technologies has been carried out. A study of the INSAT Disaster Warning system and Satellite Paging System has been made.

Patents, Copyrights, Trademarks and Designs

During the year, patent applications were for dichroic coating process, multiband compact feed system, integral black anodising on magnesium alloy, gold plating on titanium alloy, electroless nickel and gold plating on magnesium alloys.

Patents have been obtained for improvements in or relating to titanium lead dioxide anode, vacuum/electrolytic and vacuum coating of silver on glass, etc. Trademark has been received for a pultrusion machine (Spacetruder). Copyrights for SACIMAGE software library and software package and Optosoft for design of optical coatings have been registered.

Promotional Activities for Technology Transfer and Market Development

Promotional activities have been continued during the year to further progress technology transfer process and industry interface. A large number of Interest Exploration developed and those available for transfer. Announcements were made in professional journals and newspapers about the professional journals and newspapers about the availability of technologies for transfer. Demonstrations were arranged for some of the products and processes. A one-day Industry Meet on Precision the details of pressure transducer technology and to shortlist prospective industries for technology transfer.A Workshop-cum-Exhibition was also organised jointly with the Karnataka State Industrial Investment and Development Corporation (KSIDC), Bangalore, on(ISRO)Indian Space Research Organisation technologies during August 1991 at Bangalore. ISRO-Electronics industries meet was held at Ahmedabad during December 18-19, 1991 in which industries was apprised of ISRO's requirements in the field of electronics, microwaves, control systems, software, etc., over the next five years and were development of special products and systems.

The Agrophotometer, a novel instrument for measurement of agronomical parameters (chlorophyll and water stress) 'in vivo' developed by ISRO and licensed to a private firm, has been awarded Federation of Indian Chambers of

Commerce and Industry and Federation and Andhra Pradesh Chambers of Commerce and Industry awards for 1990-91. The first prize 'PARAM' has been given to ISRO and C-DAC for their joint work on the implementation of SEASAT Synthetic Aperture Radar (SAR) processor on PARAM.

Entrepreneurship Development and Venture Capital Funding

ISRO/DOS technocrats are being encouraged to venture as entrepreneurs utilising the technologies developed by ISRO/DOS through organising workshop. Scientists who have taken the lead are progressing well in their efforts for an early productionisation. DOS is coordinating with institutions such as Technology Development Information company of India. Industrial Development Bank of India and Risk Capital Finance Corporation to help the scientists and technocrats. Considering the satellite remote sensing, a scheme has been evolved for motivating scientists and engineers of DOS to venture as entrepreneurs in this area. The entrepreneurs would be assisted in their endeavours through necessary technology transfer on attractive terms including access to ISRO/DOS facilities at concessional rates.

ISRO Technical Consultancy Scheme

The Technical consultancy scheme of ISRO serves to diffuse the expertise available within ISRO to industry and research institutions. Since 1982-91 technology consultancy projects have been undertaken by ISRO. There has been a good progress in the consultancy assignments during the year include qualification and acceptance, training of personnel for specialised test facilities for carrying out environmental tests, etc.

Export Promotion of ISRO Technologies

A beginning has been made in the export promotion of space products. ISRO has successfully executed an order for supply of Optical Horizon Sensor components for satellite applications from Instituto Nacional De Pesquisas Espaciais (INPE), Brazil. The export of propellants for the Indonesian Space Agency, LAPAN, is currently being processed.

Recognising the vast potential for Indian space products abroad, steps have taken to prepare product catalogues and brochures, participate in international tenders, appointment of representatives, etc. ISRO has also advertised the availability of IRS-1B data and a number of agencies are actively considering the acquisition of IRS data directly in their countries.

Contribution from Industries

Indian industries have continued to actively participate in the ongoing space projects, namely ASLV, PSLV, GSLV, IRS, and INSAT, by way of development and fabrication of a variety of hardware and building of required ground infrastructure. Most of the flight components for ASLV like interstages, baseshroud and heatshields have been realised by Indian industry.

The Space Electronics Division (SED) of Bharat Electronics (BE), Bangalore, continues to produce avionics packages for launch vehicles, sounding rockets and ground systems. Supply of flight packages for the ASLV project has been successfully completed. These packages include PCM Remote Units, Tone Range Receiver, Telecommand Decoders, Power modules and Signal conditioners and are intended to be used in the ASLV D3 flight. DC-DC converters for the INSAT-2 project are being supplied as required. Technology transfer documents for flight packages to be used for PSLV class launch vehicles were formally handed over to SED for production during 1991-94.

A number of industries provided support through development, fabrication and supply of hardware for ISRO's payload and ground systems. Major items include fabrication of Solid State Power Amplifiers (SSPA) for INSAT-2 communication payloads by Hindustan Aeronautics Ltd. (HAL), Hyderabad, and design and fabrication of 14 m and 7 m diameter antennae by a private firm in Madras. Machining and fabrication of various boxes for communication payload, ground hardware electronics and antenna reflectors, feeds and mounts have been carried out at several work centres.

The liquid engines for the launch vehicle programme are continued to be manufactured at private industries. The fabrication, erection and testing of the expander mandrels, required for the manufacture of the divergent cone for the engine has been completed. This unique mandrel is totally designed and fabricated by a private industry and is the biggest one to have been install in India.

ASLV Launched

India successfully launched the five stage Augmented Satellite Launch Vehicle-D3 (ASLV) on May 20, 1992 from the Sriharikota range in Andhra Pradesh. The ASLV has in it incorporated a large number of new technologies including the closed loop guidance system, strap-on technology including a strap-on separator and a large number of controls which needed to be tested for the Polar Satellite Launch Vehicle to be lifted off next year and can put the one tonne Indian Remote Sensing Satellite (IRS) into the orbit.

The following (Date, Satellite, Function, Launcher and Result) are the successful launchings under India's Space Programme:

Date	Satellite	Function	Launcher	Result
March 19, 1975	Aryabhatta	Scientific	USSR	Success
June 7, 1979	Bhaskara-I	Earth observation	USSR	Success
July 18, 1980	Rohini	Earth observation	SLV-3	Success
July 19, 1981	Apple	Communication	Ariane European Space Agency	Success
November 20, 1981	Bhaskara-II	Earth observation	USSR	Success
April 17, 1983	Rohini	Scientific	SLV-3	Success
March 19, 1988	IRS-IA	Remote sensing	USSR	Success
August 29, 1991	IRS-IB	Remote sensing	USSR	Success
May 20, 1992	SROSS-III	Technology and application	ASLV	Success

ASLV'S Features

The launch of the ASLV rocket, its third developmental version, come at 6.00 a.m. from the Sriharikota rocket launching station of the Indian Space Research

Organisation (ISRO) in Andhra Pradesh. It injected the Stretched Rohini Satellite Series (SROSS) payload into space nine minutes 18 seconds later.

The 106 kg satellite orbitted the earth once every 92 minutes. An ISRO Press release described the launch as a "total success". The Satellite was tracked later from Sriharikota, the Vikram Sarabhai Space Centre in Trivandrum and Car Nicobar islands. The telemetry received showed that the satellite was performing in accordance with the expected parameters.

The third successful developmental flight of ASLV came after two failures of two rockets in the same series. The first launch on March 24, 1987, was abortive as the first stage motor failed to ignite. The second flight on July 13, 1988, failed 150 seconds after launch following failure of control systems.

Following the failures, modifications were incorporated in ASLV systems to ensure a success on recommendations of the expert review panel and failure analysis committee that went into the failure.

The separation of the SROSS-C from the spent fourth stage occurred about 500 seconds after lift-off and data from Car Nicobar tracking station showed that the separation was normal, ISRO said.

The ASLV-D3 has several modifications based on the experience of the first two unsuccessful flights. Fins were introduced on the core first stage for greater stability and the digital autopilot was redesigned for better control.

The ASLV was designed and built at the Vikram Sarabhai Space Centre in Thiruvananthapuram, India's lead centre for launch vehicles that was also responsible for vehicle integration and flight testing.

The successful launch of the five-stage ASLV today has demonstrated proper functioning of several advanced technologies needed for the PSLV and the GSLV programmes.

ASLV is designed to augment indigenous satellite launch capability and put 150-kg class satellites into low-earth orbits. It is parallel to the United States.

The 24 metre five-stage rocket has two strap-on motors. It uses solid propellants as did its predecessors, the SLV series of rockets. It incorporates major technological elements such as close loops guidance scheme, bulbous heatshield, S-band telemetry, tracking and command and navigational computers.

Facts About Agni

Type	:	Surface to Surface*
Range	:	2,500 Km
Weight	:	16 tonnes
Height	:	21 metres
Maximum Diameter	:	1 meter
Payload Capacity	:	1 tonne
Major Subsystems	:	45
Ist Test	:	May 22, 1989
Ist Test	:	May 29, 1992, 0817hrs
Testing Site	:	Interim Test Range, Chandipur-on-Sea, Orissa

* Intermediate Range Ballistic Missile (IRBM).

44.2 SCIENCE AND TECHNOLOGY

Overview

The formation of the Ministry of Science and Technology was announced through a Presidential Notification dated January 4, 1985 (74/2/1/85. Cab) contained in the 164th Amendment of the Government of India (Allocation of Business Rules, 1961; the Department of Science and Industrial Research (DSIR) forms a part of this Ministry.

Several laboratories under the Council of Scientific and Industrial Research made significant contributions.

Development of a cost-effective Shallow-well Handpump was taken up with an objective to design a cost-effective pump with increased reliability, reduction in failure rates, and reduction in human pumping effort from material available in the country. A modern Oil Expeller of 10 TPD capacity, developed by CFTRI, extracts almost 95 per cent of the oil that is present in the seeds. Other features of this expeller are its low power consumption, high reliability, lower wear and tear of critical components, and the production of clearer oil and suitable cake for animal use. Studies were carried out by NIO in the coastal waters of Andaman for setting up demonstration scale units of aquaculture production. Eight suitable areas have been identified. Technology of intense polyculture of finfishes were successfully demonstrated in the Andaman and Nicobar groups of islands. The NPL aeronomy payload to be flown abroad Indian SROSS-C satellite has been successfully fabricated, tested and qualified for space qualification and delivered to ISRO Satellite centre (ISRC), Bangalore for spacecraft integration and launch. IIP, in collaboration with Engineers India Ltd (EIL), has developed a technology for the production of food grade hexane, a solvent used for production of vegetable oils. NCL has isolated the active principles with insecticidal properties from neem seeds, and their formulations have been prepared and tested. The process has been transferred to industry for commercialisation. In the area of rural tanning, CLRI has been involved in a joint programme with the Khadi and Village Commission (KVIC) at Kallupatti in Tamil Nadu and Wardha in Maharashtra. Suitable technologies have been worked out for upgradation of low grade leathers, particularly rural tanned leathers, for getting better returns. The process for Timol Maleate, a drug widely used for glaucoma has been released to M/s FDC Ltd., Bombay for commercialisation. IICT has provided a commercially feasible process for obtaining the "S" enantimer starting D-Mennitol. CECRI has come out with an interesting process to coat a conducting polymer on insulating materials such as cloth, glass and plastics. CBRI has developed a new type of low cost load bearing large aggregate concrete block. These concrete blocks have low content cement, will reduce wall thickness and eliminate internal plastering.

CSIR is involved in the following important societal missions and national programme:

i) Provision of drinking water and water management.
ii) Development of Wastelands.
iii) Oil Seeds.

The involvement of CSIR laboratories is in the nature of water quality assessment by installation, commissioning and evaluation of Iron removal plants in Assam, Gujarat and in West Bengal.

Ten CSIR laboratories have been connected on the computer network which, at present, is supporting the INSDOC E-mail facility. Eleven user nodes and two mail nodes have been established.

Scientific Associations, Institutions, Universities and colleges, which undertake research in the area of medicine, agricultural natural and applied sciences seek approval to avail the fiscal incentives provided for pursuing such work. During the year 32 institutions were recommended for approval. A Research Review Group regularly examines the returns submitted by such research associations and institutions. On the basis of such a review, earlier approvals granted are renewed or withdrawn. Similarly institutions engaged in social science research were also examined. Six institutions were recommended for approval; the Research Review Group in the are of social science had examined the return of 44 institutions.

The Government had notified an incentive and relief to the user of knowhow developed in the country. This would be in the form of depreciation allowance at the higher rate of 50 per cent on the cost of plant and machinery installed after 1st April, 1987.

The Department intensified its activities relating to the scheme on National Register of Foreign Collaborations. A compilation of primary data on FCs for the year 1990 was brought out. Computerisation of data collected on Foreign Collaborations for the year 1981-90 has been completed. Reports on technology status of various sectors products like petroleum refining, dry process cement plants, self-advancing roof support and PTFE & PVDF have been printed. Technology status studies have been commissioned on various products which include seamless steel tubes, electrolyte, manganese dioxide, caprolactum, welding equipment and ceramic capacitors.

The scheme on, Promotion and Support to Indigenous Development of Capital Goods, was launched in the year 1990-91. The draft report of the studies of capital Goods requirement by the manmade fibre sector, mouldable polymer sector, metal forming industry and electronics industry were prepared and evaluated by expert committees. Studies of capital goods requirements by the food processing industry, packaging sector, naphtha and gas crackers, secondary steel sector and dies and moulds are in progress. Some development projects pertaining to packaging machinery and variable speed A.C. motors are considered.

The Technology Absorption and Adaptation scheme provided partial financial support to 30 firms involving over 50 Research, Design, Development and Engineering projects in the areas of absorption of imported technology. These include: import substitution of hydraulic AGC (Automatic Gauge Control) system, by MECON, Mining and Allied Machinery Corporations project related to Development of Slide Discharge loaders, Keltron Controls project related to indigenous development of custom build IC's used on computer, HCL's projects related to Plasma enhanced MCVD process and recovery of raw material used in fibre Optic Cables, Hindustan Organic Chemicals projects related to simulation bodies for the distillation train in the phenol plant, Swaraj Mazda project related to improvement of fuel consumption and emission reduction in Diesel Engine and Bharat Heavy Plates and Vessels Ltd., project related to development of flexible super insulated piping. In addition a Roster/Directory of Research and Design Experts in Technology Absorption has been commissioned in this year. Studies relating to the norms in use in certain important sectors were commissioned and this includes the sectors such as Glass, Refractories, Home Appliances, Paints, Packaging and Plastics. Under Talented Indian Engineers and Scientists Scheme a total of 82 preliminary industry profiles have been commissioned. Support has been approved to ERDA for a technology demonstration project related to Energy Efficient Motors.

The Transfer and Trading in Technology scheme has supported several activities such as: commissioning studies relating to preparation of technology profiles of developing countries; conducting studies highlighting India's technological capabilities in select industrial sectors; creation of computerised database on technologies available for transfer; organising workshops/ interaction meetings and live demonstration of exportable technologies at pilot joint ventures ion 4 South-East Asian countries was carried out. Close linkages were maintained in the area of technology transfer with international organisations such as UNCTAD, ESCAP, WIPO, and UNIDO.

The scheme relating to promotion and support to consultancy services essentially aims to strengthen consultancy capabilities for domestic and export markets. The activities have been towards: Documenting consultancy needs and capabilities in important economic sectors and at State levels; Providing institutional and programme support to CDC, Associations and other promotional agencies; Registration scheme for consultants has been initiated; an ESCAP workshop was organised at Delhi in September, 1991, to discuss promotion of cooperation in consultancy in the ESCAP region and setting up of a Regional Apex Body for the purpose; and Technology Business Incubator Programme has been launched to promote Technology based small enterprises.

CDC was promoted in January 1986 as a Non-profit society, with the support of consultancy promotion agencies, such as FIEO, ACE, NACE, with a view to implement some of the programmes of DSIR and also promote and strengthen the consultancy capabilities. It is not to undertake any commercial activities but, at the same time, earn revenues to the extent possible. The Chairman of CDC is to be Secretary in the Ministry of Science and Technology or his representative, and the Governing Body consists of representatives from Consultancy (Private and Public), Government Departments, agencies, industry, R&D and academic institutions. CDC is implementing programmes such as CDPA, computerised Databases, training and human resources development for consultancy, Registration scheme, and programmes sponsored by other agencies. DSIR is providing recurring and non-recurring support to CDC.

The National Information System for Science and Technology (NISSAT) programme envisages promotion and support to the development of a compatible set of information systems on science and technology and inter-linking of these into a network. Ten sectoral centres have been established in Leather Technology, Food Technology, Machine Tools, Drugs and Pharmaceuticals, Textiles and Allied subjects, Chemicals, Bibliometrics, Advanced Ceramics and Compact-disk. NISSAT has taken the initiative for the development of metropolitan library networks to ensure better utilisation of S&T information resources through resources sharing.

Two public undertakings namely National Research Development Corporation (NRDC) and Central Electronics Limited (CEL) attached to this Department, were engaged in important activities in the commercialisation of indigenously developed technology. Some of the major technologies licensed by NRDC during the year include: Succine Acid, Flyash Bricks, Lindane, Spice Oleoresin, Rice Husk Particle Board, Disposable Blood Bags. NRDC gave awards and presented certificates of merit to investors thereby promoting innovative efforts in the country. NRDC has been successful in promoting several projects based on their technologies in Indonesia, Vietnam and Thailand.

The activities of CEL are sharply focused in three thrust areas namely selected electronic components, electronic systems and solar photo-voltaic cells, modules and systems for a variety of applications, intensive technology development work was carried out by the company in the field of growth of multicrystalline solar cells, new SPV systems and high permeability ferrites.

TABLE 44.1: List of In-House R&D in Industry Reporting Annual Expenditure more than Rs. 100 lakhs

Sl. No.	Name of the Unit	R&D expenditure (Rs. in lakhs)
1	2	3
1.	Altos India Limited	107
2.	Armour Chemicals Private Limited	119
3.	Asea Brown Boveri Limited	101
4.	Ashok Leyland Limited	430
5.	Asian Paints (India) Limited	179
6.	Associated Cement Co. Ltd.	327
7.	Atic Industries Limited	102
8.	Atul Products Limited	130
9.	Bajaj Auto Limited	446
10.	Bajaj Tempo Limited	157
11.	Bata India Limited	157
12.	Bharat Earth Movers Limited	1217
13.	Bharat Electronics Limited	3309
14.	Bharat Heavy Electrical Ltd. (Pollution Control Res. Instt.)	184
15.	Bharat Heavy Electricals Ltd. (High Pressure Boiler Plant)	1058
16.	Boots Pharmaceuticals Ltd.	183
17.	Brakes India Limited	293
18.	Bush Boake Allen (India) Limited	147
19.	CMC Limited	436
20.	Cable Corporation of India Ltd.	434
21.	Cadila Laboratories Limited	193
22.	Central Electronics Limited	104
23.	Cibatul Limited	104
24.	Colour Chem Limited	154
25.	Crompton Greaves Limited	728
26.	Dunlop India Limited	300
27.	Eicher Goodearth Limited	181
28.	Electronic Research and Development Centre	374
29.	Electronics Corp. of India Ltd.	450
30.	Engineers India Limited	373
31.	English Electric Company of India Limited	245
32.	Escorts Limited Corporate R&D Centre	270
33.	Escorts Limited (Motor Cycle & Scooter Division)	111
34.	E.I.D. Parry (India) Limited	168
35.	Garware Plastics & Polyster Limited	155
36.	Gharda Chemicals Limited	330
37.	Glaxo India Limited	169

Contd.

TABLE 44.1 *Contd.*

1	2	3
38.	Godrej Soaps Limited	140
39.	Godrej & Boyce Mfg. Company Limited	574
40.	Grauer & Weil (India) Limited	109
41.	Gujarat Ambuja Cements Ltd.	159
42.	Gujarat Communications & Electronics Limited	296
43.	Gujarat State Fertiliser Company Limited (Polymer Unit)	450
44.	HCL Limited (Communication & Computer Division)	200
45.	HMT Limited R&D Centre (Metal Cutting Division)	472
46.	HMT Limited (Agricultural Machinery Group)	164
47.	Heavy Engineering Corporation Ltd. (Heavy Machine Tools Plant)	500
48.	Hindustan Aeronautics Limited	314
49.	Hindustan Aeronautics Limited (Hyderabad Division)	482
50.	Hindustan Aeronautics Limited (Design & Engg. Department)	212
51.	Hindustan Antibiotics Limited	200
52.	Hindustan Cables Limited	122
53.	Hindustan Ciba-Geigy Limited	280
54.	Hindustan Insecticides Limited	103
55.	Hindustan Level Limited	471
56.	Hindustan Organic Chemicals Limited	135
57.	Hindustan Photo Films Manufacturing Company Ltd.	156
58.	Hindustan Zinc Limited	468
59.	Hoechst India Limited	1150
60.	Hyderabad Allwyn Limited	170
61.	ICI India Limited	167
62.	ICI India Limited (Explosives & Fertilisers Division)	117
63.	ICI India Limited (Fibres Division)	157
64.	IDL Chemicals Limited	140
65.	IOL Limited	120
66.	ITC Limited	246
67.	Indian Aluminium Company Limited	229
68.	Indian Drugs & Pharmaceuticals Limited	202
69.	Indian Oil Corporation Limited	1000
70.	Indian Organic Chemicals Ltd.	112
71.	Indian Telephone Industries Limited	2945
72.	Instrumentation Limited	125
73.	Johnson & Johnson Limited	104
74.	Jyoti Limited	100
75.	J.K. Industries Limited	136
76.	J.K. Synthetics Limited	255
77.	Kegg Farms Limited	108
78.	Kelvinator India Limited	238
79.	Kirloskar Brothers Limited	112
80.	Kirloskar Cummins Limited	323
81.	Kirloskar Electric Company Ltd.	122
82.	Kirloskar Oil Engines Limited	101
83.	K.C.P. Limited	424
84.	Larsen & Toubro Limited	588
85.	Lubrizol India Limited	233
86.	Lucas-TVS Limited	121
87.	MRF Limited	1676
88.	Madras Refineries Limited	300
89.	Maharashtra Hybrid Seeds Company Limited	320
90.	Mahindra & Mahindra Limited (Tractor and Automotive Division)	277
91.	Malladi Drugs & Pharmaceuticals Limited	145
92.	Maruti Udyog Limited	239
93.	Metallurgical & Engineering Consultants (India) Limited	148
94.	Modi Rubber Limited	101

Contd.

TABLE 44.1 *Concld.*

1	2	3
95.	Motor Industries Co. Limited	357
96.	Mysore Kirloskar Limited	281
97.	National Mineral Development Corporation Limited	181
98.	National Organic Chemical Industries Limited	410
99.	National Thermal Power Corporation Limited	221
100.	Oil India Limited	126
101.	Oil & Natural Gas Commission (O.N.G.C.)	1294
102.	Padmashri Dr. Vithalrao Vikhe Patel Sahakari Sakhar Karkhana	304
103.	Peico Electronics & Electricals Limited	1482
104.	Pfizer Limited	159
105.	Premier Automobiles Limited	322
106.	Procter & Gamble India Limited (Formerly: Richardson Hindustan)	140
107.	Projects & Development India Limited	760
108.	Punjab Tractors Ltd.	120
109.	Rallis India Limited (Agricultural Division)	172
110.	Ranbaxy Laboratories Limited	312
111.	Reliance Petrochemicals Ltd.	611
112.	SRF Limited	165
113.	Sandoz (India) Ltd.	871
114.	Semiconductor Complex Limited	871
115.	Siemens India Limited	795
116.	Steel Authority of India Limited (R&D Centre for Iron & Steel)	3830
117.	Steel Authority of India Limited (Bokaro Steel Plant)	105
118.	S.D. Technical Services Pvt. Ltd.	150
119.	TVS-Suzuki Limited	104
120.	Tata Chemicals Ltd.	117
121.	Tata Engineering & Locomotive Company Limited	1354
122.	Tata Hydro-Electric Power Supply Company Limited	358
123.	Tata Iron & Steel Company Limited	600
124.	Tata Tea Ltd.	187
125.	Venco Research & Breeding Farm Limited	125
126.	Venkateshwara Research & Breeding Farm Limited	107
127.	Voltas Limited	411
128.	Widia (India) Limited	124
129.	Wipro Infortech Limited	336
130.	Wockhardt Limited	130
131.	Zandu Pharmaceuticals Works Limited	102

TABLE 44.2: List of In-House R&D Units in Industry Reporting Annual Expenditure in the Range of Rs. 25 Lakhs to Rs. 100 Lakhs

Sl. No.	Name of the Unit	R&D expenditure (Rs. in lakhs)
1	2	3
1.	Advani-Oerlikon Limited	39
2.	Aegis Chemical Industries	26
3.	Afco Industrial & Chemical Limited	27
4.	Alembic Chemical Works Company Limited	81
5.	Alembic Glass Industries Limited	25
6.	Alfa-Laval (India) Limited	52
7.	Ambalal Sarabhai Enterprises Limited	49
8.	Andhra Sugars Limited (Sugarcane Dev. Division)	46
9.	Andrew Yule & Company Limited	51
10.	Apollo Tyres Limited	56
11.	Applied Electronics Limited	52
12.	Arlabs Limited	34
13.	Asian Cables Ltd.	60
14.	Assam Electronics Development Corporation Limited	43
15.	Astra IDL Limited	27
16.	Audco India Limited	27
17.	Automatic Electric Limited	40
18.	BASF India Limited	65
19.	BPL Sanyo Utilities and Appliances Limited	35
20.	BPL Systems & Projects Limited	44
21.	BPL-INDIA (British Physical Laboratories)	43
22.	Bajaj Electricals Ltd.	48
23.	Bakelite Hylam Limited	48
24.	Ballarpur Industries Limited	45
25.	Balmer Lawrie & Company Ltd.	45
26.	Baroda Rayon Corporation Limited	60
27.	Bayer India Limited	73
28.	Berger Paints India Limited	44
29.	Best & Crompton Engineering Ltd.	25
30.	Bharat Aluminium Company Ltd.	25
31.	Bharat Dynamics Limited	30
32.	Bharat Forge Limited	26
33.	Bharat Heavy Electricals Ltd. (Industrial Systems Group)	72
34.	Bharat Heavy Electricals Ltd. (Electroporcelains Division)	30
35.	Bharat Heavy Plate & Vessels Limited	42
36.	Bharat Pumps & Compressors Limited	30
37.	Bharat Refractories Limited	29
38.	Bharatia Electric Steel Company Limited	29
39.	Bharatia Cutter-Hammer Limited	25
40.	Bhilai Engineering Corporation Limited	31
41.	Bhoruka Gases Ltd. (Formerly Karnataka Oxygen Ltd.)	33
42.	Bhoruka Steel Limited	28
43.	Bicycle & Sewing Machine Research & Development Centre	84
44.	Bihar Alloy Steels Limited	50
45.	Blue Star Limited	39
46.	Bombay Tyres International Ltd.	42
47.	Britannia Industries Limited	45
48.	Bush India Limited	30
49.	Cadbury India Limited (Formerly Hindustan Cocoa)	65
50.	Camphor & Allied Products Limited	56
51.	Carborundum Universal Limited	51
52.	Castrol India Ltd. (Formerly Indrol Lub. & Specialities Ltd.)	35
53.	Ceat Limited	54

Contd.

TABLE 44.2 *Contd.*

1	2	3
54.	Century Textiles Industries Limited	35
55.	Chloride Industries Limited	78
56.	Cipla Limited	42
57.	Coats of India Limited	38
58.	Cochin Refineries Limited	53
59.	Continental Device of India Limited	25
60.	Control & Switchgear Co. Ltd.	31
61.	Coromandal Prodorite Limited	39
62.	Cosmo Ferrites Limited	51
63.	Coventry Spring & Engineering Company Limited	39
64.	Cynamid India Limited	80
65.	DCM Data Products (Unit: D.C.M.) Limited	83
66.	Dai Ichi Karkaria Pvt. Ltd.	35
67.	Daurala Sugar Works (Unit of Shriram Industries Ltd.)	31
68.	Dey's Medical Stores (Mfg.) Limited	37
69.	Dharamsi Morarji Chemicals Company Limited	49
70.	Digital Electronics Limited	34
71.	Digital Equipments (India) Limited	34
72.	Dr. Beck & Company (India) Limited	27
73.	Dr. Reddy's Laboratories Ltd.	40
74.	Duphar Interfran Limited	52
75.	ESAB India Ltd.	75
76.	EWAC Alloys Limited	68
77.	East India Pharmaceutical Works Limited	27
78.	Eddy Current Controls (India) Limited	46
79.	Eimco Elicon (India) Limited	32
80.	Electronic Research Pvt. Ltd.	28
81.	Elgi Tyre & Tread Limited	25
82.	Elpro International Limited	43
83.	Emco Electronics	32
84.	Ennore Foundries Limited	28
85.	Escorts Tractors Limited (Research & Development Centre)	54
86.	Eskayef Limited	39
87.	Etermit Everest Ltd. (Formerly Everest Building)	39
88.	Ethnor Limited	31
89.	Eureka Forbes Limited	30
90.	Excel Industries Limited	27
91.	Fedders Llyod Corporation Private Limited	38
92.	Fertilizers & Chemicals Travancore Limited	37
93.	Ficom Organics Limited	25
94.	Fort Gloster Industries Limited (Cable Division)	67
95.	Franco-Indian Pharmaceuticals Private Limited	26
96.	Galaxy Organics (P) Limited	29
97.	Garware Paints Limited	31
98.	Garware-wall Ropes Limited	65
99.	Godfrey Phillips India Limited	25
100.	Goodlass Nerolac Paints Limited	90
101.	Graphite India Limited	33
102.	Greaves Foseco Limited	54
103.	Grindwell Norton Limited	77
104.	Guest Keen Williams Limited	27
105.	Gujarat Alkalies & Chemicals Limited	38
106.	Gujarat Insecticides Limited	56
107.	Gujarat Narmada Valley Fertilizers Company Limited	35
108.	HMM Limited	41
109.	HMT Limited (Watch Directorate)	92
110.	Haryana State Electronics Development Corporation Limited	54

Contd.

TABLE 44.2 *Contd.*

1	2	3
111.	Hawkins Cookers Limited	61
112.	Herdillia Chemicals Limited	37
113.	Hico Products Limited	54
114.	High Energy Batteries (India) Limited	32
115.	Himalaya Machinery Pvt. Ltd.	34
116.	Hinditron Computer Systems & Consultants Private Limited	31
117.	Hindustan Aeronautics Limited (HAL-Corporate Office)	67
118.	Hindustan Dorr-Oliver Limited	28
119.	Hindustan Motors Limited (Auto Division)	77
120.	Hindustan Teleprinter Limited	25
121.	Hyderabad Batteries Limited	40
122.	Hyderabad Industries Limited	60
123.	IBP Company Limited (Engineering Division)	58
124.	IPCA Laboratories Pvt. Ltd.	72
125.	ITI Equatorial Satcom Limited	51
126.	IVP Limited	37
127.	Incab Industries Limited	38
128.	Indchen ATL Limited	27
129.	Indchem Electronics Limited	45
130.	India Carbon Limited	30
131.	India Pistons Limited	35
132.	India Tele-Comp Limited	25
133.	Indian Dyestuff Industries Limited	61
134.	Indian Hume Pipe Company Limited	49
135.	Indo National Limited	25
136.	Indofil Chemicals Company (A Division of Modipon Limited)	29
137.	Indo-American Hybrid Seeds	34
138.	Infar (India) Limited	53
139.	Inforcom Digital Systems (P) Ltd.	33
140.	International computers Indian Manufacturers Limited	48
141.	International Data Management Limited	60
142.	Ion Exchange (India) Limited	75
143.	Jagatjit Cotton Textiles Mills Limited	37
144.	Jamna Auto Industries	25
145.	Jaya Hind Industries Limited	26
146.	Jaysynth Dyechem Private Limited	43
147.	Jenson & Nicholson (India) Ltd.	42
148.	KSB Pumps Limited	28
149.	Kasila Farms Private Limited	73
150.	Keonics Magnavision Computers Limited	56
151.	Kerala Electrical & Allied Engineering Co. Ltd.	40
152.	Kinetic Engineering Limited	77
153.	Kirloskar Pneumatic Company Limited	62
154.	Klockner Windsor (India) Limited	35
155.	Kolhapur Steel Limited	67
156.	K.E.C. International Limited	30
157.	K.G. Khosla Compressors Limited	43
158.	Lakhanpal National Limited	27
159.	Lakshmi Machine Works Limited	47
160.	Lawkim Limited	27
161.	Lona Industries Pvt. Ltd.	49
162.	Lupin Laboratories Limited	52
163.	Lyka Labs Private Limited	37
164.	Machine Tools Aids and Reconditioning	53
165.	Maharashtra Electronics Corporation Limited	60
166.	Maize Products	25
167.	Marine & Communications (I) Limited	83

Contd.

TABLE 44.2 *Contd.*

1	2	3
168.	McDowell & Company Limited	36
169.	Merind Limited	30
170.	Mirc Electronics Limited	65
171.	Modern Malleable Casting Works Limited	41
172.	Modern Woollens Limited	35
173.	Modi Xerox Limited	81
174.	Modipon Limited	61
175.	Mukund Limited	54
176.	Murphy India Limited	29
177.	M.P. Electricity Board (R&D Cell)	58
178.	NGEF Limited	30
179.	National Insulated Cable Company of India Limited	31
180.	National Peroxide Limited	56
181.	National Radio & Electronics Company Limited	73
182.	National Rayon Corporation Limited	38
183.	Navin Flouring Industries.	33
184.	Network Limited	77
185.	New Shorrock Mills (Div. of Mafatlal Ind. Ltd.)	29
186.	Neyveli Lignite Corporation Limited	38
187.	Nippon Denro Ispat Limited	35
188.	Nirlon Limited	56
189.	Nuchem Plastics Limited	30
190.	OMC Computers Limited	71
191.	Orient Papers Mills	51
192.	Orissa Cement Limited	27
193.	Orissa Industries Limited	27
194.	Orissa State Electronics Development Corporation Limited	69
195.	Otis Elevator Co. (India) Ltd.	65
196.	PSI Data Systems Limited	81
197.	Paper Products Limited	25
198.	Parke-Davis (India) Limited	40
199.	Pennwalt India Limited	27
200.	Petrofils Co-operative Limited	49
201.	Phillips Carbon Black Limited	55
202.	Pidilite Industries Ltd. (Formerly PDI Chemicals Ltd.)	25
203.	Polyolefins Industries Limited	87
204.	Pond's (India) Limited	30
205.	Pratap Steel Limited	25
206.	Premier Cable Company Limited	36
207.	Premier Instruments & Controls Limited	99
208.	Priyaraj Electronics Pvt. Ltd.	30
209.	Proagro Seed Company Limited (Formerly Pioneer Seed Co. Ltd.)	66
210.	Prototype Development Training Centre	45
211.	Punjab Anand Batteries Limited	80
212.	Punjab Wireless Systems Ltd.	43
213.	Rainbow Ink & Varnish Manufacturing Co. Limited	28
214.	Rajasthan Electronics and Instruments Limited	79
215.	Rallis India Limited (Pharmaceutical & Chemical)	55
216.	Ralliwolf Limited	54
217.	Rane (Madras) Limited	30
218.	Rashtriya Chemical & Fertilizers Limited	95
219.	Raymond Woolen Mills Ltd.	28
220.	Reckitt and Colman of India Ltd.	66
221.	Reliance Industries Ltd.	77
222.	Roche Products Limited	26
223.	Ruston and Hornsby (India) Ltd.	25
224.	R.G. Ispat Limited	60
225.	Samtel (India) Limited	26

Contd.

TABLE 44.2 *Concld.*

1	2	3
226.	Sandvik Asia Limited	79
227.	Savita Chemicals Ltd.	28
228.	Searle (India) Limited	60
229.	Shalimar Paints Limited	29
230.	Shree Synthetics Limited	37
231.	Shriram Refrigeration Industries Limited	33
232.	Simbhaoli Sugar Mills Ltd.	34
233.	Simco Engineering Limited	35
234.	Simpson and Company Limited	37
235.	Siris Limited (Formerly: South India Research Institute)	27
236.	Sirpur Paper Mills Limited	26
237.	Southern Petrochemical Industries Corporation Limited	60
238.	Sponge Iron India Limited	47
239.	Standard Industries Limited	27
240.	Standard Research Centre	39
241.	Sun Pharmaceutical Industries	82
242.	Sundram Fastners Limited	25
243.	Swadeshi Polytex Limited	37
244.	S.A.J. Froude Test Plant Private Limited	26
245.	S.H. Kelkar and Company Limited	32
246.	TIL Limited	45
247.	TVS Electronics Ltd.	46
248.	TVS Whirlpool Ltd.	92
249.	Tamil Nadu Dadha Pharmaceuticals Limited	55
250.	Tamil Nadu Newsprint and Papers Limited	54
251.	Tamil Nadu Petroproducts Ltd.	27
252.	Tata Oil Mills Co. Ltd.	41
253.	Tata Refractories Limited	79
254.	Tata-Yodogawa Limited	46
255.	Teletube Electronics Pvt. Ltd.	55
256.	Television and Components (P) Ltd.	27
257.	Thermax Limited (Chemical, Computer and Engg. Div.)	82
258.	Titan Watches Limited	29
259.	Titanium Equipments and Anode Manufacturing Company Limited	30
260.	Tractor Engineers Limited	29
261.	Transpek Industry Limited	38
262.	Tube Products of India	38
263.	T. Stanes and Company Limited	73
264.	Unichem Laboratories Limited	67
265.	Unique Chemicals (Div. of J.B. Chemicals and Pharmaceuticals Ltd.)	29
266.	Unique Pharmaceuticals Laboratories Private Limited	27
267.	United Catalysts India Ltd.	28
268.	United Phosphorous Pvt. Ltd.	40
269.	Universal Biochemicals	30
270.	Universal Cables Ltd.	59
271.	Uptron India Limited	38
272.	Usha Telehoist Limited	26
273.	U.S. Vitamin (India) Limited	57
274.	VXL India Limited	32
275.	Vidyut Metallics Limited	27
276.	Vijay Wires and Filament (P) Limited	70
277.	Vikrant Tyres Limited	27
278.	Walchandnagar Industries Limited (Copper Group)	60
279.	West bengal Electronic Industry Development Corporation Limited	27
280.	Weston Electronics Limited	40
281.	Wheels India Limited	43
282.	Worthington Pump India Limited	49
283.	Wyeth Laboratories Limited	53

TABLE 44.3: Certificate for Accelerated Depreciation Allowance Issued under Rules 5(2) of I.T. Rules vide Notification No. 133/342/86-TPL Dated 1.4.1988

S. No.	Name of Company	Lab where knowhow developed	Rs. in lakhs	Items of Manufacture
1	2	3	4	5
1.	Kapercon Sleeper Works Pvt. Ltd., Bombay	RDSO Lucknow	20	Pre-stress concrete sleepers
2.	INDCHEM Electronics Ltd. Madras	C-DOT	4	128 Port Electronic Pvt. Automatic Br. Exchange EPABX and Rural Automatic Exchange (RAX)
3.	Gharda Chemical Ltd. Bombay	In-House	9	Oxyclozanide
4.	Gharda Chemicals Ltd. Bombay	In-House	36	Insoproturon Technical Insoproturon 50% & 75% W.P.
5.	Gharda Chemicals Ltd. Bombay	In-House	11	Cypermethric Acid Chiloride & Cypermethric Technical
6.	ARLEM Electronics, Goa	C-DOT	311	28 Electronics PABX
7.	Gharda Chemicals Ltd. Bombay	In-House	22	Cypermethric Acid Chloride Cypermethrin Technical
8.	Punjab Communications Ltd., SAS Ngr.	C-DOT	36	EPABX and RAX
9.	Vijay Lakshmi Engg. Works Pvt. Ltd. Coimbatore	SIITRA	57	Two or one twister
10.	Punjab Tractors Ltd., Ltd., Ropar	In-House	730	Swaraj Agri. Tractors grey Iron Castings, Indl. Fork lifts, Harvestor Combine
11.	Webel Electronics Communication System Ltd., Calcutta	In-House	6	Automatic Message Account Equipment (AMA), Electronic Detector (ED)
12.	Isotrack Sleeper Pvt. Ltd., Bombay	RDSO	32	Prestressed concrete Sleepers
13.	Punjab Communications Ltd., Ropar	C-DOT	17	EPABX and RAX

Contd.

TABLE 44.3 *Concld.*

1	2	3	4	5
14.	Baharat Electronics Ltd. Trade Centre Bangalore	In-house	1480 1717	Professional Electronics & equipments, viz. Booster amplifier (transistorised), Regulator, Power Meter etc.
15.	BASF India Ltd. Bombay	In-House	2	Agro-Chemicals
16.	Gharda Chemicals Ltd., Bombay	In-House	152	Oxyclozanide.
17.	Gharda Chemicals Ltd., Bombay	In-House	42	Insoproturon Technical Insoproturon 50% & 75% WP
18.	Jyoti Ceramic Industries Pvt. Ltd. Bombay	In-House	34 95	High density high Aluminia ceramic grinding material and wear registering material
19.	Gharda Chemicals	In-House	13	Oxyclozanide
20.	Gharda Chemicals	In-House	83	Orthro Phenylene Diamine (OPDA)

Council of Scientific and Industrial Research

The Council of Scientific and Industrial Research established in 1942 consists of 42 National Laboratories and Research Associations covering Physical and Earth Sciences, Chemical Science, Biological Sciences, Engineering Sciences, Information Science and Industrial Research Associations.

LIST OF CSIR INSTITUTIONS

Physical and Earth Sciences Group

National Physical Laboratory, New Delhi	(NPL)
Central Electronics Engineering Research Institute, Pilani	(CEERI)
Central Scientific Instruments Organisation, Chandigarh	(CSIO)
National Geophysical Research Institute, Hyderabad	(NGRI)
National Institute of Oceanography, Dona Paula, Goa	(NIO)

Chemicals Sciences Group

National Chemical Laboratory, Pune	(NCL)
Central Electrochemical Research Institute, Karaikudi	(CECRI)
Central Salt and Marine Chemicals Research Institute, Bhavnagar	(CSMCRI)
Indian Institute of Chemical Technology, Hyderabad	(IICT)
Regional Research Laboratory, Jorhat	(RRL-Jorhat)
Indian Institute of Petroleum, Dehradun	(IIP)
Central Leather Research Institute, Madras	(CLRI)
Central Fuel Research Institute, Jealgora	(CFRI)

Biological Sciences Group

Central Food Technological Research Institute, Mysore	(CFTRI)
Central Drug Research Institute, Lucknow	(CDRI)
National Botanical Research Institute, Lucknow	(NBRI)
Indian Institute of Chemical Biology, Calcutta	(IICB)
Central Institute of Medicinal & Aromatic Plants, Lucknow	(CIMAP)
Industrial Toxicology Research Centre, Lucknow	(ITRC)
Centre for Cellular and Molecular Biology, Hyderabad	(CCMB)
Regional Research Laboratory, Jammu	(RRL-Jammu)
Institute of Microbial Technology, Chandigarh	(IMTECH)
CSIR Complex, Palampur, HP	Palampur
CSIR, Complex, for Biochemicals	(CFB)

Engineering Sciences Group

Central Building Research Institute, Roorkee	(CBRI)
Central Road Research Institute, New Delhi	(CRRI)
Central Glass and Ceramic Research Institute, Calcutta	(CGCRI)
National Metallurgical Laboratory, Jamshedpur	(NML)
Central Mining Research Station, Dhanbad	(CMRS)
Central Mechanical Engineering Research Institute, Durgapur	(CMERI)
National Environmental Engineering Research Institute, Nagpur	(NEERI)
National Aeronautical Laboratory, Bangalore	(NAL)
Structural Engineering Research Centre, Madras	(SERC-M)
Structural Engineering Research Centre, Ghaziabad	(SERC-G)
Regional Research Laboratory, Bhubaneswar	(RRL-Bhu)
Regional Research Laboratory, Trivandrum	(RRL-Triv)
Regional Research Laboratory, Bhopal	(RRL-Bhopal)

Information Science Group

Publications and Information Directorate, New Delhi	(PID)
Indian National Scientific Documentation Centre, New Delhi	(INSDOC)
National Institute of Science, Technology and Development Studies, New Delhi	(NISTADS)

Industrial Research Associations

Tocklai Experimental Station of TRA, Jorhat	(TESTRA)
Electrical Research and Development Association, Vadodara	(ERDA)

45

TRANSPORT

45.1 Civil Aviation

The civil aviation sector has two functional divisions: operational and infrastructural. On the operational side, Indian Airlines, Vayudoot and private air taxis provide domestic air services, and Air India provides international air services. Pawan Hans provides helicopter services to ONGC in its offshore operations and to inaccessible areas and difficult terrains. Infrastructural facilities are provided by the International Airports Authority of India (IAAI) and the National Airports Authority (NAA).

Air India

The net profit of Air India has increased to Rs.279.03 crore in April-December 1992 compared to Rs.77.15 crore in the same period of the previous year (Table 45.1). The load factor in April-December 1992 was 58.5 per cent in the same period of the previous year.

TABLE 45.1: Performance of Air India

				April-December*		Change over previous year		
	1989-90	1990-91	1991-92*	1991-92	1992-93	1990-91	1991-92	1992-93@
1	2	3	4	5	6	7	8	9
							(per cent)	
1 Revenue (Rs.crore)	1428.38	1747.96	2128.84	1486.28	1996.32	22.37	21.79	34.32
2 Expenses (Rs.crore)	1357.49	1666.73	2012.13	1409.13	1717.29	22.78	20.72	21.87
3 Net Surplus after tax (Rs.crore)	70.89	81.23	116.71	77.15	279.03	14.59	43.68	261.67
4 Capacity available million tonne-km)	2292	2260	2249	1462	1513	-1.40	-0.49	3.50
5 Capacity utilised (million tonne-km)	1441	1381	1493	849	874	-4.16	8.11	`2.88
6 Load factor (per cent)	62.87	61.11	66.39	58.50	58.20	-2.81	8.64	-0.51

* Provisional.
@ April-December

Air India's load factor is still low compared to other international airlines. Its share of international traffic originating from India has come down from 42 per cent in 1981 to 35 per cent in 1990-91. Air India intends to augment its aircraft and reduce the average life of its fleet by a fleet renewal and expansion plan.

Indian Airlines

The total revenue of Indian Airlines increased by 3.9 per cent in 1990-91 and 24.7 per cent in 1991-92, but the expenses by 8.2 per cent in 1990-91 and 36.6 per cent in 1991-92. The net loss tripled from Rs.64.6 crore in 1990-91 to Rs.198.65 crore in 1991-92 (Table 45.2).

TABLE 45.2: Performance of Indian Airlines

				April-December*		Change over previous year		
	1989-90	1990-91	1991-92*	1991-92	1992-93	1990-91	1991-92	1992-93@
1	2	3	4	5	6	7	8	9
							(per cent)	
1 Revenue (Rs.crore)	1125.15	1169	1457.85	1288.79	1189.06	3.90	24.71	-7.74
2 Expenses (Rs.crore)	1140.19	1234	1685.97	1341.76	1296.17	8.23	36.63	-3.40
3 Net surplus after tax (Rs.crore)	15.24	-64.59	-198.65	-52.97	-107.11	-523.82	207.56	102.21
4 Capacity available (million tonne-km)	113	926.7	1089.77	904.33	779.64	-18.28	17.60	-13.79
5 Capacity utilised (million tonne-km)	826	699.2	761.08	639.53	553.96	-15.35	8.85	-13.38
6 Load factor (per cent)	72.84	75.45	69.84	70.72	71.05	3.58	-7.44	0.47

* Provisional.
@ April-December.

Vayudoot

The loss incurred by Vayudoot was Rs.37.07 crore in 1990-91 and Rs.30.59 crore in 1991-92, was more than the revenue earned in the respective years. The loss incurred unit April-December, 1992 is Rs.15.8 crore in the same period of the previous year.

Pawan Hans Limited (PHL)

The induction of three Mi-8 helicopters on wet lease from Russia augmented the efforts of PHL in providing total helicopter support services to the oil sector. The revenue of the corporation is expected to increase by 27 per cent in 1992-93. Projected expenditure shows an increase of 15 per cent over the previous year. Net operating profit is projected to increase by about 46 per cent in 1992-93.

Air Taxi Services

The scheme for the operation of air taxi service by private sector has become operational since 1990. All citizens of India or groups of Indians including Non-resident Indians or public-sector undertakings can apply for an air taxi operator's permit. Air taxis are permitted to operate to all authorised airports and can decide their fares and flight schedules. Air taxi services can be operated both on charter and on a non-charter basis. The number of passengers carried by these air tax operators has increased from 582 in 1990 to 35018 during April-November 1992.

Certain important policy initiatives have been taken recently to accelerate the development of civil aviation in the country. The tourist charter policy has been considerably liberalised so that foreign nationals can now visit the country by specially chartered aircraft, automatic clearance for which is given by the Director General of Civil Aviation.

An open sky policy for cargo has been introduced to facilitate exports. Under this policy, any foreign or domestic airline or association of exporters or private operators can bring freighters to the country for lifting of cargo from any Customs airport.

International Airports Authority of India (IAAI)

During 1990-91 and 1991-92, IAAI fell short of performance level of 1989-90 in terms of passenger and cargo handled (Table 45.3). To some extent, this represents a slowdown in tourist arrivals and foreign trade compression of 1991-92. But it also emphasises the need for better capacity utilisation and improving the quality of facilities and services at the international airports.

TABLE 45.3: Performance of the International Airports Authority of India

				April-December*		Change over previous year		
	1989-90	1990-91	1991-92*	1991-92	1992-93	1990-91	1991-92	1992-93@
1	2	3	4	5	6	7	8	9
							(per cent)	
1 Revenue (Rs. crore)	227.83	230.89	259.92	192.82	220.22	1.34	12.57	14.21
2. Expenses (Rs. crore)	119.89	131.84	171.84	95.01	112.08	9.97	29.96	17.97
3. Net Surplus after Tax (Rs. crore)	60.94	54.05	46.08	48.59	54.27	-11.31	-14.75	11.69
4. Passengers (lakh)	199.64	177.23	188.2	140.33	146.07	-11.23	6.19	4.09
5. Cargo (thousand tonnes)	414.99	376.9	370.3	268.9	295.12	-9.18	-1.75	9.75

* Provisional.
@ April-December.

National Airport Authority

Airport Surveillance Radars (ASR) and Monopulse Secondary Surveillance Radars (MSSRR) were installed at Guwahati, Trivandrum, Hyderabad and Ahmedabad. The total capital outlay for a set of ASR and MSSR is estimated at Rs.28.15 crore including a foreign exchange content of Rs.20.66 crore.

Hindustan Aeronautics Limited (HAL)

The defence-oriented public sector unit Hindustan Aeronautics Limited (HAL) added another feather to its cap when the first multi-purpose and multi-role fully indigenous Advanced Light Helicopter (ALH) rolled out its assembly line today marking an important landmark on the Indian aviation scene.

The cost effective highly reliable twin-engine aircraft apart from meeting the staff requirements of the Indian Air Force, Navy and Army could cater to the commercial and emergency needs of the civil aviation.

Designed and developed with international market in mind, the duplex flight controlled helicopter fitted with integrated dynamic and antiresonance isolation system is ready for the skies though the maiden test flight is expected by August after a series of ground tests staring from today.

To quote the chairman of the HAL Wg. Cdr. R.N. Sharma, the advanced light helicopter is the result of high technology optimised to achieve best combination of performance, safety and versatility. Incorporation of a number of state-of-the-art technologies developed with the technical support from Eurocopter, Germany (formerly MBB, West Germany), would not only have an edge over other helicopters in the 4-5 tonne class, it may herald a new era in aviation.

Extensive use of composite fibre-glass material would result in low radar signature thus increasing the survivability in Defence applications. And with stress on computers for aerodynamics it would ensure safety in emergency evacuation operations in case of natural calamities and disaster. It was the culmination of joint effort of a team of 750 qualified scientists, engineers and technicians with the help of computer aided designs and CNC machines.

The unit has a production capacity of 36 aircrafts a year and once the production starts the indigenously developed model should be the cheapest in the world market among its kind.

The aircraft had capability to fly for 30 minutes even if all the lubricants go dry. The large verticle fin would also enable continuation of forward flight even if the tail rotor was damaged.

All these features, would enable ALH to achieve various missions with exceptionally high degree of confidence, because of easy manoeuvrability country.

Light Combat Aircraft (LCA) will take to the skies in 1996 and will be inducted into the country's air-strike wing by the next century.

45.2 **Inland Water Transport**

Inland Waterways Authority of India (IWAI)

The Inland Waterways Authority of India was set up on 27-10-1986 under IWAI Act, 1985. The Authority has been entrusted with the responsibility of development, maintenance and regulation of National Waterways in the country besides advising the Government of India on the matters relating to Inland Waterways Transportation. At present there are two National Waterways viz. Allahabad-Haldia stretch of the Ganga-Bhagirathi-Hooghly river and Sadiya-Dhubri Stretch of the Brahmaputra river. For the development of these National Waterways, the following works were undertaken:

— A navigation channel of 1.5 metre depth and 45 metre width is provided in Haldia-Ballia Stretch (1140 km) of the Gange.
— A scheme for construction of general cargo berth at Patna has been sanctioned at an estimated cost of Rs. 4.90 crore.
— The shallow draft cargo vessel "Rajagopalachari" is being operated regularly one round trip in a month between Calcutta and Patna with a view to make public awareness in making use of IWT services.
— A navigation channel of 2.25 metre depth and 45 metre width is being provided in Dhubri-Gamari stretch (520 km) of the Brahmputra.

Central Inland Water Transport Corporation Limited (CIWTC)

Central Inland Water Transport Corporation Limited was set up on 3rd May 1967. The present authorised share capital of the CIWTC is Rs. 100.00 crore with a paid-up capital of Rs. 8003.73 lakhs.

The Corporation, for the first time, has been brought under the Memorandum of Understanding Scheme in appreciation of the fact that the functioning of the Corporation is essential from the strategic view point of maintaining supplies to North-East which has chromic transport bottlenecks due to natural factors.

The MOU for 1991-92, envisages among other things reduction of cash loss to the level of Rs. 3.225 crore, cargo transportation of 1500 lakh tonne km, fleet utilisation of 42 per cent ship building to the extent of 510 MT, ship repair of Rs. 5.20 crore, acquisition of 19 more vessels, etc.

the Government has sanctioned in June, 1991 a scheme costing Rs. 3.65 crores for acquisition of a hovercraft and setting up of allied infrastructural facilities for running a superfast passenger ferry services between Calcutta and Haldia.

Protocol on Inland Water Trade and Transit with Bangladesh

The Protocol on Inland Water Transit and Trade with Government of Bangladesh was renewed on 3-10-1991 for a further period of two years 4-10-1991 to 3-10-1993.

A Centrally-sponsored Scheme for construction of five terminals for ferry services across the river Hooghly at Botanical Garden, Kidderpur, Strand Road, Panihati, Konnagar at a cost of Rs. 225.00 lakhs has been sanctioned on 25th November 1991. A scheme will be executed by the Government of West Bengal. 50 per cent of the sanctioned cost of scheme would be met by the Central Government as loan assistance.

Declaration of West Coast Canal as a National Waterway

The Government has decided to declare the Quilon-Kottapuram Stretch of the West Coast Canal and Champakara Canal and Udyogmandal Canal in Kerala as a National Waterway. A Bill for enactment of a Central Legislation in this regard, is to be introduced in the Parliament during the Budget Session.

45.3 **Railways**

The length of the railway network during 1991-92 was 62571 route kilometers. The electrified network increased at average annual rate of six per cent in the 1980s, and by eight per cent in 1991-92. The electrified network in 1991-92 was 10809 route kilometers.

TABLE 45.4: Performance of the Railways

				April-December*			Change over previous year	
	1989-90	1990-91	1991-92*	1991-92	1992-93	1990-92	1991-92	1992-93@
1	2	3	4	5	6	7	8	9
								(per cent)
1 Total revenue-earning freight traffic (million tonnes)	309.97	318.40	337.98	244.91	254.45	2.72	6.15	3.90
(i) Coal	130.15	135.16	146.43	106.56	113.82	3.85	8.34	6.80
(ii) Raw materials for steel Plants (excl.coal)	27.43	25.90	29.56	20.93	24.44	-5.58	14.13	16.77
(iii) Pig iron & finished steel from steel plants	10.15	10.01	11.44	7.96	8.80	-1.38	14.29	10.55
(iv) Iron ore for export	14.76	13.14	12.76	9.52	7.99	-10.98	-2.29	-16.07
(v) Cement	27.45	28.78	30.51	21.51	21.66	4.85	6.01	0.70
(vi) Foodgrains	23.66	25.35	27.38	19.39	19.16	7.14	8.01	-1.19
(vii) Fertilizers	16.97	18.36	18.59	14.08	14.51	8.19	1.25	3.05
(viii) POL	24.31	25.06	25.63	18.89	19.77	3.09	2.27	4.66
(ix) Balance (other goods)	35.09	36.64	35.68	26.07	24.30	4.42	-2.62	-6.79
2 Net tonne-kilometers (million)	229.60	235.78	250.24	181.30	184.82	2.69	6.13	1.94
3 Net tonne-kilometers per wagon per day (broad gauge)	1428.00	1455.00	1473.00	1380.00**	1439.00**	1.89	1.24	4.30**
4 Passenger traffic originating (million)	3653.00	3959.00	4048.00	2292.00**	2162.00**	5.61	4.92	-5.70**
5 Passenger-kilometers (billion)	280.80	295.70	314.56	186.10**	181.85**	5.31	6.38	-2.30**

* Provisional.
@ April-December.
** April-October.

Energy constitutes a little over 20 per cent of the Railways' working expenses. Therefore, priority is being given to energy-conserving measures like the accelerated phasing out of energy-inefficient steam locomotives, retrofitting fuel-efficient kits on diesel locomotives, fitting choppers and thyristors on electric locomotives, and introducing lightweight coaches and wagons.

Originating freight traffic increased by six per cent to 337.43 million tonnes in 1991-92 (Table 45.4). During the 1980s, it increased at an average annual rate of 4.8 per cent. Shortfalls from the target for moving traffic reflected the slowdown in industrial growth, specially in steel and engineering. The freight traffic carried was 254.45 million tonnes in April-December, 3.9 per cent higher than during the same period of previous year. 6000 km of gauge conversion from metre and narrow gauge to broad gauge has been targeted.

There has been a progressive decline in the share of freight carried by the Railways. Since rail transport is more energy-efficient and environment-friendly, the decline in its share of freight needs to be reversed by means of higher efficiency, lower costs and a competitive management of the Railways. The importance of road transport for shorter haulages of high-value and perishable products is well established. An optimum mix of both forms of transport needs to be developed.

The Railways employ 16 lakh workers, the largest number for any undertaking in the country. Labour productivity has been quite low. A comprehensive human resource development programme is required to upgrade skills, retrain workers and achieve higher productivity. While staff productivity in terms of net tonnes per km per wagon-day, wagon turnaround time, loco utilisation etc. Have improved over the years, there is still scope for further improvement.

Budgetary support for the Railways has declined. The prospects of extra-budgetary support by way of market borrowings are receding, resulting in further pressure on internal resource generation. Railways being a basic infrastructural facility, the scope for raising fares and freight rates is limited. Hence, they have to meet the challenge by eliminating non-essential expenditure, increasing efficiency, conserving energy and raising manpower productivity.

Railway Budget 1993-94

* No increase in fares for Second Class ordinary up to a distance of 100 km.
* Fare to go up by 10 per cent for distances beyond 100 km.
* Fares for AC First Class First Class, AC Sleeper, AC Chair Car and Second Class Mail/Express to be raised by 10 per cent for all distances.
* Exemptions from Freight increases given in the past in respect of grains and pulses, sugar diesel and oilcake to be withdrawn.
* Freight rates of all commodities to be increased by 10 per cent for distances up to 500 km and 12 per cent for distance of 501 km and above.
* A new class of travel designated as "Sleeper Class" to be introduced. The fare of this class will be 25 per cent higher than that of ordinary mail/express second class but no separate sleeper surcharge to be recovered.
* Frequency of New Delhi/Howrah Rajdhani Express from five days a week to daily.
* New Delhi-Bombay Rajdhani Express from six days a week to daily.
* Insurance scheme to cover deaths and injuries to passengers caused by terrorist attacks, dacoities and bomb blasts.
* Computerised passenger reservations being extended to 12 more stations. As a result 80 per cent of train reservations would be on computer.

* 11 new line projects and sections, totalling 319 km, targetted for opening in the current year.
* Four new line projects and sections programmed to be completed in 1993-94 totalling 269 km.

TABLE 45.5: Existing and Proposed Fares between Selected Pairs of Station

Pairs of Stations	AC First Class		AC Sleeper		First Class		AC Chair Car		Second Class (Mail/Express)	
	Existing	Proposed	Existing	Proposed	Existing	Proposed	Existing	Proposed	Existing	Proposed
New Delhi-Bombay Central	1560	1716	861	948	682	751	379	417	172	189
New Delhi-Bangalore	2410	2651	1219	1341	1053	1159	563	620	223	245
New Delhi-Trivandrum Ctrl.	2919	3211	1420	1562	1274	1402	672	740	255	281
New Delhi-Bhubaneshwar	1931	2125	1029	1132	843	928	458	504	194	213
New Delhi-Lucknow	753	829	454	500	331	365	199	219	92	101
New Delhi-Patna	1241	1366	718	790	543	598	309	340	142	162
New Delhi-Ahmedabad (BG)	1308	1439	745	820	572	630	325	358	150	165
New Delhi-Howrah	1599	1759	878	966	703	774	388	427	175	193
New Delhi-Guwahati	2039	2243	1072	1180	891	981	481	530	201	221
New Delhi-Chandigarh	450	495	279	307	199	219	124	137	54	59
New Delhi-Jaipur	504	555	308	339	224	247	137	151	63	69
New Delhi-Madras Central	2198	2418	1136	1250	961	1058	517	569	210	231
New Delhi-Secunderabad	1800	1980	979	1077	789	868	431	475	186	205
Pune-New Delhi	1738	1912	946	1041	751	827	413	455	181	199
New Delhi-Allahabad	906	997	521	574	397	437	232	256	106	117

TABLE 45.6: Fares for Rajdhani Express — and New Delhi-Bombay August Kranti Rajdhani Express Train

(*in Rs.*)

Pairs of Station	AC First Class		AC Sleeper		AC Chair Car	
	Existing	Proposed	Existing	Proposed	Existing	Proposed
1	2	3	4	5	6	7
New Delhi-Bombay Central	2030	2235	1170	1290	580	640
New Delhi-Vadodara	1605	1770	915	1010	465	515
New Delhi-Ratlam	1390	1530	780	880	420	465
New Delhi-Kota	990	1095	595	655	320	355
New Delhi-Howrah	2070	2280	1195	1315	590	650
New Delhi-Dhanbad	1830	2015	1060	1170	520	575
New Delhi-Mughalsarai	1435	1580	800	900	435	480
New Delhi-Kanpur Central	950	1055	580	640	310	345
New Delhi-Allahabad	1260	1390	750	825	385	430
New Delhi-Sawai Madhopur	865	955	520	575	285	315
New Delhi-Surat	1765	1945	1035	1140	510	565

Contd.

(*Concld.*)

1	2	3	4	5	6	7
New Delhi-Gaya	1545	1715	900	990	455	500
H. Nizamuddin-Bhopal	1170	1285	685	755	330	370
H. Nizamuddin-Nagpur	1550	1705	890	985	430	480
H. Nizamuddin-Secunderabad	2025	2230	1110	1225	520	580
H. Nizamuddin-Bangalore	2700	2970	1375	1520	670	745

Railway Finances

1	Goods earnings	66p
2	Passenger earnings	26p
3	Other coaching earnings	03p
4	Miscellaneous receipts	03p
5	Sundry other earnings	02p

This rupee was spent on

1	Staff wages and other allowances	32p
2	Dividend	08p
3	Pension fund	08p
4	Fuel	14p
5	Depreciation reserve fund	14p
6	Stores	08p
7	Lease Charges	04p
8	Development fund	03p
9	Miscellaneous	09p

Excerpts of Railway Minister's Speech

Freight Traffic: The Railways carried 338 million tonnes revenue earning freight traffic. Three million tonnes more than the Budget Estimate target of 335 million tonnes and 19.6 million tonnes more than the loading achieved in 1990-91. Thus, a growth rate of over six per cent was achieved during this year. The Railways would have surpassed even this target but for the agitation and economic blockade by Jharkhand Mukti Morcha.

Passenger Traffic: Passenger traffic also registered an impressive growth. The number of originating passengers increased by about five per cent and passenger kilometres by about 6.4 per cent.

The financial results truly reflect the good physical performance. An excess of Rs.235 crore was projected in the Budget Estimates for the year 1991-92. This excess was placed at Rs.435 crore at the Revised Estimate stage, after providing in full for the dividend liability of Rs.1,039 crore and Rs.40 crore additionally for the Pension Fund.Indian Railways not only achieved the projected excess of Rs 453 crore but augmented the Pension Fund further by Rs.90 crore and liquidated the deferred dividend liability to an extend of performance, as yet unsurpassed in the annals of Indian Railways.

The Indian Railways started the current year on an optimistic note. A general upswing in the transport demand was anticipated as a result of the bold industrial and economic reforms initiated by the Government. The originating revenue earning freight traffic was expected to go up from 338 million tonnes in 1992-93. The projected traffic from the core sectors has however, not materialised. The tragic event at Ayodhya and the disturbances thereafter have also taken their toll of the freight movement. Nevertheless, the Railways hope to carry 350 million tonnes of traffic, 12 million tonnes more than that carried last year, and this has been provided for in the Revised Estimates.

It was anticipated that, in the current year, there would be a growth of passenger traffic by about five per cent. The anticipated growth in passenger traffic has not materialised. The Ayodhya incident and the law and order situation reduction in passenger earnings.

Action Plan: As the House is aware, a detailed Action Plan was launched this year to achieve reduction in working expenses by cost control, cost reduction and economy measure besides augmenting earnings through marketing strategies and plugging leakage of revenue, though intensive checks. The Action Plan is by the Zonal Railways.

Though passenger earnings are likely to be Rs. 4,330 crore, the Budget target of Rs.10.568 crore of goods earnings is likely to be exceeded by Rs. 532 crore. The gross traffic receipts are expected to go up from, the budgeted figure of Rs.15,884 crore to Rs.16,115 crore, an increase of Rs.231 crore.

The Ordinary Working Expenses for the current financial year, 1992-93 are estimated at Rs 10,575 crore. Several post-budgetary factors such as higher dearness allowance rates, decontrol of steel prices, procurement of foreign exchange at market rates, hike in diesel prices and increase in electricity tariff have put the working expenses under a severe strain. While the Indian Railways are able to absorb most of the post-budgetary impact, it has, nonetheless, become inescapable to provide in the Revised Estimates 1992-93, an amount of Rs.115 crore over the Budget Estimates of Rs 10,460 crore.

In the Budget for the year 1992-93, provision for payment of deferred dividend of Rs.416 crore was made. Since an amount of Rs.74 crore of deferred dividend liability has already been discharged in the year 1991-92, the liability gets reduced from the budget figure of Rs. 416 crore to Rs. 342 crore.

After meeting in full the dividend liability of Rs. 1,146 crore and the deferred dividend liability of Rs. 342 crore, an excess of Rs. 575 crore is anticipated as against the budget of Rs. 564 crore. This excess of rs. 757 crore will be utilised in repayment of Development Fund loan together with interest thereon, cost of Development Fund Works and to meet part of the capital requirements of the Railways.

The House is aware that the budgetary support provided by the General Revenues to Indian Railways is declining. It has come down from 75 per cent in the Fifth Plan to 58 per cent in the Sixth Plan and 42 per cent in the Seventh Plan. It is now only 14.7 per cent in 1993-94. At the same time, the market borrowings by Indian Railways Finance Corporation to supplement the Railway Plan are becoming increasingly difficult and expensive. Thus a substantial component of the capital outlay will, from now onwards, have to be met with from out of the internally generated resources. A Memorandum has accordingly been submitted to the Railway Convention Committee to approve setting up of a

Capital Fund. Meanwhile, this new Capital Fund is being set up from this year. This fund will be financed from out of the internally generated resources and will be used to meet part of the capital requirements.

Plan Outlay: The size of the Eighth Plan has been fixed at Rs. 27,202 crore, including a budgetary support of Rs. 5,375 crore. The Eighth Plan objectives are an annual growth rate of 5 per cent in passenger traffic and a total freight traffic of 443 million tonnes in the terminal year of the Eighth Plan.

The current year, 1992-93, is the first year of the Eight Plan. The Plan size for this year is Rs. 5,710 crore including an amount of Rs. 1,200 crore to be mobilised by Indian Railway Finance Corporation through issue of bonds. Unfortunately, due to adverse bond market conditions, Indian Railway Finance Corporation has so far been able to mobilise only a meagre amount of Rs. 10.5 crore, even though the rate of interest on the bonds was increased from 9 per cent to 10.5 per cent tax-free. The Plan was in jeopardy. Since infrastructure development is crucial for economic development, I have decided to keep the Plan size intact. Out of Rs. 1,200 crore to be mobilised through bonds, an amount of Rs. 238 crore is proposed to be met through internal resource generation of Railways themselves. Indian Railway Finance Corporation has paid Rs. 530 crore from its own corpus and is making further efforts to mobilise resources.

The Railway's capacity has now reached a plateau and there is hardly any slack left in the system. Massive outlays are needed for creation of additional capacity and for replacement of assets. Development of alternative routes through gauge conversion has become a necessity for smooth flow of rail traffic and for opening up areas for development. The size of the Eighth Plan may require a mid-term upward revision.

The outlay for the Railway Plan, 1993-94 is fixed at Rs. 6,500 crore as against the Plan size of Rs. 5,710 crore for the current year. If one takes into account the general inflation and the increase in steel prices due to decontrol, the size of the Plan for 1993-94 will, in real terms, be not more than that of the current year. A notable feature of this Plan is that the budgetary support provided is only Rs. 960 crore. An amount of Rs. 4,640 crore will be met from out of the internally generated resources and the balance of Rs. 900 crore is proposed to be raised through issue of bonds. It is for the first time that more than 70 per cent of the Plan outlay is being funded by the resources generated internally, after payment of dividend in full.

Source: *Hindustan Times*, February 25, 1993.

45.4 **Roads and Road Transport**

The total road network in the country increased 20.7 per cent from 16.9 lakh km in 1985 to 20.4 lakh km at the end of 1990-91. The National Highways constitute hardly two per cent of the total road network but carry nearly 40 per cent of the total road traffic.

The National Highway network is in need of considerable improvement. About 12 per cent of the total National Highway needs widening from single to double lanes. About 56 per cent of the total length of two-lane roads have to be strengthened; 44 per cent of the National Highway network is expected to have traffic of more than 1500 passenger car units by 1995 and thus will have to be widened to four lanes. Selected corridors, traffic of more than 40, 000 passenger car units in 1995- about 3 per cent of the National Highway network-needs conversion into expressways. The estimated expenditure on the above items as worked out by the Ministry of Surface Transport will be Rs.41390 crore at 1991 prices. An outlay of Rs.2600 crore has been approved by the Planning Commission for the Eighth Plan.

All-weather accessibility of villages has improved significantly over the years. During 1990-91 and 1991-92, 93, 000 villages was connected with all-weather roads.

The present share of road traffic is about 80 per cent in passenger traffic and about 50 per cent in freight traffic.

The sixty-six State Road Transport Corporations operate a fleet of nearly 1.12 lakh buses with an investment of over Rs.3910 crore. They employ over 7.53 lakh workers and carry about 6.8 crore passengers a day.

Fleet utilisation has declined from 89 per cent in 1989-90 to 87 per cent in 1991-92. Vehicle productivity at 183 km/bus/day in 1991-92 has increased at 5 per cent per annum since 1989-90. The performance of most State transport undertakings is below the desired level. Most incur heavy losses. Their declined from Rs.167.30 crore in 1987-88 to Rs.118.90 crore in 1991-92 as a number of them revised fares.

206 km of National Highways were widened from single lane to double lane, 727 km strengthened. 25 km widened to four lane and 8 bridges completed.

Major National Highway works completed include:

(i) Strengthening existing two lane pavement of km 16 and km 30 to 35 on NH 28 in U.P. — Cost Rs. 393.31 lakhs.

(ii) Strengthening existing two lane pavement from km 156 to 186 of NH 4 in Karnataka — Cost Rs. 278.24 lakhs.

(iii) Strengthening weak and carriageway from km 318 to 343 of NH 17 in Karnataka — Cost Rs. 188.57 lakhs.

(iv) Construction of Vanasdhara bridge at km 112.8 of NH 5 in Andhra Pradesh — Cost Rs. 185.78 Lakhs.

(v) Strengthening existing two lane pavements of km 115 to 140 on NH 56 in Uttar Pradesh — Cost Rs. 284.17 lakhs.

(vi) Strengthening existing two lane pavement of km 430.5 to 448.855 on NH 1 in Punjab — Cost Rs. 268.00 lakhs.

(vii) Strengthening existing two lane pavement of km 309 to 325 of NH 24 in Uttar Pradesh — Cost Rs. 269.20 lakhs.

(viii) Strengthening two lane pavement of km 65 to 67.69, 71.72 and 110 to 115 of NH 56 in Uttar Pradesh — Cost Rs. 234.15 lakhs.

(ix) Strengthening pavement of km 148 to 170 of NH 48 in Karnataka — Cost Rs. 146.40 lakhs.

(x) Construction of bridge including approaches across Borgaon nalla at km 510/200 of NH 6 in Maharashtra — Cost Rs. 103.62 lakhs.

(xi) Construction of bridge at Km 61/6 & 72/2 on Hyderabad-Bangalore section of NH 7 in Andhra Pradesh — Cost Rs. 371.52 lakhs.

An agreement loan 2534-IN was signed with the World Bank in September, 1985 for loan assistance of US$ 200 million (Approx. Rs. 240 crore) for financing the six National Highway projects in the States of Haryana, Punjab, Uttar Pradesh, Gujarat, West Bengal and Tamil Nadu are in various stages of progress.

World Bank have also agreed to provide loan assistance for some State road projects in the States of Bihar, Maharashtra, Rajasthan and U.P. The total cost of these projects is estimated as US$ 450 million and the loan assistance is US$ 250 million (US$ 170 million Bank loan US$ 80 million IDFA credit).

World Bank Assistance (Second Loan): A Negotiations have been completed with the World Bank in July 1991 for a Second NH Loan for four-laning of National Highway Projects in the States of Haryana, Punjab, Maharashtra, Orissa, Madhya Pradesh and West Bengal. The total loan will be US$ 299 million including US$14 million for reconstruction of damaged bridges on State Roads in Orissa.

Overseas Economic Cooperation Fund (Japan): The Mission of OECF visited India from 29th July, 1991 to 9th August, 1991 for appraisal of the Project of four laning of Mathura-Agra Section of NH 2 in Uttar Pradesh. as per assessment of the Appraisal Mission, the latest cost of the project is Rs. 106.50 crores including price escalation. The amount of loan would be 4055 million Yen (Approx. US$ 34.7 million). Negotiation for loan has been held in Tokyo in December 1991.

An agreement RIP 918-IND was signed by the Asian Development Bank with the Government of India and is effective since April 1989 for a loan assistance amounting to US$ 198 million for financing road projects both in the Central and States sectors covering states of Andhra Pradesh, Haryana, Karnataka, Tamil Nadu and U.P. Work of execution have been entrusted in most of the packages on National Highways.

Negotiations were concluded with the Asian Development Bank for a loan assistance of US$ 250 million for financing 2nd Road projects in Central and State sectors covering States of Kerala, Karnataka, Rajasthan, Andhra Pradesh, Orissa, Uttar Pradesh and West Bengal. The loan agreement has been signed in May, 1991 and is effective from July, 1991. Pre-qualification of contractors for these projects has been completed and tenders have been invited for all projects except those in Kerala.

Road Transport

Road Transport Division of this Ministry is concerned with the formulation of broad policies relating to Road Transport, Motor Vehicle Legislation, Legislation relating to State Road Transport Corporations and movement of vehicular traffic with the neighbouring countries, apart from looking after the affairs of the Delhi Transport Corporation.

Road Transport plays an important role in the economic development of the country. During the recent past, there has been a phenomenal growth in vehicle population, as also the carrying of freight and passengers by road. For regulating the operation of vehicular traffic, Motor Vehicles Act, 1988 is the Chief document where the Government policy relating to Motor Vehicles is enunciated. The rule relating to prototype testing and issue of certificate of road worthiness have been notified to come into effect from 1st April, 1991. The various provisions of the Act/Rules were also reviewed during this period by a Committee constituted with representatives from the States/UTs and vehicle manufacturer's associations, etc. Comprehensive amendments in the Motor Vehicles Act and Rules are under consideration of the Government.

State Road Transport Undertakings

There are 56 State Road Transport Undertakings having a fleet of nearly 104500 vehicles providing passenger transport in various parts of the country. These public sector organisation put together 6 crores passengers every day. The physical and financial performance of these undertakings is compiled on a quarterly basis.

45.5 **Shipping**

Indian vessels carried about 38 per cent of the total sea borne cargo in 1991-92 against 37.8 per cent during 1990-91. The share of India vessels in POL was 61 per cent in 1991-92, in bulk carriers 28 per cent (long-term target: 50 per cent) and in liner traffic 17 per cent (long-term target: 40 per cent).

The fleet strength at the end of December 1992 was 430 vessels of 6.28 million Gross Registered Tonnes (GRT) against 414 vessels of 5.917 million GRT in November, 1991. Overseas trade during 1991-92 was 113.77 million tonnes against 111.03 million tonnes during 1990-91.

Acquisition of vessels by ship-owning companies is now granted automatic approval except in respect of crude tankers from September 1992. There are no restrictions on the sale of vessels by shipping companies. Foreign shipping companies are free to charter Indian vessels.

Shipping Corporation of India (SCI), a public-sector unit, which accounted for 6.36 million GRT (52.6 per cent of the fleet) in 1985-86, brought it down to 3.01 million GRT (47.9 per cent of the fleet) in 1985-86, brought it down to 3.01 million GRT (47.9 per cent of the fleet) by November 1992. It increased its gross internal resources to Rs.257 crore in 1991-92 from Rs.198 crore in 1990-91. Net Profit after tax was Rs.54.46 crore in 1990-91 and Rs.114.52 crore in 1991-92. During April-September 1992 the net profit after tax was 47.06 crore, compared to 56.18 core in the same period of the previous year.

From Independence till about 1980 the Indian fleet expanded rapidly, growing 27 times in a span of 33 years. From 1980 till 1988, there was practically no growth in the Indian tonnage but it improved qualitatively in terms of its diversification during these years. There has been a marked improvement in the Shipping scenario since 1988 and the Indian tonnage has started rising slowly.

Almost from the close of 1974, the shipping industry, the world over started experiencing a slump following the hike in oil prices and consequent cut-back in production, with too many ships chasing a progressively falling quantum of cargo. Indian shipping industry has not been an exception to this phenomenon. Government have been making continuous assessment of the shipping scenario. With the upturn in freight rates, which started towards the end of 1987, still continuing, the Indian Shipping scene has looked up during the last three and a half years.

With the conclusion of new wage agreements in the shipping industry in 1990, the continued exodus of Merchant Officers and Seamen to Foreign Ships had declined. A number of Indian ships had also been given for manning by Shipping Management Companies. Following devaluation of the rupee in July 1991, however, the disparities in salaries and wages between Indian and foreign ships in rupee terms have widened considerably. This has acted as an inducement to seek jobs on foreign vessels and Indian shipping companies are once again feeling the impact of short manning.

The prevailing balance of payment position affected the availability of foreign exchange for financing ship acquisitions from abroad. The increase in the prices of ships, both second hand and new, as also the foreign exchange crunch considerably slowed down the pace of acquisition of fresh tonnage. The restrictions imposed by the Reserve Bank of India in March, 1991, on availability of free foreign exchange for acquisition of ships brought ship acquisition to a virtual standstill.

The Government took various steps for the improvement of shipping industry. Some more fiscal incentives have been proposed for the Shipping Industry. To support them a new shipping policy has also been initiated with a view to provide rapid development of shipping. Maximise foreign exchange earnings, eliminate obstacles of procedures and increase the role of private and foreign participation.

Of the four Public Sector Units under the Shipping Wing, the Shipping Corporation of India is catering to shipping services on the mainland-islands, coastal and international routes whereas the three public sector shipyards, namely, Cochin Shipyard Limited, Cochin; Hindustan Shipyard Limited, Visakhapatnam and Hooghly Dock and Port Engineers Limited, Calcutta are engaged in Shipbuilding and Ship repair activities. CSL and HSL are catering to ocean-going sector while HDPE is mainly confined to construction of Fishing Trawlers, dumb barges, and small crafts for ports etc., in addition to building small passenger vessels for mainland-island services. In 1985 Hindustan Shipyard Limited diversified its activities to the fabrication of Offshore structures for oil exploration and production by ONGC, besides fabrication of Steel Girders for rail bridges, and, in a small way, construction of patrol vessels for Indian Navy and Coast Guard. Of these 4 Companies, only Shipping Corporation of India has continued to register profits while for a variety of reasons, the Shipyards have accumulated losses over the years.

Oil Tanker 'Jawaharlal Nehru' Launched

Ship No. 008 built by Cochin Shipyard Ltd. (CSL), a Public Sector Undertaking of the Ministry of Surface Transport, was launched recently. The ship named 'Jawaharlal Nehru', a 86,000 DWT crude oil tanker is being built for the Shipping Corporation of India (SCI). With the completion of work on the hull, it has been launched into the Cochin backwaters where the ship will undergo outboard fittings in the coming months. After engine and sea trial, 'Jawaharlal Nehru' is expected to be handed over to the SCI by December 1992.

The shipyard, incorporated as a company in 1972, was established by the Government of India with the object of augmenting ship building and ship repair capacity as well as to act as a catalyst for marine ancillary development and import substitution.

The first ship built by the yard 'M.V. Rani Padmini' was delivered to its owners SCI in July 1981. A 75,000 DWT Panamax Bulk Carrier, 'Rani Padmini' was the first biggest ship ever built in the country. Since then, four more similar vessels have been built and all of them are operating on international sea routes. The nation can certainly feel proud that CSL could build huge ships of international standard which bring fame to the yard and the country.

With the delivery of the last Panamax Bulk Carrier in 1989, the shipyard took upon the task of building mammoth crude oil tankers. One such vessel 'Motilal Nehru' (86,000 DWT) was delivered to the SCI in October 1990. 'Jawaharlal Nehru' is the second crude oil tanker being built in the same series. The tanker is 238 metres long and 38 mts wide. From keel to deck it is 21 metres high and goes up another 21 mts from the deck level.

The Union Government has also given CSL the green signal to go ahead with the construction of one more 86,000 DWT tanker for SCI. The yard, however, will not commence construction of Ship No. 009 immediately. According to Commodore S.S. Bawa, Chairman and Managing Director, CSL, the gap of almost one year between the launching and delivery of 'Jawaharlal Nehru' will be a period to concentrate more on ship repair activities. In addition to the ship repair dock, the shipyard can now utilise its building dock also for ship repairing.

The CSL which started ship repair in a limited way by attending to afloat repairs in 1978, installed full repair facilities by 1981. Today just as its building dock, the dry dock of CSL is the largest in the country capable of taking vessels up to 1,15,000 DWT for repair. There two quays with various associated shops having specialised machinery and cranes. The company is now capable of executing complex and sophisticated repair works on bulk carriers, cargo ships, tankers, single buoy mooring and oil rigs. One of the most sophisticated repair works undertaken recently was on the aircraft carrier "INS Viraat".

During 1990-91, profit from ship repair amounted to Rs. 7.84 crore. The target turnover from ship repair for the year 1991-92 is Rs. 30 crore. During January this year the shipyard carried out dry docking and repair on a foreign flag vessel earning Rs. 1 crore in foreign exchange.

The CSL is planning to set up a new ship repair complex with a capital outlay of Rs. 107.93 crore. The project provides for an additional repair dock with matching facilities. The gestation period for this new project would be five years. Work on this project is to commence during the Eighth Plan and completed during the Ninth Plan. The Government has set aside Rs. 41 crore to finance the project during the Eighth Plan. It is expected that the earnings from this project would be Rs. 50 crore per annum. The new complex can also provide direct employment to 200 persons.

The yard is also poised to diversify activities of the ship repair division into allied fields. A team of technicians has been formed exclusively to repair high-pressure boilers. The ship repair division has registered an unprecedented growth in recent months. As against the revised target of Rs. 30 crore for the current financial year, the income from ship repair has touched Rs. 28 crore on February 20.

Source: *Yojana*, June 30, 1992.

Ports

During the 7th Plan i.e. 1985-90, capacity of the major ports has increased from 132.73 Mt to 161.32 Mt (reassessed). In 8th Plan 1992-97, it is proposed to enhance the capacity to 256.49 Mt including 11.85 Mt to be added by user agencies. The Commodity-wise break-up of the capacity is given in Table 45.5.

TABLE 45.7: Commoditywise breakup of the Capacity of the Major Ports

S.No.	Commodity	Capacity in Million Tonnes as on				
		31.3.85	31.3.87	31.3.89	31.3.90 (reassessed)	31.3.97 (proposed)
1.	POL	55.25	63.25	63.25	72.15	106.15
2.	Iron Ore	41.50	41.50	41.50	41.50	45.50
3.	Fertiliser (Raw & Finished)	3.90	5.10	5.10	6.60	6.60
4.	Coal	6.25	6.25	6.25	6.50	42.00
5.	General Break Bulk Cargo	22.25	22.35	22.35	28.75	38.91
6.	Containers	3.48	3.48	3.48	5.82	17.33
	Total	132.73	141.93	141.93	161.32	256.49

Emphasis has been placed on modernisation of existing facilities. Stress is being also laid on increasing the extent of containerisation.

Objectives for the Eighth Plan

The following are the broad objectives for development of ports during the Eighth Plan:

(i) development of ports in such a way that it can move with and subserve the overall economic growth;
(ii) development of proper container handling facilities;
(iii) Port development should keep pace with change in shipping scenario especially in respect of size of ships, specialisation and automation;
(iv) deepening of drafts at selected major ports to receive larger vessels;
(v) increase in dredging capacity by replacement of averaged dredgers with modern larger capacity dredgers;
(vi) before embarking on any major investment on creation of additional infrastructural facilities, the development and modernisation of existing port facilities should receive top priority to improve overall efficiency and cargo handling productivity;
(vii) planned modernisation of port facilities and use of updated technology;
(viii) appropriate financial measures to be taken to improve the viability of ports including pooling of resources of major ports, rationalisation of ports tariff, simplification of documentation system;
(ix) encourage private sector in appropriate areas of investment such as ship repair facilities dry docking container terminal etc. to operate under the overall administration of ports; and
(x) development of inter-face transport links like rail and road to enable smooth transhipment and flow of traffic.

Outlays Proposed in Eighth Plan

An outlay of Rs. 7374.51 crore has been proposed for inclusion in 8th Plan 1992-97 for Ports Sector. Out of this, expenditure up to Rs. 3313.42 crore will be met by Port Trust out of Internal Extra Budgetary resources (Including funds to be provided by user agencies) and the balance of Rs. 4061.08 crore would be met out of budgetary support (including Rs. 1210.78 crore from foreign assistance).

There are several important projects under the Port Sector. The most important being the Jawaharlal Nehru Port Trust near, Bombay. The Port, when fully operational will have a capacity to handle 5.9 million tonnes of cargo. It will handle third generation container vessels as well as deep draft Panamax Type Bulk Carriers (60,000-80,000 DWT). The other important on-going projects in the Port Sector relate to Augmentation of Container handling facilities at Cochin, Madras and Calcutta. Construction of Second Oil Jetty at Haldia, procurement of dredger to replace Lady Willingdon and Construction of 7th Cargo Berth at Kandla are the other major on-going schemes.

During the second half of the 1980s, the cargo-handling capacity at major ports increased at an average annual rate of 4.5 per cent to reach the level of 162.77 million tonnes in 1989-90. During 1991-92, this capacity rose to 169.3 million tonnes, four per cent over the preceding year. Cargo handled at major ports during 1991-92 was 157.9 million tonnes against 152.9 million tonnes in the preceding year and a target of 155 million tonnes.

TABLE 45.8: Trends in Traffic at Major ports

				April-December*		Change over previous year		
	1989-90	1990-91	1991-92*	1991-92	1992-93	1990-91	1991-92	1992-93@
1	2	3	4	5	6	7	8	9
	(Million tonnes)					(per cent)		
1 POL	63.6	65.88	69.62	50.14	54.93	3.58	5.68	9.55
2 Iron ore	33.21	31.9	32.09	22.48	20.24	-3.94	0.60	-9.96
3 Fertiliser & raw materials	6.74	7.26	7.08	5.83	6.28	7.72	-2.48	7.72
4 Foodgrains	1.16	0.88	1.2	0.93	1.18	-24.14	36.36	26.88
5 Coal	17.6	19.65	22.5	16.82	18.1	11.65	14.50	7.61
6 Vegetable oil	0.49	0.88	0.36	0.25	0.19	79.59	-59.09	-24.00
7 Other liquids	2.26	2.75	4.43	3.28	3.25	21.68	61.09	-0.91
8 Containerised cargo	7.29	8.04	7.59	5.44	6.19	10.29	-5.60	13.79
9 Others	16.03	15.62	12.99	9.01	11.42	-2.56	-16.84	26.75
Total	148.38	152.86	157.86	114.18	121.78	3.02	3.27	6.66

* Provisional
@ April-December

During April-December 1992, the major ports handled 121.8 million tonnes of cargo against the target of 120.4 million tonnes, 6.7 per cent more than in the period last year (Table 45.6). Major increases in traffic were in respect of POL (4.79 million tonnes) coal (1.28 million tonnes) and general cargo, mostly foodgrains (3.32 million tonnes). However, iron ore traffic declined.

The composition of traffic has undergone significant changes in recent years making the item-wise capacities available at ports unrealistic (Table 45.7).

In contrast to port productivity, labour and equipment productivity are still low. Low labour productivity is mainly due to surplus labour in ports and outdated manning scales. These have to be renegotiated and made more flexible and raised in line with investment in equipment and machinery. Low equipment productivity is due to operational constraints such as equipment breakdown, time spent on surveys and deballasting, power failures etc.

In order to give a boost to container traffic and cut down transit time, the cabotage restrictions have been removed. Foreign shipping lines are now allowed to bring containers from the hinterland to a port and carry them from such a hub centre to destinations of this scheme. The Coastal trade restrictions have also been further relaxed to give foreign ships access to minor ports for break-bulk, support and import cargo.

TABLE 45.9: Commodity-wise Capacity and Actual Traffic Handled at Major Ports

Commodity	1984-85 Capacity	1984-85 Traffic	1991-92 Capacity	1991-92 Traffic
POL (Petroleum Oil and Lubricants)	55.25	49.73	78.00	69.42
Iron ore	41.50	26.00	41.50	32.09
Coal	6.25	4.50	7.0	22.50
Fertilisers	3.90	6.00	7.95	7.08
Containers	3.48	3.23	6.83	7.59
General cargo	22.35	17.28	27.95	18.98
	(Per cent share in the total)			
POL	41.6	46.6	46.1	44.1
Iron ore	31.3	24.4	24.5	20.3
Coal	4.7	4.2	4.1	14.3
Fertilisers	2.9	5.6	4.7	4.5
Containers	2.6	3.0	4.0	4.8
General cargo	16.8	16.2	16.6	12.0

Note: Foodgrains are included in general cargo.

Container Corporation of India Limited (CONDOR) provides and organises the multimodal logistics infrastructure for containerised cargo traffic for international as well as internal trade and commerce. CONCOR has now significantly diversified into domestic cargo transport. During 1991-92 CONCOR handled 1.1 lakh twenty-foot equivalent units (TEUs), 64 per more than in the previous year.

46

WELFARE PROGRAMMES: Welfare of Scheduled Castes, Scheduled Tribes, Backward Classes and Other Weaker Sections including Minorities

46.1 Scheduled Castes

The development of Scheduled Castes is being pursued through protective and developmental measures and positive discrimination in their favour in education, employment and other facilities etc. The Special Component Plan (SCP) for Scheduled Castes is at present in operation in 21 States and 3 Union Territories. The SCPs of the States are supplemented with special Central assistance with a view to creating a multiplier effect and facilitating adequate flow of resources. There are 21 State Scheduled Caste Development Corporations which extend assistance to Scheduled Caste entrepreneurs to procure loans from financial institutions for taking up bankable projects. There are several central and vulnerable sections of the population including the SCs. The target for coverage of SC & ST families under IRDP is 50 per cent from 1990-91. Against this,t he actual coverage was 51.1 per cent; 36.1 per cent for SCs and 15 per cent STs during 1991-92. Similarly under JRY, 56.2 per cent of employment generation during 1991-92 was from SC and ST beneficiaries. Under Indira Awaas Yojana (IAY), a sub-scheme of JRY, houses free of cost are constructed for SCs/STs and freed bonded labourers. During 1991-92, about 2.08 lakh houses were built under IAY. Under another sub-scheme of JRY, viz., the Million Wells Scheme (MWS), free boring of irrigation wells is done for small and marginal farmers belonging to SCs/STs and freed bonded labourers. During 1991-92, about 1.69 lakh wells were constructed under the scheme. A central sector scheme for special educational development of SC girls of low literacy level has been included in 1992-93 Plan. One of the important objectives of the Eighth Plan is elimination of scavenging and rehabilitation of scavengers. In 1991-92, a National Scheme of Liberation and Rehabilitation of Scavengers has been launched.

Special Component Plan for Scheduled Castes

The Special Component Plan (SCP) is designed to channelise the flow of outlays and benefits from the general sectors in the Plans of the states and the Central Ministries for development of Scheduled Castes, at least, in proportion to their population.

States/Union Territories

Twenty one States and three Union Territories are formulating and implementing their respective Special Component Plans.

The Special Component Plans of the States are supplemented with Special Central Assistance with a view to creating a muitiplier effect and helping fill the gaps which the normal financial flows from the Central and State Plans are not able to provide.

The Scheduled Castes Development Corporations in the States are envisaged to interface between the poor Scheduled Caste entrepreneurs and the financial institutions in respect of bankable schemes of economic development. Since February, 1989, the National Scheduled Castes and Scheduled Tribes Finance and Development Corporation has also been incorporated with the objective of promoting economic development of Scheduled Castes and Scheduled Tribes, as a supportive and conjunctional arrangement to the States'/UTs' Scheduled Castes' Development Corporations (SCDCs) and the State Tribal Development Corporations (STDCs).

Special Central Assistance

Special Central Assistance (SCA) to Special Component Plans of the States and UTs for Scheduled Caste people is linked to Government of India's strategy for the socio-economic development of these people. This Centrally Sponsored Scheme is the most important programme of the Ministry of Welfare for the alleviation of poverty among Scheduled Caste people. The underlying objective behind SCA which is hundred per cent grant to States and UTs as an additive to their Special Component Plans is that it would be used to give an added thrust to the development programmes for Scheduled Caste people with reference to their occupational pattern and the need for increasing the productivity of and income from their limited assets by taking up family oriented schemes for them. The SCA is used to fill the critical gaps and vital missing inputs in income-generating family-oriented schemes and through non-recurring items, so as to make the schemes more meaningful and effective.

This scheme was started in 1979-80 with a token provision of Rs. 5 crores.

The State Governments and UT Administrations are required to disburse Special Central Assistance to various sectors and agencies including SCDCs which are involved in the implementation of economic development programmes for scheduled castes.

This scheme has motivated the State Governments to provide larger outlays in their Special Component Plans.

The utilisation of Special Central Assistance is reviewed through Half Yearly and Annual progress reports from States/UTs.

State Scheduled Castes Development Corporations

The Scheduled Castes Development Corporations (SCDCs) are now functioning in 18 States and 3 Union Territories with significant Scheduled Castes population. These Corporations are playing a very useful role for the economic development of Scheduled Caste families below poverty line. The Corporations have been mainly functioning as catalysts and agencies for mobilising institutional finance through margin money loan programme/seed money deposits. The margin money loan recovered is added to their share capital. The SCDCs are service oriented organisations.

The Government of India is participating in the share capital investment of the SCDCs to the extent of 49 per cent as against 51 per cent investment by the State Governments.

The scheme to assist SCDCs was rationalised in July 1981 to include assistance for promotional activities and for monitoring and evaluation, technical and recovery wings. The grant-in-aid for promotional activities is subject to a maximum of one per cent of the Centre's cumulative share capital contribution, while matching grant is subject to a limit of 3 per cent of the Centre's cumulative share capital contribution.

In order to make the scale of assistance to be effective and result-oriented, the Government of India has raised the ceiling of unit cost of SCDCs Scheme to the Rs. 35,000 from October, 1989.

The SCDCs are trying to increase the per capita assistance by way of loan and grant as is evident from the above table. Efforts have been on to improve the quality of the performance on the part of the Corporations by making them take up relevant and viable economic projects for the target groups, associating them with the projects right from the formulation stage and avoiding the middlemen in executing the projects/schemes. The viability gaps in the schemes are largely met by way of support from the Special Central Assistance made available to States as an additionality to the Special Component Plans. The States also supplement the requirement mostly by infrastructure support.

National Scheduled Castes and Scheduled Tribes Finance and Development Corporation Limited

The National Scheduled Castes and Scheduled Tribes Finance and Development Corporation Ltd. (NSFDC) was incorporated on 8th February, 1989 to serve as a national institution to take and finance economically viable and technically feasible schemes for the economic development of both Scheduled Castes and Scheduled Tribes. Its role is supportive and conjunctional to the activity of the States/SC/ST Development Corporations. The NSFDC operates through the SC/ST Development Corporation largely.

Monitoring of Programmes under Point 11-A of Twenty Point Programme

Point 11-A of Twenty Point Programme (TPP) aims at giving economic benefits to SC families living below poverty line through Family Oriented Income Generating Programmes.

Central and Centrally Sponsored Schemes

(a) *Post Matric Scholarships for Scheduled Castes and Scheduled Tribes*

The Post Matric Scholarship Scheme is the most important Centrally Sponsored Scheme meant for providing financial assistance to Scheduled Caste and Scheduled Tribe students whose parents/guardians satisfy the means test and number of children prescribed under the scheme. The scheme is implemented by the State Governments/Union Territory Administrations according to the scheme framed by the Government of India and the students get the scholarships through the States/Union Territories to which they belong, irrespective of the place of their study. The scholarships are sanctioned on year to year basis.

(b) *Prematric Scholarships for the Children of those engaged in Unclean Occupations*

The objective of the scheme is to provide financial assistance to enable the children of scavengers of dry latrines, sweepers who have traditional link with scavenging, flayers and tanners to pursue pre-matric education.

(c) *Book Banks for SC/ST Students Studying in Medical and Engineering Colleges*

The Scheme is intended for the SC/ST students pursuing medical and engineering courses in the country. Under this scheme Central assistance is provided to the State Governments on 50:50 basis.

(d) *Girls Hostels for Scheduled Castes*

This scheme was started during the Third Five Year Plan. Under this scheme Central assistance is provided to the State Governments on 50:50 basis for the construction of hostel buildings for Scheduled Caste girls studying in middle and higher level of education.

(e) *Boys Hostels for SC/ST*

The Centrally Sponsored Scheme of Girls Hostels has been extended to SC/ST boys also from the year 1989-90. Central assistance is being released to the State Governments on the basis of existing scheme of Girls Hostels for SC/ST.

(f) *Coaching and Allied Scheme*

Under this scheme Central assistance is provided to the State Governments on 50:50 basis for providing coaching to SC/ST candidates through Pre-examination Training Centres to improve their representation in various posts and services under the Central/State Governments and Public Undertakings. In the case of Universities and private institutions, Central assistance is provided to them on 100 per cent basis for running the pre-examination training centres for SC/ST candidates intending to appear in the various competitive examinations.

(g) *National Overseas Scholarships*

The scheme of National Overseas Scholarships is a Non-Plan Scheme. Under this scheme, candidates belonging to Scheduled Castes, Scheduled Tribes, Denotified, Nomadic and Semi-Nomadic Tribes, Neo-Buddhists, Scheduled Castes converted to other religions and landless agricultural labourers are sent abroad for higher education i.e.. for graduate, post-graduate, Ph.D. and Post

Doctoral research in engineering, technology and other subjects for which adequate facilities are not available in the country.

(h) *Liberation and Rehabilitation of Scavengers and their Dependents*

The objective of the National Scheme of Liberation and Rehabilitation of Scavengers and their dependents is to liberate them from their existing hereditary obnoxious and inhuman occupation of manually removing night soil and filth and to provide for and engage them in alternative and dignified occupations within a period of five years.

Protection of Civil Rights Act, 1955 and the Scheduled Castes and the Scheduled Tribes (Prevention of Atrocities) Act, 1989

Under the Centrally Sponsored Scheme of strengthening of machinery for implementation of Protection of Civil Rights Act, 1955, the State Governments are given financial assistance on 50: 50 sharing basis. The Union Territories are given 50:50 sharing basis. The Union Territories are given 100 per cent assistance. An amount of 5.5 crores has been made for the current year 1991-92 for implementing both the Protection of Civil Rights Act, 1955 and the Scheduled Castes and the Scheduled Tribes (Prevention of Atrocities) Act, 1989. The State Governments have been advised to make full use of the Scheme so that proper and effective machinery is built up in the States and due measures are taken for enforcing the provisions contained in the Act.

A total number of 3,740 cases were registered by the Police during 1989 and 3,730 cases were registered during 1990 under the PCR Act, 1955.

The Scheduled Castes and the Scheduled Tribes (Prevention of Atrocities) Act, 1989

In view of the increasing trend of atrocities on the Scheduled Castes and the Scheduled Tribes, the existing laws under the Protection of Civil Rights Act had been found inadequate. A new legislation called "The Scheduled Castes and the Scheduled Tribes (Prevention of Atrocities) Act, 1989" to check and detect crimes against them committed by non-Scheduled Castes and non-Scheduled Tribes was passed and brought into force w.e.f. 30.1.1990.

46.2 **Scheduled Tribes**

The Tribal Sub-Plan (TSP) strategy has been adopted since 1974-75 for promotion of developmental activities among Scheduled Tribes and protection of their interest. This is in operation in 18 States and 2 UTs and is being implemented through 193 Integrated Tribal Development Projects (ITDPs) covering 311.97 lakh tribal population, 249 pockets of tribal concentration having coverage of 39.95 lakh tribal population, 77 clusters and 74 primitive tribal group projects. Funds for the TSP are made available from State Plans. Special Central Assistance, Sectoral Programme of Central Ministries/Departments and financial institutions. There are several central and centrally sponsored schemes for economic and educational development of STs. For promotion of education among tribal women and employment opportunities in tribal areas, two central sector schemes with focus on their education and employability through vocational training in tribal areas have been included in 1992-93. A Tribal Cooperative Marketing Development Federation (TRIFED), set up in 1987, has expanded its activities for facilitating marketing of tribal produce, especially minor forest produce. During 1991-92, 9.15 lakh ST families were economically assisted as against the target of 8.00 lakh. The target for 1992-93 is to assist 8.96 lakh families and 2.4 lakh families have been assisted up to September 1992. Under the majority poverty alleviation programme of IRDP, 3.81 lakh families i.e. 15 per cent of total families assisted during 1991-92 were STs. Under JRY, 1501.74 lakh of man-days of employment generation i.e. 18.6 per cent of total employment generation during 1991-92 was for ST beneficiaries.

A National Scheduled Castes and Scheduled Tribes Finance and Development Corporation (NSFDC) was set up in February 1989 to serve as a national institution for taking up and financing viable schemes for economic development of SCs/STs. Its role is to support the activities of State SC and ST Development Corporations. Till May 1992, it had sanctioned 208 income generating projects/schemes which are likely to benefit about 1.3 lakh SCs and STs beneficiaries.

Scheduled Tribes are spread over 26 States/UTs except in the three States of Goa, Punjab and Haryana and three Union Territories of Chandigarh, Delhi and Pondicherry. The essential characteristics of these communities are geographical isolation, distinctive culture, shyness of contact with others, economic and educational backwardness.

Tribal Sub-Plan strategy

The Tribal Sub-Plan approach, adopted from the beginning of the Fifth Five Year Plan in 1974-75, has a two-pronged strategy, namely, (i) promotion of developmental activities to raise the level of living of Scheduled Tribes and (ii) protection of their interest through legal and administrative support. The Tribal sub-plan strategy applies to 20 States and UTs where the tribals are in a minority, but inhabit well-defined areas where they constitute a sizeable population. The Tribal Sub-Plan strategy is being implemented through 193 Integrated Tribal Development Projects (ITDPs) with 311.97 lakh Scheduled Tribe population, 249 Modified Area Development Approach (MADA) Pockets with 39.95 lakh Scheduled Tribe population, 77 clusters of tribal concentration with 2.45 lakh Scheduled Tribes population. In Jammu and Kashmir, 12 communities have been notified as Scheduled Tribes and the State Government is in the process of identifying the ITDPs.

Funding of Tribal Development Programmes

Funds for the tribal development are made available from different sources, namely, (i) State Plan (ii) Special Central Assistance (iii) Sectoral Programmes of Central Ministries/Departments and (iv) Institutional Finance. The State Governments are required to quantify funds from State Plans for tribal development in proportion to their population percentage in the State. Reviews are held with the States and Central Ministries regarding implementation of policies, programmes and physical achievements.

Special Central Assistance

Special Central Assistance (SCA) to States is given by Government of India to supplement their efforts in tribal development. This has been of considerable significance in properly orienting programmes, particularly those relating to income generating family oriented schemes.

The criteria for allocation of Special Central Assistance have been fixed on the basis of the norms approved by the Planning Commission. The norms for allocation of Special Central Assistance are as under.

(A) **ITDP**: For allocation of SCA to ITDPs, the States are grouped into three categories. Category 'A' consists of States with substantial areas prominently inhabited by tribals such as (i) Andhra Pradesh (ii) Bihar (iii) Gujarat (iv) Himachal Pradesh (v) Madhya Pradesh (vi) Maharashtra (vii) Manipur (viii) Orissa (ix) Rajasthan and (x) Sikkim.

Category 'B' consists of States having dispersed tribal population with some areas of tribal concentration such as (i) Assam (ii) West Bengal (iii) Tripura.

Category 'C' consists of the States/UTs where the tribal population is by and large dispersed with very small areas of concentration such as (i) Karnataka (ii) Kerala (iii) Tamil Nadu (iv) Uttar Pradesh (v) Andaman & Nicobar Islands and (vi) Goa, Daman & Diu. The total outlay of SCA for tribal sub-Plan is allocated to the three categories on the basis of tribal population of the States/UTs included in each group. The funds are allocated to the three categories on the basis of tribal population of the States/UTs included in each group. The funds allocated to Category 'A' is then distributed to the States on three criteria, i.e., (i) 50% on the basis of Scheduled Tribes population in the Tribal sub-Plan area, (ii) 30% on the basis of geographical area of tribal sub-Plan, and (iii) 20% in inverse proportion to per capita Net State Domestic Product (NSDP) of the States with weightage to tribal population within the TSP area. For category 'B' and 'C' States, the share of individual States/UTs. is worked out on the basis of 2 criteria, i.e., 70% according to Scheduled Tribe population of the Tribal sub-Plan and 30% in inverse proportion to per capita NSDP of the States/UTs with weightage to tribal population within the TSP area. The assistance to Jammu and Kashmir is given on adhoc basis till specific areas are delineated.

(B) **MADA Pockets and Clusters of tribal concentration**: While allocating SCA for MADA programmes, 70% of the total allocation is distributed according to ST population in the MADA area and 30% in inverse proportion to per capita NSDP of the State/UT with weightage to tribal population within the pockets.

(C) **Primitive Tribes**: The distribution formula is:

(a) 40% of the amount on numerical size of the primitive tribal communities.

(b) 30% according to population depending on different occupations, namely, (i) food gathering or hunting, (ii) shifting cultivation (iii) Sedentary cultivation, and (iv) other occupations with weightage accorded in the ratio of 5:3:1:1 respectively.

(c) 15% according to number of primitive tribal communities in the States/UTs.

(d) 15% in inverse proportion to per capita Net State Domestic Product with weightage to Primitive tribe population.

Quantification of Central Ministries/Departments

As per the Government of India (Allocation of Business Rules), 1961, as amended from time to time, the Ministry of Welfare is the nodal Ministry for overall policy, planning and co-ordination of programmes of tribal development for Scheduled Castes and Scheduled Tribes. In regard to sectoral programmes and schemes of development of these communities, policy, planning, monitoring, evaluation, etc., as also their co-ordination is the responsibility of respective Central Ministries.

20-Point Programme

Point 11(b) of 20-Point Programme was aimed to give economic benefit to the Scheduled Tribes families living below the poverty line through family oriented income generating programmes in various sectors of development such as Agriculture, Rural Development, Horticulture, Minor Irrigation, Animal Husbandry, Fisheries, Forestry, Sericulture, Village and Cottage Industries, Small Business, etc., for the Seventh Plan Period. A target of 40 lakh tribal families was fixed in respect of 19 States/UTs having Tribal sub-Plan.

In regard to monitoring and evaluation of the programmes under 20-Point Programme, the Tribal Development Departments of the States/UTs concerned have by and large established monitoring and evaluation machinery at State, District, ITDP and block levels. In addition, number of agencies at the Central and State levels have been conducting evaluation of 20-Point programmes which include Directorate of Statistics/Evaluation of State Governments. Programme Evaluation Organisation of Planning Commission and the Directors for Scheduled Castes and Scheduled Tribes, National Institute of Rural Development, Hyderabad and Professional/Research Organisations which have been doing the work of evaluation and the study on impact of various programmes in tribal areas. The evaluation studies at the Central level are awarded by the Ministry of Welfare and Department of Rural Development and at the State level by the State Governments.

The incidence of poverty among STs in rural areas, where 94% of the STs live, is, higher than for the population as a whole and 5% higher as compared to SCs. The incidence of poverty among STs in urban areas is comparable to that among SCs but is much higher than the overall position.

National Policy on Rehabilitation of Displaced Tribals

Over the years, the tribals have been displaced due to various development projects undertaken in tribal areas. This has resulted in a feeling of deprivation amongst them. The Land Acquisition Act does not provide for rehabilitation of displaced persons. The guidelines issued by the Ministries/Departments fall short of the actual requirements of tribal oustees for their satisfactory relocation and rehabilitation. With this end in view, a comprehensive National Policy which will provide for complete socio-economic and cultural rehabilitation of displaced tribals is under active consideration of the Government of India. The Policy is being formulated with the objective that tribals enjoy a better standard of living after rehabilitation and their socio-economic and cultural ethos are preserved as far as possible.

Atrocities on STs

The Scheduled Castes and the Scheduled Tribes (Prevention of Atrocities) Act, 1989, was promulgated to prevent the commission of offences and atrocities against the members of Scheduled Castes and Scheduled Tribes, to provide for Special Courts for the trial of such offences and for the relief and rehabilitation of the victims of such offences.

The State Governments have been advised to set up 'Special Courts' as per provisions contained in Section 15A of Protection of Civil Rights Act 1955. A few State Governments have already set up Courts and some other State Governments are reportedly in the process of setting up of such Courts. Through a Centrally Sponsored Scheme the State Governments are given financial assistance on 50 : 50 sharing basis for strengthening the machinery for enforcement of the provisions contained in the Act. The Ministry has also set up a Control Room from 15-10-1991 in the Tribal Development Division to obtain information speedily about the atrocities against SCs/STs so that remedial measures are initiated promptly.

46.3 Other Backward Classes

In order to provide an additional channel of finance for economic development of the socially and educationally backward classes (SEBCs), Government has set up a National Backward Classes Finance and Development Corporation (NBFDC) with an authorised capital of Rs. 200 crore in January 1992. The objectives of the Corporation include promotion of self-employment and other ventures, extension of loans for pursuing general/professional/technical education or training at graduate and higher levels, and upgradation of technical and entrepreneurial skills of people belonging to Backward Classes. The Corporation will work as an apex institution for coordination and monitoring the work of Corporations/Boards set up by the State Governments and UT Administrations for the welfare of backward classes.

An Office Memorandum was issued by the Department of Personnel and Training on 13.8.90 providing 27 per cent reservation of vacancies in civil posts and services under the Government of India to be filled through direct recruitment, in favour of Socially and Educationally Backward Classes.

The order dated 13.8.1990 was challenged through a number of writ petitions filed in various High Courts as well as in the Supreme Court which were bunched together by an order of the Supreme Court and referred to a 5-Judge Constitution Bench headed by the Chief Justice for disposal. The Supreme Court, in its interim orders, directed that no steps shall be taken to implement the impugned order dated 13.8.90 excepting identification of SEBCs to be benefited until the matter is heard by the Court and the scope of the order shall not be extended without the prior leave of the Court.

In consonance with the stand of the present Government with regard to reservation for Socially and Educationally Backward Classes (SEBCs), the OM of 13-8-1990 has been amended wide Office Memorandum dated 25.9.1991 to provide for the following:

(i) within the 27 per cent of the vacancies in civil posts and services under the Government of India reserved for SEBCs, preference shall be given to candidates belongs to the proper sections of SEBCs. In case sufficient number of such candidates are not available, unfilled vacancies shall be filled by the other SEBC candidates.
(ii) 10 per cent of the vacancies in civil posts and services under the Government of India shall be reserved for other economically backward sections of the people who are not covered by any of the existing schemes of reservation.

Government is taking steps to lay down the economic criteria referred to in the Office Memorandum of 25.9.1991 after evolving, if possible, a consensus on the subject.

National Backward Classes Finance and Development Corporation

A National Backward Classes Finance and Development Corporation has been set up on 13-1-1992 under the Companies Act with an authorised Share Capital of Rs. 200.00 crores to, *inter alia*, provide an additional channel of finance and assist in the upgradation of technical and entrepreneurial skills, for the economic development of Socially and Educationally Backward Classes (SEBCs). Rs. 25 crores was also provided in the budget for 1991-92 to provide paid up Capital to the Corporation. The Corporation shall assist the following target groups of backward Classes:

(i) Persons belonging to Socially and Educationally Backward Classes (SEBCs) below the poverty line as defined by the Planning Commission from time to time, by providing financial assistance on concessional rate of interest.
(ii) Persons belonging to SEBCs who are above the poverty line, but satisfy the income/economic criteria to be prescribed by the Government of India, for self-employment schemes and other financially and economically viable schemes.

The Corporation will work as an apex institution for monitoring the working of all Corporations/Boards set up in the States and the Union Territories for the welfare of Backward Classes.

46.4 **Other Weaker Sections including Minorities**

46.4.1. **Minorities**

Minorities and the Constitution

Article 29 and 30 of the Constitution recognise the rights of minorities to con-

Note: See also Chapter 35 "Mandal Commission: Supreme Court Judgment and Follow Up".

serve their culture and establish and administer educational institutions of their choice.

Minorities and the National Integration

The Government is committed to ensure the welfare of minorities. While the Ministry of Home Affairs, through the machinery of National Integration Council has been taking steps for the integration of all sections of the society for the integration of all sections of the society irrespective of religion, language, etc., Ministry of Welfare, as the nodal Ministry has been charged with the responsibility of ensuring fuller participation and integration of the minorities in the national mainstream. This is sought to be achieved through the 15-Point Programme for the Welfare of Minorities, which is implemented through the State Governments and the concerned Ministries of the Government of India. Five communities, viz., Muslims, Christians, Sikhs, Buddhists and Zoroastrians are recognised as religious minorities at the national level for the purpose of implementation of 15-Point Programme.

15-Point Programme for the Welfare of Minorities

Point Nos. 1 to 7 of the programme lay down the measures for preventing and controlling communal disturbances, promotion of communal harmony and peace and to restore confidence among the minorities. Point Nos. 8 to 10 provide for giving special consideration to minorities in public employment, recruitment of police personnel in States and Central Police Forces, recruitment to Railways, Nationalised Banks and Public Enterprises, etc., by making the Selection Committees representative of the minority community so as to ensure that there is no discrimination. Point No. 11 of the Programme provides for coaching minority community candidates to enable them to compete for examination conducted for public employment as in the Central and State Governments, Banks, etc. Point No. 12 deals with opening of ITIs and Polytechnics in minority concentration areas to encourage candidates belonging to these communities to get job-oriented education which, ultimately, may help them to stand on their own feet. Point No. 13 is to ensure that the benefits of various developmental schemes flow to the minorities in a fair and adequate measure. Point No. 14 lays down the steps to be taken to deal with problems relating to wakf matters such as removal of encroachment from wakf properties, graveyards, etc., and other issues which sometimes lead to communal tension. Point No. 15 requires setting up of Minority Cells at Central and State level to deal with the matters relating to minorities.

Implementation of 15-Point Programme

The Programme is being implemented by States/UTs and the concerned Central Ministries/Departments. The entire Programme is monitored and its implementation watched by the Minorities Wing in the Ministry of Welfare. The Ministry calls for quarterly reports on the progress of implementation of the Programme from the State Governments/UT Administrations and the concerned Central Ministries/Departments. The format for sending quarterly reports on the progress of the implementation of the Programme has been devised with the concurrence of the State Governments. The information received is compiled, analysed and reviewed and the deficiencies noticed in the implementation of the Programme are brought to the notice of the authorities concerned for remedial action.

A Cabinet Committee on Minority Welfare has been reconstituted under the Chairmanship of the Prime Minister.

At the State level, the Programme is generally monitored by Deputy Commissioner/District Magistrate on monthly basis.

Recruitment

State Governments have been advised to ensure better representation of minorities in State police forces and also to raise composite police battalions for law and order duties. They have also been asked to organise special training/orientation programmes for police personnel for maintaining communal harmony.

Similar decision has been taken in respect of Central Police Organisations.

The Central Ministries/Departments have been requested for monitoring, through sample surveys, the status of minorities in recruitment and in Recruitment Boards/Selection Committees, etc., in the format devised by this Ministry for this purpose. The monitoring mechanism covers all Groups, i.e., A, B, C and D employees.

Employment

Instructions have been issued by the Director General Employment and Training, Ministry of Labour to the State Governments to ensure that there is no discrimination in the matter of registration and sponsoring of minority candidates for employment. State Governments were also requested to issue necessary instructions to the Employment Exchanges to take necessary steps for (a) making special drives in minority concentration areas to register as many minority candidates as possible, (b) setting up mobile registration units/sub-exchanges in minority concentration areas, (c) including a member of the minority community on the Advisory Committees attached to the Employment Exchanges at the District and Exchange level, and (d) setting up monitoring cell at the State level to monitor the progress.

A decision has also been taken that in all Selection Committees/ Recruitment Boards, there should be a representative of minority community to inspire confidence in the selection process.

Minorities Commission

The Minorities Commission was set up by a Government of India resolution in January, 1978 to safeguard the interests of minorities and with a view to preserving secular traditions and national integration. The Commission consists of a Chairman and six other Members. The Chairman and five other members belong to minority communities. One member belongs to non-minority community. The functions entrusted to the Commission are as follows:

(a) to evaluate the working of various safeguards provided in the Constitution for the protection of minorities and in the laws passed by the Union and State Governments;

(b) to make recommendations with a view to ensuring effective implementation and enforcement of all the safeguards and the laws;

(c) to undertake a review of the implementation of the policies pursued by the Union and the State Governments with respect to the minorities;

(d) to look into specific complaints regarding deprivation of rights and safeguards of the minorities;

(e) to conduct studies, research and analysis on the question of avoidance of discrimination against minorities;

(f) to suggest appropriate legal and welfare measures in respect of any minority to be undertaken by the Central or the State Governments.;

(g) to serve as a national clearing house for information in respect of the conditions of the minorities; and

(h) to make periodical reports at prescribed intervals to the Government.

47

WOMEN AND CHILDREN

47.1 Women

Women and children form a sizeable proportion of our population and they constitute the most important source for human resource development. The major thrust of the programmes of the Department of Women and Child Development is to ensure a state of well-being for women and children particularly those of the weaker sections of the society. The setting up of a separate Department of Women and Child Development in 1985, was based on an appreciation of Women's productive role in development rather than as mere beneficiaries of governmental programmes or recipients of various welfare measures. The Department continued its programmes and advocacy thrusts in these twin interrelated sectors of child and women's development for which the Department has the nodal responsibility in the Government of India. The emphasis has been on developing women's potential for participation in National Development through awareness generation, skill development and income generating activities which are expected to provide not only the desired economic independence to women but also to improve their quality of life and, through them, of the family and society. The emphasis in Child Development has been on improving the delivery of services to the children and also to achieve convergence of services available for women and children. Besides expanding the on-going programmes, the Department has evolved some innovative projects and proposed amendments in social legislations relating to women to make them more effective. It has also promoted and assisted voluntary sector significantly in the implementation of governmental policies and programmes for women and children.

The Department of Women and Child Development which was made a part of the Ministry of Welfare was again placed under the Ministry of Human Resource Development (HRD) w.e.f. 5 July, 1991.

The activities of the Department are carried out through two Bureaux (i) Nutrition and Child Development and (ii) Women's Welfare and Development; each headed by a Joint Secretary. The Secretary is the administrative head of the Department assisted by these two Joint Secretaries.

The Department has two attached organisations under it namely the National Institute of Public Cooperation and Child Development (NIPCCD) and the Central Social Welfare Board (CSWB). NIPCCD is a society registered under the Societies of Registration Act, 1860 while CSWB is a charitable company registered under Section 25 of the Indian Companies Act, 1956. These organisations are fully funded by the Government and both the organisations assist the Department in its functions including implementation of some of its programmes. The Central Technical Committee (CTC) provides technical support in the matter of monitoring and evaluation of health and nutritional components of the programmes of Integrated Child Development Services of the Department. CTC is also fully funded by Government.

Eighth Five Year Plan

The Eighth Five Year Plan (1992-97) proposals were prepared by the Department and submitted to the Planning Commission. The Planning Commission has recommended an outlay of Rs. 450 crores for the Annual Plan 1992-93.

A special set of interventions have been devised for the Adolescent Girls in the age-group 11-18 years, belonging to poor families with particular focus on school drop-outs and an effort has been made to institutionalise these interventions through ICDS infrastructure. Till the end of 1991-92, these Adolescent Girls Schemes were sanctioned in 507 ICDS Projects. These Schemes aim at covering the health, nutrition, non-formal education, literacy, social and recreational needs of these girls on the one hand and recognise their potential role as effective social animators at the village level.

LIGURIA International Technology for Development Prize for ICDS

The ICDS Programme was selected by the International Culture Centre for People's Development, Italy of the prestigious **LIGURIA International Technology for Development Prize.**

National Nutrition Policy

A draft National Nutrition Policy been prepared. The Policy identifies a number of interventions in different sectors of development both short-term as well as long term to counter the problem of under nutrition particularly for the vulnerable sections of the population such as children, women, landless labourers and urban slum dwellers.

Indira Mahila Yojana

An integrated system of services has been envisaged for the development of women and children under the proposed Indira Mahila Yojana. Drafted by the Department of Women and Child Development, Ministry of Human Resource Development, the scheme has been well received by the State Governments. The Indira Mahila Yojana aims at creating a new sense of awareness among poor women, specially in rural areas, their mobilisation and empowerment. Upgradation of skills and creation of employment are its basic components. The highlight of the draft scheme is a proposed integrated system covering ICDS, family welfare, adult education, schemes for adolescent girls and creche services. The focal point of delivery of services will be Indira Mahila Vikas Kendras each of which will cover between 1000 and 1500 people at the village level. The functionaries of a Kendra will include a worker to attend to activities related to health and to child, an organiser-cum-instructor for employment generation activities and two helpers. They will be paid a token honorarium. In additional, there will be a recipient group as distinct from the delivery system at every village.

National Commission for Women

The Government have constituted a National Commission for Women on 31.1.1991 to, *inter alia,* monitor the implementation of laws enacted for the protection of women's rights.

National Credit Fund for Women

A proposal to set up National Credit Fund for Women as national instrumentality for extending credit to needy poor women in the informal sector has been mooted.

Gender Sensitization

The Department has taken several steps for the sensitization of planners, policy makers, administrators including enforcement machinery and masses in order to enhance their perception and sensitivity towards gender issues and promote gender concerns.

Special Measures for the Development Vulnerable Girls

Secretary, Department of Women and Child Development took a meeting in 11.11.1991 with the representative of various voluntary organisation and Central and State officials from Kerala, Andhra Pradesh, Karnataka and West Bengal to discuss about the "Exploitation of young girls by way of their marriage to ineligible husbands and other related forms of exploitation". The meeting concluded with a consensus decision to support those cities/areas with income generating activities, education and training for skill development. Accordingly, the Department has extended assistance in those affected areas for intensification of existing programmes for adolescent girls to train and keep them gainfully occupied.

47.2 **Child Development**

Integrated Child Development Services (ICDS)

Under the ICDS Programme, during 1991-92, 100 Centrally Sponsored Projects been sanctioned to various States. In addition 65 ICDS projects have been sanctioned to the States of Andhra Pradesh and Orissa with the assistance of World Bank. The progressive total of Centrally Sponsored and State Sector projects sanctioned up to March 1992 was 2506 and 188 respectively i.e. a total of 2694.

The programme now covers 2761 blocks benefiting about 150 lakh children and 30 lakh pregnant and lactating mothers in 2.7 lakh villages and urban slums. During 1992-93 300 additional ICDS projects were planned.

Foreign Assistance under ICDS

UNICEF assists the ICDS programme in the sphere of consultancy services, training, certain initial supplies and equipments and in monitoring and research.

The Norwegian Agency for Development (NORAD) is assisting 58 ICDS projects in 11 Districts of Uttar Pradesh. The assistance includes expenditure on Nutrition and for construction of anganwadis.

USAID is assisting 11 ICDS projects in Panchmahals District of Gujarat and 10 ICDS projects in Chandrapur District of Maharashtra. It has also extended its assistance for Mobile-in-Service training in Vadodra District of Gujarat and for Ready-to-eat Food Plant namely : "Sukhada Processing Plant" in Chandrapur District of Maharashtra. Another Ready-to-eat Food Plant is being established in District of Mehasana in Gujarat. USAID assistance is available only up to March 31, 1992.

The Swedish International Development Agency (SIDA) is assisting 8 ICDS Projects in Chengai-Anna District of Tamil Nadu.

Food supplied by CARE and World Food Programme (WFP) is being utilised for supplementary nutrition component in a number of ICDS projects.

National Programme of Action on Children

As a signatory to the World Declaration (September, 1990) on the Survival, Protection and Development of children, India is committed to prepare a National Programme of Action on Children to achieve the goals set under the World Declaration. Accordingly this Department had set up a working group with representatives from concerned Ministries/Departments and some Voluntary Organisations. The draft National Programme of Action for Children is being finalised.

Master Plan of Operations (UNICEF)

The nodal Department of Women and Child Development and UNICEF entered into cooperation as envisaged in the Master Plan of Operations covering the period 1st January 1991 to 31st December 1995. The UNICEF allocation for India for the five year period is US $ 175 million from its general resources and US $ 290 million from supplementary resources.

World Bank Assisted ICDS Projects

The Centrally-sponsored World Bank assisted ICDS-I Project, sanctioned during 1990-91 for predominantly tribal areas of Andhra Pradesh and Orissa, continued its operation. In addition to normal ICDS facilities, the Project provides additional inputs for Women's Income Generation. Women's Integrated Learning for Life (WILL), services for adolescent girls, strengthening of Health Components, Experimentation with nutritional rehabilitation centres and therapeutic Food, construction of anganwadi buildings and godowns-cum-CDPO's offices on selective basis, and enhanced inputs in the spheres of communication, training, project management, equipment, monitoring, evaluation etc.

An Action Plan for SAARC Decade of the Girl Child (1991-2000 AD)

A meeting to formulate an Action Plan for the SAARC Decade of the Girl Child 1991-2000 AD, was held at New Delhi on 11.3.1992. The proposed Plan of Action lays its emphasis on need-based policies and programmes based on the findings of an Action Research Project on Girl Child and the Family, carried out throughout the country by the 22 Women's Study Centres affiliated to various Universities.

Support for Training and Employment Programmes (STEP)

The Programme of Support for Training and Employment gained momentum when its coverage expanded to other sectors of handloom, sericulture and handicrafts in the State of Gujarat, Haryana, Karnataka and Uttar Pradesh. The Programme made a beginning in the areas of dairying in Bihar and goat rearing in Tamil Nadu in 1987. About 3400 women below the poverty line are expected to be covered under this programme. Social inputs clubbed with income generation is the speciality of this programme. Under this programme, 81,000 women had benefitted up to December 1992.

Child Survival and Safe Motherhood Programme

The President Shankar Dayal Sharma inaugurated the Child Survival and Safety Motherhood Programme on August 28, 1992.

The Child Survival and Safe Motherhood Programme will have a positive impact on many goals of the National Health Policy. The neonatal and infant mortality rates which have been showing declining trends in recent years largely due to the successful implementation of the Immunization Mission, will be further reduced as other causes of mortality in infancy are controlled. Under the goals of the National Health Policy it is aimed to bring down the infant mortality rate to below 60 per 1000 live births by 2000 AD; the rate in 1990 was 80 per 1000 live births. The pre-school child mortality (under 5 years of age) and maternal mortality rates are targeted to be below 10 per 1000 children and 2 per 1000 live births, respectively by 2000 AD. Current accurate rates are not known and there are wide disparities between regions but rough estimates based on local studies indicate that the rates are at least two to three times higher than the goals to be reached by the end of the decade. Another important parameter of the quality of primary health care services is the reduction in the percentage of low birth weight babies (below 2500 gms) to less than 10 per cent. It is expected that by the end of the decade antenatal services would be accessible to all pregnant women and that all deliveries will be attended by trained personnel including trained dais.

The Child Survival and Safe Motherhood Programme is also important in the overall efforts to encourage a small family norm and family planning.

48

YOUTH, SPORTS AND PHYSICAL EDUCATION

There are a number of programmes/schemes to channelise the energies of youth into constructive activities like adventure, sports, education, environmental/ecological development, national integration, drug de-addiction, combating of AIDS/HIV, vocational training, youth clubs etc. These programmes/schemes have been revamped to make them more effective and result-oriented according to the given time frame. The coverage includes involvement of 10 lakh students in youth activities through the National Service Scheme (NSS), 10 lakh in National Cadet Corps (NCC) and 24 lakh in Scouts and Guides and non-student youth activities organised by 432 Nehru Yuva Kendras. Under the National Service Scheme (NSS) volunteers are involved in conducting programmes on adult literacy (including total literacy), family welfare, national integration, wasteland development etc. NSS has adopted about 5000 villages for development and community service. National Institute of Youth Development is being set up to co-ordinate and monitor youth programmes and conduct specialised youth training programmes.

Grants are given to various National Sports Federations (51 in number) for promotion and popularisation of their respective sports disciplines. Various awards have been instituted to honour outstanding sportspersons. During 1991-92, twelve outstanding sportspersons were decorated with Arjun Award. Cash awards amounting to Rs. 39.62 lakh were given to 49 medal winners in international competitions. Another 3640 sports persons were covered under different scholarship schemes for promotion of sports. To meet the standards of international competition, efforts are being made to create Olympic standard swimming pools, multipurpose indoor halls and artificial playing surfaces. During 1992-93, sportspersons continued to be covered under different scholarship schemes for promotion of sports. Cooperation of the Indian Army has been obtained in raising 13 companies of 484 boys under the Scheme of Boys' Sports Companies. Sports Authority of India (SAI) is running 31 Sports Project Development Area (SPDA) centres for 668 trainees and 17 sports hostels for 681 inmates. A total of about 1200 Nationals Sports Talent Contest (NSTC) trainees received specialised coaching in 56 SAI adopted sports schools.

Sports and Physical Education

Even though India has a long tradition in Sports and Physical activities, it was only after Independence in 1947 that attention was paid to sports with a view to develop excellence. However, a higher priority to sports was accorded only just prior to the 1982 Asian Games. The will to develop modern competitive sports with a view to compete for international recognition was firmed up in the first ever Sports Policy announced in 1984. Our efforts to foster medal winning potential in international sports is less than a decade old. The performance of the country in sports should, therefore, be viewed in this context rather than in terms of total population.

It was decided to critically examine the Sports Policy, 1984 and all on-going schemes with a view to take stock of requisite additions or alternations before start of the VIII Plan. A Committee was constituted under the Chairmanship of DG, Sports Authority of India (SAI), to review the Sports Policy as also the prevailing guidelines for National Sports Federations. Another Committee was constituted under the Chairmanship of the Secretary, Deptt. of Youth and Sports to review all schemes and programmes of Sports. This Committee was assisted by three Sub-Committees — one each for reviewing the Schemes for Development of Excellence in Sports; Board-basing of Sports; and for the review of the Schemes of Incentives, Awards and Scholarships. Follow up action will be initiated and all work completed as early as feasible.

Approach to Eighth Plan

This was finalised after a great deal of deliberations. A wide spectrum of sports programmes incorporated therein are updated/amended existing programmes and some new schemes. An allocation of Rs. 727 crores for the VIII Plan has been sought from the Planning Commission on the basis of a detailed draft plan document.

Sports Ministers' Conference

The Fourth National Conference of Ministers of Youth & Sports was organised after a gap of over two years on November 18, 1991. The recommendations of the Conference are given below:

Recommendations and Conclusions of the 4th National Conference of Ministers of Youth Affairs and Sports

SPORTS

1. *Single Agency for promotion of Sports at State Level*

Most State Governments have Department of Youth Affairs and Sports to look after various activities of promotion of sports and games. Some State Governments also have Sports Authority at State level. Some more are thinking of having such a body at their State level. It was felt that a single agency for promotion of sports at State level will help in promoting sports in the States/U.Ts. in a more coordinated manner. Such an agency will also help to generate non-government resources.

It was explained that the concept of setting up Regional Offices of SAI is to decentralise the facilities for expert coaching and to conduct the academic courses nearer to the homes of sportspersons as also to facilitate consideration of proposals of State Governments at regional level. This was appreciated by the State Governments.

2. *Scheme of Grants to State Sports Councils, etc.*

The State Governments expressed that Government of India's assistance for creation of sports infrastructure should be more liberal and States should be provided assistance to complete the long pending projects. It was also suggested that the development works should not be hindered because of these pending projects and the new approach of Government of India to release grants after spending State Government's/sponsor's share needs to be reviewed.

The importance of fully utilising the infrastructure created was stressed and the State Government agreed to take measures to optimally utilize sports infrastructure already created.

Realising that the status of pending projects in the States needs to be tackled in a result-oriented manner, it was decided that requests for enhancement of central assistance for only those projects where the first instalment of assistance has been availed of, will be considered on a case to case basis, provided further investment is proposed on essential playing facilities only. The enhancement of central assistance will not be considered where full central assistance (i.e. both the instalments as approved earlier) has been released.

3. *Grants to Rural Schools*

The scheme was appreciated and the State Government requested that the terms and conditions laid down in the scheme should be liberalised and assistance should also be made available to such schools which are not able to spend Rs. 15,000 per annum on maintenance of sports infrastructure. For this purpose, it was suggested that the amount of Rs. 15,000 be brought down.

4. *Scheme of Synthetic Tracks and Artificial Surfaces*

The State Governments requested that the quantum of assistance for this purpose should be increased because the cost of laying of synthetic track/artificial surfaces has increased due to recent devaluation of rupee. A suggestion was also given that Central Government's assistance should be 75 per cent of the cost for laying of the first of such surfaces so as to encourage the States to having at least one surface in their States.

5. *Industrial Growth Centres*

The facilities and opportunities available were noted by the States.

6. *Sports Hostels*

The position was noted by the State Governments.

7. *Sports Project Development Area Scheme*

The Scheme was appreciated by the State Governments who insisted that more and more such Centres should be made operational in their respective States.

8. *Broad-basing of Sports Tournament Calendar at State level*

The States expressed lack of resources for conducting tournaments at State level and requested for increased Central assistance.

9. *Prize Money Scheme*

It was suggested to conduct these tournaments by ensuring participation of schools in rural areas. The rural schools have failed to participate in large numbers as they have no funds to finance transportation and stay of their teams. It was also suggested that schools achieving 2nd/3rd position in district level tournaments should also be given incentive on a lesser scale.

10. *Rural Sports*

Some State Governments expressed that NYKs may not be able to do justice with this additional liability of implementation of the Scheme because of lack of State Government's control over NYKs. However, the consensus was to let Nehru Yuva Kendra handle this activity.

11. *Other Miscellaneous Schemes*

The State Governments noted the contents of other various Schemes being, operated by Department of Youth Affairs and Sports and Sports Authority of India.

12. *Indigenous Games and Martial Arts*

A suggestion was given that Central assistance should be available at 50:50 for construction of a Centre for Martial Arts in Kerala.

13. *Special Area Games*

The State Governments appreciated the Scheme and gave suggestions for setting up Special Area Games Centres promoting specified sports in their States.

14. *Coaching Camps for Juniors and Women at State level*

It was suggested that State Governments should launch their own training programmes at State level to take care of all the needs of coaching and training of junior sportspersons. The State Governments requested that SAI's support should continue to be given for such coaching and coaches should be provided by SAI.

15. *Proposal to bring Sports on the Concurrent List of Constitution of India*

The Sports Ministers from U.P., West Bengal, Tamil Nadu etc. expresseu their opposition to such a move although some other States like Mizoram supported such a move.

16. *Other Issues*

(i) The Sports should be reviewed so as to remove gap between the urban sports and rural sports. Sports in rural areas should be given more attention so as to bring it on par with sports in urban areas.
(ii) Jobs should be guaranteed to all sportspersons. Sportspersons having position of being the first hundred in every sports discipline should have such guarantee.
(iii) Adventure sports like Ice-skating, Ice-Hockey, etc. should be encouraged.
(iv) Winter Sports should not only be a tourism subject. The Sports Department should also recognise skiing as a adventure sport and this should

also be included among the recognised sports.

(v) Every Primary School Teacher should get sports and physical education reorientation.

(vi) Every State should adopt one or two sports disciplines for giving thrust in that State. Land should be reserved for playgrounds, etc.

(vii) Departments of Youth Affairs and Sports/Sports Authority of India should concentrate on promotion of sports by creation of sports infrastructure, etc. Other ways of promoting sports, preparation of teams and their participation in national and international sports events should be the responsibility of State Sports Associations and National Sports Federations. The National sports Federations should raise their own resources also.

YOUTH

Nehru Yuva Kendra Sangathan

Many States expressed the view that there is lack of coordination between the Kendras of the Sangathan and the respective State Government which is the main reason for the Sangathan. Some States were of the view that one reason for this lack of coordination is that the District Organising Committee, though headed by the District Magistrate, does not have representatives of various Departments of State Government. Some States opined that Nehru Yuva Kendras should be placed under the administrative control of the Director of Youth Services of the respective State Governments.

The consensus that emerged in the Conference was that taking into account the fact that NYKS is an autonomous organisation and hence cannot be placed directly under the State authorities, better coordination/monitoring of the work of the Nehru Yuva Kendra and its linkages with various other programmes of the State Government can be achieved by suitable arrangement with State level coordination Committee headed by the Minister incharge of Youth Services and Sport. It has also been decided that the District level Organising Committee of NYK Programmes be broad based by providing specific representation from sports culture and folk arts. This will give the district level Committee more representation to represent interests of youth. Consensus was also arrived on the necessity to establish at least one Kendra in each District immediately and Nehru Yuva Kendra in some blocks also where the districts are large in size and population.

The Department of Youth affairs and Sports has projected requirements of funds to cover all the districts. It has also recommended to the Planning Commission for establishment of Youth Development Centres catering for a cluster of 10 to 15 villages and Nehru Yuva Kendras at the District level. The Centre will conduct programmes for personality development of youth, leadership training, skill development, and prepare them for self-employment.

National Service Scheme

In order to strengthen the NSS programmes it is most important that funds are directly released to the colleges (units) through a mechanism to be worked out in consultation with the State Governments. State Governments will have to immediately look into the position regarding the unutilised Central funds lying with them because of non-release of funds for NSS programmes. A consensus was arrived at that NSS and NCC should be strengthened and expanded in all the colleges and universities to benefit the youth.

Training of Youth

The Youth Development Centres to be established in the rural areas will take up training programmes for awareness generation, upgradation of skills and training for self-employment and finally entrepreneurial development in selected youth. For this, active cooperation of the State Governments, voluntary organisations and Youth Clubs will be necessary. State Governments have been requested to take up with various banks and financial institutions in their respective areas, to ensure prompt release of soft-loans in favour of youth for starting their own small enterprise and self-employment programmes. Ministry of Finance will be requested to relax norms regarding sanction of loans for the youth self-employment projects.

A suggestion was also made that financial assistance should be given to Youth Clubs, as youngsters are attached themselves to youth clubs realisation of advances will be better.

Linkages

In order to achieve the objective for developing the personality of youth, bring awareness among them and also to prepare them for self-employment it is important that various agencies working in the field of youth should coordinate and act together. It was recommended that a State level monitoring Committee/Coordination Committees will be established. This may be called as Youth Development Council which would consist of officials/non-officials/youth leaders/representatives of voluntary organisations to establish linkages and monitor various activities for youth. An active partnership between State and Central Government is essential in exploiting the full potential of youth and provide a new thrust to all the programmes meant for the youth.

Mass Media

The Standing Inter-Departmental Committee for Mass Media to publicise and disseminate the schemes and programmes of sports of the Department and of SAI was activated.

Involvement of Public and Private Sector Enterprises

The initiative of the Minister of State, who held a two days Conference with top executives of important Private/Public Sector Enterprises to enlist the support for development of sports was a success. A Task Force was constituted under the Chairmanship of Secretary to review the follow-up work. Major industrial enterprises are being persuaded to adopt one or more sports discipline each and share the burden of establishing single discipline dedicated Sports Academies. The first meeting of the Task Force was held on February 4, 1992.

Financial Incentives

Financial incentives are available to sports persons in the form of exemption of Customs Duty on import of sports equipments, exemption of Income Tax on Awards/Prizes. However, the hesitancy of Industry/Business Enterprises to contribute generously for promotion of sports is due to lack of tax incentives for them. Fifty per cent income tax exemptions for donations to certain recognised sports bodies is presently insufficient motivation. Moreover, expenditure incurred on sports is not being allowed to be charged as legitimate expenditure. The Department has, therefore, taken the initiative to seek total exemption of Income Tax on expenditure incurred by the Enterprises/Business Houses on promotion of sports by way of Creation of Infrastructure, purchase of equipment, running of Sports Academies, sponsoring teams/individuals for training and participation in the sports events in the country or abroad, for sponsoring the hosting of the National/International Sports Tournaments in the country etc. The Deptt. has also sought full exemption of Customs Duty on Import of Sports Equipment by the Enterprises for training of elite sportspersons in the National Academies and elsewhere.

Incentives for Employment/Admission in Colleges and Universities

A Group was constituted under chairmanship of Secretary, Department of Youth Affairs and Sports to suggest incentives and special consideration to be given to sportspersons in employment as also admission to colleges and universities. A series of meetings of this group have been during the past few months and the report is being finalised.

IMPORTANT SCHEMES

Grants for Creation of Sports Infrastructure

This scheme is of vital importance and, therefore, received the highest allocation of Rs. 60 crores amongst the schemes of sports in the VIIth Plan. Higher allocations are needed in the VIII Plan to meet the ever increasing demand of Central assistance to promote sports infrastructure as also to cover the higher per unit assistance due to escalation of costs.

To date, 2045 projects have been Centrally assisted. Most of them (around 1752) are yet to be completed by the State Governments and sponsors. These are incomplete primarily due to inability of the State Government to finance the projects as per their commitments given while applying for Central assistance. This problem has been discussed exhaustively with all the State Governments. Due to all out efforts, the States are now more concerned about completing these projects. As a result, over 200 projects have been reported as completed during the last 3 years. The strategy adopted is to enhance Central assistance to those incomplete projects in which only the first instalment of Central assistance has been released. This is subject to the condition that further investment will be limited to facilities most essential for sportspersons. Where full Central assistance has already been availed of, the State Governments/Sponsors will have to complete the projects from their own resources.

Central assistance now available for projects is inadequate since the ceilings of Central assistance were last fixed in 1986, this scheme has been revised to rationalise the categories of infrastructure as well as increase financial assistance.

The most salient feature of this scheme has been the promotion of one State Sports Training Complex in each State. In the absence of such a complex the State athletes were looking to the Union Government for their training/coaching requirements. Six such complexes have been approved. It is hoped that the State Government will complete these facilities soon and begin inhouse dedicated training programmes for elite State athletes. Central assistance to upgrade sports facilities in Sports Project Development Area (SPDA) Centres is also provided under this scheme. The running and maintenance cost of these centres will be borne fully by Sports Authority of India. The first phase of infrastructural assistance for 20 SPDA Centres (out of a total 78 such centres) has already been disbursed. This scheme has great potential to promote higher standards of sports at grassroot level.

Grant to Rural Schools

This scheme is meant to promote sports facilities in rural schools. Grants up to Rs. 1 lakh are given to provide basic sports facilities in rural schools. There is no condition of matching contribution except that the State Government/School have to undertake to maintain the facilities created with this grant. Due to the very dismel status of sports in rural schools, not many schools could avail this assistance for failure to meet the eligibility criteria, which has now been relaxed with regard to requirement of land, strength of students enrolled, qualification of the Physical Education Teachers employed, and commitment for annual expenditure on sports. It is hoped that in the VIII Plan this scheme will find more takers.

This scheme has received wide publicity and has resulted in an enthusiastic response. The impact of this scheme will lead to enhanced sports activities in rural areas.

Synthetic Athletic Tracks/Artificial Surfaces

The use of synthetic playing surface is now the order of the day. While mandatory in a new disciplines, in many others it has become widely prevalent. Apart from providing safety, speed and consistency, synthetic playing surfaces help the Sportspersons to improve their performances. We call ill afford not to acquire and install such surfaces which are indispensable for acquiring a competitive edge in international tournaments. Presently, the Scheme includes Central financial assistance for installation of synthetic athletic tracks and artificial hockey surfaces only. Central assistance is given for 50 per cent of the cost of installation of the surface subject to a ceiling of Rs. 50 lakhs in each case. Besides these, there are a few other surfaces, which have been installed by SAI.

The scheme is under revision. Inclusion of synthetic playing surfaces for other disciplines like Badminton, Handball, Basketball, Volleyball, Tennis and Cricket pitch may be considered. Some of these are outdoor playing surfaces and are not manufactured indigenously. Consequent upon the devaluation of the Indian Rupees, the cost of these surfaces has increased and hence there is no alternative but to increase Central assistance. As a result of the sudden jump in prices, the Department sanctioned only two applications in the current financial year. The endeavour will also be to promote installation of a large number of cheaper surfaces which are suitable for training/practice/conduct of local championships. This will facilitate familiarisation of Indian sportspersons with synthetic playing surfaces at an early age. This will remove the impediment, facing budding sportspersons, of lack of experience of playing on synthetic surface.

Sports and Games in Universities and Colleges

This scheme, earlier known as National Sports Organisation (NSO), has been revised recently. The strategy is to tackle University Sports in three broad segments — infrastructure, inter-University tournaments and incentives/scholarships to meritorious students. Accordingly, the scheme is implemented through three different organisations, each of them covering one aspect:

(i) *University Grants Commission*: A lump sum grant is released to University Grants Commission (UGC) to provide assistance to create sports infrastructure in Universities and Colleges. Educational institutions like Engineering Colleges, Medical Colleges, Professional Institutes, not covered by UGC, are provided grants directly by the Department.

(ii) *Association of Indian Universities (AIU)* is provided grant to hold inter-University tournaments, provide coaching facilities and prepare Indian Universities' teams to participate in national and international tournaments. However, since AIU does not have standard infrastructure and facilities, this work will be entrusted to Sports Authority of India to the extent feasible.

(iii) *Sports Authority of India* is given a lump sum grant to award scholarships to talented sportspersons in Universities and Colleges.

Most of the funds under the scheme are utilised by UGC. The ceilings of Central assistance for infrastructure have recently been enhanced and consequently the assistance per project would now go up.

It is strongly felt that young sportspersons in the age group of 17-20 years are not adequately taken care of due to weak sports infrastructure in universities/colleges. The Department is finalising a strategy to specially assist a limited number of universities and colleges on the basis of their past sports performance at national level and in inter-university tournaments. Such universities/colleges will be helped to nurture two or three disciplines each. The exercise to identify such universities has been entrusted to SAI and UGC.

Association of Indian Universities conduct Inter-University tournaments. A well defined and precise scale of assistance for these tournaments has been prepared. The tournaments are conducted on zonal basis culminating into one zonal winner entering into last and final phase. The numbers of zones depend upon the popularity of various sports disciplines. Maulana Abul Kalam Azad Trophy, is provided to the overall winner University. There are precise rules/criteria laid out for determining the overall 1st, 2nd, 3rd and 4th place for universities in sports. Apart from Maulana Abul Kalam Azad Trophy to the overall winner University, cash prizes of Rs. 50,000, Rs. 20,000 and Rs. 10,000 are provided to 1st, 2nd and 3rd position in 13 specified disciplines of sports in inter-University tournaments also, cash prizes amounting to Rs. 50,000, Rs. 30,000 and Rs. 20,000 respectively are given.

Since SAI is the best equipped institution to train/coach sportspersons, it has been decided, as mentioned above, to entrust SAI with the responsibility to conduct coaching camps for the benefit of the University/College students as far as possible. SAI will also prepare the combined University teams to participate in various national/international sports tournaments. This will of course be done in close cooperation with AIU.

Every year, fresh sports scholarships of Rs.3,600 per annum each are provided to 300 students besides renewal of existing scholarships provided the holders continue to maintain a high level of achievement.

Assistance to National Sports Federation

These are autonomous organisation, which have been recognised in many disciplines of sports. There are 51 recognised National Sports Federations. The Indian Olympic Association is also treated as a Sports Federation for the purpose of support and assistance under this scheme.

The Sports Federations are financially assisted for conducting National Championships, organising coaching camps for preparing teams for participation in international tournaments and for participation of their teams in international tournaments. The Department also gives subsidy for the purchase of sports equipment by the National Sports Federations. Limited secretarial support is also given by way of reimbursement of the salary of the paid Joint/Assistant Secretary of the Federation.

The requests for assistance are processed according to the Guidelines laid down by the Department. These were formulated in 1988. The Committee headed by Director-General, SAI has been appointed to examine revision of the Guidelines.

TABLE 48.1: Schemewise Details of Financial Allocations (for 1991-92 and 1992-93)

(*Rupees in Lakhs*)

Sl. No.	Name of the Scheme	Revised Estimates 1991-92		Budget Estimates 1992-93	
		Plan	Non-Plan	Plan	Non-Plan
1	2	3	4	5	6
I.	**Youth Welfare Schemes**				
1.	National Service Scheme	674.00	442.00	987.00	440.00
2.	Nehru Yuva Kendra Sangthan	319.00	603.00	900.00	603.00
3.	Assistance to Voluntary Organisations	28.00	1.50	55.00	1.50
4.	Promotion of adventure Activities	50.00	21.00	150.00	20.75
5.	Establishment and Development of Mountaineering Institutes	11.00	10.00	30.00	10.00
6.	Scouting and Guiding	55.00	12.00	88.00	12.00
7.	National Service Volunteers Schemes	88.00	10.30	180.00	10.50
8.	National Integration Programme	185.00	20.00	270.00	19.75

Contd.

TABLE 48.1 *Contd.*

1	2	3	4	5	6
9.	Exchange of Youth Delegation	15.00	—	25.00	—
10.	Exhibitions for Youth	16.00	—	30.00	—
11.	Youth Hostels	124.00	—	210.00	—
12.	Commonwealth Youth Programme	3.00	30.10	3.00	30.10
13.	National Discipline Scheme	—	965.00	—	965.00
14.	Youth Clubs	15.00	—	50.00	—
15.	Programme of Training of Youth	80.00	—	120.00	—
16.	National Youth Award	10.00	—	10.00	—
17.	Contribution to United Nations Volunteer Programme	—	6.70	—	4.00
18.	UNV-DDS Volunteers deployed in India	—	2.40	—	2.40
19.	National Fitness Corps				
20.	Special Scheme for Promotion of Youth Activities Among Youth of Backward Tribes	80.00	—	100.00	—
21.	Compulsory National Service	1.00	—	1.00	—
22.	Evaluation	—	—	1.00	—
Total: Youth Welfare Schemes		1755.00	2125.00	3239.00	2120.00
II. Games and Sports					
1.	Sports Authority of India	2678.00	1330.00	2341.00	1330.00
2.	Grants to Universities and Colleges	151.00	—	250.00	—
3.	Grants to National Sports Federations	350.00	48.00	350.00	94.00
4.	Development of Sports through State Sports Councils, etc.	1000.00	—	624.00	—
5.	Incentives for Promotion of Sports Activities	260.00	—	300.00	—
6.	Laying of Synthetic Tracks/surfaces	100.00	—	100.00	—
7.	Exchange of Sports & Phy. Education Team Experts	100.00	—	100.00	—
8.	National Sports Championship for Women	—	55.00	—	60.00
9.	Physical Education	—	19.00	—	19.00
10.	Promotion of Sports among Women	—	—	3.00	—
11.	Sports Talent Search Scholarship Scheme	70.00	—	70.00	—
12.	Rural sports Tournaments	—	32.50	—	53.00
13.	National Welfare Fund	—	2.00	—	2.00
14.	Arjuna Award	—	6.50	—	3.00
15.	Dronacharya Award	—	—	—	2.00
16.	Travel Grants to Sports Scholars	1.00	—	1.00	—
17.	Afro-Asian Games	—	1.00	—	1.00
18.	Transfer to Asiad Property	—	1.00	—	1.00
19.	Scholarships for Training of Specialists & Outstanding Sportspersons in Sports Adventure abroad	—	—	1.00	—

Contd.

TABLE 48.1 *Concld.*

1	2	3	4	5	6
20.	Special Scheme for sports Activities among the Backward Tribes	—	—	40.00	—
21.	Assistance to Sports Clubs				
22.	Evaluation	—	—	5.00	—
	Total: Games & Sports	4710.00	1495.00	4136.00	1565.00
	Total: I and II	6465.00	3620.00	7375.00	3685.00
III.	**Other Programmes**				
1.	Expenditure on Seminars, Committees, Meetings, etc.	—	25.00	—	25.00
2.	Other Items	—	2.00	—	2.00
IV.	**Secretariat — Social Service**	20.00	167.00	25.00	168.00
	Grand Total (I + II + III)	6485.00	3814.00	7488.00	3880.00

Promotion of Sports and Games in Schools through Prize Money

This scheme was introduced in 1986 with the objective of promoting sports in Schools. Cash prizes of Rs. 10,000 each are awarded annually to Secondary/Higher Secondary Schools, which win the District Inter-School Tournaments conducted by School Games Federation of India in the disciplines of Athletics, Hockey, Basketball, Volleyball (for Boys & Girls) and Football (for Boys only). Thus, in each district a maximum of Rs. 90,000 is awarded each year to schools. The cash amounts are required to be invested by the School in direct promotion of sports like improvement/construction of playgrounds, purchase of sports equipment etc.

The basic weakness is that all the Districts are unable to conduct the tournaments in all the disciplines. A large number of schools, particularly in rural areas, are unable to participate due to lack of resources. For the same reasons they may not have teams in all the 9 disciplines of sports. The status of women sports is even worse. Partly due to social reasons many schools do not have women teams.

Despite such obstacles, the scheme is being pursued through persuasion and motivation. It has been well received and has won widespread appreciation since promotion and sports at grass-roots is its strong point.

Cash Awards to Medal Winners in International Sports Events

Awards ranging from Rs. 50,000 to Rs. 5 lakhs are given for winning medals in specified international sports events in all disciplines, which are included in the Olympics, Asian and Commonwealth Games. These awards are also given in the disciplines of Chess and Billiards/Snooker.

The basic objective of the Awards is to serve as an incentive to the achievers and as inspiration to other sports-minded youth. It is also intended to help sportspersons of outstanding excellence to be able to maintain themselves with dignity and continue to give their best in further pursuit of the sport of their choice.

These awards were introduced in 1986. The awards have been instrumental in injecting a burning desire among the sportspersons to give out their best in international sports events.

Travel Grant to Sports Scholars/Research Workers

The Scheme of "Travel Grant to Sports Scholars/Research Workers for undertaking Specialised Training/Research abroad' was introduced during the VII Five Year Plan in pursuance of the Resolution of National Sports Policy, 1984. The objective of this Scheme is to promote and encourage Research and Development in the field of Sports and Physical Education. Under this scheme, the department provides passage cost for International travel for attending important academic conferences, etc.

In the beginning the response under the scheme was very encouraging since a larger number of applications were received especially for trips connected with seminars on sports subjects.

National Welfare Fund for Sportspersons

The National Welfare Fund for sportspersons and their families was created in 1982 primarily to assist outstanding sportspersons of yesteryears, who had won glory for the country in the international sports field but are now living in indigent circumstances.

This financial support is generally in the form of monthly pension up to Rs. 1500. Lump sum grants are also given for medical treatment.

The sportspersons suffering grievous or fatal injury in the course of participation in sports events or during training are also helped.

The fund has been able to discharge its social responsibility for sportspersons to a great extent. Many a sportsperson and their families have been saved from disaster and humiliation. They have gratefully acknowledged the support of the fund. A large number of applications are now pouring in, including many which are ineligible. In deserving cases, the rules are relaxed to help them.

Arjuna Award

The Arjuna Award was instituted in 1961 as the highest national recognition of distinguished sportspersons. The awardee is given a bronze statuette of Arjuna, a Scroll and a cash award of Rs. 20,000 alongwith a monogram, a blazer and a tie.

Nominations for the award are made by National Sports Federations and the awardees are selected by a selection committee constituted by the Department. To be eligible for this award, a candidate should have displayed outstanding performances at national and international levels consistently for the three years preceding the year of the award and excellence in the year of the award and should also have a high sense of discipline, sportsmanship and outstanding qualities of leadership.

So far 391 sportspersons have been honoured with the Arjuna awards.

Fifth South Asian Federation (SAF) Games

The 5th SAF Games were held in Colombo during December 22-31, 1991. A strongest ever contingent of 223 sportspersons/officials was sent at full cost of Government. These games are held once in two years among the South Asian Association for Regional Cooperation (SAARC) countries.

India won 164 medals (64 Gold, 59 Silver, 41 Bronze) and remained on the top of the medal tally.

Highlights of Achievements in Sports

ATHLETICS

(i) In the 9th Asian Track and Field Meet held at Kuala Lumpur during October, 1991, India won two Gold, 4 Silver and 2 Bronze medals.
(ii) In the 5th International Permit Meet held at New Delhi during September, 1991 India won Bronze medals.

ARCHERY

In the 2nd Federation Cup International Archery Competition held at Calcutta during December 1991 India won the Championship.

CANOEING and KAYAKING

In the Asian Canoe Championship held at Tokyo during November 1991, Shri Johny Romal, an SAG trainee, won a Silver in 1000 mtr C-1, the first ever medal for the country.

CARROM

In the 1st World Carrom Championship held at Delhi during October, 1991, Indian men and women won the Individual and Team championships.

CHESS

Shri Vishwanathan Anand achieved a historic success by winning a very strong International Chess Tournament held at Italy during January 1992.

CRICKET (MEN)

During the Indo-Asutralia test series held at Australia, Shri Kapil Dev became the 2nd player in world and 1st Indian to get 400 test wickets.

EQUESTRIAN

In the 8th Asian Show jumping competition held at Japan during October 1991, Indian team won a Silver medal.

HANDBALL

Indian boys and girls handball teams got the 2nd position in the Commonwealth Junior Handball Championship held at New Delhi during August, 1991.

HOCKEY (MEN)

(i) Indian team participated in the Sultan Azlam Shah Hockey tournament at Malaysia during July-August 1991 and won the tournament.
(ii) Indian team participated in the Pre-Olympic Qualifying Tournament held at Auckland during October 1991 and got 2nd position by virtue of which the team qualified for the Olympics 1992.
(iii) Indian team won the 6th Indira Gandhi International Hockey Tournament held at New Delhi during January 1992.

JUDO

In the Asian Judo Championship held in Japan during November 1991, Shri Sandeep Byala won a Bronze medal.

POWERLIFTING

(i) At the World Women Powerlifting Championship held in New Delhi during June, 1991, India came third as a team.
(ii) In the 9th World Jr. Powerlifting Championship held at Abidjan during September, 1991, Indian team won 1 Silver and 2 Bronze medals.

TENNIS

Shri Leander Paes won the Junior US Open Tennis Championship held in USA during September 1991.

WEIGHTLIFTING

(i) In the Silver Dragon International Weightlifting Tournament held at Cardiff during August, 1991, Indian (Men) team won 3 Gold medals.
(ii) In the 4th (Women) & 5th (Men) Junior Asian Championship held in Indonesia during August, 1991 the Indian team won 3 Silver medals.
(iii) In the 5th World Women Weightlifting Championship held in Germany during Sept.-Oct. 1991, Indian team won a Silver medal.

WRESTLING

(i) In the 4th Commonwealth Wrestling Championship held in New Zealand during October, 1991, the Indian team won 3 Gold, 1 Silver and 5 Bronze medals and secured 2nd position out of 8 countries.
(ii) In an International wrestling tournament held during August, 1991 in erstwhile USSR, Indian team won 7 Silver and 3 Bronze medals.
(iii) In the International Greeco style Junior Wrestling Tournament held in erstwhile USSR, Indian team won 1 Silver and 1 Bronze medals.

YACHTING

(i) In the World Enterprise Championship held at Bombay, the Indian team won the Championship.

(ii) In the 6th Asian Regatta Championship held at Hongkong during October, 1991, India won 1 Gold and 1 Silver medal.

Sports Authority of India

The Sports Authority of India (SAI) was set up by Government of India on March 16, 1984 as a Registered Society with the objective of promoting sports and games in the country and to manage, maintain and ensure proper use of various infrastructure and other sports facilities created for the Asiad 1982 at Delhi.

The Sports Authority of India has the following four functional wings with specific areas of action:

(i) *Academic Wing* for training of coaches and for Research and Development (R&D) in Sports, which is located at Netaji Subhas National Institute of Sports (NSNIS), Patiala;
(ii) *Academic Wing* for physical education and R & D in physical education. This is at Laxmibai National College of Physical Education (LNCPE) Gwalior and Trivandrum;
(iii) The *Operational Wing* for general sports promotion and spotting and nurturing of young talent; and
(iv) *Teams Wing* (Training of Elite Athletes and Management Support) for long term training of elite sportspersons and for preparing of national teams in specific disciplines for targeted international competitions.

The Regional Centres of erstwhile NSNIS, Patiala were restructured in 1987 and six Regional Centres of Sports Authority of India were set up — one each at Bangalore, Gandhinagar, Calcutta, Patiala, Delhi (temporary, to be located at Lucknow) and Imphal — to ensure effective implementation and coordination of the sports development programmes in different regions of the country. The Southern Centre at Bangalore is being developed as a Centre of Excellence in collaboration with Russia and other erstwhile republics of USSR and USA. SAI has two sub-Centres also at Guwahati under the North Eastern Centre and at Aurangabad under the Western Centre. A High Altitude Training Centre at Shillaroo (near Shimla) is also coming up.

Each Regional Centre is under the charge of a Regional Director and has an Advisory Committee to oversee and advise on the implementation of various schemes and programmes of SAI and Central Government in their respective regions. To improve the functioning of the Centres and to ensure expeditious disposal of cases, SAI has decentralised operations of its various schemes and programmes and had revised the delegation of powers to the Regional Directors in 1988 making them responsible for effective implementation of various schemes in their regions.

Apart from providing training to sportspersons to become coaches, the Regional Centres at Bangalore, Calcutta and Gandhinagar also train young talented children and have become centres for holding the State regional and national level sport events and coaching camps. During the year under report, a large number of such meets and camps were held at these centres. Further, Sports facilities are being created in phases at these Centres. Several facilities, which were started recently, have already been completed and have become functional or are about to become functional.

49

SIGNIFICANT NATIONAL EVENTS

1992

Jan 7 : Manipur placed under President's rule.
Jan 12 : Renowned classical vocalist Kumar Gandharva dies at Indore.
Jan 13 : Government suspends army action against 'ULFA'.
Jan 22 : Bharat Ratna for Subash Chandra Bose and Maulana Abul Kalam Azad announced.
Jan 25 : Bharat Ratna for J.R.D. Tata.
Feb 3 : Kapil reaches the 400-mark at Perth, becomes only the second bowler in the history of Test cricket.
Feb 20 : Congress sweeps Punjab elections.
Feb 21 : Centre bank JKLF.
Feb 25 : Beant Singh is new CM of Punjab. 26-member Congress Ministry installed.
Feb 29 : Income-tax exemption limit raised to Rs. 28,000 in 1992-93 budget.
March 3 : Central rule extended in J & K again.
March 4 : Authorised dealers permitted to sell foreign exchange.
March 9 : Rao again wins trial of strength.
March 15: Well-known Urdu poet Rahi Masoom Raza dies at Bombay.
March 16: Satyajit Ray receives 'Oscar' in Calcutta hospital.
March 31: Foreign Minister Madhav Singh Solanki resigns. Sequel to media disclosure on secret note to Swiss Minister.
April 3 : Nagaland put under President's rule.
April 8 : Cong-led Manipur coalition takes oath. President's rule revoked.
April 11 : Geet Sethi wins world masters Billiards championship in New Delhi.
April 16 : Noted sports administrator Raja Bhalinder Singh dies in Delhi.
April 23 : PM denies hand in Bofors note.
May 11 : Govt orders CBI probe into stock market scam.
May 14 : India bans LTTE, steps for Prabhakaran's extradition to begin.
May 15 : BSE suspends Harshad Mehta. Bank accounts frozen.
May 20 : Indira peace prize for Rajiv Gandhi.
May 20 : ASLV launched successfully. 106 kg satellite (SROSS) put into orbit.
May 29 : 'AGNI' launched but develops snag during re-entry stage.
Jun 2 : RBI panel discovers fraud worth Rs. 3078:63 cr. Collusion of bankers, brokers exposed. Special court to try stock scam culprits. Ordinance promulgated. Custodian appointed to attach assets.
Jun 9 : Rajesh Khanna of Congress (I) wins New Delhi seat by 28,256 votes.
Jun 14 : Chairman and managing director of UCO Bank K. Morgabanthu admits Rs. 90 cr. fraud.
Jun 15 : Verma panel report submitted. Security agencies indicated.

Jun 23 : Nationwide raids by CBI. Three more FIRs filed. Bhupen Dalal, 3 others held.
Jul 6 : Stock scam extends to sale of PSU shares. Report puts amount at Rs. 3542.7 cr. Two more foreign banks involved.
Jul 9 : Minister of State of Commerce P. Chaidambaram resigns over investments in Fairgrowth.
Jul 10 : Najma Heptullah elected Rajya Sabha Dy Chairperson.
Jul 13 : HC rejects plea to stay digging at Ayodhya site.
Jul 16 : Dr. S.D. Sharma elected ninth President of India.
Jul 18 : Kanan Devi, legendary singing star of Bengali cinema dies at Calcutta.
Jul 25 : Dr. S.D. Sharma takes Oath of the President.
Jul 27 : Popular film star Amjad Khan dies at Bombay.
Aug 1 : PM dedicates Vizag Steel Plant to nation.
Aug 8 : Nehru award for Aruna Asaf Ali.
Aug 8 : JPC constituted under R.N. Mirdha to probe bank securities scam.
Aug 18 : 'Prithvi' lunch successful.
Aug 19 : K.R. Narayanan elected Vice-President of India.
Aug 25 : Third RBI report bares bankers, brokers further Syndicate Bank, two others added to scam list.
Sep 3 : Ayodhya report submitted to SC.
Sep 12 : Renowned Hindustani classical vocalist Pandit Mallikarjun Mansur dies at Dharwar (Karnataka).
Sep 29 : Andhra CM Janardan Reddy quits.
Sep 29 : SJP splits : Mulayam forms new party.
Oct 7 : K. Vijay Bhaskara Reddy is new Andhra CM.
Oct 9 : Jinda and Sukha hanged in Pune jail.
Oct 31 : Chandra Shekhar is new SJP president.
Nov 6 : L.M. Sharma named new Chief Justice.
Nov 10 : Attorney General G. Ramaswamy resigns.
Nov 16 : SC upholds VP Govt notification on job quota. Suggests exclusion of the "creamy layer". No reservation in promotions. Govt. amendment struck down.
Nov 24 : Milon Banerjee is Attorney General.
Nov 28 : SC allows symbolic Kar Seva. Observer to monitor situation.
Dec 6 : Kar Sevaks demolish disputed structure at Ayodhya.
Dec 7 : Over 200 killed in nationwide frenzy. Maharashtra, U.P. worst hit. Troops out in many areas.
Dec 8 : L.K. Advani, Joshi, Singhal and Uma Bharati arrested.
Dec 10 : Centre bans RSS, VHP, Bajrang Dal, Jamait-e-Islami and the Islamic Seva Sangh.
Dec 11 : Allahabad High Court quashes Ayodhya land acquisition.
Dec 13 : Nationwide violence toll crosses 1244 mark. Panel to probe demolition.
Dec 15 : BJP Govts in Rajasthan, MP and Himachal dismissed. Assemblies dissolved.
Dec 21 : Govt. survives BJP no-trust motion. Left supports Cong. NF abstains.
Dec 23 : Rajiv assassination (Verma) panel indicts Centre, Intelligence Bureau, Tamil Nadu police and Congress leaders.

Dec 28 : Centre to acquire land for Ram temple and mosque.
Dec 29 : Devotees allowed 'darshan', Pooja' of Ram Lalla
Dec 29 : Karnataka State Raitha Sangham attacks the Bangalore office of a seeds multinational "Cargill Seeds".

1993

Jan 8 : All regulations of the Foreign Exchange Regulation Act (FERA). done away with through a Presidential Ordinance.
Jan 15 : All controls over coal trade were lifted to enable privatization.
Feb 9 : Finance Ministry slashes heavily the customs duty on 35 items.
Mar 4 : National Front and Left submit notice to the Speaker of the Lok Sabha for the impeachment of Chief Election Commissioner T.N. Seshan.
Mar 4 : PM claims people's support for economic policies.
Mar 4 : Left parties organise nationwide protests on the economic policies of the Government.
Mar 9 : Rao Government wins trial of strength in the Lok Sabha. Amendments to Motion of Thanks to the President defeated by 262 votes to 210. Nine TDP MPS defy whip and do not turn up for voting.
Mar 17 : The Railway Minister C.K. Jaffer Sharief announces concessions while winding up the debate on the railway budget for 1992-93.
Mar 20 : 'Bharat Ratna' for noted film Producer and Director Satyajit Ray for his distinguished and excellent services.

TECHNICAL TERMS

Under-five mortality rate: number of deaths of children under five years of age per 1,000 live births. More specifically, this is the probability of dying between birth and exactly five years of age.

Infant mortality rate: number of deaths of infants under one year of age per 1,000 live births. More specifically, this is the probability of dying between birth and exactly one year of age.

GNP: gross national product. Annual GNPs per capita are expressed in current United States dollars. GNP per capita growth rates are average annual growth rates that have been computd by fitting trend lines to the logarithmic values of GNP per capita at constant market prices for each year of the time period.

Life expectancy at birth: the number of years newborn children would live if subject to the mortality risks prevailing for the cross-section of population at the time of their birth.

Adult literacy rate: percentage of persons aged 15 and over who can read and write.

Primary and secondary enrolment ratios: The gross enrolment ratio is the total number of children enrolled in a schooling level — whether or not they belong in the relevant age group for that level — expressed as a percentage of the total number of children in the relevant age group for that level. The net enrolment ratio is the total number of children enrolled in a schooling level who belong in the relevant age group, expressed as a percentage of the total number in that age-group.

Income share: percentage of private income received by the highest 20 per cent and lowest 40 per cent of households.

Low birth weight: Less than 2,500 grams.

Underweight: moderate and severe — below minus two standard deviations from median weight for age of reference population; severe — below minus three standard deviations from median weight for age of reference population.

Wasting: moderate and severe — below minus two standard deviations from mediam weight for height of reference population.

Stunting: moderate and severe — below minus two standard deviations from median height for age of reference population.

Access to health services: percentage of the population that can reach appropriate local health services by the local means of transport in no more than one hour.

DPT: diphtheria, pertussis (whooping cough) and tetanus.

ORT use: percentage of all cases of diarrhoea in children under five years of age treated with oral rehydration salts or an appropriate household solution.

Children reaching final grade of primary school: percentage of the children entering the first grade of primary school who eventually reach the final grade.

Crude death rate: annual number of deaths per 1,000 population.

Total fertility rate: the number of children that would be born per women, if she were to live to the end of her child-bearing years and bear children at each age in accordance with prevailing age-specific fertility rates.

Urban population: percentage of population living in urban areas as defined according to the national definition used in the most recent population census.

Absolute poverty level: the income level below which a minimum nutritionally adequate diet plus essential non-food requirements is not affordable.

ODA: Official development assistance.

Debt service: the sum of interest payments and repayments of principal on external public and publicly guaranteed long-term debts.

Contraceptive prevalence: percentage of married women aged 15-49 currently using contraception.

Births attended: percentage of births attended by physicians, nurses, midwives, trained primary health care workers or trained traditional birth attendants.

Maternal mortality rate: annual number of deaths of women from pregnancy related causes per 100,000 live births.

GDP : gross domestic product.

APPENDIX II

CATEGORISATION OF COUNTRIES – DEVELOPED AND LEAST DEVELOPED COUNTRIES

Middle East & North Africa:	Algeria Egypt Iran, Islamic Rep. of Iraq Jordan	Kuwait Lebanon Libyan Arab Jamahiriya Morocco Oman	Saudi Arabia Sudan Syria Tunisia Turkey	United Arab Emirates Yemen
South Asia:	Afghanistan Bangladesh	Bhutan India	Nepal Pakistan	Sri Lanka
East Asia & Pacific:	Cambodia China Hong Kong Indonesia Korea, Dem.	Peo. Rep. Korea, Rep. of Lao, Peo. Dem. Rep. Malaysia	Mongolia Myanmar Papua New Guinea Philippines	Singapore Thailand Viet Nam
Latin America & Caribbean:	Argentina Bolivia Brazil Chile Colombia Costa Rica	Cuba Dominican Rep. Ecuador El Salvador Guatemala Haiti	Honduras Jamaica Mexico Nicaragua Panama Paraguay	Peru Trinidad and Tobago Uruguay Venezuela
Least Developed Countries:	Afghanistan Bangladesh Benin Bhutan Botswana Burkina Faso Burundi Cambodia Chad	Ethiopia Gunea Guinea-Bissau Haiti Lao, Peo. Dem. Rep. Lesotho Liberia Madagascar Malawi	Mali Mauritania Mozambique Myanmar Nepal Niger Rwanda Sierra Leone Somalia	Sudan Tanzania Togo Uganda Yemen Zaire Zambia
Developed Countries:	Albania Australia Austria Belgium Bulgaria Canada Czechoslovakia Denmark	Finland France Germany Greece Hungary Ireland Israel Italy	Japan Netherlands New Zealand Norway Poland Portugal Romania Spain	Sweden Switzerland USA USSR (former) United Kingdom Yugoslavia (former)

APPENDIX III

ACRONYMS*

ACU	Asian Clearing Union
ADB	Asian Development Bank
AIDS	Acquired Immuno Deficiency Syndrome
API	Annual Parasite Index
ARM	Additional Resource Mobilisation
ASI	Annual Survey of Industries
ASR	Airport Surveillance Radar
BCCL	Bharat Coking Coal Limited
BCR	Balance from Current Revenue
BE	Budget Estimate
BG	Broad Gauge
BIFR	Board for Industrial and Financial Reconstruction
BNP	Balwadi Nutrition Programme
CAD	Command Area Development
CARE	Cooperative for American Relief Everywhere
CBI	Central Bureau of Investigation
CCA	Cumulative Command Area
CCI	Controller of Capital Issues
CCIS	Comprehensive Crop Insurance Scheme
CCS	Cash Compensatory Support
CD	Certificate of Deposit
CEA	Central Electricity Authority
CHC	Community Health Centre
CIL	Coal India Limited
CIP	Central Issue Price
CIS	Commonwealth of Independent States
COB	Carry on Business
CONCOR	Container Corporation of India
COSIP	Colleges Science Improvement Programme
CP	Commercial Paper
CPI	Consumer Price Index
CPI (AL)	Consumer Price Index for Agricultural Labourers
CPI (IW)	Consumer Price Index for Industrial Workers
CPI (UNME)	Consumer Price Index for Urban Non-Manual Employees
CRISIL	Credit Rating Information Services of India Limited
CRR	Cash Reserve Ratio
CSO	Central Statistical Organisation
DAP	Di-Ammonium Phosphate
DEL	Direct Exchange Lines
DFHI	Discount and Finance House of India
DFI	Development Finance Institution
DGCI&S	Director General of Commercial Intelligence & Statistics
DGE&T	Directorate General of Employment and Training
DOT	Department of Telecommunication
DRC	District Rehabilition Centre
DRI	Differential Rate of Interest
DTL	Demand and Time Liabilities
DVC	Damodar Valley Corporation
DWCRA	Development of Women and Children in Rural Areas

---

* used in the main text.

ECB	External Commercial Borrowing
ECE	Early Childhood Education
ECGC	Export Credit Guarantee Corporation
EEC	European Economic Community
EFF	Extended Fund Facility
EGS	Employment Guarantee Scheme
EHTP	Electronics Hardware Technology Park
EIUS	Environmental Improvement of Urban Slums
EOU	Export-Oriented Unit
EPC	Export Promotion Council
EPCG	Export Promotion Capital Goods
EPZ	Export Processing Zone
ESAF	Enlarged Structural Adjustment Facility
ESTP	Electronics Software Technology Park
EWS	Economically Weaker Section
FCNRA	Foreign Currency Non-Resident Accounts
FC(B&O)D	Foreign Currency (Banks and Others) Deposits
FERA	Foreign Exchange Regulation Act
FII	Foreign Institutional Investor
FIPB	Foreign Investment Promotion Board
GATT	General Agreement on Tariffs and Trade
GCA	General Currency Area
GDP	Gross Domestic Product
GDRM	Global Depository Receipt Mechanism
GER	Gross Enrolment Ratio
GIC	General Insurance Corporation
GRT	Gross Registered Tonnes
HFA	Health for all
HIV	Human Immuno Deficiency Virus
HSD	High Speed Diesel
HUDCO	Housing and Urban Development Corporation
HYV	High Yielding Variety
IAAI	International Airport Authority of India
IAY	Indira Awaas Yojana
IBRD	International Bank for Reconstruction and Development
ICAR	Indian Council of Agricultural Research
ICDS	Integrated Child Development Service
ICICI	Industrial Credit and Investment Corporation of India
ICOR	Incremental Capital-Output Ratio
ICRA	Investment Information and Credit Rating Agency
ICRR	Incremental Cash Reserve Ratio
IDA	International Development Agency
IDBI	Industrial Development Bank of India
IEC	Information, Education and Communication
IEM	Industrial Entrepreneurs' Memoranda
IFCI	Industrial Financial Corporation of India
IIM	Indian Institute of Management
IIP	Index of Industrial Production
ILO	International Labour Organisation
IMF	International Monetary Fund
IMR	Infant Mortality Rate
IMS	Integrated Management System
IPCL	Indian Petroleum and Chemicals Limited
IPM	Integrated Pest Management
IPRS	International Price Reiumbursement Scheme
IRBI	Industrial Reconstruction Bank of India
IRDP	Integrated Rural Development Programme
IREDA	Indian Renewable Energy Development Agency

IT ACT	Income Tax Act
ITDP	Integrated Tribal Development Project
ITI	Indian Telephone Industries
ITI	Industrial Training Institute
IUD	Intra-Uterine Device
JBRI	Japanese Bond Research Institute
JE	Japanese Encephalitis
JPC	Joint Parliamentary Committee
JRY	Jawahar Rozgar Yojana
JSN	Jana Shikshan Nilayam
KVIC	Khadi and Village Industries Commission
LDPT	Long Distance Public Telephone
LDSP	Land Development and Shelter Project
LERMS	Liberalised Exchange Rate Management System
LIC	Life Insurance Corporation
LIG	Low Income Group
LPC	Liquified Petroleum Gas
LTFP	Long-term Fiscal Policy
LTO	Long Term Operations
M3	Money Supply
MDT	Multi Drug Therapy
MFA	Multi-Fibre Arrangement
MG	Meter Gauge
MILIC	Moderately Indebted Low-Income Country
MISC	MIscellaneous
MMMF	Money Market Mutual Funds
MMTC	Mineral and Metal Trading Corporation
MOP	Muriate of Potash
MOU	Memorandum of Understanding
MPBF	Maximum Permissible Bank Finance
MSSR	Monopulse Secondary Surveillance Radar
MST	Monthly Season Ticket
MWS	Million Wells Scheme
N	Nitrogen
NAA	National Airports Authority
NABARD	National Bank for Agricultural and Rural Development
NAFED	National Agricultural Cooperative Marketing Federation
NAV	Net Asset Value
NBCG	Net Bank Credit to Government
NBFDC	National Backward Classes Finance and Development Corporation
NBO	National Building Organisation
NCC	National Cadet Corps
NCHF	National Cooperative and Housing Federation of India
NCVT	National Council of Vocational Training
NDA	Net Domestic Assets
NEER	Nominal Effective Exchange Rate
NFE	Non-Formal Eduation
NFEE	Net Foreign Exchange Earnings
NG	Narrow Gauge
NGO	Non-Governmental Organisation
NHB	National Housing Bank
NHP	National Housing Policy
NLC	Neyveli Lignite Corporation
NMEP	National Malaria Eradication Programme
NNP	Net National Product
NORAD	Norwegion Agency for Development
NPE	National Policy on Education

NRCCG	Net Reserve Bank Credit to Central Government
NRER	Non-Resident External (Rupee) Accounts
NRF	National Renewal Fund
NRI	Non-Resident Indian
NRR	Net Reproduction Rate
NRSE	New and Renewable Sources of Energy
NRY	Nehru Rozgar Yojana
NR(E)RA	Non-Residents (External) Rupee Account
NSEI	National Stock Exchange of India
NSEDC	National Scheduled Castes and Scheduled Tribes Finance and Development Corporation
NSS	National Service Scheme
NSSO	National Sample Survey Organisation
NSTC	National Sports Talent Contest
OB	Operation Blackboard
OC	Open Cast
OCB	Overseas Corporate Body
OECD	Organisation for Economic Co-operation and Development
OIL	Oil India Limited
OMS	Out per Man-Shift
ONGC	Oil and Natural Gas Commission
OPEC	Organisation of Petroleum Exporting Countries
P	Phosphorus
P & T	Posts and Telecommunications
P_2O_5	Phosphate
PACS	Primary Agricultural Credit Society
PCRA	Petroleum Conservation Research Association
PDS	Public Distribution System
PECV	Profit Earning Capacity Value
PHC	Primary Health Centre
PHL	Pawan Hans Limited
PLF	Plant Load Factor
POL	Petroleum Oil and Lubricants
PSE	Public Sector Enterprise
PSU	Public Sector Undertaking
R&D	Research and Development
RBF	Refinery Boiler Fuel
RBI	Reserve Bank of India
RCMC	Registration-cum-Membership Certificate
RCTFC	Risk Capital and Technology Finance Corporation
RE	Revised Estimate
REER	Real Effective Exchange Rate
REPOS	Repurchasing Obligations
RMP	Registered Medical Practitioner
RPA	Rupee Payment Area
RRB	Regional Rural Bank
RREC	Rural Rehabilitation Extension centre
RRTC	Regional Rehabilitation Training Centre
SAF	Structural Adjustment Facility
SAI	Sports Authority of India
SAIL	Steel Authority of India
SAL	Structural Adjustment Loan
SAP	State Advised Price
SBI	State Bank of India
SC	Scheduled Castes
SCCL	Singareni Collieries Company Limited
SCI	Shipping Corporation of India
SCICI	Shipping Credit & Investment Company of India

SCP	Special Component Plan
SDR	Special Drawing Right
SEB	State Electricity Board
SEBC	Socially and Educationally Backward Class
SEBI	Securities and Exchange Board of India
SEEUY	Scheme of Self-Employment for Educated Unemployed Youth
SEEUP	Self Employment Programme for Urban Poor
SESRU	Self Employment for Registered Unemployed
SFC	State Financial Corproation
SHASU	Scheme for Housing and Shelter Upgradation
SIA	Secretariat of Industrial Approvals
SICA	Sick Industrial Companis (Special Provisions) Act, 1985
SIDA	Swedish International Development Agency
SIDBI	Small Industries Development Bank of India
SIDC	State Industrial Development Corporation
SIDCO	Small Industries Development Corporation
SIDO	Small Industries Development Organisation
SLR	Statutory Liquidity Ratio
SMP	Statutory Minimum Price
SNP	Special Nutrition Programme
SPDA	Sports Project Development Area
SRS	Sample REgistration System
SRTC	State Road Transport Corporation
SRTU	State Road Transport Undertaking
SSI	Small-Scale Industries
ST	Scheduled Tribes
STEP	Support to Training and Employment Programme
STP	Software Technology Park
SUME	Scheme for Urban Micro Enterprises
SUWE	Scheme of Urban Wage Employment
TB	Tuberculosis
TDICI	Technology Development and Information Company of India
TDS	Tax Deducted at Source
TEI	Technical Education Institute
TEU	Twenty-Foot Equivalent
TFCI	Tourism Finance Corporation of India
TISCO	Tata Iron and Steel Company
TLC	Total Literacy Campaign
TRIFED	Tribal Cooperative Marketing Development Federation
TRYSEM	Training of Rural Yough for Self Employment
TSP	Tribal Sub-Plan
TT	Titurus Toxide
T&D	Transmission and Disruption
UBSP	Urban Basic Services for the Poor
UEE	Universalisation of Elementary Education
UG	Under Ground
UGC	University Grants Commission
UNDP	United Nations Development Programme
UNICEF	United Nations International Children and Educational Fund
UT	Union Territory
UTI	Unit Trust of India
VRC	Vocational Rehabilitation Centre
VSAT	Very Small Aperture Terminals
VSP	Visakhapatnam Steel Project

NUMERICAL UNITS

Lakh	100000
Crore	10 million

CROPS

Kharif crops planted at the outset of the southwest monsoon in June-July and harvested in September-October.

Rabi crops planted in winter, usually between October and December, and harvested in spring, between March and May.

WARABANDI

Warabandi construction of channels to carry irrigation water from canals to farms.

INDEX

CICIL LIST

CONCEPTS IN COMMUNICATION, INFORMATICS & LIBRARIANSHIP

(CICIL)

General Editor: **S.P. AGRAWAL**

CICIL-1 Development of Library Services in India: Social Science Information
S.P. Agrawal Rs. 150

CICIL-2 Development of Documentation in India: Social Science Information
S.P. Agrawal Rs. 250

CICIL-3 UNESCO and Social Sciences: Retrospect and Prospect
S.P. Agrawal and **J.C. Aggarwal** Rs. 250

CICIL-4 INDIANA : A Bibliography of Bibliographical Sources
M.K. Jain Rs. 200

CICIL-5 Dimensions of Library and Information Science: Kaula Festschrift
V. Venkatappaiah (Eds.) Rs. 600

CICIL-6 Book Numbers: Some Indian Methods
M.P. Satija and **S.P. Agrawal** Rs. 100

CICIL-7 National Policy for University Libraries in India: Problems and Perspectives
N.B. Inamdar and **L.S. Ramaiah** (Ed.) Rs. 250

CICIL-8 Media Utilisation for the Development of Women and Children
B.S. Thakur and **Binod C. Agrawal** Rs. 150

CICIL-9 Terrorism: An Annotated Bibliography
Susheela Bhan (Ed.) Rs. 275

CICIL-10 Transnational Library Relations: The Indo-American Experience
M.B. Konnur Rs. 175

CICIL-11 Geography of Marketing and Commercial Activities in India (Documentation on Research Information)
R.S. Dixit Rs. 130

CICIL-12 Information India 1988: Global View
S.P. Agrawal and **J.C. Aggarwal** Rs. 200

CICIL-13 Women's Education in India: Historical Review, Present Status and Perspective Plan
S.P. Agrawal and **J.C. Aggarwal** Rs. 360

CICIL-14 Cultural Communication in India: Role and Impact of Phonograms
J.M. Ojha Rs. 220

CICIL-15 Second Historical Survey of Educational Development in India: Select Documents 1985-1989
S.P. Agrawal and **J.C. Aggarwal** Rs. 490

CICIL-16 Documentation Encyclopaedia of UNESCO and Education
J.C. Aggarwal and **S.P. Agrawal** Rs. 800 (set of 2 parts)

CICIL-17 Attitude Towards Information: A Study of Post-Graduate Teachers and Researchers in Social Sciences
N.G. Satish (in press)

CICIL-18 Librarianship and Bureaucratic Organisation: A Study in the Sociology of Library Profession in India
P.K. Jayaswal Rs. 175

CICIL-19 Literature Search
K.A. Isaac Rs. 150

CICIL-20 Child Education in India: Index to Scholarly Writings in Indian Educational Journals and Newspapers since independence
S.P. Agrawal and **Naresh Kanta** Rs. 100

CICIL-21 Lok Sabha and Vidhan Sabha Elections in India 1989 & 1990: Process and Results with Comparative Study of Manifestos
S.P. Agrawal and **J.C. Aggarwal** Rs. 250

CICIL-22 Islamic Studies in India: A Survey of Human, Institutional and Documentary Sources
Mohamed Taher Rs. 180

CICIL-23 Panchayati Raj: An Annotated Bibliography
N.B. Inamdar, N.G. Satish and **Anil Takalkar** 290

CICIL-24 Information India 1989-90: Global View
S.P. Agrawal and **J.C. Aggarwal** Rs. 500

CICIL-25 First Handbook of Psychological and Social Instruments
Udai Pareek and **T. Venkateswara Rao** Rs. 500

CICIL-26 Educational and Social Uplift of Backward Classes: At What Cost and How? Mandal Commission and After
S.P. Agrawal and **J.C. Aggarwal** Rs. 275

CICIL-27 Mass Media and New Horizons: Impact of TV & Video an Urban Milieu
H.R. Trivedi Rs. 180

CICIL-28 Indian Writings on Education : An Indicator to Indian Educational Journals Grouped by Subject Deseriptors 1979 to 1986 (in two parts)
S.P. Agarwal Rs. 900 (per set)

CICIL-29 Nation in Crisis
S.P. Agrawal and **J.C. Aggarwal** Rs. 200

CICIL-30 Information India 1990-91: Global View
S.P. Agrawal and **J.C. Aggarwal** Rs. 500

CICIL-31 Development of University Libraries in India after Independence
O.P. Gupta Rs. 270

CICIL-32 Handbook on Child : With Historical Background
Pramila Pandit Barooah Rs. 320

CICIL-33 Weaker Section in Indian Society : Undiscovered Past, Uncertain Present and Unpredictable Future : Index to Writings in Indian Scholarly Journals and 10 National Newspapers Classified under 1500 Descriptors 1886-1990
S.P. Agrawal and **Rajeev Kumar Sharma** Rs. 600

CICIL-34 Communication Informatics and Librarianship in India : An Introductory Guide to Publications Based on a Survey of Libraries in Capital City of India
S.P. Agrawal and **Pushpa Rani Sharma** Rs. 720

CICIL-35 Problems of Collection Development in Special Libraries
M.S. Sridhar Rs. 225

CICIL-36 National Information Resources for Social Sciences in India : Mobilisation, Dispersal and International Enhancement
S.P. Agrawal Rs. 225

CICIL-37 Modern History of Punjab : A Look Back into Ancient Peaceful Punjab Focusing Confrontation and Failures Leading to Present Punjab Problem, and a Peep Ahead : Relevant Select Documents
J.C. Aggarwal and **S.P. Agrawal** Rs. 400

CICIL-38 India Information Sources : Economics and Business
Kyllikki Ruokonen and **Manohar Lal** Rs.

CICIL-39 Educational Planning in India : With a Slant to Educational Financing and Administration, Vol. 1, Reports of Committees and Commissions, Five Year Plans, Statistical Tables
J.C. Aggarwal and **S.P. Agrawal** Rs. 650

CICIL-40 Integrated Library System : Two Case Studies : Latin America and India
Maria Luiza Rigo Pasquarelli, Rosaly Favero Krzyanowski, Ines Maria M. Imperatriz and S.P. Agrawal Rs. 160

CICIL-41 Social Science Information in India: Effort towards Bibliographical Control
S.D. Vyas Rs. 300

CICIL-42 Higher Education in India Since Independence: U.G.C. and Its Approach
O.P. Gupta Rs. 360

CICIL-43 Government and Politics in India: A Bibliographical Study of Contemporary Scenario Chronicling Rajiv Gandhi Era
S.P. Agrawal and **Rajeev Kumar Sharma** Rs. 500

CICIL-44 Second Handbook of Psychological and Social Instruments
D.M. Pestonjee Rs. 300

CICIL-45 Development/Digression Diary of India; 3D Companion Volume to Information India: 1990-91
S.P. Agrawal Rs. 200

CICIL-46 Development/Digression Diary of India; 3D Companion Volume to Information India: 1991-92
S.P. Agrawal Rs. 300

CICIL-47 Information India 1991-92: Global View
S.P. Agrawal and **J.C. Aggarwal** Rs. 500

CICIL-48 Committees and Commissions in India 1974, A Concept's Project, Compiled by a team of professionals guided by **Virender Kumar** (Vol. 12) Rs. 450

CICIL-49 Committees and Commissions in India 1975, A Concept's Project, Compiled by a team of professionals guided by **Virender Kumar** (Vol. 13) Rs. 450

CICIL-50 Committees and Commissions in India 1976, A Concept's Project, Compiled by a team of professionals guided **Virender Kumar** (Vol. 14) Rs. 450

CICIL-51 Committees and Commissions in India 1977, A Concept's Project, Compiled by a team of professionals guided by **Virender Kumar** (Vol. 15) (in four parts) Rs. 450 each

CICIL-52 Committees and Commissions in India 1978, A Concept's Project, Compiled by a team of professionals guided by **Virender Kumar** (Vol. 16) (in two parts) Rs. 450 each